RELIGION AND THE STATE

Leo Pfeffer

RELIGION AND THE STATE

Essays in Honor of Leo Pfeffer

edited by
James E. Wood, Jr.

Baylor University Press
Waco, Texas

Copyright © 1985 by
Baylor University Press
Waco, Texas 76798

All Rights Reserved
Library of Congress Catalog Card Number: 85-070643
International Standard Book Number: 0-918954-29-0

Printed in the United States of America

2-24-86

CONTENTS

Part 8   Religion and World Order

Part 9   Leo Pfeffer

PREFACE

This volume is an appropriate and timely expression of gratitude for and tribute to Leo Pfeffer—America's foremost author, scholar, and jurist of church-state relations. Long recognized as one of this nation's outstanding authorities on the subject of church and state, his prodigious scholarship has earned him the respect and stature accorded few scholars at anytime, anywhere. His contributions to church and state thought are perhaps unparalleled in American jurisprudence.

Samuel Krislov writes in this volume, "Leo Pfeffer is probably *sui generis*. There are a score or so of lawyers who have litigated the majority of cases by their chosen area of expertise in front of the United States Supreme Court. A few of these have written extensively in the same area. No one comes to mind, however, to rival Pfeffer's intellectual dominance over so vital an area of constitutional law for so extensive a period in this combination of pleading and intellectualizing. . . . Remarkably, this was achieved by a one-man 'repeat player.'" Krislov then cites an acknowledgment of Pfeffer's predominance in a recent review of a book highly critical of Pfeffer in which the reviewer writes: "The book is a frontal attack on the opinions of Leo Pfeffer as expressed in *Church, State, and Freedom* and *God, Caesar, and the Constitution*. [Robert L.] Cord picked his target with good reason, for Pfeffer has argued roughly half the Establishment Clause cases to come before the Supreme Court. It is his version of that clause's meaning more than others that forms the Court's reasoning in this area."

Certainly it may be said without fear of contradiction that anyone working in the area of church-state relations during the past thirty years has been compelled to take note of the work of Leo Pfeffer, both as an author and as a jurist. His eminence and lengthening influence in this area have been taken seriously even by those holding widely divergent views from Pfeffer himself.

Born in Hungary, the son of a Jewish rabbi, Leo Pfeffer was brought to the United States by his parents when he was two years old; he became a naturalized citizen of the United States when he was seven. He received the B.S.S. degree from the College of the City of New York and the J.D. degree

from the New York University School of Law. Admitted to
the New York bar at the age of twenty-three, he has been
actively engaged in the practice of law for more than half a
century, during which time he has probably argued more
church-state cases before the United States Supreme Court
than anyone else in American history.

His professional responsibilities have included: Lecturer, New
School of Social Research, 1954-58; Lecturer, Mt. Holyoke
College, 1958-60; David W. Petergorsky Professor of Consti-
tutional Law, Yeshiva University, 1962-63; Professor of Polit-
ical Science and Chairman of the Department (1964-79), Long
Island University, 1964-85; Visiting Professor of Constitutional
Law, Rutgers University, 1965; President, Lawyers Constitu-
tional Defense Committee, 1964-66, General Counsel, 1966-
82, Emeritus Counsel, 1982-   ; General Counsel, American
Jewish Congress, 1958-64, Special Counsel, 1964-85; General
Counsel, Committee for Public Education and Religious Liberty (PEARL), 1967-82; and General Counsel for the Horace
Mann League.

In Leo Pfeffer are combined thinker and participant, theo-
retician and practitioner. Scholarship, advocacy, and juridical
skill have been inextricably intertwined and embodied in his
life and work. Through the years, he has been deeply involved in concerns for human rights and civil liberties, with
special attention given to religious rights and religious liberty
as the cornerstone upon which all other civil rights and civil
liberties ultimately rest. A lifelong champion of religious liberty and the institutional separation of church and state, he
has argued with considerable force and persuasiveness that
they are of immense importance to both religion and the state.
In the concluding words of his monumental work, *Church,
State, and Freedom*, Pfeffer wrote "Complete separation of
church and state is best for the church and best for the state,
and secures freedom for both."

Recognition of his work has come from many and varied
sources. A sampling of the awards and honors given him
include the following: L.H.D. degree from Hebrew Union
College; Trustee Award for Scholarly Achievement, Long
Island University; Thomas Jefferson Religious Freedom
Award, Unitarian-Universalist Church; Religious Freedom
Award, Americans United; Rabbi Maurice N. Eisendrath
Memorial Award, Union of American Hebrew Congregations;
Brooklyn Civil Liberties Award; Citation for Contributions to

Public Education, Horace Mann League; Townsend Harris Medal, College of the City of New York; and George Brussel Memorial Award, Stephen Wise Free Synagogue.

The appropriateness of this volume as an expression of tribute to Leo Pfeffer is not only to be found in the subject of this work but, of far more importance, in the original and timely quality of the essays themselves. Nineteen contributors from a variety of academic disciplines and religious traditions have authored essays expressly for this volume in honor of Leo Pfeffer. While each essay is offered by way of a tribute to a distinguished scholar and jurist, each essay addresses a major subject on the theme of the volume. This volume was purposely planned to cover a wide range of subjects while maintaining an organic unity for the work as a whole. The breadth and comprehensiveness of this volume, as well as the specific subjects addressed, are an appropriate expression of Leo Pfeffer's own range of interests, writings, and labors. The essays are grouped under the following topics: "No Establishment of Religion and the Free Exercise of Relegion," "The Right of Voluntary Association," "The Right of Religious Dissent," "Government Chaplaincies and Military Conscription," "Religion and Public Education," "Religion and Taxation," "Religion and Politics," and "Religion and World Order." The final section is devoted to "An Autobiographical Sketch," by Leo Pfeffer, and a "Bibliography of the Writings of Leo Pfeffer to 1984," contributed by his wife, Freda Pfeffer, his companion and collaborator for almost fifty years.

Finally, a word of profound appreciation must be expressed to the Baylor University Press for support given to the publication of this volume. As editor, I am indebted to Wanda Gilbert for her clerical skills. James Obielodan assisted in the preparation of the Index. Debra Z. Masten deserves special mention for her able and conscientious editorial assistance. Appreciation is also acknowledged to all others who in a variety of ways contributed to the final plans and preparation of this volume.

James E. Wood, Jr.

PART 1

NO ESTABLISHMENT OF RELIGION AND THE FREE EXERCISE OF RELIGION

Roger Williams and the Separation of Church and State

DAVID LITTLE

INTRODUCTION

A volume of essays honoring Leo Pfeffer, particularly since it is published just now, merits attention to Roger Williams and his views on the separation of church and state. There are several reasons for this. First, though he never treats Williams at length, Pfeffer frequently pays his respects in the course of emphasizing that "ideological influences" are every bit as important as "practical considerations" in explaining the origins of the two religion clauses of the First Amendment.[1] In *Church, State, and Freedom*, Pfeffer acknowledges the importance of Williams in no uncertain terms:

In Rhode Island, . . . religious liberty was not a practice forced on an unwilling leader by the accident of history, but an ideal founded on the concept which a century and a half later was to achieve its fullest expression in the American Constitution—the concept of the mutual independence of religion and government.

Williams' pamphlet, *The Bloudy Tenent* . . . , is an epochal milestone in the history of religious freedom and the separation of church and state. Along with Jefferson's *Act for Establishing Religious Freedom* and Madison's *Memorial and Remonstrance*, and the First Amendment, it stands as one of the cornerstones of the American experiment.

Seventeenth century America was not ready for Roger Williams. In view of the still current attack on the principle of separation of church and state, . . . we are perhaps even now not ready for those ideas. Nevertheless, they do represent the great contribution of American democracy to civilization.[2]

First, in this author's view, Pfeffer understands, better even than some eminent historians and religious thinkers, Williams's significance in the American struggle for religious liberty. Second, Williams died sometime in early 1683, and, therefore, the three-hundredth anniversary of his death has only recently passed. Finally, in what Pfeffer might well regard as but one more manifestation of "the still current attack on the principle of separation of church and state," Jerry Falwell and others on the New Right have for several years been seeking legislation of what they call "Bible-based laws" in matters of sexuality, the status of women, the role of the family, and other personal morality issues.[3] Falwell, for one, readily in-

vokes Roger Williams in support of his position, apparently
unaware of the deep discrepancies between Williams's thought
and his own.[4] There is, therefore, a special need to set the
record straight.

To reconsider Williams on the subject of church and state
yet one more time, however, should make one anxious and
unsure. So many people have notoriously failed to interpret
Williams correctly that one ought to approach his life and
writings acutely aware of the difficulties ahead. Without
doubt, Williams is an elusive figure. Much of what he had to
say is, to post-Enlightenment ears, quite alien. In the words of
one author, "Students have been known to open one of Roger
Williams' pamphlets, under the impression that they were
going to meet a familiar figure, only to shut it hastily again
with the feeling that there must have been some mistake."[5]

Nor has Williams proved an easy subject for historians,
even for so accomplished an historian as Edmund S. Morgan.
By his own admission, Morgan needed two attempts. In *The
Puritan Dilemma: The Story of John Winthrop*, Morgan depicted
Williams as something of a crackpot—a person who advocated
"an irresponsible pursuit of individual holiness" whom "the
colony was better off without."[6] Some years later, however,
when Morgan undertook to investigate the complete works of
Williams, he had second thoughts. "As I read and reread, I
gradually recognized that I had formerly misunderstood and
misjudged the man, and I thought many other historians had
done so too."[7] Consequently, Morgan published his second
(and more successful) attempt to capture Williams, *Roger Williams: The Church and the State*.

Whatever there is about his writings and his life that attracts
attention may also obscure the wider and stranger context of
concerns and circumstances in which Williams wrote and
lived. Williams was, above all, a creature of seventeenth-
century Puritan Christianity; he was unmistakably a Calvinist
in doctrine and outlook. His radical views on church-state
questions set him at odds, assuredly, with many of his conservative Puritan brethren, like John Cotton and John Winthrop
of the Massachusetts Bay Colony. It is, nevertheless, thoroughly appropriate, if somewhat unexpected, that the statue of
Roger Williams adorns the International Monument of the
Reformation in Geneva as the representative of the Calvinist
movement in early America.

To characterize Williams as a "Christian freethinker, more

concerned with social commonwealths than with theological dogmas" (as Vernon Parrington did in his well-known work, *Main Currents of American Thought*) is plainly mistaken. So is Parrington's idea that Williams was a "transcendental mystic," and, as such, a forerunner of Ralph Waldo Emerson and the Concord school, of William Ellery Channing and the Unitarians, and of Thomas Paine and the French Romantics.[8] Williams was neither mystic nor pantheist, deist nor romantic, skeptic nor Unitarian. True to his Calvinist heritage, he was committed to the authority of Scripture and the transcendence and sovereignty of God.[9] He was passionately concerned with theological dogmas to the end of his life, as he demonstrated in his heated and exhausting public disputes with the Quakers in 1672, just ten years before his death.

Williams was indeed a strong activist and man of affairs.[10] His tireless, sympathetic, and sometimes fruitful dealings with the Indians,[11] his career as trader and merchant, his efforts at organizing and administering the Rhode Island colony against fearful odds,[12] his skillful lobbying of Parliament in the 1650s in pursuit of a charter, and his leadership of the local militia during King Philip's War all attest to that. Unobservant interpreters, however, have misjudged the source and background of his activism. Williams was not a political ideologue or "irrepressible democrat" of an essentially secular stripe,[13] nor was he primarily a political thinker devoted, above all, to constructing a democratic commonwealth in Rhode Island.[14] He was, rather, a practical theologian on the Genevan and Puritan model, an "inner-wordly ascetic," as the German sociologist, Max Weber, would have described him.

His attack on the paid clergy in the pamphlet, *A Hireling Ministry, None of Christ's*, and his denunciation of the universities of his time as encouraging a "Monkish and idle course of life," where, as he said, "to wet a finger in any pains or labor, . . . is a disgraceful and unworthy act,"[15] were simply illustrations of his radical, this-worldly Calvinism. This kind of activism was undergirded, as it was for all Calvinists, by a strong and abiding belief in predestination, the depravity of human beings, and their need for, as well as the availability of, God's grace and sanctification. Whatever observations Williams made on social and political subjects were all part of this unmistakable web of belief.

If one needs to be anxious about the risks of misinterpreting Williams by forgetting what he stood for, however, one also

has a right to be expectant in his presence. Properly understood, his thought has enormous relevance for this society,
and for present attempts to work out the right relations
between church and state.

Williams's thought has had relevance, from the beginning,
because it was so much a part of the intellectual sources of the
American Revolution out of which emerged the constitutional
definition of church-state relations in this country. This point
must be stressed against the conclusions of distinguished and
normally trustworthy interpreters like Perry Miller and Mark
DeWolfe Howe. Eager to correct the distorted image of Williams portrayed by Parrington and others, Miller and Howe
succumbed to the temptation to overcompensate in the opposite direction. Williams' thought may be remote, but it is not
archane. It may be religiously oriented, but it is not, therefore, insensitive to political and social affairs. Miller claims
that Williams "actually exerted little or no influence on institutional developments in America," and that "only after the
conception of liberty for all denominations had triumphed on
wholly other grounds did Americans look back on Williams
and invest him with his ill-fitting halo."[16]

In this Miller is fully supported by the Catholic social
thinker, John Courtney Murray. From Miller's decree, Murray draws the conclusion that Williams "is to be ruled out as
the original theologian of the First Amendment. In fact, one
must rule out the whole idea that any theologian stood at the
origin of this piece of legislation."[17] These views are, however, in various ways seriously misleading.

There are at least two lines of Williams's influence upon
"institutional developments in America" that may be called
"the Lockean connection" and "the Baptist connection."
These two lines of influence on thoughts about religious liberty are certainly distinct analytically between, as it is conventional to say, the Enlightenment influence of Locke and the
Pietist influence of the Baptists and Isaac Backus. Still, it is
dangerous to overlook historical complexities when it comes
to affixing these labels. William G. McLoughlin is in danger
of making too simple a distinction when he writes: "[Backus']
was a pietistic version of the doctrine of separation, more like
that of Roger Williams, with whom he deserves to be compared, than that of Jefferson and Madison."[18]

First, Williams, as this essay shall demonstrate, has a deep
affinity with the so-called Enlightenment tradition as illus-

trated by Locke. Williams is not purely a Pietist. Second, Backus himself draws not only upon Williams but also upon Locke's views of religious liberty as well. That he does so is, of course, not surprising in the light of the affinities between Williams and Locke. Williams's influence in these matters must be seen in a much more complex way than currently seems fashionable among American historians.

THE LOCKEAN CONNECTION

While it is conventional these days to speak of Locke's thought as simply part of the "deep background" of the moving ideas of the American Revolution,[19] there are some manifestly direct links between Locke and Jefferson in respect to the development of Jefferson's influential ideas on religious liberty.[20]

The connection between Williams and Locke, in turn, is compelling, if somewhat more conjectural. There is no question that Locke's ideas on religious liberty were unoriginal.[21] Locke was simply restating many of the arguments concerning the subject that had been developed by Puritan Independents like John Milton, John Owen, John Goodwin, Henry Stubbe, and others. As Winthrop S. Hudson has demonstrated, however, the similarities between the thought of Williams and Locke on religious liberty are so evident that, quite possibly, Locke did little more than translate Williams' often tedious and rambling arguments into succinct and lucid prose. "Beyond a differing emphasis and concern, it is impossible to discover a single difference between the argument set forth by Williams and that later advanced by Locke."[22] Whether Locke consciously copied Williams's ideas or not, the close parallels in thought are of the greatest importance.[23]

Hudson has identified three general principles that Williams and Locke held in common—fallibility, segregation, and consent. According to the first, human beings are, as the result of their fallen nature, prone to error and bias in spiritual and speculative matters. They ought, therefore, to be permitted as wide a diversity of opinion and belief as is consonant with protecting everyone's basic rights so as to be able to test all teachings and alleged revelations by "chewing, and rational weighing and consideration," as Williams put it.[24] "It is the command of Christ Jesus to his scholars to try all things: and liberty of trying what a friend, yea, what an (esteemed) enemy presents hath ever (in point of Christianity)

proved one especial means of attaining to the truth of
Christ."[25] Or, as Williams says elsewhere, "Without search
and trial no man attains this faith and right persuasion."[26] It is
only by this means that *enlightened consent*—the essence of religion and conscience—is possible. There is, thus, a direct connection between Williams's view of human fallibility and his
doctrine of liberty of conscience and religion. A civil order
with a uniform and established religion necessarily prevents
free investigation and testing.

Locke frequently echoes this theme: "For the truth certainly would do well enough if she were once left to shift for
herself,"[27] which means left free to take on all comers. Truth
for Locke is strengthened by being allowed to confront and
correct itself in face of error. Locke agrees with Williams that
human beings and, perhaps especially, religious enthusiasts
are liable to error.

St. Paul himself believed he did well, and that he had a call to it, when he
persecuted Christians, whom he confidently thought in the wrong; but yet
it was he, and not they, who were mistaken. Good men are men still liable
to mistakes, and are sometimes warmly engaged in errors, which they take
for divine truths, shining in their minds with the clearest light. . . . God
when he makes the prophet does not unmake the man. He leaves all his
faculties in their natural state, to enable him to judge of his inspirations,
whether they be of divine original or no.[28]

It is no doubt true that Locke relied upon "Reason," as
"our last judge and guide in everything,"[29] to discriminate
truth from error more readily and exclusively than did Williams. As the comment about "chewing and rational weighing" indicates, however, Williams was by no means indifferent to the power of rational scrutiny in these matters. Natural
reason was not thoroughly crippled for Williams. As Perry
Miller remarks, with only some overstatement, "Williams was
always convinced that rational argument could settle everything. . . ."[30]

Moreover, for all Locke's emphasis upon reason as the last
judge and guide, the burden of his position "is not the claims
[he] advances on behalf of human reason, but rather, [his]
assertion of the meagreness of human knowledge. . . . Man
exists in a state of 'incurable ignorance' facing a universe of
'impenetrable obscurity.' "[31]

To some extent, however, the principles of segregation and
consent play an even more prominent role in the thought of
Williams and Locke. According to the principle of segregation, there is a sharp distinction to be drawn between the

"inward" world of belief, conviction, and commitment (the world of mind, spirit, and conscience) and the "outward" world of civil and social regulation (the world of external coercion and control). According to the principle of consent, the outward world ought to be arranged so as to maximize overall opportunity for the inward world to be governed, ultimately, by enlightened and free consent.

For Williams and Locke, religious persecution is the result of a conceptual or category confusion. To their way of thinking, it was perfectly appropriate for the civil authority to employ weapons of iron, wood, and steel to control civil disorders—threats to life and limb. To try to apply them, however, to inward matters is utterly wrongheaded. In Williams's words:

To take a stronghold, men bring cannons, . . . muskets, swords, pikes; and these to this end are weapons effectual and proportionable.

On the other side, to batter down idolatry, false worship, heresy, schism, blindness, hardness, out of the soul and spirit, it is vain, improper, and unsuitable to bring those weapons which are used by persecutors—stocks, whips, prisons, swords, gibbets, stakes. . . —but against these spiritual strongholds in the souls of men, spiritual artillery and weapons are proper. . . .

I observe that as civil weapons are improper in this business, and *never able to effect aught in the soul,* so . . . they are unnecessary. . . .[32]

This observation is, to Williams's mind, a compelling ground for believing in freedom of conscience: "Only let it be their souls choice, and no inforcing sword, but what is spiritual in their spiritual causes. . . . I *plead for* Impartiality *and equal* freedom, peace, *and* safety *to other* Consciences *and* assemblies, *unto which the people may as freely goe, and this according to each* conscience *be* (*not transgressing against* Civilities) *whether of* Jew *or* Gentile."[33]

Locke espoused the same view:

The care of souls cannot belong to the civil magistrate because his power consists only in outward force; but true and saving religion consists in the inward persuasion of the mind, without which nothing can be acceptable to God. And such is the nature of the understanding that it cannot be compelled to the belief of anything by outward force. . . . All the life and power of true religion consists in the inward and full persuasion of the mind; and faith is not faith without believing.[34]

Anyone may employ as many exhortations and arguments as he pleases, toward the promoting of another man's salvation. But all force and compulsion are not to be forborne. Nothing is to be done imperiously. Nobody is obliged in that manner to yield obedience unto the admonitions or injunctions of another, further than he himself is persuaded. Everyman in that has the supreme and absolute authority of judging for himself.[35]

As with Williams, so for Locke "liberty of conscience is everyman's natural right, equally belonging to dissenters as to themselves."[36] In addition, they would both concur that freedom of conscience is an *inalienable* natural right. As Locke puts it: "Nor can [individual consent in religious affairs] be vested in the magistrate by the consent of the people, because no man can so far abandon the care of his own salvation as blindly to leave to the choice of any other, whether prince or subject, to prescribe to him what faith or worship he shall embrace."[37]

With all the similarity between Williams and Locke regarding freedom of conscience, there is, nevertheless, one important discrepancy. Williams was, in fact, more liberal than Locke in respect to the extent of toleration each allowed.[38] For example, Locke wrote: "Those are not at all to be tolerated who deny the being of a God. Promises, covenants, and oaths, which are the bonds of human society, can have no hold upon an atheist. The taking away of God, though but even in thought, dissolves all. . . . "[39]

There are, however, no such restrictions in Williams's writings. Indeed, he accepted unflinchingly the possibility that religious liberty could lead, among other things, to a loss of religious belief:

If the civil state does not enforce religion, what will become of the ministry of the Gospel and the souls of men? For if each man's conscience be at liberty to come to church or not, to pay the minister or not, the prophane and loose will neither pay nor pray, but turn *atheistical and irreligious.* . . . Although the loose will be more loose (yet) possibly being at more liberty they may be put upon consideration and choice of ways of life and peace yet[;] *however it is infinitely better, that the prophane and loose be unmasked, than to be muffled up under the veil and hood of traditional hypocrisy, which turns and dulls the very edge of all conscience either toward God or man.*[40]

The central issue between Locke and Williams here concerns a conflict over whether no religion or coerced religion has the more deleterious effect upon moral capability. For Williams, the greatest danger is hypocrisy, "which turns and dulls the very edge of all conscience either toward God or man," a consequence, of course, of trying to compel belief. For Locke, belief in God is so indispensable for all knowledge, moral and intellectual, that atheism must undermine all moral and intellectual order.[41] Whether this was the only line of argument available to Locke is very much an open question.[42] Nevertheless, Locke does on several occasions incline to Williams's position that religious persecution, by trying to compel belief, serves to make "men worse hypocrites than they were before, by a new act of hypocrisy; and to corrupt the manners of the rest of the church, by their converse with these,"[43] though Locke never worries about the demoralizing effects of punishing atheists for their beliefs.

THE BAPTIST CONNECTION: ISAAC BACKUS

In regard to the second line of Williams's influence, it is necessary to consider the vital role of the Separate Baptists and, in particular, of their leader, Isaac Backus, in leading the fight against established religion in New England in the 1760s and 1770s, and in participating in the deliberations concerning church-state separation in the Continental Congress and the Constitutional Convention.[44] Bernard Bailyn, in his volume on the ideological origins of the American Revolution, exhibits "the mutual reenforcement that took place in the Revolution between the struggles for civil and religious liberty"[45] largely as the result of Backus and his Baptist brethren.

Now Backus more than once avowed his reverence for the ideas and example of Roger Williams.[46] In 1805, Backus wrote: "The liberty that . . . [Roger Williams] was for, civil and religious, is now enjoyed in thirteen of the seventeen of the United States of America. No tax for any religious minister is imposed by authority in any of the said thirteen states, and their power is much weakened in the other four."[47] In his pamphlet, *An Appeal to the Public for Religious Liberty* (1773)—a pamphlet that was enormously influential in the movement for the separation of church and state[48]—Backus simply rephrased many of the arguments in Williams's writings, especially *The Bloudy Tenent* (1644) and *The Bloudy Tenent Made Yet More Bloudy* (1652). Backus's basic proposition was that "God has appointed two different kinds of government in the world which are different in their nature and ought never to be confounded together; one of which is called civil, and the other ecclesiastical government."[49] Unfortunately, the two governments had, Backus lamented, been confounded, among others, by the Emperor Constantine, by the papacy, and by the New England Puritans, which was in all cases to the severe detriment of *both* church and state.

Williams, of course, had defended the same view in much the same way. For him, as for Backus, the key distinction was between freedom and coercion. "The church," wrote Williams, "can least of all be forced: for as it is a spiritual society, and not subject to any civil judicature, . . . so is the combination of it voluntary, and endures no civil violence."[50] The state has no business compelling people against their wills to espouse religious beliefs, engage in religious practices, or contribute financial support to religious institutions. Indeed, Williams would have agreed with Backus that direct compulsory support for religious institutions amounts to nothing more than taxation without representation.

The foundation for this understanding in both Williams and Backus was the example of the Christian church. On their reading, the early church was first and foremost a voluntary community decisively set apart from state direction and political affiliation, as well as from family and ethnic identity. At the start, one became a Christian, not because of ethnic or national connection, but solely by virtue of a personal, voluntary act, and Christians sustained their fellowship and supported its activities on that basis alone.

For Williams and Backus, then, the leading revolution in all human history was the event of sharply distinguishing and differentiating, both in theory and in practice, between spiritual and civil society and between "religion" and "secular life." They admitted that such a distinction was not drawn by the Israelites in the Old Testament. That example of "national religion," of an established church, however, was a temporary, provisional phase of God's providential plan. Since the coming of Christ and the laying down of the new covenant, the relevance of that earlier arrangement has passed. For Williams—and Backus agreed—Israel was a "None-such"[51] though, it is true, they each drew different conclusions with respect to encouraging what nowadays would be called "civil religion." Backus, the Pietist, was far more favorable to such a notion than was Williams.[52]

Modern interpreters of Williams (and no doubt of Backus, too!) have great difficulty grasping the connection between this central commitment to voluntarism in religion and the Calvinist belief in predestination, so dear to the hearts of both men.[53] Should not the idea of predestination dispose people to passive, dependent behavior and, therefore, work against any notion of free choice and self-direction?

The answer is to the contrary. The doctrine of predestination for both Williams and Backus was a way of affirming that God, and no other human authority, is finally sovereign over each person. When the state, and all other earthly rulers, are duly restricted, then the individual is free to act upon God's electing will immediately and directly. Williams did the orthodox Calvinists of his time one better. He argued that since, by the terms of the doctrine of predestination, God alone elects and directs his people, civil coercion in religious affairs serves only to confuse and distract. It dilutes the purity and ultimacy of God's word by giving people an extraneous reason for obedience.[54]

These convictions issue in an interesting and influential view of the liberty of conscience. Since the conscience is, as Williams defined it, "persuasion fixed in the mind and heart of man, which enforces him to judge . . . and to do so with respect to God, His worship, etc.,"[55] it constituted for Williams and Backus the seat of spiritual authority in each human being. Just because the conscience is something between the individual and God, it must be left free of interference by human authorities. Moreover, because the conscience binds supremely an individual's basic beliefs and commitments, and "enforces him to judge" in respect to them, it cannot be subject to civil and other forms of coercive influence. Conscientious convictions are not something a person has ready control over, nor are they something that are normally reconstituted under threat of punishment. For these reasons, one should be left free (up to a point, at least) to be "ruled by conscience"; one should be at liberty to honor *its* constraints.

"This conscience," Williams said, "is found in all mankind, more or less, in Jews, Turks, Papists, Protestants, pagans, etc."[56] The consciences of all these people should be tolerated and protected against civil interference. The "bloody tenent," according to Williams and Backus, is precisely the widespread failure of both religious bodies and governments to remember the due limits of civil coercion.

Civil coercion has its place, of course. It is there to insure civil order and peace by preventing individuals from inflicting harm or arbitrary injury upon one another. Without it the world would be, in Williams's description, "like the sea, wherein men, like fishes, would hunt and devour each other, and the greater devour the less."[57] The state is responsible for enforcing the second table of the Decalogue concerning basic social relations among human beings in the "moral and civil" sphere of life. The state is not, however, responsible for enforcing the first table regarding the relations between human beings and God. That is, of course, the religious sphere where conscience must have free reign.

Now on this scheme, the civil and moral sphere is governed by the "natural law," a moral standard that is understood to be commonly available to human beings regardless of their religious affiliation. "There is a moral virtue, a moral fidelity, ability, and honesty, which other men (beside Church-members) are, by good nature and education, by good laws and good examples, nourished and trained up in, that civil places need not be monopolized into the hands of Church-members (who are sometimes not fitted for them), and all others deprived of their natural and civil rights and liberties."[58] An analogous emphasis can be found in Backus.[59]

There are naturally points where the dictates of a religious conscience may conflict with the "natural and civil rights and liberties" that the natural law extends to all human beings. Williams contended that although "upon the very account of religion and conscience" Mexicans had sacrificed "yearly many thousands [of] infants to their bloody deities," that practice should be prohibited by civil government because to his mind it directly and grossly violates "civility" in the "bodies or goods of any."[60]

In regard to permitting conscientious objection to war on religious grounds, Williams was not as generous as the United States government. He believed there were natural requirements for defense of the state that imposed burdens upon all citizens. No able-bodied member of the society ought to be allowed to avoid those burdens, even for the sake of religious scruples, such as those the Quakers of Rhode Island had announced.[61] Whatever may be thought of Williams's judgment here, however, it is important to note that he argued his case against conscientious objection to war by appealing not to religious belief or scriptural warrant, but to natural justice or to simple fairness as he saw it. That is characteristic of this approach: Questions of civil policy must be argued and debated on the assumption that there is a shared, commonly available moral standard independent of particular religious belief.

This author is suggesting, then, that just as the symmetry between Williams's and Locke's views on the principles of fallibility, segregation, and consent indicates one important line of influence upon American church-state arrangements, so the clear similarities between Williams and Backus, regarding the separation of spiritual and civil government, liberty of conscience, Calvinistic conviction, and commitment to an independent, "secular" moral law, indicates a second line of influence. This author is further suggesting that just as these two lines of influence appear in important respects to issue conjointly from Williams, so they appear to converge again in their mutual impact—via Locke and the Separate Baptists—upon Jefferson and upon the deliberations concerning religious liberty that surrounded the formation of the constitutional provisions for freedom of religion.

This complex account of Williams's place in the background of eighteenth-century American thinking about church-state relations leads one to doubt the accuracy of Mark DeWolfe Howe's famous way of contrasting the attitudes of Roger Williams and Thomas Jefferson toward the wall of separation between church and state. Williams favored such a wall, writes Howe, "not because he was fearful that without such a barrier the arm of the church would extend its reach. It was, rather, the dread of worldly corruptions which might consume the churches if sturdy fences against the wilderness were not maintained." Jefferson, by comparison, favored the wall out of primary concern for the protection of civil and political liberties against the encroachment of the church.[62]

In fact, perhaps the severest "worldly corruption" that could, to Williams's mind, consume the church was precisely the length of the church's reach into civil affairs! A wall of separation was needed to protect the state from the church, every bit as much as the other way around. It is a mistake to believe that Jefferson was more alive to religious threats against civil and political rights than was Williams. Williams suffered personal deprivations at the hands of an overextended church far more severely than Jefferson ever did.

For Williams, religious groups are, if anything, more liable to pretension and self-importance just because they address the things of the spirit. The temptation of the church to mistake its own voice for the voice of God is keen.[63] Williams's solution, of course, is diversification: separate church and state and pluralize religious opportunities.

The primary deficiency in Howe's description, at least so far as Williams is concerned, is that Williams's position entails simultaneous respect for the integrity of both church and state. Neither will function as intended so long as one encroaches upon the proper activities of the other. It is not simply that civil authorities threaten to corrupt the spirit by regulating religious affairs, although they do. Equally as important, it is simply *"against civil justice* for the civil state or officers thereof to deal so partially in matters of God, as to permit to some the freedom of their consciences and worships, but to curb and suppress the consciences and souls of all others."[64] Against that violation of natural justice, the state needs the wall of separation to protect it, just as the wall is needed to protect, for its part, the purity of the church.

CONCLUSION

This author has endeavored to sort out and trace the lines of influence of Roger Williams on church-state thinking in the American Revolution, not simply in the interests of historical accuracy. This author has also wished to suggest by means of examining those lines of influence, that Williams's central ideas, however remote some of them may seem to be, continue to lie just below the surface of this nation's institutional commitments. It does some good, from time to time, to retrieve and reexamine those ideas. For example, Williams's belief in a shared moral standard independent of religious conviction, as the basis for civil society, and his special conception of the liberty of conscience should particularly be retrieved and reexamined.

The first notion clearly runs afoul of much New Right thinking. The idea that it is desirable to enact into law certain biblical prescriptions because they are believed to be God's word bears the marks of Williams's "bloody tenent." In a pluralistic society, the practical consequence of that idea is religious strife and persecution, since the state would explicitly favor one religious rationale over others.

The only satisfactory alternative is for the members of society to assume, as Roger Williams did, that there exists for all of them a common moral denominator based on certain shared notions of welfare and harm that do not require religious commitment in order to affirm. Religious beliefs may or may not be consonant with them. Citizens in a truly pluralistic society, however, are bound to believe that the foundations of the common moral standards *are not necessarily religious.* They are defensible and acceptable whether one adheres to a particular set of religious convictions or not.

Thus, if Williams is correct, questions of the legal rights of homosexuals, laws concerning censorship and public decency, the legal status of women, and so forth must all be argued, not on the basis of scriptural appeal or religious warrant, but in reference to these shared standards of welfare and harm. For example, whether or not "the production and distribution of any pictures of children under the age of 16 engaged in sex or lewd conduct" is a criminal act, as the Supreme Court recently upheld it to be, must not be decided on the basis of the Bible or the like, but decided with reference to a notion of harm that the Court assumes to underlie the law "civil and moral"—a notion of harm that obtains whatever one's religious convictions may be.[65]

The same is true for those who argue at present that "aggressive erotica," as it is called, has a strong influence upon violence against women and, therefore, ought to be extensively regulated. Proposals for censorship based upon claims of this sort at least "make sense" within the requirements of a pluralistic society, as perceived by Roger Williams. New Right proposals for censorship that are deduced from Scripture do not.

As to the liberty of conscience, Williams's ideas are relevant at two points. First, society continues to believe that it ought to honor a presumption, at least, in favor of an individual's right to follow the dictates of conscience because of the special sort of sovereignty and dominion that the conscience is assumed to have. Society is heavily influenced by Williams's Puritan view that, so to speak, conscience is not something one can altogether help. It constrains and coerces a person often beyond one's own immediate wishes and preferences. Conscience compels with the force of authority; however, it has in some deep sense the individual's final consent. It is not, therefore, like other compulsions that pathologically drive one against one's "better judgment." Sovereignty of that sort ought to be respected seriously.

Second, and much related to the first, society continues to believe with Williams that conscience has a special religious cast to it. Society is inclined, that is, to give exceptional legal consideration to appeals to conscience that either regard religious matters or that are based on religious or "religious-like" beliefs. When, in *United States* v. *Seeger*, the famous 1965 draft case, the Court extended conscientious-objector status to an avowedly nonreligious petitioner, it held, significantly: "The test might be stated in these words: A sincere and meaningful belief which occupies in the life of its possessor a place parallel to that filled by the God of those admittedly qualifying for the exemption comes within the statutory definition."[66]

However debatable were Williams's specific reservations regarding conscientious objection to war, the Court's pronouncement here seems fully in keeping with Williams's general teaching on conscience. Beliefs are conscientious and thus entitled to special respect, so long as they occupy the same place or carry the same weight for a person that religious convictions have for a believer. Remember that Williams defined the conscience as "a persuasion fixed in the mind and heart of man, which enforces him to judge . . . and to do so with respect to God, his worship, etc." Nothing in Williams's writings suggests that an atheist or nonbeliever could not be thought by him to have a conscience just because that person rejected belief in God, whatever Locke's views were. The only implicit stipulation is that such a person substitute a set of beliefs that are equally as grave, equally as sovereign over and binding upon that person as belief in God is for a religious believer. That is the force, this author supposes, of Williams's phrase "to judge . . . with respect to God."

Leo Pfeffer is right on two counts: Williams's basic notion of religious liberty was of profound significance in shaping the thinking during the American Revolution regarding church-state relations. Moreover, the power and relevance of Williams's ideas continue to be felt. It is time scholars began to understand how and why that is so.

NOTES

1. See, esp., Leo Pfeffer, "Freedom and/or Separation: The Constitutional Dilemma of the First Amendment," *Minnesota Law Review* 64 (1980):561, 564; idem, *Creeds in Competition: A Creative Force in American Culture* (New York: Harper & Bros., 1958), 44ff. Cf. idem, *God, Caesar and the Constitution* (Boston: Beacon Press, 1975), 163-64, for favorable mention of Williams regarding his opposition to compulsory worship attendance of any kind.
2. Pfeffer, *Church, State, and Freedom* (Boston: Beacon Press, 1967), 84, 86, 88. In idem, *The Liberties of an American* (Boston: Beacon Press, 1956), 32, Pfeffer leaves no doubt about his attitude concerning the importance of American achievements in respect to religious liberty: "The greatest single contribution made by America to contemporary civilization is the evolution and successful launching of the uniquely American experiment of religious freedom and the separation of church and state." Earlier, he argues that "religious liberty is the progenitor of most other civil liberties."
3. See, for example, Jerry Falwell, *Listen, America!* (Garden City: Doubleday, 1980), 201, 253, 259, 260.

4. For a fuller account of the differences between Falwell and Williams, see David Little, "Legislating Morality: The Role of Religion," in *Christianity and Politics*, ed. Carol Friedley Griffith (Washington, D.C.: Ethics and Public Policy Center, 1981), 39; cf. idem, "Theological Dimensions of Church-State Relations," in *Conceived in Conscience*, ed. Richard A. Rutyna and John W. Kuehl (Norfolk, Va.: Donning Co., 1983), 88.

5. Alan Simpson, "How Democratic Was Roger Williams?" *William and Mary Quarterly Review* 13 (January 1956), 53.

6. Edmund S. Morgan, *The Puritan Dilemma: The Story of John Winthrop* (Boston: Little, Brown & Co., 1958), 132-33.

7. Morgan, *Roger Williams: The Church and the State* (New York: Harcourt, Brace & World, 1976), foreword.

8. LeRoy Moore, "Roger Williams and the Historian," *Church History* 32 (December 1963), 442ff.

9. Perry Miller, *Roger Williams: His Contributions to the American Tradition* (New York: Atheneum, 1962), 28, 24lff.

10. Ola E. Winslow, *Master Roger Williams* (New York: MacMillan, 1957).

11. See, esp., Jack L. Davis, "Roger Williams Among the Narragansett Indians," *New England Quarterly* 43 (December 1970):593-604, for a generally perceptive account of Williams' remarkably respectful attitudes toward the Indians and dealings with them. Davis properly criticizes the judgment of Alden T. Vaughan, in *New England Frontier* (Boston: Little, Brown & Co., 1965), 119, that "Williams and the other Puritans differed very little in their attitude or their actions toward the natives of New England." In his guide to the language of the local Narragansett Indians, *A Key into the Language of America* (London, 1643), Williams repeatedly judges Indian civilization to be morally superior to English civilization, on both sides of the Atlantic. Such judgments were quite incomprehensible to most of Williams's compatriots! "If nature's sons both wild and tame, Humane and courteous be, How ill becomes it sons of God, To want humanity?" *Complete Writings of Roger Williams*, 7 vols. (New York: Russell & Russell, 1963), 1:39. Or, Williams goes on: "Boast not, proud English, of thy birth and blood, Thy brother Indian is by birth as good. Of one blood God made him and thee and all, As wise, as fair, as strong, as personal." Ibid., 1:81. Williams was particularly struck, in comparison with the English, by the Narragansetts' treatment of strangers and needy people: "It is a strange truth that a man shall generally find more free entertainment and refreshing among these barbarians than among thousands who call themselves Christians." Ibid., 1:46. "There are no beggars amongst them, no fatherless children unprovided for." Ibid., 1:58; cf. Davis, "Roger Williams Among," 596ff. Williams also concluded that "the Indian government was more democratic in operation than that of the Massachusetts colony." Idem, 599. Although, the Indian rulers are "absolute monarchs," they undertake no policy "that concerns all, either laws, or subsidies or wards, unto which the people are averse, and by gentle persuasion cannot be brought." *Complete Writings of Roger Williams*, 1:164.

Davis, however, misrepresents Williams as favoring "cultural relativism." Ibid., 600, 604. Williams's comparative cultural judgments as between the English and the Indians are clearly not "relativistic." They assume one general and universal moral standard according to which the Indians at many points are adjudged to be superior to the English!

12. For a highly instructive account of Williams's early struggles in Rhode Island to combine civil order with religious pluralism, see Theodore Dwight Bozeman, "Religious Liberty and the Problem of Order in Early Rhode Island," *New England Quarterly Review* 45 (March 1972): 44-64. Cf. Clinton Rossiter, "Roger Williams on the Anvil of Experience," *American Quarterly* 3 (January 1951):14. "The central fact about Williams . . . is that he not only thought, but acted. There was an unusually close tie-up in his mind and career between theory and practice."

13. Samuel H. Brockunier, *The Irrepressible Democrat: Roger Williams* (New York: Ronald Press, 1940).

14. James Ernst, *The Political Thought of Roger Williams* (Seattle: University of Washington Press, 1929); idem, *Roger Williams: New England Firebrand* (New York: MacMillan, 1932).

15. *Complete Writings of Roger Williams*, 7:170.

16. Miller, *Roger Williams*, 29. Miller does not, it is true, deny completely that Williams has a certain significance for American self-understanding; see 254ff. Still, these statements are in error and need to be corrected. Miller also needs correcting, as Morgan points out, for making the rather astounding claim that "the cast of [Williams's] mind was not social," but was "exclusively religious," as though religious thought were somehow necessarily asocial. See Morgan, *Roger Williams*, 86. "The cast of Williams' mind, Perry Miller has reminded us, was theological, rather than social or political. And theological it certainly was, if we take the statement to mean that Williams' every thought took its rise from religion. But in his writings, from which alone we can know his mind, Williams was more often concerned with ecclesiastical and political institutions than with theology." This author's view is that Mark DeWolfe Howe's brief, but widely cited, discussion of Williams in *The Garden and the Wilderness* (Chicago: University of Chicago Press, 1965) repeats essentially the same errors. Howe relies on Miller for his interpretation; see p. 6 n. 5. Howe's characterization of Williams is discussed (see text at note 62) below.

17. John Courtney Murray, *We Hold These Truths* (Garden City, N.Y.: Doubleday, 1964), 65.

18. William G. McLoughlin, *Isaac Backus and the American Pietistic Tradition* (Boston: Little, Brown & Co., 1967), xii. McLoughlin seems, to this author, simply to perpetuate this oversimplification by trading on Howe's characterization of Williams as a Pietist or evangelical, "Role of Religion in the Revolution," in *Essays on the American Revolution*, ed. Stephen G. Kurtz and James H. Hutson (New York: Norton, 1973), fn. 10, 208. In other respects, this is a very instructive essay.

19. See Bernard Bailyn, "Central Themes of the American Revolution," in *Essays on the American Revolution*, 7, 10. This emphasis is aimed, of course, against the overstatement of Locke's influence and the influence of "natural rights philosophy" upon American revolutionary thinking, as, for example, in Carl L. Becker, *The Declaration of Independence* (New York: Random House, 1942), 27. "Most Americans had absorbed Locke's works as a kind of political gospel." Bailyn's own definitive study, *Ideological Origins of the American Revolution* (Cambridge, Mass.: Harvard University Press, 1967), goes a long way toward modifying Becker's simplistic account. Still, in his study, Bailyn by no means disregards the direct influence of people like Locke on the ideas of the American revolutionaries: "In pamphlet after pamphlet the American writers cited Locke on natural rights and on the social and governmental contract," 27, cf. 30. For other evidence of Locke's direct impact on American thinking, especially *after* 1776, see Gordon S. Wood, *The Creation of the American Republic* (New York: Norton, 1969), 283ff.

20. See F. C. Leubke, "The Development of Thomas Jefferson's Religious Opinion, 1743-1800" (M.A. thesis, Claremont Graduate School, 1958). For a discussion of Jefferson's nearly total dependence upon Locke in his "Notes on Religion," which were prepared for use in legislative debates, see Luebke, "The Origins of Thomas Jefferson's Anti-Clericalism," *Church History* 32 (September 1963): 344-56. Also see LeRoy Moore, "Religious Liberty: Roger Williams and the Revolutionary Era," *Church History* 34 (March 1965): 67-68. Gary Wills, in *Inventing America* (New York: Vintage Books, 1979), 171, states: "The most vivid and traceable influence Locke had on Jefferson was in the area of religious tolerance (*Papers*, 1:544-51)." This admission is all the more important because Wills seeks otherwise to reduce Locke's influence on Jefferson (no doubt overzealously).

21. Roland H. Bainton, *Travail of Religious Liberty* (New York: Harper & Bros., 1951), 237.

22. Winthrop S. Hudson, "Locke: Heir of Puritan Political Theorists," in *Calvinism and Political Order*, ed. George L. Hunt (Philadelphia: Westminister Press, 1965), 117-18. This author has undertaken to supply references that illustrate a bit

more sharply the similarities between Williams and Locke in regard to the three principles suggested by Hudson. Cf. idem, "John Locke—Preparing the Way for the Revolution," *Journal of Presbyterian History* 42 (March 1964): 19-38.

23. Moore, "Religious Liberty: Roger Williams and the Revolutionary Era," 65ff.

24. *Complete Writings of Roger Williams*, 5:392.

25. Miller, *Roger Williams*, 170.

26. *Complete Writings of Roger Williams*, 3:13.

27. John Locke, *A Letter Concerning Toleration* (New York: Liberal Arts Press, 1955), 45.

28. John Locke, *An Essay Concerning Human Understanding* (New York: World Publishing, 1971), 432 (iv, xvii, 12).

29. Ibid.

30. Miller, *Roger Williams*, 243.

31. Richard Ashcraft, "Faith and Knowledge in Locke's Philosophy," in *John Locke: Problems and Perspectives*, ed. John Yolton (Cambridge, Mass.: Harvard University Press, 1969), 195. Cf. Locke, *An Essay Concerning Human Understanding*, 341, 343, 344; 287-88 (IV, III, 22, 25, 27: III, IV, 9, 11). Locke rather starkly develops and reemphasizes the "darkness of reason" in respect to religious and moral matters in *Reasonableness of Christianity*, ed. I.T. Ramsey (Stanford: University Press, 1958), 57-66. Both Williams and Locke appear to share a deeply ambivalent attitude toward the power of reason—a consequence, quite possibly, of their common Calvinist heritage.

32. Miller, *Roger Williams*, 131, 132; emphasis added.

33. *Complete Writings of Roger Williams*, 7:154-55.

34. Locke, *Letter Concerning Toleration*, 18.

35. Ibid., 46-47.

36. Ibid., 52.

37. Ibid., 18. It is most unfortunate that discussions of Locke's view of "inalienable rights," even the most recent, consistently overlook this reference to inalienability. Whatever one may "want" to do, Locke clearly holds that to try to surrender control over one's conscience would be "against nature" in the profoundest sense. This all needs much more exploration than it has received in the literature. For an example of this standard oversight, see A. John Simmons, "Inalienable Rights and Locke's 'Treatises,' " *Philosophy and Public Affairs* 12 (Summer 1983): 175-204.

38. Locke is also more restrictive than Williams in regard to tolerating Roman Catholics. "That church can have no right to be tolerated by the magistrate which is constituted upon such a bottom that all those who enter into it do thereby *ipso facto* deliver themselves up to the protection and service of another prince." Locke, *Letter Concerning Toleration*, 51. According to McLoughlin, Locke also had sympathy for a comprehensive national church, *Isaac Backus on Church, State, and Calvinism* (Cambridge, Mass.: Harvard University Press, 1968), 43, though it is difficult to see how such sympathy squares with Locke's definition of a church as "a voluntary society of men, joining themselves together of their own accord in order to the public worshipping of God in such manner as they judge acceptable to Him." *Letter Concerning Toleration*, 20. In any case, by contrast, Williams explicitly and repeatedly advocated the toleration of "papists," and he rejected the idea of a "national religion," as is seen. It is true that, from Williams's point of view, all religious groups, including Catholics, Anglicans, "Mohammedans," and so forth, would have to yield any claims to uniform, established control. If they would not, then Williams might have been closer to Locke than it first appears.

39. Locke, *Letter Concerning Toleration*, 52.

40. *Complete Writings of Roger Williams*, 7:181; emphasis added.

41. Ashcraft, "Faith and Knowledge in Locke's Philosophy," 205, 208ff.

42. More open, for example, than David Gauthier understands in "Why Ought One Obey God? Reflections on Hobbes and Locke," *Canadian Journal of Philosophy* (September 1977): 425-46. Contrary to Gauthier, who seems to feel Locke "had" to hold this view because he espoused a divine command theory of ethics, it is clear that

Locke's position is not reducible without remainder to such a theory. There is, therefore, considerable space for a "purely rational foundation of ethics," independent of
divine will. See W. von Leyden's "Introduction" to John Locke, *Essays on the Law of
Nature* (Oxford: University Press, 1954), 52; cf. 56-57, and see Essay VII, 199.
43.   Locke, "A Third Letter for Toleration," in *Works*, 10 vols. (London: Thomas
Tegg, 1823; Germany: Scientia Verlag Aalen, 1963); 6:379; cf. 147, 395.
44.   McLoughlin, *Isaac Backus and the American Pietistic Tradition*, 128ff.
45.   Bailyn, *Ideological Origins of the American Revolution*, 268ff.
46.   Backus' devotion to Williams developed and intensified over time. In his early
career, he paid no particular attention to Williams's thought but in the 1770s, Backus
"discovered" Williams (and Locke) and consciously employed Williams's ideas to
bolster his own case in favor of religious liberty, a case that itself grew stronger and
more elaborate as Backus matured. See McLoughlin, *Isaac Backus on Church, State
and Calvinism*, 17ff. Cf. Moore, "Roger Williams and the Historians," 445-46. Moore
indicates that Backus first turned to Williams in his *History of New England with Particular Reference to the Denomination of Churches called Baptists* (Boston: 1777-1796).
The first volume is largely a biography of Williams, and Backus undertook there to
correct many of the prevailing errors of interpretation surrounding Williams's name
by attending to information previously unknown or disregarded. Thereafter, Williams became of central significance for Backus, even though, as pointed out below,
they do diverge over the question of 'national' or 'civil' religion (see note 52, below).
47.   Cited in McLoughlin, *Isaac Backus and the American Pietistic Tradition*, 209.
48.   Ibid., 123ff.
49.   Ibid.
50.   *Complete Writings of Roger Williams*, 4:74.
51.   Ibid., 29; McLoughlin, *Isaac Backus and the American Pietistic Tradition*, 74.
Backus' use of Scripture is, in important respects, very close to Williams, particularly
in regard to the so-called "typological" interpretation. According to this method,
"type-anti-type" contrasts are oppositional. If Israel (established religion of the Old
Testament) is the "type," then "New Israel" (the sectarian religion of the New Testament) is the "anti-type." For one example of Williams's use of this method, see
Complete Writings of Roger Williams, 4:29. Whether Backus depended directly upon
Williams for this is not known, but the similarity between them is striking. Miller in
Roger Williams makes typology the key to Williams' thought, "so much so that Wil-
liams is almost represented as a prophet who owed his insights to a daring principle
of literary criticism." Simpson, "How Democratic Was Roger Williams?" fn. 10, 58.
Miller, however, clearly overdoes it. Typology, a standard device of the period, was
simply for Williams "a handy means to an end," as Simpson rightly says. For an
article illustrating the commonness of the method at that time, see Richard Reinitz,
"The Typological Argument for Religious Toleration: The Separatist Tradition and
Roger Williams," *Early American Literature* 5 (Spring 1970): 74-110.
52.   See McLoughlin, *Isaac Backus and the American Pietistic Tradition*, 233, and
McLoughlin, *Backus on Church, State, and Calvinism*, 51ff. for references to Backus'
strong support, along side his commitment to religious liberty, for "the establishment
of a Protestant Christian nation." McLoughlin, "Role of Religion in the Revolution," 208. This support included laws against blasphemy, theater-going, blue laws
and Sabbatarian restrictions, among other things. *Isaac Backus and the American Pietistic Tradition*, 212.
   In contrast, Williams' views on the subject do not leave much room for doubt. "I
am unquestionably satisfied, that there was never any national religion good in this
world but one, and since the desolation of that nation, there was never, there shall be
never any national religion good again." *Complete Writings of Roger Williams*, 4:442.
Moreover, in a most remarkable passage, Williams urged toleration for blasphemers
and apostates on grounds that "even the natural conscience and reason of all men put
a difference" between the crimes of murder, treason, and adultery, "for which although the offender repent, yet he suffers punishment," and the crimes of heresy and
blasphemy, "which upon recantation and confession are frequently remitted." Ibid.,

443. Williams's point seems to be that punishment is only appropriately applied against completed offenses and not against offenses that might yet be avoided.

53. For Backus's view on the subject, see McLoughlin, *Isaac Backus and the American Pietistic Tradition*, 172-73. For mention of Williams's view, see Miller, *Roger Williams*, 28.

54. See *Complete Writings of Roger Williams*, 3:258-59.

55. Ibid., 4:508.

56. Ibid.

57. Ibid., 3:398. In his essay, "How Democratic Was Roger Williams?" Simpson performs an undoubted service of deflating the romantic idea that Williams was, at bottom, an "irrepressible democrat," and, as such, primarily a liberal political theorist. Simpson is right: "[Williams] never wrote a pamphlet in his life to explain the principles of civil government." Whatever remarks regarding government as exist in his writings are not his central concern. Nor does Williams give evidence of favoring absolutely a democratic regime. As is typical of much Williams scholarship, Simpson overreacts in the opposite direction. While there is no theory or doctrine of natural rights in Williams, he does mention the idea often enough in connection with religious liberty and civil organization—often enough to permit the conclusion that the idea was of great moral and political significance to him. That Williams intended to apply the idea of natural rights, including the notion of "equal freedom" (in his words), to political life can fairly be inferred from his *practice* in Rhode Island. For example, he supported constitutional provisions for religious equality and freedom, legal equality and freedom (in the Code of 1647), equality in land distribution (see R.E.E. Harkness, "Principles Established in Rhode Island, *Church History* 5 [September 1936]: 225-26), and equality in government, "which spurred his relentless campaign against the pattern of feudalism that William Coddington insisted on transplanting to Newport." (See Rossiter, "Roger Williams on the Anvil of Experience," 20.) Cf. Moore, "Religious Liberty: Roger Williams and the Revolutionary Era," 62.

58. *Complete Writings of Roger Williams*, 4:365.

59. See McLoughlin, *Isaac Backus and the American Pietistic Tradition*, 143.

60. *Complete Writings of Roger Williams*, 4:243.

61. Miller, *Roger Williams*, 224-26; cf. VI, 6:278-79.

62. Howe, *Garden and the Wilderness*, 6.

63. Miller, *Roger Williams*, 242-43.

64. *Complete Writings of Roger Williams*, 4:251; emphasis added.

65. *Washington Post*, 3 July 1982, A1,9.

66. Lillian Schlissel, ed., *Conscience in America* (New York: E.P. Dutton, 1968), 265-66.

The Emergence of Religious Freedom in the Early Republic

EDWIN SCOTT GAUSTAD

All the force of history and tradition pressed upon a new nation to recognize its own national church, if not in 1776, then surely in 1787. Church-state alliance had been the pattern in the Western world for over fourteen hundred years, in England (even without the Vatican) for over three hundred years, and in such colonies as Virginia and Massachusetts for a century or more. The precedent was powerful. So also were the familiar arguments for social stability, political expediency ("no bishop, no king"), and moral certainty. Powerful at any time or place, those precedents and arguments had special force in a land where a culture was yet to be formed and in a nation whose staying power was yet to be demonstrated.

Countervailing pressures, however, also made themselves felt. Pietists who had fled from church establishment in England or on the Continent had no wish to fall again under the heavy hand of a state that, sooner or later, demanded conformity, orthodoxy, and total loyalty both in war and peace. Deists, in tune with Enlightenment refrains first heard abroad, concluded that institutional religion of any kind had repeatedly stunted or shackled the human mind and that religion's hierarchies had regularly preferred profit and power to devotion and sacrifice. Such rationalists were therefore determined never to do anything that would elevate or enhance the institutions of religion. One could, of course, find large numbers of church leaders who strongly favored a national church, with the single proviso that the church in question be their own. Congregationalists, however, would never tolerate a national Anglican Church, nor would Anglicans tolerate a national Congregational Church. In eighteenth-century America, no other candidates for the honor even came close. Besides that standoff, there were also, in the words of a contemporary, those "nothingarians" who were either totally indifferent or actively hostile to religion of any kind in any form.

Because everyone knows that the countervailing forces somehow emerged victorious, it is easy to see this outcome as the

only one possible—even easier to move lightly from a vague
and undifferentiated cause to a precise effect. Causation has
enough problems, as David Hume has written, without com-
pounding the leaps of logic by skipping all too lightly over the
surface of early American history. By what means did Americans convince themselves to stride into religious freedom—
into, that is, the unknown and, therefore, fearful modern
world? What small and hesitating steps preceded the giant and
better known ones? What persuasive examples could be
pointed to? How could history and tradition be enlisted on the
side of those favoring disestablishment? What a priori arguments, ingenuous or sound, could make the case for this special feature of modernity? Taking 1776 as the starting point,
this essay examines those actors, those actions, and those
locales that enable one to observe more closely the gradual
and often painful commitment of America to religious freedom.

In 1776, Virginia was unarguably a critical state from virtually any point of view. With the largest population of all the
colonies at this time, with the only college south of Philadelphia and with a clear chronological priority, Virginia spoke
with a voice that commanded attention. Virginia also possessed the strongest establishment of Anglicanism to be found
anywhere in North America. With respect to religious freedom, then, what Virginia did would reverberate not only
throughout the South but up and down the entire Atlantic
seaboard.

What was Virginia's religious "profile" in 1776? Since
1619, the Church of England had not only enjoyed the official
favor of Virginia's own colonial government, but had in addition received steady support, both public and private, from the
mother country. Beyond such external buttressing, this
church had now been a part of colonial Virginia for over a
century and one-half; much of that time it had functioned
without serious or sustained competition. Now, in 1776, there
was competition from Presbyterians, Baptists, and proto-
Methodists, but all these were relative newcomers and many
lived in the rural or mountainous West, well removed from
the seat of power in Williamsburg. It is not surprising, therefore, that the Church of England, with over ninety parishes
and about one hundred clergymen, would dominate Virginia
politically and socially, no less than ecclesiastically. The American Revolution, however, severely shook this entrenched

church, with two-thirds of the clergy departing and one-third of the parishes becoming "extinct or forsaken."[1] Presbyterians, Baptists, and Methodists, however, continued to experience a sharply rising growth rate from the time of the Revolution to the end of the century.[2]

Anglicanism throughout the rebellious colonies was, of course, thrown on the defensive by being so closely identified with the nation against whom a desperate and prolonged war was being waged. In Virginia itself, where the Church of England's membership was predominantly patriotic, the stance of the Church had nonetheless always been privileged and protected; sometimes it had been intolerant and persecutorial. The Church that had made many enemies suddenly found itself unguarded and deeply suspect. On that ground alone, forces favoring its disestablishment could meet and march forward together. There was, however, higher ground as well. A principled search for religious freedom sought more than mere displacement of the current favorite with another denomination or sect. In 1776, Presbyterians of Hanover, for example, petitioned the Virginia legislature for freedom "from all the incumbrances which a spirit of Domination, prejudice, or bigotry hath interwoven with most other political systems." Four years later, the Baptists of Spottsylvania expressed similar sentiments: "We hope to enjoy equal Religious as well as civil Liberty, while we demean our Selves as good Citizens and peaceable Subjects of this Commonwealth."[3] Finally, Anglicanism in Virginia also found itself besieged by those whose chief concern was not religion but politics—the health and general welfare of the civil estate. In the view of these powerful few, steps must be taken to keep the state from being trampled, bound, or blinded by the Church—any church. Exponents of this perspective exercised an influence out of all proportion to their numbers, but men such as Thomas Jefferson and James Madison were not carried about on the tides of public opinion. Rather, they shaped that opinion and thereby made history.

Both the Presbyterian and the Baptist petitioners, noted above, included in their petitions a laudatory comment about an action already taken in May of 1776 by Virginia's delegates to their state convention. The Presbyterians had reinforced their call for religious freedom by adding: "This we are the more strongly encouraged to expect, by the *Declaration of Rights*, so universally applauded for that dignity, firmness, and

precision with which it delineates, and asserts the privileges of
society, and the prerogatives of human nature. . . ." The Baptists, in arguing specifically against a law that granted to
Anglican ministers alone the right to perform marriages,
asked for a new law that would sanction marriages that were
"solemnized by Dissenting Ministers . . . haveing [*sic*] great
confidence in the present Honourable Assembly's principals
for equal Liberty. . . ."[4] What had happened in May 1776?
In the midst of revolutionary activity and even before a Declaration of Independence had been adopted in Philadelphia,
Virginia delegates had adopted a Declaration of Rights written mainly by George Mason. The final (sixteenth) article, as
amended on a motion by Madison, asserted that "all men are
equally entitled to the free exercise of religion."[5] Dissenters
all over the state helped make clear what they understood by
"free exercise" even as the newly elected Virginia Assembly
struggled in the autumn of that year to determine just what
that phrase did mean, especially in the context of a still-
established Church of England. Jefferson, back from his significant labors in Philadelphia, argued for what seemed to
him to be the obvious and logical demand of "equality" and
"free exercise"; namely, the placing of *all* religious bodies on
precisely the same legal footing vis-à-vis the state. The state
had no right to demand a specific religious obedience, partly
because in forming a government one should surrender as little as possible. Also, however, since religion is totally a matter
between the individual and God, the state becomes an offensive intruder into what should be a purely private entente.
Crude efforts to demand conformity in both thought and practice, moreover, are—one must always remember—the work of
fallible men.[6] Civil rights are the only rights with which civil
government is legitimately concerned; religious rights are
among those inalienable rights never to be delivered into the
hands of another.

In his own notes for the crucial legislative debate on this
issue, Jefferson observed that the Established Church in Virginia was too strong "for any 1 sect, bt. too weak agt. all."[7]
The overwhelming probability, however, is that even the united opposition of all the groups against Anglicanism would not
have prevailed without the critical and timely efforts of both
Jefferson and Madison. Beginning in 1776, and never resting
until victory was theirs a decade later, these two men wrote,
debated, lobbied, and maneuvered for a full freedom in reli-

gion that would enable them to hold up this new state as a model of enlightened and emancipated government.

During that busy decade, the Anglican Church and its many influential supporters (e.g., Edmund Pendleton and Robert Carter Nicholas) resisted each removal of privilege and favor and protested each intrusion of "an over pious or misguided enthusiasm."[8] The Church's allies railed against the dangerous heresy that civil society could long survive without the sober, orderly ministrations of that society's official institution of religion. The more they pleaded, however, the more the opposition seemed to grow. All around them alliances of convenience or conviction arose and gathered strength. How could they break this united if somewhat accidental combination of forces arrayed against Virginia's true church? Perhaps a sensible strategy would be to broaden the notion of "establishment" to include the Christian religion in general. Such a move would never appease the deists, of course, but possibly the noisy dissenters could be persuaded to soften their harsh rhetoric and think of the common good: social order, civic virtue, pious education, and Christian morals. Between 1776 and 1786, the chief legislative threat to freedom of religion was the repeated effort to establish Christianity as the official religion of the state of Virginia.

Patrick Henry, Richard Henry Lee, John Marshall, and others favored a "general assessment bill" that would tax all the citizens on behalf of religion and virtue. More specifically, the bill provided that "the Christian Religion shall in all times coming be deemed and held to be the established Religion of this Commonwealth; and all Denominations of Christians demeaning themselves peaceably and faithfully, shall enjoy equal privileges, civil and Religious."[9] It then became necessary, of course, to give legislative precision to the phrase, "Christian religion," as well as to assert the necessity of public worship and to affirm "that the Holy Scriptures . . . are of divine inspiration, and are the only rule of Faith." The proposed legislation even entered into the details of the minister's duties and decorum, his necessity to be diligent in prayer, and his obligation to see that he along with his family present themselves as "wholesome examples and patterns to the flock of Christ."[10] State coercion in religion—a coercion to be enforced by fallible men—would in no way be moderated by this bill but would only be generalized to include a somewhat broader segment of the population than that of Anglicans

alone. In general, the dissenters were no more charmed by a
state-operated and state-defined "general assessment" than
they had been by a state-supported and state-manipulated single church. For as the Presbyterians noted in 1777, the power
to tax, which is also the power to control, opens the way for
Virginia to "revive the old Establishment in its former extent;
or ordain a new one for any Sect they may think proper."[11]
In the ensuing years, Presbyterians did not always hold steady
on this point, their vacillation both alarming and angering
Madison.

On the legislative floor, the burden of battle by 1785 fell
upon the shoulders of the thirty-four-year-old James Madison.
Jefferson, in many respects even more ready for battle, was
removed from the scene by virtue of his duties as minister to
France. Madison, however, who would soon be deeply involved in writing and defending a new national constitution,
proved to be no timid warrior. He conceded that religion may
be necessary for the state, but was certain that the state was
not necessary for religion. (Jefferson in earlier debates had
even quoted the biblical assurance that the gates of hell would
never prevail against the Kingdom of God.) State establishment of religion, moreover, never turned out to be the friend
of religion, but sooner or later only its seducer and corrupter.
While other states in the new union had already embraced
religious freedom, would Virginia take a step backward into a
pre-Enlightenment, pre-Reformation world? Madison's words
were matched by deeds, such as helping to "promote" Patrick
Henry to the office of governor, a position of little power at
this time and a position that removed the fiery orator from his
legislative role as chief sponsor of "general assessment."
Richard Henry Lee, moreover, was off with the Continental
Congress. While many proassessment voices remained in the
legislature to be heard, none could match Madison in careful
reasoning and persistent force.

Those virtues were evident in purest form in Madison's
Memorial and Remonstrance (first presented anonymously), a
now classic writing that was designed specifically to defeat the
assessment bill. As the bill through compromise and constant
revision appeared to some more innocuous, even more appealing, Madison moved with dispatch and force.[12] Anglicans
unthinkingly came to his aid. In an ill-timed move, the reor-
ganized Episcopal Church in Virginia applied to the state for
incorporation. In calmer times, such action would seem inof-

fensive and unobjectionable. These, however, were not calm times either politically or religiously. The Anglican/Episcopal action was widely perceived as but the first step to return the new Church to the same favored and protected status enjoyed by the old Church. A potential alliance between Presbyterians and Episcopalians quickly fell apart; a newly organized Methodist Church further weakened the Episcopal Church from within and competed with that Church from without; neither Baptists nor deists had ever been tempted by general assessment; and public sentiment broadly began to waver on the wisdom of the Patrick Henry proposal.

To give all those groups a standard around which they might rally, Madison, in fifteen carefully crafted paragraphs, explained (persuading as he explained) just what the issue was all about. Arguing from the dictates of reason, the state of nature, the examples of history, the essence of religion, the best interests of Virginia, and on any other ground that might seem suitable or just nearby, Madison made the case for a full freedom in religion. Religion, a private duty that men owe to their Creator, "must be left to the conscience and conviction of every man." One betrays the "late Revolution" if one fails "to take alarm at the first experiment on our liberties." Today we are asked to establish Christianity to the "exclusion of all other Religions"; tomorrow, what is to prevent our being asked to establish "any particular sect of Christians, in exclusion of all other Sects?" Christianity, moreover, needs no political defense or artificial support; indeed, the long history of state-supported Christianity is quite enough to give one pause, for the general result has been "pride and indolence in the Clergy; ignorance and servility in the laity; in both, superstition, bigotry, and persecution." Let us keep our land free, Madison urged, keep it as a haven for the oppressed, "an asylum to the persecuted." The very appearance of this assessment bill, the young Virginian noted, has transformed Christian love and forebearance into pervasive animosity and jealousy. This is but a small sample of what will follow in its train if such a bill should actually be passed and become law. Let it, therefore, be defeated that "the liberties, the prosperity and the Happiness of the Commonwealth" may be preserved for generations to come.[13]

By the fall of 1785, the Virginia Assembly had received more than one hundred petitions on the religion issue—about nine-tenths of these opposed assessment.[14] Perhaps the time had now come to abandon consideration of Patrick Henry's long-discussed bill in favor of Thomas Jefferson's long-delayed one: a Bill for Establishing Religious Freedom. In the waning days of 1786 that bill was passed by the Assembly. Delayed for a time by the more aristocratic, more Anglican Senate, the bill within a month had become law. Virginia had turned away from entanglement of its civil and ecclesiastical estates and had turned toward a separation that soon found favor in national deliberations. For the next forty years, Jefferson took a special satisfaction in his authorship of and agitation for a legislative act that provided that "no man shall be compelled to frequent or support any religious worship, place or ministry whatsoever, nor shall be enforced, restrained, molested, or burthened in his body or goods, nor shall otherwise suffer, on account of his religious opinions or belief, but that all men shall be free to profess, and by argument to maintain, their opinions in matters of religion, and that the same shall in no wise diminish, enlarge, or affect their civil capacities."[15]

Pennsylvania, though founded more than two generations after Virginia, had moved swiftly to become the latter's rival in wealth and free population by 1776. Philadelphia, moreover, was clearly the cultural capital of all the colonies as it would become, for a time, the political capital of the thirteen states. Unlike Virginia, Pennsylvania in the revolutionary era faced no great crisis of disestablishment nor did it require fresh and powerful arguments on behalf of religious liberty. A century before, William Penn, while still in England, had written *The Great Case of Liberty of Conscience* (1670). Protesting against England's harsh persecution of dissenters generally and of Quakers specifically, Penn argued for a liberty for not only religious opinions but for religious actions as well; namely, "the exercise of ourselves in a visible way of worship." Like Jefferson, Penn believed "that Almighty God hath created the mind free"; unlike Jefferson, however, he believed that a proper religious worship was "indispensably required at our hands," and that to neglect such worship is to "incur divine wrath." Like Madison, Penn declared mere fallible men to be incompetent to judge the affairs of other men's souls, but, unlike Madison, he believed in the scriptural promise that "faith is the gift of God." Like both Jefferson and Madison, Penn called upon as many arguments on as many grounds as seemed capable of convincing as many people as possible that government must leave conscience alone.

So, in 1682, this Quaker libertarian established a great colony, launching the Holy Experiment that society could succeed where every person shall "freely and fully Enjoy his or her Christian Liberty without any Interruption. . . ."[16]

By 1776, Quaker dominance in the affairs of Pennsylvania had long since ceased. The consequences of Penn's bold principle, however, were by that time all too evident: Germans, Swiss, Scots, Swedes, Welsh, Scotch-Irish, Africans, as well as English; Quakers, Presbyterians, Anglicans, Baptists, Mennonites, Moravians, Lutherans, German Reformed, Roman Catholics, Methodists, Jews, New Lights, Dunkers, and on the list could go. Pennsylvania had proved to be America's most hospitable haven for diversity and dissent, its doors to liberty were opened the widest, and its opportunities for land and livelihood were the most generous. The resulting heterogeneity was so unfamiliar, so visible, and indeed so flaunting as to scandalize many, especially the Anglicans who were growing in numbers, prestige, and anxiety. In Lancaster County, the Society for the Propagation of the Gospel missionary, Thomas Barton, spoke for many of his fellows when he complained in 1770 that "national religion & common sense have been rejected & forsaken." Everyone regards himself as equally inspired (the heritage of Penn's Inner Light) and as equally competent in matters of faith; there is no order, no stability, no approved ministry, and no supported and truly English Church. "In short the raving notions & ridiculous freaks that are every day spread & acted upon among us under the name of Religion is beyond the power of description."[17]

At the very time that Virginia was moving toward greater equality in religion, Pennsylvania under Anglican goading was in danger of retreating toward the hoary ideal: a national church. If a national church might be effectively installed in Pennsylvania, what would happen then? Would a revolution be forestalled or aborted? Would an ecclesiastical pattern be widely emulated up and down the Atlantic coast? Would a society be safely English and rescued from all raving notions and ridiculous freaks? Difficult as it must be for a later age to comprehend, it is in this very period of the late 1760s and early 1770s that Pennsylvania Anglicans pressed hardest for an English bishop to come into their midst. Joining with their coreligionists in New York and New Jersey, these Church of England clergy made their "strong and convincing" case for a bishop who could then unify the Church in America, reform

the morals, stem the madness, and save the colonies. By
August of 1776, however, Pennsylvania Anglican Philip Reading glumly announced that "the Church of England has now
no longer an existence in the United Colonies of America."
Explaining that he writes neither in exaggeration nor "in-
temperate heat," Missionary Reading adds: "I look upon the
King's supremacy and the constitution of the Church of England to be so intimately blended together that whenever the
supremacy is either suspended or abrogated, the fences of the
Church are then broken down and its visibility is destroyed."[18]
After a Declaration of Independence in July, there could be
no Church of England in August. The alliance of church and
state was so intimate that the fall of one necessitated the fall of
the other. The only alternative, then, is for raving notions and
ridiculous freaks to continue to have their way in Penn's large
and now clearly doomed land.

That was, however, the marvel of Pennsylvania. It refused
to wither and die; perversely, it went from strength to
strength. It not only survived, it prospered! To answer all of
those clichés about the indispensable presence of an official
church and about the necessary connection between establishment and order and between hierarchy and political stability there stood defiant and wealthy and growing Pennsylvania
declaring so eloquently, if silently, "It isn't so." As early as
1707 the deputy governor of North Carolina, John Archdale,
contended for religious freedom in that colony on the empirical grounds that it has already proved workable in Pennsylvania. Dissenters, Archdale wryly noted, can kill wolves or
bears every bit as well as Anglicans are able to do; dissenters
can also "Fell Trees and Clear Ground for Plantations" with
an efficiency equal to that of the most distinguished churchman. "Surely Pennsylvania can bear witness to what I write."
All this is so obvious and so common sensical, that the
wonder is that people ever behaved or believed otherwise.
That they so behave and believe can only be because a "passionate and preposterous Zeal . . . stupefies . . . the Rational
Powers."[19]

Seventy years later the evidence was even more convincing
as rationality bid fair to overcome stupefying zeal. Pennsylvania was a conspicious success, a prosperous land, a cultural
center, and an invitation to emulation. Thus, Penn's colony
made its most vital contribution to religious liberty by simply
being there. It was an example of religious liberty at work,

and at work successfully. In 1786, Virginia sailed out onto uncharted water; not so, Pennsylvania. There religious liberty, even when joined with strongly pacifist aggregations, had not subverted the state, had not destroyed the market place, and had not eaten away the connecting social tissue. Here religious liberty was not an elusive dream to be grasped; it was a historical reality—available for export.

Of course, Pennsylvania in the eighteenth century was not the very model of a modern civil order. It took seriously, for example, the inculcation and enforcement of virtue, even passing laws against what might be seen as minor vices. To eschew a national church was not to disdain a national (or regional) civility. The state or the school or both may well assume this responsibility. In Virginia, one of the legislators who supported Madison argued the case for education. John Breckinridge, a Presbyterian opposing state religion, declared: " 'Tis Education alone that makes the Man, and is the parent of every Virtue; it is the most sacred, the most useful, and at the same time, the most neglected thing in every Country."[20] In Pennsylvania, however, most relied on the state to enforce laws against drinking, swearing, defaming, card-playing, dice-throwing, and the like. All this was seen as no violation of liberty of conscience; on the contrary, such vices weakened the health of the society and thereby weakened the state.[21] Government had its own legitimate reasons for the suppression of vice and the promotion of virtue; an established church was not essential to the pursuit of these ends. Only be sure, as in Penn's arguments a century earlier, that the mind is left free, that conscience is left free, and that the state is kept free from that which is not appropriate to its finitude and its fallibility.

Pennsylvania required no Memorial and Remonstrance; it suffered no constitutional crises; it endured no legislative battles where religion was the paramount issue. It embraced a cultural and religious pluralism that was wary of narrow dogma in places of power. Benjamin Franklin, its most famous citizen in the revolutionary period, reflected this benign comprehensiveness: "I believe in one God," Franklin wrote in 1790, and that "the most acceptable service we render to him is doing good to his other children." Franklin believed that "the soul of man is immortal, and will be treated in justice in another life respecting its conduct in this. These I take to be the fundamental principles of all sound religion . . . in whatever sect I meet with them.''[22] The state of Pennsylvania glided gracefully from the world of its founder and his cry on behalf of conscience, through or around the concerted Anglican effort to make it an Anglican fortification and model, into the world of its elder statesman and his call for and example of charity in all things religious.

New England's voyage into modernity was not nearly so smooth, nor were constitutional crises so easily bypassed. The date for setting sail, moreover, was long delayed, the favorable wind and tide not appearing in the revolutionary era at all, but long after. Both in Massachusetts and Connecticut, the tradition of church establishment was almost as old as that in Virginia. In this instance, however, the establishment was more deep-seated and durable. First, it was Congregational, not Anglican. Second, it was controlled from within and not dependent upon English aid or subject to England's ecclesiastical control. Third, the major motivation for emigration to New England in the 1620s and 1630s was religious, so that the new arrivals, both clerical and lay, set about their "errand into the wilderness" with a vigor and dedication that made establishment not so much a matter of law as of life. Thus, it became possible to speak of a "New England Way" or a "New England Mind" that had no counterpart in the other colonies. However strong the drive was from within, this was not sufficient of itself to maintain the homogeneity that is the goal of all establishment. Both Massachusetts and Connecticut, in other words, found it necessary to levy fines, fill jails, whip offenders, bore tongues, crop ears, exile "strangers," and take lives. In New England as in Old, the price of conformity came high. In the seventeenth century, none could doubt the commingling of the civil and the ecclesiastical; none could deny the active employment of compulsion and coercion in matters of religion.

In eighteenth-century New England, some tentative steps toward toleration—not liberty—were taken, these steps often to be followed by a hasty retreat toward safer and securer ground. The turbulence and "enthusiasm" of the Great Awakening, for example, actually resulted in a diminishing of toleration. In the Revolution itself a generation later, the establishment held on, grudgingly yielding ground when hard pressed to do so, but never throughout that century yielding on the major point of the state's proper and necessary involvement with the church. This essay shall follow the slow progress toward separation as it unfolded in Connecticut—the historical development there presenting a marked contrast to that observed in either Virginia or Pennsylvania.

Only in the aftermath of the Revolution and its promise of liberty and equality did Connecticut manage to pass an Act of Toleration in 1784. This act somewhat reduced the liabilities under which dissenters labored, though it can in no way be compared with the declaration that the Virginia legislature debated in 1785 and passed the following year. Dissenters—at this time in Connecticut they consisted chiefly of Baptists, Methodists, and Episcopalians—were obliged to obtain a "certificate" giving evidence of their membership in and regular contribution to another recognized religious body. When so certified, the dissenter was excused from paying taxes to support the Congregational establishment. Nonbelievers, nonattenders, and noncontributors continued, of course, to support that establishment. Being identified as a "certificate man" carried with it, moreover, some social stigma and clear political liability. Even after 1784 the public school system remained unmistakably Congregational in its bias, in its instruction, and in its supervision. Yale remained the only institution of higher education recognized by the state, while gatherings of Congregational clergy informally determined who should stand for state offices in that year's forthcoming elections. Even as Anglican clergy had tenaciously held the right to perform marriages to be theirs alone, so Congregational Connecticut disdained to recognize marriages where only dissenting ministers officiated.

So matters stood even while a national constitution that prohibited all religious tests was ratified in 1789, and even while an amendment that restrained the federal Congress from taking any steps toward religious establishment or any steps away from free exercise was adopted in 1791. What prevented matters from standing there indefinitely was the appearance of a new and unanticipated phenomenon on the American scene: political parties. With the election of Thomas Jefferson in 1800 (an election that Connecticut did all within its power to forestall), the reality of political parties could no longer be gainsaid, even in Connecticut. Soon the Jeffersonian Republicans organized themselves into a faction that would press hard for complete separation of Congregationalism from the political arm of the state. Condemning clerical manipulation and control, these radicals—for so they

were regarded—adopted "liberty and constitution" as their
slogan—the second being necessary in their view to a securing
of the first. The traditional elite and establishment power-
brokers came to think of themselves as the party of "religion
and order." Thus, Federalists, to use the national name, were
arrayed against Republicans on grounds that, in Connecticut,
had unmistakable church-state implications. The party split
also had unmistakable religious followings.

The Congregational clergy, virtually to a man, supported
the Federalist party; indeed, failure to do so became grounds
for removing a minister or questioning his ordination. Baptists
and Methodists quickly made common cause with the more
egalitarian and more libertarian Republicans. They saw their
security much more in "liberty and constitution" than in
"religion and order," knowing precisely which religion the
Federalists had in mind and precisely what order they were
prepared to enforce. Lyman Beecher, Conneticut's most active
Congregationalist leader and organizer at this time, saw this
Republican alliance in the darkest terms. These radicals
gather to themselves, he observed, every disaffected, dis-
gruntled, and disorderly element in the state of Connecticut.
"The democracy, as it rose, included nearly all the minor
sects, besides the Sabbath-breakers, rum-selling tippling folk,
infidels, and ruff-scuff generally, and made a dead set at us of
the standing order."[23]

The only way in which religious liberty could ever be made
secure in Connecticut, the Republicans argued, was for there
to be a written constitution in which the explicit guarantees
were given. Nonsense, the Federalists replied. Connecticut's
constitution, like England's, is well known, if unwritten; the
vast majority of the state's population knows its metes and
bounds as well as any good Connecticut farmer knows his
own land. There is no need for a "fine spun constitution,
spread over abundance of paper, and consisting of divers chapters and sections and of numerous articles and nice definition."[24] The dissenters who had seen even toleration wax and
wane for decades, however, felt otherwise. Likewise, Jeffer-
sonians who had placed their faith in written documents—a
declaration in 1776, a bill in 1786, a constitution in 1789, and
a spelling out of inalienable rights in 1791—also saw the
necessity of explicit assurances. Together then, dissenters and
Jeffersonian Republicans worked for votes year by year, precinct by precinct, and office by office.

Nationwide the Federalists did not do well in the election of 1800 and even more poorly in Jefferson's reelection in 1804. In Connecticut, however, some of Jefferson's policies, particularly in the second term, proved so very unpopular (the Embargo Act, for example) that Republicans made little gain in that state. Then in the War of 1812, "Mr. Madison's War," Connecticut was alienated even further from any sentiment associated with the party of Jefferson or Madison. "Liberty and constitution" seemed to be getting nowhere in the first decade or so of the nineteenth century. With fine timing, Congregational leaders also took this occasion to help launch a counterattack against secularism, infidelity, Jacobinism, French radicals, and American deists. Connecticut's Second Great Awakening, a great crusade for and revival of religion, "had very practical ends in view—Christianity, the Standing Order, and Federalism . . . [Timothy] Dwight could not dissociate true religion from the established church—he could hardly dissociate Christianity from Federalism."[25]

Against such formidable opposition and disaffection, dissenters began to lose heart. Then, in 1816, help came from a most unexpected source. Episcopalians, unaccustomed to being associated with the "ruff-scuff generally," had heretofore cast their lot with the Federalists. Now, because of a mishandling of funds by the party in power, the Episcopalians decided to cast their lot with the other "outsiders" to challenge the entrenched state church, even perhaps to question the easy identification of Federalism with social and moral respectability. In the election of 1818, Republicans—now calling themselves in Connecticut the "Toleration Party"—were voted in while the Federalists, in the words of Lyman Beecher, were slung "out like a stone from a sling."[26] The election sermon that May was delivered for the first time in the state's history by a minister who was not a Congregationalist.

Four months later, in August of 1818, a constitutional convention was called in Hartford. In September, the state's document was completed, and, in October, it was submitted to the voters for their approbation or repudiation. The vote was close: 12,364 against the constitution (and thus against all those "numerous articles and nice definitions") and 13,918 for adoption (and thus for "liberty," which in the minds of many meant specifically a liberty in the realm of religion). Hardly a lopsided victory in the land of steady habits, this constitutional

ratification was nonetheless a victory. Article VII of the document, devoted wholly to religion, read in part: "No person
shall be compelled to join or support, nor by law be classed
with, or associated to any congregation, church or religious
association. And each and every society or denomination of
Christians in this State, shall have and enjoy the same and
equal powers, rights and privileges. . . . "[27]

In faraway Monticello, Thomas Jefferson, long retired from
the presidency of the United States, wrote to a fellow retiree
in Massachusetts, John Adams. Though the two men had disagreed on much, they were at this time of their lives philosophically sympathetic on many fronts. Massachusetts had not
yet fully severed all ties between church and state, but now
Jefferson had new hope "after the resurrection of Connecticut
to light and liberality." Connecticut, Jefferson had assumed,
would be "the last retreat of Monkish darkness, bigotry, and
abhorrence of those advances of the mind which had carried
the other states a century ahead of them." The sage of Monticello added: "They seemed still to be exactly where their forefathers were when they schismatised from the Covenant of
works, and to consider, as dangerous heresies, all innovations
good or bad. I join you therefore in sincere congratulations
that this den of the priesthood is at length broken up, and
that a protestant popedom is no longer to disgrace American
history and character."[28] All of the arguments that Jefferson
had hurled against an Anglican establishment in Virginia
some forty years earlier he found equally applicable to a Congregational establishment in Connecticut. There should be no
"popedom," Protestant or Catholic, foreign or domestic, subtle or severe.

Of course, 1818 marked a beginning in Connecticut, not an
ending, just as the adoption of the First Amendment in 1791
only set the nation on its road without determining its final
destination. The road chosen, however, was made possible and
plausible by such as Virginia's deists and dissenters, Pennsylvania's Pietists and pragmatists, Connecticut's political partisans, and those grown intolerant of mere toleration. From the
early years of the Republic, it is evident that there was no
single road to religious liberty. Each state had its own unique
history, its own agenda for the future, and its own quite distinct constituencies and constellation of attitudes. These three
states, however, along with many more, helped the nation to
begin a perilous if promising journey. Those joining in the

journey shared the conviction that Almighty God hath created the mind—and, yes, the spirit and the conscience—free. Two centuries after Jefferson's bill made its tortuous way through the legislative processes of Virginia, one is more aware of how it all began, but no more certain of precisely where it all will end.

NOTES

1. F. L. Hawks, *Contributions to the Ecclesiastical History of the United States of America: Virginia* (New York: Harper & Brothers, 1836), 153-54.

2. See the useful and revealing maps in Lester J. Cappon, ed., *Atlas of Early American History* (Princeton, N.J.: Princeton University Press, 1976), 39, 71. Note especially the large number of Methodist circuits in Virginia in 1790, only six years after the Methodist Episcopal Church was formally constituted in Baltimore. This was also less than two decades after Methodism had been introduced into the colony.

3. Julian P. Boyd, ed., *The Papers of Thomas Jefferson* (Princeton, N.J.: Princeton University Press, 1950), 1:526; H. J. Eckenrode, *Separation of Church and State in Virginia* (Richmond, Va.: Superintendent of Public Printing, 1910), 66.

4. Ibid.

5. Thomas E. Buckley, *Church and State in Revolutionary Virginia, 1776-1787* (Charlottesville: University of Virginia Press, 1977), 18. This able study provides excellent detail on shifting alliances, demographic and voting patterns, and individual legislators.

6. Buckley, *Church and State in Revolutionary Virginia, 1776-1787*, 33; Boyd, *The Papers of Thomas Jefferson*, 1:537.

7. Boyd, *The Papers of Thomas Jefferson*, 1:537.

8. Buckley, *Church and State in Revolutionary Virginia, 1776-1787*, 49.

9. Eckenrode, *Separation of Church and State in Virginia*, 58.

10. Ibid., 59.

11. Buckley, *Church and State in Revolutionary Virginia, 1776-1787*, 39.

12. At the last minute, promoters of the general assessment changed the title of their bill to read as follows: A Bill for Establishing a Provision for Teachers of the Christian Religion. The use of the word "Teachers" was a ploy to broaden support for assessment by gathering the educational dimension under the canopy of the Christian religion. The bill did, in fact, allow those who wished to specify that their tax monies would go entirely to education. See all of Chapter III in Buckley, *Church and State in Revolutionary Virginia, 1776-1787.*

13. *The Papers of James Madison* (Chicago: University of Chicago Press, 1973), 8:298-304.

14. Buckley, *Church and State in Revolutionary Virginia, 1776-1787*, 145.

15. Boyd, *The Papers of Thomas Jefferson*, 2:545-47.

16. For relevant segments from this treatise of Penn's, see *The Select Works of William Penn*, 3rd ed. (London: James Phillips, 1782), 3:1-13. The presence of the "his or her" may strike the reader as a modernizing of or tinkering with an eighteenth-century text. The reader must recall, however, that women were as prominent as men in the structure and operation of the Quaker religion. For an excellent analysis of Penn's views and their early application in his colony, see J. William Frost, "Religious Liberty in Early Pennsylvania," *The Pennsylvania Magazine of History and Biography* CV:4 (October 1981): 419-51.

17. William S. Perry, *Historical Collections Relating to the American Colonial Church* (Hartford: privately printed, 1871), 2:448-51.

18.   Ibid., 483-84.
19.   Alexander S. Salley, Jr., *Narratives of Early Carolina, 1650-1750* (New York: Charles Scribner's Sons, 1911), 305.
20.   Quoted in Buckley, *Church and State in Revolutionary Virginia, 1776-1787*, 105.
21.   Frost, "Religious Liberty," 428-29.
22.   F. B. Dexter, ed., *The Literary Diary of Ezra Stiles* (New York: Charles Scribner's Sons, 1901), 3:387. Franklin's letter to Ezra Stiles is dated 9 March 1790; he died the following month.
23.   Lyman Beecher, *Autobiography, Correspondence, etc.* (New York: Harper & Brothers, 1864), 1:342. The depth of partisan feeling is further revealed in the diary of Thomas Robbins, a Connecticut minister who in 1800 wrote concerning Jefferson and the forthcoming election: "I do not believe that the Most High will permit a howling atheist to sit at the head of this nation." Quoted in R. J. Purcell, *Connecticut in Transition 1775-1818* (Washington, D.C.: American Historical Association, 1918), 313.
24.   Quoted in Purcell, *Connecticut in Transition 1775-1818*, 269. For an extraordinarily careful discussion of the process by which disestablishment came about in Connecticut, with particular attention to perspective of the dissenters, see William G. McLoughlin, *New England Dissent, 1630-1833: The Baptists and the Separation of Church and State* (Cambridge, Mass.: Harvard University Press, 1971), 2:915-1062.
25.   Sidney E. Mead, *Nathaniel William Taylor* (Chicago: University of Chicago Press, 1942), 48.
26.   Beecher, *Autobiography, Correspondence, etc.*, 1:343. The religious profile in Connecticut at this time was as follows: Baptist churches, 85; Episcopal churches, 74; Methodist churches, 53; and for the Establishment, 204 churches. As McLoughlin points out, "By 1818, the dissenting churches outnumbered the Congregational" (*New England Dissent, 1630-1833*, 2:919; also note 7.) It should also be remembered that it was to Connecticut Baptists (Danbury Association) that Thomas Jefferson in 1801 wrote the famous letter in which, in an even more famous phrase, he quoted the First Amendment, adding "thus building a wall of separation between Church and State."
27.   Quoted in Purcell, *Connecticut in Transition 1775-1818*, 401.
28.   Lester J. Cappon, ed., *The Adams-Jefferson Letters* (Chapel Hill: University of North Carolina Press, 1959), 2:512. Jefferson's letter is dated 5 May 1817 as he anticipates the constitutional change with a victorious election in 1817 of his "tolerationists." Adams, a month earlier (19 April), had written Jefferson to congratulate him on the "late Election in Connecticutt." "Several causes have conspired," Adams wrote, to bring this epochal change about. He gave the devil credit for inspiring someone "to print a new Edition of "The independent Whig' even in Connecticutt. . . ." (A London publication of the early 1720s, *The Independent Whig*, was often reprinted in the colonies as a warning against powerful, Roman Catholic-leaning bishops in the Church of England.) John Adams added to his old friend: "These Volumes . . . have produced a Burst of Indignation against Priestcraft Bigotry and Intollerance, and in conjunction with other causes have produced the late Election."

The Original Meaning of the Establishment Clause of the First Amendment

LEONARD W. LEVY

The First Amendment begins with the clause against an establishment of religion: "Congress shall make no law respecting an establishment of religion." There are two basic interpretations of what the framers meant by this clause.

The United States Supreme Court advanced the broad interpretation most authoritatively in *Everson* v. *Board of Education* in 1947. Justice Hugo Black, speaking for the majority, declared:

> The "establishment of religion" clause of the First Amendment means at least this: Neither a state nor the Federal Government can set up a church. Neither can pass laws which aid one religion, aid all religions, or prefer one religion over another. Neither can force nor influence a person to go to or to remain away from church against his will or force him to profess a belief or disbelief in any religion. No person can be punished for entertaining or professing religious beliefs or disbeliefs, for church attendance or non-attendance. No tax in any amount, large or small, can be levied to support any religious activities or institutions, whatever they may be called, or whatever form they may adopt to teach or practice religion. Neither a state nor the Federal Government can, openly or secretly, participate in the affairs of any religious organizations or groups and vice versa. In the words of Jefferson, the clause against establishment of religion by laws was intended to erect "a wall of separation between Church and State."[1]

The dissenting justices in the *Everson* case, while disagreeing with the majority on the question of whether the "wall of separation" had in fact been breached by the practice at issue, concurred with the majority on the historical question of the intention of the framers. Justice Wiley Rutledge's opinion, endorsed by all the dissenting justices, declared: "The Amendment's purpose was not to strike merely at the establishment of a single sect, creed or religion, outlawing only a formal relation such as had prevailed in England and some of the colonies. Necessarily it was to uproot all such relationships, but the object was broader than separating church and state in this narrow sense. It was to create a complete and permanent separation of the spheres of religious activity and civil author-

ity by comprehensively forbidding every form of public aid or
support for religion."[2] Thus, the heart of this broad interpretation is that the First Amendment prohibits even government
aid impartially and equitably administered to all religious
groups.

The second or narrow interpretation of the Establishment
Clause holds that it was intended to prevent government recognition of a single state church that would have preferences of
any sort over other churches. According to this interpretation,
the members of the First Congress understood "establishment
of religion" as "a formal, legal union of a single church or
religion with government, giving the one church or religion
an exclusive position of power and favor over all other
churches or denominations."[3] Advocates of this view reject
Justice Rutledge's contention that every form of public aid or
support for religion is prohibited; they also reject Justice
Black's opinion that government cannot aid all religions. In
their view, the wall of separation was intended merely to keep
the government from abridging religious liberty by discriminatory practices against religion generally or against any particular sects or denominations. The wall was not intended,
however, to create a sharp division between government and
religion or to enjoin the government from fostering religion
in general.

These two interpretations of the Establishment Clause are
patently irreconcilable, yet almost every writer who has ex-
plored the evidence has concluded that the interpretation of
his choice is historically "right" or "wrong." The subject,
apparently because of its implications for current public policy
in the field of education, seems to transform into partisans all
who approach it. The issue is certainly more debatable than
partisans on either side would have us believe, however, and
historical investigation is hampered by the fact that the known
sources are often unclear and always disappointingly incomplete. A preponderance of the evidence indicates that the
Supreme Court's interpretation is historically the more accurate one.

THE BACKGROUND
THE CONSTITUTIONAL CONVENTION

The Constitutional Convention of 1789 gave only slight
attention to the subject of a Bill of Rights and even less to the
subject of religion. In contrast to the Declaration of Inde-

pendence and to many acts of the Continental Congress, the Constitution contained no references to God; the Convention did not even invoke divine guidance for its deliberations. Its only reference to religion was in reference to qualifications for federal officeholders.[4] On 20 August, Charles Pinckney proposed that "no religious test or qualification shall ever be annexed to any oath of office under the authority of the U.S."[5] The proposal was referred to the Committee on Detail without debate or consideration by the Convention. When the committee reported ten days later, it ignored Pinckney's proposal. From the floor of the Convention, he moved it again. The chairman of the committee, Roger Sherman of Connecticut, stated that such a provision was "unnecessary, the prevailing liberality being a sufficient security against such tests."[6] Two delegates, however, in unreported speeches, "approved the motion" by Pinckney, and when put to a vote without further debate it passed.[7] Rephrased by the Committee on Style, it was incorporated into Article 6, clause 3 of the Constitution: "No religious test shall ever be required as a qualification to any office or public trust under the United States."

This clause "went far," according to one scholar, "in thwarting any State Church" in the United States.[8] The reasoning behind this thought is that in the absence of the clause, Congress might have had the power to require subscription to the articles of faith of some particular church,[9] or to Protestantism, or to Christianity generally. The scope of the protection, however, was not defined by anyone at the time; that is, the implied ban against an establishment of religion is no aid in explaining the meaning of such an establishment.

No other references to the subject of religion occurred at the Constitutional Convention. When George Mason of Virginia expressed a wish that the new Constitution "had been prefaced with a Bill of Rights," he offered no suggestions as to the contents of such a bill. Nor did Elbridge Gerry of Massachusetts who, agreeing with Mason, moved for a committee to prepare a Bill of Rights. This motion aroused opposition on the ground that the state bills of rights "being in force are sufficient." Mason rejoined, "The Laws of the U.S. are to be paramount to State Bills of Rights," but without further debate the motion that a Bill of Rights be prepared was defeated 10 to 0, the delegates voting as state units.[10] Thus, on its face, the record of the Constitutional Convention is no guide to discerning the understanding of the framers as to establishments of religion.

The failure of the Convention, however, to provide for a Bill of Rights should not be misunderstood. The members of the Convention did not oppose personal liberties; in the main, they simply regarded a Bill of Rights as superfluous. The new national government possessed only limited powers; no power had been granted to legislate on any of the subjects that would be the concern of a Bill of Rights. Because no such power existed, none could be exercised or abused and, therefore, all provisions against that possibility were unnecessary. Of the many statements of this argument,[11] the most widely publicized was that of Alexander Hamilton in *The Federalist* where he concluded, simply: "For why declare that things shall not be done which there is no power to do? Why, for instance, should it be said that the liberty of the press shall not be restrained, when no power is given by which restrictions may be imposed?"[12]

The framers of the Constitution have left abundant evidence of their belief that Congress was bereft of any authority over the subject of religion.[13] Congress was powerless, therefore, even in the absence of the First Amendment, to enact laws that benefited one religion or church in particular or all of them equally and impartially. Although it is important to try to understand the Establishment Clause of the First Amendment, this effort must be viewed within the larger framework of the Constitution.

THE RATIFICATION CONTROVERSY

From late 1787 through the following year, the proposed Constitution submitted to state conventions for ratification engrossed the political attention of the country. A torrent of speeches, essays, articles, and pamphlets poured forth from partisans on both sides. Opponents of ratification feared most of all that the centralizing tendencies of a consolidated national government would extinguish the rights of states and individuals. They objected most particularly to the failure of the instrument to provide for a Bill of Rights, and the Constitution probably would not have received the requisite number of state votes for ratification had not James Madison and other Federalist leaders pledged themselves to seek amendments constituting a Bill of Rights as soon as the new government went into operation. Indeed, six of the thirteen original states ac-

companied their instruments of ratification with recommendations for amendments that would secure specific personal
liberties.[14]

In the light of these facts, it is astonishing to discover that
the debate on a Bill of Rights was conducted on a level of
abstraction so vague as to convey the impression that Americans during 1787-88 had only the most nebulous conception
of the meanings of the particular rights they sought to insure.
The insistent demands for the "rights of conscience" or "trial
by jury" or "liberty of the press" by the principal advocates of
a Bill of Rights were unaccompanied by a reasoned analysis of
what these rights meant, how far they extended, and in what
circumstances they might be limited. In addition, many opponents of ratification had discovered that denouncing the omission of a Bill of Rights provided a useful mask for less elevat-
ing, perhaps even sordid, objections relating to such matters
as taxation and commerce.

One cannot assume that the existence of widely known and
agreed upon definitions of specific rights precluded the necessity for discussion of their meanings. They did not. Even trial
by jury, which was protected by more state constitutions than
any other right, differed in meaning and scope from state to
state.[15] Moreover, the states differed substantially in the character and number of the rights they guaranteed.[16] Several state
conventions in ratifying the Constitution even recommended
amendments to protect rights not known in their own constitutions.[17] Whatever the explanation, the tens of thousands of
words exchanged on the subject of a Bill of Rights during the
ratification controversy do not illuminate the understanding
and content attached at that time to particular rights.

This generalization applies to the subject of establishments
of religion. An awareness of the need for precision and analysis in discussing the subject might be expected, considering
the variety of historical experiences with establishments before
and after independence and considering the diversity of relevant state constitutions and statutory provisions. At the very
least, one would expect frequent expressions of fear and concern on the subject. Amazingly, however, it received rare and
then only brief mention. One searches in vain for a definition
in the rhetorical effusions of leading advocates of a Bill of
Rights.

The debates of the state ratifying conventions offer no help
either.[18] The perfunctory reports of the ratifying conventions

of Delaware, New Jersey, and Georgia reveal nothing of value. Moreover, each ratified unconditionally and without proposing any amendments. Nothing, therefore, can be said of opinion in those states.

In Connecticut, which also ratified without recommendations for amendments, the fragmentary record of the debates shows only that Oliver Wolcott, briefly mentioning the value of the clause against test oaths, said: "Knowledge and liberty are so prevalent in this country, that I do not believe that the United States would ever be disposed to establish one religious sect, and lay all others under legal disabilities."[19] Similarly, Oliver Ellsworth referred in a tract to the fact that religious tests for office were always found in European nations where one church was established as the state church.[20] Neither Ellsworth nor Wolcott, both Federalists, believed that Congress could legislate on the subject of religion.

In Pennsylvania, the Convention ratified unconditionally, after voting against a series of amendments constituting a Bill of Rights proposed by the minority. These defeated amendments, while protecting the "rights of conscience," contained no provision respecting an establishment of religion,[21] which Pennsylvania never experienced. Antiratificationists from the town of Carlisle proposed that "none should be compelled contrary to his principles or inclination to hear or support the clergy of any one established religion."[22] "Centinel" (probably Samuel Bryan), who also recommended a Bill of Rights, proposed more broadly in the language of the state constitution that "no man ought, or of right can be compelled to attend any religious worship, or erect or support any place of worship, or maintain any ministry, contrary to or against his own free will and consent. . . . "[23]

Massachusetts, which maintained an establishment of religion at the time of ratification, was the first state to ratify with amendments, but the only rights mentioned were those of the criminally accused.[24] Isaac Backus, agent for the New England Baptists and a delegate to the Massachusetts ratifying convention, described the Constitution as a door "opened for the establishment of righteous government, and for securing of equal liberty, as never before opened to any people upon earth."[25] Backus, and Baptists generally, passionately opposed the Massachusetts church-state system, by which the state mandated support for all Protestant churches. Clearly, he had not the slightest suspicion that the federal government could do likewise. No person in the state convention believed that the new government would have any power in religious matters.

Maryland ratified without amendments, although fifteen had been recommended, including a proposal "that there be no national religion established by law; but that all persons be equally entitled to protection in their religious liberty."[26] Maryland's constitution permitted an establishment of religion, though none existed. All fifteen defeated amendments were designed chiefly to protect state governments from infringement by the national government.[27] They failed not because the Federalist-dominated convention of Maryland disagreed with them, but because it wished to ratify unconditionally for the purpose of demonstrating confidence in the new system of government.[28] The same may be said of Pennsylvania and all the other states that ratified without recommending amendments.

In South Carolina, Rev. Francis Cummins made the only reference to an establishment of religion when he condemned "religious establishments; or the states giving preference to any religious denomination."[29] The convention's recommendations for amendments, however, mentioned nothing about a Bill of Rights.[30] At the time, South Carolina proclaimed the "Christian Protestant . . . religion to be the established religion of this state." No churches received public financial support, but those that subscribed to a stated set of beliefs were "considered as established."[31]

New Hampshire's debates are nonexistent. Though the state maintained an establishment, its instrument of ratification included among recommendations for amendments the following: "Congress shall make no laws touching Religion, or to infringe the rights of Conscience."[32]

In Virginia, where the most crucial struggle against establishments of religion had ended in victory just three years before the state ratifying convention met, only two speakers during the course of the lengthy debates alluded to an establishment. Edmund Randolph, defending the Constitution against Patrick Henry's allegation that it endangered religious liberty, pointed out that Congress had no power over religion and that the exclusion of religious tests for federal officeholders meant "they are not bound to support one mode of worship, or to adhere to one particular sect." He added that there were so many different sects in the United States "that

they will prevent the establishment of any one sect, in prejudice to the rest, and forever oppose all attempts to infringe
religious liberty."[33] James Madison, also addressing himself to
Henry's general and unsupported accusation, argued at this
time that a "multiplicity of sects" would secure freedom of
religion, but that a Bill of Rights would not. He pointed out
that the Virginia Declaration of Rights (which guaranteed
"the free exercise of religion, according to the dictates of conscience") would not have exempted people "from paying to
the support of one particular sect, if such sect were exclusively
established by law." If a majority were of one sect, liberty
would be poorly protected by a Bill of Rights. "Fortunately
for this commonwealth," he added, "a majority of the people
are decidedly against any exclusive establishment. I believe it
to be so in the other states. There is not a shadow of right in
the general government to intermeddle with religion. Its least
interference with it would be a most flagrant usurpation. . . . A
particular state might concur in one religious project. But the
United States abound[s] in such a variety of sects, that it is a
strong security against religious persecution; and it is sufficient to authorize a conclusion that no one sect will ever be
able to outnumber or depress the rest."[34]

Nonetheless, Madison and his party could not muster sufficient votes to secure Virginia's ratification of the Constitution
without accepting a recommendation for amendments, which
were first submitted by Patrick Henry. Henry's amendments,
including a Declaration of Rights, were read before the Convention, but not recorded in its record of proceedings; the
reporter stated that they "were nearly the same as those ultimately proposed by the Convention"[35] after perfunctory endorsement by a committee on amendments. Among the recommended amendments was a provision that "no particular
religious sect or society ought to be favored or established, by
law, in preference to others."[36]

In New York, Thomas Tredwell, an antiratificationist, in
his speech favoring a Bill of Rights, made the only reported
reference to an establishment: "I could have wished also that
sufficient caution had been used to secure to us our religious
liberties, and to have prevented the general government from
tyrannizing over our consciences by a religious establishment—a tyranny of all others most dreadful, and which will
assuredly be exercised whenever it shall be thought necessary
for the promotion and support of their political measures."[37]

The New York debates were fully reported until the closing days of the Convention, when John Lansing, an antiratificationist leader, introduced a Bill of Rights to be prefixed to the Constitution. Although debate on this subject began on 19 July 1788 and continued intermittently through 25 July, when Lansing's Bill of Rights was adopted, not a single word of the debate is reported.[38] Accordingly, the Convention members left no explanation of what they understood by their recommendation "that no Religious Sect or Society ought to be favored or established by Law in preference of others."[39] This wording matched that used in the state constitution of 1777, which abolished establishments of religion in New York.

North Carolina, which had abolished its establishment in 1776, recommended an amendment like that of Virginia and New York.[40] The subject first arose in the Convention when Henry Abbot, a delegate expressing concern about the possibility of the general government's infringing religious liberty, asserted that "some people" feared that a treaty might be made with foreign powers to adopt the Roman Catholic religion in the United States. "Many wish to know what religion shall be established," he added. He was "against any exclusive establishment; but if there were any, I would prefer the Episcopal." In the next breath, he expressed a belief that the exclusion of religious tests was "dangerous," because Congressmen "might all be pagans."[41]

James Iredell responded to Abbot's fears by pointing out that the exclusion of a religious test indicated an intent to establish religious liberty. Congress was powerless to enact "the establishment of any religion whatsoever; and I am astonished that any gentleman should conceive they have. Is there any power given to Congress in matters of religion? . . . If any future Congress should pass an act concerning the religion of the country, it would be an act which they are not authorized to pass, by the Constitution, and which the people would not obey."[42] Governor Samuel Johnston agreed with Iredell and concluded: "I hope, therefore, that gentlemen will see there is no cause of fear that any one religion shall be exclusively established."[43] David Caldwell, a Presbyterian minister, then spoke in favor of a religious test that would eliminate "Jews and pagans of every kind."[44] Samuel Spencer, the leading Antifederalist, took Caldwell's statement as endorsing the establishment of "one particular religion," which Spencer feared would lead to persecution. He believed that religion should stand on its own "without any connection with temporal authority."[45] William Lenoir agreed with Spencer, but warned that federal ecclesiastical courts might be erected, and they "may make any establishment they think proper."[46] Richard Dobbs Spaight, who had been a delegate to the federal Convention, answered: "As to the subject of religion, I thought what had been said [by Iredell] would fully satisfy that gentleman and every other. No power is given to the general government to interfere with it at all. Any act of Congress on this subject would be a usurpation."[47]

When Rhode Island's convention tardily met to ratify the Constitution, eight states had already ratified the Bill of Rights. Thus, Rhode Island's recommendation for an amendment against an establishment,[48] modeled after those of New York, Virginia, and North Carolina, was a superfluous flourish that had no effect on the framing of the First Amendment.

CONCLUSIONS

Scanty as they are, the relevant data drawn from the period of the ratification controversy have been described in full. What conclusions do they yield?

1. No state or person favored an establishment of religion by Congress. On those few occasions when a Convention delegate or a contemporary writer mentioned an establishment of religion, he spoke either against its desirability and/or against the likelihood that there would be one.

2. The evidence does not permit a generalization as to what was meant by an establishment of religion. To be sure, most of the few references to an establishment expressly or in context referred to the preference of one church or sect or religion above others. Clearly, however, this fact taken by itself proves little. Madison, for example, was simply saying to those who believed that religious liberty was endangered by the proposed national government, "Not even your least fears shall come to pass." As for the recommendations for amendments by Virginia, New York, North Carolina, and Rhode Island, they are not clarifying. They do not even necessarily indicate that preference of one sect over others was all that was comprehended by an establishment of religion. They do indicate the preference of one sect over others was something so feared that to assuage that fear by specifically making it groundless became a political necessity.

3. The members of the Constitutional Convention and Americans throughout the states shared a widespread understanding that the new central government would have no power whatever to legislate on the subject of religion either to aid one sect exclusively or to aid all equally. Many contemporaries, especially in New England, believed that governments could and should foster religion, or at least Protestant Christianity. All agreed, however, that the matter pertained to the realm of state government and that the federal government possessed no authority to meddle in religious matters.

DRAFTING AND RATIFICATION OF THE ESTABLISHMENT CLAUSE

In the first United States Congress, Madison championed a Bill of Rights. Only after considerable prodding, however, did he succeed in getting a House preoccupied with what it considered the more important subject of getting the government organized to turn its attention to this matter.[49] Madison's determination represented a change of heart on his part. Originally he opposed a Bill of Rights on several grounds. He thought it unnecessary because the Constitution gave the national government no power to interfere in matters touching personal freedoms; he believed that liberty would be best protected not by "paper barriers," but by competition and a multiplicity of interests in society and sects in religion. In addition, he feared that a Bill of Rights might even endanger liberty by implying that the federal government possessed powers not specifically denied it.[50]

A number of factors combined to change his mind. He realized that acceding to the demand for a Bill of Rights would deflate the movement for a new Convention and assist in the ratification of the Constitution.[51] Moreover, his friend Thomas Jefferson, as well as the Virginia Baptists, whose support he needed to be elected to Congress, insisted on the need for a Bill of Rights. Jefferson, then American minister to France, sent back to Madison a steady stream of commentary on the need for a Bill of Rights, including a statement to ensure that "religious faith shall go unpunished."[52] Jefferson has left ample evidence of his understanding of the proper relationship between church and state, especially in his Bill for Establishing Religious Freedom. Considered by Jefferson himself as one of the three crowning achievements of his life, the Act forbade Virginia's government to meddle in religion in any

way. None could be "compelled to frequent or support any
religious worship, place or ministry whatsoever." Nor could
the government even demand that a citizen support a minister
of his own choice.[53]

The First Amendment as passed perfectly satisfied Jefferson's desire for the protection of religious liberty on the
national level, as was demonstrated by his famous statement to
the Danbury (Connecticut) Baptist Association in 1802: "I
contemplate with sovereign reverence the act of the whole
American people which declared that their legislature should
'make no law respecting an establishment of religion, or prohibiting the free exercise thereof,' thus building a wall of separation between church and state."[54]

Virginia's Baptists, too, insisted vehemently that religion be
supported only by voluntary, not by tax, contributions. They
reasoned that if "the State provide a Support for Preachers of
the gospel, and they receive it in Consideration of their Services, they must certainly when they Preach act as officers of
the State."[55] Alarmed by Antifederalist propaganda, they
feared that Madison had reneged on his former position and
that religious liberty was in danger. When John Leland, one
of their most influential ministers, represented Baptists' fears
to Madison personally, he assured them of his constancy and
promised to work for a Bill of Rights including a protection
for religious liberty.[56] Consequently, Madison felt himself
"bound in honor" to secure amendments; hence his persistence in doing so.[57] That the amendment in its final form
"completely satisfied" both Jefferson and the Baptists[58] lends
strong support to the argument that the parties most interested in its passage saw it as prohibiting the government from
interfering in religious matters in order to aid either one or
many sects or religions.

On 8 June 1789, at the first session of the first United States
Congress, Representative Madison proposed for House approval a series of amendments to the Constitution.[59] He accompanied his presentation with a lengthy speech explaining his
action and defending the value of a Bill of Rights, but he did
not discuss the proposal relating to an establishment of religion. The section on religion read: "The civil rights of none
shall be abridged on account of religious belief or worship,
nor shall any national religion be established, nor shall the
full and equal rights of conscience be in any manner, or on
any pretext, infringed."[60]

Proponents of the narrow interpretation of the Establishment Clause see in the word "national" proof of their contention that Madison intended nothing more than a prohibition against the preference for one church or religion over others. This argument presumes a drastic change of opinion on Madison's part for which no evidence exists. He had been one of the principal leaders in the fight against a general assessment in Virginia in 1785. Although that plan proposed tax support not for one religion exclusively but for all Christian religions, Madison, in his famous Memorial and Remonstrance, referred to it repeatedly as an "establishment of religion."[61] That same year, the Continental Congress attempted unsuccessfully to set aside a section of land for the "support of religion" in the Western territories. Madison described this non-preferential aid to religion as "unjust in itself, so foreign to the authority of Congress, . . . and smelling so strongly of antiquated bigotry."[62]

His subsequent actions show that he became, if anything, even more scrupulous on church-state separation. As president, he vetoed a land-grant bill intended to remedy the peculiar situation of a Baptist church that had, through a surveying error, been built on public land. Congress sought to rectify the error by permitting the church to have the land rather than buy it or be dispossessed. Here was no making of broad public policy, yet President Madison saw a dangerous precedent, and he vetoed the bill on the ground that it "comprises a principle and precedent for the appropriation of funds of the United States for the use and support of religious societies, contrary to the article of the Constitution which declares that 'Congress shall make no law respecting a religious establishment.' "[63] He also vetoed a bill that would have incorporated a church in the District of Columbia.

In his "Detached Memoranda," written in 1817 after he had retired from the presidency, Madison expressed his disapproval of presidential proclamations of days of thanksgiving and of tax-supported chaplains for Congress and the armed services. Significantly, he described these as "establishments" or "the establishment of a national religion." He commented: "If religion consists in voluntary acts of individuals, singly, or voluntarily associated, and it be proper that public functionaries, as well as their Constituents should discharge their religious duties, let them like their Constituents, do so at their own expense."[64] Years earlier, at the Virginia ratifying con-

vention, Madison had cited his "uniform conduct" on the
subject of religious liberty.[65] Clearly, he remained constant on
this subject all his life. The evidence points to the conclusion
that in 1789, as in 1817, he used the phrase "national establishment" to signify not a preference for a single religion but
national action on behalf of one or all religions. Indeed, the
fact that he followed his statement limiting the national
government in religion with one that read, "No state shall
violate the equal rights of conscience,"[66] adds further weight
to this interpretation.

Without debate, Madison's recommendations for amendments were referred for consideration to a select committee of
the House, composed of one member from each state, including Madison himself.[67] Although nothing is known of the
committee's week-long deliberations, its report to the House
shows that Madison was the dominating figure, because his
amendments were kept intact with only slight changes in
phraseology in the interests of brevity. From the proposal on
religion, the committee deleted the clause on "civil rights"
and the word "national." The proposed amendment then
read: "No religion shall be established by law, nor shall the
equal rights of conscience be infringed."[68] The report of the
select committee to the House was merely a redrafting of the
original proposals; no explanation of changes was included.

Sitting as a Committee of the Whole, the House began and
ended its debate on the amendment on 15 August. The only
account of the debate, in the *Annals of Congress*, is probably
more in the nature of a condensed and paraphrased version
than it is a verbatim report. The account is brief enough to be
given here in full:

Saturday, August 15

AMENDMENT TO THE CONSTITUTION

The House again went into a Committee of the Whole on the proposed
amendments to the constitution, Mr. Boudinot in the chair.

The fourth proposition being under consideration, as follows:

Article 1. Section 9. Between paragraphs two and three insert "no religion
shall be established by law, nor shall the equal rights of conscience be
infringed."

Mr. Sylvester had some doubts of the propriety of the mode of expression
used in this paragraph. He apprehended that it was liable to a construction different from what had been made by the committee. He feared it
might be thought to have a tendency to abolish religion altogether.

Mr. Vining suggested the propriety of transposing the two members of the
sentence.

Mr. Gerry said it would read better if it was, that no religious doctrine shall be established by law.

Mr. Sherman thought the amendment altogether unnecessary, inasmuch as Congress had no authority whatever delegated to them by the constitution to make religious establishments; he would, therefore, move to have it struck out.

Mr. Carroll.—As the rights of conscience are, in their nature, of peculiar delicacy, and will little bear the gentlest touch of governmental hand; and as many sects have concurred in opinion that they are not well secured under the present constitution, he said he was much in favor of adopting the words. He thought it would tend more towards conciliating the minds of the people to the Government than almost any other amendment he had heard proposed. He would not contend with gentlemen about the phraseology, his object was to secure the substance in such a manner as to satisfy the wishes of the honest part of the community.

Mr. Madison said, he apprehended the meaning of the words to be, that Congress should not establish a religion, and enforce the legal observation of it by law, nor compel men to worship God in any manner contrary to their conscience. Whether the words are necessary or not, he did not mean to say, but they had been required by some of the State Conventions, who seemed to entertain an opinion that under the clause of the constitution, which gave power to Congress to make all laws necessary and proper to carry into execution the constitution, and the laws made under it, enabled them to make laws of such a nature as might infringe the rights of conscience, and establish a national religion; to prevent these effects he presumed the amendment was intended, and he thought it as well expressed as the nature of the language would admit.

Mr. Huntington said that he feared, with the gentleman first up on this subject, that the words might be taken in such latitude as to be extremely hurtful to the cause of religion. He understood the amendment to mean what had been expressed by the gentleman from Virginia; but others might find it convenient to put another construction upon it. The ministers of their congregations to the Eastward were maintained by the contributions of those who belonged to their society; the expense of building meeting-houses was contributed in the same manner. These things were regulated by by-laws. If an action was brought before a Federal Court on any of these cases, the person who had neglected to perform his engagements could not be compelled to do it; for a support of ministers, or building places of worship might be construed into a religious establishment.

By the charter of Rhode Island, no religion could be established by law; he could give a history of the effects of such a regulation; indeed the people were now enjoying the blessed fruits of it. [Intended as irony.] He hoped, therefore, the amendment would be made in such a way as to secure the rights of conscience, and a free exercise of the rights of religion, but not to patronize those who professed no religion at all.

Mr. Madison thought, if the word national was inserted before religion, it would satisfy the minds of honorable gentlemen. He believed that the people feared one sect might obtain a pre-eminence, or two combine together, and establish a religion to which they would compel others to conform. He thought if the word national was introduced, it would point the amendment directly to the object it was intended to prevent.

Mr. Livermore was not satisfied with that amendment; but he did not wish them to dwell long on the subject. He thought it would be better if it was altered, and made to read in this manner, that Congress shall make no laws touching religion, or infringing the rights of conscience.

Mr. Gerry did not like the term national, proposed by the gentleman from Virginia, and he hoped it would not be adopted by the House. It brought to his mind some observations that had taken place in the conventions at the time they were considering the present constitution. It had been insisted upon by those who were called anti-federalists, that this form of Government consolidated the Union; the honorable gentleman's motion shows that he considers it in the same light. Those who were called antifederalists at that time complained that they had injustice done them by the title, because they were in favor of a Federal Government, and the others were in favor of a national one; the federalists were for ratifying the constitution as it stood, and the others not until amendments were made. Their names then ought not to have been distinguished by federalists and antifederalists, but rats and antirats.

Mr. Madison withdrew his motion, but observed that the words "no national religion shall be established by law," did not imply that the Government was a national one; the question was then taken on Mr. Livermore's motion, and passed in the affirmative, thirty-one for, and twenty against it.[69]

Present-day proponents of both the narrow and the broad interpretations of the Establishment Clause are quick to see in this House debate conclusive proof for their respective points of view. In fact, however, it proves nothing conclusively. It was apathetic and unclear: ambiguity, brevity, and imprecision in thought and expression characterized the comments of the few members who spoke. That the House understood the debate, cared deeply about its outcome, or shared a common understanding of the finished amendment is doubtful.

Not even Madison himself, dutifully carrying out his pledge to secure amendments, seems to have troubled to do more than was necessary to get something adopted in order to satisfy popular clamor and deflate Antifederalist charges. Indeed, he agreed with Sherman's statement that the amendment was "altogether unnecessary, inasmuch as Congress had no authority whatever delegated to them by the constitution to make religious establishments." The difficulty, however, lies in the fact that neither Sherman, Madison, nor anyone else took the trouble to define what "religious establishments" were. What did the select committee on amendments intend by recommending that "no religion shall be established by law"? Madison's statement that the words meant "that Congress should not establish a religion" hardly showed the clar-

ity for which one might have hoped. Livermore's motion for a
change of wording apparently expressed what Madison meant
by his use of the word "national" and satisfied the Committee
of the Whole. The proposed amendment, adopted by a vote of
thirty-one to twenty, then read: "Congress shall make no laws
touching religion, or infringing the rights of conscience." A
few days later, however, on 20 August, when the House took
up the report of the Committee of the Whole and voted clause
by clause on the proposed amendments, an additional change
was made. Fisher Ames of Massachusetts moved that the
amendment read: "Congress shall make no law establishing
religion, or to prevent the free exercise thereof, or to infringe
the rights of conscience."[70] Without debate this was adopted
by the necessary two-thirds of the House. Apparently there
was a feeling that the draft of the clause based on Livermore's
motion might not satisfy the demand of those who wanted
something said specifically against establishments of religion.
The amendment as submitted to the Senate reflected a stylistic
change that gave it the following reading: "Congress shall
make no law establishing religion, or prohibiting the free
exercise thereof, nor shall the rights of conscience be infringed."

The Senate began debate on the House amendments on 3
September and continued through 9 September. The debate
was conducted in secrecy and no record of it exists except for
the bare account of motions and votes in the *Senate Journal.*
According to the record of 3 September, three motions of special interest here were defeated on that day.[71] These motions
were clearly intended to restrict the ban in the proposed
amendment to establishments preferring one sect above others. The first motion would have made the clause in the
amendment read: "Congress shall make no law establishing
one religious sect or society in preference to others." After the
failure of a motion to kill the amendment, a motion was made
to change it to read: "Congress shall not make any law infringing the rights of conscience, or establishing any religious sect
or society." The last defeated motion restated the same
thought differently: "Congress shall make no law establishing
any particular denomination of religion in preference to another."[72]

The failure of these three motions, each of which clearly
expressed a narrow intent, would seem to show that the
Senate intended something broader than merely a ban on

preference to one sect. If anything is really clear about this problem of "meaning" and "intent," however, it is that nothing is clear. When the Senate returned to the clause six days later, the House amendment was changed to read: "Congress shall make no law establishing articles of faith or a mode of worship, or prohibiting the free exercise of religion." Like the three previously defeated motions, this has the unmistakable meaning of limiting the ban to acts that prefer one sect over others or which, to put it simply, establish a single state church.

Americans are indebted to the Senate's wording for provoking the House to action that would make *its* intent clear, as the next step in the drafting of the amendment reveals. In voting on the Senate's proposed amendments, the House accepted some and rejected others. Among those rejected was the Senate's article on religion. To resolve the disagreement between the two branches, the House proposed a joint conference committee. The Senate refused to recede from its position, but agreed to the proposal. The committee, a strong and distinguished one, consisted of Madison as chairman of the House conferees, joined by Sherman and Vining, and of Ellsworth as chairman of the Senate conferees, joined by Paterson and Carroll. Four of the six men had been influential members of the Constitutional Convention. The House members of the conference committee flatly refused to accept the Senate's version of the amendment on religion, indicating that the House would not be satisfied with merely a ban on preference of one sect or religion over others. The Senate conferees abandoned the Senate version, and the amendment was redrafted to give it its present phraseology. On 24 September, Ellsworth reported to the Senate that the House would accept the Senate's version of the other amendments provided that the amendment on religion "shall read as follows: 'Congress shall make no law respecting an establishment of religion, or prohibiting the free exercise thereof.' " On the same day, the House sent a message to the Senate verifying Ellsworth's report. On the next day, 25 September, the Senate by a two-thirds vote accepted the condition laid down by the House. Congress had passed the Establishment Clause.[73]

CONCLUSIONS

The outstanding fact that emerges from this review of the drafting of the amendment is that Congress very carefully considered and rejected the phraseology spelling out the narrow interpretation. Through its rejection of the Senate's version of the amendment, rather than through its own ambiguous and imprecise debates, the House showed its intent *not* to frame an amendment that banned only Congressional support to one sect, church, denomination, or religion. The amendment was definitely intended to mean something broader than the narrow interpretation some scholars have given it. At bottom, the amendment was an expression of the fact that the framers of the Constitution had not intended to empower Congress to act in the field of religion. The "great object" of the Bill of Rights, as Madison explicitly said when introducing his draft of amendments to the House, was to "limit and qualify the powers of Government"[74] for the purpose of making certain that the powers granted could not be exercised in forbidden fields, such as religion.

The history of the drafting of the Establishment Clause does not provide any understanding of what was meant by "an establishment of religion." To argue, however, as proponents of the narrow interpretation do, that the amendment permits Congressional aid and support to religion in general or to all churches without discrimination leads to the impossible conclusion that the First Amendment added to Congress' power. Nothing supports such a conclusion. Every bit of evidence goes to prove that the First Amendment, like the others, was intended to restrict Congress to its enumerated powers. Since the Constitutional Convention gave Congress no power to legislate on matters concerning religion, Congress had no such power even in the absence of the First Amendment. It is, therefore, unreasonable to believe that an express prohibition of power—"Congress shall make no law respecting an establishment of religion"—creates the power, previously nonexistent, of supporting religion by aid to one or all religious groups. The Bill of Rights, as Madison said, was not framed "to imply powers not meant to be included in the enumeration."[75]

RATIFICATION OF THE FIRST AMENDMENT

The deliberations of the state legislatures to which the amendments to the Constitution were submitted for ratification shed little light on the meaning of the Establishment Clause. Records of state debates are nonexistent; private correspondence, newspapers, and tracts are of no help.

By mid-June of 1790, nine states had summarily approved
the Bill of Rights.[76] Georgia, Connecticut, Massachusetts, and
Virginia had not yet taken action; indeed, the first three states
did not ratify the Bill of Rights until 1939, on the sesquicentennial anniversary of the Constitution.

Of these states, Georgia took the position that amendments
were unnecessary until experience under the Constitution
demonstrated the need for them.[77] Connecticut's lower house
voted to ratify in 1789 and again the following year, but the
state senate, apparently in the belief that a Bill of Rights was
superfluous, adamantly refused to do so. Yankee Federalists in
Connecticut seem to have thought any suggestion that the
Constitution was not perfect would add to the strength of the
Antifederalists. The same sentiment was prevalent in Massachusetts. There Federalist apathy to the Bill of Rights was
grounded on satisfaction with the Constitution as it was, una-
mended, while Antifederalists were more interested in amendments that would weaken the national government and strength-
en the states than in efforts to protect personal liberties. With
the Bill of Rights thus caught between conflicting party interests, Massachusetts failed to act on the proposed amendments.

The circumstances surrounding ratification in Virginia are
of particular interest for this discussion. Ratification there was
held up for nearly two years while the amendment was
attacked as inadequate. The eight state senators who opposed
it explained their vote publicly in these words: "The 3d amendment [now First Amendment] recommended by Congress
does not prohibit the rights of conscience from being violated
or infringed: and although it goes to restrain Congress from
passing laws establishing any national religion, they might,
notwithstanding, levy taxes to any amount, for the support of
religion or its preachers; and any particular denomination of
christians might be so favored and supported by the General
Government, as to give it a decided advantage over others,
and in process of time render it as powerful and dangerous as
if it was established as the national religion of the country
. . . . This amendment then, when considered as it relates to
any of the rights it is pretended to secure, will be found totally
inadequate."[78]

Taken out of context and used uncritically, this statement
by the eight Virginia state senators has been offered as proof
that the Establishment Clause carried only the narrowest
intent, that the Virginia legislators so understood it, and that

the state ultimately approved it only in that narrow sense. Because the eight senators who favored a broader ban were ultimately defeated, the conclusion is drawn that the amendment did not purport to ban government aid to religion generally or to all sects without discrimination. Examination of the intricate party maneuverings and complex motives in the Virginia ratification dispute, however, sheds a different light on the senators' statement.

Virginia's Antifederalists, led by Patrick Henry and United States Senators Richard Henry Lee and William Grayson, had opposed the ratification of the Constitution for a variety of reasons. Chief among these was the belief that it established too strong a central government at the expense of the states. For example, the Antifederalists wanted amendments to the Constitution that would restrict Congress' commerce and tax powers. It is true enough that they were also in the forefront of the movement for amendments that would protect personal liberties, but there is considerable reason to suspect that many deplored the absence of a Bill of Rights primarily for the purpose of defeating the Constitution itself. Antifederalists in the first session of Congress sought to secure amendments that would aggrandize state powers, but they failed in this effort. Then, in order to force Congress to reconsider the whole subject of amendments, Virginia's Antifederalists attempted to defeat the proposed Bill of Rights. Virginia's Federalists, however, eagerly supported the Bill of Rights in order to prevent additional amendments that might hamstring the national government.

On 30 November 1789, Virginia's lower house, dominated by the Federalists, "and without debate of any consequence," quickly passed all the amendments proposed by Congress. The opposition party, however, controlled the state senate. "That body," reported Randolph to Washington, "will attempt to postpone them [the amendments]; for a majority is unfriendly to the government."[79] As a member of the Virginia lower house reported to Madison, the senate was inclined to reject the amendments not from dissatisfaction with them, but from apprehension "that the adoption of them at this time will be an obstacle to the chief object of their pursuit, the amendment on the subject of direct taxation."[80] As Randolph had predicted, the senate, by a vote of eight to seven, did decide to postpone final action on what are now the First, Sixth, Ninth, and Tenth Amendments until the next session of the legislature, thereby allowing time for the electorate to express itself. It was on this occasion that the eight senators in question made their statement on the alleged inadequacy of the First Amendment, bidding for electoral support against an allegedly weak Bill of Rights by presenting themselves as champions of religious liberty and advocates of separation between government and religion.

Madison remained unworried by this tactic, confidently predicting that the action of the senators would boomerang. "The miscarriage of the third article [the First Amendment], particularly, will have this effect," he wrote to Washington.[81] His confidence is explainable on several counts.

First, Madison knew that the First Amendment had the support of the Baptists, the one group most insistent upon the voluntary support of religion.[82] Second, he knew that the eight senators did not come before the electorate with clean hands. Like Henry and Lee, who laid out their strategy for them, they had consistently voted against religious liberty and in favor of taxes for religion. Their legislative record on this score was well known. By contrast, the seven senators who favored ratification of the First Amendment had stood with Jefferson and Madison in the fight from 1779 to 1786 against a state establishment of religion and for religious liberty.[83] Finally, Madison reasoned that the statement by the eight senators was an inept piece of propaganda with little chance of convincing anyone, because it was obviously misleading and inaccurate. The eight senators alleged that "any particular denomination of Christians might be so favored and supported by the general government, as to give it a decided advantage over others,"—a construction of the First Amendment that not even proponents of the narrow interpretation would accept—and the same senators also asserted that the amendment "does not prohibit the rights of conscience from being violated or infringed"—whereas anyone might read for himself the Amendment's positive statement that Congress shall not abridge the free exercise of religion.

In the end, Madison's confidence proved justified. On 15 December 1791, after a session of inaction on the Bill of Rights, the state senate finally ratified it without a record vote. In the context of Antifederalist maneuverings, there is every reason to believe that Virginia supported the First Amendment with the understanding that it had been misrepresented by the eight senators. There is no reason to believe that Virginia ratified with the understanding that the Amendment permitted any government aid to religion.

What conclusions can one come to, then, in connection with ratification of the First Amendment by the states? In Virginia, the one state for which there is some evidence, one can arrive only at a negative conclusion: The evidence does not support the narrow interpretation of the Establishment Clause. In nine other states there was perfunctory ratification, with no record of the debates, and in the remaining three states there was inaction. In the absence of other evidence, therefore, it is impossible to determine solely on the basis of ratification just what the general understanding of the Establishment Clause actually was.

MEANING OF THE CLAUSE

By now the difficulty of trying to explain exactly what was intended by the Establishment Clause should be obvious. What was meant by an establishment of religion? Was the prohibition in the First Amendment intended only to ban preference for one church? Or was it designed to ban nondiscriminatory government support to all religious bodies and to religion generally? Here an examination of the American experience with establishments of religion is essential.

This experience was in many respects unique, for it did not always follow the pattern of European precedent. Some scholars have arbitrarily assigned to the phrase "an establishment of religion" its European meaning only. James O'Neill, one of the first advocates of the narrow interpretation, without examining establishments of religion in colonial America or the establishments that existed after the Revolution and at the time of the framing of the First Amendment, concluded in capital letters that an establishment of religion has always and everywhere meant "A SINGLE CHURCH OR RELIGION ENJOYING FORMAL, LEGAL, OFFICIAL, MONOPOLISTIC PRIVILEGE THROUGH A UNION WITH THE GOVERNMENT OF THE STATE."[84]

Other scholars[85] who insist that the First Amendment only banned a single privileged state church also fail to deal with the history of colonial and revolutionary periods, which provide repeated examples demonstrating that establishment of religion in America commonly meant something different than it did in Europe. Indeed, at the time of the framing of the Bill of Rights all state establishments that still existed in

America were *multiple* establishments of *several* churches, something unknown in European experience.

THE COLONIAL EXPERIENCE

On the eve of the Revolution, establishments of religion in the European sense existed only in the Southern colonies of Virginia, Maryland, North Carolina, South Carolina, and Georgia, where the Church of England or Episcopalian Church was the state church. All persons, regardless of belief or affiliation, were taxed for its support as the official church of these colonies. Taxes so collected were spent to build and maintain church buildings and pay salaries of Episcopalian clergy. These Southern establishments were, therefore, comparable to European counterparts.

The record in Rhode Island, Pennsylvania, Delaware, and New Jersey is equally clear; these four colonies never experienced any establishment of religion. In the colonies of New York, Massachusetts, Connecticut, and New Hampshire, however, the pattern of establishment was diversified and uniquely American.

New York's colonial history of church-state relationships provides the first example of an establishment of religion radically different from the European type, an establishment of religion in general—or at least of Protestantism in general—and without preference to one church over others. When the English conquered New Netherlands in 1664, renaming it New York in honor of its new proprietor, the Duke of York (James II), they found that the Dutch Reformed Church (Calvinist) was exclusively established as the state church. After the colony passed to English control, however, this church lost its government support. In 1665, the people of Long Island agreed to what came to be known as the "Duke's Laws," which made provisions for the regulation of churches in that area. Any church of the Protestant religion could become an established church. In a sense, of course, this was an exclusive establishment of one religion, Protestantism; but the system involved a multiple establishment of several different Protestant churches, in sharp contrast to European precedents, which provided for the establishment of one church only.

Under the "Duke's Laws," every township was obliged publicly to support some Protestant church and a minister. The denomination of the church did not matter. Costs were to be met by a public tax: "Every inhabitant shall contribute to all charges both in Church and State."[86] A local option system prevailed. On producing evidence of ordination "from some Protestant bishop or minister,"[87] the minister selected by a town was inducted into his pastorate by the governor representing the state. In other words, this was an establishment of religion in which there was a formal, legal, official union between government and religion on a nonpreferential basis and without the establishment of any individual church. In 1683, the New York Assembly enacted a "Charter of Liberties" that adopted the Long Island system of multiple establishments and extended it to the whole colony.

Following the Glorious Revolution of 1688, the English government expected and instructed its governors of New York to implement an establishment of Anglicanism there.[88] In 1693, Governor Benjamin Fletcher managed to have a recalcitrant legislature, composed almost entirely of non-Anglicans, pass "An Act for Settling a Ministry & raising a Maintenance for them" in the four counties of New York, Richmond, Queens, and Westchester. The law called only for "a good and sufficient Protestant Minister" and nowhere mentioned the Church of England.[89] The royal governors, together with most Anglicans, asserted that the Act had established their church; but many non-Anglican New Yorkers disagreed. Thus, in 1695, the legislature agreed with the New York City vestry that according to the terms of the 1693 act, it was entitled to select a "Dissenting Protestant Minister," i.e., a non-Anglican one, although the governor refused to permit this.[90] A few years after, in 1699, Lewis Morris, a staunch Anglican and later chief justice of the province, wrote: "The People were generally dissenters [and] fancied they had made an effectual provision for Ministers of their own persuasion by this Act."[91]

In 1703 and 1704, Anglicans, with the assistance of Lord Cornbury, the highhanded governor of the colony, managed to gain possession of the church and parsonage in the town of Jamaica, Long Island. These buildings had been erected at public expense, and the town had chosen a Presbyterian minister. The Anglicans' action set off a long and bitter controversy. The Presbyterians refused to pay the salary of the Anglican minister because, as the Church of England townspeople reported, "they [the Presbyterians] stick not to call themselves the Established Church."[92] In 1710, the Presbyterians man-

aged to seize and retain the parsonage, and, in 1727, they
brought suit for the recovery of the church, which the provincial court, in an unreported decision, awarded them.[93] For
much of the remainder of the colonial period, Anglicans managed to pry a minister's salary out of the reluctant inhabitants,
but not without constant complaints and a further attempt,
defeated by the courts in 1768, to withhold the minister's
salary.[94] Elsewhere on Long Island, the inhabitants supported
the non-Anglican town ministers chosen by the majority.
Brookhaven certainly supported such a minister, and given
the scarcity of Anglicans and Anglican ministers in the colony, most towns probably reached their own accommodations
with the minister of their choice.[95]

In the 1750s, the organization of King's (later Columbia)
College provoked a fierce controversy over the nature of New
York's establishment. Anglicans demanded that they control
the new school because they enjoyed "a preference by the
Constitution of the province."[96] Non-Anglicans rejected both
claims. A young lawyer, William Livingston, and two asso-
ciates, William Smith, Jr. and John Morin Scott, organized
the opposition. The Triumvirate, as the three came to be
known, specifically denied that the Anglican Church was exclusively established in the colony. They publicized this refuta-
tion in their paper, *The Independent Reflector*, and Smith
devoted a section to it in his *History*.[97] The Triumvirate
insisted that the establishment "restricted no particular Protestant Denomination whatsoever," and that the people were
to choose which ministers to establish.[98] Here again is evidence that the concept of a multiple establishment of religion
was not only understood by but also engaged the attention of
the inhabitants of colonial New York.

Although New York Anglicans claimed an exclusive establishment of their church, a large number of the colony's population understood the establishment set up by the Act of 1693
not simply as a state preference for one religion or sect over
others, but as allowing public support for many different
churches to be determined by popular vote. Thus, in 1775,
Alexander Hamilton, New York's leading citizen, was able to
define "an established religion" as "a religion which the civil
authority engaged, not only to protect, but to support."[99]

Massachusetts, the major and archetypal New England colony, proclaimed no establishment of the Congregational
church by name after 1692. That year the general court pro-

vided for an establishment of religion on a town basis by simply requiring every town to maintain an "able, learned and orthodox" minister, to be chosen by the voters of the town and supported by a tax levied on all taxpayers.[100] By law, several different denominations could benefit from the establishment. In fact, Congregationalists, since they constituted the overwhelming majority in nearly every town, reaped the benefits of the establishment of religion. Except in Boston, where all congregations were supported voluntarily, the law operated to make the Congregational Church the privileged one, which unquestionably was the purpose of the statute, and non-Congregationalists, chiefly Episcopalians, Baptists, and Quakers, were for a long time taxed for the support of Congregationalism.

The growing number of dissenters, however, forced Congregationalists to retreat and make concessions. The retreat began in 1727, when the Episcopalians won the statutory right of having their religious taxes applied to the support of their own churches.[101] By coincidence, the Connecticut legislature passed a similar act on behalf of the Episcopalian churches in the same year.[102] In 1728, Massachusetts exempted Quakers and Baptists from taxes for the payment of ministerial salaries. Then, in 1731 and 1735, each denomination was respectively exempted from sharing the taxes for building new town churches.[103] After those dates tax exemption statutes on behalf of Quakers and Baptists were periodically renewed, so that members of these denominations were not supposed to pay religious taxes for the benefit of either Congregational churches or of their own.

As a result of a variety of complicated legal technicalities, as well as outright illegal action, frequent abuses occurred under the system of tax exemption, which also prevailed in Connecticut. In both colonies many Quakers and Baptists were unconscionably forced to pay for the support of Congregational churches, and even Episcopalians who lived too far from a church of their own denomination to attend its services were taxed for support of Congregational ones. These abuses of both the letter and spirit of the law, however, do not alter the basic fact that after 1728 the establishments of religion in both colonies meant government support of two churches, Congregationalist and Episcopalian, without specified preference to either.

These injustices arose out of the overwhelming numerical

superiority of Congregationalists. Although Congregationalists
in fact made up the establishment in New England, prominent spokesmen among them understood that they did not
constitute an exclusive establishment. Cotton Mather wrote
that "the Person elected by the Majority of the Inhabitants
. . . is . . . the King's Minister," and he went on to state that
the minister elected by each town was the official minister and
as such entitled to the taxes of the place.[104] Benjamin Colman
declared: "If any Town will chuse [sic] a Gentleman of the
Church of England for their Pastor . . . he is their Minister
by the Laws of our Province as much as any Congregational
Minister."[105] Near the end of the colonial period, Johnathan
Mayhew made the most explicit statement of all on this subject. Massachusetts, he explained, did not establish a single
church, but rather "protestant churches of various denominations." He understood that "an hundred churches, all of different denominations . . . might all be established in the same
. . . colony, as well as one, two, or three."[106] Thus did three
of the most prominent New England ministers of the eighteenth century specify their understanding that the Massachusetts establishment was something other than an exclusive
preference for one church. In fact, two groups, Congregationalists and Episcopalians, received tax support for their
churches, and all agreed that were it not for the fact that Congregationalists constituted a majority in the towns, ministers
of other churches could be elected and be established according
to the laws of the colony. Massachusetts, and Connecticut to a
lesser extent, clearly proclaimed not an exclusive but a dual or
plural establishment of religion.

   The situation did not substantially differ in New Hampshire. Down to the middle of the eighteenth century, the
town system of establishment operated to benefit the Congregational Church exclusively. New Hampshire, however, did
not systematically require the payment of rates by dissenters
nor concern itself with the support of their ministers. Quakers, Episcopalians, Presbyterians, and Baptists were exempt
from supporting the local established church, which was usually Congregationalist. In some towns, however, Episcopalians
and Presbyterians were authorized to establish their own parishes and to use town authority to collect taxes for their
churches. By the eve of the Revolution, the pattern of establishment had become bewilderingly diverse. Some towns maintained dual establishments, others maintained multiple estab-

lishments, with free exercise for dissenters.[107]

No New England colony maintained a single provincial establishment supported by all, or even by the taxes of its own members alone. In Massachusetts, Connecticut, and New Hampshire, other groups apart from Congregationalists were eligible for and received public tax support for religion. Clearly New Englanders understood that an individual town could decide which denomination would be established within its precincts.

EARLY STATE CONSTITUTIONS

In the wake of the American Revoultion and its attendant atmosphere of liberty, those exclusive establishments of religion inherited from the colonial period collapsed. States that had never had establishments renewed their barriers against them, except for Rhode Island, which did not adopt a new state constitution.

New Jersey provided by its constitution of 1776 that no person should "ever be obliged to pay tithes, taxes, or any other rates, for the purpose of building or repairing any other church or churches, place or places of worship, or for the maintenance of any minister or ministry, contrary to what he believes to be right, or has deliberately or voluntarily engaged himself to perform."[108] Delaware adopted a similar article.[109] Both states, however, banned an establishment of "one sect in preference to others."[110] Pennsylvania's provision in its constitution of 1776 was equally broad: "No man ought or of right can be compelled to attend any religious worship, or erect or support any place of worship, or maintain any ministry, contrary to, or against, his own free will and consent."[111]

In New York, where a multiple establishment had been maintained in New York City and three adjoining counties, the long history of an insistence by the Church of England that it was rightfully the only established church influenced the writing of the clause against establishments in the constitution of 1777. The system of multiple establishments of religion was ended by the following words, reflecting the stubborn determination of non-Episcopalians never to admit, even by implication, that there had ever been an exclusive or preferential establishment of the Church of England: "That all such parts of the said common law, and all such of the said statutes and acts aforesaid, or parts thereof, *as may be construed to establish or maintain any particular denomination of Christians*

*or their ministers . . . be, and they hereby are, abrogated and
rejected.*"[112]

Nowhere in America after 1776 did an establishment of
religion restrict itself to a state church or to a system of public
support of one sect alone; instead, an establishment of religion
meant public support of several or all churches, with preference to none. The six states that continued to provide for public support of religion were careful to make concessions to the
spirit of the times by extending their establishments to embrace many different groups.

Three of these six states were in New England. Massachusetts adopted its constitution in 1780. Article 3 of its Declaration of Rights commanded the legislature to authorize the
"several towns, parishes, precincts, and other bodies politic, or
religious societies, to make suitable provision, at their own
expense, for the institution of the public worship of God, and
for the support and maintenance of public Protestant teachers
of piety, religion, and morality." Clause 2 of Article 3 empowered the legislature to make church attendance compulsory.
Clause 3 provided that the towns and parishes were to have
the right of electing their ministers. Clause 4 was the principal one relevant to the problem under inquiry. It stated: "And
all moneys paid by the subject to the support of public worship, and all the public teachers aforesaid, shall, if he require
it, be uniformly applied to the support of the public teacher or
teachers of his own religious sect or denomination, provided
there be any on whose instructions he attends; otherwise it
may be paid towards the support of the teacher or teachers of
the parish or precinct in which the said moneys are raised." A
fifth clause even provided that "no subordination of any one
sect or denomination to the other shall ever be established by
law."[113] In the context of Article 3, the fifth clause, against
preference, proves that constitutionally speaking the several
churches of the establishment were on a nonpreferential basis.
Clearly, establishment in Massachusetts meant government
support of religion and of several different churches in an
equitable manner. As in colonial days, the Congregationalists
were the chief beneficiaries of the establishment, primarily
because they were by far the most numerous and because they
resorted to various tricks to fleece non-Congregationalists out
of their share of religious taxes. The fact remains, however,
that Baptist, Episcopalian, Methodist, Unitarian, and even

Universalist churches were publicly supported under the establishment after 1780.[114] The establishment in Massachusetts lasted until 1833.

In New Hampshire, the state constitution of 1784, by Article 6 of its Declaration of Rights, created a statewide multiple establishment with the guarantee that no sect or denomination should be subordinated to another.[115] As in Massachusetts, which was the model for New Hampshire, all Protestant churches benefited. The multiple establishment ended in 1819.

Connecticut's story is also like that of Massachusetts. Like Rhode Island, the state adopted no constitution at this time; its establishment was regulated by the "Act of Toleration" of 1784, which was in force when the Bill of Rights was framed. By this statute each town was to choose which minister to support, and no sect was to be subordinated to any other. Those who did not belong to the majority established church were exempted from paying towards its support as long as they contributed to their own congregation. The establishment lasted until 1818.[116]

In Maryland, Georgia, and South Carolina, "an establishment of religion" meant very much what it did in the three New England states that maintained multiple establishments. In Maryland, where the Church of England had been exclusively established, the constitution of 1776 provided that no person could be compelled "to maintain any particular place of worship, or any particular ministry," thus disestablishing the Episcopalian Church. The same constitution, however, provided for a new establishment of religion: "Yet the Legislature may, in their discretion, lay a general and *equal tax*, for the support of the Christian religion; leaving to each individual the power of appointing the payment over of the money, collected from him, to the support of any particular place or worship or minister."[117] "Christian" rather than "Protestant" was used in Maryland because of the presence of a large Catholic population, thus insuring nonpreferential support of all churches existing in the state. In 1785, the Maryland legislature sought to exercise its discretionary power to institute nonpreferential support, but "a huge uproar arose against the measure," and it was denounced as a new establishment and decisively beaten.[118] In 1810, the power to enact a multiple establishment was taken from the legislature by a constitu-

tional amendment providing that "an *equal* and *general* tax or
any other tax . . . for the support of *any religion*" was not
lawful.[119]

Georgia's constitution of 1777 tersely effected the disestablishment of the Church of England while permitting a multiple establishment of all churches without exception: "All persons whatever shall have the free exercise of their religion; . . .
and shall not, unless by consent, support any teacher or
teachers except those of their own profession."[120] "This, of
course, left the way open for taxation for the support of one's
own religion," said the historian of eighteenth-century church-
state relationships in Georgia, "and such a law was passed in
1785,"[121] although similar bills had failed in 1782 and 1784.
According to the 1785 law, all Christian sects and denominations were to receive tax support in proportion to the amount
of property owned by their respective church members, but it
is not clear whether this measure ever went into operation.
What is clear is that an establishment of religion meant
government tax support to all churches, with preference to
none. The constitution in effect at the time of the framing of
the Bill of Rights was adopted in 1789. Its relevant provision
declared that no persons should be obliged "to contribute to
the support of any religious profession but their own," thereby permitting a multiple establishment as before. In the state
constitution adopted in 1798, however, Georgia separated
church and state by a guarantee against any religious taxes
and by placing the support of religion on a purely voluntary
basis.[122]

South Carolina's constitution of 1778 was the sixth state
constitution providing for a multiple establishment of religion.
Article 28 most elaborately spelled out the details for the
maintenance of the "Christian Protestant religion" as "the
established religion of this State." Adult males forming themselves into any religious society of a Protestant denomination
were declared to be "a church of the established religion of
this State," on condition of subscribing to a belief in God,
promising to worship him publicly, a belief in Christianity as
"the true religion," and a belief in the divine inspiration of
the Scriptures. Pursuant to this law, Baptists, Independents,
Methodists, and Anglicans qualified as "Established" churches.
The state also specifically guaranteed that "no person shall,
by law, be obliged to pay towards the maintenance and
support of a religious worship that he does not freely join in,
or has not voluntarily engaged to support."[123] In 1790, South

Carolina, reflecting the influence of the federal Bill of Rights, adopted a new constitution with no provisions whatever for public support of religion.[124]

The constitutions of North Carolina and Virginia did not provide for an establishment of religion of any kind. In 1776, North Carolina banned state support for religion and disestablished the Church of England.[125] By contrast, Virginia's constitution of 1776 was noncommittal on the subject of an establishment. At the close of 1776, the Church of England was for all practical purposes disestablished in Virginia by a statute that forever exempted all nonmembers from taxes for its support, and that suspended for one year the collection of any taxes from Church of England members. The suspension of religious taxes for members was renewed in 1777 and 1778; in 1779, the old colonial statute levying those taxes was repealed. Thus, the Church of England received no government support after 1776. The statute of 1776 that initiated the end of the exclusive establishment, however, expressly reserved for future decision the question whether religion ought to be placed on a private, voluntary basis or be supported on a non-preferential basis by a new "general" assessment.[126]

In 1779, a bill for support on a nonpreferential basis was introduced; at the same time, however, Jefferson's Bill for Establishing Religious Freedom was introduced, providing, in part, "that no man shall be compelled to frequent or support any religious worship, place, or ministry whatsoever."[127] The principle underlying this provision was Jefferson's belief that religion was a personal matter between the individual and God and not rightfully a subject under the jurisdiction of the civil government. By contrast, the "General Assessment Bill" was predicated on the supposition, expressed in its preamble, that the state must encourage religion. This bill stipulated that the Christian religion should be "the established religion," that societies of Christians organized for the purpose of religious worship should in law be regarded as churches of the established religion, each to have its own "name or denomination" and each to share the tax proceeds assessed on tithable personal property and collected by county sheriffs. Every person was to designate the church of his membership, and that church alone would receive his taxes; money collected from persons not designating membership was to be divided proportionately among all churches of his county.[128]

Confronted by two diametrically opposed bills, the Virginia legislature deadlocked, and neither bill could muster a major-

ity. In 1784, Patrick Henry reintroduced the general assessment plan under the title "A Bill Establishing a Provision for
the Teachers of the Christian Religion," in which the stated
purpose was to require "a moderate tax or contribution annually for the support of the Christian religion, or of some
Christian church, denomination or communion of Christians,
or for some form of Christian worship."[129] A resolution in
favor of the bill was passed against the opposition of a minority led by Madison.

Only the notes of Madison's speech against the measure
remain. These show that he argued that religion is a matter of
private rather than civil concern, and that taxes in support of
religion violated religious liberty. The true question, he declared, was not "Is religion necessary?" but rather "Are religious establishments necessary for religion?," to which he
argued in the negative.[130] Through masterly political maneu-
vering, Madison got Henry out of the legislature by supporting his election as governor and then managed to get a final
vote on the bill postponed until the next session of the legislature, nearly a year later, in November of 1785. In the meantime, he brought his case to the people by writing his famous
"Memorial and Remonstrance Against Religious Assessments." This widely distributed pamphlet acted as a catalyst
for the opposition to the assessment bill and resulted in the
election of a legislature with an overwhelming majority against
it. The new legislature let the bill die unnoticed, and by a
vote of sixty-seven to twenty enacted instead Jefferson's bill
for religious freedom with its provision against government
support of religion.

CONCLUSIONS

The struggle in Virginia outlined above is usually featured
in accounts of the history of separation of church and state in
America. No doubt historians focus their attention on the
Virginia story because the sources are uniquely ample,[131] the
struggle was important and dramatic, and the opinions of
Madison, the principal framer of the Bill of Rights, not to
mention those of Jefferson, were fully elicited. As a result, the
details of no other state controversy over church-state relationships are so familiar. If, however, one is concerned with
attempting to understand what was meant by "an establishment of religion" at the time of the framing of the Bill of
Rights, the histories of the other states are equally important.

Indeed, the abortive effort in Virginia to enact Patrick Henry's assessment bill is less important than the fact that five states actually had constitutional provisions authorizing general assessments for religion, and a sixth (Connecticut) provided for the same by statute. Had the assessment bill in Virginia been enacted, it would simply have increased the number of states maintaining multiple establishments from six to seven.

Clearly the provisions of these six states show that to understand the American meaning of "an establishment of religion" one cannot arbitrarily adopt a definition based on European experience. In every European precedent of an establishment, the religion established was that of a single church. Many different churches, or the religion held in common by all of them, i.e., Christianity or Protestantism, were never simultaneously established by any European nation. Establishments in America, however, both in the colonial and early state periods, were not limited in nature or in meaning to state support of one church. *An establishment of religion in America at the time of the framing of the Bill of Rights meant government aid and sponsorship of religion, principally by impartial tax support of the institutions of religion, the churches.*

In no state or colony, of course, was there ever an establishment of religion that included every religion without exception. Neither Judaism, nor Buddhism, nor Islam, nor any but a Christian religion was ever established in America. In half of the six multiple establishments existing in 1789, Protestantism was the established religion; in the other half, Christianity was. No member of the First Congress came from a state that supported an exclusive establishment of religion; no such example could have been found in colonial America. Of those states that provided public support for religion, half of them had provided for such at least theoretically since the early eighteenth century; the remainder did so from the time of the American Revolution. Their experience told the legislators in 1789 that an establishment of religion meant not simply state preference for one religion but nonpreferential support for any or all.

NOTES

The author is pleased to acknowledge the indispensable assistance of Thomas Curry, whose own work on this topic, when published as a book, will surely become the standard and definitive scholarly treatment.

1.   *Everson* v. *Board of Education*, 330 U.S. 1:15-16 (1947).
2.   Ibid., 31-32.
3.   J. M. O'Neill, *Religion and Education Under the Constitution* (New York: Harper and Row, 1949), 56. See Also Edwin S. Corwin, "The Supreme Court As National School Board," *Law and Contemporary Problems* 14 (Winter 1949):10, 20. Chester James Antieau, Arthur L. Downey, and Edward C. Roberts, *Freedom from Federal Establishment. Formation and Early History of the First Amendment Religion Clauses* (Milwaukee: Bruce Publishing Company, 1964), is the most completely documented presentation of this point of view, which can also be found in Walter Berns, *The First Amendment and the Future of American Democracy* (New York: Basic Books, Inc., 1976); Michael J. Malbin, *Religion and Politics: The Intentions of the Authors of the First Amendment* (Washington: American Enterprise Institute, 1978); and Robert L. Cord, *Separation of Church and State: Historical Fact and Current Fiction* (New York: Lambeth Press, 1982).
4.   Several scholars declare that the germ of the Establishment Clause derived from a proposal allegedly advanced by Charles Pinckney of South Carolina on 29 May: "The legislature of the United States shall pass no law on the subject of religion." See Leo Pfeffer, *Church, State, and Freedom* (Boston: Beacon Press, 1967), 123; Anson Phelps Stokes, *Church and State in the United States*, 3 vols. (New York: Harper & Brothers, 1950), 1:526-27. Pinckney's proposal appears in Madison's *Notes* as part of a comprehensive plan of union submitted to the Convention by Pinckney. Jonathan Elliot, ed., *The Debates in the Several State Conventions on the Adoption of the Federal Constitution In Five Volumes* (Philadelphia: J.B. Lippincott and Company, 1941), 5:131. The Pinckney plan, however, has been revealed to be spurious. Neither it nor the proposal banning laws on religion was ever presented to the Convention; in 1818 or later, a copy of the Pinckney plan was added by Madison to his original *Notes*, which were not published until 1840. Charles Warren, *The Making of the Constitution* (Boston: Little, Brown and Company, 1928), 142-43. Pfeffer's book, mentioned above, is particularly recommended to readers as the most authoritative constitutional history of America's experience with the double-faceted principle of religious liberty and separation of government and religion.
5.   Elliot, *Debates*, 5:446.
6.   Ibid., 5:498.
7.   Ibid.
8.   Stokes, *Church and State*, 1:527. See also Pfeffer, *Church, State, and Freedom*, 123.
9.   See Madison to Edmund Randolph, 10 April 1788, James Madison, *The Papers of James Madison*, ed. Robert A. Rutland et al. (Charlottesville: University of Virginia Press, 1976), 11:19.
10.   Elliot is in error on this point; see Charles C. Tansill, ed., *Documents Illustrative of the Formation of the Union of the American States* (Washington: Government Printing Office, 1927), 716.
11.   For example: Elliot, *Debates*, 3:203-4, 450, 600 (Randolph and Nicholas in Virginia); 4:149 (Iredell in North Carolina); 4:315-16 (C. C. Pinckney in South Carolina); and 2:78 (Varnum in Massachusetts). For the very influential statements by Wilson of Pennsylvania, see ibid., 2:436 and 453; also *Pennsylvania and the Federal Constitution, 1787-1788*, ed. John Bach McMaster and Frederick D. Stone (Lancaster, Pa.: Historical Society of Pennsylvania, 1888), 313-14. See also McKean in ibid., 377; Ellsworth in *Essays on the Constitution of the United States*, ed. Paul L. Ford (Brooklyn: The Historical Printing Club, 1892), 163-64; Williamson, "Remarks," in ibid.,

398; and Hanson, "Remarks on the Proposed Plan," in *Pamphlets on the Constitution
of the United States*, ed. Paul L. Ford (Brooklyn: The Historical Printing Club, 1888),
241-42. See also *The Documentary History of the Ratification of the Constitution*, ed.
Merrill Jensen et al., 4 vols. to date (Madison: State Historical Society of Wisconsin,
1976-   ). The volumes published to date cover Pennsylvania, Delaware, New Jersey, Georgia, and Connecticut.
12.   *The Federalist*, any edition, no. 84.
13.   The whole concept of a federal system of distributed powers, with the national
government possessing only limited, delegated powers, forms the principal evidence.
In addition, consider the following specific comments that are illustrative rather than
exhaustive. Wilson of Pennsylvania, in response to the allegation that there was no
security for the rights of conscience, said: "I ask the honorable gentlemen, what part
of this system puts it in the power of Congress to attack those rights? When there is
no power to attack, it is idle to prepare the means of defense." Elliot, *Debates*, 2:455.
Randolph of Virginia asserted that "no power is given expressly to Congress over
religion," and added that only powers "constitutionally given" could be exercised.
Elliot, *Debates*, 3:204 and 469. Madison of Virginia commented: "There is not a
shadow of right in the general government to intermeddle with religion." Elliot,
Debates, 3:330. Iredell of North Carolina said: "If any future Congress should pass an
act concerning the religion of the country, it would be an act which they are not
authorized to pass, by the Constitution, and which the people would not obey."
Elliot, *Debates*, 4:194. Spaight of North Carolina added: "As to the subject of religion . . . No power is given to the general government to interfere with it at all. Any
act of Congress on this subject would be a usurpation." Elliot, *Debates*, 4:208.
14.   Massachusetts, New Hampshire, Virginia, New York, North Carolina, and
Rhode Island.
15.   See Elliot, *Debates*, 2:112, 114 (Gore and Davis in Massachusetts); 3:468 (Randolph in Virginia); 4:145, 150 (Iredell and Johnston in North Carolina); see also Wilson of Pennsylvania in McMaster and Stone, eds., *Pennsylvania and the Federal Constitution*, 309, 353, 406. On the variety of early state procedures concerning the rights of
accused persons, see generally Charles Fairman, "The Supreme Court and Constitutional Limitations on State Government Authority," *University of Chicago Law
Review* 21 (Autumn 1953):40-78, passim. Charles Warren points out that in civil
cases, the citizens of four states had been deprived of jury trial in the seven-year
period before the Constitution was framed, in *Congress, the Constitution and the
Supreme Court* (Boston: Little, Brown and Company, 1925), 81.
16.   For example, only seven of the thirteen states had separate Bills of Rights in
their constitutions; several states maintained establishments of religion that were
prohibited by others; and six states did not constitutionally provide for the right to
the writ of habeas corpus. See generally Francis Newton Thorpe, *The Constitutional
History of the United States* (Chicago: Callagan & Co., 1901), 2:199-211, for a table on
state precedents for the federal Bill of Rights. See also Edward Dumbauld, "State
Precedents for the Bill of Rights," *Journal of Public Law* 7 (January 1958):323-44.
17.   For example, Massachusetts recommended the right to indictment by grand jury
but did not provide for it in its own constitution; Virginia and North Carolina
recommended constitutional protection for freedom of speech that they did not protect in their respective constitutions; and New York recommended protections against
compulsory self-incrimination and double jeopardy, neither of which were constitutionally protected by New York.
18.   Elliot, *Debates*, reports in detail the debates of five states (Massachusetts, New
York, Virginia, North Carolina, and South Carolina) and in very fragmentary fashion
reports the debates of three others (Maryland, Pennsylvania, and Connecticut).
McMaster and Stone collected the extant Pennsylvania debates, together with pamphlets and essays from that state, while P. L. Ford collected important essays and
pamphlets from all the states. See also Jensen, *Ratification*.
19.   Elliot, *Debates*, 2:202.

20. Ford, *Essays on the Constitution*, 168.
21. McMaster and Stone, *Pennsylvania and the Federal Constitution*, 421, 424, 461, 480.
22. Ibid., 502.
23. Ibid., 589.
24. Tansill, *Documents*, 1018-20.
25. Elliott, *Debates*, 2:236.
26. Elliott, *Debates*, 2:553.
27. Philip A. Crowl, *Maryland During and After the Revolution* (Baltimore: Johns Hopkins Press, 1943), 156; Albert W. Werline, *Problems of Church and State in Maryland* (South Lancaster, Mass.: The College Press, 1948), 143-68.
28. Werline, *Problems*, chap. 6, passim.
29. *City Gazette or Daily Advertiser of Charleston*, 26 May 1788, quoted in Antieau, *Freedom*, 106.
30. Tansill, *Documents*, 1022-24.
31. *The Federal and State Constitutions, Colonial Charters, and Other Organic Laws of the States, Territories, and Colonies*, ed. Francis Newton Thorpe, 7 vols. (Washington: Government Printing Office, 1909), 6:3255. *South Carolina Laws, Charleston, 1785, 1786, 1787, 1790*, in Charles Evans, *American Bibliography: A Chronological Dictionary of All Books, Pamphlets and Periodical Publications Printed in the United States of America from the Genesis of Printing in 1639 down to and Including the Year 1820*, 14 vols. (Chicago: Charles Evans, 1903-1959), microcard, no. 19750, p. 8; no. 19998, p. 43; no. 20715, p. 48; no. 22895, p. 11 (hereafter cited as Evans, *Early American Imprints*). John Wesley Brinsfield, *Religion and Politics in South Carolina* (Easley, S.C.: Southern Historical Press, Inc., 1983), 122-27.
32. Tansill, *Documents*, 1026.
33. Elliot, *Debates*, 3:204.
34. Ibid., 3:330. See also the similar statement by Zachariah Johnson at 3:645-46.
35. Ibid., 3:593.
36. Ibid., 3:659, and Tansill, *Documents*, 1031.
37. Elliot, *Debates*, 2:399.
38. Ibid., 2:410-12.
39. Tansill, *Documents*, 1035.
40. Ibid., 1047, and Elliot, *Debates*, 4:244.
41. Elliot, *Debates*, 4:191-92.
42. Ibid., 194.
43. Ibid., 198-99.
44. Ibid., 199.
45. Ibid., 200.
46. Ibid., 203.
47. Ibid., 208.
48. Tansill, *Documents*, 1053.
49. For Madison's persistence, see *The Debates and Proceedings in the Congress of the United States. Compiled from Authentic Materials*, comp. Joseph Gales (Washington: Joseph Gales, 1834), 2:444, 459, 460, 733 (hereafter cited as *Annals*).
50. James Madison to Thomas Jefferson, 17 October and 8 December 1788, *Madison Papers*, 11:295, 381; *The Federalist*, no. 51; *Annals*, 1:456.
51. James Madison to Thomas Jefferson, 8 December 1788, James Madison to Tench Coxe, 24 June 1789, James Madison to George Eve, 2 January 1789, *Madison Papers*, 11:390, 12:257, 11:404.
52. Thomas Jefferson to James Madison, 31 July 1788, *Madison Papers*, 11:213.
53. *The Statutes at Large*, ed. E. W. Hening, 13 vols. (Richmond: S. Pleasants, Jr., 1809-1823), 12:84-86.
54. Quoted in *Stokes*, 1:335. Available in any edition of Jefferson's writings.
55. "Declaration of the Virginia Association of Baptists," in Thomas Jefferson, *The Papers of Thomas Jefferson*, ed. Julian P. Boyd (Princeton: Princeton University Press, 1950-   ), 1:660-61.
56. James Madison, *The Writings of James Madison*, ed. Gaillard Hunt, 9 vols. (New

York: G.P. Putnam's Sons, 1900-1910), 5:105. Madison to George Eve, George Nicholas to James Madison, Benjamin Johnson to James Madison, *Madison Papers*, 11:404, 405, 408, 424, 442. L.H. Butterfield, "Elder John Leland, Jeffersonian Itinerant," *American Antiquarian Society Proceedings* 62 (June 1952):188.
57. *Annals*, 1:441.
58. *Madison Papers*, 12:453.
59. *Annals*, 1:448-49.
60. *Annals*, 1:451.
61. *Madison Papers*, 8:298-306.
62. Madison to Monroe, 29 May 1785, *Madison Papers*, 8:280. Irving Brant, *James Madison, the Nationalist* (Indianapolis: Bobbs-Merrill Company, 1948), 353.
63. *A Compilation of the Messages and Papers of the Presidents*, comp. James D. Richardson, 10 vols. (Washington: Government Printing Office, 1896-1899), 1:490.
64. "Madison's 'Detached Memoranda,' " ed. Elizabeth Fleet, *William and Mary Quarterly* 3 (1946): 554-59.
65. *Madison Papers*, 11:130.
66. *Annals*, 1:452.
67. In addition to Madison, the committee included three other signers of the Constitution: Abraham Baldwin of Georgia, Roger Sherman of Connecticut, and George Clymer of Pennsylvania. Also on the committee were Aedanus Burke of South Carolina, the only Antifederalist; Nicholas Gilman of New Hampshire; Egbert Benson of New York; Benjamin Goodhue of Massachusetts; Elias Boudinot of New Jersey; and John Vining of Delaware, who was chairman. *Annals*, 1:691.
68. *Annals*, 1:757.
69. *Annals*, 1:757-59.
70. *Annals*, 1:796.
71. *Documentary History of the First Federal Congress of the United States of America*, ed. Linda Grant DePauw, 3 vols. (Baltimore: John Hopkins University Press, 1977), 1:151.
72. Ibid., 166. It is interesting, however, to note that a Baptist memorial of 1774 used similar language: "The magistrate's power extends not to the establishing any articles of faith or forms of worship, by force of laws." The Baptists opposed, however, nondiscriminatory government aid to all sects—proving once again how infuriatingly ambiguous language can be. For the Baptist statement, see Pfeffer, *Church, State, and Freedom*, 91. For Baptist views, see Stokes, *Church and State in the United States*, 1:306-10, 353-57, 368-75.
73. DePauw, *Documentary History*, 1:186, 189, 192.
74. *Annals*, 1:454.
75. Madison to Jefferson, 17 October 1788, *Madison Papers*, 11:295.
76. David M. Matteson, "The Organization of the Government under the Constitution," in Sol Bloom, director general, *History of the Formation of the Union Under the Constitution* (Washington, D.C.: United States Sesquicentennial Commission, 1943), 317-19.
77. Ibid., 325-28.
78. *Journal of the Senate of the Commonwealth of Virginia; Begun and Held in the City of Richmond, on Monday, the 18th Day of October, 1789* (Richmond 1828) *[Binder's title, Journal of the Senate, 1785 to 1790]*, 62, quoted by John Courtney Murray, in "Law or Prepossessions," *Law and Contemporary Problems*, 14:43, and quoted by Corwin, "Supreme Court as National School Board," ibid., 12. See also, Antieau, *Freedom*, 144. The statement by the eight Virginia senators was revived and quoted by an advocate of the narrow interpretation of the Establishment Clause in "Brief for Appellees," 51-54, filed in the case of *McCollum* v. *Board of Education*, 333 U.S. 203 (1948). Both Murray and Corwin drew their conclusions on this matter from the brief alone, without investigating the context of the statement by the eight senators.
79. E. Randolph to Washington, 6 December 1789, quoted by Matteson, "The Organization of the Government," 321.
80. Hardin Burnley to Madison, 5 December 1789, *Madison Papers*, 12:460.
81. Matteson, "The Organization of the Government," 321-22; Madison to Washing-

ton, 20 November 1789, quoted in Irving Brant, *Madison, Father of the Constitution* (Indianapolis: Bobbs-Merrill, 1948), 287.
82. Brant, *Madison, Father of the Constitution*, 287.
83. Ibid., 286-87 and 491, note 16, for the voting records.
84. O'Neill, *Religion and Education*, 204.
85. Antieau, *Freedom*, 202 and passim. Cord, *Separation of Church and State*, 3-15.
86. Sanford Cobb, *The Rise of Religious Liberty in America* (New York: Macmillan Company, 1902), 236. John Webb Pratt, *Religion, Politics, and Diversity. The Church-State Theme in New York History* (Ithaca, N.Y.: Cornell University Press, 1967), 27-29.
87. *Ecclesiastical Records of the State of New York*, ed. Hugh Hastings and Edward T. Corwin, 7 vols. (Albany: J.B. Lyon, State Printer, 1901-1906), 1:571.
88. Pratt, *Religion*, 39.
89. *Ecclesiastical Records*, 2:1073-78. Pratt, *Religion*, 40-42. Carl Bridenbaugh, *Mitre and Sceptre. Transatlantic Faiths, Ideas, Personalities, and Politics 1689-1775* (New York: Oxford University Press, 1962), 117-18.
90. *Ecclesiastical Records*, 2:1114.
91. E. B. O'Callaghan, ed., *Documents Relative to the Colonial History of the State of New York*, 15 vols. (Albany: Weed, Parsons, Printers, 1853-1887), 5:323. Bridenbaugh, *Mitre*, 118.
92. *The Documentary History of the State of New York*, ed. E. B. O'Callaghan, 4 vols. (Albany: Weed, Parson, Printers, 1848-1849), 3:278.
93. Ibid., 3:309-11. The Jamaica controversy can be followed in this work, 205-302. See also Pratt, *Religion*, 54:61-62.
94. O'Callaghan, *Documentary History*, 3:311, 330. Pratt, *Politics*, 62.
95. *Ecclesiastical Records*, 2:1392, 3:1589, 1591, 1695, 2141.
96. William Smith, *A General Idea of the College of Mirania* (New York: J. Parker and W. Weyman, 1753. Evans, *Early American Imprints*, no. 7121, microcard), 84. Pratt, *Politics*, 67-71.
97. *The Independent Reflector*, ed. Milton Klein (Cambridge, Mass.: Harvard University Press, 1963), 171-78 and passim. William Smith, Jr., *The History of the Province of New York*, ed. Michael Kammen (Cambridge, Mass.: Harvard University Press, 1972).
98. Klein, *Independent Reflector*, New York Mercury, 26 May 1755, 26; William Livingston, *Address to Sir Charles Hardy* (New York: Hugh Gaine, 1755), vii-viii.
99. "Remarks on the Quebec Bill," *Works of Alexander Hamilton*, ed. J. C. Hamilton, 2:131, quoted in Stokes, 1:510.
100. *Acts and Resolves, Public and Private of the Province of Massachusetts Bay (1692-1786)*, 21 vols. (Boston: Wright and Potter, 1869-1922), 1:62. Susan M. Reed, *Church and State in Massachusetts 1691-1740* (Urbana: University of Illinois Press, 1914), 19-35. William G. McLoughlin, *New England Dissent 1630-1833. The Baptists and the Separation of Church and State*, 2 vols. (Cambridge, Mass.: Harvard University Press, 1971), 1:113-27.
101. Reed, *Church and State*, 180. McLoughlin, *New England Dissent*, 1:221.
102. M. Louise Greene, *The Development of Religious Liberty in Connecticut* (Boston: Houghton, Mifflin, Co., 1905), 200-201; McLoughlin, *New England Dissent*, 1:269.
103. McLoughlin, *New England Dissent*, 1:225-43.
104. Cotton Mather, *Ratio Disciplinae* (Boston: S. Gerrish, 1726). Evans, *Early American Imprints*, no. 2775, microcard, 20.
105. Ebenezer Turell, *The Life and Character of Benjamin Colman* (Boston: Rogers and Fowle, 1749). Evans, *Early American Imprints*, no. 6434, microcard, 138.
106. Jonathan Mayhew, *A Defense of the Observations* (Boston: Draper, 1763). Evans, *Early American Imprints*, No. 9442, 46-47.
107. Charles B. Kinney, *Church and State: The Struggle for Separation in New Hampshire, 1630-1900* (New York: Teachers College, Columbia University, 1955), 58-62, 72-82. McLoughlin, *New England Dissent*, 2:833-43.
108. Thorpe, *Federal and State Constitutions*, 5:2597.

109. *Delaware Convention Proceedings* (Wilmington: J. Adams, 1776). Evans, *Early American Imprints*, no. 43018, microcard, 14.
110. Thorpe, *Federal and State Constitutions*, 1:567, 5:2597.
111. Ibid., 5:3082
112. Ibid., 5:2636. Italics added.
113. Ibid., 3:1890-91.
114. See Jacob Conrad Meyer, *Church and State in Massachusetts to 1833* (Cleveland: Western Reserve University Press, 1930) for details, beginning with chap. 4. McLoughlin, *New England Dissent*, 2:697-722.
115. Thorpe, *Federal and State Constitutions*, 4:2454. See Kinney, *Separation*, 83-108. McLoughlin, *New England Dissent*, 2:844.
116. McLoughlin, *New England Dissent*, 2:923.
117. Thorpe, *Federal and State Constitutions*, 3:1689.
118. Allan Nevins, *The American States During and After the Revolution* (New York: Macmillan Company, 1927), 431; Werline, *Problems of Church and State*, 169-86. John C. Rainbolt, "The Struggle to Define 'Religious Liberty' in Maryland, 1776-1785," *Journal of Church and State* 17 (Autumn 1975):448.
119. Thorpe, *Federal and State Constitutions*, 3:1705.
120. Ibid., 2:784.
121. Reba C. Strickland, *Religion and the State in Georgia in the Eighteenth Century* (New York: Columbia University Press, 1939), 164, 166.
122. Thorpe, *Federal and State Constitutions*, 2:789.
123. Ibid., 2:801. Evans, *Early American Imprints*, microcard, no. 19750, p. 8; no. 19998, p. 43; no. 20715, p. 48; no. 22895, p. 11-12. Brinsfield, *Religion and Politics*, 122-27.
124. Thorpe, *Federal and State Constitutions*, 6:3253-57. Brinsfield, *Religion and Politics*, 134.
125. Thorpe, *Federal and State Constitutions*, 6:3264.
126. Ibid., 5:2793. Thomas Buckley, *Church and State in Revolutionary Virginia, 1776-1787* (Charlottesville: University of Virginia Press, 1977).
127. Stokes, *Church and State*, 1:393. Jefferson in 1776 had written a draft of a constitution for Virginia that included a similar provision: "Nor shall any be compelled to frequent or maintain any religious institution." Boyd, *Jefferson Papers*, 1:344.
128. Hamilton J. Eckenrode, *The Separation of Church and State in Virginia* (Richmond: D. Bottom, 1910), 58-61. For the actual bills, see Buckley, *Church and State*, 185-88, 190-91.
129. Eckenrode, *Separation*, 86. Buckley, *Church and State*, 188-89 for the text of the bill.
130. *Madison Papers*, 8:197. See Brant, *James Madison, the Nationalist*, 344-45.
131. In 1785, the same year the general assessment bill was debated in Virginia, both Maryland and Georgia also considered general assessment bills; comparatively little is known about their history.

The Wall of Separation:
The Supreme Court as
Uncertain Stonemason

A. E. DICK HOWARD

Thomas Jefferson brought the "wall of separation" into the permanent lexicon of American relations between church and state when, in 1802, he wrote a letter (often quoted) to the Danbury Baptist Association on his understanding of the meaning of the First Amendment's religion clauses:

Believing with you that religion lies solely between man and his God, that he owes account to none other for his faith or his worship, that the legislative powers of government reach action only, and not opinions, I contemplate with solemn reverence that act of the whole American people which declared that their legislature should "make no law respecting an establishment of religion, or prohibiting the free exercise thereof," thus building a wall of separation between church and state.[1]

Much ink has been spilled by lawyers and judges and by historians and theologians over the wall of separation on whether the concept fairly expresses the purpose of the First Amendment, or whether the wall is in fact as absolute and impervious as the language suggests, and how the separation of church and state is to evolve as new demands vie with old traditions.

THE SUPREME COURT AND FREE EXERCISE

In light of the founding fathers' concern over religious freedom, the average citizen today might be surprised to learn that virtually all of the significant gloss placed on the First Amendment's religion clauses by the United States Supreme Court has arisen from litigation in the past half century. The reasons may be readily assigned. In the first place, the Supreme Court ruled in 1833 that the provisions of the Bill of Rights were not enforceable against the states.[2] In 1845, the Court applied this reasoning so as to reject the appeal of a Louisiana priest who had been convicted of conducting funeral services at a chapel unlicensed under state law.[3] Thus, insofar as one's religious liberty might be threatened by state law, it was to state constitutions that the aggrieved party must look. In fact, as state constitutions were revised during the nineteenth century, the trend was toward increasingly stringent separation of church and state.[4]

The First Amendment did apply, of course, to federal legislation. Even here, however, it was 1878—nearly a century after the First Amendment's adoption—before the Supreme Court first had occasion to construe the religion clauses of the First Amendment. In that case, *Reynolds* v. *United States*, the Court affirmed the conviction, under federal bigamy laws, of a Mormon practicing polygamy in Utah.[5] Chief Justice Morrison R. Waite looked to Jefferson for guidance. In his letter to the Danbury Baptists, Jefferson had declared that "the legislative powers of government reach actions only and not opinions."[6]

Although Jefferson himself had not been at the Philadelphia convention or in the first Congress—he was at that time minister to Paris—Waite looked to Jefferson's Virginia Bill for Establishing Religious Freedom as being, in effect, part of the legislative history of the First Amendment.[7] Quoting several passages from the preamble to Jefferson's Bill, Waite said, "Coming as this does from an acknowledged leader of the advocates of the measure [the First Amendment], it may be accepted almost as an authoritative declaration of the scope and effect of the amendment thus secured." Waite seized on Jefferson's distinction between opinion and conduct to conclude that "Congress was deprived of all legislative power over mere opinion, but was left free to reach actions which were in violation of social duties or subversive of good order."[8] Polygamy, whatever its religious impetus, was safely within Congress's power to forbid.[9]

Thus, in the Supreme Court's initial look at the First Amendment's religion clauses, was born the notion of looking to ideas and events in postrevolutionary Virginia to give meaning to the First Amendment. In 1878, Justice Waite turned to Jefferson; in 1947 (as elaborated below), Justice Hugo Black turned to James Madison.[10]

Other than having to deal with the Mormons—there was another Mormon case in 1890 involving an Idaho oath requiring voters to forswear membership in any organization advocating bigamy[11]—the Supreme Court had little further occasion to explore the First Amendment's religion clauses until the 1940s. Then it was the Jehovah's Witnesses whose effort to be different brought them into conflict with the law.[12] The nadir of free exercise, in the view of some commentators,[13] came in 1961, when the Court rejected the efforts by Orthodox Jewish merchants (who closed their shops on Saturday) to have Sunday Closing Laws struck down on First Amendment grounds.[14]

Free exercise made a sudden, and controversial, comeback two years later. In *Sherbert* v. *Verner*,[15] the Court ruled that South Carolina was obliged to pay unemployment compensation benefits to a Seventh-day Adventist who could not get a job because she was unwilling to work on Saturdays. The dissenters objected that the Court was requiring a state to give a preference to those whose unavailability for work was based on religious grounds over those unavailable for nonreligious reasons.[16]

The Burger Court's most noted free exercise decision is *Wisconsin* v. *Yoder* (1972).[17] Members of the Amish religion in Wisconsin had resisted sending their children to public schools after the eighth grade, and Chief Justice Warren E. Burger ruled that the state's effort to enforce its public school attendance laws against the Amish violated their rights of free exercise of religion. The fact that Wisconsin's statute was neutral on its face and was motivated by legitimate and important state interests did not save it. Nor was the statute immunized from free exercise challenge by the state's characterizing the law as regarding "conduct" rather than "belief." To the argument that to allow the Amish to opt out of the state's compulsory education requirement would effect an establishment of religion, Burger replied that accommodating the religious beliefs of the Amish "can hardly be characterized as sponsorship or active involvement." As in *Sherbert* v. *Verner*, Burger saw such accommodation as being nothing more than "neutrality in the face of religious differences."[18] Burger's opinion, in short, represents a decision to prefer a free exercise claim in the face of establishment implications—a choice he has been unsuccessful in pressing on his brethren in some of the later parochiaid cases.

THE SUPREME COURT AND ESTABLISHMENT

As to the Establishment Clause, the seminal case in the modern Court is *Everson* v. *Board of Education* (1947).[19] Though much First Amendment law has been written in the subsequent three decades, Justice Hugo Black's majority opinion remains the starting point for any consideration of the current

Court's approach to religious liberty. A man self-taught in the
Greek and Roman classics and in British and American History, Black was fond of advising his law clerks to read Tacitus
or *Fox's Book of Martyrs*. Black took a preeminently Whig
view of history, and *Everson* is an example.[20]

The specific holding in *Everson* was that New Jersey had
not violated the Establishment Clause by authorizing local
boards of education to reimburse parents for the cost of having
their children ride the public buses to school, including to a
parochial school. The opinion is of wider interest, however,
for its effort to provide a roadmap for the reading of the First
Amendment.

After reviewing the history of religious persecution, Black
went straight to Madison and Jefferson for inspiration. Pointing to Madison's "great Memorial and Remonstrance" and
Jefferson's Bill for Establishing Religious Freedom, Black
declared that "the provisions of the First Amendment, in the
drafting and adoption of which Madison and Jefferson played
such leading roles, had the same objective and were intended
to provide the same protection against governmental intrusion
on religious liberty as the Virginia statute." Then Black laid
down surely the most famous dictum in any Supreme Court
opinion on the meaning of the Establishment Clause:

> The "establishment of religion" clause of the First Amendment means at
> least this: Neither a state nor the Federal Government can set up a church.
> Neither can pass laws which aid one religion, aid all religions, or prefer one
> religion over another. Neither can force nor influence a person to go to or
> remain away from church against his will or force him to profess a belief or
> disbelief in any religion. No person can be punished for entertaining or pro-
> fessing religious beliefs or disbeliefs, for church attendance or non-
> attendance. No tax in any amount, large or small, can be levied to support
> any religious activities or institutions, whatever they may be called, or what-
> ever form they may adopt to teach or practice religion. Neither a state nor
> the Federal Government can, openly or secretly, participate in the affairs of
> any religious organizations or groups and *vice versa*. In the words of Jeffer-
> son, the clause against establishment of religion by law was intended to
> erect "a wall of separation between church and State." *Reynolds* v. *United
> States*, supra at 164.[21]

Notwithstanding his use of the "wall of separation" metaphor, Black was able to sustain the New Jersey law—which
he admitted approached the "verge" of the state's constitutional power—by viewing it as general public welfare legislation—a statute to help children get safely to school, public
or private. The First Amendment, Black thought, "requires
the state to be a neutral in its relations with groups of reli-

gious believers and non-believers; it does not require the state
to be their adversary."[22]

Everson has been an important and influential opinion. To
begin with, it settled (on this the justices apparently were
unanimous) that the Establishment Clause applies to the states.
This was not a foregone conclusion. In the same year of Everson, Justice Black, dissenting in Adamson v. California, had
argued that the Fourteenth Amendment applies to the states
all the provisions of the Bill of Rights—a proposition that Justice Felix Frankfurter and other critics on and off the bench
derided.[23] Moreover, as to establishment, some wondered how
the Court could apply to the states a provision that, they
argued, was put in the Constitution primarily to keep Congress from interfering with state establishments existing at the
time the First Amendment was proposed.[24]

Everson's influence went beyond interpretation of the federal Constitution. State constitutions have often been interpreted by state courts even more restrictively of state aid to
private schools than the First Amendment.[25] Everson's "child
benefit" theory offered a way to soften some of those state
provisions, and the doctrine thus found its way into the decisions of some state courts.[26]

Everson spawned much academic comment, much of it critical. Paul Freund has called the dichotomy between pupil
benefit and benefit to the school "a chimerical constitutional
criterion."[27] Erwin Griswold has ridiculed Black as an "absolutist,"[28] and, as to Black's use of history, Paul G. Kauper
concluded, "Nothing in the historical research to date lends
authority to Justice Black's broad interpretation."[29]

Everson was only the opening shot in the war over the reach
of the Establishment Clause. Subsequent years have seen
repeated occasions for the Supreme Court to assess the applications of separationism. The "wall of separation," as Justice
Jackson once remarked, has been as serpentine as the walls at
Mr. Jefferson's University of Virginia.[30] In 1948, the Court
struck down an Illinois "released time" program under which
religious instructors were permitted to come into public classrooms, but four years later the justices upheld a New York
program that released students during school hours to receive
religious instruction off the school grounds.[31]

The Court came down against prayers and Bible reading in
the public schools.[32] The Court thought it unnecessary to ask
whether unwilling children were coerced into taking part in

these exercises. A finding on coercion (relevant to a free exercise claim) is not a prerequisite to showing that the Establishment Clause has been violated.[33] The "wall," however, was found not to have been breached when states enacted Sunday closing laws; notwithstanding the laws' religious origins, it was enough that they now served a secular purpose.[34] Nor was there a breach when New York lent textbooks to students in parochial schools (*Board of Education* v. *Allen*), even though textbooks are far more central to the educational process than was schoolbus transportation in *Everson*.[35]

The justices' opinions reflected the difficulties they encountered in construing the Establishment Clause. Justice Potter Stewart, dissenting in the first of the school prayer cases (1962), complained of the "uncritical invocation of metaphors like the 'wall of separation,' a phrase nowhere to be found in the Constitution."[36] Some justices seemed to take a wavering course. Justice William O. Douglas joined in approving the New Jersey bus transportation plan and, in 1952, wrote the majority opinion permitting "released time" programs off school premises. Said Douglas, "We are a religious people whose institutions presuppose a Supreme Being."[37] Douglas, however, subsequently became one of the Court's strictest separationists. Concurring in the 1962 prayer decision, Douglas confessed that he had changed his mind about *Everson*—a holding that, he said, "seems in retrospect to be out of line with the First Amendment."[38] In 1968, Douglas dissented from the New York textbook decision.[39]

As they groped for ways to apply the Establishment Clause, the justices devised additional tests. The major innovation between *Everson* and the advent of the Burger Court was the test stated by Justice Tom Clark in the 1963 Bible reading and Lord's Prayer cases, *Abington School District* v. *Schempp* and *Murray* v. *Curlett*. Clark said that two questions had to be asked about a challenged law: What is the enactment's purpose, and what is its primary effect? In order to be valid, "there must be a secular legislative purpose and a primary effect that neither advances nor inhibits religion."[40] The purpose and effect tests quickly became a boiler plate in Establishment Clause opinions, both during the Warren years and since.[41]

AID TO CHURCH-RELATED EDUCATION

In Warren Burger's first term on the Court, the new chief

justice wrote *Walz* v. *Tax Commission*, a nearly unanimous decision (only Douglas dissenting) upholding property tax exemptions for religious property. Noting that all fifty states provide for tax exemptions for places of worship, Burger saw the First Amendment as permitting "benevolent neutrality" by government toward religion. Burger found "deeply embedded in the fabric of our national life" the principle that government could fashion policies grounded in benevolent neutrality towards religion "so long as none was favored over others and none suffered interference." Tax exemptions, he reasoned, did not constitute sponsorship as the government does not transfer revenue to churches "but simply abstains from demanding that the church support the state."[42]

Walz fanned hopes of greater state aid for education that had been ignited by the Court's 1968 *Allen* opinion. Catholic educators and parents saw in the language of "benevolent neutrality" the opportunity to carry *Everson*'s general welfare legislation notion quite beyond such narrow aids as bus transportation or textbooks. Indeed, even before *Walz*, in the late sixties state legislatures had begun to enact significant programs of aid to private education—among them supplements to teachers' salaries, money to pay for textbooks and instructional materials, appropriations for maintenance and repair of schools, tuition grants to parents, and income tax credits. Opponents of such aid promptly went to court, and the stage was set in the early seventies for a major round of Supreme Court decisions on aid to church-related schools.

In 1971, in *Lemon* v. *Kurtzman*, the Court passed on aid programs from Rhode Island and Pennsylvania.[43] Rhode Island's statute provided for a 15 percent salary supplement to be paid to teachers in nonpublic schools. Pennsylvania's act authorized the "purchase" of "secular" educational services from private schools, reimbursing those schools for teachers' salaries, textbooks, and instructional materials. Both states, conscious of the sensitive First Amendment questions raised by such aid, had laced the programs about with safeguards and restrictions. For example, Pennsylvania required that reimbursement be limited to courses in specified secular subjects, that textbooks and materials must be approved by the state, and that payment was not to be made for any course having religious content.

The safeguards proved the programs' undoing. To the purpose and effect test of establishment used in the 1963 prayer

cases, Burger in *Walz* had added a third test—that a program
not result in an "excessive governmental entanglement with
religion."[44] The property tax exemptions in *Walz* had passed
that test, but the Pennsylvania and Rhode Island school aid
programs in *Lemon* failed it. The very fact that the state had
"carefully conditioned its aid with pervasive restrictions"
meant that "comprehensive, discriminating, and continuing
state surveillance" would be necessary to ensure that the
schools honored the restrictions; the result would be "excessive and enduring entanglement between state and church."[45]

The chief justice had yet another ground for striking down
the Pennsylvania and Rhode Island programs—their "divisive
political potential." Burger saw political division along religious lines one of the principal evils against which the First
Amendment was directed. State programs channeling money
to a relatively few religious groups—Roman Catholics were
the overwhelming beneficiaries of the challenged programs—
would, Burger thought, intensify political demands along religious lines.[46]

Undaunted, the proponents of parochiaid kept trying. The
result was another round of major Supreme Court decisions,
in June 1973. In the principal case, *Committee for Public Education and Religious Liberty* v. *Nyquist*, a divided Court struck
down three New York programs—direct grants to private
schools for "maintenance and repair" of facilities and equipment, a tuition reimbursement plan for low-income parents of
children in private schools, and tax deductions for parents
who did not qualify for tuition reimbursement.[47] In the 1971
decisions, it had been "entanglement" that proved fatal for
the Pennsylvania and Rhode Island programs. In 1973, it was
the "effect" test that was fatal; the three programs were found
to have the effect of advancing religion.[48] Justice Lewis F.
Powell, who wrote the majority opinion in *Nyquist*, found it
unnecessary to consider whether the New York program
would result in entanglement of state and religion. He did,
however, bolster his opinion by invoking the political entanglement argument—that the programs carried a "potentially
divisive political effect."[49]

The years since *Nyquist* have seen the Court able to wring
surprisingly divergent decisions from the application of the
test laid down in that case. In *Meek* v. *Pittenger* (1975),[50] the
Court reviewed three Pennsylvania programs—the loan of
textbooks to students in private schools, the loan to the school

themselves of instructional equipment and materials, and the provision of "auxiliary" services, such as counseling, testing, speech and hearing therapy, and similar services. Only the textbook program passed muster—and even that dispensation passed largely on the strength of the precedent set by *Allen*.

The Court relaxed the barriers somewhat, but only slightly, in *Wolman* v. *Walter* (1977). Reviewing several Ohio programs, the Court refused to permit the state to lend instructional materials and equipment for use in sectarian schools or to pay for field trips. The Court did, however, permit the state to provide specialized diagnostic guidance and other services to students in nonpublic schools, as the services were not performed on school premises.[51]

While policing aid to sectarian schools at the primary and secondary level, the Court proved strikingly more deferential on aid to church-related colleges. The same day that the Court ruled against parochiaid in *Lemon* v. *Kurtzman*, the justices upheld federal construction grants to four church-related colleges in Connecticut. The federal statute placed limits on the purposes for which grants could be used, among them the exclusion of facilities to be used for sectarian instruction or religious worship. Writing for a five-man majority, Chief Justice Burger, in *Tilton* v. *Richardson*, concluded that the grant program satisfied all the Court's establishment tests—purpose, effect, entanglement, and political divisiveness. Key to the decision were the differences Burger noted between higher education and primary and secondary schools. College students, he thought, are less impressionable and less susceptible to religious indoctrination than younger students. Moreover, other forces, such as traditions of academic freedom, operate to create a more open climate at the college level.[52]

All four of the Connecticut colleges were controlled by religious orders, and the faculty and student body at each were predominantly Catholic. Nevertheless, Burger noted that non-Catholics were admitted as students and were given faculty appointments. None of the colleges required students to attend religious services. Although all four schools required students to take theology courses, it was stipulated that the courses covered a range of religious experience and were not limited to Catholicism. In fact, some of the required courses at two of the colleges were taught by rabbis. In short, Burger was able to conclude that, although the colleges had "admittedly religious functions," their predominant educational mission was to provide their students with a secular education.[53]

The Court has continued to distinguish between aid to sectarian primary and secondary schools and aid at the level of higher education. In 1973, in *Hunt* v. *McNair*, the Court rejected First Amendment challenges to the issuance by a South Carolina state authority of revenue bonds to help a Baptist college borrow money for capital improvements.[54] No state money was involved, but having the authority's backing enabled the college to borrow money at more favorable interest rates. Justice Powell, who wrote the majority opinion, noted that the college's board of trustees was elected by the South Carolina Baptist Convention, that its charter could be amended only by the Convention, and that the Convention's approval was required for certain financial transactions. Powell concluded, however, that the college was not "pervasively sectarian" and that South Carolina had laid down sufficient safeguards to ensure that aid did not flow to religious activities.[55]

Another case, decided in 1976, also reflects the majority's ability to be more permissive toward aid to church-related colleges than to primary and secondary education. In that decision, *Roemer* v. *Board of Public Works*, the Court upheld Maryland's appropriation, on an annual basis, of noncategorical grants to private colleges, some of them with religious affiliations.[56] For each full-time student (not including seminary and theology students), a college received an amount equal to 15 percent of the state's appropriation for full-time students in the state college system. At issue were appropriations to four Roman Catholic colleges. The district court had concluded that the four colleges were not "pervasively sectarian," and Justice Harry Blackmun, reviewing findings as to curriculum, faculty, and other factors, held that the lower court's conclusion was not "clearly erroneous." Moreover, Maryland's system operated to ensure that aid would go only to "the secular side" of the college's activities. Nor, finally, was there "excessive entanglement" between government and religion.[57]

In 1983, a sharply divided Court (five to four) signaled a potential relaxation of the standards to be applied in reviewing state programs challenged as aiding sectarian schools at the elementary and secondary level. In *Mueller* v. *Allen*, the Court upheld a Minnesota statute allowing taxpayers to deduct from their state tax payments expenses for tuition, textbooks, and transportation of their children attending elementary or secondary schools.[58] Justice William H. Rehnquist, writing for the majority, had to explain why *Nyquist* did not require the statute's invalidation, in light of the manifest similarities between the New York law struck down in that case and the Minnesota law now being upheld.

Rehnquist made much of the fact that Minnesota, unlike New York, allowed the deduction to be taken for educational expenses incurred by parents of children attending public schools as well as those in private schools.[59] The dissenters were little impressed by this argument, responding in turn that public schools in Minnesota charge tuition only for students accepted from outside the district and that in the 1978-79 school year only seventy-nine students out of about eight hundred fifteen thousand in public schools paid such tuition.[60]

A key to the *Mueller* opinion lies in Rehnquist's observation as that parochial schools make "special contributions" by offering an "educational alternative" to and "wholesome competition" with public schools.[61] Also central to the opinion is Rehnquist's argument, essentially one grounded in equity, that the seeming disproportion of parochial schools beneficiaries under the Minnesota program should be regarded "as a rough return" for the benefit conferred upon the state's taxpayers by private schools' educating students who otherwise would have to be educated at public expense.[62]

Rehnquist's opinion in *Mueller* might have been broader but for the need to sidestep *Nyquist*. The 1983 decision does not overrule that of ten years earlier. The two decisions, however, are not easily reconciled. In *Nyquist*, Chief Justice Burger, dissenting in part, thought that "simple equity" supported aid to parents who sent their children to private schools and that giving such aid would promote a "wholesome" diversity in education.[63] That philosophy seems to gain new life in *Mueller*.

THE SEARCH FOR "TESTS"

The uninitiated observer who seeks to make sense of the Supreme Court's rulings in Establishment Clause cases is in for a shock. Looking simply at the results in the aid-to-education cases, he will find that a state may reimburse parents for the cost of bus transportation to parochial schools but may not reimburse them for the cost of field trips, even though the destination of the former trip is a school permeated with religious instruction and the destination of the latter may be a museum or the state capitol (not usually

thought of as a place wherein one seeks spiritual guidance).
He will learn that a state may lend textbooks to students in
parochial schools but may not lend other kinds of instructional equipment, such as tape recorders and maps. Therapeutic and diagnostic health services may be given at state expense
to parochial school students in a mobile unit parked next door
to the school but may not be given in the parochial school
itself, even though the services be rendered in either case by
public employees.[64] He is also, of course, confronted by the
Court's invalidating New York's program of tax deductions
for tuition payments while upholding that of Minnesota.[65]
The casual reader of opinions that draw such seemingly fine
distinctions may be forgiven if he thinks that he has stumbled
into the forest of Hansel and Gretel, the birds having eaten all
the crumbs that mark the way out.[66]

One explanation—though perhaps not justification—for such
curious distinctions in the cases would turn on the fact that
some of the decisions just mentioned were handed down at
different points in the Court's search for standards or "tests"
by which to measure violations of the Establishment Clause.
Some years after *Everson*, the Warren Court's effort to articu-
late standards yielded the "secular legislative purpose" and
"primary effect tests." To these yardsticks, Chief Justice
Burger in *Walz* added the excessive entanglement test. Beginning with Justice John M. Harlan's concurring opinion in
Walz, there emerged the "political divisiveness" test.

The proliferation of tests has hardly clarified the issues.
Entanglement, for example, has operated as a kind of Catch-
22. Aware of the need to avoid allowing state aid to be used to
support parochial schools' religious functons, Pennsylvania
and Rhode Island took elaborate steps to ensure that only secular instruction benefited. Having taken those steps, the two
states ran headlong into the entanglement test in *Lemon* v.
Kurtzman. When the majority invoked the entanglement test
in *Meek* v. *Pittenger*, Justice Rehnquist, in dissent, commented
that school authorities "are left to wonder . . . whether the
possibility of meeting the entanglement test is now anything
more than"—quoting the late Justice Robert H. Jackson—"a
promise to the ear to be broken to the hope, a teasing illusion
like a munificent bequest in a pauper's will."[67]

Philip B. Kurland derides the Court's entanglement test as
being "either empty or nonsensical."[68] Jesse Choper objects to
the entanglement principle on the ground that avoiding ad-

ministrative entanglement between government and religion neither can, nor should, be a value to be judicially secured by the Establishment Clause. Indeed, he submits, scrupulous avoidance of administrative entanglement between church and state might well require abandonment of virtually all regulation of religious activities, even those having such desirable purposes as ensuring minimal educational standards in private as in public education.[69]

Some justices have proposed scrapping some or all of the tests now being used. While he concurred with the Court's judgment in *Roemer*, upholding Maryland's annual grants to private colleges, Justice Byron R. White voiced his dislike for the entanglement test, which he found "curious and mystifying." White would stick to purpose and effect: "As long as there is a secular legislative purpose, and as long as the primary effect of the legislation is neither to advance nor inhibit religion," White saw no reason to take the constitutional inquiry further.[70] Justice John Paul Stevens is another critic of the Court's tests, although Stevens reaches more separationist results than does White. In a 1977 opinion, Stevens ventured that the Court, having failed to improve on the *Everson* test, had simply encouraged the states "to search for new ways of achieving forbidden ends." Therefore, Stevens would throw out the three-part test (purpose, effect, and entanglement) altogether and return to Black's *Everson* standard.[71] Thus, somewhat over thirty years after *Everson* one finds at least one justice coming full circle.

"POLITICAL DIVISIVENESS"

In *Lemon* v. *Kurtzman*, Chief Justice Burger portrayed the dangers of voters' dividing along religious lines because of proposals to aid church-related schools. Granting that political debate and divisions are normal and healthy in a democratic system, Burger maintained that "political division along religious lines was one of the principal evils against which the First Amendment was intended to protect." Burger saw competition among religious groups for public funds as a "threat to the normal political process."[72]

Whether political divisiveness is an independent ground of decision or simply used to reinforce other tests is not clear. In *Lemon*, Burger referred to divisiveness as a "broader base of entanglement of yet a different character."[73] In *Nyquist*, having found the challenged New York laws to have the imper-

missible effect of advancing religion, Powell did not consider
whether such aid would result in entanglement of state and
religion. He went on to say, however, that "apart from any
specific entanglement of the State in particular religious programs, assistance of the sort here involved carries grave potential for entanglement in the broader sense of continuing strife
over aid to religion." Nevertheless, Powell stopped short of
saying that political divisiveness could stand by itself as a
ground of decision: "And while the prospect of such divisiveness may not alone warrant the invalidation of state laws that
otherwise survive the careful scrutiny required by the decisions of this Court, it is certainly a 'warning signal' not to be
ignored."[74] At least three justices—William J. Brennan, Douglas, and Thurgood Marshall—appear to have elevated the political divisiveness principle to independent status. In *Meek*,
Brennan cited *Lemon* as having added "a significant fourth
factor to the Establishment Clause test"—political divisiveness.
Brennan invoked that test to argue for striking down Pennsylvania's loan of textbooks to students in parochial schools.
Brennan thought *Allen* (which he had joined) not controlling,
as it had been decided before the Court began using the political divisiveness factor.[75]

In a separate opinion in *Walz*, Justice Harlan said that
"history cautions that political fragmentation on sectarian lines
must be guarded against."[76] Both Harlan in *Walz* and Burger
in *Lemon* cited a comment by Professor Paul Freund in the
Harvard Law Review, where Freund has said that "political
division on religious lines is one of the principal evils that the
First Amendment sought to forestall."[77] Freund did not elaborate. Other than citing Freund (as Powell also did in *Nyquist*),
the Burger Court, in speaking of political divisiveness, has
contented itself with resting on the Court's own opinions.

Justice Rehnquist's opinion in *Mueller* v. *Allen* takes aim at
the "political divisiveness" argument. With characteristic
adroitness, Justice Rehnquist relied on language in *Lemon* that
distinguished that case from *Everson* and *Allen*. Rehnquist
then concluded that political divisiveness would only apply in
cases similarly distinguishable—that is, cases where "direct
financial subsidies are paid to parochial schools or to teachers
in parochial schools."[78] While Rehnquist's logic here may not
be compelling, his message is unmistakable: he would like to
eliminate political divisiveness from the Court's toolbox.

Justice Brennan, however, would retain political divisiveness in the Court's establishment analysis. In *Marsh* v. *Chambers*, he turned to "political divisiveness"—framed as a subcategory of "entanglement"—in arguing that Nebraska's practice of paying a chaplain to open legislative sessions had split the state legislature on a religious issue.[79]

The notion of political divisiveness as a limit on governmental involvement with religion has roots in James Madison's concerns about factions. In the Federalist No. 10, Madison defined a faction as "a number of citizens, whether amounting to a majority or minority of the whole, who are united and actuated by some common impulse of passion, or of interest, adverse to the rights of other citizens, or to the permanent and aggregate interests of the community." Relief from the danger of factions, he thought, is only to be sought in the means of "controling its effects."[80] Following Madison's advice, government does enact legislation to regulate factions, at least where they take the form of self-interest groups. Labor legislation is an example. The First Amendment, however, stands in the way of regulating religious groups as factions. Hence, for want of the normal governmental mechanism for controlling factions, the Court's political divisiveness formula may address the dangers of faction when it is religious groups that are acting as self-interest interest groups.[81]

Madison's Memorial and Remonstrance Against Religious Assessments bear even more directly on the modern Court's political divisiveness doctrine. In objecting to the bill's assessing taxpayers for the support of religion, Madison declared that the bill would "destroy that moderation and harmony which the forbearance of our laws to intermeddle with Religion has produced among its several sects. . . . The very appearance of the Bill has transformed 'that Christian forbearance, love and charity,' which of late mutually prevailed, into animosities and jealousies, which may not be soon appeased."[82] Even though the avoidance of religious divisions did not become a full-blown feature of the Court's First Amendment doctrine until the Burger Court's parochiaid cases, this Madisonian principle had informed decisions of individual justices as early as Justice Wiley Rutledge's dissent in *Everson*.[83]

Despite the Madisonian credentials, the political divisiveness doctrine rests somewhat uncomfortably alongside the norms of the Court's free speech opinions. In a case arising under the First Amendment's speech clause, the Court would reject out of hand a state's argument that a statute—say, a law

stifling unpopular speakers—ought to be upheld because what
the speaker would say might be "divisive." When an Alabama jury awarded a local official a sizeable libel judgment
against civil rights leaders and against the *New York Times*
(which had carried a civil rights advertisement), Justice Brennan wrote the Court's opinion overruling that judgment. The
principle at stake, Brennan said, was "a profound national
commitment to the principle that debate on public issues
should be uninhibited, robust, and wide-open. . . ."[84] It is
hard to see why that principle should not apply to arguments
about aid to religion as to other questions. The kind of argument, however, that the Court will not hear as supporting restrictions on speech, it will use itself to decide what kinds of
issues people ought not to be debating lest the dispute proceed
along religious lines. Why the country can survive rancorous
debate over race or the use of American troops abroad but is
threatened by disputes over aid to religion is not self-evident.

In short, notwithstanding the roots of the political divisiveness doctrine in the thinking of so central a First Amendment
figure as Madison, there remains something unsettling about
the Court's deciding which issues are suitable for public debate
and which are not. As one commentator has said, "If there is
any single large public question that has been debated more
politely in legislative chambers and litigated more respectfully
through the courts than the matter of public aid to parochial
school it is hard to think of it."[85] If the Court is to talk of
political divisiveness, it is well that the Court has done so
largely in the context of records where other tests, such as
finding an effect of advancing religion, have been met. So
long as the political divisiveness doctrine is used in a more
cautious and supplementary manner, it can be more readily
confined. Should it become an independent norm, there would
be more cause for concern.

The Tension Between Free Exercise and Establishment

Securing free exercise of religion and prohibiting an establishment of religion are two ways of attaining a common
object—religious liberty. Freedom to worship as one chose
and freedom from exactions to support a religious establishment were implicit in Madison's proposal for a religious freedom section in Virginia's first Bill of Rights. Neither Jefferson nor Madison thought the fight for religious liberty complete in Virginia until both rights were secure. It was natural,

therefore, that the First Amendment should contain both a free exercise and an establishment clause.

It is now seen that though the two clauses may complement each other, they sometimes conflict.[86] Concurring in the Court's 1963 ruling against prayers and Bible reading in public schools, Justice Brennan noted this conflict. There are some practices, he thought, which, though questionable under the Establishment Clause, might be permissible in the interest of free exercise. Brennan's examples included provision of chaplains and places of worship for prisoners and soldiers cut off from civilian opportunities for public communal worship.[87]

In several cases the Burger Court has had to worry about how to reconcile potential tensions between free exercise and establishment. The possibility of conflict seemed not to trouble the Court in *Yoder*. There Chief Justice Burger granted the establishment implications of allowing a religious group an exemption from general laws. He concluded, however, that enforcing the compulsory attendance laws on the Amish would have such a telling impact on their religious practices that the Court came down on the side of free exercise.

Other cases have proved more troublesome to the justices. Programs of aid to parochial schools have provoked the sharpest quarrels among the justices. In *Nyquist*, Justice Powell read the Court's precedents as requiring that, in order to resolve the tension that "inevitably exists" between free exercise and establishment, the state must maintain "an attitude of 'neutrality,' neither 'advancing' nor 'inhibiting' religion."[88] For Powell and the majority, that approach meant striking down New York's efforts to relieve the financial pinch felt by parents whose children were in private schools. The dissenters, however, saw free exercise interests imperiled by the Court's ruling. Justice White argued that in light of the free exercise clause, a state "should put no unnecessary obstacles in the way of religious training for the young."[89] Likewise, Chief Justice Burger thought that "where the state law is genuinely directed at enhancing a recognized freedom of individuals . . . the Establishment Clause no longer has a prohibitive effect."[90]

"Benevolent Neutrality"—
The Accommodation of Religion

Of all the themes in the religion cases perhaps none had greater appeal than "neutrality." Justice Black appealed to that standard in *Everson* when he said that the First Amendment "requires the state to be a neutral in its relations with groups of religious believers and non-believers."[91] Like the "wall of separation" metaphor, "neutrality" has proved an elusive standard, difficult of application to concrete facts. Black thought government was being neutral when it reimbursed parochial school parents for the cost of bus transportation. When Justice Douglas, however, in *Zorach*, invoked the neutrality principle in upholding New York City's released time program, Black dissented: "The freedom and separation clauses should be read as stating a single precept: that government cannot utilize religion as a standard for action or inaction because these clauses, read together as they should be, prohibit classification in terms of religion either to confer a benefit or to impose a burden."[92] Philip B. Kurland's notion of neutrality leads him to endorse government aid to parochial schools.[93] Paul Freund also points to neutrality as a central premise of the religion clause. Freund's idea of neutrality, however, brings him to oppose parochiaid.[94]

In an age of limited government—before government began to play a role in ordering such a vast range of social and economic activities—it mattered less precisely what one meant by "neutrality." Strict separationists, such as Jefferson and Madison, would have argued that the neutrality ordained by the First Amendment required that the government give no aid of any kind to religion. Two hundred years later, in an age of positive government, equating neutrality with a strict "no-aid" position invites a more spirited argument. Donald Giannella has maintained that the founding fathers expected religion to play a part in the established social order but also assumed that the state would play a minimal role in forming that order. In the present time, his argument runs, the question of how to treat religious groups and interests "has become a fundamentally different one" from that confronting the founders. Political equality for religious groups requires that they be able to participate in and have access to the benefits of government programs on the same terms as other groups.[95] Were the Supreme Court to adopt Giannella's reasoning, a "no-aid" theory—of the kind Justice Black had in mind— would have to give way to "neutrality" of the sort conceived by Professor Kurland. The implications of such a shift would be the most marked in education cases, notably those involving aid at the elementary and secondary level of private education.[96]

On the Court, Chief Justice Burger himself has been an especially active spokesman for neutrality—or, as he puts it, "benevolent neutrality." His first religion opinion, *Walz* v. *Tax Commission*, turns on this principle. Rejecting what he called "absolute" readings of the First Amendment, Burger seems to have joined the ranks of those, on the Court and off, who have criticized the "absolutist" Justice Black and, specifically, Black's opinion in *Everson*. Cautioning against relying on "too sweeping utterances" in earlier cases, Burger in *Walz* argued for "play in the joints productive of a benevolent neutrality which will permit religious exercise to exist without sponsorship and without interference."[97]

In the context of tax exemptions, Burger had little difficulty in lining up his brethren in support of "benevolent neutrality" (only Douglas dissented in *Walz*). Subsequent cases, however, have shown Burger (along with White and Rehnquist) to be emphatically more of an accommodationist than the majority of his colleagues. Granted, Burger wrote for the majority in *Lemon* v. *Kurtzman* invalidating the Pennsylvania and Rhode Island aid programs. Rather than resting his holding on the programs having an impermissible effect of aiding religion, however, he relied on the excessive entanglement likely to result from the states' need to police the programs to prevent aid to parochial schools' religious functions.[98]

Burger's commitment to accommodating religion became clear in *Nyquist*. Burger, dissenting in part, saw tuition grant and tax relief programs as "general welfare" statutes—sustainable, as in *Everson*, on the theory that it was individual parents, not the parochial schools, who should be viewed as the beneficiaries of the aid. Burger adopted the argument traditionally put forth by Catholic proponents of parochiaid—a principle of equal treatment for Catholic parents who must pay tuition costs for their own children while also paying taxes to support public schools.

It is beyond dispute that the parents of public school children in New York and Pennsylvania presently receive the "benefit" of having their children educated totally at state expense; the statutes enacted in those States and at issue here merely attempt to equalize that "benefit" by giving to parents of private school children, in the form of dollars or tax deductions, what the parents of public school children receive in kind. It is no more than simple equity to grant partial relief to parents who support the public schools they do not use.[99]

Indeed, it is hard to escape the conclusion that, apart from the bare question of the constitutionality of help for the patrons of private schools, Burger agrees with the policy underlying aid programs. That agreement is reflected in the closing paragraph of Burger's *Nyquist* dissent, where he invoked the "debt owed by the public generally to the parochial school systems" and praised the "wholesome diversity" those schools make possible.[100]

Justices White and Rehnquist have also taken the accommodationist point of view. Indeed, White was in that camp in the parochiaid cases even before Burger; White dissented in part in *Lemon* v. *Kurtzman*.[101] Invoking the principle of benevolent neutrality, Rehnquist is disturbed that the Court should "throw its weight on the side of those who believe that our society as a whole should be a purely secular one."[102] Rehnquist's opinion in *Mueller*, upholding Minnesota's system of tax deductions for tuition and other educational expenses of parents, represents at least a limited victory for the proponents of benevolent neutrality. Both in finding a secular purpose in the Minnesota statute and in refusing to hold that the statute had a primary effect of advancing religion, Rehnquist made much of the public interest in a pluralistic system of education and the essential fairness of recognizing the burden lifted from taxpayers' shoulders by patrons of private schools.[103]

THE SHIFTING WALL: LINE-DRAWING IN THE AID TO EDUCATION CASES

The Court's response to these analytical difficulties has been less than satisfying. Rather than restructure its analysis, the Court has often reached results by adroit characterization of the fact situations it faces. A willingness to characterize as distinct situations that a casual observer might think were similar explains much of the inconsistency in the Court's approach in aid to education cases.

Consider the techniques used by the Court to achieve the distinction it has made between programs aiding nonpublic elementary schools and those aiding private colleges, including colleges that are church-related.[104] The Court has created two different patterns of cases by applying the same rule to cases whose contours it shaped differently—much as a child making paper snowflakes can create strikingly different shapes by making the same straight cuts in paper he has folded differently.

One way the Court approaches the cases differently is in deciding whether to take prophylactic action based on speculation about potential future problems. In First Amendment cases generally, it is not unusual for the Court to test the constitutionality of a statute by looking not merely at how the statute has been applied on the facts of the case at bar but also at how it might be applied in other situations. Thus, in speech cases, a litigant may be able to argue a statute's "chilling" effect—that, apart from its impact on his speech, it may operate to discourage others from expressing themselves.

One might expect the Court to take a similarly prophylactic approach in the religion cases, policing the "wall of separation" by measuring the potential, as well as actual, hazards of a state program. In this respect the contrast between how the Burger Court decides parochiaid cases and how it handles college cases is striking.

Chief Justice Burger's opinion in *Lemon* v. *Kurtzman* illustrates the prophylactic approach. Several Rhode Island teachers had testified that they did not inject religion into their secular classes. Burger thought it enough, however, that the state's program carried "potential" hazards. He had no need to assume that teachers would be unsuccessful in attempting to keep their religious beliefs out of their secular teaching. Because of the "potential" for impermissible fostering of religion, the state had to condition its aid with pervasive restrictions—surveillance giving rise to entanglement of government and religion. Similarly, although the district court in *Lemon* had found only one instance in which the state had had to examine a school's records to determine which expenditures were religious and which were secular, Burger relied on the state's power to conduct audits as creating "an intimate and continuing relationship between church and state."[105] Justice White, in dissent, complained of the Court's striking down the Rhode Island statute on its face. Nothing in the record, he said, indicated that any participating teacher "had inserted religion into his secular teaching or had had any difficulty in avoiding doing so. The testimony of the teachers was quite the contrary."[106] White, in short, wanted the case to turn on the facts as found. The majority was more willing to speculate on what might happen under the statute's operation—and to strike it down on the basis of the potential hazards.

This willingness to speculate is missing from the majority

opinions when the Court has reviewed aid to church-related colleges and universities. In *Hunt*, Justice Powell noted the "sweeping powers" conferred upon the South Carolina authority by its enabling statute, such as powers to fix and collect fees and charges for the use of or services furnished by an aided project and to establish rules and regulations for the use of a project. Were there a "realistic likelihood" that these powers would be exercised fully, Powell conceded that there might be entanglement problems. Under the actual lease agreement with the Baptist College at Charleston, however, the authority could not take action unless the college defaulted in its obligation. Possibly some of those actions, such as setting rates and charges, would offend the Establishment Clause, but, Powell said, "we do not now have that situation before us."[107]

The Court could, of course, have taken a tougher line toward the dangers of entanglement in *Hunt*. It could, as in *Lemon*, have emphasized the dangers of what might happen, rather than looking only at the facts as developed in the case before the Court. Justice Brennan, dissenting in *Hunt*, thought the Court should be more influenced by what the authority had the power to do: "Indeed, under this scheme the policing by the State can become so extensive that the State may well end up in complete control of the operation of the College, at least for the life of the bonds."[108]

In narrowing issues in higher education cases, the Court takes a college-by-college approach—again, a sharp contrast to the parochial school cases. The parties challenging the federal construction grants to the Catholic colleges in *Tilton* asked the Court to accept a "composite profile" of the "typical sectarian" institution of higher education. Chief Justice Burger, however, refused to "strike down an Act of Congress on the basis of a hypothetical profile." Assuming that some church-related colleges did fit such a profile, it would be enough to deal with those situations "if and when challenges arise with respect to particular recipients and some evidence is then presented to show that the institution does in fact possess these characteristics."[109] Similarly, in *Hunt*, Justice Powell said that, in considering the "primary effect" of the South Carolina program, "we narrow our focus from the statute as a whole to the only transaction presently before us"—the arrangement with the Baptist Church of Charleston.[110]

In the parochial school cases, by contrast, the Court has

painted with a broader brush. In *Lemon* v. *Kurtzman*, Justice White, dissenting in part, complained that the Court "accepts the model for the Catholic elementary and secondary schools that was rejected for the Catholic universities or colleges in the *Tilton* case." It was wrong, thought White, for the Court to strike down the Rhode Island statute on the Court's "own suppositions and unsupported views of what is likely to happen in Rhode Island parochial school classrooms. . . ."[111]

The higher education cases turn heavily on assumptions that the Court makes about church-related institutions and, as a corollary, how the Court assigns burdens of proof. The Court takes nonsectarianism at private colleges to be the norm. Generalizing in *Tilton*, Chief Justice Burger took this norm to include the skepticism of college students, the internal disciplines of courses of instruction, commitment to academic freedom, and an atmosphere of open inquiry.[112]

The plaintiff challenging a program aiding private colleges will find himself being obliged to show, on the facts of the particular case, that a given college departs from the assumed form. In *Tilton*, Chief Justice Burger found that the "record here would not support a conclusion that any of these four institutions departed from this general pattern."[113] In *Hunt*, Justice Powell was even more explicit about the burden of proof: "The burden rests on appellant to show the extent to which the College is church-related. . . ." Powell concluded that the program's challenger had failed to show that the Baptist College at Charleston was "any more an instrument of religious indoctrination than were the colleges and universities involved in *Tilton*."[114]

Roemer, the Maryland case, reflects the Court's unwillingness to second-guess a district court that has found an aided college not to be "pervasively sectarian." Justice Blackmun, having restated the trial court's findings, said he could not characterize those findings as "clearly erroneous."[115]

Formal ties between a college and a religious body—such as a church's power to appoint trustees or to approve charter amendments—do not make the college "pervasively sectarian." All four of the colleges in *Tilton* were governed by Catholic religious organizations.[116] In *Hunt*, the South Carolina Baptist Convention elected the college's trustees, had a veto over certain financial transactions, and had to approve any charter amendments.[117] The colleges in *Roemer* had a "formal affiliation with the Roman Catholic Church," which was represented on their governing boards.[118] Nevertheless, the Court approved the aid programs in all three cases.

The Court directs its inquiry, therefore, to a college's actual operations—its admissions and faculty hiring policies, compulsory chapel, required religion courses, and the like. The Court has not been notably stringent in reviewing these factors. The faculty and student body at the four colleges in *Tilton* were predominantly Catholic, but the Court was satisfied by the finding that non-Catholics were admitted as students and given faculty appointments. All four institutions required students to take theology courses, but Chief Justice Burger noted that courses were taught according to the academic requirements of the subject matter and the teacher's concept of professional standards and that the courses covered a range of human experience not limited to Catholicism.[119] In *Roemer*, some classes were begun with prayer but the Court accepted the trial court's finding that this was left up to each instructor and was not a matter of "actual college policy."[120] On such records the Court has been able to conclude that the colleges' basic mission was secular rather than sectarian education.

The Court does insist on safeguards, even in the college cases. Even when satisfied, as in both *Tilton* and *Hunt*, with the basic contours of an aid program, the Court looks for evidence that there are devices to prevent public funds from being channeled to religious uses. In *Tilton*, Chief Justice Burger thought it important that the federal act had been drafted to ensure that federally subsidized facilities would be used for secular and not religious functions and that these restrictions were being enforced in the act's actual administration.[121] Likewise, in *Hunt*, no aid could be used for facilities used for religious purposes—a ban backed up by clauses in each lease forbidding religious use and allowing inspections to enforce the agreement.[122] Without these limitations and safeguards, it is hard to imagine that a majority could have been mustered in either *Tilton* or *Hunt* to uphold the respective statutes.

The Court, in brief, takes a pragmatic approach to programs aiding church-related colleges. The dissenters, especially Brennan, would take a tougher line on such aid. Brennan found impermissible entanglement in both *Tilton* and *Hunt*; he complained in *Hunt* that the Court has "utterly failed to explain how programs of surveillance and inspection of the kind common to both cases differ from the Pennsylvania and

Rhode Island programs" invalidated in *Lemon*.[123] While the majority, however, do require safeguards to prevent aid being used to support religious functions at church-related colleges, they have been clearly less concerned than in the parochiaid cases about either entanglement or political divisiveness. The Court finds less danger of entanglement because church-related colleges pursue a secular objective similar to that sought by other colleges and because the atmosphere and attitudes on college campuses, church-related or not, gives less opportunity for religious indoctrination than does the parochial school environment. Likewise, the Court is less apprehensive about political divisiveness where the aid is to colleges, as the student constituency is more diverse, aid goes to private colleges generally (more than two-thirds of which have no religious affiliation), and a church-related college is likely to be more autonomous than a parochial school.[124]

After the Court's 1975 *Meek* decision, John Nowak said that the majority "will use any 'test' necessary to invalidate any program granting aid to parochial elementary or secondary schools or aid to the students who attend them." Indeed, he concluded, *Meek* signaled "the end of the use of 'tests' to determine the legitimacy" of such programs.[125]

The Court's 1983 decision in *Mueller* v. *Allen*, however, blurs the de facto distinction between the justices' prophylactic approach to elementary and secondary education cases and the Court's more deferential posture in reviewing aid at the college level. *Mueller* has unmistakable qualities of deference about it. In weighing the validity of Minnesota's tax deduction for tuition and educational expenses, Rehnquist invoked traditional notions about legislators' having "broad latitude" in distributing the tax burden—a principle of deference not usually associated with Establishment Clause attacks on legislation. More striking as a departure from earlier cases like *Nyquist* is Rehnquist's concluding that, the Minnesota statute's being "facially neutral," he was unwilling to look into the "extent to which various classes or private citizens claimed benefits under the law."[126] This tack permitted Rehnquist to deflect the force of the fact that, of those taxpayers eligible for the deduction, 96 percent send their children to religious schools.[127]

In earlier parochiaid cases such as *Nyquist*, the Court did not stop at the statute's face; instead the majority looked at the law's actual operation. The question there was whether the

statute's primary benefit ran to those who send their children
to sectarian schools. In pulling up short, as he did in *Mueller*,
Rehnquist wrote an opinion much more in the spirit of the
Court's decisions upholding aid benefiting church-related colleges and universities.

Only time will tell whether the justices' decision in *Mueller*
portends a shift in approach. Earlier parochiaid precedents
stand, but the tension between the 1983 decision and the earlier cases is evident. Certainly Mueller must give new hope to
advocates of tuition credits and other forms of aid to private
education, both in Congress and in the states.

The Porous Wall: *Marsh v. Chambers*

Relaxing the Court's three-part establishment test is but one
avenue for accommodating state recognition of religion.
Another road is to bypass that test altogether. This is what the
Court did in another 1983 case, *Marsh v. Chambers*. There
Chief Justice Burger rejected an Establishment Clause challenge to Nebraska's long-standing practice of paying a chaplain to open legislative sessions.

The Court of Appeals for the Eighth Circuit had applied in
Marsh the traditional three-part test and had concluded that
Nebraska's practice violated all three prongs of that test.[128] In
looking to history, however, Burger sidestepped the three-
part test altogether. Burger found Nebraska's practice to be
"deeply imbedded in the history and tradition of this country." That history included the action of the First Congress—
the same session that voted to submit the First Amendment to
the states for ratification—in appointing a chaplain to open
sessions with a prayer.[129]

Marsh's inquiry into history and tradition carves out an
exception to the Court's usual approach to Establishment
Clause cases. Justice Brennan, in dissent, thought the exemption a "narrow" one, posing little threat (he said hopefully)
"to the overall fate" of the Establishment Clause. Brennan
went through the motions of applying the conventional three-
part test, but he devoted many more pages and much more
effort to resting his arguments on the "underlying function"
of the Establishment Clause.[130]

Marsh reflects an air of a pragmatic concern about other
cases that might be brought before the Court. The majority's
invocation of history may signal a concern over their being
pestered with suits challenging the use of "In God We Trust"

on coins or the opening of sessions of court with the cry "God save the United States and this Honorable Court." In an age in which Americans are quick to take a remarkable range of issues to court, religious and otherwise, the Court has some reason to wonder what religious practice will surface in the next round of cases.

Indeed, the ink was hardly dry on *Mueller* and *Marsh* before the Court, early in the next term, heard arguments in a challenge to Pawtucket, Rhode Island's display of a crèche at the Christmas season. In *Lynch* v. *Donnelly*, the Justices split five to four in upholding the display.[131] Chief Justice Burger, who wrote the Court's opinion, observed that the crèche (owned by the city and erected in a privately owned park) was displayed alongside more secular seasonal figures, such as Santa Claus and his reindeer. Burger concluded that the crèche, rather than carrying an explicitly sectarian message, served to engender "a friendly community spirit of good will in keeping with the season."[132]

The chief justice's opinion in *Lynch* carries something of the flavor of both *Marsh* and *Mueller*. Burger did apply the three-part establishment test, but he wasted few words in finding all three aspects of the test satisfied in *Lynch*. At the same time, however, he characterized the Court as having shown an "unwillingness to be confined to any single test or criterion in this sensitive area." He devoted a fair proportion of the *Lynch* opinion to history, an approach that recalls his opinion in *Marsh*.[133]

The chief justice may have had a broad agenda in mind in *Lynch*. The passages devoted to history are not confined to the practice of displaying crèches. Instead, Burger developed a more general thesis of "an unbroken history of official acknowledgement by all three branches of government of the role of religion in American life from at least 1789." In so doing, he supplied examples of the proclamation of Christmas and Thanksgiving as official holidays, of references to God on coins and in the pledge of allegiance, and of public galleries' display of religious art.[134] Throughout, Burger's opinion is characterized by a distaste for "absolutist" readings of the Establishment Clause and by an effort to accommodate the nation's religious traditions.

Justice Brennan wrote for the four dissenters in *Lynch*. Dissenting opinions have a way of wavering between hope and fear, and Brennan's opinion is no exception. On the hopeful side, he saw *Lynch* as reaching "an essentially narrow result" turning largely upon the particular way in which Pawtucket displayed the crèche. He saw as an open question, for example, the constitutionality of the display of a crèche by itself or the erection of other religious symbols such as crosses.[135]

On the fearful side, however, Brennan showed obvious concern that the Court's tendency to accommodation presaged a weakening of the traditional limits implicit in Establishment Clause jurisprudence. He was concerned that the Court's "less than vigorous application" of the three-part test suggested that the majority were not really committed to that standard. Moreover, he was troubled by the Court's "broader and more troubling theme"—the scope and range of practices that government might "acknowledge" despite what Brennan saw as the danger that, in so doing, government would be implying approval of or favoritism toward one set of religious beliefs.[136]

In *Lynch*, as in *Marsh*, the majority had signaled their unwillingness to uproot practices that, while carrying strong religious symbolism, have become widely absorbed into the civic consciousness of Americans. The struggle, of course, goes on. In the term of Court following in which *Lynch* was decided, the Court set no fewer than seven religion cases for argument. Several of these cases promised to add significant gloss to religion clause doctrine. One case involved an Alabama law permitting public school teachers to start the school day with a moment of silence "for meditation and voluntary prayer." A second case posed for review a Michigan school district's "shared time" program, in which public school teachers were sent into parochial schools to teach remedial and enrichment classes. On the same day as the Michigan case was argued, the Court also heard arguments in a challenge to the use of federal funds to pay public employees to teach remedial courses and perform other services on the premises of church schools. In yet another case, the Court had before it a Connecticut law giving employees in the private sector a right not to work on a day the employee designated as the Sabbath.[137] In each of these four cases, appellate courts had struck down the statutes as amounting to an establishment of religion. In all four cases, the Reagan administration filed briefs defending the statutes. The Court's decisions will tell much about how far the Court will go in the direction marked out by *Mueller*, *Marsh*, and *Lynch*.

PRAGMATISM AND DOCTRINE IN THE SUPREME COURT

Justices of the Supreme Court often seek to anchor their opinions in history. In the Court's first interpretation of the Free Exercise Clause, *Reynolds* v. *United States*, Chief Justice Waite looked to the writings of Jefferson for an "authoritative" understanding of the First Amendment.[138] In *Everson*, Justice Black looked to the fight led by Madison and Jefferson in disestablishment in Virginia as having had the "same objective" as the First Amendment.[139]

Historians are not slow to criticize the Court's use of history. Mark DeWolfe Howe voiced his disenchantment with the justices' efforts to play historians. "The judge as statesman, purporting to be the servant of the judge as historian, often asks us to believe that the choices that he makes—the rules of law that he establishes for the nation—are the dictates of a past which his abundant and uncommitted scholarship has discovered." Howe thought that "illusion born of oversimplification" has brought the Court to favor the Jeffersonian version of the "wall of separation"—a political principle grounded in rationalism—over Roger Williams's version, which is a theological concern to preserve the "garden of the church" in the "wilderness of the world." Modern liberals, according to Howe, have not sufficiently recognized the complexities of motive that fashioned the policy of separation. Howe was concerned that the Court's "current inclination to extract a few homespun absolutes from the complexities of a pluralistic tradition" would stand in the way of accommodating the religious strands in American life.[140]

The years since *Everson* have brought so much gloss on the First Amendment that the Court has fallen into the habit—natural to judges as to lawyers—of putting gloss on gloss. Thus, it becomes more important to reconcile an opinion with *Allen* or *Lemon* than to go back to first principles. Moreover, the tradition of a "living Constitution"—a continuing process of reinterpretation—affects religion decisions as much as any other. Finally, the justices—again, like lawyers—often seem more comfortable with immediate, real-life problems than with theory and abstract principle. Thus, they get the feel of the issue before them—aid to parochial schools, or whatever—and try their hand at what seems like a workable approach to the problem. As a result, one sees the Court's evolving pragmatic decisions in which aid to primary and secondary schools is one thing, and aid to colleges is another. Even where an opinion looks explicitly to history (as Burger did in *Marsh*) or revisits fundamental principles (as Brennan saw himself doing in his *Marsh* dissent), whiffs of pragmatism hang in the air.

Justice Oliver Wendell Holmes once remarked that a "page of history is worth a volume of logic."[141] The modern Court often seems to have paraphrased Holmes to read that "a page of experience is worth a volume of history." With the advent of the Burger Court, constitutional adjudication seems to have taken on a more ad hoc, episodic quality—in constitutional cases generally, not just in religion cases.[142] Since so much of the case law on establishment, especially aid to education, comes from the Burger era, the present Court's pragmatic instincts have particular importance in understanding judicial glosses on the First Amendment's religion clauses. The justices are by no means oblivious to the origins of the First Amendment. The contours of the religion cases, however, often owe as much to pragmatic institutions as to doctrine grounded in historical judgments.

NOTES

This paper is adapted and updated from an earlier essay, "Up Against the Wall," which appeared in *Church, State, and Politics* (Washington, D.C.: Roscoe Pound-American Trial Lawyers Foundation, 1981).

1. Thomas Jefferson to Committee of the Danbury Baptist Association, 1 January 1802, reprinted in Adrienne Koch and William Peden, *The Life and Selected Writings of Thomas Jefferson* (New York: Modern Library, 1944), 332-33. See also Joseph Martin Dawson, *Baptists and the American Republic* (Nashville: Broadman Press, 1956), 38.

2. *Barron* v. *Baltimore*, 7 Pet. (32 U.S.) 243 (1833).

3. *Permoli* v. *New Orleans*, 44 U.S. 589 (1845).

4. Especially was this true of provisions banning appropriations to aid nonpublic education.

5. *Reynolds* v. *United States*, 98 U.S. 145 (1878).

6. Thomas Jefferson to Committee of the Danbury Baptist Association, 1 January 1802, see note 1.

7. In 1784, Virginia's General Assembly considered two bills, both supported by Patrick Henry, to levy a general assessment for the support of teachers of religion and to incorporate the Episcopal Church. It was against the assessment bill that Madison wrote his famous Memorial and Remonstrance against Religious Assessments. The memorial evoked an avalanche of petitions and the assessment bill was tabled. In its place emerged Thomas Jefferson's Bill for Establishing Religious Freedom, which declared that no one should be compelled "to frequent or support any religious worship, place, or ministry whatsoever. . . ." See Julian P. Boyd, ed., *The Papers of Thomas Jefferson*, 20 vols. to date (Princeton, N.J.: Princeton University Press, 1950-), 2:545-47.

8. *Reynolds* v. *United States*, at 164.

9. See David Little, "Thomas Jefferson's Religious Views and Their Influence on the Supreme Court's Interpretation of the First Amendment," *Catholic University Law Review* 26 (1976):57.

10. See *Everson* v. *Board of Education*, 330 U.S. 1, 11-13 (1947). See also Justice Rutledge's even lengthier reliance on Madison in his dissent in *Everson*, at 33-43 (Justice Wiley Rutledge, dissenting).

11. *Davis* v. *Beason*, 133 U.S. 33 (1890).

12. See, e.g., *Cantwell* v. *Connecticut*, 310 U.S. 296 (1940).

13. E.g., Leo Pfeffer, "The Supremacy of Free Exercise," *Georgetown Law Journal* 61 (1973):1115, 1127.

14. *Braunfeld* v. *Brown*, 366 U.S. 599, 606 (1961).

15. *Sherbert* v. *Verner*, 374 U.S. 398 (1963).

16. Ibid., at 420 (Justice John M. Harlan, dissenting).

17. *Wisconsin* v. *Yoder*, 406 U.S. 205 (1972).

18. Ibid., at 234-35 n.22, quoting *Sherbert* v. *Verner*, at 409.

19. See note 10.

20. A. E. Dick Howard "Mr. Justice Black, the Negro Protest Movement, and the Rule of Law," *Virginia Law Review* 53 (1967):1030, 1068-69.

21. *Everson* v. *Board of Education*, at 15-16.

22. Ibid., at 18.

23. *Adamson* v. *California*, 332 U.S. 46, 59 (Justice Felix Frankfurter, concurring), 68 (Justice Hugo Black, dissenting) (1947); see Charles Fairman, "Does the Fourteenth Amendment Incorporate the Bill of Rights? The Original Understanding," *Stanford Law Review* 2 (1949):5.

24. *Abington School District* v. *Schempp*, 374 U.S. 203, 309-10 (1963) (Justice Potter Stewart, dissenting).

25. A. E. Dick Howard, *State Aid to Private Higher Education* (Charlottesville, Va.: Michie Co., 1977), 27; Howard, "State Courts and Constitutional Rights in the Day of the Burger Court," *Virginia Law Review* 62 (1976):873, 907-12.

26. Howard, *State Aid to Private Higher Education*, 29.

27. Paul A. Freund, "Public Aid to Parochial Schools," *Harvard Law Review* 82 (1969):1680, 1682.

28. Erwin N. Griswold, "Absolute Is in the Dark—A Discussion of the Approach of the Supreme Court to Constitutional Questions," *Utah Law Review* 8 (1963):167.

29. Paul G. Kauper, "*Everson* v. *Board of Education*: A Product of the Judicial Will," *Arizona Law Review* 15 (1973):307, 317.

30. *McCollum* v. *Board of Education*, 333 U.S. 203, 238 (1948) (Justice Robert H. Jackson, concurring).

31. *McCollum* v. *Board of Education*; and *Zorach* v. *Clauson*, 343 U.S. 306 (1952).

32. *Engel* v. *Vitale*, 370 U.S. 421 (1962) (Regents' prayer); *Abington School District* v. *Schempp*, 374 U.S. 203 (1963) (Bible readings, Lord's Prayer).

33. *Engel* v. *Vitale*, at 430.

34. *McGowan* v. *Maryland*, 366 U.S. 420 (1961).

35. *Board of Education* v. *Allen*, 392 U.S. 236 (1968).

36. *Engel* v. *Vitale*, at 445-46 (Justice Potter Stewart, dissenting).

37. *Zorach* v. *Clauson*, at 313.

38. *Engel* v. *Vitale*, at 443 (Justice William O. Douglas, concurring).

39. *Board of Education* v. *Allen*, at 254 (Justice William O. Douglas, dissenting).

40. *Abington* v. *Schempp*, at 222.

41. In *Larson* v. *Valente*, 456 U.S. 228 (1982), the Court observed that the three-part "test" is meant to apply where a challenged law affords a uniform benefit to *all* religions. Where a law is perceived to grant a preference or discriminate *among* religions, the law is treated as "suspect" and subjected to "strict scrutiny," at 246, 252.

42. *Walz* v. *Tax Commission*, 397 U.S. 664, 675, 677 (1970).

43. *Lemon* v. *Kurtzman*, 403 U.S. 602 (1971).

44. *Walz* v. *Tax Commission*, at 674.

45. *Lemon* v. *Kurtzman*, at 619.

46. Ibid., at 622-24.

47. *Committee for Public Education and Religious Liberty (PEARL)* v. *Nyquist*, 413 U.S. 756 (1973).

48. *Sloan* v. *Lemon*, 413 U.S. 825 (1973); *Levitt* v. *Committee for Public Education*, 413 U.S. 472 (1973).
49. *PEARL* v. *Nyquist*, at 795.
50. *Meek* v. *Pittenger*, 421 U.S. 349 (1945).
51. *Wolman* v. *Walter*, 433 U.S. 229 (1977).
52. *Tilton* v. *Richardson*, 403 U.S. 672, 686 (1971).
53. Ibid., at 687.
54. *Hunt* v. *McNair*, 413 U.S. 734 (1973).
55. Ibid., at 743-44.
56. *Roemer* v. *Board of Public Works*, 426 U.S. 736 (1976).
57. Ibid., at 755-67.
58. *Mueller* v. *Allen*, 51 USLW 5050 (U.S. 29 June 1983).
59. Ibid., at 5053.
60. Ibid., at 5055 (Justice Thurgood Marshall, dissenting).
61. Ibid., at 5054, quoting *Wolman* v. *Walter*, at 262 (Justice Lewis F. Powell, Jr., concurring and dissenting).
62. *Mueller* v. *Allen*, at 5054.
63. *PEARL* v. *Nyquist*, at 803, 805 (Chief Justice Warren Burger, dissenting in part).
64. Compare *Wolman* v. *Walter* with *Meek* v. *Pittenger*.
65. Compare *PEARL* v. *Nyquist* with *Mueller* v. *Allen*.
66. Jesse Choper has observed that application of the Court's three-pronged test with school aid cases "has generated ad hoc judgments which are incapable of being reconciled on any principled basis." Choper, "The Religious Clauses of the First Amendment: Reconciling the Conflict," *University of Pittsburgh Law Review* 41 (1980):673, 680. Nathan Lewin characterizes the Court's establishment decisions as a "drunkard's reel." Lewin, "Disentangling Myth from Reality," *Journal of Law and Education* 3 (1974):107, 108.
67. *Meek* v. *Pittenger*, at 394, quoting *Edwards* v. *California*, 314 U.S. 160, 186 (1941) (Justice Robert H. Jackson, concurring).
68. Philip B. Kurland, "The Irrelevance of the Constitution: The Religion Clauses of the First Amendment and the Supreme Court," *Villanova Law Review* 24 (1978-79):3, 19. For a further critique of the entanglement test, see Kenneth F. Ripple, "The Entanglement of the Religion Clauses—A Ten Year Assessment," *U.C.L.A. Law Review* 27 (1980):1195.
69. Choper, "The Religious Clauses of the First Amendment," 681-83. See also Choper's criticisms of the Court's establishment cases at 52 USLW 2228-29 (1983).
70. *Roemer* v. *Public Works*, at 768 (Justice Byron R. White, concurring).
71. *Wolman* v. *Walter*, at 265-66 (Justice John Paul Stevens, concurring and dissenting).
72. *Lemon* v. *Kurtzman*, at 623.
73. Ibid., at 622.
74. *PEARL* v. *Nyquist*, at 794, 797-98, quoting *Lemon* v. *Kurtzman*, at 602, 625 (Justice William O. Douglas, concurring).
75. *Meek* v. *Pittenger*, at 374 (Justice William J. Brennan, concurring and dissenting).
76. *Walz* v. *Tax Commission*, at 695 (opinion of Justice John M. Harlan).
77. Freund, "Public Aid to Parochial Schools," 1680, 1692.
78. *Mueller* v. *Allen*, at 5054 n.11.
79. *Marsh* v. *Chambers*, 51 USLW 5167 (U.S. 5 July 1983). See also Justice Brennan's majority language in *Larson* v. *Valente*, at 252-55, quoting Justice Harlan's language in *Walz* and arguing that the statute at issue in *Larson* should be overturned to avoid political fragmentation along religious lines.
80. Jacob E. Cooke, ed., *The Federalist* (Middletown, Conn.: Wesleyan University Press, 1961), 57, 58.
81. Leo Pfeffer distinguishes between groups of people organizing to protect and advance their own position in society and organizing to promote a shared attitude. In

the former instance, they act as a self-interest group; in the latter, as an ideological interest group. The trade union movement, organizing to improve wages and working conditions is an example of the former; a league to abolish capital punishment is an example of the latter. Pfeffer submits that the Court "rejects the church as a self-interest group but accepts it as an ideological interest group." Pfeffer, *God, Caesar, and the Constitution: The Court As Referee of Church-State Confrontation* (Boston: Beacon Press, 1975), 62.

82. Robert Rutland and William Rachal, eds., *The Papers of James Madison*, 14 vols. to date (Chicago: University of Chicago Press, 1962-   ), 8:302-3.
83. *Everson* v. *Board of Education*, at 28, 33-41 (Justice Wiley Rutledge, dissenting).
84. *New York Times* v. *Sullivan*, 376 U.S. 254, 270 (1964).
85. Lewin, "Disentangling Myth from Reality," 111. For other criticisms of the political divisiveness doctrine, see Choper, "The Religion Clauses of the First Amendment," 683-85; Kurland, "The Irrelevance of the Constitution," 19; John E. Nowak, "The Supreme Court, the Religion Clauses, and the Nationalization of Education," *Northwestern University Law Review* 70 (1976):883, 905-8.
86. See Choper, "The Religion Clauses of the First Amendment."
87. *Abington* v. *Schempp*, at 296 (Justice William J. Brennan, concurring).
88. *PEARL* v. *Nyquist*, at 788.
89. Ibid., at 814 (Justice Byron R. White, dissenting).
90. Ibid., at 802 (Chief Justice Warren Burger, dissenting in part).
91. *Everson* v. *Board of Education*, at 18.
92. *Zorach* v. *Clauson*, at 315-20 (Justice Hugo Black, dissenting).
93. Philip B. Kurland, *Religion and the Law* (Chicago: University of Chicago Press, 1962), 112, Professor Kurland continues to stick by his guns. See Kurland, "The Irrelevance of the Constitution," 22, 24.
94. Freund, "Public Aid to Parochial Schools," 1680, 1686.
95. Donald A. Giannella, "Religious Liberty, Nonestablishment, and Doctrinal Development, Part II: The Nonestablishment Principle," *Harvard Law Review* 81 (1968):513, 514-15.
96. Michael J. Malbin argues that, under the "original meaning" of the Establishment Clause, federal aid to private schools would have been allowed, perhaps even aid limited to religious schools, depending upon there being a secular purpose and upon how one defined "religion." Malbin, *Religion and Politics: The Intentions of the Authors of the First Amendment* (Washington, D.C.: American Enterprise Institute, 1978), preface. See also Walter Berns, *The First Amendment and the Future of American Democracy* (New York: Basic Books, 1976), 1-32.
97. *Walz* v. *Tax Commission*, at 669.
98. *Lemon* v. *Kurtzman*, at 619-21.
99. *PEARL* v. *Nyquist*, at 803 (Chief Justice Warren Burger, dissenting in part).
100. Ibid., at 805.
101. *Lemon* v. *Kurtzman*, at 661 (Justice Byron R. White, concurring and dissenting).
102. *Meek* v. *Pittenger*, at 395 (Justice William H. Rehnquist, concurring and dissenting).
103. *Mueller* v. *Allen*, at 5052, 5054.
104. See generally, Howard, *State Aid to Private Higher Education*.
105. *Lemon* v. *Kurtzman*, at 619, 622, and at 608 n.2.
106. Ibid., at 667 (Justice Byron R. White, concurring and dissenting).
107. *Hunt* v. *McNair*, at 749.
108. Ibid., at 752 (emphasis supplied) (Justice William J. Brennan, Jr., dissenting).
109. *Tilton* v. *Richardson*, at 682.
110. *Hunt* v. *McNair*, at 742.
111. *Lemon* v. *Kurtzman*, at 667-68 (Justice Byron R. White, concurring and dissenting).
112. *Tilton* v. *Richardson*, at 685-87.
113. Ibid., at 686.

114. *Hunt* v. *McNair*, at 746, 746-47 n.8.
115. *Roemer* v. *Public Works*, at 758.
116. *Tilton* v. *Richardson*, at 686.
117. *Hunt* v. *McNair*, at 743.
118. *Roemer* v. *Public Works*, at 755.
119. *Tilton* v. *Richardson*, at 686-87.
120. *Roemer* v. *Public Works*, at 756.
121. *Tilton* v. *Richardson*, at 682-84.
122. *Hunt* v. *McNair*, at 744.
123. Ibid., at 743 (Justice William J. Brennan, Jr., dissenting).
124. See *Tilton* v. *Richardson*, at 765-66.
125. Nowak, "The Supreme Court, the Religion Clauses, and the Nationalization of Education," 883, 891-92.
126. *Mueller* v. *Allen*, at 5052-54.
127. See ibid., at 5055-56 (Justice Thurgood Marshall, dissenting).
128. *Marsh* v. *Chambers*, 675 F.2d 228, 234-35 (8th Cir. 1982).
129. Ibid., 51 USLW at 5163-64.
130. Ibid., at 5165-73 (Justice William J. Brennan, Jr., dissenting).
131. *Lynch* v. *Donnelly*, No. 82-1256 (5 March 1984).
132. Slip opinion, p. 15.
133. Ibid., 4-9.
134. Ibid., 5-8.
135. Ibid., 1 (Justice William J. Brennan, dissenting).
136. Ibid., 2, 20.
137. See *Wallace* v. *Jaffree*, No. 83-812; *Smith* v. *Jaffree*, No. 83-929; *School District of City of Grand Rapids* v. *Ball*, No. 83-990; *Aguilar* v. *Felton*, Nos. 84-237, 84-238, 84-239; *Estate of Thornton* v. *Caldor, Inc.*, No. 83-1158.
138. *Reynolds* v. *United States*, at 164.
139. *Everson* v. *Board of Education*, at 13.
140. Mark DeWolfe Howe, *The Garden and the Wilderness: Religion and Government in American Constitutional History* (Chicago: University of Chicago Press, 1965), 4-10, 174.
141. *New York Trust Co.* v. *Eisner*, 256 U.S. 345, 349 (1921).
142. See A. E. Dick Howard, "The Burger Court: A Judicial Nonet Plays the Enigma Variations," *Law and Contemporary Problems* 43 (1980):7.

The Deity in American Constitutional History

LEO PFEFFER

Invocation of the deity or deities to authenticate the commands of those who decreed the acts of state goes back long before the biblical era and encompasses not only the Western world but the Eastern as well. In ancient Israel, and its offsprings Christianity and Islam, every important act of state was accompanied by a prayer to the deity and an attestation that the particular act was commanded or at the very least sanctioned by him. The crowning of a king,[1] the going out to war and the coming back from it, whether in success or defeat,[2] the establishment of communities and the fixing of their borders,[3] the regulation of what today would be deemed strictly secular affairs, such as the determination of the compensation to be received by one whose ox was gored by his neighbor's[4]—all these and an infinite number of others were determined in accordance with what the particular governmental body, national or local, executive, legislative, or judicial, asserted was the will of God.

When, therefore, the Christians from the Old World settled on these shores, it was taken for granted that they would be governed by the laws of God as set forth in his Bible and transmitted to them through the appropriate organs of government, theocratic for a time in New England or secular elsewhere. It was quite natural too, that, in the enactment of statutes or the judicial enforcement of laws, the deity should be invoked, not merely in respect to those dealing with obviously religious matters, such as heresy or blasphemy (which included utterance of "any reproachful speeches concerning the Holy Trinity or the Virgin Mary" and which was punishable by death),[5] but also with those dealing with what today would be deemed purely secular matters.[6]

There were, of course, dissenters, not in respect to the basic premise that ultimately all valid laws, religious or secular, came from God, but rather as to the assumption that it was his will that secular tribunals should have jurisdiction over sacred matters.[7] The incorrectness of this assumption, according to Roger Williams, was witnessed by the doctrine of the two tables, i.e., that it was the business of the civil magistrate to enforce the second table of the Decalogue which concerned man's dealings with his fellow men, but that the punishment of offenses against the first table, governing man's relations with God, was not within the sphere of state authority.

Williams's influence on American constitutional history is manifest in the writings of Baptists such as Isaac Backus, who asserted that "religion is a concern between God and the soul with which no human authority can intermeddle,"[8] and John Leland[9] among others. All in all the Baptists were by far, but by no means the only conventional major religious group that could claim credit for the exclusion of religion and man's relationship to God from the jurisdiction of civil government; Presbyterians[10] and Lutherans[11] among others shared in this successful endeavor.

Parallel to the efforts of Baptists and other religious groups, and leading to the end result were those of individuals, generally called Deists, whose religious commitments were almost diametrically opposite those of the pietistic Baptists. As Baptists inherited the spirit of Williams, the Deists, such as Thomas Jefferson, James Madison, and Thomas Paine, inherited and reflected the views of John Locke. It was through them that the principles expressed in Locke's Letter Concerning Toleration became the foundation of the Constitution's ban on religious tests for governmental office and the First Amendment's exclusion from governmental authority of laws respecting an establishment of religion or forbidding its free exercise.[12]

The social contract theory, popularized by Locke, became so widely accepted as to be deemed a self-evident truth to the signers of the Declaration of Independence. That comparatively short document, penned by Jefferson, however, contained no less than four references to or invocations of the Deity—"God," "Creation," "Supreme Judge of the World," and "divine Providence."

The explanation, it may be suggested, lies in the reality of political life dictating that so revolutionary a document addressed "to the opinions of mankind," must appeal to and be accepted by the greatest number of the American people. Ironically, this felt necessity impelled Jefferson to violate the principles, expressed a decade later by his disciple Madison in his Memorial and Remonstrance Against Religious Assessment, that government may not "employ religion as an engine of civil policy."[13] The tensions between principle and political reality are manifest in the duality of "nature" and "nature's God" in the opening paragraph of the Declaration.

The multiplicity of references to the Deity in the Declaration reflects similar invocations in the proclamations and other state papers of the Continental Congress. These unabashedly exhibited a belief in Trinitarian Protestantism. Congress continually invoked, as sanction for its acts, the name of "God," "Almighty God," "Nature's God," "God of Armies," "Lord of Hosts," "His Goodness," "God's Superintending Providence," "Providence of God," "Providence," "Supreme and Universal Providence," "Overruling Providence of God," "Creator of All," "Indulgent Creator," "Great Governor of the World," "The Divinity," "Supreme Disposer of All Events," "Holy Ghost," "Jesus Christ," "Christian Religion," "Free Protestant Colonies," and other expressions of devout Christian Protestantism.[14]

In stark contrast is the document penned some eleven years after the Declaration of Independence and adopted as the Constitution of the United States. Neither the preamble, which set forth the purpose of the proposed national government, nor the body of the document makes any reference to the Deity. The only reference to religion in it, and that in an exclusionary rather than endorsing context, is found at the end of the last operative section, which forbids religious tests as a qualification for public office.

The omission of a reference to the Diety was not inadvertent; nor did it remain unnoticed. A delegate to the Connecticut ratifying convention stated in a letter to Oliver Ellsworth (later chief justice of the United States) that he would have required "an explicit acknowledgment of the being of God, his perfections and his providence . . . in the following or similar terms, viz. 'We the people of the United States, in a firm belief of the being and perfection of the one living and true God, the creator and supreme Governor of the world, in his universal providence and the authority of his laws . . . do ordain, etc.' "[15] At a meeting of Congregationalists in June 1788 a request was presented "that some suitable Testimony might be borne against the sinful omission in the late Federal Constitution in not looking to God for direction, and of omitting the mention of the name of God in the Constitution."[16]

These were not the only expressions of dissatisfaction with

the omission of the name of God in the Constitution, but it was not this omission that was the major fault found with the document. On the contrary, what concerned them most was the omission of a Bill of Rights, and it was only in reliance upon the defenders' promise that a bill would be added after ratification that the requisite number of states voted for ratification. To meet the situation and fulfill the promise, a legislative committee, under Madison's leadership, drafted the Bill of Rights which was to become the first ten amendments to the Constitution. The opening words of the bill, "Congress shall make no law respecting an establishment of religion, or prohibiting the free exercise thereof," constituted a seal of approval rather than a repudiation of the absence of reference to the Deity in the Constitution.[17]

It should be noted that references to the Deity in state constitutions today are common, and included among them are the constitutions of states which were part of the Union when it was originally established as well as those who joined thereafter.[18] As a practical matter there is no way by which the constitutionality of this practice can be challenged in the federal courts, since its mere presence, as its presence on American coins and currency, in a legal sense injures no one. In any event, it is quite clear that irrespective of the practice in the state constitutions, the American people are not eager to amend the federal Constitution to incorporate a reference to an invocation of the Deity.

Efforts to achieve this have, during America's history, been tried from time to time.[19] Some have been limited to an invocation addressed to God; others sought to frame it in terms of Jesus Christ. In 1863, representatives from eleven Protestant denominations organized the National Reform Association[20] (later known as the Christian Amendment Movement[21]) with the purpose, among others, of amending the Constitution so as to "declare the Nation's allegiance to Jesus Christ and its acceptance of the moral laws of the Christian religion, and to indicate that this is a Christian nation, and place all Christian laws, institutions and usages of our government on an undeniably legal basis in the fundamental law of the land."

The proposal to declare the United States "a Christian nation" was in a sense a progressive step, for it encompassed not only Protestant heretics, such as Roger Williams, Anne Hutchinson, and the Quakers, but even Roman Catholics (who, having become so numerous, could hardly be ignored).

It was predicated on the assumption, strongly contested by Jefferson (who condemned it as a "judicial forging" and a "conspiracy between church and state"),[22] that Christianity is part of the common law, and, therefore, is recognizable as such in the American legal system, which is based upon the common law. As will be noted later, as recently as 1978 the Kentucky legislature enacted a law declaring that the Ten Commandments are part of the common law of the United States.

Nor should it be assumed that this assertion was entirely without judicial acceptance. It had the imprimatur of a unanimous Supreme Court, speaking through Joseph Story in the case of *Vidal* v. *Girard's Executors*,[23] decided in 1843. In his opinion, Story, whose monumental *Commentaries on the Constitution of the United States* was for a century deemed by courts and scholars to be the most authoritative study of constitutional law, left no doubt as to his views on the status of Christianity and its Deity in the Constitution and laws. To Story it was clear that "the Christian religion is part of the common law," and he cited in support of this assertion the provision in the constitution of Pennsylvania where the *Girard* case arose, that "all men have a natural and indefeasible right to worship Almighty God according to the dictates of their own consciences."

The case involved a testamentary grant for the establishment of an educational institution for orphans with the proviso that "no ecclesiastic, missionary, or member of any sect whatsoever, shall ever hold or exercise any station or duty whatever in said college." The Supreme Court upheld the validity of this provision on the ground that Girard had not impugned or repudiated Christianity, nor had he barred the teaching of the Christian religion, but directed only that the teaching not be done by clergymen but rather by adequately trained and competent lay teachers.

It is worthwhile here to recall the somewhat lengthy extract from the Court's opinion:

It is also said, and truly, that the Christian religion is a part of the common law of Pennsylvania. But this proposition is to be received with its appropriate qualifications, and in connection with the bill of rights of that state, as found in its constitution of government. The constitution of 1790 . . . expressly declares, "That all men have a natural and indefeasible right to worship Almighty God according to the dictates of their own consciences; no man can of right be compelled to attend, erect, or support any place of worship or to maintain any ministry against his consent; no human authority can, in any case whatever, control or interfere with the rights of conscience; and no preference shall ever be given by law to any religious establishments or modes of worship.'' Language more comprehensive for the complete protection of every variety of religious opinion could scarcely be used; and it must have been intended to extend equally to all sects, whether they believed in Christianity or not, and whether they were Jews or infidels. So that we are compelled to admit that although Christianity be a part of the common law of the state, yet it is so in this qualified sense, that its divine origin and truth are admitted, and therefore it is not to be maliciously and openly reviled and blasphemed against, to the annoyance of believers or the injury of the public. . . . It is unnecessary for us, however, to consider what would be the legal effect of a device in Pennsylvania for the establishment of a school or college for the propagation of Judaism, or Deism, or any other form of infidelity. Such a case is not to be presumed to exist in a Christian country; and therefore it must be made out by clear and indisputable proof.

This essay will later comment on "Judaism or Deism or any other form of infidelity" and the presumption that a bequest to them "is not to be presumed to exist in a Christian country." It is, however, necessary to point out here that in this case Story was speaking about the constitution of Pennsylvania rather than that of the United States. That his views in respect to the latter were not different is evidenced by the following:[24]

Probably at the time of the adoption of the Constitution, and of the [first] amendment to it now under consideration, the general if not the universal sentiment in America was, that Christianity ought to receive encouragement from the state so far as was not incompatible with the private rights of conscience and the freedom of religious worship. An attempt to level all religions, and to make it a matter of state policy to hold all in utter indifference, would have created universal disapprobation, if not universal indignation. . . .

The real object of the amendment was not to countenance, much less to advance, Mahometanism, or Judaism, or infidelity, by prostrating Christianity; but to exclude all rivalry among Christian sects, and to prevent any national ecclesiastical establishment which should give to an hierarchy the exclusive patronage of the national government.

A half century after the *Vidal* case was decided, the Court again declared that this nation and its Constitution reflect commitment to the Christian religion and its deity. In the case before it, *Church of Holy Trinity* v. *United States*,[25] the Court ruled that an act of Congress prohibiting the importation of foreigners "under contract or agreement to perform labor in the United States" was not intended to prohibit a church from contracting with an English clergyman to migrate to this country and act as its rector and pastor. The statute, the Court said, was aimed at the breakdown of domestic wage standards by the importation of foreign manual laborers under contract to work off their passage at an agreed substandard rate.

Again in an unanimous opinion, however, the Court felt it necessary to reaffirm the determination that Americans are a Christian people and that recognition of the Christian deity comports fully to American tradition and constitutional standards. In support of this assertion the Court referred, with obvious approval, to typical provisions in state constitutions. Among these was the Mississippi Constitution of 1832 which stated that "no person who denies the being of a God, or a future state of rewards and punishments, shall hold any office in the civil departments of this State." Another was the following oath required in the Delaware Constitution of all state employees: "I profess faith in God the Father, and in Jesus Christ His only Son, and in the Holy Ghost, One God, blessed for evermore, and I do acknowledge the Holy Scriptures of the Old and New Testament to be given by divine inspiration."

Following the example of Justice Story, the Court's opinion in *Church of Holy Trinity* sets forth a list of instances establishing that "this is a Christian nation": among others, the provision in Article I, Section 7 of the federal Constitution that excepts Sunday in the ten-day period during which the President may approve or veto a bill of Congress; the universally prevailing form of oath of office concluding with an appeal to the Almighty ("so help me God"); the custom of opening sessions of all deliberative bodies and most conventions with prayer; the prefatory words of all wills, "In the name of God, amen"; and the laws respecting the observance of the Sabbath.

The next litany witnessing the godliness of this nation and its Constitution came from a rather surprising source. In the history of the Supreme Court there has probably been no member more absolutist in his views regarding the First Amendment's mandates of church-state separation and the free exercise of religion than Justice William O. Douglas. He was the sole dissenter in the decisions upholding the constitutionality of Sunday closing laws.[26] He alone dissented from the Court's 1970 decision in *Walz* v. *Tax Commission*[27] upholding the constitutionality of laws exempting church-owned properties from taxation. While he concurred in the Court's 1947 decision in *Everson* v. *Board of Education* upholding the constitutionality of laws authorizing state payments for the costs of transporting pupils to parochial schools, he thereafter regretted his concurrence (saying in his concurring opinion in *Engel* v. *Vitale*[28] that the "Everson case seems in retrospect to be out of line with the First Amendment") and steadfastly voted against any measure aimed at extending the *Everson* holding beyond subsidization of school transportation, such as, for example, by public financing of secular textbooks for parochial school use.[29]

Despite all this, Justice Douglas was the author of the majority opinion in the 1952 case of *Zorach* v. *Clauson*,[30] upholding the constitutionality of a statute authorizing the release during school hours of pupils wishing to participate in religious instruction conducted off public school premises. A good distance had been traveled since the assertions were made in the earlier cases that this is a Christian nation. "We are," he said instead, "a religious people,"[31] thus broadening the boundaries of permissible governmental beneficence in legislation to encompass adherents of "Judaism, Deism, or any other form of infidelity," to whom Justice Story was not ready to accord equal treatment under the First Amendment.

The use by Douglas of the term "religious people" rather than "Christian people," merits noting. As late as 1931, in the case of *United States* v. *Macintosh*,[32] in holding that a religiously motivated pacifist could be denied citizenship for refusing to take an oath that he would in all cases bear arms in defense of the nation, asserting rather that he would do so only in instances where he believed the war to be morally justified, the Supreme Court ventured into the arena of theology and undertook to correct Macintosh on what really was the will of God. The Court said:

> When he speaks of putting his allegiance to the will of God above his allegiance to the government, it is evident, in the light of his entire statement, that he means to make *his own interpretation* of the will of God the decisive test which shall conclude the government and stay its hand. We are a Christian people, according to one another the equal right of religious freedom, and acknowledging with reverence the duty of obedience to the will of God. But, also, we are a nation with the duty to survive; a nation whose Constitution contemplates war as well as peace; whose government must go forward upon the assumption, and safely can proceed upon no other, that unqualified allegiance to the nation and submission and obedience to the laws of the land, as well those made for war as those made for peace, are not inconsistent with the will of God.[33]

The *Macintosh* case will be examined further later in this essay. It is quoted here only to note the assertion that this is a

Christian nation, a claim which today is heard considerably less frequently than in earlier years. One hears instead that this is a pluralistic society, but almost invariably today the term "Judeo-Christian" is used synonymously for "pluralistic." The frequent use of this term indicates the great influence that the Jews, notwithstanding their small percentage of the population, have exercised on American political and cultural values. Yet, it may be suggested, to say that the United States is a Judeo-Christian nation is as inconsistent with the spirit of the First Amendment as to say it is a Christian nation. Roger Williams asserted that "no civil state or country can be truly called Christian, although the Christians be in it."[34] Likewise, no civil state or country committed to the First Amendment can be called Judeo-Christian, although Christians and Jews be in it.

Returning to Justice Douglas's opinion in *Zorach* v. *Clauson*, note should be taken of his statement in it that "we are religious people whose institutions presuppose a Supreme Being." To support this assertion and the constitutionality of its recognition in the public school system he states that were this not so:

Municipalities would not be permitted to render police or fire protection to religious groups. Policemen who helped parishioners into their places of worship would violate the Constitution. Prayers in our legislative halls; the appeals to the Almighty in the messages of the Chief Executive; the proclamations making Thanksgiving Day a holiday; "so help me God" in our courtroom oaths—these and all other references to the Almighty that run through our laws, our public rituals, our ceremonies would be flouting the First Amendment. A fastidious atheist or agnostic could even object to the supplication with which the Court opens each session: "God save the United States and this Honorable Court."[35]

Less than a month after the Court handed down its decision in *Zorach* v. *Clauson*, it announced its decision in *Burstyn* v. *Wilson*,[36] wherein it interpreted the First Amendment in respect to the divinity in an opinion that points in a direction opposite to its ruling in *Zorach* v. *Clauson* and in the other cases that have been discussed here.

The colonists who settled on these shores found no difficulties in promulgating laws against blasphemy and sacrilege, even though many of them came here to escape such laws in England. These laws became quite common in the United States, and although the Court had stated in the 1872 case of *Watson* v. *Jones* that in this country "the law knows no heresy and is committed to the support of no dogma,"[37] this was not deemed to proscribe laws aimed at blasphemy or sacrilege.

Burstyn v. *Wilson* involved such a law. Its terms required the granting of a license to all films except those that were in whole or part "obscene, indecent, immoral, inhuman [or] sacrilegious." Acting under that law, the New York authorities revoked a license that had been issued for the exhibition of a motion picture entitled *The Miracle.* The picture dealt with a poor, simple-minded girl who had been seduced and impregnated by a bearded stranger she believed to have been Joseph, the husband of Mary, the mother of Jesus. The license was revoked after a strong denunciation of the film and its licensing by Francis Joseph Cardinal Spellman and by Catholic organizations that condemned it as blasphemous in that it impugned the virgin birth of Jesus.[38]

The revocation was challenged in the courts on the ground that it violated the First Amendment's guaranty of freedom of speech and its prohibition of laws respecting an establishment of religion and forbidding its free exercise. The Court chose to base its decision, annulling the revocation, on the freedom of speech rather than on the religious clauses. As to the latter, however, it noted that under the standard of "sacrilege,"

the most careful and tolerant censor would find it virtually impossible to avoid favoring one religion over another, and he would be subject to an inevitable tendency to ban the expression of unpopular sentiments sacred to a religious minority. Application of the "sacrilegious" [*sic*] test, in these or other respects, might raise substantial questions under the First Amendment's guaranty of separate church and state with freedom of worship for all. However, from the standpoint of freedom of speech and the press, it is enough to point out that the state has no legitimate interest in protecting any or all religions from views distasteful to them which is sufficient to justify prior restraints upon the expression of those views. It is not the business of government in our nation to suppress real or imagined attacks upon a particular religious doctrine, whether they appeal in publications, speeches, or motion pictures.[39]

It bears noting that New York's highest court, in upholding the statute authorizing the revocation, stated that there was "nothing mysterious" in it. What was meant by the word "sacrilegious" was that "no religion as that word is understood by the ordinary, reasonable person, shall be treated with contempt, mockery, scorn or ridicule."[40] Yet as far as is known, neither the New York statute nor any similar one has ever been invoked in New York or elsewhere against any religion other than the Christian faith. In any event, *Torcaso* v. *Watkins,*[41] decided in 1961, made it clear that no divinity, Christian, Jewish, or other, could constitutionally receive governmental protection against blasphemy, sacrilege, or atheism.

Maryland's constitution, challenged in that case, copied Article VI of the federal Constitution in providing that "no religious test ought ever be required for any office of profit or trust in this State," but qualified it by adding the words "other than a declaration of belief in the existence of God." Torcaso, an atheist, was appointed to the office of Notary Public but was refused his commission to serve because he would not declare a belief in the existence of God. Appealing to the Supreme Court, Torcaso cited its 1948 decision in the case of *McCollum* v. *Board of Education*.[42] There, the Court, in invalidating under the Establishment Clause a law providing for the devotional teaching of religion in the public schools, declared that "no person can be punished for entertaining religious beliefs or disbeliefs, for church attendance or non-attendance."[43] The Maryland Court of Appeals, in upholding the denial of the commission asserted that the *McCollum* decision had been overruled in *Zorach* v. *Clauson* and cited in support of this ruling the statement in Justice Douglas's opinion in that case that "we are a religious people whose institutions presuppose a Supreme Being."[44]

If a personal note may be interjected here, this writer was Torcaso's attorney in this case and he saw (or perhaps imagined he saw) Justice Douglas wince when the state's attorney general read that sentence in his oral argument to the Court. In any event, Justice Hugo Black, the author of the *McCollum* opinion (holding unconstitutional religious instruction in the public schools) who shared Justice Douglas's commitment to the absolute separation of church and state, would not accept it. In the opinion that he wrote for the Court in Torcaso's case, he quoted the sentence in *Zorach* v. *Clauson* that "we follow the McCollum case."

We repeat and again reaffirm [he said] that neither a State nor the Federal government can constitutionally force a person to profess a belief or disbelief in any religion. Neither can constitutionally pass laws or impose requirements which aid all religions as against non-believers, and neither can aid those religions based on a belief in the existence of God as against those religions founded on different beliefs.[45]

In a footnote at this point, Justice Black said: "Among religions in this country which do not teach what would generally be considered a belief in the existence of God are Buddhism, Taoism, Ethical Culture, Secular Humanism and others."[46]

This footnote was hardly relevant to Torcaso's case, since he did not claim to be an adherent of any of these religions or of any other. It is, however, relevant to this article, which deals with the subject of the Deity in American constitutional history, in that it accords equal protection to deistic and non-deistic religions.

A year after the *Torcaso* ruling, the Court handed down its decision in *Engel* v. *Vitale*. That case dealt with the constitutionality of the recitation by public school pupils of a twenty-two-word prayer formulated by the New York State Board of Regents. The prayer read as follows: "Almighty God, we acknowledge our dependence upon Thee, and we beg Thy blessings upon us, our parents, our teachers and our country."

The prayer had been cleared in advance with authoritative New York representatives of Protestantism, Catholicism, and Judaism, and was accordingly characterized by the Regents as being "nonsectarian." In view of the footnote already cited in the *Torcaso* case, this would seem to be hardly relevant. Nor, in view of the *McCollum* decision, would it be relevant that pupils' participation in the prayer recitation was purportedly entirely voluntary, in that dissenting children could remain silent or be excused from the room. Nevertheless, the New York Court of Appeals upheld the practice on these grounds.[47]

The Supreme Court decided otherwise. Neither of these facts, it held, immunized the practice from nullification under the Establishment Clause. Nor, the Court said, was it either sacrilegious or antireligious "to say that each separate government in this country should stay out of the business of writing or sanctioning official prayers and leave that purely religious function to the people themselves and to those the people choose to look to for religious guidance."[48]

A year later, in the case of *Abington Township School District* v. *Schempp*,[49] the Court was again faced with the need to pass upon the constitutionality of invoking the Divinity through prayer in the public schools. Also involved in that case was a challenge to the practice of reading verses from the Bible at the opening of public school sessions each morning. Somewhat surprisingly, but perhaps understandably in view of Justice Potter Stewart's dissent in *Engel* v. *Vitale*[50] and the hostile reaction that decision received in many parts of the United States and particularly in the South,[51] Justice Thomas Clark, in his opinion for the Court, felt it necessary to recite the ritual litany of godliness in governmental actions. (Justice Stewart's dissent in *Engel* had recited the stanza in the national anthem stating that "in God we trust," the 1954 act of Congress which added the words "under God" in the Pledge of Allegiance, the presence of the phrase "In God We Trust" on U.S. coins, and the act of Congress calling upon the president to proclaim each year a National Day of Prayer.[52])

The fact [the Court's opinion in the *Schempp* case said] that the Founding Fathers believed devotedly that there was a God and that the unalienable rights of man were rooted in Him is clearly evidenced in their writings, from the Mayflower Compact to the Constitution itself. This background is evidenced today in our public life through the continuance in our oaths of office from the Presidency to the Alderman of the final supplication, "So help me God." Likewise each House of Congress provides through its Chaplain an opening prayer, and the sessions of this Court are declared open by the crier in a short ceremony, the final phrase of which invokes the grace of God. Again, there are such manifestations in our military forces, where those of our citizens who are under the restrictions of military service wish to engaged in voluntary worship. Indeed, only last year an official survey of the country indicated that 64% of our people have church membership, while less than 3% profess no religion whatever. It can be truly said, therefore, that today, as in the beginning, our national life reflects a religious people who, in the words of Madison, are "earnestly praying, as . . . in duty bound, that the Supreme Lawgiver of the Universe . . . guide them into every measure which may be worthy of his [blessing . . .]." Memorial and Remonstrance Against Religious Assessments.[53]

Justice Clark's reference to God in the Constitution is puzzling. It may refer to the provision excluding Sundays in counting the ten days in which the president has to veto an act of Congress. Perhaps it also referred to the following paragraph that appears after the text of the Constitution: "Done in convention by the unanimous consent of the States present the Seventeenth day of September in the year of our Lord one thousand seven hundred and eighty seven, and of the independence of the United States of America the Twelfth. In witness whereof we have hereunto subscribed our names." If these are what Justice Clark had in mind, they seem to exclude not only Jews, who do not accept Jesus Christ as "our Lord," but also those Christians who observe Saturday as the divinely ordained day of rest.

Notwithstanding this ritual recitation, the Court in its decision determined that both practices, reciting the Lord's Prayer and reading the Bible, violated the First Amendment. The Court paid little attention to the efforts made by counsel for school authorities to prove that the *Engel* holding should be distinguished in that the prayer involved therein was formulated by the state Board of Regents, whereas the Lord's Prayer was in the Bible, universally acknowledged as a great work of literature. It was obvious to the Court that the recitation and reading were acts of worship and not exercises in literature.

Prayer that was neither church-formulated (as in *Schempp*) nor government-formulated (as in *Engel*) fared no better. In *DeKalb School District* v. *DeSpain*,[54] a federal court in 1967 frowned upon what was known as the "cookie prayer," so called because it was recited by the kindergarten children before their morning snack. The work of an anonymous poet of unknown religious affiliation, its simple words were as follows:

> We thank you for the flowers so sweet;
> We thank you for the food we eat;
> We thank you for the birds that sing;
> We thank you, God, for everything.

The kindergarten teacher in Elwood Public School in DeKalb County, Illinois, was no lawyer, but she must have had some inkling of the *Engel* and *Schempp* decisions, for she sought to make the prayer constitutionally permissible by making it Godless. The words of the prayer that she led her pupils in reciting were:

> We thank you for the flowers so sweet;
> We thank you for the food we eat;
> We thank you for the birds that sing;
> We thank you for everything.

This revision obviously sacrificed the rhythm of the original and must have left at least some of the children puzzled as to who was the "you" they addressed. The sacrifice, however, proved futile; the court issued an injunction against the now presumably Godless prayer and the Supreme Court refused to upset the decision.

Relevance to the subject of this paper, the Deity in American constitutional history, requires mention of the Supreme Court's 1968 decision in *Epperson* v. *Arkansas*.[55] Like the present-day crusade by Senator Jesse Helms (Rep., N.C.), the Moral Majority, and others to nullify the *Engel* and *Schempp* decisions and restore prayer to the public schools, efforts to reintroduce what is essentially the biblical account of creation under the title "scientific creationism" as an alternative to the theory of evolution indicate that the issue is a live one today.[56] In the *Epperson* case, the Court held violative of the First Amendment's Establishment Clause a state statute making it unlawful for a teacher in any state-supported school or university to teach theory or doctrine that mankind ascended or descended from a lower order of animals, or "to adopt or use in any such institution a textbook that teaches" this theory.

Just as the "cookie prayer" in the *Dekalb School* case sought, unsuccessfully, to avoid judicial invalidation by omitting the word "God" from the challenged prayer, so the Arkansas legislature sought to reach the end by making no direct reference to the Deity. The effort was no more successful than the earlier one, as is indicated by the following paragraph from the *Epperson* decision.

In the present case, there can be no doubt that Arkansas has sought to prevent its teachers from discussing the theory of evolution because it is contrary to the belief of some that the Book of Genesis must be the exclusive source of doctrine as to the origin of man. No suggestion has been made that Arkansas' law may be justified by considerations of state policy other than the religious views of some of its citizens. It is clear that fundamentalist sectarian conviction was and is the law's reason for existence. Its antecedent, Tennessee's "monkey law," candidly stated its purpose: to make it unlawful "to teach any theory that denies the story of the Divine Creation of man as taught in the Bible, and to teach instead that man has descended from a lower order of animals." Perhaps the sensational publicity attendant upon the Scopes trial induced Arkansas to adopt less explicit language. It eliminated Tennessee's reference to "the story of the Divine Creation of man" as taught in the Bible, but there is no doubt that the motivation for the law was the same: to suppress the teaching of a theory which, it was thought, "denied" the divine creation of man.[57]

Attention must also be given to the subject of the Deity and military service in war and in peace. As noted in the *Macintosh* case the Court dismissed as presumptuous and unacceptable the assertion that an individual may make his own interpretation of God's will and that it is the government alone that may rightfully make such a claim.[58]

This may be true in respect to England where the head of the state is simultaneously the head of the church and perhaps could claim infallibility in that capacity. It is obviously not true in respect to a nation whose constitution forbids laws respecting an establishment of religion or prohibitions on its free exercise. American policy is predicated upon the principle that in order to secure a republican form of government it is necessary to separate secular powers among its three branches, but none of them nor all of them together are competent to discern or legislate what is the will of the Deity. If the First Amendment and the ban on religious tests for governmental office mean anything, they mean that no agency of government has the constitutional power to determine what is God's will and translate that will into the law of the land.

This, indeed, was what the Supreme Court ruled in the 1872 case of *Watson* v. *Jones*, wherein it held that no legislature or court may constitutionally determine which of two factions in a church schism truly represents the will of God according to the doctrines of the particular church. There the Court said: "In this country the full and free right to entertain any religious belief, to entertain any religious principle, and to teach any religious doctrine which does not violate the laws of morality and property, and which does not infringe personal rights, is conceded to all. The law knows no heresy, and is committed to the support of no dogma, the establishment of no sect."[59]

What, then, did the Court have in mind with respect to the statement made in the *Macintosh* case? It is simply this: there are certain arenas where the government may intervene and overrule an individual's claim to the free exercise of religion. Child sacrifice is an obvious example, and the courts have universally held that the states have the power to authorize blood transfusions where necessary to save the life of a child even though the parents believe that the procedure would violate God's command forbidding the drinking of blood.[60] If religious conscience and commitment to God's will can be overruled where necessary to save the life of one child, the same is certainly true where the life of a nation is at stake.

Yet, from the earliest days of this nation (and even before that, in Cromwell's England), persons whose religious doctrine forbade participation in armed conflict were exempt from military service by the laws in some states and by the Continental Congress. This, however, the Court has ruled, was a matter of legislative grace, not constitutional right, and what Congress gives Congress can take back or can limit or qualify.[61] Thus, the first national exemption of conscientious objectors adopted by Congress during the Civil War was limited to members of well-recognized religious denominations whose articles to faith forbade the bearing of arms.[62]

So, too, was the exemption accorded by the conscription law enacted at the time of America's entry into World War I. Exemption was allowed only to those who were affiliated with well-recognized religious groups, the creed or principles of which forbade their members to participate "in war in any form." Lest new groups arise to provide a shelter for unwilling draftees, the law limited the exemption to groups already existing at the time it was enacted, and to prevent existing groups from altering their doctrine for the same purpose, the law also required that the creed of principle against military service be in existence when the law was passed.[63]

The intended beneficiaries of these exemption laws were the long-established peace denominations, such as the Friends and Mennonites. Yet the genius of American freedoms is individualistic rather than corporate; the opening words of the Bill of Rights reflect a suspicion of, if not antipathy to, religious establishments. The 1940 selective service law, enacted upon the eve of America's entry into World War II, liberalized the exemption to make it more consistent with the American genius. It no longer required membership in a particular sect, but granted the exemption to anyone who by "reason of religious training and belief" possessed conscientious scruples against "participation in war in any form."

Congress, however, had no intention of extending the mantle of protection to political, intellectual, humanist, or other nonreligious objectors to war. To make this clear, it again amended the law in 1948 to state explicitly that "religious training and belief in this connection means an individual's belief in a relation to a Supreme Being involving duties superior to those arising from any human relation, but does not include essentially political, sociological, or philosophical views or a merely personal moral code."

So amended, the law gave rise to some difficult constitutional questions. In the first place, religion and belief in God are not necessarily synonymous. As has been noted, the Court was later to point out in *Torcaso* v. *Watkins,* there are ancient, well-recognized religions that are not theistic, such as Buddhism, Taoism, and Confucianism. A military exemption law limited to adherents of the Christian faith would obviously be unconstitutional; so too would be one which specifically excluded Buddhists, Taoists, and Confucianists. Yet this was what was affected by requiring a belief in God as a condition to exemption. The concept of God as generally understood in this country is basically Judeo-Christian (and Islamic), and, under the Establishment Clause of the First Amendment, Congress could no more prefer these religions over nontheistic faiths than it could prefer Christianity over Judaism or Protestantism over Catholicism.

A second constitutional difficulty arose from the fact that the law imposes upon civil officials the duty of making theological determinations and, moreover, gives them no standards or guidelines by which to make them. How is a draft board to decide whether that in which a particular applicant for exemption believes is a "Supreme Being?" Does he have to

believe in the God of the Old Testament or the New Testament or the Koran or all three? Does his belief have to be
fundamentalist in essence or may it be liberal and modernist?

Finally, even if the draft boards were to take a liberal position as to what constitutes God and were also to accept as religious training and belief, within the meaning of the exemption, training and belief in nontheistic religions, a constitutional problem would still remain. The Establishment Clause,
the Court has held on numerous occasions, does not impose a
mandate of neutrality merely as among different religions, but
also as between religion and nonreligion. The government
may not prefer all religions over nonreligions any more than
it may prefer one or some religions over others.[64]

These were some of the difficulties facing the Court in 1965
in three cases decided under the name of *United States* v.
Seeger.[65] Before considering these cases, something should be
said about the meaning of the phrase conditioning exemption
on possession of conscientious scruples against "participation
in war in any form."

The issue arose in 1955 in *Sicurella* v. *United States*,[66] involving a member of the Jehovah's Witnesses and thus "in the
Army of Christ Jesus serving as a soldier of Jehovah's appointed Commander Jesus Christ." Inasmuch as the war weapons of the soldier of Jesus Christ were not carnal, he was not
authorized by his Commander to engage in the carnal warfare
of this world. The literature of the Jehovah's Witnesses, however, extolled the ancient wars of the Israelites, asserted that
Witnesses would engage in a "theocratic war" if Jehovah so
commanded them, and declared that they would fight at
Armageddon.

On the basis of this evidence, the draft board ruled that
Sicurella was not entitled to exemption, but the Supreme
Court felt otherwise. As to theocratic war, the Court stated
that his willingness to fight on the orders of Jehovah was
tempered by the fact that, as far as is known, the Witnesses'
history records no such command since biblical times and
their theology does not contemplate one in the future. While
the Witnesses expected to fight at Armageddon, they would
do so without carnal weapons, and Congress had in mind real
shooting wars—"actual military conflicts between nations of
the earth in our time—wars with bombs and bullets, tanks,
planes and rockets."[67]

Returning to the difficulties facing the Court in the *Seeger* case, it appears that the explanation lies in the fact that it met them by first taking God out of religion and then taking religion out of religion. Seeger, in applying for exemption, admitted his "skepticism or disbelief in the existence of God," but avowed a "belief in and devotion to goodness and virtue for their own sakes and a religious faith in a purely ethical creed," and cited Plato, Aristotle, and Spinoza in support of such belief. Jakobson, another applicant, stated a belief in "Godness horizontally through Mankind and the World," rather than "vertically, towards Godness directly." The third applicant, Peter, avowed a commitment to religion defined as "the supreme expression of human nature; man thinking his highest, feeling his deepest, living his best."

The Court held that all three applicants were entitled to exemption since all had the requisite "religious training and belief in relation to a Supreme Being." By using the term "Supreme Being" rather than "God," the Court said, Congress intended something much broader than the traditional personal Deity. As for the term "religious belief," that is one which "is sincere and meaningful and occupies a place in the life of its possessor parallel to that filled by the orthodox belief in God of one who clearly qualifies for the exemption."[68]

What this meant is that depth and sincerity can be substituted for dogma and creedal affiliation. The decision assumed the importance of being earnest, but not necessarily of being religious, at least as that word would be understood by the man in the street. By holding that the three applicants all qualified under the exemption, the Court was able to avoid deciding whether the exemption itself was constitutional. Yet it is doubtful that Congress really meant what the Court said it did. The terms "God" and "Supreme Being" are generally considered synonymous. The Declaration of Independence uses the terms "Nature's God," "Creator," "Supreme Judge of the World," and "divine Providence," and certainly did not mean different things in each case.

Why, then, did not the Court unambiguously adjudge unconstitutional a law that accords a privilege to believers in God, by whatever synonym Congress chooses to use, and denies it to those who do not? As already noted, this, indeed, is just what the Court did in the *Torcaso* case decided four years ealier. The answer in the concurring opinion of Justice Douglas is stated with the frankness characteristic of him; were the Court to have interpreted the exemption as Congress

intended, it probably would have had to invalidate it just as it
had done in the *Torcaso* case:

The legislative history of this Act leaves much in the dark. But it is, in my
opinion, not a *tour de force* if we construe the words "Supreme Being" to
include the cosmos, as well as an anthropomorphic entity. If it is a *tour de
force* so to hold, it is no more so than other instances where we have gone to
extremes to construe an Act of Congress to save it from demise on constitutional grounds. In a more extreme case than the present one we said that
the words of a statute may be strained "in the candid service of avoiding a
serious constitutional doubt."[69]

Ironically, even under the Court's finding of a legislative
intent to differentiate between Supreme Being and God, at
least two of the three draftees, Seeger and Peter, would not
have qualified for exemption since both refused to answer
affirmatively the question whether they believe in a Supreme
Being.

Yet, the troublesome question of constitutionality will not
go away. At the present writing there are two cases now
before the Supreme Court as yet undecided which may ultimately require it to pass upon that issue.

The first of these is the case of *Thomas* v. *Indiana Employment Security Division*.[70] It involves a Jehovah's Witness who
left his job because the company for which he worked became
engaged primarily in the manufacture of weapons. The Court
will have to decide whether a state can constitutionally deny
unemployment compensation benefits to one who, by reason
of his religious conscience, will not participate in the manufacture of weapons of war.[71]

The second case is *Rostker* v. *Goldberg*.[72] That involves a
challenge to the draft registration law enacted in 1980 upon
the recommendation of President Jimmy Carter. The president asked that the registration be required of persons of both
sexes and it made no exception in respect to those whose religious conscience forbade participation in any action relating
to armed conflict, including registration. Congress, however,
chose to limit the registration to males, and it is only this
issue of sexual discrimination that is now before the Court in
the *Rostker* case.

The Court may uphold the statute as written; or it may
agree with the American Civil Liberties Union, which is
representing Goldberg, that it is invalid on the ground of sexual discrimination. Should the latter alternative eventuate, it is
almost certain that in view of the present tensions in respect
to the Soviet Union and other Communist countries, Con-

gress will amend the law to include women. In either event, the issue whether requiring registration on the part of those who believe that God forbids participation not only in war but in preparation for war is permissible will still remain to be decided. This writer has been instructed by the Jewish Peace Fellowship and the Fellowship of Reconciliation, in whose behalf he filed an amicus brief in the *Thomas* case, to institute a suit challenging as violative of the Free Exercise Clause the compulsory registration imposed upon conscientious objectors.

In view of the Court's disposition of the constitutional issue in the *Seeger* case, it can be assumed that the Court will be able to find a way to avoid deciding that issue in either the *Thomas* case or in the one that will be brought in behalf of the Jewish Peace Fellowship and the Fellowship of Reconciliation, should it wish to do so.

The efforts to return God to the public schools through prayer have been discussed earlier in this essay. Prayer, however, is not the only means through which this end has been pursued. The most recent opinion that the Supreme Court has issued on the subject concerns not prayer but the Ten Commandments.[73] At issue was a 1978 law enacted by the Kentucky legislature providing that a copy of the Ten Commandments be posted on the wall of every elementary and secondary public school classroom in the state. Perhaps in an effort to exorcise the spirit of unconstitutionality, the legislature added two sections to the measure. The first read: "In small print below the last commandment shall appear a notation concerning the purpose of the display, as follows: 'The secular application of the Ten Commandments is clearly seen in its adoption as the fundamental legal code of Western Civilization and the Common Law of the United States.' " The second read: "The copies required by this Act shall be purchased with funds made available through voluntary contributions made to the state treasurer for the purposes of this Act."

It should be noted that the two provisions really contradict each other. If the purpose of the law was secular, there was no reason to mandate that tax-raised funds not be used in achieving it. If it was religious, however, then, as the Court later said in its decision holding the law unconstitutional, "The mere posting of the copies under the auspices of the legislation provide[d] the official support of the State" in violation of the Establishment Clause. Echoing Roger Williams's Law of the Two Tables, in respect to man's obigations to the Divinity, the Court said:

The Commandments do not confine themselves to arguably secular matters, such as honoring one's parents, killing or murder, adultery, stealing, false witness, and covetousness. See Exodus 20:12-17; Deuteronomy 5:16-21. Rather, the first part of the Commandments concerns the religious duties of believers: worshipping the Lord God alone, avoiding idolatry, not using the Lord's name in vain, and observing the sabbath day. See Exodus 20:1-11; Deuteronomy 5:6-15.[74]

While the effort to return the Deity to governmental institutions is most prevalent and persistent in respect to public education, that is by no means the only arena of conflict. Nor is it, by any means, always unsuccessful. The words "under God" in the Pledge of Allegiance were added by Congress in 1954 as the result of a sermon preached by Rev. George Daugherty of the New York Avenue Presbyterian Church in Washington, D.C., on an occasion when President Dwight Eisenhower was present. Daugherty objected that the Pledge was one that a Russian school child could utter by merely substituting "USSR" for "USA." He observed that something was wrong when a pledge could be used equally well in a "godless" nation and in this country. Accordingly, he urged addition of the words "under God" to the Pledge. President Eisenhower endorsed the proposal and it was approved by Congress without any dissent.[75]

A decade later a suit was brought in New York by Joseph Lewis, an avowed and somewhat flamboyant atheist, to declare the law unconstitutional. The attorney for the New York Department of Education, with the support of the thirty states that joined in an amicus curiae brief in opposition to Lewis, argued that the Pledge, including the 1954 addition, was not a religious exercise but was designed to promote patriotism.[76]

It is somewhat difficult to accept this argument in view of the statement in Madison's Memorial and Remonstrance, which has often been recognized by the Supreme Court as a foundation of the Establishment Clause, that the civil authority's effort to employ religion as an engine of civil policy was "an unhallowed perversion of the means of salvation." In any event, in the case of *Lewis* v. *Allen*,[77] the Supreme Court refused to set aside the decision of a New York court upholding the statute's constitionality.

Using the terms "evangelical" and "crusade" in a somewhat broader sense than is to be found in most standard dictionaries, note may be taken of some evangelical efforts of

Madalyn Murray O'Hair, exceeding in flamboyance and lack
of success those of Lewis, in her crusade against God. Among
these were her attempts to obtain a court injunction forbidding the astronauts to pray to God on the *Apollo VIII* space
flight, or at least forbidding telecasting them while they were
engaged in prayer;[78] to delete "So help me God" from judicial
oaths;[79] and to forbid the use of a national mall for the celebration of a Mass by Pope John Paul II.[80]

To bring this account as close to the present as practicable,
attention should be called to the Supreme Court's decision in
the case of *Bradshaw* v. *Hall*.[81] In that case, a federal court
ruled that the official North Carolina state highway map violated the Constitution in printing on it the "Motorist's
Prayer," which asked the blessings of "our heavenly Father
as we take the wheel of our car." In doing so, it rejected the
state's argument that the prayer was no more offensive than
the nondenominational invocation common at public meetings, a practice which (if not exercised in public schools during school hours) the courts had consistently refused to enjoin.[82] Logic and consistency might have supported this argument, but the federal court refused to accept it and held that
the prayer was an impermissible government sponsorship of
religion. On 2 March 1981, the Supreme Court, without opinion, rejected the state's appeal.

The substance of this article may be summarized as follows.
From the initial landing of the Pilgrims on these shores, up to
the time of the Declaration of Independence, invocation of the
Deity in official governmental acts was a practically universal
practice. Thereafter it continued and still continues to be
acceptable in state constitutions; indeed it is to be found today
in almost all state constitutions. Those who wrote and those
who adopted our national Constitution and its Bill of Rights,
however, made a deliberate determination not to invoke the
Diety therein. The Supreme Court, however, for more than a
century and half, showed no reticence in invoking the Deity
in its own decisions. In the course of this period, however, it
expanded the meaning of the term to encompass the nontrin-
itarian Deity of the Unitarians and Universalists and by using
the term "Judeo-Christian," to include the Deity of the Jews.
In its most recent relevant decisions it has employed the
amorphous and almost boundaryless term "Supreme Being"
as that term is interpreted by each individual for himself.
Finally, while it will not exercise its judicial power to inhibit

invocation of the Deity outside the arena of public education, it will not sanction denial of privileges such as governmental employment to those who deny the existence of a deity.

NOTES

1.   1 Sam. 15:1.
2.   Deut. 20:4.
3.   Num. 34:1ff.
4.   Exod. 21:35.
5.   Leo Pfeffer, *Church, State and Freedom*, rev. ed. (Boston: Beacon Press, 1967), 83.
6.   E.g., becoming a notary public; *Torcaso* v. *Watkins*, 367 U.S. 488 (1961).
7.   Pfeffer, *Church, State and Freedom*, 84-85, fn. 5.
8.   Anson Stokes and Leo Pfeffer, *Church and State in the United States*, rev. one-vol. ed.(New York: Harper & Row, 1964), 486.
9.   Ibid., 63.
10. Ibid., 69.
11. Ibid., 68.
12. Ibid., 4, 52, 576.
13. The Memorial is set forth as an appendix to the dissenting opinion of Justice Wiley B. Rutledge in *Everson* v. *Board of Education*, 330 U.S. 1 at 63 (1947).
14. Edward F. Humphrey, *Nationalism and Religion in America, 1774-1789* (Boston: Chipman Law Publishing Co., 1924), 407.
15. Ibid., 406.
16. Ibid.
17. Irving Brant, *James Madison*, 6 vols. (New York: Bobbs-Merrill Co., 1941-61), 3:271.
18. Stokes and Pfeffer, *Church and State in the United States*, 155-56, fn. 8.
19. Ibid., 565-67.
20. Ibid., 566.
21. Ibid., 567.
22. Pfeffer, *Church, State and Freedom*, 247, fn. 5.
23. *Vidal* v. *Girard's Executors*, 2 How 127 (1843). The anticlericalism, or at least suspicion of clericalism, manifested in this case was quite common in the early days of the Republic; see *McDaniel* v. *Paty*, 435 U.S. 618 (1978), wherein the Court invalidated an early Tennessee statute disqualifying clergymen from serving in the state legislature.
24. Joseph Story, *Commentaries on the Constitution of the United States*, 3 vols. (Boston: Hilliard, Gray and Co., 1833), 3:725.
25. *Church of Holy Trinity* v. *United States*, 143 U.S. 457 (1892); see also *Church of Jesus Christ of Latter-day Saints* v. *United States*, 136 U.S. 1 (1890), wherein the Court said, "The organization of a community for the spread and practice of polygamy is, in a measure, a return to barbarism. It is contrary to the spirit of Christianity and the civilization which Christianity has produced in the Western World" (at 49).
26. *McGowan* v. *Maryland*, 366 U.S. 420 (1961); *Two Guys from Harrison-Allentown* v. *McGinley*, 366 U.S. 582 (1961).
27. *Walz* v. *Tax Commission*, 397 U.S. 664 (1970).
28. *Engel* v. *Vitale*, 370 U.S. 421 (1962).
29. *Board of Education* v. *Allen*, 392 U.S. 236 (1968).
30. *Zorach* v. *Clauson*, 343 U.S. 306 (1952).
31. Ibid., at 313.
32. *United States* v. *Macintosh*, 283 U.S. 605 (1971).
33. Ibid., at 625.
34. Cited in James E. Ernst, *The Political Thought of Roger Williams* (Seattle: Univer-

sity of Washington Press, 1929), 244; John M. Mecklin, *The Story of American Dissent* (New York: Harcourt, Brace and Co., 1934), 89.
35. *Zorach* v. *Clauson*, 343 U.S. at 312-13.
36. *Burstyn* v. *Wilson*, 343 U.S. 495 (1952).
37. *Watson* v. *Jones*, 13 Wall. (80 U.S.) 679 at 728 (1872).
38. Pfeffer, *Church, State and Freedom*, 671, fn. 5.
39. *Burstyn* v. *Wison*, at 505.
40. *Burstyn* v. *Wilson*, 303 N.Y. 242 at 258.
41. *Torcaso* v. *Watkins*, 367 U.S. 488 (1961).
42. *McCollum* v. *Board of Education*, 333 U.S. 203 (1948).
43. Ibid., at 210-11.
44. *Zorach* v. *Clauson*, at 313.
45. *Torcaso* v. *Watkins*, at 495.
46. Ibid.
47. *Engel* v. *Vitale*, 10 N.Y. 2d 174 aff'g 11 A.D. 2d 340 aff'g 18 Misc. 2d 659.
48. *Engel* v. *Vitale*, 370 U.S., at 425.
49. *Abington Township School District* v. *Schempp*, 374 U.S. 203 (1963).
50. *Engel* v. *Vitale*, 370 U.S., at 444.
51. Pfeffer, *Church, State and Freedom*, 466-68, fn. 5.
52. *Engel* v. *Vitale*, 370 U.S., at 440 et seq.
53. *Abington* v. *Schempp*, at 213-14.
54. *Dekalb School District* v. *DeSpain*, 255 F. Supp. 655, 384 F. 2d 836; certiorari denied 390 U.S. 906 (1968).
55. *Epperson* v. *Arkansas*, 393 U.S. 97 (1968).
56. Wendell R. Bird, "Freedom of Religion and Science Instruction in Public Schools." *Yale Law Journal* 87 (January 1978):533, fn. 87.
57. *Epperson* v. *Arkansas*, at 107-9.
58. See above, 223.
59. *Watson* v. *Jones*, at 728.
60. *People ex rel Wallace* v. *Labrenz*, 411 Ill. 618 (1952); certiorari denied 344 U.S. 824 (1952).
61. *Arver* v. *United States*, 245 U.S. 366 (1918); *United States* v. *Macintosh*, 283 U.S. 605 (1931), overruled on other grounds; *Girouard* v. *United States*, 328 U.S. 61 (1946).
62. Stokes and Pfeffer, *Church and State in the United States*, 475, fn. 8.
63. Selective Service Act of 1917.
64. *Everson* v. *Board of Education*, at 1, 15; *McCollum* v. *Board of Education*, at 203, 211.
65. *United States* v. *Seeger*, 380 U.S. 163 (1965).
66. *Sicurella* v. *United States*, 348 U.S. 385 (1955).
67. Ibid., at 391.
68. *United States* v. *Seeger*, at 165-66.
69. Ibid., at 188.
70. No. 79-852.
71. Since the above was written, the Supreme Court reversed the lower court's decision and ruled in favor of the claimant on First Amendment grounds, relying primarily on *Sherbert* v. *Verner*, 374 U.S. 398 (1963); see *Thomas* v. *Indiana Employment Review Board*, 49 L.W. 4341 (1981).
72. *Rostker* v. *Goldberg*, 101 S.Ct. 1 (1980).
73. *Stone* v. *Graham*, 101 S.Ct. 192 (1980).
74. Ibid., at 194.
75. Stokes and Pfeffer, *Church and State in the United States*, 570-71, fn. 8.
76. *Lewis* v. *Allen*, 379 U.S. 923 (1964).
77. Ibid.
78. *O'Hair* v. *Paine*, 312 F. Supp. 434 (D.C. Tex., 1969), aff. 432 F. 2d 66, appeal dismissed 397 U.S. 531, certiorari denied 401 U.S. 955.
79. Ibid.
80. *O'Hair* v. *Andrus*, 613 F. 2d 931 (U.S. App. D.C., 1979).

81. *Bradshaw* v. *Hall*, 101 S.Ct. 1480, 450 U.S. 956 (1981).
82. See, e.g., *Bogen* v. *Doty*, 598 F. 2d 1110 (C.A. Minn., 1979).

PART 2

THE RIGHT OF
VOLUNTARY ASSOCIATION

The Problem of a Constitutional Definition of Religion

MILTON R. KONVITZ

I

The terms "religion" and "religious" appear in the United States Constitution but are not defined. The First Amendment reads simply that "Congress shall make no law respecting an establishment of religion, or prohibiting the free exercise thereof"; and the original Constitution (Art. VI, Cl. 3) contains the provision that "no religious test shall ever be required as a qualification to any office or public trust under the United States." Until fairly recently, it was assumed that the words "religion" and "religious" had rather limited and conventionally acceptable meanings; today, however, the courts have a much more sophisticated approach. They are aware of the much greater complexity that the domain of religious thought and religious life presents than was the case in the nineteenth century.

In the leading case involving the Mormon Church, decided in 1878, the Supreme Court stated: "The word 'religion' is not defined in the Constitution. We must go elsewhere, therefore, to ascertain its meaning, and nowhere more appropriately, we think, than to the history of the times in the midst of which the provision was adopted."[1] The Court, however, proceeded to examine the history not in order to define the word "religion" but to discover what was the religious freedom that was intended to be guaranteed. The Court's opinion contains no definition of religion. Twelve years later, however, in another case involving the Mormon Church, the Court did define the term "religion." The term, it said, "has reference to one's views of his relations to his Creator, and to the obligations they impose of reverence for his being and character, and of obedience to his will."[2] In a case decided two years later, in 1892, the Court went a step further and practically identified religion with Christianity. In that case the Court said that "we are a religious people" and that "this is a Christian nation."[3]

The chief effort to examine the historical record, in order to determine the framers' intent in the framing of the First Amendment, was made in two cases that were decided in the late 1940s: *Everson* v. *Board of Education*[4] and *McCollum* v. *Board of Education*.[5] Neither case, however, attempted a definition of religion. Justice Hugo Black's opinions for the Court in these cases did, however, free the concept of religion from a Christian monopoly. In *Everson*, the Court said that neither a state nor the federal government "can pass laws which aid one religion, aid all religions, or prefer one religion over another. Neither can force nor influence a person to go to or remain away from church against his will or force him to profess a belief or disbelief in any religion." The Court held that a state "cannot exclude individual Catholics, Lutherans, Mohammedans, Baptists, Jews, Methodists, Non-believers, Presbyterians, or the members of any other faith, *because of their faith, or lack of it*, from receiving the benefits of public welfare legislation."[6] Similarly in the *McCollum* case, the Court's opinion made it clear that the religion clauses use the term religion to comprehend all religions, "any or all religious faiths or sects . . . or religious teachings."

The Court in the Mormon Church cases or in the *Everson* and *McCollum* cases had no need to define religion. The Church of Jesus Christ of Latter-Day Saints was unquestionably a religious organization;[7] the only question was whether "those who make polygamy a part of their religion" are excepted from the operation of a statute that made polygamy a criminal offense. In *Everson*, the question was whether New Jersey could reimburse to parents the bus fares for the transportation of their children attending a Roman Catholic parochial school without violating the Establishment Clause. In *McCollum*, the question was whether there was a breach in the wall of separation between church and state when, under a released-time arrangement, religious instruction classes were conducted during regular school time within a public school building by a Protestant minister, a Catholic priest, and a rabbi. The purpose of the released-time program was precisely to afford an opportunity to offer instruction in what was admittedly religion or religious beliefs.

By enumerating a number of religious denominations, and placing "Non-believers" between Methodists and Presbyterians, Justice Black, in his *Everson* opinion, can be understood as intending to say that the words "religion" and "religious" in the Constitution must be taken in their widest reach; that the religion clauses are for the protection of even those who deny religious belief. How "religion" can be defined so as to include nonbelief as well as belief, lack of faith as well as faith, and "Non-believers" no less than Catholics was not explained.

In 1961, the Supreme Court considered the provision of the Maryland Constitution that required a declaration of belief in God as a qualification for public office. The Court unanimously held that this requirement invaded freedom of religion and was a violation of the First Amendment.[8] In his opinion for the Court, Justice Black said: "We repeat and again reaffirm that neither a State nor the Federal Government can constitutionally force a person 'to profess a belief or disbelief in any religion.' Neither can constitutionally pass laws nor impose requirements which aid all religions as against non-believers, and neither can aid those religions based on a belief in the existence of God as against those religions founded on different beliefs." At this point, Justice Black wrote a footnote that reads as follows: "Among religions in this country which do not teach what would generally be considered a belief in the existence of God are Buddhism, Taoism, Ethical Culture, Secular Humanism, and others. . . . "

Again, there was no attempt at a definition but an enumeration of instances that, by the method of induction, may contribute to a definition. One might say that the approach was similar to that which Socrates made famous: a consideration of individual cases in order to obtain a definition that would be a complete and adequate expression of the nature of all the individual instances sharing in the class name.[9] Once again, the term religion is used as a wide net to include the extremes of Catholicism and "Secular Humanism." (It may be assumed that Justice Black advisedly used capital letters for "Non-believers" and "Secular Humanism," to give them the same dignity and the same constitutional status accorded to Catholics and Presbyterians.) This is a far cry from the Supreme Court's definition of religion as a term that "has reference to one's views of his relations to his Creator. . . . " Justice Black cited examples of what the term religion must include, but he failed to state what it is that Catholicism and Secular Humanism, or Methodism and Ethical Culture, have in common so as to make them all equally religions. The one definite result of Justice Black's opinions for the Court in the cases thus far considered was a greatly expanded idea of what religion is when it is considered under the Constitution. That this expansion, wherever the boundaries may be drawn, is in the interests of religious liberty, cannot be doubted; and it may well be that this result or benefit was the uppermost consideration for the Court. This expansion is an accommodation to the greatly increased complexity in the social scene of religion with the countless variety of denominations, sects, cults, churches, chapels, and temples.

II

The congressional and judicial changes, with respect to the position of the conscientious objector to war, offer the best opportunity to see the evolution of a line of thought as to the meaning of religion in a constitutional context. Although there is no constitutional right to be relieved of military duty by reason of religious conviction, Congress may grant the privilege of exemption.[10] In defining conscientious objection, however, Congress must act in a way that would not violate the guarantees of the First Amendment and of the Fifth Amendment.[11]

The first military exemption act, enacted in 1864, exempted members of the historic pacifist churches, such as the Mennonites and the Friends, those who are "prohibited from [bearing arms] by the rules and articles of faith and practice of said religious denominations."[12] In 1917, Congress broadened the scope to include "any well-recognized religious sect or organization . . . whose existing creed or principles forbid its members to participate in war in any form and whose religious convictions are against war."[13] The 1940 Selective Training and Service Act went a step further to include in the exemption anyone "who, by reason of religious training and belief is conscientiously opposed to war in any form."[14]

What did Congress mean by "religious training and belief"? Federal courts of appeal gave various interpretations, some liberal and some restrictive. The interpretation given in *United States* v. *Berman*,[15] in the ninth circuit, apparently played a crucial role. The court in this case said that the purpose of Congress in using the phrase "by reason of religious training and belief" was to distinguish "between a conscientious social belief, or a sincere devotion to a high moralistic philosophy, and one based on an individual's belief in his responsibility to an authority higher and beyond any worldly one." The court quoted from the dissenting opinion of Chief Justice Charles

Evans Hughes in a case decided in 1931,[16] in which it was said that "the essence of religion is belief in a relation to God involving duties superior to those arising from any human relation." The Court in *United States* v. *Berman* (1946) underscored this proposition and said that a claimant to the status of conscientious objector does not satisfy the statutory requirements if his philosophy, morals, and social policy are "without the concept of deity," for what lacks "the concept of deity" "cannot be said to be religion in the sense of that term as it is used in the statute."

Perhaps in an attempt to eliminate the confusion—and perhaps with the intent to both broaden and to restrict the classification of conscientious objection—Congress in 1948 defined "religious training and belief" as "an individual's belief in a relation to a Supreme Being involving duties superior to those arising from any human relation, but does not include essentially political, sociological or philosophical views or a merely personal moral code."[17] Congress obviously took some of the phraseology that was used by Chief Justice Hughes but substituted "Supreme Being" for "God." It can also be said that Congress substituted "Supreme Being" for "the concept of deity" that was used in the *Berman* opinion. Congress obviously also intended to mark off religious belief (as expressed in conscientious objection) from "political, sociological or philosophical views or a merely personal code."

In the consolidated case of *United States* v. *Seeger*,[18] in 1965, the Supreme Court once again tried to clarify the meaning of "religious training and belief," and to interpret the phrase "belief in relation to a Supreme Being" in light of the assumption that Congress intended to conform to the spirit of the religion clauses and the Fifth Amendment.[19] One of the men claiming conscientious objection status, Arno S. Jakobson, said that he believed in "Godness," but that the relation to Godness was not vertical but horizontal; that is, a movement through mankind and the world. A second man, Forest B. Peter, stated that he accepted as his definition of religion "the consciousness of some power manifest in nature which helps man in the ordering of his life in harmony with its demands . . . [it] is the supreme expression of human nature; it is man thinking his highest, feeling his deepest, and living his best."[20] He attributed the source of his conviction to reading and meditation "in our democratic American culture," which derives its values from the "western religious and philosophi-

cal tradition." As to his belief in a Supreme Being, Peter
hedged by saying that he supposed "you could call that a
belief in the Supreme Being or God. These just do not happen
to be the words I use." The Supreme Court held that both
these men were entitled to the statutory exemption. The third
man, Daniel A. Seeger, perhaps "did not clearly demonstrate,"
said the Court, "what his beliefs were with regard to the usual
understanding of the term 'Supreme Being.'" He had been
brought up in a devout Roman Catholic home, but derived
much of his thought from Quaker teachings. The Court held
that Seeger, too, had met the statutory requirements for
exemption from military service.

In his opinion for a unanimous Court, Justice Tom Clark
stated that the question before the Court was "the narrow
one: Does the term 'Supreme Being' as used in [the statute]
mean the orthodox God or the broader concept of a power or
being, or a faith, 'to which all else is subordinate or upon
which all else is ultimately dependent'? *Webster's New International Dictionary.*" Justice Clark added that in considering
this question, "We resolve it solely in relation to the language
of [the statute] and not otherwise." That is, the Court intended only to say what Congress meant; it was not defining
the term "Supreme Being" except in the context of its use in
the statute enacted by Congress. The Court candidly recognized "the elusive nature of the inquiry," for, significantly,
Congress did not "elaborate on the form or nature of this
higher authority which it chose to designate as 'Supreme
Being.'" It was clear to the Court, however, that the intent
of Congress in substituting Supreme Being for God was to
broaden the meaning of "religious training and belief." Now,
then, said Justice Clark, all that is required is a conviction
based on religious training and belief. What, however, does
that mean? Justice Clark answered the question in the following passage which is the central focus of the opinion: "Within
that phrase would come all sincere religious beliefs which are
based upon a power or being, or upon a faith, to which all
else is subordinate or upon which all else is ultimately dependent. The test might be stated in these words: A sincere
and meaningful belief which occupies in the life of its possess-
or a place parallel to that filled by the God of those admittedly
qualifying for the exemption comes within the statutory definition." The Court added that this definition or construction
avoids imputing to Congress an intent to classify different

religious beliefs, exempting some and excluding others, for such an intent might spell a denial of equal treatment.

In giving this broad construction to the meaning of "religious training and belief," the Court said that it was reflecting "the ever-broadening understanding of the modern religious community." For some indications of that understanding, the Court quoted from the writings of Paul Tillich; John A. T. Robinson, Bishop of Woolwich and author of *Honest to God*; David Saville Muzzey, leader in the ethical culture movement; and the Schema of the recent Ecumenical Council—all of them stating, in one way or another, that there has been movement in religious thought, that (in the words of the above-mentioned Schema) "religions in an advanced culture have been able to use more refined concepts and a more developed language in their struggle for an answer to man's religious questions."

In a crucial passage, the Court, in commenting on Seeger's testimony, said that his beliefs "occupy the same place in his life as the belief in a traditional deity holds in the lives of his friends, the Quakers." At this point Justice Clark quoted from Tillich's *The Shaking of the Foundations* as follows: "And if that word [God] has not much meaning for you, translate it, and speak of your life, of the source of your being, of your ultimate concern, *of what you take seriously without any reservation.* Perhaps, in order to do so, you must forget everything traditional that you have learned about God."[21]

By giving this construction to the definition of "religious training and belief," the Court concluded that the statute satisfied the guarantees of the Free Exercise and Establishment Clauses of the First Amendment and the equal protection guarantee contained in the Due Process Clause of the Fifth Amendment. The Court also found nothing constitutionally objectionable in the provision that excluded from the exemption persons whose beliefs are based on essentially political, sociological, or economic considerations. "These judgments have historically been reserved for the Government," said the Court, "and in matters which can be said to fall within these areas the conviction of the individual has never been permitted to override that of the State."

The Court made no significant comment on the exclusion of persons whose beliefs are based on "a merely personal moral code," for none of the applicants involved in the consolidated cases could be said to have failed to meet the religious-beliefs test as formulated by the Court. "Indeed," said Justice Clark, "at the outset each of them claimed in his application that his objection was based on religious belief. We have construed the statutory definition broadly and it follows that any exception to it must be interpreted narrowly. The use by Congress of the words 'merely personal' seems to us to restrict the exception to a moral code which is not only personal but which is the sole basis for the registrant's belief and is in no way related to a Supreme Being."

It is important to note, in the context of this discussion, that the Court in *Seeger* did not address the question of the definition of "religion" or "religious" as the terms are used in the Constitution. The Court purported only to elucidate the meaning of the statutory phrase "religious training and belief." In performing this task, however, the Court interpreted this phrase in a way that would vindicate the constitutionality of the congressional enactment. Indirectly, therefore, and by implication, the Court, at least partially, defined the constitutional term "religion." It in effect said: "If Congress wishes to grant exemption to persons who are conscientious objectors because of their religious beliefs, then *this* is what Congress must mean by religion or religious belief."

In order to avoid condemnation of the statute as a violation of the Free Exercise or the Establishment Clause, or as a denial of equality under the Fifth Amendment, the Court gave the statute the broadest possible meaning. The test, said the Court, is "a sincere and meaningful belief which occupies in the life of its possessor a place parallel to that filled by the God of those admittedly qualifying for the exemption." This may be thought of as the *parallel test*. If one takes a Mennonite or a Quaker as the model, then if the applicant claims that his "religious belief" plays the same role in his life that the "religious belief" plays in the life of the Quaker, then he is equally entitled to the exemption.

This, of course, is no definition of religion. It is, indeed, an attempt to avoid making a definition so as to steer clear of a collision with the religion clauses of the Constitution.

The Supreme Court, however, did not stop with *Seeger*. In 1970, in *Welsh* v. *United States*,[22] the Court diluted further the meaning of "religious training and belief." In his opinion for the Court, Justice Black gave an interpretation of the opinion in *Seeger* that substantially attenuated the meaning of the term "religion." Justice Black noted that although both Seeger and

Elliott A. Welsh had been brought up in religious homes and had attended church in their childhood, in neither case was the church one that belonged to a pacifist denomination. Neither of the men continued into manhood any religious ties. When Seeger filled out his Selective Service forms, he struck out "religious training" and left in only "religious belief" but placed quotation marks around the word "religious"; Welsh left in only the word "belief" and struck out "religious training and."

In *Seeger*, Justice Black said, the Court stated that the phrase "religious training and belief" embraced "*all* religions." That, however, said Justice Black, still left the "more serious problem of determining which beliefs were 'religious' within the meaning of the statute." The Court in *Seeger*, said Justice Black, held that the task was to decide whether the beliefs professed by a registrant are, "*in his own scheme of things*, religious," This meant, said Justice Black, "whether these beliefs play the role of a religion and function as a religion in the registrant's life." These beliefs need not be confined, said Justice Black, "to traditional or parochial concepts of religion." What is required, under *Seeger*, is that the registrant's opposition to war "stem from the registrant's moral, ethical, or religious beliefs about what is right and wrong and that these beliefs be held with the strength of traditional religious convictions." A crucial passage in the Court's opinion in *Welsh*, interpreting *Seeger*, reads as follows:

If an individual deeply and sincerely holds beliefs which are purely ethical or moral in source and content but which nevertheless impose upon him a duty of conscience to refrain from participating in any war at any time, those beliefs certainly occupy in the life of that individual "a place parallel to that filled by . . . God" in traditionally religious persons. Because his beliefs function as a religion in his life, such an individual is as much entitled to a "religious" conscientious objector exemption under Sec. 6(j) as is someone who derives his conscientious opposition to war from traditional religious convictions.

As has been seen, Welsh denied that his views were "religious." Does that take him out of the embrace of the statute? Not at all, said Justice Black. A registrant's own interpretation of his beliefs is not at all conclusive if he states that his beliefs are nonreligious, for very few registrants "are fully aware of the broad scope of the word 'religious' as used in Sec. 6(j), and accordingly a registrant's statement that his beliefs are nonreligious is a highly unreliable guide. . . ."

In considering the statutory exclusion of persons with "essen-

tially political, sociological, or philosophical views or a merely
personal code," Justice Black said that these words should be
read so as to exclude only two classes of persons; namely,
those whose beliefs are not deeply held, and those whose
objection to war rests solely upon considerations of policy or
expediency. Furthermore, once the Selective Service System
has determined, under the tests enunciated in *Seeger* and
Welsh, that the registrant is a "religious" conscientious objector, "it follows that his views cannot be essentially political,
sociological or philosophical.' Nor can they be a 'merely personal moral code.' " Justice Black concluded that the statute
"exempts from military service all those whose consciences,
spurred by deeply held moral, ethical, or religious beliefs,
would give them no rest or peace if they allowed themselves to
become a part of an instrument of war."

The *Welsh* opinion, interpreting *Seeger*'s interpretation of
the statute interpreted against constitutional limitations—super-
commentary upon super-commentary—resulted in a functional
test of "religious training and belief": whatever is perceived as
performing the function of a religion in the life of a person is
that person's religion. This, of course, is no definition. It
assumes that there is something like a Platonic idea of religion, or that there are orders of beliefs, like Roman Catholicism or Presbyterianism or Quakerism, against which a person's beliefs can be tested, but tested not for content of beliefs,
not for substance, but for the role the beliefs play in the person's life. These beliefs need not to be rooted in any traditional religion. They need be only "moral, ethical, or religious beliefs," and they must be held deeply and sincerely.

In *Seeger*, the Court said that the task of local draft boards
and of the courts is "to decide whether the beliefs professed
by a registrant are sincerely held. . . . " In *Welsh*, the Court
said that the statute excludes from exemptions "those whose
beliefs are not deeply held," and protects those whose consciences are "spurred by deeply held moral, ethical, or religious beliefs."

The Court in these cases apparently was persuaded by Chief
Justice Harlan F. Stone's opinion[23] that the sincerity of one's
religious beliefs is a question of fact that may be passed upon
by a court or jury without violating the person's religious liberty. "The state of one's mind is a fact," said Chief Justice
Stone, "as capable of fraudulent misrepresentation as is one's
physical condition or the state of his bodily health." The

question of sincerity of religious beliefs, however, which Chief Justice Stone and other members of the Court debated in the *Ballard* case, decided in 1944, cannot be gone into here where the concentration is on the question of definition of religion, though the question of sincerity cannot be altogether avoided.

It should be noted that the *Seeger* case was decided in 1965. In 1967, Congress amended the legislation to eliminate the reference to a Supreme Being. The passage in the 1948 act that defined "religious training and belief" as "an individual's belief in a relation to a Supreme Being involving duties superior to those arising from any human relation" was entirely omitted. The new phraseology, in the 1967 act, provided that no person shall be subject to combatant service if he, "by reason of religious training and belief, is conscientiously opposed to participating in war in any form. As used in this subsection, the term 'religious training and belief' does not include essentially political, sociological, or philosophical views, or a merely personal moral code."[24]

III

Justice John M. Harlan's concurring opinion in *Welsh* deserves consideration, for although in this opinion he spoke only for himself, his intellectual and professional stature during the sixteen years of his service on the Court (1955-1971) enjoyed general recognition.

Justice Harlan stated that he had joined the Court's opinion in *Seeger* only with the gravest misgivings as to whether that opinion was a legitimate exercise in statutory construction. The decision in *Welsh* convinced him that he had made a mistake. The statute expressed the intention of Congress to limit draft exemption to those opposed to war because of theistic beliefs. This construction of the statute would lead to the conclusion that it violated the religion clauses of the First Amendment. Justice Harlan agreed with the test as rewritten by the Court, however, not as a matter of statutory construction, but as a way of salvaging the longstanding congressional policy of exempting conscientious objectors.

In considering the statutory language, Justice Harlan consulted the *New International Dictionary, Unabridged* (2d ed., 1934) and said that of the five pertinent definitions four include the notion of either a Supreme Being or an organized group pursuing a common purpose together. In the statute, Congress restricted the meaning to its conventional sense. In the act, Congress included not only a reference to a Supreme Being but also contrasted religious beliefs with beliefs that are "essentially political, sociological, or philosophical" and with a "personal moral code." "This exception," said Justice Harlan, "certainly is, at the very least, the statutory boundary, the 'asymptote,' of the word 'religion.' " Congress did not intend to have the word "religion" embrace "individual principles acquired on an individualized basis but was adopting, at least, those meanings that associate religion with formal, organized worship or shared beliefs by a recognizable and cohesive group."

This construction of the statute, however, Justice Harlan declared, would compel him to conclude that the statute was unconstitutional. Congress need not exempt anyone for conscientious objection, but if it chooses to grant exemption it cannot draw the line between theistic and nontheistic religious beliefs, on the one hand, and secular beliefs, on the other hand. Any such distinction would violate the Establishment Clause. The statute excludes from its scope adherents of nontheistic religions (such as those mentioned by Justice Black in *Torcaso*), and individuals who are guided by "an inner ethical voice that bespeaks secular and not 'religious' reflection." To withstand attack under the Establishment Clause, the exemption must include "those whose beliefs emanate from a purely moral, ethical, or philosophical source. The common denominator must be the intensity of moral conviction with which a belief is held."

Justice Harlan found that the policy of exempting religious conscientious objectors was one of longstanding tradition in the United States. The tradition, dating back to colonial times, has been phrased in religious terms because ethics and morals have traditionally been matters taught by organized religion, and because for most persons spiritual and ethical teachings were derived from religion. It also reflected the assumption that beliefs emanating from a religious source are probably held with great intensity. Because the policy has roots so deeply embedded in history, the Court correctly hazarded the "patchwork of judicial making that cures the defects of underinclusion in Sec. 6(j)." The Court was, therefore, right in not throwing out as unconstitutional the statute but instead choosing to build upon it.

The importance of Justice Harlan's concurring opinion lies in his underscoring the accomplishment of *Torcaso;* namely, that the term "religion" in the First Amendment must be read so as to include nontheistic as well as theistic religions, and even secular beliefs such as Ethical Culture and Secular Humanism. A constitutional term like "speech" or "religion," said Justice Harlan, is to be construed "in light of evolving needs and circumstances."

Justice Harlan was probably right in his position that the Court in *Seeger* and *Welsh* had not construed but had rewritten the act of Congress in order to save its constitutionality. His opinion, however, underscores the tenuous, amorphous character of the term "religion" as it appears in the First Amendment; for no definition, apparently, can withstand the charge that it is in conflict with the Establishment Clause. If to define is to exclude, then definition means an *establishment* of religion as defined.

Two years after Justice Harlan had written his concurring opinion in *Welsh*, Chief Justice Warren E. Burger, in his opinion for the Court in the Amish school case—*Wisconsin v. Yoder*,[25] rejected the proposition that to meet the demands of the First Amendment the exemption must include those "whose beliefs emanate from a purely moral, ethical, or philosophical source"; that is, that "religious belief" must be understood broadly enough to encompass beliefs grounded on sources that are "purely moral, ethical, or philosophical."

The Wisconsin compulsory school attendance law required parents to send their children to a public or private school until they reach the age of sixteen. The Old Order Amish religion forbade attendance at school beyond the eighth grade. The Court unanimously held that, *as applied to the Old Order Amish parents*, the law violated the Free Exercise Clause of the First Amendment. Chief Justice Burger wrote:

A way of life, however virtuous and admirable, may not be interposed as a barrier to reasonable state regulation of education if it is based on purely secular considerations; to have the protection of the Religion Clauses, the claims must be rooted in religious belief. Although a determination of what is a "religious" belief or practice entitled to constitutional protection may present a most delicate question, the very concept of ordered liberty precludes allowing every person to make his own standards on matters of conduct in which society as a whole has important interests. Thus, if the Amish asserted their claims because of their subjective evaluation and rejection of the contemporary secular values accepted by the majority, much as Thoreau rejected the social values of his time and isolated himself at Walden Pond, their claims would not rest on a religious basis. Thoreau's choice was philosophical and personal rather than religious, and such belief does not rise to the demands of the Religion Clauses.

The only dissenter in the case was Justice William O. Douglas, and it was precisely this point that he chose to emphasize by dissenting from it. The Court, he said, "retreats when in reference to Henry Thoreau it says his 'choice was philosophical and personal rather than religious, and such belief does not rise to the demands of the Religion Clauses.' That is contrary to what we held in *United States* v. *Seeger*." He went on to say that he adhered to the *Seeger* and *Welsh* decisions or definition of "religion," and saw "no alternative to them now that we have become a Nation of many religions and sects, representing all of the diversities of the human race."

Quite obviously, the matter of a constitutional definition of religion remains largely unresolved. It still continues to "present a most delicate question."

IV

In trying to explain what a philosophy of law includes, Benjamin N. Cardozo, in his Yale lectures on *Growth of the Law*, stated that he wished to circumvent the difficulties of definition that philosophy of law shares with philosophy in general. He quoted William Windelband's statement that the moment you attempt to define the subject matter of philosophy, "You find the philosophers themselves failing you. There is no such thing as a generally received definition of philosophy, and it would be useless to reproduce the innumerable attempts that have been made to provide one." Then Cardozo added significantly: "Description may serve where definition would be hazardous."[26]

Generally, the Supreme Court has followed this advice. To cite only a single example, as a typical instance of this policy to avoid definition of important constitutional terms, a brief look at the *Penn Central Transportation* case,[27] decided by the Court in 1978, will be helpful. The Fifth Amendment provides simply that "private property" shall not be "taken for public use, without just compensation." What is a "taking" against which the Constitution offers some protection? Countless cases have dealt with this question.[28] In the 1978 case cited above, however, Justice William J. Brennan said, in the opinion for the Court: "The question of what constitutes a 'taking' for purposes of the Fifth Amendment has proved to be a problem of considerable difficulty . . . this Court, quite simply, has been unable to develop any 'set formula' for determining when 'justice and fairness' require that economic injuries caused by public action be compensated by the government, . . . Indeed, we have frequently observed that whether a particular restriction will be rendered invalid by the government's failure to pay for any losses proximately caused by it depends largely 'upon the particular circumstances [in that] case.' " In such cases, Justice Brennan observed, the Court engages in what he called "ad hoc, factual inquiries," but the Court has, he added, identified several factors that it considers particularly significant. Thus, while the cases cannot all be rationalized under a single, comprehensive principle, some guidelines have in fact evolved.

The constitutional sense of "taking" is a relatively simple matter when compared with the word "religion," the sense or essence of which has eluded not only judges and legal scholars but philosophers and students of religion as well. Even someone whose mind and heart were wholly immersed in religious inquiry, Søren Kierkegaard, insisted on religion as something "subjective and passionate, and therefore recalcitrant to all definition. . . ."[29] In interpreting crucial constitutional terms, the Supreme Court has, on the whole, taken seriously the counsel implied in the observation of Justice Oliver Wendell Holmes that "a word is not a crystal, transparent and unchanged; it is the skin of a living thought and may vary greatly in color and content according to the circumstances and the time in which it is used."[30] All this was implied in Justice Harlan's statement, in his concurring opinion in *Welsh*, that when the Court needs to consider a phrase in the Constitution like "religion" or "speech," the Court needs to construe it "in light of evolving needs and circumstances."[31]

The inability to define such terms as "religion," "speech," or "taking" and such phrases as "due process of law," "equal protection of the laws," or "privileges or immunities of citizens" has not meant, and does not mean, that these and similar words and phrases are without meaning or significance. Who can give a definition of "justice" or "beauty" or "goodness" that would be universally accepted, yet who can avoid using these words? Despite all the difficulty encountered in trying to define the meaning of the religion clauses, one must think of how different would be the face of the United States if those clauses had not been written into the Constitution.

When the First Amendment was adopted by Congress in 1789 and was ratified by the states in 1791, the word "religion" may have had a relatively definite meaning, just as the phrase "to regulate commerce with foreign nations, and among the several States, and with Indian tribes," in Article I of the Constitution, may have had a meaning that could have been simply stated. The justices of the Supreme Court, however, do not sit as a body of lexicographers nor as an academy of historians. They sit as justices charged with the duty to perform a judicial function. They are, perforce, ever mindful of the saying of Chief Justice John Marshall, in a case decided in 1819, only thirty years after the adoption of the Constitution: "We must never forget," he wrote for the Court, "that it is a *constitution* that we are expounding." He went on to explain that the Constitution was "intended to endure for ages to come, and consequently, to be adapted to the various *crises* of human affairs."[32]

The important constitutional aspect of the word "religion" is in its denotative use, its employment in extension. Justice Black in *Torcaso* found it fairly easy to name certain religions, to point to them as examples of what the word "religion" in the First Amendment means. There is nothing logically wrong with this way of thinking, in which all men engage daily and hourly.

The *Seeger* interpretation of the phrase "belief in relation to a Supreme Being" as encompassing any sincere belief occupying "a place in the life of its possessor parallel to that filled by the orthodox belief in God of one who clearly qualifies for the exemption" is not essentially different from the way scientists sometimes proceed in the way they "define" a term. For example, a recent book on animal thought has been summarized by a critic as follows:[33]

The first problem to be confronted by anyone interested in the mental life of animals is a definitional one. Just what is meant by such terms as "thought," "perception," "awareness," and the like? Without some account of how these terms are to be used, we do not know what is being asked when we ponder whether animals can think or perceive. [Stephen] Walker's approach to this problem is, I think, exactly right. He makes no attempt to give abstract or theoretical definitions. Rather, he stipulates that questions about the mental lives of animals are to be understood as asking how similar their mental lives are to our own. "Questions about thought in animals" are to be rephrased "in the form 'To what extent are animals like us?' . . . We can thus ask a number of separate questions, such as: 'Do animals have visual systems which work like ours?' 'Do animals have mental imagery like ours?' 'Do animals have hopes and fears like ours?' " In effect, Walker is proposing that we anchor our questions about the mental life of animals by analogy to our own case. Fido has thoughts or images or fears if he undergoes something like we do when we describe ourselves as having thoughts or images or fears.

Now, this is very much like the standard formulated in *Seeger* and *Welsh:* Does this person, who claims to be an adherent of the Ethical Culture movement, have an order of beliefs that plays the role in his life that the Methodist's order of beliefs plays in his? This approach makes use of the vagueness of the term "religion" positively as a value to be cherished. The vagueness of the terms in the First Amendment is part of their virtue. The imprecision gives the constitutional words the promise of a future. Their meaning and reach are not confined to what the words meant in the past. The terms are inherently elastic precisely because they need a future and not only a history. They bring with them a tradition but their main value is in the future that they make possible. Perhaps it is good fortune that an exact statement of the nature of religion cannot be made. From the standpoint of constitutional development, it is not desirable—as it is not possible—that there always be a precise definition. The imprecision may not satisfy some logicians, but it is much more serviceable in law than would be terms that lend themselves to precise definition. The meaning of a constitutional term like "religion" must be a product of past usage and history and of its present content and reach. It may contain even elements of prophecy as to its future embodiment. Its nuances and suggestiveness are subject to constant change and enlargement. Judges cannot be indifferent to the changes. This is why the Supreme Court is involved in constant elucidation of the meaning of words and principles and is ever ready to develop them further.

Over fifty years ago, in his dissenting opinion in the *Coronado* case,[34] Justice Louis D. Brandeis distinguished cases that involved applying the Constitution from cases that involved interpreting the Constitution. In cases that come up under the Due Process Clause or the Equal Protection Clause, when the question is whether a statute is unreasonable or whether there is any reasonable basis for a statutory classification, the issues resemble fundamentally that of reasonable care in negligence cases, the determination of which is ordinarily left to the jury. In all such cases, said Justice Brandeis, "the decision, in the first instance, is dependent upon the determination of what in legal parlance is called a fact, as distinguished from the declaration of a rule of law. When the underlying fact has been found, the legal result follows inevitably. The circumstances that the decision of that fact is made by a court, instead of by a jury, should not be allowed to obscure its real character."

Applying this reasoning to the question of what is religion in constitutional contemplation, one can see that the question may be differently answered at different times, for the question involves a determination of fact, which does not have the dignity of a rule of law or a constitutional doctrine. Adapting further the opinion of Justice Brandeis, one should note that the judgment of the Court in an earlier case may have been influenced by prevailing views as to religion or policy that have since been abandoned. "In cases involving constitutional issues of the character discussed," said Justice Brandeis, "this Court must, in order to reach sound conclusions, feel free to bring its opinions into agreement with experience and with facts newly ascertained, so that its judicial authority may, as Mr. Chief Justice [Roger B.] Taney said, 'depend altogether on the force of the reasoning by which it is supported.' "

NOTES

1. *Reynolds* v. *United States*, 98 U.S. 145 (1878; re-decided, 1879).
2. *Davis* v. *Beason*, 133 U.S. 333 (1890).
3. *Church of Holy Trinity* v. *United States*, 143 U.S. 457 (1892). Cf. *United States* v. *Macintosh*, 283 U.S. 605 (1931), in which Justice George Sutherland said for the Court: "We are a Christian people."
4. *Everson* v. *Board of Education*, 330 U.S. 1 (1947).
5. *McCollum* v. *Board of Education*, 333 U.S. 203 (1948).
6. Italics in original.
7. See case cited in note 3.
8. *Torcaso* v. *Watkins*, 367 U.S. 468 (1961).
9. James E. Creighton, *An Introductory Logic*, 5th ed. (New York: Macmillan, 1932), 83.
10. Milton R. Konvitz, *Expanding Liberties* (New York: Viking Press, 1966), 11. See *United States* v. *Macintosh*, at 605.
11. See Robert L. Rabin, "When Is a Religious Belief Religious? *United States* v. *Seeger* and the Scope of Free Exercise," *Cornell Law Quarterly Review* 51(1966):231, 240.
12. Act of 2 February 1864, ch. 13, sec. 17, 40 Stat. 9.
13. Act of 18 May 1917, ch. 15, 40 Stat. 76.
14. 54 Stat. 885, sec. 5(g).
15. *United States* v. *Berman*, 156 F. 2d 377, cert. den. 329 U.S. 795 (1946).
16. *United States* v. *Macintosh*, at 605. The case involved a petition for naturalization, in which the applicant stated that he would bear arms only if he felt "morally justified" to do so. The Court held that this was insufficient to satisfy the statutory requirements. It also held that exemption of conscientious objectors was not a matter of constitutional right but rather of legislative grace.
17. Selective Service Act of 1948, 62 Stat. 604, sec. 6(j).
18. *United States* v. *Seeger*, 380 U.S. 163 (1965).
19. The Due Process Clause of the Fifth Amendment has the force of an Equal Protection Clause in cases involving action by the federal government. *Bolling* v. *Sharpe*, 347 U.S. 497 (1954).

20.   Forest B. Peter quoted this definition of religion by John Haynes Holmes, Unitarian minister of the Community Church, New York City.
21.   Italics supplied by the Court, quoted from Paul Tillich, *The Shaking of the Foundations* (New York: Charles Scribner and Sons, 1948).
22.   *Welsh* v. *United States.* 398 U.S. 333 (1970). The decision was five to three; Justice Harry Blackmun did not participate. The Court's opinion was by Justice Hugo Black, in which Justices William O. Douglas, William J. Brennan, and Thurgood Marshall joined. Justice John M. Harlan wrote a concurring opinion. Justice Byran R. White wrote a dissenting opinion, in which Chief Justice Warren E. Burger and Justice Potter Stewart joined.
23.   *United States* v. *Ballard,* 322 U.S. 78 (1944). Justice Douglas wrote the opinion for the Court. Chief Justice Harlan F. Stone wrote a dissenting opinion in which he was joined by Justices Owen J. Roberts and Felix Frankfurter. Justice Robert H. Jackson wrote a separate dissenting opinion, in which he said that it was impossible to try the question of religious sincerity severed from the question of the truth of religious beliefs.
24.   50 U.S.C. sec. 456(j) (Supp. 1973), 81 Stat. 104. The *Welsh* case was decided on the basis of the statute prior to its amendment.
25.   *Wisconsin* v. *Yoder,* 406 U.S. 205 (1972). Justice Stewart wrote a concurring opinion, joined by Justice Brennan. Justice White wrote a concurring opinion, joined by Justices Brennan and Stewart. Justice Douglas dissented in part. Justices Powell and Rehnquist did not participate.
26.   Benjamin N. Cardozo, *The Growth of the Law* (New Haven: Yale University Press, 1924), 24.
27.   *Penn Central Transportation Co.* v. *New York City,* 438 U.S. 104 (1978), rehearing den. 58 L. Ed. 2d 198 (1978).
28.   Annot., "Just Compensation: Taking Property," 57 L. Ed. 2d 1254 (1978).
29.   Miguel de Unamuno, *The Tragic Sense of Life* (Princeton, N.J.: Princeton University Press, 1972); notes by editor, 379.
30.   *Towne* v. *Eisner,* 245 U.S. 418 (1918).
31.   *Welsh* v. *United States,* at 333.
32.   *McCulloch* v. *Maryland,* 4 Wheaton 316 (1819).
33.   Stephen Stich, review of Stephen Walker, *Animal Thought, Times Literary Supp.,* 29 April 1983, 424.
34.   *Burnet* v. *Coronado Gas & Oil Co.,* 285 U.S. 393 (1932).

Corporate Free Exercise:
The Constitutional Rights of
Religious Associations

SHARON L. WORTHING

Although the scope of the application of the First Amendment religion clauses to religious activities has been analyzed in many cases dating from the 1940s, it is clear that religious activities depend on the protections provided by the Bill of Rights as a whole, not just on the First Amendment religion clauses. Although a primary focus of constitutional analysis of religious activities has been the rights of the individual believer, the religious institution may be in some cases the more important vehicle for the expression of constitutional rights. Recent governmental attempts to regulate church institutions have resulted in an increasing awareness of the need to establish a clear standard of constitutional rights for religious institutions as well as for the individual believer. Such a standard would need to encompass not only the protections and limitations on government established by the First Amendment religion clauses, but also the rights in the rest of the Bill of Rights.

A number of models have been used in determining the proper constitutional standard applicable to the church institution. In the instance of the receivership imposed on the Worldwide Church of God by the California attorney general in 1979, the state argued that because the church was a charitable organization, it was subject to the law of charitable trusts, and that the attorney general, as representative of its charitable beneficiaries, had total power over the organization. Such an extreme view may seem to derive from charitable trust principles but has no real precedent in actual case law relating to churches as charitable trusts. The case was eventually dropped by the attorney general without any authoritative pronouncement by a court on the validity of his charitable trust theory.

Another model that may be used to determine the proper scope of constitutional rights for church institutions is the business corporation. Many church institutions are incorporated under state law. In some states, the laws governing the corporate structure and activities of incorporated church institutions are similar in many ways to those governing business corporations. Although there should be distinctions between the constitutional rights possessed by those engaged in commercial activity and those engaged in constitutionally protected expression, the law relating to the constitutional rights of business corporations nevertheless provides helpful examples with respect to church institutions.

A third model to be studied in the analysis of the proper scope of a church institution's constitutional rights is the constitutional rights afforded to private individuals. These rights have been extensively analyzed by the courts. Although a church institution is different from a private individual in important ways, it is also true that a private individual may not be able to exercise his or her religion apart from a church institution. Consequently, to some extent the church institution embodies the constitutional rights of the individual and should be accorded similar constitutional protections.

After these models have been examined, one may determine what are the appropriate boundaries for the constitutional rights of church institutions. When these boundaries have been established, they can provide a framework for judicial decisions. This framework would take into account the unique nature of church institutions as a vehicle for the exercise of constitutional rights, and it would relate in reasonable ways to the standards of constitutional rights that have been established for other types of associations or persons in this society.

Principles Deriving from Charitable Trust Law

The law relating to charitable trusts in this country has its origins in the law of England, first codified in the Statute of Charitable Uses of Elizabeth I. This statute listed various uses—or purposes—deemed to be charitable, and provided for the oversight and enforcement of bequests for charitable purposes through the Court of Chancery. Where a charity had its own governors under a charter, the Court of Chancery would not exercise control over the charity unless evidence showed that the governors had abused their trust.[1]

In describing what purposes had been considered charitable and what had not under this English statute, the United

States Supreme Court wrote:

It is clear, that no superstitious uses are within its purview, such as gifts of money for the finding or maintenance of a stipendiary priest, or for the maintenance of an anniversary or obiit, or of any light or lamp in any church or chapel, or for prayers for the dead, or to such purposes as the superior of a convent or her successor may judge expedient. But there are certain uses, which, though not within the letter, are yet deemed charitable within the equity of the statute; such as money given to maintain a preaching minister; to maintain a schoolmaster in a parish; for the setting up a hospital for the relief of poor people; for the building of a sessions house for a city or county; the making a new or repairing an old pulpit in a church, or the buying of a pulpit cushion or pulpit cloth; or the setting up of new bells, where none are, or amending of them, where they are out of order.[2]

In some cases, the testator would indicate a charitable intention, but the actual bequest would be contrary to law. The Court of Chancery would then order the property applied to a charitable purpose permitted by law: "Thus a sum of money bequeathed to found a Jews' synagogue, has been taken by the Court, and judicially transferred to the benefit of a foundling hospital!! And a bequest for the education of poor children in the Roman Catholic faith has been decreed in Chancery to be disposed of by the King at his pleasure, under his sign manual."[3] As the law of charitable trusts has been carried over into the United States, the supervisory powers formerly exercised by the Court of Chancery are now generally vested in the state attorneys general. These attorneys general represent the charitable beneficiaries, who are the public at large.

At the time a receivership was imposed upon the Worldwide Church of God on the application of the California attorney general's office, representatives of the attorney general stated that because of his charitable enforcement powers, there were "no private interests," that records the state sought from the Church and related organizations were "public records" and that the assets of the organizations were "public assets."[4] Because of this "public" character of the Church and related organizations, the attorney general took the position that he, as representative of the public, did not need to follow procedural due process that would apply to businesses or other private interests. In effect, he took the position that the state owned the Worldwide Church of God and was entitled to run it if it felt that was necessary. In fact, a court-appointed receiver did run the Church on behalf of the state for some two-and-a-half months.[5]

To have a state running a church is at least novel in the American system, not to mention unconstitutional. The Su-

preme Court has stated that "neither a state nor the Federal
Government can set up a church. . . . Neither a state nor the
Federal Government can, openly or secretly, participate in the
affairs of any religious organizations or groups. . . . "[6] Nevertheless, this was the outcome of the California attorney general's charitable trust theory. As mentioned earlier, there is no
authoritative judicial validation of such a theory as applied to
churches.

In discussing what charitable trust status can mean for
churches, Charles Whelan observed that when confronted
with internal church disputes over property or doctrine, the
Supreme Court has generally tried to intervene as little as possible.[7] Thus, in *Watson* v. *Jones*[8] and *Presbyterian Church in the
United States* v. *Mary Elizabeth Blue Hull Memorial Presbyterian
Church*,[9] the Supreme Court held that civil courts could not
examine church doctrine to determine who was the proper
holder of disputed church property. In *Jones* v. *Wolf*,[10] the
Supreme Court held that only if relevant church documents
(such as deeds, constitutions, and charters) and state statutes
did not clearly show that the property of a local church was
held in trust for the parent church could a court award the
property to a local congregation that has seceded from the
parent church. The Court said such a determination was
reached through the application of "neutral principles." In
Serbian Orthodox Diocese v. *Milivojevich*,[11] the Supreme Court
reversed a decision of the Supreme Court of Illinois that invalidated a decision of the highest authority of the Serbian Eastern Orthodox Church to defrock a bishop and reorganize
church structure in the United States. The Supreme Court
held that the First Amendment, as applied to the states
through the Fourteenth Amendment, forbade such a judicial
intrusion. Far from considering churches to be "owned" by
the state and governable at its will, the Court has erected barriers around the degree to which governmental authorities
may affect church decisions.

PRINCIPLES DERIVING FROM CORPORATE LAW

Many churches in this country are organized as corporations.[12] New York has a Religious Corporations Law that sets
forth procedures for the incorporation of different kinds of
church bodies: Roman Catholic, Episcopalian, Methodist, Presbyterian, Greek Orthodox, and many others. Some religious
organizations, such as certain religious orders, are incorpo-

rated under the New York Not-for-Profit Corporation Law. One could then ask to what extent the fact that a church is a corporation makes it subject to the will of the state in which it is incorporated. If the state, through granting the privilege of incorporation, has in effect "created" the church, the argument could be made that the church is dependent upon and subject to the state's will. State attorneys general exercise supervisory authority over charitable corportions as they do over charitable trusts.

In the classic Supreme Court case of *Trustees of Dartmouth College* v. *Woodward*,[13] the Court was confronted with the extent to which Dartmouth College, a "religious and literary institution," was subservient to the will of the State of New Hampshire. The college had been chartered in 1769 by the English Crown, and the charter created a board of trustees empowered to select a president and replace its own members. In 1816, the New Hampshire legislature passed a law changing the name of the institution to Dartmouth University; increasing the trustees from twelve to twenty-one, all to be appointed by the governor and council; creating a body of twenty-five overseers, twenty-one of whom would be appointed by the governor and council, and who would have power to veto acts of the trustees; requiring the president to report annually to the governor; and empowering the governor and council to inspect the college every five years and report on it to the legislature. When the law was passed, the trustees in office brought a suit that challenged the statute on constitutional grounds.

In analyzing the nature of the chartered institution, Chief Justice John Marshall framed the issue as follows:

If the act of incorporation be a grant of political power, if it create a civil institution to be employed in the administration of the government, or if the funds of the college be public property, or if the State of New-Hampshire, as a government, be alone interested in its transactions, the subject is one in which the legislature of the State may act according to its own judgment, unrestrained by any limitation of its power imposed by the constitution of the United States.

But if this be a private eleemosynary institution, endowed with a capacity to take property for objects unconnected with government, whose funds are bestowed by individuals on the faith of the charter; if the donors have stipulated for the future disposition and management of those funds in the manner prescribed by themselves; there may be more difficulty in the case, although neither the persons who have made these stipulations, nor those for whose benefit they were made, should be parties to the cause.[14]

The Court found that although the omnipotent British parlia-

ment could have changed the college's charter in the manner
in which the State of New Hampshire had changed it, the
state was barred from doing so by the constitutional provision
forbidding any state from passing a law impairing the obligation of contracts. Chief Justice Marshall stated, "The will of
the State is substituted for the will of the donors, in every
essential operation of the college. This is not an immaterial
change."[15] In writing about the effect of this decision, Justice
Joseph Story said, "An impregnable barrier is thus thrown
around all rights and franchises derived from the states, and
solidity and inviolability are given to the literary, charitable,
religious, and commercial institutions of the country."[16] The
case is significant because it recognizes that even though the
governmentally chartered college was charitable and the
donors retained no private interest in its property, it did not
thereby become a creature of the state. "It is no more a State
instrument, than a natural person exercising the same powers
would be," Chief Justice Marshall wrote.[17]

The courts have also examined whether a business corporation may be prevented from asserting constitutional rights
against the state by the fact that the corporation owes its corporate existence to the state or has been granted privileges by
the state. In evaluating the rights of the Morton Salt Company and other salt producers under the Fourth and Fifth
Amendments, the Supreme Court stated in 1950: "The Federal Government allows them [corporations] the privilege of
engaging in interstate commerce. Favors from government
often carry with them an enhanced measure of regulation."[18]
The Court held that the reports the government was requiring
of the corporations did not exceed constitutional bounds, and
stated that corporations did not possess a right to privacy
commensurate with that of individuals.

In 1978, the Supreme Court examined whether the State of
Massachusetts could constitutionally enforce against national
banking associations and business corporations a criminal statute prohibiting such corporations from making contributions
or expenditures to influence voters on a question not mate-
rially affecting the corporations' business. The appellant associations and corporations claimed that this statute abridged
their freedom of speech in violation of the First and Fourteenth Amendments. The Court discussed the impact that the
appellants' status as other than natural persons had on their
claims to constitutional rights: "The Massachusetts court did
not go so far as to accept appellee's argument that corpora-

tions, as creatures of the State, have only those rights granted them by the State. The court below recognized that such an extreme position could not be reconciled either with the many decisions holding state laws invalid under the Fourteenth Amendment when they infringe protected speech by corporate bodies, or with decisions affording corporations the protection of constitutional guarantees other than the First Amendment."[19]

The question then arises as to why corporations have the constitutional rights they do. In the above case, *First National Bank* v. *Bellotti*, the Court emphasized that a commercial advertisement is protected not so much because it relates to the business of the seller, but because it advances society's interest in a free flow of information. In the case at issue, the Court seemed at least in part to be protecting a public right to hear rather than a corporate right to speak. The Court held the the corporate identity of the speaker did not allow government to impede the speech. Such an interpretation makes sense in light of the wording of the First Amendment, which provides, "Congress shall make no law respecting an establishment of religion, or prohibiting the free exercise thereof; or abridging the freedom of speech, or of the press. . . . " If the First Amendment, as made applicable to the states by the Fourteenth Amendment, is seen as purely a prohibition on government, the status of the speaker under the Constitution becomes irrelevant, because the First Amendment describes an area in which government may not act.

One then enters upon different territory when examining the extent to which corporations may claim constitutional rights granted to "persons." At that point, a corporation's status as a "person" would determine whether the corporation was entitled to that constitutional right. The Court in *Bellotti* stated that "it has been settled for almost a century that corporations are persons within the meaning of the Fourteenth Amendment."[20] Nevertheless, corporations are not entitled to all the constitutional protections provided to natural persons. The applicability of a particular protection to a corporation is dependent on "the nature, history, and purpose of the particular constitutional provision."[21] The Court rejected the idea that the states were free to determine the rights of the corporations they created without constitutional restriction, because corporations are clearly entitled to certain constitutional rights.

The status of an entity as a "person" under the law is a

very important one, because much can be done by defining a particular entity or individual as other than a person and therefore not coming within the law's scope. Certain classes of physical persons have at times been defined as other than natural persons by the law—such as slaves in the United States before the Civil War—so that the Constitution could operate in full without ever benefiting these individuals. A denial of rights through defining the affected entity as other than a person can work even more effectively than an explicit denial of rights.

<h2 style="text-align:center">PRINCIPLES DERIVING FROM RIGHTS
OF INDIVIDUALS</h2>

The protections of the Bill of Rights find their primary expression in the rights that have been held to apply to natural persons. The United States provides a very high degree of liberty and protection from governmental intrusion for natural persons within its borders. A question may then arise as to the extent to which natural persons carry their individual constitutional rights with them when they act as a corporate unit rather than as individuals.

In *NAACP* v. *Button*,[22] the Supreme Court dealt with a constitutional challenge to the application to the NAACP of a Virginia law that prohibited the solicitation of legal business. The NAACP had been holding meetings explaining how desegregation could be achieved through litigation and had paid the legal fees of persons who became plaintiffs in these actions. The individual plaintiffs were seeking redress for infringement of their constitutional rights; what then of the NAACP? The NAACP was a nonprofit corporation incorporated in New York and licensed to do business in Virginia, where it had eighty-nine active unincorporated branches.

The Supreme Court held that the NAACP could challenge the law by asserting the constitutional rights of its members. Thus, the Court was effectively holding that the constitutional rights of natural persons were transferred to the corporation through which expression was given to those constitutional rights. The only right clearly transferred here was the right to challenge unconstitutional racial segregation. The Court also stated that the NAACP could assert on its own behalf the right of the NAACP and its members and lawyers to associate in order to assist those who sought to vindicate their constitutional rights. The reason given was that even though the NAACP was a corporation, it was directly engaged in activities claimed to be protected by the Constitution, which the statute would limit.

One could derive two constitutional principles from this case: (1) Where a corporation serves as the means of expression of particular individual constitutional rights, the corporation will be able to assert the constitutional rights of the individuals it represents against any effort to limit its activities in furtherance of these rights. Thus, the corporation effectively possesses the constitutional rights sought to be furthered to the same degree as the individuals it represents. (2) Such a corporation may assert in its own right a freedom of association to further the rights sought to be protected. In the constitutional area at issue, then, the corporation has a double set of constitutional rights: its own and those of its members. Nevertheless, one could assert that in constitutional areas other than those the corporation serves to promote, such a corporation possesses only the rights of a corporation in general. In those other areas, therefore, the constitutional standing of the corporation would not be affected by the fact that it is an expression of individual constitutional rights.

APPLICATION OF THESE MODELS
TO CHURCH INSTITUTIONS

With a role analogous to that of the NAACP in the above case, church institutions are a collective expression of the constitutional rights of individuals to the free exercise of religion. As such, these institutions should be able to assert the constitutional rights of their members to free exercise of religion, as well as an institutional right of freedom of association for religious purposes. Any state action against the institution that limited the free exercise of religion should be subject to challenge by the institution on both of these grounds.

In *Surinach* v. *Pesquera de Busquets,*[23] the United States Court of Appeals for the First Circuit dealt with a challenge by the president of the Inter-Diocesan Secretariat for Catholic Education of Puerto Rico and various superintendents of Roman Catholic schools in Puerto Rico to an order of the secretary of Consumer Affairs of Puerto Rico for the production of documents relating to the costs of parochial school education. Although the plaintiffs in this case were individu-

als, the constitutional issues as treated by the court related to
the church schools as well as to the right of the individuals to
conduct their mission of religious education. Although the
court did not focus on the corporate status of the schools or
the nature of their constitutional rights, the court made clear
its concern for the order's "palpable threat of state interference with the internal policies and beliefs of these church
related schools."[24] The court stated that the schools were "an
integral part of the Catholic Church and as such 'involve substantial religious activity and purpose,' "[25] and proceeded to
examine whether the order tended to establish or infringe
upon religious beliefs or practices. Resting its decision "solely
on the free exercise clause,"[26] the court determined that the
order was unconstitutional. Accordingly, without examining
the issue, the court indicated that the church school possessed
the constitutional right to free exercise of religion. The court
in no way indicated that such a right was less or different
than that which would be possessed by an individual. Accordingly, the court's approach was in harmony with that in
NAACP v. *Button*, which found the corporation to be able to
assert the constitutional rights it served to promote.

Because religious establishment has historically occurred
through powerful church institutions, the Establishment
Clause plainly must apply to these institutions. It is a fact that
most Establishment Clause litigation has focused on state aid
to parochial schools. The question then arises as to whether a
church institution may assert a right to be free from religious
establishment. May a church institution that does not receive
public funds challenge the distribution of such funds to
another church institution? The answer to this question is
probably not. In order to challenge a governmental action in
court (or have judicial "standing"), one must allege a specific
injury. The United States Supreme Court has permitted taxpayers to challenge expenditures of government funds that
may constitute an establishment of religion.[27] Nevertheless,
the Court has drawn the borders rather narrowly around the
power of taxpayers to challenge governmental expenditures,
ruling that a disposition of property by the federal government
under the property clause of the Constitution, as opposed to
an expenditure of funds appropriated under the taxing and
spending clause of the Constitution, may not be challenged by
a taxpayer.[28]

Because church institutions do not generally pay taxes, taxpayer standing would probably not be available to them. A church institution could claim that it felt aggrieved by the support given by government to another institution, but such a sense of grievance would probably not be accepted by the courts as sufficient to enable the institution to bring suit. In *Valley Forge Christian College* v. *Americans United for Separation of Church and State, Inc.*,[29] the United States Court of Appeals for the Third Circuit indicated that an organization's concern for church-state separation and its members' sense of injury when that separation was violated provided a basis for standing in Establishment Clause litigation. The Supreme Court reversed the third circuit court's ruling and held that the organization did not have standing because it could not show sufficient injury. The Supreme Court's decision in this case might easily apply to a church institution that tried to enforce the Establishment Clause judicially. Its own sense of grievance could be found to be insufficient injury for it to litigate the matter.

A church institution, then, a vehicle for the collective exercise of the right of free exercise, would appear to have its own right of free exercise and to be able to challenge any state infringement upon that right. Moreover, the Establishment Clause applies to church institutions as entities. It is probable that a church institution could not assert an Establishment Clause violation on the basis of funding given to another church institution.

What then of the rights outside the religion clauses contained in the Bill of Rights? To what degree are these possessed by church institutions? In answering this question, it is important to note the Supreme Court's statement in *First National Bank* v. *Bellotti* that the important issue was not to what extent the corporations and national banking associations had constitutional rights, but whether particular actions were within the power of the state. Nevertheless, it seems that some determination as to whether the plaintiff is in a class protected by the Constitution is necessary in evaluating its constitutional claim. In addition, the institution must be able to show injury under the statute objected to sufficient to grant it standing in court. It is not enough that the government may not do a particular thing; the plaintiff must be injured by the government's action.

The remaining rights in the First Amendment after the religion clauses are freedom of speech, freedom of the press,

the right to peaceably assemble, and the right to petition the
government for a redress of grievances. Freedom of speech
and of the press have been applied in innumerable cases to
news corporations, which clearly enjoy these constitutional
rights. In the *Bellotti* case, the Supreme Court found that business corporations and banking associations had a right to
freedom of speech even when that speech did not relate to
their businesses. The Court indicated that when government
makes a law penalizing speech, the fact that the speakers to
whom the law applies are corporations and banking associations is not constitutionally significant. The consequence of
the Court's approach is that when the government seeks to
restrain speech by any speaker, the government must adhere
to the standard that it would apply in seeking to restrain
speech by a private individual. In *Consolidated Edison Company*
v. *Public Service Commission*,[30] the Supreme Court wrote that
the status of Consolidated Edison as a privately owned but
governmentally regulated monopoly did not prevent it from
asserting First Amendment rights. This status did not "de-
crease the informative value of its opinions on critical public
matters"[31]—a statement reminiscent of *Bellotti* that again
raises the question as to the extent to which the Court is relying on a public right to hear rather than a corporate right to
speak.

Because speaking and publishing are an inherent element of
religious activity, and because commercial corporations possess
rights in these areas, it seems clear that church institutions are
entitled to these constitutional rights as well. Many significant
cases involving religious activity have actually been decided on
free speech grounds. Based on the *Bellotti* decision, one could
assert that church institutions are entitled to these rights to
the same degree as private individuals. One could also make
this argument on the theory that church institutions express
the collective rights to freedom of speech and of the press of
their members, and that, therefore, the institutions can assert
these rights under the rationale of *NAACP* v. *Button*. The
right of peaceable assembly is essential for church institutions
as a general matter because many of these institutions by definition relate to a company of believers. A church that may not
assemble is a contradiction in terms. The right of petition is
necessary for church institutions to have full expression within society.

Other rights besides the protection of expression accorded

by the First Amendment have been held applicable to business corporations: the right to protection from unreasonable searches and seizures[32] (although a business corporation's right to privacy is less than that of a private individual);[33] security against double jeopardy,[34] but not the privilege against compulsory self-incrimination;[35] and the right to due process[36] and the equal protection of the laws.[37] Private individuals, of course, have all these rights in full measure. One may then ask to what extent special considerations applicable to church institutions dictate the applicable standard of constitutional rights in these areas. Is a church institution entitled to the same rights as private individuals? Greater rights? The same rights as business corporations? Fewer rights than business corporations? What factors determine the rights to which church institutions are entitled?

As discussed above, the California attorney general's office in imposing a receivership on the Worldwide Church of God and related institutions argued that because the institutions were subject to the attorney general's supervision as charitable organizations, enjoyed governmental "subsidies" in the form of tax exemptions, and were presumed to benefit the public generally, which he represented, there were "no private interests" and due process of law was not required. His representatives made it plain that they considered the Worldwide Church of God and its institutions to be entitled to less constitutional protection than a commercial business would be. The Supreme Court has taken a noninterventionist approach when dealing with church disputes, however. Furthermore, Chief Justice Marshall made it plain in the *Dartmouth College* case that the fact that a charitable institution was governmentally chartered did not convert it into a public institution. The college retained its private character that could not be abridged by government. Although business corporations have a number of constitutional rights, the granting of privileges by government such as the privilege of engaging in interstate commerce has been stated by the Supreme Court to constitute a basis for government regulation.

As organizations formed for the collective exercise of constitutional rights, church institutions should logically have a higher degree of constitutional rights in these non-First Amendment areas than do business corporations. The basic reason behind these rights—to protect persons from official misconduct—applies to a greater degree where constitutional rights are being exercised than when commercial activity is being undertaken. The argument that tax exemption, supervisory powers exercised by an attorney general, or the deemed general public benefit provided by a church institution make the church institution a creature of the state, so that the state can do what it wills with church property regardless of constitutional restraints, flies in the face of the Establishment Clause. If churches have become arms of government, something is very wrong with the legal structure that got them there. Instead, it is proposed that these elements do not make church institutions arms of government, just as the corporate charter discussed in the *Dartmouth College* case did not do so. In considering whether churches should in all cases have the same constitutional protections as individuals, one could argue that the fact that the individuals are exercising their constitutional rights collectively should not deprive that collective expression of any constitutional protections the individuals would have as natural persons. Actual determinations in these matters must await additional line-drawing by the courts as these issues come to them for resolution.

Conclusion

Although the constitutional rights to which natural persons and business corporations are entitled have been analyzed by the courts in some detail, the constitutional rights to which church institutions are entitled are a subject of debate. Any standard that is developed in this area must take into account the noninterventionist approach courts have adopted when dealing with church institutions. Various models are available in examining constitutional standards to be applied to church institutions; the rights accorded to individuals, the strongest level of constitutional protections, would serve to safeguard church institutions from government intervention and would ensure that individuals did not relinquish constitutional rights by associating for religious purposes.

NOTES

1. *Trustees of Dartmouth College* v. *Woodward*, 17 U.S. (4 Wheat.) 518, 21 app. (1819).
2. Ibid., 9 app. (footnotes omitted).
3. Ibid., 11 app. (footnotes omitted).
4. *California ex rel. Timmons* v. *Worldwide Church of God, Inc.*, No. C 267 607, report-

er's transcript of proceedings at 3, 7 (California Superior Court, Los Angeles County, 2 January 1979).

5. For a more extended treatment of the receivership imposed on the Worldwide Church of God by the State of California, see Sharon L. Worthing, "The State Takes Over a Church," *The Annals of the American Academy of Political and Social Science* 446 (November 1979):136-48.

6. *Everson* v. *Board of Education*, 330 U.S. 1, 15-16 (1947).

7. Charles M. Whelan, "Who Owns the Churches?" in *Government Intervention in Religious Affairs*, ed. Dean M. Kelley (New York: The Pilgrim Press, 1982), 57.

8. *Watson* v. *Jones*, 80 U.S. (13 Wall.) 679 (1871).

9. *Presbyterian Church in the United States* v. *Mary Elizabeth Blue Hull Memorial Presbyterian Church*, 393 U.S. 440 (1969).

10. *Jones* v. *Wolf*, 443 U.S. 1595 (1979).

11. *Serbian Eastern Orthodox Church* v. *Milivojevich*, 426 U.S. 696 (1976).

12. For a legal treatment of religious corporations in the United States and their history, see Paul G. Kauper and Stephen C. Ellis, "Religious Corporations and the Law," *Michigan Law Review* 71 (August 1973):1499-1574.

13. *Trustees of Dartmouth College* v. *Woodward*, 17 U.S. (4 Wheat.) 518 (1819).

14. Ibid., at 629-30.

15. Ibid., at 652.

16. Joseph Story, *Commentaries on the Constitutions of the United States*, 3rd ed. (Boston: Little, Brown and Company, 1858), 2:296 (footnote omitted).

17. *Trustees of Dartmouth College* v. *Woodward*, at 518, 636.

18. *United States* v. *Morton Salt Company*, 338 U.S. 632, 652 (1950).

19. *First National Bank* v. *Bellotti*, 435 U.S. 765, 778 n. 14 (1978) (citations omitted).

20. Ibid., 780 n. 15, citing *Santa Clara County* v. *Southern Pacific Railroad Company*, 118 U.S. 394 (1886).

21. *First National Bank* v. *Bellotti*, at 765, 778 n. 14. For a discussion of this case and of the various theories of the nature of a business corporation that may give rise to a finding of particular constitutional rights, see Note, "Constitutional Rights of the Corporate Person," *Yale Law Journal* 91 (July 1982):1641-58.

22. *NAACP* v. *Button*, 371 U.S. 415 (1963).

23. *Surinach* v. *Pesquera de Busquets*, 604 F.2d 73 (1st Cir. 1979).

24. Ibid., at 76-77.

25. Ibid., at 76; quoting *Lemon* v. *Kurtzman*, 403 U.S. 602, 616 (1971).

26. *Surinach* v. *Pesquera de Busquets*, at 79 n. 6.

27. *Flast* v. *Cohen*, 392 U.S. 83 (1968).

28. *Valley Forge Christian College* v. *Americans United for Separation of Church and State, Inc.*, 454 U.S. 464 (1982).

29. Ibid.

30. *Consolidated Edison Company* v. *Public Service Commission*, 447 U.S. 530 (1980).

31. Ibid., at 534 n. 1.

32. *G.M. Leasing Corp.* v. *United States*, 429 U.S. 338 (1977).

33. *United States* v. *Morton Salt Company*.

34. *United States* v. *Martin Linen Supply Company*, 430 U.S. 564 (1977).

35. *Hale* v. *Henkel*, 201 U.S. 43 (1906).

36. *Mississippi Railroad Commission* v. *Mobile & Ohio Railroad Company*, 244 U.S. 388 (1917).

37. *Santa Clara County* v. *Southern Pacific Railroad Company*, 118 U.S. 394 (1886).

PART 3

THE RIGHT OF
RELIGIOUS DISSENT

New Religions and the
First Amendment:
"The Law Knows No Heresy"

JAMES E. WOOD, JR.

For more than two decades, there has been a resurgence of
new religions throughout America. Commonly referred to by
the pejorative term of "cults," these new religions have been
generally met with widespread hostility in what has been
called the "anti-cult" movement. Those who may be inclined
to assume that this resurgence of new religions in America
during recent decades is essentially a new phenomenon of
American culture are ignoring a recurring characteristic of
this nation's religious history. As Sidney Ahlstrom observed,
"American civilization from the beginning and each passing
century has been continuously marked by extraordinary religious fertility, and continues to exhibit this propensity to the
present day."[1] Far from being a new phenomenon, the emergence of new religions is a regular and salient feature of religion in America—the inevitable consequence of the constitutional guarantees of religious liberty and the separation of
church and state.

Religious pluralism has been, and remains, an integral part
of the American experience and the American character, a
clue to understanding both the character and the freedom of
religion in America. The extraordinary diversity of religion,
in both its formal and informal expressions, has been one of
the most distinctive features of America throughout its history. Some historical perspective, therefore, is needed in understanding the phenomenon of new religions in America today.

I

From the beginning, religious diversity characterized the
colonies. French and Spanish explorations brought the Roman
Catholic faith to the New World in the sixteenth century. In
the seventeenth century, English colonists were planted in the
New World. Unlike the French and Spanish, English colonial authorities did not impose a pattern of religious uniformity in any of the colonies other than in Virginia. A deliberate

policy of toleration on the part of the British authorities inevitably encouraged religious diversity throughout the English colonies, since it offered to religious dissenters of England and the continent a greater measure of freedom in the New World than they had known in their homelands.

Although the policy of toleration by the British authorities was by no means always reflected among the colonists themselves, as in the case of those in Massachusetts Bay, it did contribute enormously to the religious diversity of the colonies. Commercial interests required that the widest appeal possible be made to English as well as to non-English colonists if the economic advantages of colonization were to be completely realized. These economic interests are evident in the grants that were made to Lord Baltimore and William Penn, but nowhere is this motivation as a contributing factor to religious pluralism perhaps more evident than in a communication from the Lord of Trade in London to the Council of Virginia: "A free exercise of religion . . . is essential to enriching and improving a trading nation; it should be ever held sacred in His Majesty's colonies. We must, therefore, recommend it to your care that nothing be done which can in the least affect that great point."[2]

Although religious diversity was not something sought by the settlers in the New World, the absence of religious uniformity characterized colonial America from the beginning. During the seventeenth century, colonists included members of the national churches of England, Scotland, Germany, Holland, and Sweden. New religious movements, such as the Puritans in Massachusetts, the Baptists in Rhode Island, and the Quakers in Pennsylvania, contributed significantly to the religious diversity of colonial America. Beyond the mere fact of multiplicity of religious groups was the prominent presence among the colonists of religious dissenters and schismatics from the religious establishments of Europe. As Edwin Scott Gaustad has written, "Schismatics came from Switzerland and France, from Austria and Germany, from Britain and the Netherlands, Huguenots fled to Saint Augustine and to Charleston, Moravians to North Carolina and Pennsylvania, Mennonites and Quakers to the Middle Colonies, Lutherans to Savannah, and Pilgrims to Plymouth. Schism was, quite early, an American way of life."[3]

By and large, religious immigrants to the New World belonged mainly to religious groups or shared religious beliefs that were discriminated against in the Old World: Puritans, Baptists, Calvinists, Irish Catholics, Mennonites, Jews, Dunkers, Moravians, Pietists (Puritanic Lutherans), and Scotch-Irish Presbyterians. One description of religious pluralism in the colonies at the end of the seventeenth century is as follows: "A traveler in 1700 making his way from Boston to the Carolinas would encounter Congregationalists of varying intensity, Baptists of several varieties, Presbyterians, Quakers, and several other forms of Puritan radicalism; Dutch, German, and French Reformed; Swedish, Finnish, and German Lutherans; Mennonites and radical pietists, Anglicans, Roman Catholics; here and there a Jewish congregation, a few Rosicrucians; and, of course, a vast number of the unchurched— some of them powerfully alienated from any form of institutional religion."[4]

Within the colonies, religious pluralism was rampant. In Rhode Island, where religious liberty was first made a part of organic law, it was said that "hardly any two Rhode Islanders shared the same beliefs."[5] By 1644, the governor of New Amsterdam reported that eighteen different languages could be heard on the island of Manhattan and the surrounding area. The religious diversity of New York was vividly described in a 1687 report by Governor Dongan: "New York has first a chaplain . . . of the Church of England; secondly, a Dutch Calvinist; thirdly, a French Calvinist; fourthly, a Dutch Lutheran. Here be not many of the Church of England; few Roman Catholics; abundance of Quaker preachers, men, and women especially; Singling Quakers; Ranting Quakers; Sabbatarians; Anti-Sabbatarians; some Ana-baptists; some Jews; in short, all sorts of opinion there are some, and the most part none at all."[6] By the eighteenth century, Pennsylvania was not only a denominational stronghold for Quakers, but also for Presbyterians, Episcopalians, Baptists, and the German Reformed Church.

The colonists came from many lands and differing cultural and religious backgrounds. An analysis of the census of 1790 indicates that the population at that time was composed of national stocks with English barely 60 percent of the population, with the remainder of the colonists divided as follows: German—8.6 percent, Scots—8.1 percent, "Ulster Irish"—5.9 percent, "Free State Irish"—3.6 percent, Dutch—3.1 percent, French—2.3 percent, Spanish—.8 percent, Swedish—.7 percent, and unassigned—6.8 percent. Not only did religious pluralism prevail throughout the colonies, but the vast majority of the population in each of the colonies was unchurched, described as "the largest proportion of unchurched in Christendom."[7] Understandably, there was no pattern of uniformity among the colonies regarding a religious establishment. While some form of religious establishment in the New World largely followed the pattern of the Old, at least in nine of the thirteen colonies, four of the colonies—Rhode Island, Pennsylvania, New Jersey, and Delaware—did not have established churches. Perhaps even more significant is the fact that no single church was established in more than five of the thirteen colonies. In Massachusetts, Connecticut, and New Hampshire, the Congregational Church was established by law; while in Maryland, Virginia, North Carolina, South Carolina, Georgia, and New York City and three neighboring counties, the Anglican Church was established.

Admittedly, the religious pluralism of colonial America was not without open religious conflicts and frequent acts of intolerance. While some of the persecutions of colonial America are generally well known, including the banishments from Massachusetts of Roger Williams and Anne Hutchinson, all too often those acts are not seen as rooted in the right of religious dissent that would later become an essential and pervasive trait of the American character. Colonial America was both anti-cult and anti-sect.

In many of the colonies, even established churches from Europe faced persecution and legal acts of discrimination against them. Puritans in New England banished and persecuted Anglicans, Baptists, and Quakers, among others, while Anglicans hounded the Puritans and the Baptists who came to Virginia. Jews were banished from Manhattan and Huguenots from Florida. Roman Catholics met resistance almost everywhere they settled, except in Maryland where they constituted a majority. Catholics were not represented in Connecticut until the latter part of the 1820s. Acts of toleration were passed excepting "irregular ministers and exhorters," dissenters, and certain sectarians. In a landmark church-state case in 1947, the United States Supreme Court appropriately characterized religion in colonial America as follows:

Practices of the old world were transplanted to and began to thrive in the soil of the new America. The very charters granted by the English Crown to the individuals and companies designated to make the laws which would control the destinies of the colonials authorized these individuals and companies to erect religious establishments which, whether believers or nonbelievers, would be required to support and attend. An exercise of this authority was accompanied by a repetition of many of the old-world practices and persecutions. Catholics found themselves hounded and proscribed because of their faith; Quakers who followed their conscience went to jail; Baptists were peculiarly obnoxious to certain Protestant sects; men and women of varied faiths who happened to be a minority in a particular locality were persecuted because they steadfastly persisted in worshipping God only as their own consciences dictated. And all of these dissenters were compelled to pay tithes and taxes to support government-sponsored churches whose ministers preached inflammatory sermons designed to strengthen and consolidate the established faith by generating a burning hatred against dissenters.[8]

As already indicated, although religious pluralism was not something desired by the American colonists, nor was this religious pluralism generally met by toleration in the colonies, the absence of religious uniformity contributed immeasurably to the guarantees of religious freedom in the founding of the American Republic. It was, in fact, this diversity or "multiplicity," as James Madison expressed it, that was the best guarantee against the tyranny of a majority, whether that majority be characterized as secular or religious. For this reason, Madison wrote in *The Federalist*, the new country should secure civil and religious rights since both belong to the coin of freedom, guaranteeing "the multiplicity of interests" on the one side and "the multiplicity of sects" on the other side.[9] In the absence of any religious establishment and in the presence of religious liberty as a matter of organic law in the formation of the early Republic, religious diversity was assured.

The very motto on the seal of the United States, *E Pluribus Unum* ("from the many, one"), testifies not to bigness but to multiplicity. Selected in 1776 by Benjamin Franklin, John Adams, and Thomas Jefferson, this motto has been both descriptive and a normative expression of America as a pluralistic society. Perhaps in no area of American life has multiplicity of interests been more manifest than in the area of religion.

At the time of the nation's founding, an establishment of religion was both practically and ideologically an impossibility if the ideal of *E Pluribus Unum* were to be realized. At the same time, religious freedom was eloquently championed by religious and political leaders alike. Religion is to be free of the state and government is to be denied the right of jurisdiction over religion. As Madison wrote, "The religion . . . of every man, must be left to the conviction and conscience of every man. . . . We maintain, therefore, that in matters of

religion no man's right is to be abridged by the institution of
civil society; and that religion is wholly exempt from its cog-
nizance."[10] Or, as one renowned Baptist minister, Isaac Backus, expressed it: "The free exercises of private judgement, and
the unalienable rights of conscience, are of too high a rank
and dignity to be submitted to the decrees of councils, or the
imperfect laws of fallible legislators."[11] Diversity of religious
opinion was recognized not only as the natural and inevitable
consequence of religious freedom, but also as beneficial to
religion. Thomas Jefferson wrote, "Difference of opinion is
advantageous in religion. The several sects perform the office
of a *censor morum* over each other."[12] In any event, America's
religious pluralism seemed assured. In the year of the nation's
official independence (1783), Ezra Stiles in his famous sermon, "The United States Elevated to Glory and Honour,"
confidently predicted that America would "embosom all the
religious sects and denominations in Christendom" and "give
complete freedom to all."[13] By the middle of the nineteenth
century, Phillip Schaff observed that America was already "a
motley sampler of all church history."[14]

Meanwhile, it was argued, a person's religious opinions
were not in any way to be related to the exercise of his civil
liberties. As Jefferson stated it in the Bill for Establishing
Religious Freedom in Virginia, "All men shall be free to profess, and by argument to maintain, their opinion in matters of
religion, and that the same shall in no wise diminish, enlarge,
or affect their civil liberties."[15] This document became the
primary source of other state statutes and the First Amendment. As a result of these developments, scarce consideration
was even given to the subject of religion at the Constitutional
Convention at Philadelphia in May 1787. Article VI, "No
religious test shall ever be required as a qualification to any
office or public trust under the United States," was the only
reference to religion in the original document. This itself was
a profound acknowledgment of the secular character of the
state and an expression of the constitutional assurance that
religious identity or opinions should have no bearing upon
one's qualifications for holding a position of public trust. From
dissenters, especially the Baptists and the Presbyterians, came
the demand in the form of a Bill of Rights to guarantee the
separation of church and state and to provide some explicit
assurance of the free exercise of religion. Consequently, establishment of religion, at least on a national level, was in 1789

clearly prohibited and official acknowledgment was thereby made as to the secular and the pluralistic character of the new nation. Ratification of the First Amendment in 1791, in effect, constitutionally confirmed the pluralistic character of the new Republic.

In spite of this constitutional achievement that would provide an indissoluble link in America between religious freedom and religious pluralism, the nineteenth century is replete with examples of widespread bigotry and intolerance toward Catholics and Jews as well as toward new religions. Religious discrimination against Catholics and Jews was felt in both social and political areas, reenforced in many instances by state laws and constitutions. The Nativist or "Know Nothing" party seized control of numerous state legislatures and succeeded in passing laws against Catholic immigrants. In some states, as in Delaware and Pennsylvania, public office was limited to Christians (Catholics or Protestants), while in New Jersey and North Carolina public office was limited just to Protestants. Only gradually was religious pluralism legally guaranteed in the states, and only after the ratification of the Fourteenth Amendment in 1868, followed by a lengthy history of "incorporation" (i.e., specifically "incorporating" the religion clauses of the First Amendment into the Fourteenth Amendment and, thus, applying these religion clauses to the states). As Gaustad observed of nineteenth-century America, "Religious non-conformity found its path to public acceptance paved with legal obstacles and illegal harassment."[16]

In America, religious pluralism is both a constitutional right as well as a historical or social reality. This pluralism is not an aberration to be tolerated, but rather a right to be guaranteed religion and irreligion. With the enactment of the First Amendment, "Congress shall make no law respecting the establishment of religion or prohibiting the free exercise thereof," the entanglement of government in religious affairs was constitutionally prohibited. Full religious liberty, it was reasoned, required a secular state in which the people have excluded the authority and jurisdiction of the state from religious affairs and all churches are to be equal in the sight of the state, with no church having any advantages or disadvantages of establishment. Strictly speaking, in America, the state knows neither churches nor sects, as used historically in Europe, but only "denominations" (a distinctly American term). No religious group is to be the object of privilege or discrimination under the law. The most militant atheist, along with the most fervent theist within one of the most socially accepted denominations, is to be assured full rights of citizenship and equal protection under the law. So long as one's free exercise of religion does not infringe upon the rights of others or contravene the just civil laws of the state or threaten public health and order, both the rights of religious dissent and the free exercise of that dissent are guaranteed to all citizens.

To be sure, these broad principles have not always conformed to historical reality, any more than other civil rights have applied to all citizens without regard to race or sex. Furthermore, as in the past, some formal relationships between religion and the state do exist in the United States. Chaplains in state and federal legislatures, presidential religious proclamations, and congressional actions in recent years adopting "In God We Trust" on all currency, "One Nation Under God" as the nation's motto, and the phrase "under God" in the formal pledge of allegiance to the American flag, among others, testify to the formal ties of religion to this nation, notwithstanding the prohibitions of the First Amendment. It should be noted, however, that virtually all of these formal relationships are ceremonial acts without requirements of acquiescence or formal compliance on the part of the citizens.

Since minority rights are perennially endangered by the will of majorities, marginal religious groups have simultaneously sought with mainline religions judicial redress rather than legislative remedy in their struggle for their religious rights and equality under the law. As Leo Pfeffer so aptly expressed it, "The smaller the minority, the more likely it is to need constitutional protection; the greater it is, the more likely it is to obtain the protection it needs through legislative exemption rather than judicial intervention."[17] This is amply reflected in the disproportionate number of church-state cases to reach the United States Supreme Court on behalf of religious groups outside of the mainline religious denominations. These include, among others, the Church of Jesus Christ of Latter-day Saints, Jehovah's Witnesses, Seventh-day Adventists, the "I Am" movement, Black Muslims, Amish, the Hare Krishna movement, the Worldwide Church of God, the Unification Church, and the Church of Scientology.

Religious diversity in America has helped to ensure the primacy of the voluntary principle in religion and to reenforce the concept of this nation as a free, secular state. Religious diversity is seen, in turn, as the natural corollary of freedom. The corollary of religious liberty is nothing less than the right of dissent. As former Chief Justice Charles Evans Hughes of the United States Supreme Court expressed it more than five decades ago, "When we lose the right to be different, we lose the right to be free."[18] The integration of religious pluralism into American constitutional law has been accomplished primarily by the Supreme Court's repeated emphasis on the state's neutrality, not only toward various religious denominations but also toward "groups of religious believers and non-believers."[19] In so ruling, the Court has necessarily held that a policy of neutrality forbids both government sponsorship and support of religion or religious beliefs. This neutrality the Court enunciated more than a century ago in *Watson* v. *Jones* (1872), in which the Court declared:

In this country the full and free right to entertain any religious belief, to practice any religious principle, and to teach any religious doctrine which does not violate the laws of morality and property, and which does not infringe personal rights, is conceded to all. The law knows no heresy, and is committed to the support of no dogma, the establishment of no sect. The right to organize voluntary religious associations to assist in the expression and dissemination of any religious doctrine, and to create tribunals for the decision of controverted questions of faith within the association, and for the ecclesiastical government of all the individual members, congregations and officers within the general association is unquestioned.[20]

American religious pluralism is rooted in freedom and equality, not toleration. Integral to the American concept of religious freedom is that in this nation, "all religions are equal and none is less or more equal than others."[21] The First Amendment serves to protect all religions, both marginal and mainline, old and new, popular and unpopular, against government harassment, injury, and discrimination, whether such actions are initiated from the public or private sector of society. It is in this context that marginal and new religions are to be viewed before the law and their rights are to be assured. Equality before the law is as essential to religious liberty as to all other civil rights when applied to race, sex, ethnic origin, and socioeconomic status.

II

Although sectarianism is characteristic of all religions, even those that are highly eclectic and inclusive in character, it is in a free and secular state such as the United States that religious sectarianism is able to flourish and to enjoy legal protection and the legal guarantee of equality among differing faiths. America's religious diversity has stemmed from two sources: those religions that originated in older cultures and emigrated to America, first from the Old World and more recently from the East, and those that originated in America, either as new expressions of older religious traditions or as indigenous faiths from out of the American milieu.

The constitutional phrase "prohibiting the free exercise" of religion not only affirms that religious belief or affiliation is to be voluntary, but that the *activity* of religious conscience is not to be abridged by the state. While Americans gradually came to accept the freedom to believe or disbelieve, "the free *exercise*" of religion, with its secular consequences, has been far more difficult to gain acceptance. From his study of religious conflict in America, Pfeffer observed that it is this perceived threat of new religions to secular norms not to theological orthodoxy that results in the tension that arises between marginal or new religions and American society.[22] The problem is that constitutional rights, whether civil or religious, are not to be conditioned upon social acceptance or the majority opinions of society.

Perhaps in no area of American life is this problem more manifest than in the nation's religious history. The very emergence of the concept of "denominationalism" seriously "weakened the hold of strict confessionalism and encouraged departure from tradition,"[23] and thereby contributed further to religious pluralism in America. Democratic principles, once they were carried over to religion and to religious institutions, fostered religious individualism, on the one hand, and eroded the traditional structures of ecclesiastical authority over the adherents, on the other hand. With political independence came religious independence not only from the state but from many authoritarian patterns of religious belief and practice. For many, freedom of religion came to mean freedom from the strictures of religious orthodoxy and tradition.

Less than a century and a half ago, Mormonism provoked violent reactions, first in New York, then in Ohio, and later in Illinois. Its founder and leader, Joseph Smith, and his brother were murdered by a mob in 1844, while awaiting trial for treason. Under the leadership of Brigham Young, Mormons undertook a trek westward to escape further harassment and religious persecution and to establish a religious colony of their own, the "State of Deseret" in the Great Salt Lake area. The first major church-state confrontation in America involved the Mormons in *Reynolds* v. *United States* (1878),[24] in which the United States Supreme Court unanimously sustained an act of Congress outlawing polygamy. By contrast, today the Church of Jesus Christ of Latter-day Saints is one of the largest and most influential of America's indigenous faiths. No longer viewed as a threat to the secular norms of American society, Mormonism has achieved a social acceptance and status far beyond what could have been envisioned in the mid-nineteenth century. It has become, in effect, one of America's mainline denominations. The legitimation of Mormonism may be an appropriate reminder that all faiths were once "new" religions and only gradually were they able to gain social acceptance and a status of influence to the degree that they are no longer perceived to be a threat to the secular norms of society.

Marginal or new religions have contributed significantly to American understanding as well as to judicial interpretations of religious liberty, far out of proportion to their numerical membership or institutional strength. No better example of this fact may be cited than in the case of Jehovah's Witnesses, a group that has been responsible for more court cases concerned with religious liberty than any other religious group in America. As a result of many of these cases, substantial contributions have been made in American constitutional law and substantial gains have been obtained for religious liberty. In a landmark church-state case, *Cantwell* v. *Connecticut* (1940),[25] the Supreme Court unanimously upheld the right of Jehovah's Witnesses to propagate their faith in public and to engage in door-to-door solicitation without a permit or "certificate of approval." The Court declared, "Freedom of conscience and freedom to adhere to such religious organization or form of worship as the individual may choose cannot be restricted by law." Aside from the victory won by the Jehovah's Witnesses, for the first time the Court specifically incorporated the Free Exercise Clause into the Fourteenth Amendment, thus making it applicable to the states. Three years later, in *Murdock* v. *Pennsylvania* (1943),[26] the Court upheld the proselytizing activities of the Witnesses through the distribution of their literature as integral to their free exercise of religion. "The hand distribution of religious tracts," the Court said, ". . . occupies the same high estate under the First Amendment as do worship in the churches and preaching from the pulpits. It has the same claims to protection as the more orthodox and conventional exercises of religion."

The confrontation of the Jehovah's Witnesses with the state were never more dramatically manifest than in the refusal of Jehovah's Witness children to salute and recite the pledge of allegiance to the American flag. Three years after deciding overwhelmingly to uphold the expulsion of Witness children from the public schools in *Minersville School District* v. *Gobitis* (1940),[27] the Supreme Court reversed its position in *West Virginia State Board of Education* v. *Barnette* (1943).[28] Speaking for the Court, Justice Robert H. Jackson declared, "If there is any fixed star in our constitutional constellation, it is that no official, high or petty, can prescribe what shall be orthodox in politics, nationalism, religion, or other matters of opinion or force citizens to confess by word or act their faith therein. If there are any circumstances which permit any exemption, they do not now occur to us."

In *United States* v. *Ballard* (1944),[29] the Supreme Court addressed the claims of the truth or falsity of religious beliefs or doctrines. The case involved the organizers of the "I Am" movement, Guy W., Edna W., and Donald Ballard, all of whom were charged with using the mail to defraud by claiming that they had supernatural powers to heal diseases and injuries. The Court ruled that no agency of the state has the competence or the power to determine "the truth or falsity of the beliefs or doctrines" of anyone even though those beliefs "might seem incredible, if not preposterous to most people." Speaking for the majority, Justice William O. Douglas wrote:

Heresy trials are foreign to our Constitution. Men may believe what they cannot prove. They may not be put to the proof of their religious doctrines, or beliefs. Religious experiences which are as real as life to some may be incomprehensible to others. Yet the fact that they may be beyond the ken of mortals does not mean that they can be made suspect before the law. Many take their gospel from the New Testament. But it would hardly be supposed that they could be tried before a jury charged with the duty of determining whether those teachings contained false representations. The miracles of the New Testament, the Divinity of Christ, life after death, the power of prayer are deep in the religious convictions of many. If one could be sent to jail because a jury in a hostile environment found those teachings false, little indeed would be left to religious freedom. . . . The religious views espoused by respondents might seem incredible, if not preposterous, to most people. But if those doctrines are subject to trial before a jury charged with finding their truth or falsity, then the same can be done with the religious beliefs of any sect. When the triers of fact undertake that task, they enter a forbidden domain. The First Amendment does not select any one group or any one type of religion for preferred treatment.

In defending the constitutional rights of even a religious group whose views the society at large may view as "preposterous," the Court noted that in the Constitution, "Man's relation to his God was made no concern of the state. He was granted the right to worship as he pleased and to answer to no man for the verity of his religious beliefs." For the secular court, the only issue is whether the affirmed religious beliefs are actually *believed* to be true.

Ever since the *Reynolds* decision more than a century ago, the Supreme Court has affirmed that while freedom to believe is absolute, freedom to act on that belief is not absolute. As Chief Justice Morrison Waite wrote in *Reynolds*, "Laws are made for the government of actions, and while they cannot interfere with mere religious belief and opinions, they may with practices." Subsequently, in adjudicating the "free exercise" of religion, the Court has attempted to set forth some judicial standards for regulating actions based on religious beliefs. Two standards established by the Court are the "compelling interest" rule and the "alternate means" test.

The first specific Supreme Court case to "balance" freedom of religion with compelling public or state interest came in *Prince* v. *Commonwealth of Massachusetts* (1944),[30] in which the Court upheld a state child labor law and thereby denied the right of a Jehovah's Witness to have her nine-year-old niece accompany her in selling religious literature on the street. The Court did so, in the words of Justice Wiley Rutledge, in order to uphold the prior claim of "the interest of society to protect the welfare of the children."

Another judicial criterion for determining the limits of the "free exercise" provision came almost two decades later in the "alternate means" test. First advanced in *Braunfeld* v. *Brown* (1961),[31] the test was used in *Sherbert* v. *Verner* (1963)[32] to invalidate the denial of unemployment compensation by the state of South Carolina to Adell Sherbert, a Seventh-day Adventist, because she refused to work on Saturday. The state's unwillingness to find "alternate means" readily available to it, the Court said, imposed a religious burden on the appellant in that it forced her to choose between following her religious convictions and, thus, forfeiting her employment compensation or abandoning her religious principles in order to accept employment. "Only the gravest abuses," the Court said, "endangering paramount interest, give occasion for permissible limitation" of the "free exer-

cise" of religion. "The *Sherbert* doctrine," as John Richard
Burkholder observed, "stands as the highwater mark in the
Supreme Court's interpretation of the scope of free exercise of
religions. . . . its full potential impact is yet to be realized."[33]
Similarly, in *Thomas* v. *Review Board* (1981),[34] the Supreme Court
declared unconstitutional the denial of unemployment compensation benefits to a Jehovah's Witness for refusing employment
on religious grounds in a plant making weapons for war.

In their struggle for religious freedom, America's marginal or
new religions have increasingly sought legitimation of their
claims as bona fide religions and, thereby, equality with other
religions in the "free exercise" of their beliefs and teachings.
Many court cases involving the Black Muslims have been illustrative of this pattern, most of them arising out of grievances that
Black Muslim prison inmates were denied their religious rights
of holding services, receiving Black Muslim religious literature, eating pork-free meals, wearing of beards, and obtaining
the services of Black Muslim clergy. In *Cooper* v. *Pate* (1964),[35]
the Supreme Court reversed two lower courts' decisions that
denied the rights of a Black Muslim prison inmate to obtain his
Koran and other Black Muslim literature, to attend Black Muslim religious services, and to have contacts with Black Muslim
clergy. The Court rejected the argument of the attorney general
of Illinois that the "Black Muslim Movement, despite its pretext
of a religious facade, is an organization that, outside of prison
walls, has for its object the overthrow of the white race, and inside
prison walls, has an impressive history of inciting riots and violence." In a brief per curiam opinion, the Court held that it was
unconstitutional to deny a prisoner religious privileges enjoyed
by other inmates of mainline denominations simply because of
his religious beliefs.

The Black Muslim struggle for legitimation may also be seen
in the prolonged effort of Muhammad Ali (earlier known as
Cassius Clay, Jr.) to avoid induction into military service. In *Clay*
v. *United States* (1971),[36] the Supreme Court overruled the Fifth
Circuit Court of Appeals that had accepted the ruling of the
Justice Department and the Appeal Board that Ali's refusal to
enter military service was based on "grounds which primarily are
political and racial" and did not constitute a "general scruple
against participation in war in any form." The Supreme Court
declared that the Justice Department "was simply wrong as a
matter of law in advising that the petitioner's beliefs were not
religiously based and were not sincerely held." After several

decades of Black Muslim struggle in the courts, some have seen this decision "as a clear legitimation of the Black Muslim faith."[37]

Still other confrontations with the state have occurred with new religions that have emerged in more recent decades, among these are the Church of Scientology, the International Society for Krishna Consciousness (ISKCON) or the Hare Krishna movement, and the Unification Church, all of which have been viewed with much disfavor as they have succeeded in winning numerous converts from mainline Christian denominations as well as the Jewish community. Crucial to all confrontations of new religions with the state is the issue of equality under the law, as applied to both religion clauses of the First Amendment. As the Supreme Court declared in *Everson*, no government, state or federal, "can pass laws which . . . prefer one religion over another."[38] In response to an amendment to Minnesota's Charitable Solicitation Act directed against new religions, particularly the Unification Church, the Supreme Court in *Larson* v. *Valente* (1982)[39] found the statutory amendment unconstitutional, as violative of both the Establishment Clause and the Free Exercise Clause of the Constitution. Speaking for the majority opinion, Justice William J. Brennan wrote, "The constitutional prohibition of denominational preference is inexorably connected with the continuing vitality of the Free Exercise Clause."

Unfortunately, all too often new religions have not enjoyed the same legal rights and tax privileges as have Catholic, Protestant, and Jewish groups. A recent case in point is to be found in *Moon* v. *United States* (1984),[40] which resulted in the conviction of Rev. Sun Myung Moon, the founder of the Unification Church, by a federal court of income-tax evasion. The key issue in this case came to light early, namely the selective prosecution of Moon for doing what many other religious leaders of mainline groups have done through the years. Moon expressed a view shared by many when he declared, "I would not be standing here today if my skin were white and my religion were Presbyterian." A point of view shared by the judge in the case. "I am not so naive," the judge said, "as to believe that if Reverend Moon was a noncontroversial person whose religion was Pollyannish, who nobody took exception to, that the government would not have had as much interest in looking at his taxes as they did. . . ." The United States Supreme Court declined to overturn the lower court's conviction and, thus, the conviction was upheld and Moon was sentenced to prison.

III

The mushrooming of new religious movements during the past few decades, in some cases accompanied by phenomenal numerical growth, has become one of the major features of contemporary American religious life. To be sure, some new religions have emerged and largely disappeared within the span of a decade, while others have demonstrated sustained appeal and remarkable institutional and numerical growth. Generally, the growth of new religions has been accompanied by intense missionary activity and a lifestyle of radical separation of converts from the mainstream of American civil and religious life, the latter often resulting in the alienation of youthful converts from their parents and their families' religious traditions. Social hostility toward new religions has been widespread, largely born out of conflicts of the new religions with secular interests. The Jonestown massacre, on 18 November 1978, of 917 adults and children of the People's Temple movement by means of cyanide-laced Kool-Aid involving the charismatic and erratic Jim Jones, greatly accelerated the antipathy of the anti-cult movement toward America's new religions.

By the late seventies, especially in the wake of the Jonestown tragedy, popular support was given to demands for federal, state, and local governments to investigate the new religious "cults," so as to determine their possible threat to society and the political order. Within a few weeks after the Jonestown massacre, Senator Robert Dole of Kansas called for an inquiry into the tax-exempt status of all "cults." In a letter to the chairman of the Senate Finance Committee, Dole wrote, "The question surrounding the Jonestown incident and the continuous activity of the Unification Church require action. . . . The public needs protection from unscrupulous operations that flout the law for their own purposes." "The tragedy in Guyana [Jonestown]," Dole wrote, "presents sufficient cause for a full-scale investigation of . . . this group [i.e., the People's Temple] and much closer scrutiny of other such religious cults."[41] In response to political pressure, a special congressional hearing on "The Cult Phenomenon in the United States," chaired by Senator Dole, was held in February 1979.[42] The hearing was conducted by an ad hoc congressional committee comprised of both members of the Senate and the House of Representatives. Subsequently, similar hearings on "cults" or new religions were convened by various state legislatures, including California, Connecticut, Illinois, Maryland,

Michigan, Minnesota, New Jersey, Pennsylvania, Rhode Island, and Wisconsin. Joint resolutions in state legislatures generally called for the appointment of a special committee "to study cults and similar movements." In the New York Assembly, a bill was even introduced, although never enacted into law, to amend the state's penal codes so as to make "promoting a pseudo religious cult" a felony.[43]

There are many reasons behind the political appeals for government investigations of new religions in America. Charges of tax abuses are leveled at unpopular religious groups by persons in both the public and private sectors. Alleged acts of coercion, subversion, and violence are made the basis of the necessity for government action against unpopular new religions, many of which are seen as undermining the laws and morals of the country. Substantial pressure is repeatedly put on lawmakers and government officials, from both anguished parents of converts to the new religions and irate citizens intolerant of new religions in conflict with secular interests, to investigate and regulate the activities of religions that advocate unconventional beliefs and practices not in harmony with traditional societal norms and teachings of mainline religious denominations. Ironically, the demands for government investigations of the new religions in the late 1970s came at the very time of repeated government intrusions into the internal affairs of mainline churches themselves, intrusions the churches met with almost uniform resistance.[44]

Government hearings and investigations of any particular religious group or groups raise serious First Amendment issues. This is not because religious groups, new or old, are to be free from appropriate forms of scrutiny by government. If, for example, the Internal Revenue Service has, in the language of the courts, "probable cause" to believe that a religious organization has unreported income from the operation of an unrelated business enterprise, under §512 of the Internal Revenue Code of 1954 the Service may require the organization to account for the suspect income. Similarly, when a religious group is alleged to have violated any civil or criminal law, it is in the same position as any other group, for no religion enjoys immunity from legal prosecution when it violates any law. Here again, however, government can only act on "probable cause," which the United States Supreme Court has said, in *Draper* v. *United States* (1959),[45] "exists where 'the

facts and circumstances within their [the arresting officers']
knowledge and of which they had reasonably trustworthy
information [were] sufficient in themselves to warrant a man
of reasonable caution in the belief that' an offense has been or
is being committed." The government cannot act on the basis
of mere allegations and innuendos and it must not act in a
discrimatory manner.

For government to initiate an investigation of a religious
group without probable cause is to risk a witch hunt and to
violate both the Equal Protection Clause and the Establishment Clause of the First Amendment. To single out any religious group(s) for special government scrutiny, without probable cause, is to discriminate against that religion or group of
religions, a practice the United States Supreme Court has
often and expressly forbidden.[46] Without some compelling
state interest there can be no legitimate government intrusion
into religious affairs, either for purposes of investigation or
regulation.

Nor can government legitimate hearings or investigations
concerning a religious group because its teachings are unconventional or unpopular, any more than it can accept innuendos and unsubstantiated charges against a religious group because hostile citizens (even if a majority) feel that the group
does not share the traditional ethos or values of society. As
Judge John J. Leahy of the New York Supreme Court declared in *People* v. *Angus Murphy and ISKCON, Inc.*, "The
freedom of a religion is not to be abridged because it is
unconventional in beliefs and practices, or because it is approved or disapproved of by the mainstream of society or more
conventional religions."[47] The demand for government intervention when a group supports unpopular causes that conflict
with traditional values, short of violation of the law, is in conflict with the very guarantees that the religion clauses of the
First Amendment are intended to protect. Without verifiable
evidence that a given religion has violated the law, demands
for government investigations of that religion should be denied.

Government action against new and unpopular religions
requires close scrutiny in order to ensure that the First Amendment is applied without discrimination between mainline and
new religions. When government summarily initiates such
action against new religions, defenders of religious liberty
understandably raise their voices in concern. In 1979, for
example, officials from a variety of major church offices in

Washington, D.C. expressed strong opposition to congressional hearings on religious "cults."[48] They represented, among
others, the offices of the Baptist Joint Committee on Public
Affairs, the Lutheran Council in the U.S.A., the National
Council of Churches, the Synagogue Council of America, the
United Methodist Church, and the United Presbyterian
Church in the U.S.A. These officials did so because of their
concern that "all the witnesses scheduled appear[ed] to have
definite positions in support of regulation of 'cult' activity or
efforts to 'deprogram' members of such groups" and because
no strong advocates for religious liberty were represented,
although "vital First Amendment concerns" were, the church
officials said, "at the heart of the debate about so-called
'cults.' " Such a congressional hearing, they warned, is in
danger of becoming a government witch hunt for new religions. Such an investigation without probable cause, they concluded, "can do nothing but inflame the public and obscure
the delicate, complex issues which surround the activities of
[religious] minority groups." Not to be ignored, they argued,
is the chilling effect the holding of such hearings by state or
federal governments would inevitably have on the free exercise of religion.

   With no evidence that a law has been violated, serious constitutional questions are raised whenever government calls for
an investigation of any group(s) that is based on religious
belief. As the Supreme Court declared recently in *Thomas* v.
Review Board (1981), "Only beliefs rooted in religion are protected by the Free Exercise Clause, which, by its terms, gives
special protection to the exercise of religion. The determination of what is a 'religious' belief or practice is more often
than not a difficult and delicate task. . . . However, the resolution of that question is not to turn upon a judicial perception of the particular belief or practice in question; religious
beliefs need not be acceptable, logical, consistent, or comprehensible to others in order to merit First Amendment protection." Any effort, therefore, on the part of government to
control or monitor new religious groups lies beyond the
bounds of legitimate governmental authority. In the words of
J. Stillson Judah: "Although one may express disapproval
concerning some of the proselytizing practices of some of the
new religions, so long as they perform no overt illegal acts, to
censor them by new laws would be a severe blow to religious
freedom of all Americans."[49]

   The widespread practice on the part of public officials of

even referring to the new religions as "cults" raises serious questions of discrimination and the entanglement of government with religion. The very use of the term "cult" arises out of a value judgment that has no place in American law. Actually, the term "cult" is a pejorative word used to denigrate religions other than one's own and is popularly applied to new religions so as to reenforce their deviation from the more socially established religious traditions. Government is not competent and has no authority to judge which religions are churches and which are "cults" or which religions are good and which are bad any more than it can determine which religions are true and which are false.

With the emergence of a strong anti-cult movement in the late sixties, new religions were often charged with employing tactics of "brainwashing" and "mind coercion." The charges have been primarily directed against those new religions that have made substantial numerical gains, such as the Church of Scientology, the Hare Krishna movement, and the Unification Church. In this mounting assault, the new religions are broadly denounced for alienating youthful converts from their parents and the religious traditions of their families. The assault has come from both religious and antireligious sources and from both public and private sectors of American society. The alleged goal of the anti-cult movement has been to restore family ties and traditional social values to converts of the new religions. Abduction and deprogramming have been widely used by parents in an effort to recover their adult children from membership in and from the influence of the new religions.

By definition, deprogramming is the forcible abduction (kidnapping) and "deprogramming" of a religious convert to get him or her to recant and, in most cases, to return to the convert's former religious identity. The permissibility of deprogramming when it has been upheld in the courts has been either by finding not guilty the defendants who were charged with the deprogramming and the abduction or by appointing a family member of the convert as a guardian or conservator with the right of physical custody of the convert. One widely publicized case deserves special mention. On 24 March 1977, a California Superior Court Judge, S. Lee Vavuris, upheld religious deprogramming of five young adults of the Unification Church and placed them in the custody of their parents for thirty days. Judge Vavuris ruled, in effect, that parents do

have rights over their children even after they have reached
majority. He wrote, "The child is the child even though a
parent may be 90 and the child is 60."[50] Later, a California
court of appeals, in *Katz* v. *Superior Court* (1977),[51] found the
provisions of California conservatorships to be unconstitutionally vague and released the five young adults from their parents' custody in the absence of any evidence that any of the
adults could be regarded as incompetent or dangerous. The
court declared its unwillingness to uphold deprogramming
since it would mean "to license kidnapping for the purpose of
thought control." The court ruled that temporary conservatorships violated both the rights of voluntary association and
the free exercise of religion. "In the absence of such actions,"
the court said, "as render the adult believer gravely disabled
as defined in the law of this state, the process of this state
cannot be used to deprive the believer of his freedom of action
and to subject him to involuntary treatment."

Guardianship bills in the form of legislation involving deprogramming have been introduced in Connecticut, Delaware,
Kansas, New York, Ohio, Oregon, and Texas. Increasingly,
the courts have recognized the right of converts to new religions to file suits against deprogrammers for abduction and
assault and battery. Among the successful cases against deprogrammers on behalf of religious converts to the new religions
are: *Mandelkorn* v. *Patrick* (1970),[52] *Baer* v. *Baer* (1978),[53] *Rankin* v. *Howard* (1978),[54] and *Ward* v. *Conner* (1981).[55]

No matter how well intentioned its motives, deprogramming raises fundamental First Amendment issues both with
respect to the Establishment Clause and the Free Exercise
Clause. Basic to religious liberty is the right of any person
voluntarily to join any religious group and thereby to adhere
to any religious beliefs without any legal restraints. Furthermore, no one should be denied the practice of one's religion
so long as no law has been violated or no crime has been
committed. Freedom of belief, to be sure, is legally separate
from the freedom to act on those beliefs; the former is absolute while the latter may be circumscribed, but only circumscribed if government can demonstrate a compelling state interest that cannot be achieved by a less restrictive means.
Meanwhile, the guarantees of the First Amendment must be
fully applicable to all religious groups without discrimination
or political advantage or disadvantage.

For almost two decades, deprogramming has constituted a

serious assault on many of the guarantees of the First Amendment, but nowhere more so than on the right to religious liberty, the right to believe and practice the religion of one's own choosing, a right that is fundamental to the American experience. Deprogramming is predicated on the notion of "mind coercion," a term that remains undefined and unsubstantiated in referring to converts of new and unpopular religions. It should be noted, however, that deprogramming has not been limited to converts to new religions, but has also been employed on converts to older or mainline churches. "The tragedy for many who have been abducted without any due process of law," Judah observed, "has been that deprogramming has been done without any psychological examination, but often on the assumption that conversion to one of the new religions or even to one of the established churches signified the effects of coercive mind control." Unfortunately, "invariably each subject is programmed to believe he or she was coercively mind controlled whether this was true or not."[56]

Any statute designed to legitimize deprogramming and thereby harass, limit, or prohibit any religious belief or permit the use of physical or psychological coercion to cause a recanting of religious belief, as evidenced in recent years by the rash of bills on temporary guardianships introduced in numerous state legislatures, is contrary to the guarantees of the religion clauses of the First Amendment. No government, whether state or federal, can justify using the power and prestige of its legislative branch to encourage distraught parents to violate the religious liberty of their offspring. Deprogramming needs to be seen for what it is, a criminal act against the person. The problem of deprogramming has been exacerbated by the continued introduction of bills into state legislatures providing for court-appointed guardians to protect persons of whatever age from "a substantial behavioral change" resulting from "a systematic course of coercive persuasion," as expressed in a bill submitted recently to the New York Assembly.[57]

Conversions to new and dissenting religions have rarely been greeted with tolerance. Converts to Anabaptism were both feared and ridiculed for their beliefs. Quakers were despised and denigrated by many of the early American colonists. Seventeenth and eighteenth-century Baptists, who constituted a small and disinherited sect, were jailed in Massachusetts and Virginia because they preached a message that did not have the approval of the state. Just as the state was not a competent judge of which religions should be approved in an earlier day, so it is not competent to do so today. Subsequently, the persecution of the Mormons, the vigorous anti-Catholic campaigns by Nativists, and the struggle of Jehovah's Witnesses for religious liberty, as noted earlier, should all provide valuable lessons today toward defending the rights of contemporary new religions in the United States. Unlike many other parts of the world, the United States has no ministry of religious affairs and, therefore, no religion can be required to obtain a "Good Housekeeping" seal of approval from the state in order to enjoy the protection of the First Amendment.

Thus, the presumed right of temporary guardianship over adults, legitimated by state statutes and admittedly aimed at converts to new religions, should be viewed with alarm. Such legislation seriously threatens civil liberties in general and religious liberty in particular. Deprogramming adults through statutory authorization of temporary guardianship, because of a person's conversion to an unconventional or socially unacceptable religious group, is incompatible with the First Amendment—the free exercise of religion, freedom of speech, freedom of press, and freedom of assembly. Anti-conversion legislation simply has no place in a free society.

The anguish of parents over the conversion of their children to alien faiths may be understandable, but parental anguish does not justify the denial of religious liberty to converts who have become estranged from their parents. Every person should be free to affirm, change, or deny his or her religious identity, no matter how unacceptable a given faith may appear to be to one's parents or family. Any use of physical coercion by any religion is subject to the same prosecution any other organization would face. Religion enjoys no exemption from compliance with the civil or criminal laws of the state. Without trustworthy and verifiable evidence, however, mere allegations of possible wrongdoing do not permit any government the right to search or seize religious property, to hold hearings on religious groups, or to appoint temporary guardians for religious adherents.

The denial of religious liberty to any one group is a threat to the religious liberty of all. To abridge the religious rights of any one religious adherent is to imperil the rights of all religious adherents. For this reason, if for no other, no religion can be denied the protection of the First Amendment simply because its beliefs are socially unacceptable or are unconventional. As Harvey Cox has written, "The basic issue is still that of religious freedom. As bizarre as some of the new religious movements may seem . . . (and some of them appear bizarre indeed), it is hard for people to see that oddness or distastefulness has nothing to do with a religious movement's claim to religious freedom. It is precisely *un*popular movements that most need due process of law, the supposition of innocence until proven otherwise, and the protection guaranteed by the Constitution."[58]

Guardianship legislation to justify deprogramming of adults easily becomes a terrorist activity that inhibits the right of religious liberty. Today, vigorous and strong opposition is needed to counter sweeping statutory authority given to the guardianship of adults; such authority gives license to deprogrammers who participate in acts of abduction and involuntary guardianship of adult converts. To sanction, without probable cause, government investigations of new religions and to provide statutory authorization for deprogramming and temporary guardianship of adult converts to new religions are fraught with the dangers of the inevitable erosion of religious liberty and the diminution of a free society.

NOTES

1. Sydney E. Ahlstrom, "From Sinai to the Golden Gate: The Liberation of Religion in the Occident," in *Understanding New Religions*, ed. Jacob Needleman and George Baker (New York: Seabury Press, 1978), 6. There are those, as exemplified by sociologists David G. Bromley and Anson D. Shupe, Jr., who insist that there is no real resurgence of rapidly growing new religions in America. "In fact," they maintain, "there are more such groups existing today than there have been at any other time in our recent history"; David G. Bromley and Anson D. Shupe, Jr., *Strange Gods: The Great American Scare* (Boston: Beacon Press, 1981), 3-4.
2. Quoted in Anson Phelps Stokes, *Church and State in the United States*, 3 vols. (New York: Harper and Brothers, 1950), 1:255.
3. Edwin Scott Gaustad, *Dissent in American Religion* (Chicago: University of Chicago Press, 1973), 8-9.
4. Sydney E. Ahlstrom, *A Religious History of the American People* (New Haven: Yale University Press, 1972), 4.
5. Samuel Eliot Morison, *The Oxford History of the American People* (New York: Oxford University Press, 1965), 68.
6. William Warren Sweet, *Religion in Colonial America* (New York: Charles Scribner's Sons, 1942), 323.
7. Ibid., 334.

8. *Everson* v. *Board of Education*, 330 U.S. 1 (1947).
9. See Sweet, *Religion in Colonial America*, 339.
10. Joseph L. Blau, ed., *Cornerstones of Religious Freedom in America* (New York: Harper and Row, 1964), 84-85.
11. Alvah Hovey, *A Memoir of the Life and Times of the Reverend Isaac Backus* (Boston: Gould and Lincoln, 1858), 205-6; see also Edward F. Humphrey, *Nationalism and Religion in America, 1774-1789* (Boston: Chipman Law Publishing Co., 1924), 331-32.
12. Thomas Jefferson, Bill for Establishing Religious Freedom (1779); see Blau, *Cornerstones of Religious Freedom in America*, 78.
13. Ezra Stiles, *The United States Elevated to Glory and Honour* (New Haven: n.p., 1783).
14. Philip Schaff, *America: A Sketch of the Political, Social, and Religious Character of the United States of North America* (New York: C. Scribner, 1855), 80. Among many of the old-line Protestant clergy, the growth of religious pluralism far beyond mainline Protestants was unsettling. Lyman Beecher observed that "democracy as it rose, included nearly all the minor sects, besides the Sabbath-breakers, rum-sellers, tippling folk, infidels, and ruff-scuff generally, and made a deadly set [?] at us of the Standing Order," quoted in Richard J. Purcell, *Connecticut in Transition: 1775-1818* (Middleton, Conn: Wesleyan University Press, 1963).
15. See Blau, *Cornerstones of Religious Freedom in America*, 78.
16. Edwin Scott Gaustad, *Religious Issues in American History* (New York: Harper & Row, 1968), 246.
17. Leo Pfeffer, *Church, State, and Freedom*, rev. ed. (Boston: Beacon Press, 1967), 616.
18. Quoted in Stokes, *Church and State in the United States*, 2:462.
19. See *Everson* v. *Board of Education*, 330 U.S. 1 (1947), and *McCollum* v. *Board of Education*, 333 U.S. 203 (1948).
20. *Watson* v. *Jones*, 13 Wall. 679 (1872).
21. Leo Pfeffer, "The Legitimation of Marginal Religions in the United States," in *Religious Movements in Contemporary America*, ed. Irving I. Zaretsky and Mark P. Leone (Princeton, N.J.: Princeton University Press, 1974), 9.
22. Ibid., 10.
23. Ahlstrom, "From Sinai to the Garden Gate," 10.
24. *Reynolds* v. *United States*, 98 U.S. 145 (1878). Other cases decided against the Mormons by the United States Supreme Court were *Davis* v. *Beason*, 133 U.S. 333 (1890), and *Church of Jesus Christ of Latter-day Saints* v. *United States*, 136 U.S. 1 (1890). In the former, the Court denied that Mormonism was a religion and, in the latter, the Court upheld congressional acts that voided the charter of the Mormon Church and declared its property forfeited.
25. *Cantwell* v. *Connecticut*, 310 U.S. 296 (1940).
26. *Murdock* v. *Pennsylvania*, 319 U.S. 105 (1943).
27. *Minersville School District* v. *Gobitis*, 310 U.S. 586 (1940).
28. *West Virginia State Board of Education* v. *Barnette*, 319 U.S. 624 (1943).
29. *United States* v. *Ballard*, 322 U.S. 78 (1944).
30. *Prince* v. *Commonwealth of Massachusetts*, 321 U.S. 158 (1944).
31. *Braunfeld* v. *Brown*, 366 U.S. 599 (1961).
32. *Sherbert* v. *Verner*, 374 U.S. 398 (1963).
33. John Richard Burkholder, " 'The Law Knows No Heresy': Marginal Religious Groups and the Courts," in *Religious Movements in Contemporary America*, 36.
34. *Thomas* v. *Review Board*, 450 U.S. 707 (1981).
35. *Cooper* v. *Pate*, 378 U.S. 546 (1964).
36. *Clay* v. *United States*, 403 U.S. 698 (1971).
37. Burkholder, " 'The Law Knows No Heresy,' " 43.
38. *Everson* v. *Board of Education* (1947).
39. *Larson* v. *Valente*, 456 U.S. 228 (1982).
40. *Moon* v. *United States*, 104 S.Ct. 2344 (1984), denying cert. in 718 F.2d 1210.

Massive support for Moon came from a large number and a wide variety of organiza-
tions in the form of *amicus curiae* briefs, perhaps unprecedented in both number and
diversity including: the American Civil Liberties Union; the National Association of
Evangelicals; the National Bar Association; the National Council of Churches of
Christ in the U.S.A.; the Catholic League for Religion and Civil Rights; Church of
Jesus Christ of Latter-day Saints; the American Association of Christian Schools; the
Southern Christian Leadership Conference; the Center for Judicial Studies; and the
Institute for the Study of American Religion. In addition, *amicus curiae* briefs were
submitted by the States of Hawaii, Oregon, and Rhode Island and by Orrin G.
Hatch, chairman of the Subcommittee on the Constitution, United States Senate
Committee on the Judiciary. For complete texts, see Herbert Richardson, ed., *Consti-
tutional Issues in the Case of Rev. Moon: Amicus Briefs Presented to the United States
Supreme Court* (New York: Edwin Mellen Press, 1984).

41. *Washington Post*, 2 December 1978.

42. See *Transcript of Proceeding, Information Meeting on the Cult Phenomenon in the
United States* (Lexington, Mass.: American Family Foundation, Inc., 1979). Three
years earlier, Senator Dole arranged "unofficial" public meetings in Washington,
D.C., 18 February 1976, between representatives of federal agencies, parents, and
"ex-cult" members. These meetings came to be referred to as the "Dole hearings."

43. New York Bill AB 9566-A was introduced by New York Assemblyman Robert
Wertz.

44. As a consequence of this widespread concern, perhaps the most inclusive gathering of religious groups ever assembled in the United States formally convened a conference in February 1981 in Washington, D.C. on "Government Intervention in
Religious Affairs." The sixteen papers presented at the conference were later published. See Dean M. Kelley, *Government Intervention in Religious Affairs* (New York:
Pilgrim Press, 1982). Note, particularly, Sharon L. Worthing, "The Use of Legal
Process for De-Conversion," 165-69.

45. *Draper v. United States*, 352 U.S. 307 (1959).

46. *Everson v. Board of Education* (1947).

47. *People v. Angus Murphy and ISKCON, Inc.*, 98 Misc. 2d 235 and 413. N.Y.
Supp. 2d 540 (1977).

48. From a jointly signed letter sent to Senator Dole and members of the ad hoc
committee, dated 28 January 1979.

49. J. Stillson Judah, "New Religions and Religious Liberty," in *Understanding
New Religions*, 204.

50. *Katz v. Superior Court*, 73 Cal. App. 3d 952, 141 Cal. Rptr. 234, modified, 74
Cal. App. 3d 582 (1977).

51. Ibid.

52. *Mandelkorn v. Patrick*, 359 F.Supp. 692 (1973).

53. *Baer v. Baer*, 450 F.Supp. 481 (N.D.Cal. 1978).

54. *Rankin v. Harvard*, 457 F.Supp. 70 (1978).

55. *Ward v. Conner*, No. 80-1336, 50 U.S.L.W. 2111 (4th Cir., Aug. 1981).

56. Judah, "New Religions and Religious Liberty," 205.

57. Out of the growing volume of literature on deprogramming, see Dean M. Kelley, "Deprogramming and Religious Liberty," *The Civil Liberties Review* 4 (July/Au-
gust 1977):23-33; John E. LeMoult, "Deprogramming Members of Religious Sects,"
Fordham Law Review (March 1978):599-640; Anson D. Shupe, Jr. and David G.
Bromley, *The New Vigilantes: Deprogrammers, Anti-Cultists, and the New Religions*,
Sage Library of Social Research, vol. 113 (Beverly Hills, Calif.: Sage Publications,
1980); David G. Bromley and James T. Richardson, eds., *The Brainwashing/Depro-
gramming Controversy: Sociological, Psychological, Legal and Historical Perspectives*, Studies
in Religion and Society, vol. 5 (New York: Edwin Mellen Press, 1983).

58. Cox, "Introduction," *Strange Gods: The Great American Scare*, xii.

The State and the
Christian Day School

JAMES C. CARPER and NEAL E. DEVINS

Since the mid-1960s, and particularly during the last decade, evangelical Protestants and their churches, only a few of which are affiliated with mainline denominations, have been founding Christian day schools at an unprecedented rate. The growth of these institutions, though more robust in the West and the South, is clearly a national phenomenon. Not only do these schools currently constitute the most rapidly expanding segment of formal education in the United States, but they also represent the first *widespread* secession from the public school pattern since the establishment of Catholic schools in the nineteenth century.[1]

Due to the unorganized, grass-roots growth of the Christian day schools and the refusal of some of these institutions to either join one of the national Christian school associations or report enrollment figures to government agencies, there is considerable variation in the estimates of the number of schools and their enrollment. On the basis of the best available data, it seems reasonable to estimate that between eight and ten thousand of these schools have been established since 1965, with a current student population of approximately 1 million (kindergarten through twelfth grade).[2]

Accompanying the proliferation of Christian day schools and the explicit repudiation of public education they represent, there has been a growing controversy concerning whether and to what extent the state should regulate these institutions. While Catholic, Jewish, and other Protestant schools generally abide by state accreditation requirements, some Christian day schools argue that to comply with certain state-prescribed "minimum standards" and licensing procedures would violate their religious convictions. These schools and parents who send their children to them maintain that the Free Exercise Clause of the First Amendment exempts them from submitting to regulations that they deem objectionable on religious grounds. Furthermore, Christian day school officials also claim that state regulations violate the Fourteenth

Amendment right of parents to direct their children's upbringing and the First Amendment's prohibition of government efforts to "establish" religion. Christian day schools,
they conclude, need not comply with expansive state procedures that govern the content of Christian education.[3]

State authorities, however, assert their right to impose
"reasonable" regulations on religious schools in order to
ensure that every child in the state receives an adequate education.[4] These officials contend that existing regulations are
both necessary and unobtrusive. As far as the state is concerned, institutions that do not conform to these regulations
are not schools. Therefore, parents sending their children to
them are not in compliance with compulsory school attendance laws and, therefore, subject to prosecution.[5] Additionally,
the state contends that it can prohibit these "schools" from
continued operation.[6] During the past ten years, these conflicting assertions of state interest in education and First
Amendment rights have bred significant litigation in at least a
dozen states, and legislative action in several others.

THE CONTROVERSY

The dispute between these Christian school educators and
the state pits the educators' belief that education is inherently
religious against the state's contention that its regulatory
scheme is a necessary means to ensure that every child in the
state receives an adequate education. This controversy has
been played out in negotiations between Christian day school
educators and state education officials, in the halls of the state
legislatures, and, finally, in the courts. In fact, it is not unusual for controversy to be spread over these three domains for
the strategy of Christian educators is often "negotiate, legislate, litigate."[7]

The belief of Christian day school supporters in the religious nature of education manifests itself in their refusal to
comply with the broad-based regulations that allegedly would
make the state "lord over their schools." Additionally, they
view many of the regulations as antithetical to quality education.

The basis of the religious-based objection to state regulations is twofold. First, these Christian day school advocates
believe that the state educational bureaucracy is hostile to the
religious mission of their schools. In support of this contention, they allege that the educational bureaucracy has been

unduly influenced by anti-Christian thinkers.[8] Christian educators thus believe that when the state uses its regulatory
power to make private schools like public schools, it is more
difficult for Christian schools to fulfill their religious mission.

The second reason that these Christian educators refuse to
follow many state regulations is that they view their schools as
God's property. For them to concede that the state has ultimate authority to regulate their schools would breach the
New Testament command to "render, therefore, to Caesar the
things that are Caesar's and to God the things that are
God's."[9]

These Christian educators, in addition to these religious-
based claims, also contend that many state regulations serve
no useful educational purpose. To support this claim, they
point to the fact that their students generally perform as well
or better on nationally recognized achievement tests than their
public school counterparts.[10] This contention, as shall be
demonstrated, is significant since Free Exercise Clause analysis demands that the state prove that its regulatory scheme is
the least restrictive means available to achieve some compelling state interest.

Education is one of a state's most compelling responsibilities. The state's interest in education was noted by the great
educational reformer, Horace Mann, who asserted that "the
true business of the schoolroom connects itself, and becomes
identical, with the great interest of society."[11] In a similar
view, the Supreme Court noted in *Brown* v. *Board of Education:* "Today, education is perhaps the most important function of the state and local government. Compulsory school
attendance laws and the great expenditures for education
demonstrate our recognition of the importance of education to
our democratic society. . . . In these days, it is doubtful that
any child may reasonably be expected to succeed in life if he
is denied the opportunity to an education."[12] The centrality of
the state's interest in ensuring the provision of an adequate
education to all youngsters vests in the state the authority to
establish reasonable regulations governing both public and
private schools.

The Christian day school issue raises the question of what
kinds of rules and regulations serve a valuable educational
function. There is little doubt as to the sensibility of core curriculum requirements (reading, writing, and computation) and
fire, health, and safety standards. More controversial, how-

ever, are broad curriculum, teacher certification, and licensing requirements, which many Christian day school officials assert bear no rational relationship to the quality of education.[13]

THE PATH TO THE COURTHOUSE

When the state's interest in education conflicts with Christian day school advocates' religious convictions, the general strategy of these educators is one of negotiation, legislation, and, if all else fails, litigation.[14] The issue of state accreditation of Christian day schools in Maine provides a prime example of this strategy.

In Maine, Christian educators were represented by a statewide organization called the Maine Association of Christian Schools (MACS). MACS, after unsuccessful negotiations with state department of education officials, proposed House Bill 1817 in the 1980 state legislature. This legislative proposal was intended to address two issues of general concern to MACS member schools: state teacher certification and licensing requirements.

In introducing this bill, MACS described their purposes as follows: "The present law requires that all schools be approved by [the state], including church-operated schools. Because our church schools are integral, inseparable ministries of our churches, in approving our schools the [state] is, in effect, approving our churches."[15] To rectify this situation, Bill 1817 would have permitted church-affiliated schools to exempt themselves from state approval procedures merely by informing the Commissioner of Education that approval procedures conflict with religious beliefs.

MACS backed their legislative proposal in several ways. First, MACS provided state legislators with information about their cause. Second, they sought news media exposure. Third, constituents of their member churches wrote letters and made phone calls to their area legislators in support of the proposal. Fourth, MACS arranged for educators, lawyers, and law professors to testify in favor of their proposal. Finally, MACS sought to enter into a compromise legislative proposal to garner additional support for their bill. Despite all this, a modified version of 1817 was defeated in the state legislature.

Following this defeat, MACS felt compelled to seek recourse through the courts. In October 1981, the Association brought a declaratory action against the state in an attempt to have Maine's school approval law declared unconstitutional.

In December 1983, U.S. District Court Judge Conrad Cyr ruled in *Bangor Baptist Church* v. *State* that Maine education officials were without statutory authority to close down unapproved schools.[16]

In several other states negotiation precluded judicial proceedings. In 1981, for example, Christian school administrators persuaded the Colorado Board of Education to lay aside proposed regulations placing Christian day schools under the jurisdiction of local public school districts. Negotiation also proved fruitful in Iowa, where state officials agreed to accept attendance reports from parents rather than the challenged practice of demanding such reports directly from several Christian day schools.[17]

The question of state regulation of Christian day schools has also been the focus of considerable legislative activity since the late 1970s. In 1979, for instance, the North Carolina legislature rendered moot an ongoing legal proceeding against several Christian schools by effectively deregulating religious educational institutions. Taking unprecedented action, the legislature repealed all state regulation except for health, safety, and attendance reporting requirements, and mandated instead school-selected standardized skills and competency tests for students at various grade levels (often called "proof in the pudding standards").[18] Other state legislatures have followed suit. In 1982 and 1983, Alabama, Arizona, Vermont, and West Virginia exempted religious schools from licensing, teacher certification, and curriculum requirements.[19]

Efforts on the part of Christian day school officials to obtain legislative relief from requirements that they believe either burden free exercise of religion or entangle the state in religious affairs have not always succeeded. During recent legislative sessions in Illinois, Pennsylvania, Iowa, and Michigan, bills designed to reduce state control of religious schools were introduced but not enacted. When such efforts fail, only one avenue remains open to those who object to the state's regulatory scheme—the courts.[20]

ISSUES BEFORE THE COURT

The right of parental control. The rights of parents to direct the upbringing of their children date back to *Meyer* v. *Nebraska*,[21] a 1923 Supreme Court decision involving Nebraska's requirement that English be the language of instruction in *all* schools in the state through the eighth grade. Under this reg-

ulation, a private school teacher had been held criminally cul-
pable for teaching German to an elementary school student.
The Court found the regulation unconstitutional because, "[a
teacher's] right to teach and the right of parents to engage
him to instruct their children . . . are within the liberty of the
[fourteenth] amendment."[22]

Expanding on *Meyer*, the 1925 Supreme Court decision in
Pierce v. *Society of Sisters*[23] held unconstitutional an Oregon
statute that mandated that all children attend public school.
The Court ruled that the state could not outlaw private
schooling: "The fundamental theory of liberty upon which all
governments in this Union repose excludes any general power
of the state to standardize the children by forcing them to
accept instruction from public teachers only. The child is not
the mere creature of the state; those who nurture him and
direct his destiny have the right, coupled with the high duty,
to recognize and prepare him for additional obligations."[24]
The *Pierce* decision, however, did not abridge the authority of
the state to make reasonable regulations governing nonpublic
schools. To the contrary, the Court recognized: "No question
is raised concerning the power of the state reasonably to regulate all schools, to inspect, supervise, and examine them, their
teachers and pupils; to require that all children of proper age
attend some school, that teachers shall be of good moral character and patriotic disposition, that certain studies plainly
essential to good moral character be taught, and that nothing
be taught which is manifestly inimical to the public welfare."[25] Presently, the Supreme Court explicitly recognizes
the constitutionality of reasonable state regulations of private
schools. In the 1976 decision *Runyon* v. *McCrary*,[26] for example, the Court observed that "while parents have a constitutional right to send their children to private schools and . . .
to select private schools that offer specialized instruction, they
have no constitutional right to provide their children with
private school education unfettered by reasonable government
regulation."[27] In other words, "If the State must satisfy its
interest in secular education through the instrument of private
schools, it has a proper interest in the manner in which those
schools perform their secular educational function."[28]

The Free Exercise Clause. The resolution of the conflict
between the Christian day school leaders and the state is
primarily based in the First Amendment Free Exercise
Clause. The Free Exercise Clause prohibits the government

from unnecessarily interfering in religiously-based practices. The Supreme Court has devised a test to determine whether regulation of religiously motivated conduct violates the Free Exercise Clause. This test involves a three-part determination: (1) whether the challenge is motivated by and rooted in a legitimate and sincerely held religious belief; (2) whether and to what extent state regulations burden free exercise rights; and (3) whether any such burden is justified by a sufficiently compelling state interest.[29]

Government regulation that significantly burdens the free exercise of religion cannot withstand constitutional challenge, unless it represents "the least restrictive means of achieving some compelling state interest."[30] The exemption of a religious activity from regulation, however, is not constitutionally required where it would "unduly interfere with the fulfillment of the (compelling) government interest."[31]

The starting point in any Free Exercise Clause analysis is a recognition that although laws cannot interfere with mere religious beliefs and opinions, they may interfere with practices. In *Reynolds* v. *United States*,[32] the Supreme Court explained, in upholding the conviction of a Mormon under a federal antipolygamy statute, that "laws are made for the government of actions, and while they cannot interfere with mere religious belief and opinions, they may with practices."[33] In other words: "The Amendment embraces two concepts, freedom to believe and freedom to act. The first is absolute but, in the nature of things, the second cannot be. Conduct remains subject to regulation for the protection of society. The freedom to act must have appropriate definition to preserve the enforcement of that protection."[34]

Thus, while some degree of government regulation over religious activities is permissible, striking a balance between legitimate governmental regulation and impermissible government dominion is a task that the judiciary confronts. Free Exercise Clause analysis is triggered when some state action infringes upon an individual's right to practice freely his religion.[35]

The line distinguishing permissible from impermissible government conduct that infringes on religious freedom is not clearly drawn.[36] This confusion results from a standard of review in which free exercise litigation is structured so as to grant the fact finder great discretion in determining both the nature of the infringement on religious liberty and whether the state is using the least restrictive means available to it to further some compelling government interest.[37] Under this standard the government clearly cannot justify a particular regulatory scheme by the mere assertion that it has jurisdiction over the subject matter in question. According to Professor Laurence Tribe: "In applying the least intrusive alternative—compelling interest requirement, it is crucial to avoid the error of equating the state's interest in denying an exemption with the state's usually much greater interest in maintaining the underlying rule of program for unexceptional cases. Only the first interest—that in denying an exemption—is constitutionally relevant when an exemption is sought."[38]

The ultimate issue in distinguishing permissible from impermissible government action is the degree of proof required in applying the free exercise test.[39] If the government need only demonstrate that its regulation is arguably the least restrictive means available to achieve some compelling government interest, the state will have considerable discretion in promulgating regulations that have an impact on religious freedom. If the government must introduce "clear and convincing" evidence that its regulatory scheme satisfied the least restrictive means compelling interest standard, however, the state will be forced to act very cautiously when it promulgates regulations that have an impact on religious liberty interest.[40]

The Establishment Clause. In addition to the Free Exercise Clause, many Christian school lawsuits involve Establishment Clause challenges to state regulations. The Establishment Clause, in part, bars the state from fostering an excessive governmental entanglement with religion.[41] In determining whether there is excessive entanglement, the question is "whether particular acts in question are intended to establish or interfere with religious beliefs and practices or have the effect of doing so."[42] For the most part, an unconstitutional entanglement involves "the government's continuing monitoring or potential for regulating the religious activity under scrutiny."[43]

Some degree of governmental entanglement is permissible. Churches, for example, are presently subject to both tax and audit in regard to their business income.[44] Once government involvement has been established, the state must demonstrate that its regulatory scheme meets the least restrictive means compelling interest test.[45] In *Surinach* v. *Pesquera de Busquets*,[46] the Court of Appeals for the First Circuit stated: "In the sensitive area of First Amendment religious freedoms, the burden is upon the state to show that implementation of a regulatory scheme will not ultimately infringe upon and entangle it in the affairs of a religion to an extent to which the Constitution will not countenance."[47]

The entanglement issue, although properly a part of Christian school lawsuits, has not proven to be dispositive in any of these court cases.[48] It is also noteworthy that the Christian Law Association—one of the leading participants in this type of litigation—refuses to let its lawyers raise the entanglement issue, claiming "that an argument against 'excessive' entanglement implies that some entanglement is legal."[49]

Court cases. Lawsuits involving Christian schools and the state have arisen in twelve different areas of regulation, namely: (1) fire, health, and safety; (2) curriculum; (3) textbook selection; (4) instructional time; (5) teacher certification; (6) zoning; (7) consumer protection; (8) student reporting; (9) testing; (10) state licensing; (11) community interaction; and (12) guidance requirements.[50] Among these regulations, the most likely source of controversy between the Christian schools and the state involves programmatic regulations that govern actual teaching practices in nonpublic schools, including curriculum, textbook, and teacher certification.

The courts thus far have been unable to provide consistent guidance either to the states or to the schools involved in state regulation lawsuits. Courts have upheld state procedures in Michigan, North Dakota, Nebraska, Hawaii, Massachusetts, and Iowa. Christian educators have successfully challenged state procedures in Vermont, Ohio, New Hampshire, Kentucky, and Maine. Many of the court decisions on this issue are totally at odds with each other, and this involves decisions from the same court and decisions involving identical regulations—all applying the "same" legal standards.[51]

The most striking example of the inconsistency of judicial rule-making on the Christian school issue concerns varying judicial perceptions of teacher certification requirements. In *Kentucky State Board* v. *Rudasill*,[52] the Kentucky Supreme Court held the state's certification requirement unconstitutional. The court asserted: "It cannot be said as an absolute that a teacher in a nonpublic school . . . will be unable to instruct children to become intelligent citizens. . . . The receipt of 'a bachelor's degree from a standard college or university' . . . is not a sine qua non the absence of which establishes that private and parochial school teachers are unable to teach their students to intelligently exercise their elective franchise."[53] Similarly, in *State* v. *Whisner*,[54] the Ohio Supreme Court held unconstitutional a teacher certification requirement. According to the court: "In the face of the record before us, and in light of the expert testimony . . . it is difficult to imagine a state interest of sufficient magnitude to override the interest claiming protection under the free exercise clause. . . .We will not, therefore, attempt to conjure up such an interest in order to sustain application of the 'minimum standards' to these appellants."[55]

In stark contradiction of these two decisions, the Nebraska Supreme Court upheld a teacher certification requirement in *State* v. *Faith Baptist Church*.[56] Here, the court claimed: "We think it cannot be fairly disputed that such a requirement is neither arbitrary nor unreasonable; additionally, we believe it is also a reliable indicator of the probability of success in that particular field. We believe that it goes without saying that the state has a compelling interest in the quality and ability of those who are to teach its young people."[57] The North Dakota Supreme Court, in *State* v. *Shaver*,[58] also upheld a teacher certification law. It noted that:

> . . . courts are ill-equipped to act as school boards and determine the need for discrete aspects of a compulsory school education program. The courtroom is surely not the best arena for the debate of issues of educational policy and the measurement of educational quality. Although North Dakota's minimal requirements for state approval of a private or parochial school may be imperfect, without the regulations the state would have no reasonable assurance that its recognized interest in providing an education for its youth is being protected.[59]

Poor lawyering on the part of some state prosecutors and Christian day school attorneys offers partial explanation for this judicial failure.[60] Varying regulatory schemes are also at issue.[61] More significantly, however, these cases often present courts with an apparently hopeless entanglement of fact, judgment, secular values, and religious convictions.

Despite the inconsistency of the courts in their review of several types of regulations, certain regulations appear clearly constitutional and others appear clearly unconstitutional.[62] Courts will always uphold reasonable student reporting requirements; reasonable fire, health, and safety standards; core curriculum requirements; and regulations governing the number of school days per academic year and length of each school day. Courts, however, will always find unreasonable state efforts to prescribe textbook selection, community interaction requirements, and guidance service requirements. Courts have been inconsistent in their review of regulations that govern teacher certification, zoning, and state licensing as well as expansive curriculum requirements.

Ohio and Nebraska: Examples of Conflicting Resolutions of the Christian Day School Issue

Court decisions on the Christian day school issue frequently provoke strong responses from both the state and Christian educators. There are too many of these "stories" to permit a detailed discussion of each case. Events surrounding decisions by the Ohio and Nebraska Supreme Courts, however, embody many themes common to all these cases and illustrate conflicting approaches to the issues raised by these lawsuits.

In the 1976 *State* v. *Whisner* decision, the Ohio Supreme Court, in upholding the rights of Christian educators, gave careful consideration to a conflict involving state accreditation requirements and free exercise of religion and parental rights. Events leading up to this significant decision commenced in 1973. Before opening Tabernacle Christian School, Pastor Levi Whisner obtained a copy of *Minimum Standards for Ohio Elementary Schools*, which outlined detailed and comprehensive requirements with which all public and private schools had to comply in toto in order to be chartered or licensed by the state. Since Whisner and members of the school board concluded that as a matter of religious principle they could not conform to *all* of the standards, they decided to open the school without applying for a charter. As a result, Whisner and other parents sending their children to Tabernacle Christian School were arrested and prosecuted for violating Ohio's compulsory education law. After being convicted by a state trial court and having those convictions upheld by a court of appeals, they successfully appealed those decisions to the Ohio Supreme Court.[63]

In overruling the lower court decisions, the Ohio Supreme Court first determined that the appellants' religious beliefs were "sincerely held." Noting that in order to sustain a free exercise case, one not only had to demonstrate sincere religious convictions, but also to "show the coercive effect of the enactment as it operates against him in the practice of his religion," the court examined the appellants' objections to minimum standards requiring precise allocation of instructional time (inadequate time for religious training), conformity of all school activities to policies of the local board ("blank check" for state control), and school-community cooperation (abandonment of separated policy). Here, the court agreed that the minimum standards not only burdened the appellants' First Amendment free exercise rights, but also their Ninth and Fourteenth Amendment rights because: "These standards are so pervasive and all-encompassing that total compliance with each and every standard by a nonpublic school would effectively eradicate the distinction between public and nonpublic education, and thereby deprive these appellants of their traditional interest as parents to direct the upbringing and education of their children."[64]

It has been established that the state *may* exert "reasonable" regulation over private schools. When regulations collide with the free exercise of religion, however, the state is obligated to "show more than just a reasonable relation to some valid purpose within its competency." As the *Whisner* Court pointed out, in order to override a free exercise claim, it was incumbent upon the state to demonstrate a "compelling interest" in mandating total compliance to the minimum standards on the part of a religious school. The state, concluded the Court, failed to establish such a compelling interest.[65]

In reversing the lower courts and in effect declaring unconstitutional many of the state's provisions for chartering and regulating independent, religious schools, the Ohio Supreme Court gave strong recognition to parental and free exercise rights and was extremely critical of the state's assumption that its compelling interest in regulation and control was self-evident. Affirming the primacy of these rights, the court noted that when religious liberty conflicts with state interest in regulating education the state is not only required to prove a compelling interest, but is also obligated to employ the *least burdensome* means to satisfy its interest, thus precluding pervasive and all-encompassing regulation. Perhaps as significant as its recognition of the "first order" nature of individual rights vis-à-vis state interests, was the court's observation that a quality education could be obtained at a school that did not conform to the state's minimum standards.[66]

The Ohio situation has been fairly stable since the issuance of the *Whisner* decision in 1976. In 1980, however, the Ohio Supreme Court issued a decision that undercut much of the *Whisner* rationale. This decision, *State ex rel. Nagle* v. *Ohio*,[67] invalidated the conviction of a parent who sent his child to a religious school that did not satisfy pre-*Whisner* regulations. Although claiming to be bound by *Whisner* to reverse the conviction, the Ohio Supreme Court indicated that it would uphold a regulatory scheme that required that "(1) all teachers are legally certified, (2) courses are offered in a prescribed range of secular subjects, and (3) the school is in compliance with all municipal and state health, fire, and safety laws."[68] At present, the *Nagle* decision has not led to a restructuring of Ohio's private school regulations. At the same time, private school interest groups, such as the Ohio Catholic Conference, have encouraged the state to adopt some sort of regulatory scheme. These groups fear that state legislators will change their views, and in turn will be less receptive to aiding private schools.[69]

In 1981, the Nebraska Supreme Court in *State ex rel. Douglas* v. *Faith Baptist Church*[70] considered issues similar to those raised in *Whisner*. Its findings, however, differed considerably. The court upheld the state's regulatory scheme in a strongly worded opinion.

Events leading up to this widely publicized decision and its aftermath date back to 1977 when Faith Baptist Church of Louisville opened a school without state approval. The leadership of the church maintained that "the operation of the school is simply an extension of the ministry of the church, over which the State of Nebraska has no authority to approve or accredit." Asserting that the state has no "right to inspect God's property," Pastor Everett Sileven and the church officers refused to (1) provide a list of the students enrolled in the school; (2) seek approval for the educational program; (3) employ certified teachers; and (4) seek approval to operate the institution.[71] The state sought to enjoin the operation of the school because of noncompliance with state regulations. A lower state court ruled in favor of the state. The defendants then appealed to the Nebraska Supreme Court.

The Nebraska Supreme Court focused on the claim that the accreditation process violated free exercise and parental rights. Though acknowledging that the defendants' educational practice was of less than two years' duration, the court assumed, with some reservation, the sincerity of their convictions concerning their religious education independent of state control. The court, however, concentrated its attention on the state's compelling interest in education. The court asserted that the

state's teacher certification and curriculum approval requirements were minimal, that testing alone could not protect the
state's interest in education, and that the state had the power
to impose "reasonable regulations for the control and duration
of basic education." In rather terse language the court concluded: "The refusal of the defendants to comply with the
compulsory education laws of the State of Nebraska as applied
in this case is an arbitrary and unreasonable attempt to thwart
the legitimate, reasonable, and compelling interests of the
State in carrying out its educational obligations, under a claim
of religious freedom."[72]

The *Faith Baptist* holding was, in part, a result of the
inability of the church's lawyers to introduce evidence into
the trial record that supported their claims.[73] Considering the
record, and the often quasi-anarchistic position taken by Faith
Baptist, several Christian day school supporters urged Sileven
not to risk appealing the decision to the United States Supreme
Court. These individuals believed that if the high court heard
the case it would uphold the state and, thus, set a "disastrous"
constitutional precedent.[74] An appeal was filed, however. In
October 1981, the Supreme Court dismissed the appeal for
lack of a substantial federal question.[75]

The aftermath of the Nebraska Supreme Court decision,
however, has drawn more attention than the nearly three
years of litigation. Since the school could no longer lawfully
operate in Nebraska, it operated both in an Iowa church and
"underground" in Nebraska until January 1982 when Sileven
reopened the school at Faith Baptist Church. Refusing to
close the institution because of his religious convictions, he
was sentenced in February 1982 to four months in jail for
contempt of court. He was released in early March after the
church voted to close the school. Two weeks later, however,
the school was reopened. Though no legal action was taken
during the few weeks remaining in the school year, Sileven
was warned not to open the unapproved school in the fall. In
the meantime, the Nebraska legislature considered, but ultimately rejected, proposed legislation deregulating Faith Christian and similar schools.[76]

When Faith Christian School reopened in August without
state approval, Sileven was arrested and returned to jail to
complete the contempt of court sentence. To prevent continued operation of the school, the state, in October 1982, padlocked the church on weekdays. This, however, precipitated a

protest involving upwards of eight hundred persons. The
school continued to operate under the supervision of a pastor
from Cleveland, Ohio.[77]

Amidst threats of prosecution, Faith Christian School and
as many as twenty-five other "non-approved" institutions
operated throughout 1983. Efforts at compromise during the
fall of 1983 again failed, and in November seven fathers of
Faith Christian students were jailed (and remained jailed until
February 1984) for refusing to answer a judge's questions
concerning the school. Their wives and children then fled the
state to avoid prosecution.[78]

Through all this, Nebraska became the subject of national
publicity, frequently negative, for its jailing of individuals who
acted on the basis of religious conscience. In January 1984,
for example, Jerry Falwell and Jesse Jackson visited, on separate occasions, the Faith Baptist School.[79] Possibly in response
to this publicity and possibly just unwilling to keep jailing
Christian educators, Nebraska Governor Robert Kerry established a four-member panel to examine and report on the public policy questions surrounding the Christian school issue.
On 26 January 1984, the governor's panel issued its report,
concluding, among other things, that "some accommodation
to the First Amendment freedom of religion claims of the
Christian school supporters must be recognized." The panel
thus recommended: "If parents agree, standardized tests could
be offered to students in place of [teacher] certification and
curriculum requirements. Parents choosing that procedure
would give the State a written statement saying that their religious beliefs dictated their choice, and they consent to testing."[80] Interestingly, the panel's conclusions contradicted the
Nebraska Supreme Court's 1981 ruling in the *Faith Baptist*
case.

The state legislature acted on the panel's recommendations
and enacted legislation in April 1984.[81] The new law does not
require schools to provide any information to state officials.
Instead, parents who elect to send their children to a school
that does not apply for state approval must provide the state
with information about the education their children are receiving.

On 16 August 1984, the State Board of Education determined what information they will demand from these parents.[82] Under these procedures, parents, who find existing
state regulations in conflict with their religious beliefs, can

satisfy state compulsory education laws by submitting an
"information statement" that declares that their children
attend school for 175 days a year and that they are instructed
in core curriculum subjects. That, believe it or not, is the
extent of Nebraska's current standards governing these schools—
no teacher certification requirements and no competency
exams.

The Nebraska situation is instructive to an understanding of
the future of Christian day school regulation. Although the
state has a compelling interest in ensuring that children
receive an adequate education, the costs of enforcing expansive regulations are too high. Initially, the state runs the risk
of having its procedures invalidated in the courts. If they win
in the courts, they will face massive resistance by Christian
day school educators. As Nebraska demonstrates, tremendous
pressure is placed on the state through this massive resistance.
In the long run, Christian day school educators will win in a
game of chicken with the state; for whatever wrong Christian
day school educators might be guilty of, it is a wrong that
does not justify the padlocking of churches, the jailing of ministers and parents, or the state's assuming custody of children.
Combined with this, the authority of the state and the soundness of state education regulations are subject to public
scrutiny.

Michigan and Maine: The Future of Christian Day School Litigation

Over the past year, two Christian day school lawsuits of
potentially great national significance appear to have been
resolved. On 20 December 1983, U.S. District Judge Conrad
Cyr ruled in *Bangor Baptist Church* v. *State* that Maine cannot
close church schools that refuse to seek state approval because
of religious conviction.[83] An opposite result, however, was
reached in the *Sheridan Road Baptist Church* v. *State* decision.[84]
On 7 February 1984, the Michigan Court of Appeals upheld
as constitutional state teacher certification and licensing requirements.[85]

The *Bangor Baptist* and *Sheridan Road* cases, when filed,
were of potentially great national significance. These cases
represented the most extensive trial on the religious freedom
issue in the Christian day school context ever to have taken
place. Unlike earlier Christian day school litigation character-

ized by poor lawyering on the part of some state prosecutors and Christian school attorneys, lawyers in *Bangor Baptist* and *Sheridan Road* introduced evidence to support their claims, and raised all possible legal arguments that would support their position. Consequently, these cases promised a more definitive ruling on the Christian day school issue.

The *Bangor Baptist* case also appeared significant because it was the first Christian day school lawsuit to be resolved in the federal court system. All previous Christian day school cases were initiated in state courts. Since federal court opinions are generally accorded more precedential value than out-of-state court decisions, Christian day school attorneys will emphasize their legal victory in Maine in future litigation in other states.

It is important, however, to realize the possible limitation of the *Bangor Baptist* case. Judge Cyr's ruling was based on statutory grounds, not constitutional grounds.[86] Since Maine's statutory scheme varies in significant respects from regulatory schemes of other states, the *Bangor Baptist* decision does not directly repudiate the authority of state officials to promulgate teacher certification, curriculum, and many other types of regulations. Instead, Judge Cyr merely held that Maine education officials were without statutory authority to shut down unaccredited church schools.[87]

Unlike the *Bangor Baptist* case, the *Sheridan Road* court resolved the constitutional issues presented to it. That court upheld—on constitutional grounds—regulations quite similar to those utilized in Maine. For the Michigan Court: "Any burden [that state procedures place on the fundamentalist's religious] beliefs is not constitutionally significant."[88]

The *Sheridan Road* case, despite its ruling on the constitutional issue, may prove of minimal precedential significance. The court deciding the case, the Michigan Court of Appeals, simply is not accorded much deference by other courts. Without a decision by the Michigan Supreme Court (or U.S. Supreme Court), it is unlikely that the *Sheridan Road* decision will sway other courts.

Sheridan Road, however, may set the stage for another high noon showdown between Christian day school educators and the state. Christian educators affected by the *Sheridan Road* decision have publicly stated that under no circumstances will they comply with Michigan's law. What will happen next in Michigan is difficult to predict. Conversations with state attorneys indicate, however, that although the state will seek to enforce its judgment, Michigan does not want another Nebraska-like situation.

Bangor Baptist and *Sheridan Road*, taken together, point to the need for some definitive resolution of the Christian day school issue. Over the past five years, at least twelve state courts have issued decisions on this matter. These decisions as a whole, are quite inconclusive as to the rights and responsibilities of both the state and Christian day school educators. This varied body of court decisions suggests that this issue will likely remain unresolved until the United States Supreme Court addresses this matter.

NOTES

*Portions of this chapter have been adapted from essays that have been or will be published in *Journal of Church and State, Journal of Legislation*, and *Journal of Thought*.

1. For a discussion of the character and context of the Christian day school movement, see James C. Carper, "The Christian Day School," in *Religious Schooling in America*, ed. James C. Carper and Thomas C. Hunt (Birmingham: Religious Education Press, 1984), 110-29.

2. Ibid. See also Bruce S. Cooper, "The Changing Demography of Private Schools," *Education and Urban Society* 16 (August 1984):429-36.

3. Christian educators, for the most part, recognize that the state has the authority to promulgate fire, health, and safety standards as well as prescribe core curriculum requirements. See William B. Ball, "Religious Liberty: New Issues and Past Decisions," in *A Blueprint for Judicial Reform*, ed. Patrick McGuigan and Randall Rader (Washington, D.C.: Free Congress Research and Education Foundation, 1981), 327-49. Some fundamentalists, however, are strict separationists and, thus, refuse to comply with any government regulations. See "The Police Lock a Baptist Church," *Christianity Today*, 12 November 1982, 54-60.

4. The federal government, in an effort to ensure equal educational opportunity, has also placed restrictions on private day school operations. At present, commercial private schools cannot deny admission to a student because of race under the right to contract provision of the Civil Rights Act of 1866. See *Runyon* v. *McCrary*, L127 U.S. 160 (1976); and *Brown* v. *Dade Christian Schools, Inc.*, 556 R.2d 310 (5th Cir. 1977). Additionally, tax-exempt private schools must comply with IRS nondiscrimination standards. See *Bob Jones University* v. *United States*, 103 S.Ct. 2017 (1983). Finally, private schools receiving federal aid must comply with the various nondiscrimination requirements of the 1964 Civil Rights Act.

5. See, for example, *State* v. *LaBarge*, 357 A.2d 121 (Vermont 1976); and *State ex rel. Nagle* v. *Olin*, 64 Ohio St. 2d 341 (1980).

6. See, for example, *State ex rel. Douglas* v. *Faith Baptist Church*, 207 Neb. 802 (1981); and *Kentucky State Board* v. *Rudasill*, 589 S.W. 2d 877 (1979).

7. Interview with Ralph Yarnell, Director, Maine Association of Christian Schools, 10 August 1982.

8. See discussion of John Dewey in John W. Whitehead, *The New Tyranny* (Fort Lauderdale: Coral Ridge, 1982), 14.

9. Matt. 22:21.

10. See, for example, *On Further Examination: Report of the Advisory Panel on the Scholastic Aptitude Test Decline*, College Entrance Examination Board (Princeton, N.J.: College Entrance Examination Board, 1977).

11. Lawrence A. Cremin, ed., *The Republic and the School: Horace Mann on the Education of Free Men* (New York: Teachers College, Columbia University, 1957), 80.

12. *Brown* v. *Board of Education*, 347 U.S. 483, 494 (1954).

13. The effectiveness of state regulation is debated in "State Regulation of Private Schools: Three Views," *Education Week*, 9 November 1983, 18-19, 24. See also Donald A. Erickson, "Bad Fences Make Bad Neighbors: A Look at State Regulation of Private Schools," in *Religious Schooling in America*.

14. See generally, Francis A. Schaeffer, *A Christian Manifesto* (Westchester, Ill.: Crossway Books, 1981).

15. Interview with Ralph Yarnell, Director, Maine Association of Christian Schools, 10 August 1982.

16. *Bangor Baptist Church* v. *State*, 576 F. Supp. 1299 (D. Me. 1983).

17. James C. Carper, "The *Whisner* Decision: A Case Study in State Regulation of Christian Day Schools," *Journal of Church and State* 24 (Spring 1982):301.

18. In stark contrast to this legislative provision, North Carolina prohibits home instruction. For a discussion of legal standards governing the home instruction issue, see Neal Devins, "A Constitutional Right to Home Instruction?" *Washington University Law Quarterly*, forthcoming.

19. Carper, "The *Whisner* Decision," 301. Legislative actions are monitored in *The Briefcase*, a publication of the Christian Law Association, Cleveland, Ohio; *The AACS Newsletter*, a publication of the American Association of Christian Schools, Normal, Illinois; and *Education Week*.

20. Carper, "The *Whisner* Decision,"301. See also "Fundamentalist Schools Defy State Laws," *Church and State* 35 (February 1982):14-15; and Alex Heard, "Church-Related Schools: Resistance to State Control Increases," *Education Week*, 17 February 1982, 1, 10, 18. For a discussion of the legal issues raised in the Christian school controversy, see Neal Devins, "State Regulation of Christian Schools," *Journal of Legislation* 10 (Summer 1983):363-73.

21. *Meyer* v. *Nebraska*, 262 U.S. 390 (1923).

22. Ibid., at 400.

23. *Pierce* v. *Society of Sisters*, 268 U.S. 510 (1925).

24. Ibid., at 535. Expanding upon *Meyer* and *Pierce*, the Supreme Court—in its 1927 *Farrington* v. *Tokushige* decision—held unconstitutional a statute that sought to promote the "Americanism" of pupils attending foreign language schools in the territory of Hawaii; 273 U.S. 284 (1927). This legislation, among other things, empowered the territorial government to prescribe the school's course of study, entrance and attendance qualifications, and textbooks; to require their teachers to satisfy certain standards; and to limit hours of operation and the pupils who may attend them. In invalidating this legislation, the Court noted that "the Japanese parent has the right to direct the education of his own child." Ibid., at 298.

25. *Pierce* v. *Society of Sisters*, at 534.

26. *Runyon* v. *McCrary*, 427 U.S. 160 (1978).

27. Ibid., at 178.

28. *Board of Education* v. *Allen*, 392 U.S. 236, 247 (1968). For discussion of other Supreme Court decisions that have recognized the rights of states to impose reasonable regulations on private schools, see Cynthia West, "The State and Sectarian Education: Regulation to Deregulation," *Duke Law Journal* (1980):801, 811-12, n. 59.

29. See *Wisconsin* v. *Yoder*, 406 U.S. 205, 215 (1972). The Supreme Court has also articulated a slightly different standard to govern free exercise analysis, namely, once a showing has been made that religious practice is burdened by a governmental program, the state must demonstrate both that its regulation furthers some compelling interest and that the regulation is the least restrictive means available for furthering that interest. See *Thomas* v. *Review Board*, 450 U.S. 707, 718 (1981). This essay utilizes this standard.

30. Ibid., at 713.

31. *United States* v. *Lee*, 71 L.Ed.2d 127, 137 (1982).

32. *Reynolds* v. *United States*, 98 U.S. 145 (1878).

33. Ibid., at 166-67.

34. *Cantwell* v. *Connecticut*, 310 U.S. 296, 303-4 (1940).

35. There is some conflict among the federal courts concerning the threshold issue of whether state action interferes with religious practice. The Fifth and Sixth United States Circuit Court of Appeals have suggested that free exercise analysis will be triggered if the belief (1) is clearly expressed in the literature or traditions of religion; and (2) is central to their religion. See *Brown* v. *Dade Christian Schools, Inc.*, 556 F.2d 310 (5th Cir. 1980); and *Sequovah* v. *Tennessee Valley Authority*, 620 F.2d 1159 (6th Cir. 1980). Supreme Court decisions support a less restrictive definition of sincere religious belief. In *United States* v. *Ballard*, the Court held that "the truth or verity of religious doctrines or beliefs" could not be considered by a judge or jury without violating the free exercise clause; 322 U.S. 78, 86 (1944). Similarly, in *Fowler* v. *Rhode Island*, the Court held that "it is not the business of the courts to say what is a religious practice or activity for one group is not religious under the protection of the First Amendment"; 345 U.S. 67, 69-70 (1953).
36. See *Thomas* v. *Review Board*, at 720-27 (Justice Rehnquist dissenting).
37. See Neal Devins, "A Fundamentalist's Right to Education?" *National Law Journal*, 21 February 1983, 13.
38. Laurence Tribe, *American Constitutional Law* (Mineola, N.Y.: Foundation Press, 1978), 855.
39. See Lee Boothby, "Government Entanglement with Religion: What Degree of Proof Is Required?" *Pepperdine Law Review* 7 (October 1980): 613.
40. For a discussion of the "clear and convincing" proof standard, see Devins, "State Regulation of Christian Schools," 377-81.
41. In addition to this prohibition of excessive government entanglement, the Establishment Clause also requires that government action "must reflect a clearly secular legislative purpose . . . [and] must have a primary effect that neither advances nor inhibits religion." *Committee for Public Education and Religious Liberty* v. *Nyquist*, 413 U.S. 756, 773 (1973) (citations omitted). If any prong of this test is violated, a court will invalidate the government program.
42. *Walz* v. *Tax Commission*, 397 U.S. 664, 669 (1970).
43. 549 F. Supp. 1208, 1221 (D.Me. 1982) (Summary judgment denied).
44. See Karla Simon, "The Tax-Exempt Status of Racially Discriminatory Religious Schools," *Tax Law Review* 36 (Summer 1981):507; and Sharon Worthing, "Government Surveillance of Religious Organizations," *Journal of Church and State* 23 (Autumn 1981):551.
45. See *Surinach* v. *Pesquera de Busquets*, 604 F.2d 73, 79-80, (1st Cir. 1979); and *Bangor Baptist Church*, 549 F. Supp. at 1222. See also *Thomas* v. *Review Board;* and *Sherbert* v. *Verner*, 374 U.S. 398 (1963).
46. *Surinach* v. *Pesquera de Busquets.*
47. Ibid., at 75-76. This term the Supreme Court will hear a case, *Grand Rapids School District* v. *Ball,* that may significantly alter the entanglement test.
48. In *Surinach* v. *Pesquera de Busquets,* however, a Catholic school successfully challenged Puerto Rico's extensive consumer protection regulations solely on entanglement grounds. Entanglement concerns, however, do temper Christian lawsuits. Additionally, the entanglement question has proven a source of controversy between attorneys representing Christian school interests.
49. Tom Minnery, "Does David Gibbs Practice Law as Well as He Preaches Church-State Separation?" *Christianity Today*, 10 April 1981, 48.
50. For an inventory of these cases, see Devins, "State Regulation of Christian Schools," 361-62.
51. The Ohio Supreme Court, for example, recognized the propriety of teacher certification and other requirements in the 1980 *State ex rel. Nagle* v. *Olin* decision; 415 N.E. 2d 279 (1980). Four years earlier, however that court invalidated an expansive regulatory scheme that included, among other things, a teacher certification requirement. *State* v. *Whisner*, 351 N.E.2d 750 (1976).
52. See note 6
53. *Kentucky State Board* v. *Rudasill*, at 884.
54. *State* v. *Whisner.*
55. Ibid., at 771.

56. *State ex rel. Douglas* v. *Faith Baptist Church*, 301 N.W.2d 571 (Neb. 1981).
57. Ibid., at 579.
58. *State* v. *Shaver*, 294 N.W.2d 883 (1980).
59. Ibid., at 899-900.
60. The Christian Law Association, which refuses to raise the excessive entangle-ment issue, lost significant cases in Nebraska, North Dakota, and Massachusetts. See Minnery, "Does David Gibbs Practice Law as Well as He Preaches Church-State Separation?" On the state side, courts in Ohio and Michigan have held against the state, in part, because of the failure of government attorneys to introduce evidence that supports their claim. *State* v. *Whisner*, at 771 (1976); and *State* v. *Nobel*, S. 791-0114-A (Allegan Cty., Mich.) slip op. at 8.
61. For a description of state procedures governing the operation of nonpublic schools, see Paul Kinder, "The Regulation and Accreditation of Non-Public Schools in the United States" (Ph.D. diss., University of Missouri at Columbia, 1982). See also Devins, "State Regulation of Christian Schools," 360, n. 67.
62. For a category by category reference to these court decisions, see ibid., 361-62.
63. Carper, "The *Whisner* Decision," 281-93.
64. *State* v. *Whisner*, at 764-70. Four major decisions recognize the primacy of paren-tal authority in the direction of their children's education and circumscribe the state's power in education matters touching on religious conviction. *Meyer* v. *Ne-braska; Pierce* v. *Society of Sisters; Farrington* v. *Tokushige;* and *Wisconsin* v. *Yoder.*
65. Carper, "The *Whisner* Decision," 297-98.
66. Ibid., 298-99. The implementation of new "minimum standards" in Ohio in 1984 may set off another round of negotiation, legislation, and perhaps litigation. See recent issues of the Christian Law Association *Briefcase.*
67. *State ex rel. Nagle* v. *Ohio*, 415 N.E.2d 279 (Ohio 1980).
68. Ibid., at 288.
69. See Letter from Nelson Harper (Executive Secretary for Education, Catholic Conference of Ohio) to Neal Devins, 3 August 1982.
70. See note 56.
71. Ibid., at 571, 573-74. See also Timothy J. Binder, "*Douglas* v. *Faith Baptist Church* Under Constitutional Scrutiny," *Nebraska Law Review* 61 (Spring 1982):77-81.
72. *State ex rel. Douglas* v. *Faith Baptist Church*, at 578-82.
73. See Minnery, "Does David Gibbs Practice Law as Well as He Preaches Church-State Separation?"
74. Ibid.
75. "Nebraska Private School Control Stands," *CAPE Outlook*, November 1981, 2.
76. Alex Heard, "Christian School Defies Court Rule, Is Still Operating," *Educa-tion Week*, 3 March 1982, 6. Portions of the commentary on the aftermath of *Faith Baptist* were adapted from a speech by Neal Devins given before the Second Confer-ence on Government Intervention in Religious Affairs, 13 September 1984, New York, New York.
77. Rodney Clapp, "Christian Conviction or Civil Disobedience," *Christianity Today*, 4 March 1983, 27-31.
78. For a comprehensive discussion of recent events in Nebraska, see Randy Frame, "In Nebraska the War Between Church and State Rages On," *Christianity Today*, 17 February 1984, 32-34.
79. In addition to this publicity Nebraska seemed destined to be the subject of fed-eral scrutiny. In December 1983, the Departments of Justice and Education consid-ered intervening in the Nebraska case. Jeremiah O'Leary, "U.S. Keeps Hands Off Nebraska Rhubarb," *Washington Times*, 19 December 1983, 1-A.
80. "The Report of the Governor's Christian School Issue Panel," Lincoln, Ne-braska, 26 January 1984, 2-3.
81. See Cindy Currence, "Sileven v. State of Nebraska: Who Won?" *Education Week*, 23 May 1984, 1.
82. "Nebraska Revises Hiring Rules for Church Schools," *New York Times*, 19 August 1984, 21-A.
83. Maine did not appeal this decision.

84. *Sheridan Road Baptist Church* v. *State*, C.A. No. 69050 slip op. (Cp.App. Mich. 7 Feb. 1984).
85. On 31 August 1984, the Michigan Supreme Court refused to hear the case. The case is now on appeal to the U.S. Supreme Court. It is unlikely, however, that the Supreme Court will grant certiorari to a lower state court opinion.
86. Judge Cyr found controlling the fact that no Maine law "prohibits private schools from operating merely because they are unapproved or refuse to seek or accept approval." 576 F.Supp. at 1320. The judge felt that "if the legislature had meant to ban the operation of unapproved private schools, 'it would have said so in clear and unmistakeable language.' " Ibid., at 1321.
87. Judge Cyr, however, suggested that even if state officials had statutory authority to shut down unaccredited Christian schools, "grave constitutional problems" and "serious constitutional difficulties" would be raised relating to religious liberty, rights to enterprise, and prior restraints on First Amendment grounds to grant the state the right to shut down unaccredited Christian schools without a trial on the merits. Ibid., at 1318.
88. C.A. No. 69050 slip op. (Cp. App. Mich. 7 Feb. 1984), p. 7.

PART 4

GOVERNMENT CHAPLAINCIES
AND MILITARY CONSCRIPTION

Government Chaplaincies and the Separation of Church and State

JOHN M. SWOMLEY, JR.

The military chaplaincy in the United States is not a product of the Constitutional Convention or of the Congress or any other group that considered its church-state implications. Rather, the military chaplaincy evolved in the context of wars against the French and Indians (1755-63) and the War of Independence (1775-81). The churches, particularly in New England, were often the center of community life and the place for community meetings. News of the need for armed men was conveyed through the churches. "Many of the towns' armed men began marching . . . under the lead of their pastor," as Anson Phelps Stokes observed, "so the chaplaincy grew naturally out of local ties between pastor and congregation."[1]

Some chaplains were chosen by the officers; some were appointed by the state legislature, notably in Virginia. Some visited the camps as preachers or evangelists and returned to other duties.[2]

The Constitutional Convention of 1787 had no chaplain. On 28 June 1787, Benjamin Franklin moved that "henceforth prayers imploring the assistance of Heaven, and its blessings on our deliberations, be held in this Assembly every morning before we proceed to business, and that one or more of the clergy of this City be requested to officiate in that service." There was some opposition. James Madison, who recorded this episode, said: "After several unsuccessful attempts for silently postponing the matter by adjourng. the adjournment was at length carried, without any vote on the motion."[3] In April 1789, the House and Senate approved the appointment of chaplains, and there have been government chaplaincies ever since.

James Madison frequently stated his opposition to the use of public funds to pay clergymen both in the Congress and in the armed forces. If the government felt it needed to provide religious services for men far from home, such as on a ship at sea, Madison saw "advantage in a religiously motivated and morally exemplary officer serving effectively instead of a paid ordained chaplain."[4]

Although there were advocates and opponents of government chaplaincies in early American history, such discussions provide no clear guidance whether such chaplaincies violate the constitutional separation of church and state.

When the Constitution was adopted it was understood as a "bill of powers" or a social contract. As the Tenth Amendment asserts, "The powers not delegated to the United States by the Constitution nor prohibited by it to the states, are reserved to the states respectively or to the people." The Constitution gives to the federal government no power or authority to enlist or employ ministers, priests, or rabbis to hold religious services either for military personnel or for civilians employed by the government or otherwise under government care.

A Religious Test

Not only was the government given no power to employ persons for religious duties, it was specifically forbidden to choose personnel on the basis of their religion or to use religious qualifications for such employment. Article VI of the federal Constitution states that "no religious test shall ever be required as a qualification to any office or public trust under the United States." Appointment to the chaplaincy clearly involves religious tests. Certain religious denominations are authorized to sponsor military chaplains, others are not. Chaplains chosen by the military must belong to a Christian church or a Jewish synagogue and be endorsed by those religious bodies. If there were no religious test, lay ministers, atheists, humanists, Hindus, Buddhists, and Muslims could be chaplains on the same basis as they are qualified for employment in any government agency.

In the army, according to a letter from the office of chief of chaplains in June 1941, there were 136 army chaplains chosen from only twenty religious denominations. There were more than twelve hundred reserve chaplains representing about thirty some denominations.[5] In 1941, there were more than two hundred religious denominations.

There are ecclesiastical endorsing agencies through which "the respective religious body provides chaplains to the armed forces and to the Veterans Administration, and sometimes to other federal, as well as state and municipal, institutions."[6]

Even in the case of reserve chaplains ordered into active duty "the respective religious bodies have had to endorse the application of these chaplains for Reserve commissions."[7] The armed forces, therefore, not only use a religious test but require institutional religious endorsement before a minister, priest, or rabbi may qualify as a chaplain.

Normally religious bodies determine their own selection and assignment of clergy, but the armed forces have, for many years, engaged in their own recruiting of chaplains by sending recruiting agents into selected theological schools to recruit students before they have graduated or been approved by their denomination for ordination.

Although clergy must be endorsed by their religious denomination, all clergy are not equally considered. The armed forces have imposed certain educational requirements that make it virtually impossible for those without formal college and theological education to become chaplains. The test for public office is not only religious, but one that tends to exclude smaller denominations that do not require formal or theological education. Lay ministers are also unable to qualify as government chaplains even though a number of churches use lay ministers rather than ordained clergy in their own institutional work.

The armed forces also use a quota system for chaplains. The quotas are based on ratios drawn from the *Yearbook of American Churches.*[8]

An Establishment of Religion

A second constitutional statement that provides a standard for evaluating the military chaplaincy is the Establishment Clause of the First Amendment: "Congress shall make no law respecting an establishment of religion."

The evidence of a military establishment of religion is seen in the following: (1) There is state subsidy of religion through the salaries of chaplains and the financing of chapels. (2) There is state promotion of religious personnel by the armed forces to various officer ranks such as major, colonel, and general. The mere fact that chaplains are officers institutionalizes them. (3) The government publishes religious materials such as hymnbooks. (4) The armed forces have established a religious hierarchy in each branch. In the army, for example, there is a general as the chief of chaplains and a chain of command reaching down to the lowest ranking chaplain. (5)

The "chaplain is a military officer rather than a rabbi, minister, or priest in the military," wrote a Jewish chaplain, Martin
Siegel. "He is subject to military discipline and military ambi-
tion. . . . The chaplain knows that if he ever takes the commandments of God over those of his commanding officer,
whatever effectiveness he might have will quickly disappear."[9]

The following excerpts from the *New York Times* illustrate
some of the "establishment" problems:

Lutheran leaders were warned today against what was described as a tendency within the armed forces to develop a "military church."

The warning was voiced by the Rev. Dr. Engebret O. Midboe, head of
the Bureau of Service to Military Personnel of the National Lutheran
Council.

Dr. Midboe took particular exception to what is known in the armed
forces as the "general Protestant devotional service." This, he charged, has
little if any connection with the doctrine of the civilian denomination with
which the chaplain may be affiliated.

In some instances, he noted, "one would not dare deviate from what has
already been set down for fear that there would be administrative consequences."

Dr. Midboe told the council that a newly arrived chaplain finds himself
confronted with a hymnal published jointly by the three services. At the
same time, the Lutheran official declared, it has "almost become a law" that
chaplains make use of the Component List of Religious Facilities prepared
by a committee of the Joint Chaplain Board.

Some chaplains, Dr. Midboe noted, are faced by command criticism on
the content of their sermons.

"In a day in which churches have been singing their Te Deums to God
for his holy spirit's moving in the hearts of men to bring about a desire for
church unity," Dr. Midboe commented, "there is at the same time taking
place a separation between the service church and the civilian denomination.

"It is not suggested that anyone is maliciously encouraging this schism. It
is rather a general drift away from the denominational moorings into a type
of religious community which seems to operate with the least tension in the
military services."[10]

Robert McAfee Brown reports as evidence of the establishment nature of the chaplaincy that United States chaplains in
Vietnam did not report war crimes or atrocities committed by
officers and soldiers during the Vietnam War. He wrote: "On
an issue of the greatest moral sensitivity on which the representative of the churches could have been expected to speak
forthrightly and prophetically, why were the chaplains so
silent? . . . Why is it that young enlisted men and line officers
have raised the moral issue, rather than the chaplains?"[11]

During the army's campaign for Universal Military Training (UMT) when the churches were solidly opposed to peacetime conscription, the army thought of chaplains as agents for

the military point of view by expecting them to influence the churches to accept UMT. A report issued 12 May 1947 by Col. Patrick J. Ryan, acting chief of chaplains, stated: "Upon the advice of the Legislative and Liaison Division, the Office of Chief of Chaplains sent representatives from each of the Army areas and the Air Defense Command to the Experimental Unit for UMT at Fort Knox, Kentucky, 26-28 April 1947. The purpose of this meeting was to orientate the chaplains on the aims of UMT *so that they may be properly prepared to represent this program to ministerial and denominational conventions as they take place in the United States this year*" (emphasis added).[12] The UMT campaign was not an exception. The *Army Information Digest* pointed out that the "chaplain's activities are centered in six main fields." The first field listed is "public relations."[13]

The establishment of religion in the military is evident also in the way religion is used to bolster political and military goals such as conscription or specific wars. During one of the army's campaigns for peacetime conscription, an army chaplain was quoted in the *New York Post* as saying of military training: "I know of no similar situation where so much can be done spiritually in so short a time for our youth."[14]

The chaplaincy legitimates the military enterprise by giving continuous religious support to the state and its military activity. This is accomplished in various ways, such as scriptural and sermonic support for military discipline, and through linking very closely "religious and politico-military symbols . . . beginning with the symbols worn by the chaplain himself on his uniform."[15]

Prison and other institutional chaplaincies of the government violate the Establishment Clause in that these chaplains receive their pay from the government and serve as members of the staff of the governmental institution. The American Civil Liberties Union notes that "the exercise of pervasive control by federal, state and local correctional officials over the chaplaincy in matters of selection, compensation and scope of duties has resulted in an establishment of religion." The ACLU also said: "The absence of any alternative for the prison population to the state supported chaplaincy, and the prominence accorded religious observances in evaluating a prisoner's success in conforming to the rehabilitative model at the core of the parole process, tends to result in an establishment of religion and to inhibit free exercise."[16]

The Free Exercise of Religion

The chief justification for the military and other nonlegislative governmental chaplaincies is that they are necessary for the free exercise of religion. In *Abington School District* v. *Schempp*, Justice William J. Brennan, in a concurring opinion, referred to the military chaplaincy. He wrote that provisions for such chaplaincy "may be assumed to contravene the Establishment Clause, yet be sustained on constitutional grounds as necessary to secure to the members of the Armed Forces . . . those rights of worship guaranteed under the Free Exercise Clause. Since government has deprived such persons of the opportunity to practice their faith at places of their choice, the argument runs, government may, in order to avoid infringing the free exercises guaranteed, provide substitutes where it requires such persons to be."[17]

The argument that government has deprived persons in the military or in prison or veterans' hospitals of the opportunities to practice their faith is a spurious one if they have access to worship services and to religious counselors. Most persons in the armed forces can attend churches in cities and towns near their post or base. The exceptions to this are ships at sea and combat zones. The navy, however, does not provide chaplains for every small vessel but only for the larger ones. No more than 20 percent of the army in World War II, Korea, and Vietnam were in combat and these were not always at the same time.

Even if it were argued that some chaplains were needed on board ship, it does not follow that an entire system with a chain of command including a general or admiral as chief of chaplains and gradations of rank and pay are necessary for the free exercise of religion. In special circumstances such as ships at sea and war combat zones, the armed forces have provided access by plane to civilian clergy to minister to sailors and soldiers. This can be done on a regular basis as well as during holiday seasons. Lay ministers representing such groups as Christian Scientists and the Mormons have had an effective ministry in combat and on board ship although they have had no status, pay, or rank of chaplains.

It is not correct to say that Protestants in uniform who are members of more than two hundred denominations are freely exercising their religion when the Protestant chaplain selected by the government is a minister of some church they do not want to attend or to join. For example, Southern Baptist or Assembly of God members are not exercising their religious choice when an Episcopalian or Lutheran is their assigned chaplain and vice versa. The assumption that government assignment of chaplains, not the choice of military or prison or hospital personnel, provides for free exercise is itself a violation of the right of free exercise that results when one or two chaplains are the only chaplains for a wide variety of denominational members represented therein. Free exercise is always or almost always denied when government establishes religion in any form.

The American Civil Liberties Union notes that "the process of selecting prison chaplains, favoring organized majority religious groups disproportionately, has resulted in discrimination against the minority and nonconforming beliefs more typical of the prison population and in infringement of prisoners' rights to free exercise of religion."[18]

In *Cruz* v. *Beto*, a Buddhist prisoner, Fred A. Cruz, was deprived of free exercise, such as use of the prison chapel and denial of access to a Buddhist religious adviser. In this and other Texas prisons, the state provided Catholic, Jewish, and Protestant chaplains, Jewish and Christian Bibles, and merit points toward early parole consideration and desirable job assignments as a reward for attending religious services of the major established religions. The United States Supreme Court held that Cruz was denied the free exercise of his religion.[19]

The military chaplain is not free to perform only religious functions. He also serves as a morale officer, citizenship instructor, and so forth, thus confusing or obscuring the purely religious aspect of his work. Many persons prefer to choose a religious adviser or minister who is not at the same time an agent of the armed forces. Similarly, a chaplain who is an employee of the prison system is often suspect as a government agent.

If Justice Brennan is right that the armed forces require chaplains in their work place, presumably other government employees such as those working in the Postal Service, the Department of Agriculture, and in Health or Environmental Protection Agencies also should be required to employ chaplains in their government buildings. The great bulk of those in the armed forces are no more deprived of access to churches of their choice than are other government employees.

Even those soldiers who are sent overseas, against their free choice, to places remote from their own religious house of worship are not essentially different from embassy and other State Department personnel, Peace Corps workers, or other government employees who are sent to other countries.

Randolph N. Jonakait uses an illustration of a Southern Baptist employee working in Ashland, Alabama, who "may be transferred to Sheboygan, Wisconsin, where there may not be a Southern Baptist church. Can the government, instead of requiring the employee to make a choice between his desired religious practices and his job, furnish him with a suitable chaplain in his new location? Unless little is to be left of the establishment clause, the answer must be no."[20]

Some argue that there is a difference between the volunteer and the draftee because the drafted soldier is compelled to enter the armed forces, as convicted persons are forced to enter a prison. The drafted portion of the armed forces, even during the war in Vietnam, was insubstantial, only 17 percent of the total in the armed forces. Jonakait notes the similarity between compulsory military training and compulsory education. School children are required to attend public school and "while they are fulfilling that duty in public school their opportunities for normal religious worship are abridged." The Supreme Court, however, did "not justify an establishment of religion through the institution of prayers and bible readings in the public schools" so that "the presence or absence of coercion" is not the determining factor in establishing a chaplaincy.[21]

Actually, questions of free exercise are civilian questions designed to provide a "civil libertarian" rationale for the chaplaincy. The military rationale for chaplains is that they perform military duties and give religious legitimacy to a brutalizing, death-dealing machine that Willard Waller called "a machine designed for violent action." The "army," he wrote, "must partly annihilate and partly ignore the soldier's private will."[22] There is little doubt that the armed forces would fight to keep the military chaplaincy even if they were convinced that all the religious needs of their members could be met by civilian clergy given access to military posts and bases.

The real issue in the free exercise of religion in the armed forces, prisons, and hospitals is whether there is periodic or regular access to a religious counselor and to religious services. There does not have to be hourly access during the workday or in the workplace by a military chaplain if there is access on weekends or on other occasions when leaves are available. In fixed installations overseas, there can be an American church or churches at or near the base as there is in the Canal Zone or in the United States. In prisons, access can be provided to clergy from the community or to those appointed by religious communities or churches.

The American Civil Liberties Union, after long study of the problem, decided that "adequate provision for the right of free exercise for members of the armed services can be better realized through a constitutionally neutral policy of free access to a minister of the person's denomination, and the ministry's rights, derived therefrom to be present in the military environment."[23]

With respect to prisons, the ACLU, in advocating the abolition of the chaplaincy, said: "The adoption of a policy of free access of the prisoner to a religious or ethical counselor of his or her choice, and recognition of the religious or ethical counselor's right to enter the prison environment to minister to the needs of the prisoner, better accords with the First Amendment's scheme for the preservation of individual religious liberty. . . . Moreover, it will [be] subject to independent scrutiny infringements of individual religious rights which the present system largely institutionalizes and renders immune from such oversight."[24]

There are a number of alternatives to the government-aided and government-controlled chaplaincy in the military, in prisons, and in veterans' hospitals. Among these are religious services over television and radio, the media that millions of elderly citizens use when they cannot go to church. Closed circuit television can be used for religious services or teaching. Other options include civilian religious seminars at appropriate times for those in the armed forces or other institutions who want to attend; visits by civilian ministers, priests, and rabbis; services and counseling by lay ministers who are themselves members of the armed forces. Civilian ministers can be accredited for visits to military bases or prisons in much the same way as press representatives are accredited.

Anson Phelps Stokes in his monumental three-volume study, *Church and State in the United States*, reported that Virginia's system of institutional chaplaincies "carries out the separation of church and state in a stricter way than is customary elsewhere." Religious work in prisons, hospitals, and other institutions is "in charge of a Church body known as

the Interdenominational Religious Work Foundation, supported by eleven denominations. This organization has a full-
time director, assisted by seven staff members who serve as
chaplains at the larger institutions. This paid staff is assisted
by 200 ministers, each giving service in conducting worship
and counseling on one day a month. The organization also
aids prisoners get a new start when they are released."[25] In
brief, the churches provide the chaplains and the state's function is to provide the churches access to the residents of the
institutions.

The key to the free exercise of religion is not an establishment of religion in the form of a government chaplaincy, but
the employees and wards of the state access to religious counselors and services, and religious agencies access to government institutions. Free exercise cannot be guaranteed by an
official chaplaincy or any other establishment of religion.
When religious personnel are chosen by the government and
religious exercises are sponsored by the government, they are
not freely chosen by the individual. They are frequently, if
not usually, drawn from religious traditions other than those
to which the soldier, prisoner, or other ward of the state is
accustomed. The chaplaincy, in other words, violates the
Establishment Clause, the Free Exercise Clause, and the constitutional ban on requiring a religious test for the holding of
any office or position of public trust under the United States.

NOTES

1. Anson Phelps Stokes, *Church and State in the United States*, 3 vols. (New York:
Harper and Brothers, 1950), 1:269.
2. George H. Williams, "The Chaplaincy in the Armed Forces of the United States
of America in Historical and Ecclesiastical Perspective," in *Military Chaplains, From a
Religious Military to a Military Religion*, ed. Harvey G. Cox, Jr. (New York: American
Report Press, 1971), 19.
3. Stokes, *Church and State in the United States*, 1:455.
4. Williams, "The Chaplaincy," 30.
5. Evarts B. Greene, *Religion and the State* (Ithaca, N.Y.: Cornell University Press,
1959), 96-97.
6. *The Chaplain* 29 (Spring 1972):82.
7. Ibid.
8. Williams, "The Chaplaincy," 54.
9. Martin A. Siegel, "Being a Chaplain in Today's Military," in *Military Chaplains*,
110.
10. *New York Times*, 31 January 1957.
11. Robert McAfee Brown, "Military Chaplaincy as Ministry," in *Military Chaplains*, 144.
12. *Conscription News*, 29 May 1947, 4.
13. *Army Information Digest* (Fort Slocum, N.Y.: Department of the Army, 1952).
14. *New York Post*, 16 April 1947.

15. Peter Berger and Daniel Pinard, "Military Religion: An Analysis of Educational Materials Disseminated by Chaplains," in *Military Chaplains*, 91.
16. American Civil Liberties Union Policy Guide, Policy 85. Board Minutes, 27-28 September (hereafter cited as ACLU Policy 85).
17. *Abington School District* v. *Schempp*, 374 U.S. 203 at 297-98 (1963).
18. ACLU Policy 85.
19. *Cruz* v. *Beto*, 405 U.S. 319 (1972).
20. Randolph N. Jonakait, "Is the Military Chaplaincy Constitutional," in *Military Chaplains*, 134.
21. Ibid., 134-35.
22. Willard Waller, *The Veteran Comes Back* (New York: Dryden Press, 1944), 19.
23. ACLU Policy 84 Board Minutes, 17-18 February 1973.
24. ACLU Policy 85.
25. Stokes, *Church and State in the United States*, 3:141.

Conscientious Objection and the Liberal State

KENT GREENAWALT

Despite the advent of a volunteer army in the United States, questions about the treatment of conscientious objectors remain unanswered. Some persons already in the military continue to seek relief from their committed terms of service on the ground that they have developed a conscientious opposition to participation in war; and reintroduction of the draft is distinctly possible. What Congress and the courts should do about claims of exemption from military service thus remains an important public issue. Similar claims are raised against the application of other existing obligations and conditions, including the present obligation of young men to register.[1] Further, issues about conscientious objection illumine general concerns about the interpretation of the religious clauses of the First Amendment.

This essay has highly selective aims. It develops a broad approach to exemptions for conscientious objectors in a modern liberal state, proceeding without reference to the distinctive contribution of constitutional principle.[2] The major practical conclusion is that exemptions should be self-selecting whenever feasible; if accepted, this approach would drastically alter the shape of an exemption from military service.

THE JUSTIFICATION FOR EXEMPTIONS

COMPARISON WITH OTHER EXEMPTIONS FROM LIABILITY

In making an individual's own moral appraisal of a legal duty determine whether he is subject to that duty, exemptions for conscientious objectors differ radically from other privileges conferred by the law. The law contains many justifications for actions that would otherwise be wrongful. Whether these justifications are cast relatively narrowly, however, in terms like self-defense, or much more generally, in terms of a balance of evils, the underlying idea is that the actions covered are regarded as not wrongful in the eyes of the community. The legally critical judgment about wrongfulness is made not by the individual actor but by prior legislative or judicial cate-

gorization or by a jury's or judge's evaluative weighing after
the event.

The law also contains privileges that depend on particular
relationships between the actor and another, and excuses the
actor from what would otherwise be a legal duty; the privilege
of one spouse not to testify against the other is an example.
Again, the critical legal judgment, here about the importance
of the relationships and the privileges that should attach to
them, are made by public representatives rather than the
actor.

Yet another basis for relief from liability is that the actor
was not responsible for what he has done because he was
mentally ill or under duress. Such relief does depend on evaluation of the actor's particular condition, but the determination concerns his ability to comply with the law.

None of these three kinds of defenses to liability, justifications, excuses, and relational privileges permit a person to
interpose his own deliberate judgment about appropriate behavior against the deliberate judgment of the community.
Thus, the appropriateness of these defenses hardly establishes
that exemptions for conscientious objectors are warranted.

CONSCIENTIOUS OBJECTION AND THE PURPOSES OF PUNISHMENT

To understand why such exemptions may be called for, one
needs to examine the forcefulness of justifications for punishment as they apply to conscientious objectors. Many of these
reasons have little or no application to persons who break the
law from a strong sense of moral duty, rather than because
they are pursuing their own advantage or fail to exercise
self-control.

Deterrence and education. A dominant purpose of punishment
is the deterrence of illegal acts. Since a person's course of self-
advantage will rarely include imprisonment, the fear of being
imprisoned may inhibit acts that would otherwise appear prof-
itable. Less directly, concern about harmful consequences
helps people develop self-control over time and may exercise
some restraining influence when destructive impulses are the
strongest.

The firmly convinced conscientious objector is not likely to
be deterred. He believes that suffering very severe consequences is preferable to performing the abhorrent acts that the
law requires. A typical pacifist thinks he should accept his
own execution rather than kill others in war. Perhaps for less

momentous acts one can count as a conscientious objector without believing death to be better than performing the acts, but one would need to believe that accepting more mundane criminal penalities would be better.

This simple point about deterrence does not apply to all those who have a moral objection to performing required acts. For many in this broader class, prescribed penalties can significantly affect their views about morally preferable action. Daniel might believe that his moral obligations to his family outweigh the state's need to conscript him.[3] If the option were between two years of military service or two years at home, he would say his moral duty was to stay home. By removing the option to stay home, criminal penalties drastically alter Daniel's moral equation. He might well conclude that submission to a draft was morally preferable to wasting time in prison.

Even some conscientious objectors are susceptible to deterrence. Not every one of them would actually be willing to suffer death or go to jail rather than join the army. Deterrence can work with genuine conscientious objectors who lack the will to act on their convictions, but it does so at a terrible price. Their feeling that they have yielded to compulsion and violated their most deeply held beliefs and principles will involve profound resentment and loss of self-respect. Such reactions are less likely among persons whose sense of morality of performing an act is influenced by the state's elimination of a possible alternative. Unless these persons believe that the state has no business using coercion in this way, they will not resent it strongly for changing the moral balance. This begins to suggest why individual exemptions from liability, when they are given at all, are granted only to conscientious objectors, not to everyone who has a moral objection to performing a required action.

Serious criminal penalties not only frighten people, they educate them about behavior the community deems to be acceptable. Although existing conscientious objectors are not easily deterred, young people growing up in a society that does not exempt objectors and that does not accord the recognition to autonomy that an exemption reflects may be subtly but substantially influenced against adopting a position that has been placed outside the range of the socially tolerable. Many other factors undoubtedly matter greatly, but a systematic refusal to exempt will affect how many people find themselves opposed in conscience to performing particular legal duties.

Incapacitation. The usefulness of isolating a conscientious objector from society will depend on his crime. If his moral convictions lead to continued violations of the rights of others—say he steals because of a moral conviction that private property is an outrage—then putting him behind bars serves a purpose. If he refuses to perform a single sort of positive act, such as submitting to military service, separating him from society is not needed.

Reform. Whatever the realistic possibilities of criminal punishment reforming the character of offenders in a positive way, that debatable aim of punishment has little relevance for conscientious objectors. Jail is not an apt means for encouraging thoughtful reevaluations of firm moral conviction.

Moral blameworthiness. Ordinarily, serious criminal penalties should be imposed only upon people whose acts occasion substantial moral blame; and, in this respect, the conscientious objector is on a different footing from most other offenders. Rather than seeking to advance his own interests or giving vent to his own impulses in disregard of the legitimate claims of others, he responds to a perceived moral duty, often believing that his refusal to comply will better serve his fellows than would the behavior that the state requires. At least if his underlying beliefs strike sympathetic chords in nonadherents,[4] a conscientious objector will seem morally blameless, or much less to blame than those who break the law in self-interest.

Vengeance. The satisfaction of justified anger may be one legitimate, if subsidiary, purpose of punishment. One who understands the bases for a conscientious objector's refusal to obey a law will not be likely to regard anger as an appropriate response. Perhaps others who are less understanding will feel anger, but the satisfaction of *unjustified* anger should rarely be an aim of criminal penalties.

Fairness and perceived fairness. The fairness of exempting conscientious objectors is somewhat more complex and warrants fuller discussion. If onerous burdens must be borne on behalf of society, a sharing of the burden that is equal in some sense will be most fair, barring some countervailing reason.[5] What exactly will constitute a roughly equal sharing or its closest feasible approximation will often be a subject of intense debate, but one can conceive of universal military service as based on a principle of equal sharing realized in terms of equal contributions of time. Should equal sharing among those capable of rendering service not be possible, a lottery imposing an equal risk would be a second best fair distribution.

If someone is incapable of performing the task that would constitute his share, fairness does not demand a pointless effort to make him perform. The allocation of burdens, however, will be fairer if he is imposed upon in some other way than if he is simply relieved altogether. A system is fairer if persons physically unable to engage in combat are given desk jobs than if they are excused altogether from service.

This general conclusion about fairness applies to conscientious objectors. Their morally grounded unwillingness to contribute may be viewed as making them incapable in a special sense, or at least as making the burden much more onerous for them than for others. Among friends engaged in a common endeavor, say a camping expedition, a person will not be forced to engage in a task he abhors—say killing animals for meat—but other burdens will be allocated in a manner designed to equalize sharing overall. Excusing conscientious objectors is not unfair to those who carry the burden the objectors refuse, but excusing the objectors altogether is less fair than requiring them to bear some roughly equal alternative burden. This principle underlies the rule that those who object only to combatant military service must perform noncombatant duty and the rule that those who object to all military duty must perform alternative civilian service. Since time in jail is a fate most people deem more unpalatable than military service, criminal punishment may itself be viewed as one method of equalizing burdens. A method, however, that conveys harsh condemnation wastes social resources and involves maximum interference with personal liberty is much worse than permitting objectors to make a positive contribution that is alternative to the task they reject.

Those who decide upon systems for allocating burdens must worry about perceived fairness as well as actual fairness. When citizens must bear onerous burdens, their sense that no unfair share is imposed upon them is important. Perhaps some people who submit to the risks and rigors of military service, themselves lacking any options, may not believe any noncriminal alternative task is equally onerous. Their belief that anyone exempted is "getting off too easy" is not by itself a sufficient reason for punishing conscientious objectors as criminals, but the presence of such perceived unfairness is socially undesirable.

Administrability. Concerns about fairness are magnified in any system requiring determinations whether particular persons are conscientious objectors. Ordinarily, some organ of the government must stand ready to say whether a claimant's stated views amount to conscientious objection of the sort that qualifies for an exemption and are sincerely held.[6] Such determinations not only involve some cost, but also risks of inaccuracy. So long as some of those who do not qualify for an exemption have a powerful incentive to seek it, instances of successful fraud will occur, as will instances of mistaken denial to claimants who really do qualify. Faulty determinations reduce the overall fairness of any system of exemptions; and when those compelled to perform the primary task believe that faulty determinations are frequent the system will be perceived as unfair in practice, however fair it may appear in theory.

Summary. This survey of the purposes of punishment and their relevance for conscientious objectors has indicated that certain bases for punishment do apply to conscientious objectors, but that good reasons exist for excusing them from some otherwise common obligations. When objectors are excused from shared burdens, fairness is enhanced by imposing on them some roughly equal burden.

TYPES OF LEGAL REQUIREMENTS AND POSSIBLE EXEMPTIONS FOR CONSCIENTIOUS OBJECTORS

General considerations about punishment obviously do not establish whether an exemption is warranted from any particular legal requirement. Some types of laws lend themselves much more comfortably to that possibility than do others; and an exercise in rough classification can illuminate important differences. Conscientious objectors may be unwilling to comply with four different sorts of standards: (1) rules that protect others directly from harm; (2) rules that impose shared burdens, like taxes or military service; (3) rules that protect actors from doing harm to themselves; and (4) rules that establish conditions for the receipt of benefits or the acquisition of licenses or privileges.

RULES PROTECTING OTHERS DIRECTLY FROM HARM

Reflection on laws protecting life, liberty, and property

quickly reveals why no universal principle of exemption for conscientious objectors would be appropriate. One may face some initial difficulty understanding what conscientious objection even means in this context. Almost no one thinks he is bound in conscience constantly to violate particular legal rights of other people, but a person may feel bound in conscience to violate such rights on particular occasions. For example, a person might think God has ordered him to kill a heretic or that family honor demands personal vengeance. Societies cannot afford to excuse persons who inflict injuries out of conviction. Civil law properly does not take account of idiosyncratic moral perceptions when it imposes the cost of injuries on the person who intentionally causes them. Criminal law properly declines to sacrifice maximum possible deterrence and educational effect by exempting classes of persons who violate the rights of others.

If this point seems obvious in respect to violations of personal rights, it may seem less so when violations of the "rights" of the government and large private organizations are involved. Conceivably people who trespass on public or corporate property could be excused if they act out of conscience. Deciding whether persons with some point to make feel bound in conscience to make it at a single place and time, however, will usually be very difficult. Further, if it is assumed that trespassers may be forcibly removed from property, exempting objectors from criminal punishment would create an anomaly. As soon as they were released, having established the basis for their exemption, they could return to the property to recommence their trespassing.[7] Though more might be said about this problem, it is assumed that even for such violations no exception based on conscience is appropriate.[8]

Another possible exception to the principle that no exemptions should be given from rules that protect others directly from harm concerns violations of duties of care by actors who seek the welfare of those to whom the duties are owed. Some parents refuse to procure medical treatment for their children because they believe that such treatment is less efficacious than spiritual healing, or will jeopardize the child's immortal soul. Even if one grants that the state should ensure appropriate medical treatment for children when it can, the appropriateness of imposing criminal liability on parents who fail to fulfill their duty of care does not follow. Perhaps the propensity of some people to accept bizarre ideas about what is good for them and their loved ones is so great that the law must, for educative purposes, insist on uniform minimal standards of appropriate physical treatment. Parents have such an intense concern for the physical welfare of their children, however, that an exemption for those with strong convictions against medical treatment may promote little imitation.

RULES IMPOSING SHARED BURDENS

Because refusals to comply do not directly violate the rights of others and because alternative tasks are usually possible, laws imposing shared burdens are more apt candidates for exemptions than laws forbidding infliction of harm. When some people conscientiously refuse to perform burdens, like taxes, jury duty, or military service, their share must be borne by others or the total amount of benefits will be slightly reduced. Increased shares of burdens or reduced benefits may be spread among all participants or borne by particular individuals, who, for example, may be called to serve only because conscientious objectors have declined to serve. Even in the latter instance, the individual called will have no right to be free of the burden; and, ordinarily, he will not identify himself as one who has replaced a conscientious objector. In any event, so long as conscientious objectors would go to jail rather than perform, a perfectly administered exemption itself does not affect what others must do; either someone else would end up performing the objector's share or benefits would be reduced. Since a belief that one should never perform an act may be established more easily than a belief that one must perform a certain act on a particular occasion, identifying conscientious objectors will generally be simpler when the government requires acts than when it prohibits acts.

If the law imposes a duty not to infringe the rights of others, no alternative restraint or action can offset a violation; but performance of alternative acts is a way for conscientious objectors to bear burdens equal to those carried by persons who comply with rules imposing shared responsibilities. Finally, a person's claim against being enlisted by society to do what he finds abhorrent may simply be more powerful than his claim to perform some act he thinks is right but which society deems wrongful.[9]

PATERNALISTIC LAWS

Some laws, such as those forbidding the use of drugs, are mainly designed to protect the persons whose acts are forbidden; since violation of these laws affects other persons only indirectly, generous acknowledgment of conscientious objection may seem apt. This conclusion about paternalistic laws, however, would be too hasty. Most paternalistic legislation would not be adopted unless substantial numbers of people wanted to perform the forbidden acts. Those who wish to perform the acts typically will regard them as not dangerous or harmful,[10] and often will feel the government has no business forbidding them. Were everybody to be given an exemption because they believed that they have a moral right to engage in such acts, prohibitive legislation would have little point. Strong beliefs about rights to perform self-regarding acts are indeed a very good reason for legislatures to forego paternalistic measures. Once the judgment is made that legislation is valuable enough to override this consideration, however, no broad exemption will appear warranted. Whether some narrow exemption can be justified and formulated in an administrable manner depends on the particular subject involved.

RULES ESTABLISHING CONDITIONS FOR BENEFITS AND PRIVILEGES

Conditions on benefits, such as workmen's compensation, and privileges, such as driving, do not pose the same direct conflict between law and conscience as do the three kinds of rules just discussed. Willingness to work on Saturday may be a prerequisite for receiving public money, but one who objects to Saturday work has the option of simply giving up the benefits. From this perspective, the need for an exemption for conscientious objectors appears less strong. Some benefits and privileges are very important to people, however, and granting them to objectors harms no one.[11] Unless the condition that the objector will not perform is generally regarded as onerous, attempted fraud will be minimal; and the objector's failure to satisfy a condition ordinarily will not leave any burden to be borne by someone else. For these reasons, the state interest in denying an exemption will usually be less great than in respect to other sorts of rules.

THE SCOPE OF EXEMPTIONS—THE PLACE OF RELIGION

The discussion so far has suggested that even when an exception is appropriate, it should not be extended to everyone who has any sort of moral objection to performing the acts required by law. Immunity should not ordinarily be extended to those whose moral judgment about what they should do will be sharply altered if an unpleasant consequence follows noncompliance.[12] This essay has proceeded on the assumption that if an exemption is to be granted to a class of persons, the class should be cast in terms of conscientious objectors. As will be seen, that assumption needs revision for some contexts; but the question addressed here is the possible role "religion" might play in defining the eligible class. Of course, if every conscientious claim is automatically regarded as "religious" in some broad sense,[13] the question loses importance, but religion is discussed here in a narrower sense that would not include all conscientious claims.

The focus in this essay is on a modern liberal state. Though the author confesses to being disturbed by the growing secularization of much of American society and to the divorce between religious conviction and attitudes toward politics and law may rightly be considered matters of concern,[14] nonetheless, this essay takes as a starting point that a liberal state, composed of people with widely diverse religious beliefs, should not have as a purpose the promotion of any particular religion or the promotion of religion in general as compared with nonreligion. Such a state should not make the judgment that a belief is better or more accurate simply because it has some religious underpinning. If these premises are granted, the connection of a belief to religion does not in and of itself confer any special claim to be accommodated.[15]

Despite this conclusion, religion, judged in terms of an individual's beliefs or his membership in a religious denomination, might play a role in how exemptions are formulated and administered. Conceivably, only persons with some religious identity would be thought likely to have a particular kind of conscientious objection, say to receiving a vaccination, and an exemption might be restricted to them on this ground. Or, nonreligious objectors might be barred from an exemption on the basis that those with religious scruples have, in some psychological sense, stronger reasons not to perform than they do. Even were it assumed that some nonreligious persons had objections as powerful as some deriving from religious belief, they might be excluded to minimize problems of accurate administration and perceived unfairness. Finally, were an exemption cast in other than religious terms, religious ties might still be used as evidence of sincerity and as a means of construing the views of inarticulate claimants.

Applying the General Considerations

It remains now to address some particular problems concerning conscientious objection and to try to propose their appropriate resolution by applying the principles thus far suggested.

MILITARY SERVICE

The problem of exemptions from compulsory military service has understandably dominated discussion of conscientious objection. The demand that people stand ready to kill others and to sacrifice their own lives is the most severe demand a society can place on its citizens. The first part of that demand, the readiness to kill others, is in tension with the Christian religious tradition that has largely underlain American culture. That is not to say that most Christians at any time in the country's history have believed killing in war is morally wrong, only that the perfectionist ethics of the gospels and the pacifist inclinations of the early church pose a serious question about whether such killing can be justified. Throughout American history some Christian groups have been pacifist, and their pacifist views have been thought worthy of some accommodation.

If compulsory military service is ever reintroduced, a sharp break with the traditional approach to conscientious objection is called for. What is needed is a self-selecting alternative to military duty. This essay will defend and amplify that position, but first there is need to examine how an exemption should be cast if the traditional approach, which requires proof of eligibility, is followed. This discussion has significance partly because such an approach may continue to be used,[16] and it has significance partly because some exemptions in other areas must necessarily demand proof of eligibility. The main reason for engaging in this exercise is to demonstrate how troublesome drawing eligibility lines in respect to military service can be and, thus, to promote receptivity to a radically different treatment of the problem.

An exemption with limited eligibility. The requirement that a person need be a conscientious objector in order to be exempt from military service has not occasioned controversy; and it will be assumed that an exemption for which one must qualify should not be extended to those who have "weaker" objections to performing military service. It will also be assumed that an exemption is properly tailored to the scope of the objection, that one who objects only to combatant military service should be given noncombatant military service, and that only those who object to all military service should be wholly exempt. The troublesome questions are concerned with whether the exemption must be grounded in religious belief or whether it should be restricted essentially to pacifists.[17]

A religious criterion for eligibility could be cast in terms of personal belief or membership in a pacifist sect. Though eligibility for an exemption from combatant military service was limited in the United States as recently as World War I to members of pacifist churches, few would now suggest reversion to that position. Some traditionally pacifist groups, notably the Society of Friends, have such a wide diversity of beliefs that one's membership in this group is hardly an assurance of his pacifism; and many who adhere to other religious groups or to none are also pacifists. Limiting an exemption to those affiliated with pacifist denominations would make administration simpler, but it would unjustly exclude others with virtually identical convictions, and would inappropriately encourage people to join particular religious groups.[18]

Whether an exemption should be limited to religious believers is more difficult. The Supreme Court, in two landmark cases,[19] has construed a statutory exemption orginally aimed at religious believers who accept a Supreme Being to include all of those who are truly conscientious. Though constitutional objections to the lines Congress intended may well have underlay these exercises in construction, nonetheless it formally remains open to Congress to try again to narrow the category of exempted objectors, and some justices would undoubtedly accept the fruits of such an effort.[20] The focus here is not in constitutionality but whether such an effort would be appropriate for a legislature free to make it.

One can reject fairly quickly two possible arguments for limiting an exemption to claimants whose beliefs are religious in a sense narrower than one covering all conscientious objections. The first is that such a limit would enhance public acceptability. Some citizens may resent the ability of nonreligious objectors to avoid military service, but their attitude is a doubtful basis for public policy. In any event, since the country exempted nonreligious objectors during the latter years of the Vietnam War, an exemption of that breadth is clearly tolerable, and a slight increase in acceptability would be an inadequate reason for confining it. The second argument is that administering the exemption for nonreligious objectors is too difficult. Measurements of administrative ease are hard to come by, and whether difficulties there become too great is a delicate matter of judgment. It is the opinion of this author, based on reviewing substantial numbers of draft cases,[21] that determinations of sincerity are somewhat more troublesome when persons lack religious belief and affiliation.[22] Nonetheless, some administrative difficulty is not a weighty basis for narrowing the exemption, particularly if most people are not willing to lie about their deepest convictions.

A third, more interesting argument for confining the exemption is that religious objectors are special, that they face a more painful choice than other objectors. This essay will consider arguments that belief in "extratemporal consequences" or a transcendent source of moral truth make the claim of a religious person more powerful than that of a nonbeliever.

Jesse Choper has urged that conflicts between legal demands and conscience have a particular cruelty for the religious believer because of the extratemporal consequences he thinks will ensue if he violates his conscience.[23] Acknowledging the impossibility of empirical proof, Choper writes that "intuition and experience affirm that the degree of internal trauma on earth for those who have put their souls in jeopardy for eternity can be expected to be markedly greater than for those who have only violated a moral scruple."[24] Although Choper's comments are directed to how religion should be defined for constitutional purposes, the basic argument he puts forward is also relevant for legislative choice.[25]

The quotation in the preceding paragraph, and Choper's discussion generally, suggests that he has in mind persons who believe that harmful extratemporal consequences will ensue if they violate their consciences. As Choper recognizes, just such beliefs may make it easier for an objector to suffer jail if he sticks to conscience since he has an assurance, absent for the nonbeliever, that his present sacrifice will eventually be redeemed for his own benefit.[26] Choper is probably right, however, in supposing that what matters most for a possible exemption is not how much a class of persons will suffer if they violate a law but how much they will suffer if they comply with the law and violate their consciences.

The major problem with his approach is that the distinction based on extratemporal consequences loses force as soon as one considers the diverse views taken by adherents of this country's traditional religions. Choper is on strong ground when he says that those who fear that a choice will lead to eternal damnation will find that choice particularly painful. For many practicing Christians and Jews, however, the connection between grave moral wrongs and possible extratemporal consequences is much less direct or is highly uncertain. Many persons believe that most or all sins are within God's loving forgiveness, and that a contrite heart can wash them of potential extratemporal consequences. Many persons suppose that sins will result in definite negative consequences in this life or a next existence, such as purgatory, but that a penitent person may avoid damnation as a consequence. Other persons who believe in extratemporal consequences may not think they relate to particular sins. A strict Calvinist, for example, may suppose that election to heaven is determined on some basis beyond human comprehension.[27] Some persons simply disbelieve in divine eternal punishment or any divine punishment while retaining belief in divine love and an afterlife. Others confess uncertainty about exactly what will happen after death, while expressing faith in the continuing power of God's love. Many religious persons are deeply unsure about the precise relation of sins in this life to the nature of existence in a possible afterlife.

This summary survey exposes serious objections to using a standard of extratemporal consequences. Many persons who accept a connection between potential harmful extratemporal consequences and particular sins do not think these consequences are inevitable or eternal. It is far from clear that such persons will suffer more torment from violating conscience than will someone who thinks he has done a terrible wrong in the only life he has to live. For persons who are uncertain about extratemporal consequences or perceive no strong link between them and particular sins, the likelihood that the possibility of life after death will produce special torment appears even weaker. The rationale underlying Choper's basic distinction would largely evaporate if a crucial part of the test for an exemption from military service were whether one believed in the possibility of an afterlife. There is little reason to suppose that members of a class defined in that way suffer more pain from violating conscience than persons outside the class. If a tighter connection between moral wrongs and extratemporal consequences were demanded, administrative bodies and courts would be put in the impossible position of sorting out the immense variety of beliefs that are found in traditional religious denominations and of trying to settle just how close the believed connection would have to be before an exemption were granted. Such an approach might well exclude many pacifist members of the Society of Friends and members of other mainline churches.

An alternative approach would be to repeat Congress's earlier attempt to exempt only those whose pacifism is connected to belief in a transcendent being.[28] The theory would be that persons who think they violate the norms of a higher power will feel more severely disturbed than those who think that they breach moral principles without such transcendent significance. As with the broader version of an extratemporal consequence standard, the basic problem with such a limit is that belief in a transcendent being probably does not correlate sharply with intensity of feeling that one should not violate one's convictions. The firm conviction against killing in war is one that can arise outside of belief in a transcendent being, and many pacifists who do not believe in a transcendent being have convictions as intense as those who do.

The argument that only religious objectors should receive an exemption can be put in a more plausible way than has yet been conceded. The claim may be that *most* nonreligious people sincerely opposed to participation in war have less intense feelings against participation than most pacifists who are religious (in terms of belief in a transcendent being or extratemporal consequences). A substantial percentage of nonreligious pacifists, when forced, would choose military service before jail without feeling terrible remorse. Since these persons cannot be identified in advance, they can be successfully drafted only if the exemption is withheld from all nonreligious pacifists. Even if the factual predicates of this argument for exempting only religious objectors are granted, the argument is far too weak to justify punishing the many nonreligious objectors who do have intense feelings against military service and will go to jail rather than submit. Thus, if an exemption is to be given to pacifist conscientious objectors, no religious restriction should be adopted.

Another dilemma, sharply exposed by the Vietnam War, is whether an exemption should include nonpacifists who object to participation in a particular war, i.e., selective conscientious objectors. In 1971, the Supreme Court, in accord with the plain intent of Congress, construed the statute to exclude selective objectors and also declared that Congress could permissibly distinguish them from persons who object to participation in all wars.[29] A number of reasons support limiting an exemption to the latter group. Selective objectors much more closely resemble persons who have ordinary political objections to particular wars; many grounds for selective objection are subject to change over time; objection to a particular war is much less closely tied to objection to performing military service away from that war than objection to all wars is tied to objection to all military service. Much more often than with pacifists, a person opposed to a particular war may not be sure he is really a conscientious objector if his alternative is civilian service rather than jail; and selective conscientious objectors will be more difficult for others to identify. Nevertheless, the same powerful reasons that support an exemption for pacifists apply to genuine selective objectors, and these reasons seem strong enough to justify legislative extension of the exemption.[30]

An exemption for selective objectors might conceivably be limited to those whose convictions are rooted in some traditional religious belief. The aims would be to enhance accurate identification and temper resentment by those who serve in unpopular wars that persons not so different from themselves are being exempted. Such a limitation, however, would raise many of the objections already discussed in connection with pacifism. Further, since many religious persons adduce essentially the same reasons for concluding that a war is immoral as do many nonreligious persons, tricky questions about the required connection between one's religious beliefs and one's opposition to a particular war would be raised. Finally, were nonreligious pacifists to be exempted, restricting eligible selective objectors to religious believers would be both odd and confusing.

Self-selection: a far better alternative. The preceding comments about who might be exempted reveal how imperfect is each possible formulation of the eligible class. This society, however, can handle conscientious objections to military service in a manner that effectively circumvents all the difficulties that accompany even the best test of eligibility. Should a draft have to be reinstituted, Congress should establish an alternative civilian service that anyone can choose. Since the draft's aim is to get soldiers, the conditions of civilian service need to be set so that the great majority of people will prefer military service.[31] That would not be difficult. Civilian service could carry substantially less pay and subsidiary benefits or be for a longer period of time, or both. If a lottery were used for military service, young men (and perhaps young women)[32] might choose between a certainty of two years of civilian service and a chance of two years of military service. For a more nearly universal draft, the choice might be between two years of military service and three years of civilian service. Someone already serving in the military (or previously chosen by lot) could transfer to civilian service by accepting a period of work substantially longer than his remaining military duty.

This approach exhibits powerful advantages over any version of a traditional exemption. It eliminates worry about how to draw the lines of exemption and the nagging sense that any lines incorporate elements of unfairness. It eliminates the incredible practical problems of identifying sincere conscientious objectors accurately. Beyond its great expense, potential for delay, and intrusiveness concerning personal convictions, the administration of a limited exemption must inevitably excuse some who are not really eligible and refuse to excuse others who are eligible; it must inevitably breed resentment among those wrongly denied exemptions and among those who serve believing that the system of exemptions is unfair. No one in the military could feel unfairly treated by the choice of others to do civilian work, so long as he could have made the same choice himself.

Conceivable objections to such a plan prove to be insubstantial. Concern might be raised that too many people would opt for civilian service. If the country were not engaged in a war or fighting in a fairly popular one, a relatively small percentage would opt for a civilian service with conditions substantially less favorable than those of military service. In any event, the United States since World War II has never needed anywhere near all those of conscriptable age in the military; the increasing technological sophistication of modern warfare should ensure a continuation of this pattern (which the conscription of women would accentuate further). Ample personnel for the military would remain even if substantial numbers chose civilian service. No doubt, adjustments in institutions would be needed to accommodate a great number of persons in civilian service, but there is plenty of work that they could usefully perform. The value of that work should be sufficient to cover the modest salaries of the workers and administrative costs.

A different sort of objection, that the less favorable terms of civilian service are unfair to genuine objectors, is also misconceived. Roughly equal burdens are justified to achieve fairness between those who accept military service and those whose conscience forbids them from doing so. Since risk of death and prolonged separation from loved ones characterize much military service, some adjustment in ordinary terms (pay, benefits, or period of duty) for civilian service is needed to strike a fair balance. Additional unfavorableness in civilian service, needed to lead most persons to prefer military duty (or a chance of military duty), is required to make the system work and to avoid the serious injustice of jailing whole classes of objectors, or of making uncertain judgments about eligibility for an exemption that may be fraudulently claimed.[33]

REGISTRATION

Resolving the proper treatment for those whose conscience forbids even registration for conscription is more difficult but room exists for more accommodation than has yet been afforded. Congress traditionally has not granted any exemption for persons who refuse to register, and a good many pacifists unwilling to cooperate with the draft system even to this degree have gone to jail. The country's present registration requirement[34] also lacks any exemption based on conscience.

For some people, the potential conflict between conscience and a registration requirement may be avoidable. In a system permitting anyone to choose civilian service as an alternative to military duty, persons should be permitted to register directly for civilian service. Though some persons would consider any such registration as unacceptable cooperation with military conscription, others who would not register for a draft might register for civilian service. A more general device for avoiding the conflict between conscience and draft registration would be to accomplish a person's registration without his cooperation. Schools, employers, and unemployment offices, for example, could report all persons who reached eighteen. Although such a system might manage to register virtually all young people, as a general substitute for self-reporting it would carry significant costs. Military service involves a momentous relation between the individual and his government; the natural and simplest way of determining who is eligible is for individuals to report to the government. That method, which symbolizes an individual's willingness to undertake shared burdens of citizenship, should not be altered because some people are conscientiously opposed to registering. Though jury lists are compiled, uncontroversially, without individual cooperation, such a procedure for military conscription may even derogate from the autonomous choice of those who refuse to have themselves registered. A system should permit indirect reporting for individuals who find that more acceptable than registering themselves; but indirection should not circumvent an individual's own unwillingness to have himself registered by any means.

For those situations in which the conflict between conscience and registration requirements cannot be avoided, appropriate resolution depends on the context of nonregistration. Presently, registration exists without conscription. The existence of persons who are conscientiously opposed to registering is one powerful reason for abandoning a program whose benefit to the country is extremely conjectural. If that step is not taken, proof that one cannot in conscience register should be made a defense to a criminal charge of nonregistration. The person who has refused to register would have to persuade the prosecutor or the jury not only that he could not in conscience submit to military service but that registration alone would conflict with his deepest convictions.[35] This defense would create no unfairness to those who do register, since simple registration imposes no serious burden on them.

A person who refuses to register when registration is linked to an actual draft should not have a similar defense, since he has taken an important step to avoid or decline a very serious obligation placed on others. If he can establish, however, at some time before the sentence, that his grounds for refusal were conscientious, and he also expresses his willingness to perform civilian service, any criminal penalty should be suspended while he performs civilian service, and the penalty should be erased upon his satisfactory completion of that service. The objector unwilling to perform civilian service should be imprisoned. This outcome is tragic for those whose total noncooperation is required by conscience, but fairness to those who serve at great cost requires that no one be able by personal choice, however motivated, to escape altogether the obligation to serve.

The payment of taxes is a basic but onerous responsibility of citizens. A complete escape from liability cannot properly be granted to those with strong moral objections to contributing, but governments could do more than they have to work out alternatives that meet public needs and satisfy claims of conscience. Since most people strenuously dislike paying taxes and many believe that their own taxes are unfairly high, any scheme to lift the burden from the shoulders of conscientious objectors would create a tremendous temptation to fraud and would subtly influence many people toward an honest conviction that they could not, in conscience, pay. Administrative difficulties would be immense and high levels of unfairness and perceived unfairness would be generated. For those reasons conscientious exemption from tax liabilities has never seemed a serious option. Moreover, in respect to taxes, the state need not worry, as it must in regard to pacifist soldiers, that successful coercion will produce ineffective performance; money collected under protest buys as much as money cheerfully given.

Some people, however, are appalled that contributions coerced from them are used for evil purposes. They may feel that their payment of taxes unacceptably involves them in military efforts, or in publicly funded abortions they consider murder, or they may believe that the very practice of coerced payments to the government is morally abhorrent. Such views may lead persons to believe they should not pay taxes at all, should not pay the percentage of assessed liability that goes to the purpose they consider evil, or should not pay any money to be used for that purpose.[36]

Without granting any formal exemption, the government can make some accommodation to those whose refusal to pay taxes is obviously conscientious. It can proceed to collect the amount owed without the objector's full cooperation, garnishing pay checks or a bank account, while reserving criminal prosecution for persons who dishonestly attempt to evade taxes. Though occasional prosecutions have been mounted in the United States against prominent people who conscientiously refuse to pay taxes, one has the sense that persons who openly declare their liabilities and balk at payment are less likely to be the subjects of criminal proceedings than those whose declarations are false.[37]

For major taxes, like the income tax and property tax,[38]

governments could make a formal and more serious effort to meet the claims of conscientious objectors, and they could do so without engaging in the worrisome task of determining eligibility. If people wished not to have their own taxes go for some abhorrent purpose, the government could direct their particular payments elsewhere, charging in return a substantial fee, one high enough to cover administrative expenses for this bookkeeping operation and to discourage most people from wishing to exercise this option. If people refused to pay all or a share of their taxes, they could be permitted as an alternative to direct their money to private causes, such as hospitals and other charities. The cost of this privilege would be a significant addition to the sum owed, say 10 percent. Since few people would willingly undertake this added expense, not many would take advantage of such a program unless they had strong moral convictions about taxpaying.

Because paying taxes against conscience may not portend the moral horror that the pacifist feels about the possibility of killing, the case for formal accommodation in respect to taxes is less pressing than in respect to military service. The intense indignity some people feel about the use of their taxes, however, is sufficient to justify such a program. Proposals offered thus far have been cast in terms of particular uses of tax money, namely military expenditures.[39] That limitation is a mistake, at least it is a mistake if the aim is really to accommodate conscience, rather than label military endeavors suspect. A program permitting optional choices about the direction of payments for one's tax liabilities should stand neutral among government uses of money, representing a general concession to strong moral convictions instead of acknowledging the moral dubiousness of particular kinds of expenditures.

JURY DUTY

The few people conscientiously opposed to jury duty should be excused.[40] Though imposing some alternative donation of time on them would be fair, the administrative effort is almost certainly not worthwhile. False claims of conscientious opposition to jury service will be rare, and persons called for jury service will not feel the system of selection is unfair because an insignificant number of conscientious objectors is excused or because an exemption for them provides an infrequently used opportunity for fraud.[41]

DRUG USE—PATERNALISM

Thus far, this essay has examined requirements that impose shared burdens. The inquiry now turns to paternalistic legislation, with drug laws used as an example. Of course, the conclusions reached here cannot be applied to other paternalistic laws without careful analysis of similarities and differences, but thinking about possible exemptions from drug laws does suggest problems whose scope is much broader.

When the state forbids the use of a substance like marijuana, should any class of potential users be afforded an exemption? A class defined in terms of conscientious objection would be inapt. No one is likely to believe that he is under an absolute duty to ingest a particular substance; after all, the substance might be unavailable. Someone might think he must use a substance if it is physically possible to do so; but that seems a strange position, barring some special religious significance to its use. Someone's defying a threat of death to perform a religious ceremony is comprehensible, but one cannot imagine someone's believing that despite a threat of death he has a moral duty to ingest a drug in a nonreligious setting. Many people do think the government has no business barring use of marijuana, and some of these think they have a moral right to use it, but these opinions may be held by persons who never or rarely use marijuana or regard its use as no more satisfying or uplifting than a great many other activities. Perhaps a more promising class for an exemption would be persons who believe that marijuana use produces deep insights about ultimate truths. Just what sorts of insights would be reached, however, and how unique would marijuana use have to be regarded as a source of truth for a claimant to be exempted? So long as the focus remains on individual reasons for personal use, the difficulties of categorization appear insurmountable, even in theory. When one asks how any such an exemption would be administered, he realizes that any attempted application of some amorphous standard to individual cases[42] would work serious injustice and would quickly undermine the efficacy of the general prohibition.[43] This latter result may not disturb those critical of the law's existence, but it will hardly commend itself to legislators persuaded that a broad prohibition is desirable.

Any feasible exemption would need to be cast in terms of specialized use. One such use is medical. For that, objective requisites would suffice; a person whose physical condition qualified him would not also need to have a particular moral view about the necessity of the drug's use. Another specialized use is in the context of religious services. An exemption that reaches persons who use drugs in corporate religious services, but does not cover either nonreligious group use or individual religious use, can be defended. One argument for distinguishing religious from nonreligious use is that a person who thinks he needs a drug to maintain a connection with a transcendent being, or to understand ultimate reality, makes a claim to use that is of a different dimension from the claim of a person who seeks pleasure, or personal adjustment, or even generally enhanced perception. Accompanying the basic claim that access to higher reality is simply a more compelling interest is a related point about the inappropriateness of government determination, even by indirection, of how people seek such reality. Of course, the state should generally be hesitant to cut people off from what they perceive to be sources of happiness and fulfillment, and occasionally it must prohibit extremely self-destructive acts that participants believe bear a close connection to higher reality. Still, the point remains that among paternalistic exercises the state should be particularly wary of limiting the search for a higher reality and the maintenance of perceived connections with that reality.

A second argument for excluding nonreligious use from an exemption concerns administrability, and that argument also supports the distinction between corporate religious use and individual religious use. Were it granted that some nonreligious persons had reasons for use as compelling as those engaged in religious use, still, separating use for pleasure from use for deep insight or some other compelling purpose would be too difficult. An administrable exemption could not go beyond religious use. Further, given the impossibility of assessing individual claims that purely personal religious pursuit leads to marijuana use, exempted religious use must be corporate, or at least closely tied to corporate religious practices.[44] If the general desire to use a drug is widespread, and serious enforcement efforts support a legislative prohibition, claims based on corporate religious practices will have to be reviewed with some stringency, so that groups of drug users will not succeed by creating bogus religions to cover their use.[45] Once the genuineness of the religion and an individual user's bona fide membership in the religious community were established, no further inquiry would be called for into his particular convictions about the use of marijuana.

CONDITIONS ON BENEFITS—SATURDAY EMPLOYMENT
AND REFUSALS TO PERFORM ABORTIONS

Many acts that are not absolutely required may have to be performed if a person is to receive particular benefits. Since the person may forego the benefits involved, these conditions do not pose an absolute conflict between duty and conscience. The benefits are often important enough, however, so that the strain of complying with conscience is considerable if the cost is loss of benefits. If the benefits are provided by the government, the issue regarding accommodation concerns possible concessions to conscience by the government itself.[46] The discussion concentrates on that subject, not the more complex question of when the government should compel private persons and organizations to make accommodations.[47]

The conceivable conflicts of condition and conscience are almost infinite. Refusal to work on Saturday is representative of the tension between a claim of conscience and ordinary conditions of employment; refusals to perform abortions might be a ground for withholding monetary support that would otherwise be provided or even for denying a medical license. What emerge as central to the question of possible accommodations are the dangers of unfairness, or independent harm, to others and the incentives to fraud.

Members of some Sabbatarian denominations believe that they should not work on Saturday, which God has ordained as a day of rest. The issue in a notable Supreme Court case, *Sherbert* v. *Verner*,[48] was whether a state that conditioned eligibility for unemployment compensation on availability for Saturday work could withhold that compensation from someone whose religious convictions forbade work on that day. Whether or not one endorses the Supreme Court's conclusion that the state's action was unconstitutional, the legislative question is relatively straightforward. Most people would strongly prefer working permanently to receiving unemployment benefits that may last only a temporary period,[49] so they have little incentive to feign an unwillingness to work on Saturday. Granting unemployment benefits to people like Mrs. Sherbert involves no hardship or unfairness to other individuals; and the slight drain on the public treasury is a small price to pay for the accommodation. No one is likely to have a non-religious belief that work on a particular day is absolutely wrong; but a person might have strong moral grounds, based, say, on family responsibilities, against working on Saturday. Also, Saturday employment may render attendance at religious services difficult or impossible for members of groups that worship on that day but do not regard work on that day as wrongful. Whether unemployment benefits should be afforded people who refuse Saturday work for principled reasons that do not amount to a conscientious opposition to such work is troublesome; but given the propensity of most people to want to work, the extension of benefits is warranted. As far as members of Sabbatarian groups are concerned, trying to distinguish individuals who believe Saturday work is wrong in principle from those who merely think Saturday worship is very important might prove complicated.

A more difficult question still is whether as employer the government should exempt from Saturday work persons who would otherwise work on that day but cannot do so out of conviction. Typically, freedom from Saturday work will be based on seniority; an exemption would give a preference to those who qualify over more senior nonqualifying employees.[50] In any event, if some persons are exempted, others will bear a heavier share of Saturday work, so a question of fairness is posed. Ideally, the "benefit" of freedom from Saturday work might be balanced by some corresponding detriment (lower wages, longer hours); but such precise refinements in working conditions may not be feasible. When a choice must be made between accommodation, with its accompanying unfairness, or placing a heavy burden on those whose conscience forbids Saturday work, this author's judgment is that the interest in accommodation predominates; but the exemption in this setting should be limited to those who combine membership in a Sabbatarian group with a strong conviction against Saturday work.

The belief of a large number of doctors that abortion is tantamount to murder presents at least a potential conflict between conscience and benefit or privilege.[51] If a medical license were conditioned on a willingness to perform accepted medical techniques including abortions, a person unwilling to perform abortions might lose his license or fail to get one. Alternatively, a hospital whose owners were committed to that view might be deprived of funds otherwise available. As a general principle, doctors should be free to decline to engage in treatment to which they are conscientiously opposed, so long as patients can get the treatment elsewhere and are aware of its availability. No inquiry into stated objections to abortions need be undertaken, since neither doctors nor hospitals have any apparent reason to make false claims that they find abortion morally unacceptable. The setting of conditions for medical licenses and grants of funds for medical facilities should accommodate conscientious conviction up to the point that it seriously compromises the capacity of patients to take advantage of accepted medical practice.

CONCLUSION

This brief survey of various contexts in which issues of conscientious objection may arise gives a fair indication of the complexity of the questions. It suggests that liberal societies should make greater efforts to accommodate conscience than have yet been achieved. It also suggests the general desirability of using self-selection between alternatives, rather than administration of eligibility requirements, when that course is feasible. In some areas, judgments about eligibility are unavoidable. What exactly are the appropriate standards of eligibility depend sharply on the nature of the activity from which the exemption is sought and the possibilities of fraud and other unfairness.

NOTES

1. 50 U.S.C. app. § 453 (1977) establishes "the duty of every male citizen of the United States, and every other male person residing in the United States . . . between the ages of eighteen and twenty-six, to present himself for and submit to registration . . . in such manner, as shall be determined by proclamation of the President. . . ." Registration, at present, is governed by Proclamation No. 4771, 45 F.R. 45247 (1980), reprinted in 50 U.S.C. § 453 app. at 887 (Supp. V, 1982).
2. Of course, reasons that influence wise legislation overlap with those of constitutional relevance.
3. This way of putting the matter oversimplifies the moral question. Once the state passes a conscription law, a new duty to comply with laws will also come into play.
4. Some sorts of moral beliefs—e.g., in favor of killing members of a particular race or religion—are so unacceptable that blame is not withheld from those who act on these beliefs.
5. This sentence skirts the complicated question whether norms cast in terms of equality are meaningful. This author's views on that subject are developed in Greenawalt, "How Empty Is the Idea of Equality?" *Columbia Law Review* 83 (1983):1167.
6. This essay does not pause here over possible surrogates for these inquiries, such as whether a claimant belongs to a group most of whose members have sincere beliefs that qualify.

7. The anomaly could be avoided were it acknowledged that the state could remove and detain people in these circumstances whom it could not lawfully punish.

8. This essay does not address the related issue whether some actions that would otherwise be trespassory should be permitted (by statute or constitutional interpretation) because they are a form of political expression. Such permissions would not turn on whether politically expressive acts were grounded in conscience.

9. See Harlan Fiske Stone, "The Conscientious Objector," *Columbia University Quarterly* 21 (1919):253, 268; Michael Walzer, *Obligations: Essays on Disobedience, War, and Citizenship* (Cambridge: Harvard University Press, 1970), 135-36. Although they do not enlist private persons in the performance of official tasks in the manner of jury duty and military service, duties of care toward children do require parents to perform certain acts.

10. In some instances, an element of increased danger (say in driving a motorcycle without a helmet) will be recognized, but the benefits of the act, an increased feeling of freedom, will be thought to outweigh the danger.

11. Of course, the grant of benefits often represents an overall drain on public resources. If objection is to establishing one's competence to perform a licensed act (say by taking a driving test), the grant of a license to an objector might create a danger to others.

12. See note 3 and accompanying text. See generally, Greenawalt, "Religion as a Concept in Constitutional Law," *California Law Review* 72 (1984):753.

13. See the plurality opinion in *Welsh* v. *United States*, 398 U.S. 333 (1970).

14. See generally Harold J. Berman, *The Interaction of Law and Religion* (Nashville, Tenn.: Abingdon Press, 1974).

15. A written constitution might, of course, give religious claims some special status; at least in some respects, the Constitution of the United States does so.

16. The rules regarding conscientious objection to military service, 50 U.S.C. app. 456(j) (1977), are incorporated into the Military Selective Service Act, ch. 625, 62 Stat. 604 (1948), codified as amended at 50 U.S.C. app. 451-473 (1977). Presidential authority to induct men into active military service expired in 1973, 50 U.S.C. app. 471(a) (1977), but may be renewed by act of Congress.

17. In the United States, the exemption has included persons who believe they should never fight in a war even if they think it is all right for others to fight. Such persons are not strictly pacifists. What exactly makes a person a pacifist or opposed to participating in any war is itself troublesome when either concept is applied to a person who thinks some historical wars may have been justified but believes that, given modern weaponry, no war, or no war fought by this country, can now be justified.

18. On the basis of the Supreme Court's decisions under the religion clauses, such a limitation would almost certainly be unconstitutional.

19. *Seeger* v. *United States*, 380 U.S. 163 (1965); and *Welsh* v. *United States*. In *Welsh*, only four of eight justices found the claimant eligible under the statute; Justice Harlan thought him excluded by the statute but considered that exclusion to be unconstitutional. 398 U.S. at 344.

20. See the dissenting opinion of Justice Byron White, in *Welsh* v. *United States*, at 367. Indeed, the overruling of *Welsh* is a possibility, in which event continuance of the old statutory standard would limit the exemption to persons religious in a sense narrower than that adopted by the plurality opinion in that case. After *Seeger*, Congress had amended the Selective Service Act to drop the requirement of belief in a Supreme Being. Pub L. No. 90-40 § 1(5), 81 Stat. 100-102, 104 (1967), codified as amended at 50 U.S.C. app. 456(j) (1977).

21. Reviewing such cases was part of this author's job as Deputy Solicitor General in 1971-72.

22. Very likely in this respect, religious affiliation is the most important element. Even if draft boards and others had more *trouble* determining the sincerity of nonreligious objectors, that does not establish that sincerity was really more difficult to determine. Conceivably, some persons who are insincere fool administrators by feigning religious belief and establishing religious affiliation.

23.   Jesse Choper, "Defining 'Religion' in the First Amendment," *University of Illinois Law Review* 1982 (1982):579.

24.   Ibid., 598.

25.   In an excess of caution, it might be added that one might find Choper's analysis completely persuasive as to how religion should be defined for constitutional purposes and still conclude that nonreligious conscientious objectors have a strong enough interest in obtaining an exemption so they should be granted it. Reasons for rejecting Choper's approach at the constitutional level are developed in Greenawalt, "Religion as a Concept in Constitutional Law," 803-6.

26.   If those who believe in extratemporal consequences tend to have greater confidence in their moral judgments than do nonbelievers, that would be another reason why the choice to abide by conscience would be less painful for them.

27.   A frequent strand of this position has, however, been that a good life is *evidence* of election. A Calvinist who took this view might find commission of a grave wrong particularly painful because it constitutes evidence of his nonelection.

28.   In 1948, Congress restricted the exemption to those who believed in a "Supreme Being." Section 6(j) of the Military Selective Service Act of 1948, c. 625, 62 Stat. 613. The effect of the restriction was largely gutted by *United States* v. *Seeger*, and the restriction was removed from the Act two years later. See note 20.

29.   *Gillette* v. *United States*, 401 U.S. 437, 454-56 (1970).

30.   The arguments on both sides are developed at greater length in Greenawalt, "All or Nothing At All: The Defeat of Selective Conscientious Objection," *1971 The Supreme Court Review*, 31, 47-66. Were an exemption to be granted to selective objectors, it should go no further than the scope of the objection: a person who in conscience could serve outside the theater of the war to which he objects should not be excused altogether from military service (except on possible grounds of administrative convenience).

31.   Similarly, anyone should be able to choose noncombatant service in the military to combatant service, by accepting somewhat less favorable conditions of work.

32.   Though the point is not developed in this essay, what is said about fairness points to the injustice of conscription limited to males.

33.   Another conceivable concern might be class differentiations between those who chose military service and those who chose alternative service. Very likely, among those choosing alternative service, a high percentage would come from the middle and upper classes. Still, most young persons from those classes would choose military service; and the resulting composition of the military would be much less skewed toward poorer people than is true with the volunteer army.

34.   50 U.S.C. app. § 453 (1977). See note 1.

35.   The phrasing of the sentence in text in this way is not meant to indicate that the so-called burden of persuasion as to this issue would necessarily lie on the defendant, though such a shift in the ordinary burden of persuasion for criminal cases might be justified on the ground that the government will be hard put to disprove conscientious motivation once a defendant has put forward any claim to it.

36.   The arguments in favor of granting some exemption are developed in Comment, "The World Peace Tax Fund Act: Conscientious Objection for Taxpayers," *Northwestern University Law Review* 74 (1979):76.

37.   Of course, tax prosecutions of violators in all classes is so highly selective, one cannot be confident that the percentage of conscientious refusers prosecuted is actually less than the percentage of evaders prosecuted.

38.   This author does not think accommodation is feasible for sales taxes, etc.

39.   See Comment, "The World Peace Tax Fund Act."

40.   See *In re Jenison*, 267 Minn. 136, 120 N.W.2d 515 (1963), on remand from 375 U.S. 14 (1963); *United States* v. *Hillyard*, 52 F.Supp. 612 (E.D. Wash. 1943). Both cases upheld a constitutional claim to refuse to serve.

41.   A sense of unfairness is much more likely to arise because of broader categories of excuses from jury service or because of feelings that one's time is wantonly wasted.

42.   The claim for an exemption might be made in the form of an application for a

license to use or as a defense to criminal prosecution.

43. In passing on constitutional claims to use drugs, courts have been sensitive to the problems that exceptions would undermine the effectiveness of prohibitions. See, e.g., *Leary* v. *United States*, 383 F.2d 851, 859-62 (5th Cir. 1967), rev'd on other grounds, 395 U.S. 6 (1969); *United States* v. *Middleton*, 690 F.2d 820 (11th Cir. 1982).

44. Cases granting constitutional exemptions from prohibitions have involved corporate religious practice. *People* v. *Woody*, 61 Cal. 2d 716, 394 P.2d 813, 40 Cal. Rptr. 69 (1964); *In re Grady*, 61 Cal.2d 887, 394 P.2d 728 (1964), 39 Cal. Rptr. 912 (1964); *State* v. *Whittingham*, 14 Ariz. App. 27, 504 P.2d 950 (1973), cert. denied, 417 U.S. 946 (1974). Use might be individual but closely tied to corporate practice if a tenet of a religious group was that individual use on some occasion was required or recommended.

45. Enforcement of marijuana laws is now so relaxed in most jurisdictions that people would probably not take the trouble to create bogus religions to exempt their use of that drug.

46. In a federal system, of course, one question is whether the federal government should mandate concessions by state governments.

47. An example of such legislation is the Title VII requirement that employers make reasonable accommodation to the religious requirements of employees, involved in *T.W.A.* v. *Hardison*, 432 U.S. 63 (1977).

48. *Sherbert* v. *Verner*, 374 U.S. 398 (1963).

49. Regular unemployment benefits usually run from thirteen to twenty-six weeks. See, e.g., N.C. Gen. Stat. § 96-12(d) (1981). During the recessions of the seventies and eighties, recipients who have exhausted their eligibility for regular state unemployment benefits have been able to receive extended benefits for additional periods under supplementary federal funding. These additional benefits, however, are contingent on ad hoc Congressional appropriations and the existence of a relatively high unemployment rate, computed on the basis of the employment rate among employees covered by unemployment insurance programs in the first place. See. e.g., N.C. Gen. Stat. § 96-12(e) (1981).

50. This is on the assumption that the needs of the government as employer are not thwarted by a person's nonavailability for Saturday work.

51. As far as this author is aware, no such conflict has yet arisen. The ninth circuit has ruled, in accord with existing legislation, that the failure of a Catholic hospital to perform sterilizations is not grounds for denial of its federal funding. *Chrisman* v. *Sisters of St. Joseph of Peace*, 506 F.2d 308 (9th Cir. 1974).

PART 5

RELIGION AND
PUBLIC EDUCATION

Religion and Schools:
The New Political Establishment

NORMAN REDLICH

The so-called social issues agenda of the Reagan administration has been directed toward reversing, or at least restricting, United States Supreme Court decisions in four areas— abortion, school prayer, government aid to religious schools, and court-ordered busing. While not all of these areas deal directly, or even indirectly, with the principle of separation of church and state, it is obvious that a religious constituency fuels the political engine that drives the "social issues" agenda forward. The intrusion of a fundamentalist, almost evangelical, element into the political arena has raised serious questions about the proper role of religion in political life. It has generated new pressures on previously well-established constitutional principles enforcing the First Amendment's command that "Congress shall make no law respecting an establishment of religion or prohibiting the free exercise thereof."

Surprisingly, very few of the constitutional cases on the "social issues" agenda of the Reagan administration and its allies were decided by the overtly liberal Earl Warren Court. The Warren E. Burger Court (with six justices appointed by Presidents Richard M. Nixon, Gerald R. Ford, and Ronald Reagan) has not retreated on the issue of school prayer,[1] and has been responsible for major decisions on abortion,[2] aid to religious schools,[3] and school busing.[4] Dismantling this constitutional structure has been a major goal of the Reagan presidency.

In the area of church-state relations, the political pressures have been most intense, coming not only from evangelical groups like the Moral Majority, but also from a broad spectrum of Americans who sincerely believe that religion should play a greater role in this society and who look to government to support that view. Some believe that religious exercises are desirable in public schools; others seek financial relief from the heavy burden of private religious education for their children. They do not consider these positions as a threat to anyone's religious freedom. Indeed, living in a country with more religious freedom and diversity than any nation on earth, proponents of government aid to religion can easily overlook the crucial link between those freedoms and their constitutional source. As so often occurs with those who propound a religious message (usually their own), opposition to governmental support is often confused with opposition to religion itself. Sympathizers depict proponents of governmental aid as being on the side of God and religion, while the opponents are easily characterized as atheistic proponents of secular humanism. In such a political atmosphere, the rational defense of constitutional principles becomes increasingly difficult, and religious freedom and diversity are seriously threatened. Not surprisingly, the constitutional principle that forms the first line of defense is the one specifically designed for times such as these—the principle that church and state are best served by separation rather than by fusion.

The Supreme Court, despite the unpopularity of many of its decisions, has repeatedly reaffirmed its adherence to the concept of separation of church and state, even in its recent opinions upholding one form of tax assistance for private school tuition,[5] the hiring of chaplains by legislatures,[6] and the use of public funds for the construction of a nativity scene as part of a city's Christmas celebration.[7] These recent decisions, however, are cause for serious concern. Regardless of the limitations expressed by the Court, they will be viewed by many as creating new opportunities for governmental endorsement of religious beliefs and institutions. In both courtroom and legislature, more pressure on the wall of separation can be expected.

THE SCHOOL PRAYER CONTROVERSY

Nowhere has this assault on constitutional principles been more intense than in the controversy over school prayer. In 1962, in *Engel* v. *Vitale*, the Supreme Court held invalid a so-called nondenominational New York State Regents prayer.[8] The eight-to-one decision, written by Justice Hugo Black, did not ban prayers in public schools. Individual children or teachers remain free to pray, as presumably many do for exams, or at the start of the day, or at occasions where individual conscience compels such observance. In this case, and in a similar case involving Bible reading one year later,[9] the Court did hold invalid a state-sponsored religious observance that inevitably stamped the imprimatur of the state in support of religion. Such state support of religion, especially in the public schools, posed all of the dangers that the religion clauses of the Constitution were designed to avoid. Prayers could never be "neutral" among religions. No single prayer could satisfy all religious beliefs, thus leading to controversy among religions as to the nature of the prayer to be recited. The selection of any one prayer would throw the power of the state behind a particular set of religious beliefs and behind religion as against nonreligion. Edmond Cahn, a profoundly religious man and a constitutional scholar, pointed out at the time that the so-called nondenominational prayer in *Engel* v. *Vitale* was theologically offensive to many religious faiths.[10] A government-supported religious exercise is inevitably coercive toward those who, for reasons of personal conviction, elect not to participate.

Thus, *Engel* v. *Vitale* did not break entirely new ground, although the controversy it generated created the impression that the Court had departed from, rather than followed, long-standing constitutional principles. A series of cases in the 1940s and 1950s had established the principle that the Establishment Clause of the First Amendment was intended not merely to prevent the creation of a state religion, as some proponents of state support for religion had argued, but rather to prevent state support for *all* religions as well as any particular religion. These Court decisions, dealing with the use of school facilities for religious instruction[11] or with the reimbursement to parents for bus transportation to religious schools,[12] had traced the historical origins of the Establishment Clause and concluded that separation of church and state, and not merely avoidance of state religion or the requirement that all religions be treated alike, was the guiding principle of interpretation of the Establishment Clause. Indeed, the decision of a sharply divided Court in *Everson* v. *Board of Education*,[13] which upheld government reimbursement for bus transportation to parochial schools, was based on the Court's conclusion that such expenditures were not in support of religion but rather a kind of safety-and-welfare measure designed to help children travel to school without having to run the risk of walking along crowded highways.

Of course, as *Everson* indicated, there could be strong disagreement about whether a government program was an impermissible aid to religion or a general welfare measure, such as police and fire protection, where the exclusion of religious

institutions would itself raise serious problems under the Free
Exercise Clause. The bus transportation case demonstrated
that the line was not always easy to discern since the Court
agreed on the constitutional principle but divided five to four
on the application. Similarly, differences could arise as to
whether a practice or exercise, such as the singing of Christmas carols or the placing of Christmas trees in a public area,
was religious or secular. A prayer read in school assemblies or
in each class at the start of the day was clearly a religious
exercise, as was the devotional reading of excerpts from the
Bible, or the recitation of the Lord's Prayer, held unconstitutional in the *Schempp* case, decided one year after *Engel*.

In the prayer cases, the Court started to evolve its three-part
test in evaluating whether a government practice violates the
Establishment Clause. The practice must have a secular purpose; its principal or primary effect must neither advance nor
inhibit religion; and it must not foster an excessive government entanglement with religion.[14] A challenged practice must
pass all three tests to be valid. State-sponsored prayer in the
public schools fails all three.

In the more than two decades since the school prayer cases
were decided, there has been an almost unbroken line of court
decisions applying the principles of these cases to a wide range
of practices in different factual contexts. Clearly religious
practices, such as a cross in the county seal,[15] the placing of
the Ten Commandments in classrooms,[16] or the placing of a
cross or other religious symbol in a public area,[17] have been
held to be establishments. The singing of Christmas songs,[18]
the objective teaching of religion,[19] the study of the Bible as
literature,[20] and the exemption from the reach of Sunday closing laws for those whose religion requires Saturday observance[21] have been held constitutional, and, in some instances, a
desirable accommodation to protect the free-exercise claims of
certain minorities. None of these cases has called into question
the underlying principles enunciated in the school prayer cases
of the early 1960s.

Proponents of state-sponsored school prayer received their
first glimmer of judicial hope on 5 July 1983 when the
Supreme Court, in *Marsh* v. *Chambers*, decided that paid legislative chaplains and opening prayers at the start of each session were not violations of the Establishment Clause. Chief
Justice Burger's majority opinion, however, was based almost
entirely on a historical analysis, emphasizing the fact that

these practices were adopted by the very Congress that approved the First Amendment in 1789. Moreover, there was a reference to the fact that the complaining party was an adult. Justice William J. Brennan's dissent was probably correct, therefore, in observing that the majority's "limited rationale should pose little threat to the overall fate of the Establishment Clause." The chief justice's opinion, however, contains some language that could be seized on by those who seek to narrow or overturn the decisions concerning religious practices in the schools. Although based on history, the opinion did not view the practice simply as a historical exception to Establishment Clause doctrine. Rather, it described the practice as "simply a tolerable acknowledgment of beliefs widely held among the people of this country." Such language, lifted out of the context of the opinion, could be used to argue in favor of public displays of nativity scenes, or other religious symbols, or even prayer. Indeed, this past term echoes of this language appeared in Chief Justice Burger's majority opinion in *Lynch* v. *Donnelly*.

The current intensive effort to reestablish state-sponsored prayer in public schools has been spearheaded by religious leaders such as Jerry Falwell and his so-called Moral Majority and, for the first time, has had the active support of the president of the United States. Previous presidents have either supported, or accepted, the Supreme Court decisions. Indeed, America's first Roman Catholic president, John F. Kennedy, commented shortly after the *Engel* case that he always thought that the proper setting for prayer was either at home or in church. President Reagan's election in 1980 as a vociferous proponent of returning prayer to the schools has provided a new and strong political impetus for the overturning of the school prayer cases. The president rarely misses an opportunity to criticize the Court and to urge the return of prayer to the public schools. Thus, school prayer has become an intense political issue, with all of the opinion polls appearing to show strong support for the general concept of school prayer, although it is difficult to know whether abstract support for school prayer would be sustained when some of the hard issues of implementation would have to be faced.

The attack on the school prayer decisions has taken several forms, the most direct being an attempt to reverse them by constitutional amendment.[22] Fortunately, the supporters of a constitutional amendment differ in their proposed solutions.

An amendment that would permit so-called nondenominational prayer might have wide public support, but its proponents realize that every organized public prayer, whether sponsored by or permitted by the state, would be subject to litigation, involving the courts in a hopeless inquiry over the meaning of "nondenominational." If, however, a constitutional amendment were to prescribe a prayer, the debate over the amendment would create a similar controversy, i.e., which prayer to use, but in a forum—Congress—which the legislators would wish to avoid.

In an effort to pass the buck to the future, the administration had originally proposed an amendment that would simply provide that the Constitution shall not prevent organized public prayer, leaving it to each local or state government, or local school authorities, to prescribe the form of prayer.[23] The administration then modified its proposal by adding a sentence that would bar the federal government or any state from composing an official prayer. Of course, this leaves unanswered the question of whether schoolteachers, principals, elected officials, school boards, or other state and local officials could read or compose prayers.

The administration proposal has spawned the opposition of some opponents of school prayer, like Senator Orrin G. Hatch of Utah, a Mormon and a person sensitive to the rights of religious minorities. He has proposed an amendment that would permit silent devotion, a position that does not satisfy those whose religious convictions require public and vocal expressions of faith. On 14 July 1983, the Senate Judiciary Committee sent both the administration and Hatch proposals to the Senate floor. The Senate debate began on 5 March 1984, and on 20 March, after more than two weeks of discussion, the Senate voted fifty-six to forty-four in favor of the administration proposal.[24] Although the "voluntary" school prayer amendment was thus defeated for want of the required two-thirds majority, the debate has already raised the specter of what may be expected in the future if school prayer is legalized. Americans have already witnessed divisive debate over questions of the form and content of prayer and whether majority sentiment in each community should be able to determine the nature of public prayer. The adoption of a school prayer amendment by the Congress would transfer this debate to the state legislatures and ultimately to school boards and individual schools throughout the country. It is inevitable

that the rights of religious minorities, and those who profess
no religious faith, will be chipped away in the process. With
the reelection of President Reagan, a new attempt to reintroduce a school prayer amendment in the Ninety-ninth Congress will doubtless be made.

Apart from mounting this frontal threat, by way of constitutional amendment, the proponents of state-sponsored public
school prayer have devised other techniques, legislative and
judicial, to try to undercut the thrust of the Court's decisions.
One type of proposal that has gained broad support, and for
which an arguable case can be made for validity, would permit, or require, a period of silence.[25] The legislative proposals
vary as to what would occur during this period of silence.
Some call for a simple period of silence, some call for meditation, some call for prayer, and some call for a combination of
all of them. A New Mexico law, which allows a moment of
silence in the public schools for "contemplation, meditation,
or prayer," was held unconstitutional by a United States district court as a "devotional exercise" that had the effect of
"the advancement of religion."[26] New Jersey's law requires
principals and teachers to "permit students to observe a one-
minute period of silence solely at the discretion of the individual student." The federal district court in New Jersey has
held the law unconstitutional and the state is not appealing.[27]

During its 1984 term, the Supreme Court will rule on the
constitutionality of an Alabama statute that provides for a one-
minute period of silence to be used for meditation or voluntary prayer. In *Jaffree* v. *Wallace*,[28] the Eleventh Circuit Court
of Appeals overturned a district court decision premised on
the theory that the Fourteenth Amendment was not intended
to apply the Establishment Clause of the First Amendment to
the states. Although the district court conceded that its holding ran counter to the entire body of United States Supreme
Court and eleventh circuit court precedent, it justified its
action because, in its opinion, "the United States Supreme
Court ha[d] erred in its reading of history." The circuit court
roundly criticized the district court for disregarding Supreme
Court precedent: "Judicial precedence serves as the foundation of our federal system. . . . If the Supreme Court errs, no
other court may correct it." The circuit court then proceeded
to find both Alabama prayer statutes unconstitutional. There
was no saving secular purpose to be found in prayer that the
court found to be "quintessential religious practice."

Regardless of the wording,[29] these laws should be viewed by the courts simply as substitutes for state-supported religion. In light of the legislative history that surrounds the adoption of these statutes, it is virtually impossible to ignore the fact that these laws have little to do with creating a peaceful moment at the start of the day, or permitting a period of inward reflection. Were it not for the controversy over the unconstitutionality of state-sponsored prayer, there would be no pressure for a moment of silence or meditation.

Moreover, unlike such activities as the singing of Christmas carols or ceremonial references to God at school assemblies or graduations, which by the very context in which they occur are most unlikely to be converted into a religious exercise, the moment of silence is almost certain to be used for such a purpose. The adoption of such practices, either by statute or school board resolution, constitutes an act of public hypocrisy. It is as if the public officials were winking to millions of school children and saying, "We'll show you how to get around the Constitution." It sends a message that a fundamental constitutional value—separation of church and state—can be circumvented by a phony gesture. Nothing could be more damaging to the concept of respect for constitutional rights.

A New Approach:
Student Religious Clubs and "Equal Access"

Another attempt to reintroduce a form of state-supported prayer in the public schools derives from the misguided reliance on that provision of the First Amendment that guarantees freedom of speech and the free exercise of religion. That school children have a right to pray is unquestioned. The Court has held that children cannot be compelled to salute the flag or recite the Pledge of Allegiance if such observances violate the student's religious beliefs.[30] Permitting students to be excused, on religious grounds, from an otherwise secular observance is not an establishment of religion. Rather, it is a necessary accommodation by the state to the individual's religious freedom.[31]

There are, moreover, situations where government interference with religious activity on public property would be unconstitutional. For example, if the public is permitted to gather at a park or at a facility such as the Mall in Washington, D.C., groups of individuals may not be prevented from similarly assembling if their purpose is to join in prayer.[32] The principle is that once the state creates a public forum, it may not deny the use of that forum to religious groups, providing, the state does not extend funds for a religious observance, as was the case with a recent visit by the pope to Philadelphia.[33] Indeed, recently, in *Widmar* v. *Vincent*,[34] the Supreme Court held that if a state university makes its campus available for meetings by political and social groups, the university could not deny access to student religious groups even if such groups engage in religious worship. Thus, there will be occasions where religious exercises on public property are not only permissible, but are compelled by the Free Exercise Clause of the Constitution.

Some proponents of school prayer have sought to build on these decisions by requiring school officials to set aside time during the day to permit students in the public schools to organize groups for religious purposes, including engaging in prayer. One could argue that permitting student-initiated prayer clubs to meet during a school's "student-activity" period may not constitute an establishment of religion, and may, indeed, be required as an exercise of the student's rights to free speech and free exercise of religion. It is more likely, however, that setting aside time during each school day for student-initiated prayer constitutes the placing of an imprimatur of the state behind a religious exercise. By July 1984, all four federal courts of appeal that had considered the issue held varying forms of equal access to be unconstitutional.[35] These courts distinguished *Widmar*, finding that unlike a university campus or a public park, where a wide variety of individuals and groups meet to express divergent views on political, and possibly religious, issues, a public secondary school has few of the characteristics of a public forum. Moreover, the process by which such student meetings or prayer sessions are organized could easily involve the type of official support that the school prayer cases sought to prevent. For example, this kind of official support was found by the court in *Lubbock*,[36] where the policy on religious meetings in schools was part of an official statement setting forth guidelines for religion in the schools, and not part of a policy relating to free speech or student groups generally.

As these appeals courts reached unanimity regarding the unconstitutionality of allowing student religious groups and prayer clubs to meet on public school premises on school time, however, the public clamor over school prayer led Congress to seek a legislative solution to the problem.[37] The proposals that were introduced were appealingly phrased in free-speech "equal access" terms and they required that all public schools that generally permit student groups to meet shall not discriminate against any group on the basis of the religious content of the speech at the meeting.

In May 1984, the House rejected an equal access bill that would have denied federal funds to school districts that refused to allow its high school students to hold religious meetings during noninstructional time on school premises. The final Senate version eliminated a number of the features that had made the earlier House draft so unappealing. It eliminated the cutoff of federal funds from noncomplying school districts, the virtually unlimited access to these student groups by outsiders and the bar to equal access for student religious groups that did not meet a numerical threshold. More importantly, however, the language of the Senate bill was broadened to extend protection not only to religious, but also to political, philosophical, and other speech at student meetings. This made the legislation more palatable to a variety of groups that had energetically opposed the earlier House version, and the Equal Access Act was overwhelmingly approved,[38] both by many who had fought against President Reagan's proposed school prayer amendment and by many civil libertarians who sincerely believe that the bill will serve the interests of student free speech.

There are, however, serious problems with this legislative solution. The constitutionality of the Equal Access Act is questionable, and the educational policy behind the desire to transform the high school into a public forum is misguided. The Equal Access Act requires secondary schools to do what *Widmar* requires of state universities, ignoring the fact that the principles of the *Widmar* case are not of universal applicability, even in the state university setting. Many valid distinctions may be drawn between the state university students in *Widmar* and the secondary students affected by Equal Access. High school students are younger and are likely to be more sensitive to suggestions by their school officials, even to suggestions that they participate in religious activities. Thus, there is serious doubt whether organized religious activities in public schools can ever be accomplished without impermissible state support. This is the essential teaching of the *McCollum* case. Unlike their university counterparts, high school students are subject to mandatory attendance requirements, and their educational programs are strictly controlled. High schools have traditionally not been open to all forms of collective speech and activity, but, rather, only to those programs that local school officials believe to be educationally sound. A high school is not London's Hyde Park. Finally, it is necessary to remember that the doctrine of the separation of government and religion stems not from hostility to religion or discrimination against it, but rather from a recognition that only a clear separation between the two is adequate to protect both the state and church from domination by the other.

FINANCIAL SUPPORT FOR RELIGIOUS SCHOOLS

While school prayers and other religious exercises raise the most highly charged emotional and religious issues, the question of financial assistance to religious schools is, in the long run, probably of greater importance to the cause of sectarian education. Here, the Burger Court has created a body of case law that, thus far, has barred most forms of significant financial assistance to church-related schools.

In 1969, when Chief Justice Burger acceded to his present position, there was great uncertainty as to how the Court would rule on the controversial question of whether states could pay the salaries of teachers of secular subjects in religious schools. Indeed, an opinion by the Court in 1968,[39] upholding a state program for lending secular books to students in religious schools, raised the possibility that the Court might justify government support of religious schools either by drawing a distinction between secular and religious functions of religious schools, or by expanding the notion that the aid was for the benefit of the child rather than for the religious school itself.

In one of this country's major constitutional decisions maintaining the separation of church and state, Chief Justice Burger, in *Lemon* v. *Kurtzman*, wrote for a near-unanimous Court in striking down two state laws that provided for the payment of salaries for teachers of secular subjects in parochial schools. The doctrines developed in this and later cases emphasize that any program of government assistance to church schools must avoid excessive entanglements of government and religion (including political divisiveness along religious lines), and that the program must have a secular purpose and a primary effect that neither advances nor inhibits religion. Applying these principles, the Court has struck down expenditures for instructional materials, maintenance and repair costs, field trip expenses, and therapeutic and remedial services performed on the premises of the religious school.[40]

Other types of government assistance have been upheld: the cost of state-mandated testing and test scoring as part of a system presumably to determine the adequacy of instruction at the religious school,[41] remedial programs conducted off school premises,[42] and construction grants to church-related colleges for facilities devoted exclusively to secular educational purposes.[43] Regardless of one's views about any particular decision of the Court since the *Lemon* case, the effect of the Court's decisions in the past decade has been to cut off any significant direct government financial assistance to religious schools, leaving the contest for public funds to be fought along rather narrow grounds, such as whether remedial programs are conducted on or off school premises, or whether the tests for which reimbursement is sought are prepared by the state or by the teacher. These are fine distinctions but represent the kinds of lines that courts must draw as they apply broad principles to specific cases.

AID THROUGH TAX BENEFITS

The Supreme Court has agreed to review two cases during the 1984 term that could seriously undermine the delicate balance preserved by these earlier cases. *Americans United for Separation of Church and State* v. *School District of the City of Grand Rapids*[44] involves "shared time" and community education programs in which instruction on nonpublic school premises was provided by parochial school teachers whose salaries were paid from tax funds. The sixth circuit affirmed the district court's determination that this arrangement was unconstitutional. In its application of the *Lemon* analysis, the court found that the program did have a secular purpose; however, the factors that create the potential for the advancement of religion are so strong that they necessitate a degree of government surveillance that results in an impermissibly excessive entanglement.

Similarly, in *Felton* v. *Secretary, U.S. Department of Education*,[45] the second circuit upheld a taxpayer challenge to New York City's use of federal funds to send public school teachers and other professionals into religious schools to provide remedial instruction and clinical and guidance services. The fact that the renderers of these services were public school employees rather than parochial school teachers did not obviate the necessity for a "comprehensive, discriminating and continuing state surveillance" which "itself is a constitutionally excessive entanglement of church and state." The monitoring of taxpayer-supported programs in religious schools, whether taught by public or parochial school teachers, involves such a significant entanglement of church and state that it is hard to see where the Court would draw the line in the future if it does uphold these practices next term.

One form of assistance—the granting of tax benefits[46] to help offset the cost of tuition to religious schools—promises to be the major legal and political testing ground in the years ahead for the issue of government support of sectarian education. In the recent case of *Mueller* v. *Allen*, the Supreme Court upheld a Minnesota plan that granted limited tax deductions to parents for the costs of tuition and other expenses, such as textbooks and transportation, incurred for the education of their children in public or private schools. While reaffirming all prior cases involving government aid to religious schools, including a case striking down a similar New York program,[47] the Court's decision adds a new dimension to the "tuition tax credit" controversy, even though the Minnesota plan was different in several major respects from the programs now being pushed in many states and in Congress.

The *Mueller* case was decided amid strong efforts by the Reagan administration to enact a national tuition tax credit program. The Court's approval has intensified this campaign as well as the pressure for state programs similar to the Minnesota plan. Earlier Supreme Court cases appeared to have ruled out programs where the principal beneficiaries are parents of children attending religious schools and where the financial assistance is in the form of an actual credit against the tax as distinguished from a deduction from taxable income. In a leading case from New York, *Committee for Public Education and Religious Liberty* v. *Nyquist*, and in a companion case from Pennsylvania,[48] the Court appeared to have concluded that, regardless of labels, if the state uses the tax system to reimburse a taxpayer for a fixed amount of money where the credit is earned primarily by those paying tuition to religious schools, then the primary purpose is to aid religion.

These decisions, however, involved only programs for attendance at private schools in states where the actual effect of the expenditure was to provide benefits almost entirely to those attending religious schools. Moreover, since they involved specified cash benefits to individual taxpayers, the tax savings could easily be calculated and passed along to the private religious school in the form of higher tuition. The possibility was raised, therefore, that if the class of individuals who were benefited could be broadened beyond those attending private schools (the overwhelming majority being religious schools) and if the benefits could be primarily in the form of a deduction from taxable income, rather than a specified dollar credit against the tax, the Supreme Court might distinguish its earlier cases and uphold a tuition tax credit plan.

Rhode Island[49] and Minnesota[50] exploited these possibilities by enacting laws that provided for a deduction from taxable income of up to $500 in some grades and $700 in others. The deductions were available not only to parents of children attending private schools, but also to parents of public school students. Expenses could be deducted for such items as tuition paid by public school children to attend school outside their home district, summer school tuition, tuition for instruction provided for the physically handicapped, and costs of textbooks and transportation. These differences were found decisive by the Court majority in *Mueller* even though it was estimated that anywhere from 84 percent to 96 percent of the families eligible for the tax deductions were sending their children to religious schools. The *Mueller* case was a disappointment to opponents of aid to religious schools, but it is too early to tell whether it will lead to a significant diversion of public funds to private religious education. The Court majority (five to four) set forth certain new constitutional limits that, while permitting the Minnesota plan to stand, may make it difficult for other types of programs to be upheld. The Minnesota plan itself may be very difficult to duplicate on a national scale.

Of particular importance was the fact that the Minnesota plan created a tax deduction that was available to parents of students in public schools as well as private schools. Moreover, the program was a part of a general policy of tax deductions and not a tax credit of a specified amount. The tax benefits of a deduction to an individual parent are more difficult to calculate and are not so easily passed along to the school.[51]

While the *Mueller* case will encourage the adoption of sim-

ilar state programs, those aspects of the Minnesota plan that
the Court emphasized may render the decision of very limited
value to the proponents of tuition tax credits. Congressional
proposals for a nationwide program of tuition tax credit differ
in several major respects from the program upheld in *Mueller*.
The central idea of the Reagan proposal, and those like it,
would permit a credit against tax liability of an amount equal
to fifty percent of tuition expenses to private schools, subject
to statutory maximums ($300 in the bill proposed by the
administration in 1983).[52] These proposals have met with
strong resistance from supporters of public education, who
argue that a national program of tuition tax credits would
drain billions of dollars from public education into private
(primarily sectarian) schools. Supporters of public education,
and defenders of separation of church and state, have found
strong allies in those concerned with mounting federal deficits.

To meet the standard set by the Court in *Mueller*, a program would, at a minimum, have to be available to children
in public as well as private schools. This would sharply esca-
late the cost by allowing deductions for tuition and other
expenses that some states, like Minnesota, may presently
charge public school parents. It would also tempt public
schools to charge for some expenses that are now free, since a
significant part of the cost would be borne by the federal
government in the form of the tax deduction. Moreover, there
would be some difficult political fallout from the inclusion of
public school expenses, since in many states there are constitutional and statutory barriers against any charges for public
school students. Thus, a program of federal tax deductions for
such expenses would benefit parents unevenly, depending on
the laws of their particular state.

The emphasis placed by the Court on the fact that the
Minnesota plan involved a deduction and not a specified credit
could raise other problems. The proposals in Congress clearly
do not meet this test. If they are altered to provide for a tax
deduction, the benefits to parents will be unequal, depending
on their income tax brackets. Any effort by states and private
schools to pick up the exact amount of the deduction by raising tuition to private schools, or by imposing charges for public school expenses in an amount equal to the actual value of
the tax deduction, will be challenged on grounds that the program is an impermissible direct benefit to the religious institution.

There is no doubt that the Court has opened the door to government support of religious schools through the tax benefit route. The programs permitted by the Court, however, may be far more costly than present proposals being contemplated and they may encounter administrative difficulties that could impair their validity, particularly if the tax deduction is converted into a de facto credit.

Nevertheless, pressures will mount for the enactment of programs like those in Minnesota and Rhode Island, and courts will be urged to allow still more deviations from the constitutional standard that was created in the *Nyquist* case and weakened in *Mueller* v. *Allen*. Interestingly enough, it was a proposal in Virginia, in the early 1780s, to provide public funds for religious education in church schools that inspired James Madison's famous Memorial and Remonstrance against Religious Assessments.[53] Promulgated in 1785, it was an eloquent and prophetic warning against government support of religion. The Remonstrance was the historical antecedent for the Establishment Clause proposed by Madison as the very first protection guaranteed by the Bill of Rights.[54] Two hundred years later, the dangers that Madison predicted in starting down the road of financial support for religion are even more apparent. It is useful to recall the following plea by James Madison in opposition to tax support for religious education:

That the same authority which can force a citizen to contribute three pence only of his property for the support of any one establishment, may force him to conform to any other establishment in all cases whatsoever. . . . Because it will destroy that moderation and harmony which the forbearance of our laws to intermeddle with Religion, has produced among its several sects. Torrents of blood have been spilt in the old world, by vain attempts of the secular arm to extinguish Religious discord, by proscribing all difference in Religious opinions. . . . At least let warning be taken of the first fruits of the threatened innovation. The very appearance of the Bill has transformed that "Christian forbearance, love and charity," which of late mutually prevailed, into animosities and jealousies which may not soon be appeased.

RELIGIOUS PRESSURES IN SCHOOL CURRICULUMS

It is only natural that religious groups should be concerned with the content of education in the public schools. As parents and as citizens who are concerned with the inculcation of certain moral values in the education of their children, members of religious sects have a right to influence curriculum decisions through school board elections, choice of administrators and principals, and through the many avenues by which citizens affect educational decisions in a country where local control of education is a vital tradition. When this influence extends to the point of mandating a religious observance, like a school prayer, Establishment Clause values come into play. When the same pressures seek to impart religious doctrine into school curriculums, the result is at least as troubling as mandated school prayers, but more difficult to control through the judicial mechanism.

Obviously, not every successful effort by religious groups to influence education policy can be viewed as an establishment of religion. To do so would deprive these groups of their First Amendment rights of freedom of speech. Jewish organizations are free to urge that the Holocaust be taught, or that courses on anti-Semitism be offered. On the political level, laws exempting Jews from Sunday closing laws are valid, even though enacted with strong Jewish organizational support. Courts have properly rejected the argument that laws denying public funds for abortions be held unconstitutional simply because they represent the views of the Catholic Church.[55] Catholics, and others, have the right to seek to enact laws that reflect their moral values about abortion, quite apart from the ultimate validity of those laws.

Religious groups may not, however, impose their purely religious beliefs, as distinct from their moral values, as part of the public school curriculum. Thus, in 1968, in *Epperson* v. *Arkansas*,[56] the Supreme Court held invalid a state law banning the teaching of evolution in the public schools because the law was based on the conclusion that the subject matter—evolution—was contrary to favored religious beliefs. The most recent effort to influence school curriculums has been the movement to require that "scientific creationism" be taught in the schools in order to balance the teachings of Darwin's theory of evolution. The Arkansas creation-science law was properly held by a district court to be an unconstitutional establishment of religion after a lengthy trial that demonstrated that the so-called "science" had no scientific basis and was derived from fundamentalist religious teachings.[57]

Litigation, however, is probably of limited value in dealing with the efforts of religious groups to infuse their beliefs into school curriculums. Control over curriculum is traditionally the right of local school board officials who have broad powers to determine its content. In a recent widely heralded case, the

Supreme Court struck down an extreme and clumsy effort by a local school board to remove a number of well-recognized books deemed offensive by the local authorities.[58] The Court ruled that the board was creating a "pall of orthodoxy" of belief, but the case may demonstrate less the limits of school board authority than the broad discretion that school board officials may exercise before those limits are reached. The "creation science" movement represents a religious and political force that has the ability to affect classroom teaching in ways that the courts cannot reach.

THE BROADER ISSUE:
THE ROLE OF RELIGION IN POLITICS

The cases involving school curriculum decisions point to an issue that is difficult to resolve through constitutional litigation and that underlies the resurgence of legislation and litigation in the church-state area. It is the emergence of a strong religious-political force in American life that seeks to impose a conservative religious orthodoxy in such matters as prayer, books in school libraries, motion pictures, sex education in schools, sexual conduct, television programs, and so forth. There is nothing new in the presence of strong forces advocating such positions in American society. Indeed, the right of individuals to advocate these positions is constitutionally protected. The peculiar threat of the 1980s derives from the linking of these positions with a fundamentalist religious position that equates the conservative position on a wide range of controversial issues with a morality based on religious belief, thereby creating disagreements along religious, rather than political, philosophical, or moral grounds. Followers of the Moral Majority consider themselves part of a religious crusade. Their opponents are no longer the objects of a political disagreement; rather, they are nonbelievers.

This development threatens to bring about the very evils that the religion clauses of the Constitution were designed to prevent—the enactment of religious doctrine into law and the fractious division of the country along political-religious lines. The recent five-to-four Supreme Court decision in *Lynch* v. *Donnelly*, which involved a nativity scene erected by the city of Pawtucket, Rhode Island, in front of its city hall, epitomizes the gravity of the present danger. This obviously religious symbol creates a preference for one religion over others, excludes religious minorities and nonbelievers from the official family of religion, divides a community along religious lines, and demeans the very religion it purports to support by tending to secularize a profoundly religious observance. Two lower federal courts had held the construction and display of the crèche unconstitutional.[59] That the United States Justice Department should reach out and, in an amicus brief, urge the Supreme Court to approve this religious establishment demonstrates how far the country's chief law enforcement officials have wandered from their central role of defending constitutional rights.

Chief Justice Burger's opinion, for the five-to-four majority, has, for the first time, upheld direct state support for an avowedly religious symbol that relates to one faith only—Christianity. Although the opinion seeks to justify the result as an "accommodation" to religion, or as a recognition of the secular nature of the Christmas holiday, the result is an affront to religious Christians because it trivializes a profoundly religious symbol, and is a disturbing threat to non-Christian faiths because it condones direct government support for the dominant religious majority.

This term the Supreme Court will decide whether, in the light of *Lynch* v. *Donnelly*, a municipality is precluded from barring the display of a privately financed nativity scene on public property. The second circuit recently overturned a pre-*Lynch* district court decision holding that the exhibition of Scarsdale's crèche constituted an "impermissible state advancement of religion."[60] The cornerstone of the appeals court decision was *Lynch*'s determination that any advancement of religion arising from the display would merely be "indirect, remote or incidental." It would be tragic if, under the rubric of free speech, the Supreme Court subverted Establishment Clause principles and afforded constitutional protection to the installation of a religious structure on public property. A crèche is a far cry from a religious meeting, and governments should not be powerless to bar such overtly religious endorsements.

The situation is further aggravated by the fact that another issue—a woman's reproductive freedom—is also dividing the country along religious lines. Clearly, the First Amendment protects the right of religious groups to try to enact laws that reflect their moral position on an issue such as abortion. When such laws restrict a woman's constitutionally protected right to terminate a pregnancy, they can be challenged on that basis. Moreover, there is a difference between a law regulating conduct, which embodies a moral position rooted in religious belief, and a law that directly imposes that belief in the form of religious observances, courses taught in schools, or financial support for religion. Nevertheless, it has to be recognized that the abortion controversy has created religiously based tensions in American political life.

Thus, society finds itself in an era where the traditional church-state controversies deal with only one part of the broader problem. Some of these tensions are inevitable, particularly in an era when many of the institutions and the legal structures are adjusting to the changing role of women in American life. At this time, it is particularly important that the constitutional principle of separation of church and state be maintained in those areas of the law where it is directly applicable, such as the teaching of religion, government support of religious observances, or government financial aid to religious institutions. The Reagan administration has sought to fuse a broad coalition of groups into a political force on the basis of strongly held religious beliefs. That coalition, containing diverse groups with varying objectives, could very easily wipe away many of the constitutional protections that have guaranteed religious liberty in this country.

On both the legislative and judicial levels, the wall of separation between church and state is under severe pressure. With some important exceptions, the overall record of the courts has been good. How long the judicial branch can withstand the intense pressure from religiously inspired and politically active groups, enthusiastically led by the president of the United States, is a troubling question to those who value religious freedom and the constitutional principles on which it rests.

NOTES

This essay is based on a chapter originally published in *Our Endangered Rights: The ACLU Report on Civil Liberties Today*, ed. Norman Dorsen (New York: Pantheon Books, 1984).

1. See the Supreme Court's summary affirmance of a lower court decision invalidating a Louisiana voluntary prayer law; *Karen B.* v. *Treen*, 653 F.2d 897 (5th Cir. 1981), aff'd mem., 455 U.S. 913 (1982).

2. *Roe* v. *Wade*, 410 U.S. 113 (1973), and the cases, decided in 1983, holding invalid a series of local laws that sought to restrict a woman's ability to carry out the decision to abort her pregnancy; *City of Akron* v. *Akron Center for Reproductive Health*, 103 S. Ct. 3481 (1983); *Planned Parenthood Association of Kansas City, Inc.* v. *Ashcroft* (1983); *Simopoulos* v. *Virginia*, 103 S.Ct. 2532 (1983). 103 S.Ct. 2517.

3. E.g., *Lemon* v. *Kurtzman*, 403 U.S. 602 (1971), and *Committee for Public Education and Religious Liberty* v. *Nyquist*, 413 U.S. 756 (1973).
4. *Swann* v. *Charlotte-Mecklenburg Board of Education*, 402 U.S. 1 (1971), and *Keyes* v. *School District No. 1, Denver, Colo.*, 413 U.S. 189 (1973).
5. *Mueller* v. *Allen*, 103 S.Ct. 3062 (1983).
6. *Marsh* v. *Chambers*, 103 S.Ct. 3330 (1983).
7. *Lynch* v. *Donnelly*, 104 S.Ct. 1355 (1984). See discussion of *Lynch*, p. 296.
8. *Engel* v. *Vitale*, 360 U.S. 421 (1962). The Regents prayer reads as follows: "Almighty God, we acknowledge our dependence upon Thee, and we beg Thy blessings upon us, our teachers and our country."
9. *Abington School District* v. *Schempp*, 374 U.S. 203 (1963).
10. Edmond Cahn, "On Government and Prayer," *Annual Survey of American Law* (1962) 705-6, appearing in *Confronting Injustice* (Boston: Little, Brown, 1966), 189-201.
11. *Illinois ex rel. McCollum* v. *Board of Education*, 343 U.S. 203 (1948); compare *Zorach* v. *Clauson*, 343 U.S. 306 (1952).
12. *Everson* v. *Board of Education*, 330 U.S. 1 (1947).
13. Ibid.
14. The third part of the test was propounded in *Walz* v. *Tax Commission*, 397 U.S. 664 (1970).
15. *Johnson* v. *Board of County Commissioners*, 528 F. Supp. 919 (D.N.M. 1981).
16. *Stone* v. *Graham*, 449 U.S. 39 (1980).
17. *American Civil Liberties Union* v. *Rabun County Chamber of Commerce*, 510 F. Supp. 886 (N.D. Ga. 1981), aff'd, 678 F.2d 1379 (11th Cir. 1982).
18. *Florey* v. *Sioux Falls School District*, 619 F.2d 1311 (8th Cir. 1980).
19. Holiday observances "presented objectively as part of a secular program of education" were condoned by Justice Tom Clark in his majority opinion in *Schempp*, at 225.
20. *Wiley* v. *Franklin*, 468 F. Supp. 133 (E.D.Tenn. 1979). See further litigation at 474 F. Supp. 133 (E.D.Tenn. 1979), and 497 F. Supp. 390 (E.D.Tenn. 1980).
21. See *Braunfield* v. *Brown*, 366 U.S. 599 at 608 (1961).
22. See generally hearings on proposed constitutional amendment to permit voluntary prayer, before the Committee of the Judiciary, United States Senate, 97th Cong., 2d Sess., Serial No. J-97-129. For the 1984 voluntary school prayer amendment debate, see *Congressional Record* 130 (22 March 1984): S.2901ff. A silent prayer amendment was tabled prior to the above debate. See *Congressional Record* 130 (15 March 1984): S.2901.
23. The proposed amendment submitted by President Reagan provides: "Nothing in this Constitution shall be construed to prohibit individual or group prayer in public schools or other public institutions. No person shall be required by the United States or by any state to participate in prayer."
24. See *Congressional Record* 130 (20 March 1984): S.2901.
25. An excellent summary of the laws in eighteen states dealing with moments of silence or meditation is found in Note, "Daily Moments of Silence in Public Schools," *New York University Law Review* 58 (1983):365. A constitutional amendment to allow silent meditation has also been proposed.
26. *Duffy* v. *Las Cruces Public Schools*, 557 F. Supp. 1013 (D.N.M. 1983). Many scholars have supported the constitutionality of moments of silence. See sources cited on Note, "Daily Moments of Silence in Public Schools," 368-69. Cert. denied, *Sub. nom. New Mexico* v. *Burciaga* (D.N.M.) 83-9, 11/14/83, Ruling below, 10th Cir. 4/8/83 unreported).
27. See *May* v. *Cooperman*, Civil No. 83-89, Slip op. (D.N.J. 1983) (declaring the New Jersey law unconstitutional and issuing a permanent injunction).
28. *Wallace* v. *Jaffree*, 705 F.2d 1526 (11th Cir. 1983), 83-812 (prob. jur. noted, 04/02/84).
29. A moment of silence for the purpose of "Prayer or Meditation" was upheld in Massachusetts in *Gaines* v. *Anderson*, 421 F. Supp. 337 (D. Mass. 1976), and a similar law enacted in Tennessee was held invalid in *Beck* v. *McElrath*, 548 F. Supp. 1161

300   RELIGION AND THE STATE

(M.D. Tenn. 1982). Alabama's prayer statute, which also permitted teacher-led meditation, was recently struck down. See *Jaffree* v. *Wallace*.
30.   *West Virginia State Board of Education* v. *Barnette*, 319 U.S. 624 (1943); *Lipp.* v.
Morris, 579 F.2d 834 (3d Cir. 1974).
31.   *Church of God* v. *Amarillo Independent School District*, 511 F. Supp. 613 (N.D.
Tex. 1981), aff'd, 670 F.2d 46 (5th Cir. 1982).
32.   See *O'Hair* v. *Andrus*, 613 F.2d 931 (D.C. Cir. 1979).
33.   *Gilfillian* v. *City of Philadelphia*, 637 F.2d 934 (3d Cir. 1980); apart from the
expenditure of funds there was also extensive involvement by the city with Catholic
Church officials in promoting the event, such as the sale of tickets.
34.   *Widmar* v. *Vincent*, 454 U.S. 261 (1981).
35.   *Lubbock Civil Liberties Union* v. *Lubbock Independent School District*, 669 F.2d
1038 (5th Cir. 1981); *Brandon* v. *Board of Education of Guilderland Central School District*, 635 F.2d 971 (2d Cir. 1980) cert. denied, 454 U.S. 1123 (1981); *Bender* v. *Wil-
liamsport Area School District*, 741 F.2d 538 (3d Cir. 1984); *Nartowicz* v. *Clayton
County School District*, 736 F.2d 646 (11th Cir. 1984).
36.   *Lubbock Civil Liberties Union* v. *Lubbock Independent School District*, note 35.
37.   Senator Mark Hatfield of Oregon has introduced legislation, S. 815 in the
ninety-eighth Congress, similar to an earlier bill offered in the ninety-seventh Congress, which provides in part: "It shall be unlawful for a public secondary school
receiving federal financial assistance, which generally allows groups of students to
meet during noninstructional periods, to discriminate against any meeting of students
on the basis of the religious content of the speech at such meeting, if (1) the meeting
is voluntary and orderly, and (2) no activity which is in and of itself unlawful is permitted." *Congressional Record* 129, no. 32, 15 March 1983. A similar proposal has been
introduced as a constitutional amendment. Senator Jeremiah Denton's bills are not
limited to secondary schools. See S. 425 and S. 815, 98th Cong., 1st Sess.
38.   In the early summer of 1984, by a vote of eighty-eight to eleven, the Senate
approved the Denton-Hatfield amendment (No. 3152) as modified. See *Congressional
Record* 130 (27 June 1984): S.8370. The House then approved the Equal Access Act as
Title VIII of the Senate amendment to H.R. 1310, the Emergency and Science Education and Jobs Act. See *Congressional Record* 130 (25 July 1984): H.7740-41. President
Reagan signed the Equal Access Act, P.L. 98-377, — U.S.C. —, into law on 11
August 1984.
39.   *Board of Education* v. *Allen*, 392 U.S. 236 (1968).
40.   *Committee for Public Education and Religious Liberty* v. *Nyquist*, 413 U.S. 756
(1973); *Meek* v. *Pittenger*, 421 U.S. 349 (1975); *Wolman* v. *Walter*, 433 U.S. 229
(1977); *Public Funds for Pub. Schools* v. *Marburger*, 358 F. Supp. 29 (D.N.J. 1973),
aff'd mem., 417 U.S. 961 (1974).
41.   *Committee for Public Education and Religious Liberty* v. *Regan*, 444 U.S. 646
(1980).
42.   *Wolman* v. *Walter*.
43.   *Tilton* v. *Richardson*, 403 U.S. 672 (1971). See also *Roemer* v. *Maryland*, 426 U.S.
736 (1976).
44.   *Americans United for Separation of Church and State* v. *School District of the City of
Grand Rapids*, 718 F.2d 1384 (6th Cir. 1983).
45.   *Felton* v. *Secretary, U.S. Department of Education*, 739 F.2d 48 (2d Cir. 1984).
46.   See Note, "Laws Respecting an Establishment of Religion: An Inquiry into
Tuition Tax Benefits," *New York University Law Review* 58 (1983):207.
47.   *Committee for Public Education and Religious Liberty* v. *Nyquist*, see note 3.
48.   *Sloan* v. *Lemon*, 413 U.S. 825 (1973).
49.   See *Rhode Island Federation of Teachers* v. *Norberg*, 630 F.2d 855 (1st Cir. 1980)
(Held invalid).
50.   For the lower court decision upholding the Minnesota law, see *Mueller* v. *Allen*,
676 F. 2d 1185 (8th Cir. 1982).
51.   In an earlier case, the third circuit relied on *Nyquist* in holding invalid a New
Jersey law that provided a deduction rather than a credit. The Supreme Court

RELIGION AND SCHOOLS 301

affirmed without opinion. *Public Funds for Public Schools* v. *Byrne*, 590 F. 2d 514 (3d Cir. 1979), aff'd mem., 442 U.S. 907 (1979).
52. S. 528, 98th Cong., 1st Sess., *Congressional Record* 129 (17 February 1983): S.1335-38. In November of 1983, the Senate rejected the president's proposed tuition tax credit program, *New York Times*, 17 November 1983, p. 1, col. 1.
53. Reprinted in *Everson* v. *Board of Education*, at 63 (dissenting opinion of Justice Rutledge).
54. Irving Brant, *James Madison: The Nationalist, 1780-1787* (Indianapolis: Bobbs-Merrill, 1948); Cahn, "The 'Establishment of Religion' Puzzle," *New York University Law Review* 36 (November 1961):1274.
55. *Harris* v. *McRae*, 448 U.S. 297 (1980).
56. *Epperson* v. *Arkansas*, 393 U.S. 97 (1968).
57. *McLean* v. *Arkansas*, 529 F. Supp. 1255 (E.D. Ark. 1982).
58. *Board of Education, Island Trees Union Free School District* v. *Pico*, 102 S.Ct. 1799 (1982).
59. *Donnelly* v. *Lynch*, 525 F. Supp. 1150 (D.R.I. 1981), aff'd, 691 F.2d 1029 (1st Cir. 1982).
60. *McCreary* v. *Village of Scarsdale*, 739 F.2d 716 (2d Cir. 1984).

Religion, the State, and the Public University

DAVID FELLMAN

In the 1920s, if a university dean invited a student to pack his bags and go home after an *ex parte* determination of a violation of the institution's rules, it was completely unthinkable for the student to rush to a lawyer and seek the protection of a court of law, or even to demand an administrative hearing. The courts were as reluctant to interfere in the internal affairs of the college or university as they were unwilling to interfere in the internal affairs of a family. Indeed, a commonly held view was that since the students were away from home and housed on or near the campus, the institution stood *in loco parentis*, which was translated to mean that "courts have no more authority to interfere than they have to control the domestic discipline of a father in his family."[1] Furthermore, courts regarded the relations between student and college as contractual in character, and, thus, "There is an implied condition that the student knows and will conform to the rules and regulations of the institution, and for a breach of which he may be suspended or expelled."[2] In addition, courts tended to look upon attendance at a public college or university as a privilege, not a constitutional right, from which it followed that the institution was free to insist upon whatever binding conditions of behavior it deemed appropriate.

Thus, in the leading *Hamilton* v. *Regents of the University of California* (1934) case,[3] the Supreme Court ruled that religious conscientious objectors had no federal cause of action to challenge the admissions policy of a state university that required every male student to participate in ROTC courses. Justice Pierce Butler pointed out that California did not draft or call the protesters to attend the university, and that "the 'privilege' of attending the university as a student comes not from federal sources but is given by the State. It is not within the asserted protection" of the Fourteenth Amendment.[4] Similarly, in 1915, the Court sustained the validity of a Mississippi statute that prohibited Greek-letter fraternities in all of the state's colleges and universities, noting that the right to attend

the University of Mississippi was not an absolute, but was at
best a conditional right.[5] As recently as 1959, the Court of
Appeals for the Second Circuit upheld the summary dismissal
of a student from Brooklyn College on the ground that "the
'privilege' of attending the College as a student comes not
from federal sources but is given by the State."[6] A concurring
judge stated that the plaintiff had "entered Brooklyn College
not as a matter of right but as a matter of grace after having
agreed to conform to its rules and regulations. . . ."[7]

In 1957, Professor Warren A. Seavey of the Harvard Law
School protested that it was shocking to deny students the
procedural protection given to pickpockets.[8] His notion that
students were entitled to the protection of constitutional due
process of law was soon to become the prevailing rule of law
in the courts. The former distinction between rights and privileges has been abandoned.[9] The Court made it clear in the
Brown case[10] that educational opportunity is not a mere privilege, but a valuable right safeguarded by the Fourteenth Amendment. The privilege concept in student dismissal cases was
abandoned by the federal courts beginning with the *Dixon*
case,[11] decided by the Court of Appeals of the Fifth Circuit in
1961. In an appeal from a dismissal of several black students
who had participated in a peaceful sit-in of a publicly owned
luncheon grill located in the basement of a county courthouse,
the court ruled squarely that due process requires notice of
charges and a hearing before students at a tax-supported college can be expelled for misconduct. Judge Richard T. Rives
asserted, in a notable opinion, that because a student attends
the university voluntarily does not mean that he waived his
right to notice of charges and a hearing, and pointed out that
"the State cannot condition the granting of even a privilege
upon the renunciation of the constitutional right to procedural
due process."[12] The judge argued that "it requires no argument to demonstrate that education is vital and, indeed, basic
to civilized society. Without sufficient education the plaintiffs
would not be able to earn an adequate livelihood, to enjoy life
to the fullest, or to fulfill as completely as possible the duties
and responsibilities of good citizens."[13] Judge Rives added:
"In the disciplining of college students there are no considerations of immediate danger to the public, or of peril to the
national security, which would prevent the Board from exercising at least the fundamental principles of fairness by giving
the accused students notice of the charges and an opportunity

to be heard in their own defense."[14]

The view that prevails today was stated by Justice Abe Fortas in an oft-quoted passage in the opinion in *Tinker* v. *Des Moines Independent School District*,[15] which held that the wearing of black armbands by high school students as a symbol of protest against the Vietnam War was constitutionally protected speech. Said Justice Fortas: "It can hardly be argued that either students or teachers shed their constitutional rights to freedom of speech or expression at the schoolhouse gate. . . . In our system, state-operated schools may not be enclaves of totalitarianism. School officials do not possess absolute authority over their students. Students in school as well as out of school are 'persons' under our Constitution. They are possessed of fundamental rights which the State must respect, just as they themselves must respect their obligations to the State."[16] Similarly, in *Healy* v. *James* (1972),[17] which affirmed the students' right of association on the campus, Justice Lewis F. Powell asserted that "state colleges and universities are not enclaves immune from the sweep of the First Amendment."[18] The Court ruled, however, that the institution may deny recognition to a student group that poses a substantial threat of material disruption or that is unwilling to abide by reasonable time, place, and manner regulations.

The right of students to associate on the campus for religious purposes was thoroughly reviewed by the Supreme Court in *Widmar* v. *Vincent* (1981).[19] This decision was an extension of the public forum doctrine that was initiated by the Supreme Court in *Hague* v. *CIO* (1939)[20] and in *Cox* v. *New Hampshire* (1941)[21] wherein the Court ruled that if a state provides any sort of forum for First Amendment activity, such as public streets, it must do so on a content-free basis.[22] The *Widmar* case involved a regulation of the University of Missouri at Kansas City, a state institution that prohibited the use of university buildings or grounds "for purposes of religious worship or religious teaching." A small registered student group known as Cornerstone was denied permission to conduct both religious worship and religious discussion in a university building, although, generally speaking, the university made its facilities available to all registered students groups. The State of Missouri insisted in litigation before the federal district court that its regulation was both justified and required by the Establishment Clauses of the First Amendment and of the Missouri Constitution. The district court

upheld the challenged regulation,[23] but the court of appeals
reversed, holding that the regulation was content-based discrimination against religious speech.[24] It also ruled that the
primary effect of the Cornerstone's activity would not be to
advance religion, but rather to further the neutral purpose of
developing the social and cultural awareness of students, as
well as their intellectual curiosity. The Supreme Court, with
only Justice Byron R. White dissenting, affirmed the ruling
of the court of appeals. Speaking for the Court, Justice Powell
held that having created a forum generally open for use by
students groups, the university has assumed an obligation to
justify its discriminations and exclusions. He noted that since
"students enjoy First Amendment rights of speech and association on the campus," the denial of campus facilities for meetings and other appropriate purposes must be subjected to the
level of scrutiny appropriate to any form of prior restraint.[25]
He went on to say that engaging in religious discussion and
worship "are forms of speech and association protected by the
First Amendment."[26] Thus, to justify this discrimination, the
university must satisfy the standard of review appropriate to
content-based exclusions. "It must show that its regulation is
necessary to serve a compelling state interest and that it is
narrowly drawn to achieve that end."[27] The Court agreed
with the university's claim that it has a compelling state interest in maintaining a strict separation of state and church,
derived from the Establishment Clauses of both the federal
and state constitutions, but it held that an equal access policy
was not incompatible with the rule against establishment. The
Court held that maintaining a public forum open to all forms
of discourse would not advance religion, and that if religion
benefitted, the benefit was only incidental. "An open forum
in a public university," Justice Powell wrote, "does not confer
any imprimatur of State approval on religious sects or practices . . . ," any more than it does so when it permits the
Young Socialist Alliance or any other group to meet in the
institution's buildings.[28] He also noted that since the forum
was available to over one hundred students groups, there was
no empirical evidence that religious groups would dominate
the forum. In addition, Justice Powell argued that the state's
interest in the separation of church and state is limited by the
Free Exercise Clause and the Free Speech Clause. In concluding his opinion, Justice Powell said: "The basis for our decision is narrow. Having created a forum generally open to stu-

dent groups, the University seeks to enforce a content-based exclusion of religious speech. Its exclusionary policy violates the fundamental principle that a state regulation of speech should be content-neutral, and the University is unable to justify this violation under applicable constitutional standards."[29]

In a concurring opinion, Justice John Paul Stevens maintained that in using the terms "public forum" and "compelling state interest," the Court was needlessly undermining the academic freedom of public universities. He asserted that the facilities of public colleges and universities are not open to the public, as are streets and parks, but are mainly for the benefit of the students and faculty. He could not see why a state university has to establish a "compelling state interest" to defend its decision to permit one group to use a facility, and not another, for the choice regarding the use of academic facilities should be made by academicians rather than by federal judges. Even so, said Justice Stevens, the university must have a valid reason for denying a facility to one student group as compared with the treatment of other groups. In this instance he could find no sufficient justification. He saw no danger of violating the Establishment Clause since the university was not sponsoring any particular religion, and student participation in Cornerstone was wholly voluntary. He observed that since students are free to discuss anticlerical doctrine, the same treatment ought to be extended to religious groups.

Arguing in dissent, Justice White agreed that a state university may permit its property to be used for purely religious services without violating the First and Fourteenth Amendments, but he insisted that the Establishment Clause does not require the state to do that. Just as there is room under the religious clauses for state policies that may have some beneficial effect on religion, there is also room for state policies that may incidentally burden religion. In other words, Justice White thinks that the state is a good deal freer to formulate policies that affect religion in various ways than the Court majority believes. He also rejected the Court's view that because religious worship uses speech, it is protected by the Free Speech Clause. If, he maintained, religious worship is not different from any other variety of protected speech, then in his judgment the religious clauses would be emptied of any independent meaning. Justice White insisted that there must be a line between verbal acts of worship and secular speech. He also noted that there was no serious burden on the ability of Cornerstone's members to worship as they please. The university's regulation, Justice White insisted, promoted a permissible state end, namely, avoiding the public support of religious worship.[30]

The notion that religious worship is a form of speech and association protected by the Free Speech Clause of the First Amendment has raised many eyebrows. Counsel for the University of Missouri has observed that the Court's analysis is "confusing at best."[31] This may be the first time that the Court has ever ruled that religious worship is speech within the meaning of the Free Speech Clause. What consequences will flow from this proposition remain to be seen.

At about the same time that the Court was dealing with the *Widmar* case, another case was working its way through the federal courts that involved a similar issue. This was the case of *Brandon* v. *Board of Education of Gilderland School District*, which involved a decision by a school superintendent to refuse permission to several high school students to conduct communal prayer meetings in a classroom immediately before the school day commenced. A federal district court granted summary judgment on the basis of the Establishment Clause of the First Amendment, holding that granting the request would impermissibly advance religion and lead to an excessive entanglement with religion because faculty surveillance would be necessary to assure that the meetings were voluntary.[32] The court ruled that the compelling state interest in maintaining the separation of church and state justified this restriction on religious freedom. The Court of Appeals for the Second Circuit affirmed on the ground that prayer in a high school does not pose the same issues that grow out of prayer in a university.[33] These high school students, the court noted, were free to pray anywhere else, and high school students are younger and more impressionable than college students. Prayer at public universities is a different matter because students both study and reside on the campus, and are often unable to hold prayer meetings off campus. For university students have special problems like those of members of the armed forces and prison inmates, for whom the state may provide facilities for religious worship. The appeals court went on to say, however:

To an impressionable student, even the appearance of secular involvement in religious activities might indicate that the state has placed its imprimatur on a particular religious creed. This symbolic inference is too dangerous to permit. . . . An adolescent may perceive 'voluntary' school prayer in a different light if he were to see the captain of the school's football team, the student body president, or the leading actress in a dramatic production participating in communal prayer meetings in the 'captive audience' setting of a school. . . . Misconceptions over the appropriate roles of church and state learned during one's school years may never be corrected.[34]

The court concluded that in a high school "the prayer meetings would create an improper appearance of official support, and the prohibition against impermissibly advancing religion would be violated."[35] In addition, there would be an unacceptable entanglement of the state with religion, because continuing administrative supervision of nonsecular activity would be required. Thus, a university may be a "public forum," but a high school is different, since there the symbolic effect on immature pupils is greater.

It is of interest to note that the Supreme Court decided the *Widmar* case on 8 December 1981. It denied certiorari in the *Brandon* case on 14 December 1981[36] and denied a rehearing on 22 February 1982.[37] The willingness of the Court to let the *Brandon* decision stand is not surprising, for in several previous decisions the Court had called attention to the differences between grade school and high school students, on the one hand, and college and university students, on the other hand. In *Tilton* v. *Richardson* (1971),[38] which upheld the constitutionality of the Federal Higher Education Facilities Act of 1963, Chief Justice Warren E. Burger pointed out the significant differences between church-related colleges and secondary and elementary schools. College students are older, more mature, more skeptical, and live in an atmosphere of greater academic discipline and academic freedom.[39] Accordingly, the Court approved of one-time, single-purpose construction grants to church-related colleges on the ground that the support of higher education is a legitimate secular goal that can be achieved without extensive entanglement of church and state in the form of continuing governmental inspection.

Similarly, in *Roemer* v. *Maryland Public Works Board* (1976),[40] a five-to-four decision, the Court upheld a Maryland statute that authorized noncategorical funding for all accredited colleges and universities, except those that grant only theological or seminarian degrees. The statute provided that no money so appropriated shall be used for sectarian purposes. The *Roemer* litigation involved disbursements to four Catholic church-related colleges. The Court majority accepted the findings of the district court that these colleges had much institutional autonomy, that they did not require chapel attendance, that religious indoctrination was not a substantial activity, that there is intellectual freedom in the colleges, that classroom prayers were found to be peripheral to the subjects taught, that—except for theology—faculty hiring was on a nonreligious basis, and that students were chosen without regard to religion. The Court accepted the conclusion of the trial court that these colleges were not so permeated by religion that the secular side could not be separated from the sectarian. Finally, the Court concluded that there was no excessive entanglement in this case between state and religion. Colleges are different from secondary and primary schools; the student constituency in the college is not local, the colleges are substantially autonomous, and not in fact controlled by denominational authorities. Indeed, most private colleges are not religious at all, and, in any event, it is easy to separate the secular from the sectarian activities in them.

As Leo Pfeffer pointed out in his noteworthy treatise, *Church, State, and Freedom:* "The college student has achieved his basic religious training in his home or church and is thus ready for exploration of other religious or even nonreligious beliefs. Moreover—unlike the elementary school child—he no longer accepts as incontrovertible truths all he hears from his teacher or reads in a textbook. Finally, unlike the elementary school child, he does not lack opportunity to hear a nonreligious approach to ultimate reality—as any member of the usual college science or philosophy class can attest."[41]

There have been several decisions in recent years in lower courts that suggest a willingness on the part of courts to recognize the differences between higher education and elementary and high school education. Thus, in 1969, a federal district court in Mississippi ruled that a board of trustees' regulation that provided that no student group may invite outside speakers to discuss religious topics on the campus violated the equal protection of the laws.[42] In 1975, the Supreme Court of Delaware ruled that permitting Roman Catholic students to conduct masses in a dormitory common room at the University of Delaware constituted a neutral accommodation of religion.[43] It took the position that to refuse permission placed a legal burden on the right of students to exercise their constitutional right to the free exercise of religion. "Neutrality," said the court, "is the safe harbor in which to avoid First Amendment violations: neutral 'accommodation' of religion is permitted, . . . while 'promotion' and 'advancement' of religion are not."[44] Since the room in question could be used for every other student activity, a regulation barring use for religious purposes "impedes the observance of religion," and, thus, the regulation burdens freedom of religion. The Court of Appeals for the District of Columbia ruled, however, in 1972, that the U.S. service academies must eliminate their mandatory chapel attendance rule because it conflicts with the Establishment Clause of the First Amendment.[45] The Supreme Court let the decision stand by denying certiorari.[46] Chief Judge David L. Bazelon wrote: "Compulsory church attendance was one of the primary restrictions on religious freedom which the Framers of our Constitution sought to abolish."[47]

It is clearly established in the jurisprudence of the Supreme Court that the Establishment Clause prohibits states from supplying funds for the construction of buildings devoted to seminarian or other theological purposes.[48] It is also clear that public colleges and universities are free to give courses about religion that are not designed for indoctrination purposes. While the Supreme Court has not yet ruled squarely on the point, many justices have gone out of their way, in *obiter dicta,* to say as much. Thus, in his concurring opinion in *McCollum* v. *Board of Education,*[49] Justice Robert H. Jackson noted that it is neither possible nor desirable

to isolate and cast out of secular education all that some people may reasonably regard as religious instruction. Perhaps subjects such as mathematics, physics or chemistry are, or can be, completely secularized. But it would not seem practical to teach either practice or appreciation of the arts if we are to forbid exposure of youth to any religious influences. Music without sacred music, architecture minus the cathedral, or painting without the scriptural themes would be eccentric and incomplete, even from the secular point of view. . . . Certainly a course in English literature that omitted the Bible and other powerful uses of our mother tongue for religious ends would be pretty barren. And I should suppose it is a proper, if not an indispensable, part of preparation for a worldly life to know the roles that religion and religions have played in the tragic story of mankind.

Similarly, in *Abington School District* v. *Schempp,*[50] Justice Tom C. Clark, who spoke for the Court majority in outlawing devotional Bible-reading in the public schools, observed that "one's education is not complete without a study of comparative religion or the history of religion and its relationship to the advancement of civilization. It certainly may be said that the Bible is worthy of study for its literary and historic qualities. Nothing we have said here indicates that such study of the Bible or of religion, when presented objectively as part of a secular program of education, may not be effected con-

sistently with the First Amendment." In a concurring opinion filed in the *Schempp* case,[51] Justice William J. Brennan declared that "the holding of the Court today plainly does not
foreclose teaching *about* the Holy Scriptures or about the differences between religious sects in classes in literature or history. Indeed, whether or not the Bible is involved, it would be
impossible to teach meaningfully many subjects in the social
sciences or the humanities without some mention of religion."
Such matters, said Justice Brennan, should be left "very largely to the experienced officials who superintend our Nation's
public schools. They are experts in such matters, and we are
not." As Justice Hugo L. Black observed in the school prayer
case,[52] "The history of man is inseparable from the history of
religion."

The leading state case[53] on this point was decided by the
Supreme Court of the State of Washington in 1967, when it
held that the historical and literary study of the Bible in the
state university, in a course entitled "The Bible as Literature," offered in the English department, did not violate the
state constitutional prohibition of state-sponsored religious
instruction.[54] The United States Supreme Court made this
decision final by refusing certiorari.[55] The Washington court
noted that the state constitution refers to religious instruction
that is devotional in character, and that is designed to induce
faith and belief in the student. It does not forbid "open, free,
critical, and scholarly examination of the literature, experiences, and knowledge of mankind."[56] The court insisted that
the Bible can be taught in a completely objective manner.[57]
Thus, as Professor Paul Kauper once pointed out: "It is
impossible to exclude all consideration of religion, religious
ideas, and religious institutions from any course of study at
the university level, whether this course centers in the natural
sciences, the social sciences, philosophy, literature, or art.
Religion has played too large a part in man's history and
thinking to be completely excised from academic consideration."[58] To comply with the requirements of U.S. constitutional law, however, Professor Kauper cautioned that student
participation in courses having a religious content should be
wholly voluntary. The courses should deal fairly and equally
with all religious groups, and the instructor must observe the
distinction "between the teaching of religion to promote
knowledge and understanding and that type aimed deliberately at indoctrination and commitment to religious faith."[59]

In addition, state universities may not discriminate against students because of their religious or nonreligious beliefs; students should not be obliged to attend religious services; and courses with religious content should be wholly optional. In other words, public universities and colleges must be alert to observe the distinction between the promotion of knowledge and indoctrination.[60] There are many safeguards that apply to higher education that are not available in the elementary and secondary schools: attendance is voluntary; with the elective system most courses are optional; the sheer size of the public institutions of higher learning tends to reduce tensions; the students are more mature and more skeptical; and there is a general atmosphere of free and critical inquiry nurtured by traditions of academic freedom.[61]

Actually, American colleges and universities offer many courses having a religious content. Writing in 1967, Professor Pfeffer noted that about sixty of the hundred state universities and land-grant colleges offer instruction on religion on an academic credit basis; seventeen have chairs on religion financed by the state universities; and fifteen universities have independent schools of religion affiliated in some way with them.[62] The University of Iowa led the way in establishing a school of religion in 1923. Today, this school has a faculty of fourteen who are appointed in the same way and with the same criteria that apply to all other members of the faculty; its credits are fully accepted in the institution; and it offers undergraduate majors and minors, and M.A.'s and Ph.D.'s at the graduate level. The school is located in the College of Liberal Arts and is subject to the normal administrative authority of the college dean; its professors are paid salaries by the university, as in the case of all other professors. Graduate work is offered in five areas—Jewish and Christian scriptures, history of Christianity, theology and ethics, Asian religions, and religion and personality.

While the University of Wisconsin does not have a separate department of religion, the current catalogue of the College of Letters and Science lists sixty-three courses that deal with religious experience, literature, or history. There are courses, now customarily given in American universities, on the philosophy of religion, the sociology of religion, the anthropology of religion, the place of religion in American politics, the Protestant Reformation, and biblical texts. In addition, there are courses with substantial religious content in a wide variety of

departments, such as African studies, art history, classics, East
Asian studies, English, Hebrew and Semitic studies, history,
history of science, Scandinavian studies, and South Asian studies. It cannot be said that the world's religious experience is
ignored at the University of Wisconsin.[63]

That the Supreme Court is unwilling to permit a state to
force a particular brand of religious belief upon high school or
college students is reflected in *Epperson v. Arkansas* (1968).[64]
In this case, a unanimous Court ruled unconstitutional an
Arkansas statute that made it unlawful for any teacher in a
state-supported school or university "to teach the theory or
doctrine that mankind ascended or descended from a lower
order of animals," or "to adopt or use in any such institution
a textbook that teaches" this theory. The state supreme court
held that this antievolution statute was a proper exercise of the
state's power to specify the curriculum in its public schools.
The United States Supreme Court disagreed, holding that the
challenged statute violates both of the religious clauses of the
First Amendment in that it forbids a particular body of
knowledge for the sole reason that it is deemed to conflict
with a particular religious doctrine, i.e., "a particular interpretation of the Book of Genesis by a particular religious
group."[65] Said Justice Fortas: "Government in our democracy, state and national, must be neutral in matters of religious theory, doctrine, and practice. It may not be hostile to
any religion or to the advocacy of no-religion; and it may not
aid, foster, or promote one religion or religious theory against
another or even against the militant opposite. The First
Amendment mandates governmental neutrality between religion and religion, and between religion and. nonreligion,"[66]
Justice Fortas added: "There is and can be no doubt that the
First Amendment does not permit the State to require that
teaching and learning must be tailored to the principles or
prohibitions of any religious sect or dogma."[67] While he conceded that the state had an undoubted right to prescribe the
curriculum in its public schools, he went on to assert that that
"does not carry with it the right to prohibit, on pain of criminal penalty, the teaching of a scientific theory or doctrine
where that prohibition is based upon reasons that violate the
First Amendment."[68] Since the only reason for the statute was
a "fundamentalist sectarian conviction," it is not an act of the
sort of religious neutrality the Constitution requires.

The latest attempt of fundamentalists to denigrate the theory of evolution has taken the form of demanding balanced treatment in the schools for creationism along with the theory of evolution. In March 1981, the Arkansas legislature adopted a statute, the first sentence of which stated its central purpose: "Public schools within this State shall give balanced treatment to creation-science and to evolution-science." The statute was made applicable only to secondary and elementary schools, and not to colleges and universities. On 5 January 1982, Judge William R. Overton of the federal district court in Arkansas ruled that the statute violates the Establishment Clause.[69] In an exhaustive opinion, he concluded that creationism was an aspect of fundamentalism, a central premise of which has always been a literal interpretation of the Bible. Clearly, he held on the basis of legislative history that the statute is a product of a religious crusade, and was enacted for the specific purpose of advancing religion. He noted that the essential characteristics of a science are as follows: (1) it is guided by natural law; (2) it has to be explanatory by reference to natural law; (3) it is testable against the empirical world; (4) its conclusions are tentative, i.e., not necessarily the final word; and (5) it is falsifiable.[70] Thus, he observed that "a theory that is by its own terms dogmatic, absolutist and never subject to revision is not a scientific theory."[71] Futhermore, "There is no way teachers can teach the Genesis account of creation in a secular manner."[72] Judge Overton also pointed out that creationism is not accepted by the scientific community, and that not a single scientific journal has ever published an article espousing it.

Judge Overton concluded that the statute must fall under the three-pronged test that now applies in Establishment cases. The statute does not have a secular purpose; it is designed to advance particular religious beliefs, since creation science is not a science but a concept based on "supernatural intervention"; and its enforcement would require excessive entanglement of the state in religious matters, such as the screening of texts and the monitoring of classroom discussions. Finally, Judge Overton rejected the argument that public opinion polls demonstrated wide public support for creationism, since the content and application of the First Amendment are not determined by public opinion polls or by majority votes. Judge Overton said: "No group, no matter how large or small, may use the organs of government, of which the public schools are the most conspicuous and influential, to foist its religious beliefs on others."[73]

While the Court has asserted that it is committed to a "strict separation" of church and state,[74] and indeed that the wall of separation between church and state must be kept "high and impregnable,"[75] an absolute separation of church and state is simply not possible. As Chief Justice Warren E. Burger wrote in a 1970 opinion that held valid tax exemption of church property: "The course of constitutional neutrality in this area cannot be an absolutely straight line; rigidity could well defeat the basic purpose of these provisions, which is to insure that no religion be sponsored or favored, none commanded, and none inhibited."[76] Considerable difficulty arises from the fact that the two religious clauses of the First Amendment often conflict, and, thus, some choice must be made. As Professor Lawrence H. Tribe observes in his impressive treatise on constitutional law, there is a "zone which the free exercise clause carves out of the establishment clause for permissible accommodation of religious interests. This carved-out area might be characterized as the *zone of permissible accommodation*."[77] Clearly, the subject of religion and higher education lends itself to a considerable amount of "permissible accommodation."

NOTES

1. *Stetson University* v. *Hunt*, 88 Fla. 510, 516, 102 So. 637, 640 (1925). See also *Gott* v. *Berea College*, 156 Ky. 376, 379, 161 S.W. 204, 206 (1913).
2. Ibid., 102 So. 640. See also *Behrend* v. *State*, 55 Ohio App. 2d 135, 9 O.O. 3d 280, 379 N.E.2d 617 (Ohio App. 1977). "Generally it may be stated that when a student enrolls in a college or university, pays his or her tuition and fees, and attends such school, the resulting relationship may reasonably be construed as being contractual in nature" (379 N.E.2d 620); *State* v. *Fenton*, 68 App. Div. 2d 951, 414 N.Y.S. 2d 58 (1979), suit for unpaid tuition and fees is time-barred, according to the statute of limitations applying to contractual obligations. See also *Anthony* v. *Syracuse University*, 224 App. Div. 487, 231 N.Y.S. 435 (1928), student is contractually bound, by his act of registration, to observe all rules, whether or not he was aware of the rules.
3. *Hamilton* v. *Regents of the University of California*, 293 U.S. 245 (1934).
4. Ibid., at 261. In 1933, the Supreme Court of Maryland sustained the validity of a statute providing for compulsory ROTC at the state university on the privilege theory (*University of Maryland* v. *Coale*, 165 Md. 224, 167 A. 54 [1933]), and the U.S. Supreme Court dismissed an appeal from this decision on the ground that it did not present a substantial federal question, 290 U.S. 597 (1933).
5. *Waugh* v. *Board of Trustees of University of Mississippi*, 237 U.S. 589 (1915).
6. *Steier* v. *N.Y. State Educ. Comm'r.*, 271 F.2d 13, 16 (2nd Cir. 1959).
7. Ibid., at 20.
8. Warren A. Seavey, "Dismissal of Students: Due Process," *Harvard Law Review* 70 (June 1957):1406-10, 1406-7. See also idem, Note, "Students' Constitutional Rights on Public Campuses," *Virginia Law Review* 58 (March 1972):552-83.

9. See William Van Alstyne, "The Demise of the Right-Privilege Distinction in Constitutional Law," *Harvard Law Review* 81 (May 1968):1439-64.

10. *Brown* v. *Board of Education*, 347 U.S. 483, 493 (1954).

11. *Dixon* v. *Alabama State Board of Education*, 294 F.2d 150 (5th Cir. 1961), cert. denied, 368 U.S. 930 (1961). See William Van Alstyne, "Procedural Due Process and State University Students," *University of California at Los Angeles Law Review* 10 (January 1963): 368-89.

12. *Dixon* v. *Alabama*, at 156.

13. Ibid., at 157.

14. Ibid. Charles Alan Wright ("The Constitution on the Campus," *Vanderbilt Law Review* 22 [October 1969]:1027-88, 1032) has remarked: "The opinion by Judge Rives had the force of an idea whose time had come and it has swept the field."

15. *Tinker* v. *Des Moines Independent School District*, 393 U.S. 503 (1969). See also *Burnside* v. *Byars*, 363 F.2d 744 (5th Cir. 1966). A regulation prohibiting high school students from wearing "freedom buttons" proclaiming "one man, one vote," is arbitrary and unreasonable in the absence of any evidence of interference with educational activity.

16. *Tinker* v. *Des Moines*, at 506, 510.

17. *Healy* v. *James*, 408 U.S. 169 (1972).

18. Ibid., at 180. See Note, "Beyond *Tinker* and *Healy:* Applying the First Amendment to Student Activities," *Colorado Law Review* 78 (December 1978):1700-13.

19. *Widmar* v. *Vincent*, 454 U.S. 263 (1981). See Note, "The Rights of Student Religious Groups under the First Amendment to Hold Religious Meetings in the Public University Campus," *Rutgers Law Review* 33 (Summer 1981):1008-53; Lisa M. Newell, "Use of Campus Facilities for First Amendment Activity," *Journal of College and University Law* 9 (No. 1, 1982-83):27-39; Don Howarth and William D. Connell, "Students' Rights to Organize and Meet for Religious Purposes in the University Context," *Valparaiso University Law Review* 16 (Fall 1981):103-43.

20. *Hague* v. *CIO*, 307 U.S. 496 (1939).

21. *Cox* v. *New Hampshire*, 312 U.S. 569 (1941).

22. See also *Police Department of Chicago* v. *Mosley*, 408 U.S. 92 (1972), holding that equal protection is denied if all forms of picketing are forbidden in a particular public place except for labor picketing. See the remarks of Judge Roger J. Traynor of the California Supreme Court in *Danskin* v. *San Diego Unified School District*, 28 Cal. 2d 536, 171 P.2d 885, 891 (1946): "The state is under no duty to make school buildings available for public meetings. . . . If it elects to do so, however, it cannot arbitrarily prevent any members of the public from holding such meetings." See also the opinion of Judge Stanley H. Fuld in *East Meadow Community Concerts, Inc.* v. *Board of Education*, 18 N.Y.2d 129, 272 N.Y.S.2d 341, 219 N.E.2d 172 (1966).

23. *Chess* v. *Widmar*, 480 F. Supp. 907 (W.D. Mo. 1979). The Court relied mainly on the authority of *Tilton* v. *Richardson*, 403 U.S. 672 (1971).

24. *Chess* v. *Widmar*, 635 F.2d 1310 (8th Cir. 1980).

25. *Widmar* v. *Vincent*, at 268, n. 5. There has been a great deal of litigation on the right of various student groups to be recognized officially and to use institutional facilities. See, e.g., *Hudson* v. *Harris*, 478 F.2d 244 (10th Cir. 1973) (antiwar group at a state college); *Shamlov* v. *Mississippi State Board of Trustees*, 620 F.2d 516 (5th Cir. 1980) (right of Iranian students to demonstrate); *Bazaar* v. *Fortune*, 476 F.2d 570 (5th Cir. 1973), cert. denied, 416 U.S. 995 (1974) (distribution of student literary magazine); *Joyner* v. *Whiting*, 477 F.2d 456 (4th Cir. 1973) (state funding of student newspaper). Many courts have affirmed the right of homosexual organizations to function on the campus as recognized student associations: *Gay Students Org.* v. *Bonner*, 509 F.2d 652 (1st Cir. 1974); *Gay Lib.* v. *University of Missouri*, 558 F.2d 848 (8th Cir. 1977), cert. denied, 434 U.S. 1080 (1977), rehearing denied, 435 U.S. 981 (1978); *Student Coalition for Gay Rights* v. *Austin Peay State University*, 477 F. Supp. 1267 (M.D. Tenn. 1979). On this point the cases are collected and reviewed by David Adamany, "The Supreme Court at the Frontier of Politics: The Issue of Gay Rights," *Hamline Law Review* 4 (January 1981):185-285.

26. *Widmar* v. *Vincent*, at 269.

27. Ibid., at 270. In *Spartacus Youth League* v. *Board of Trustees of Illinois Indus. University*, 502 F. Supp. 789 (N.D. Ill. 1980), the U.S. District Court held that the Student Union (called Civic Center) of the Chicago Circle Campus of the University of Illinois was a public forum, from which no group may be barred unless the state shows a compelling governmental interest.

28. *Widmar* v. *Vincent*, at 274.

29. Ibid., at 277.

30. See Newell, "Use of Campus Facilities for First Amendment Activity."

31. T. D. Ayres, "*Widmar* v. *Vincent:* The Beginning of the End for the Establishment Clause?" *Journal of College and University Law* 8 (No. 4, 1981-82):511-17, 511.

32. *Brandon* v. *Board of Education of Gilderland School District*, 487 F. Supp. 1219 (N.D.N.Y. 1980).

33. *Brandon* v. *Board of Education of Gilderland School District*, 635 F.2d 971 (2nd Cir. 1980).

34. Ibid., at 978.

35. Ibid., at 979.

36. 454 U.S. 1123.

37. 71 L.Ed. 2d 695.

38. The vote of the Court was five to four.

39. Compare the remarks of Circuit Judge H. Emory Widener, Jr. in *Williams* v. *Spencer*, 622 F.2d 1200, 1205 (4th Cir. 1980). He observed that while secondary students do not shed their constitutional rights at the schoolhouse gate, "neither are their First Amendment rights necessarily co-extensive with those of adults."

40. *Roemer* v. *Maryland Public Works Board*, 426 U.S. 736 (1976).

41. Leo Pfeffer, *Church, State, and Freedom*, rev. ed (Boston: Beacon Press, 1967), 507-8.

42. *Stacy* v. *Williams*, 306 F. Supp. 963 (N.D. Miss. 1969).

43. *Keegan* v. *University of Delaware*, 349 A.2d 14 (Del. 1975), cert. denied, 424 U.S. 934 (1976). Justices William J. Brennan and Harry Blackmun dissented from the denial of review by certiorari.

44. *Keegan* v. *Delaware*, 349 A.2d 16.

45. *Anderson* v. *Laird*, 151 App. D.C. 112, 466 F.2d 283 (1972).

46. *Anderson* v. *Laird*, 409 U.S. 1076 (1972). One of three-judge panel dissented, arguing that compulsory chapel was essential to train military leaders.

47. *Anderson* v. *Laird*, 466 F.2d 286. In *North* v. *Board of Trustees of the University of Illinois*, 137 Ill. 296, 27 N.E. 54 (1891), the Supreme Court of Illinois upheld compulsory, nonsectarian chapel services at the state university as a reasonable regulation for the inculcation of moral and religious principles. The court stressed that students could be excused from chapel for good cause. Such a decision is highly unlikely today. In *State ex rel. Sholes* v. *University of Minnesota*, 236 Minn. 452, 54 N.W.2d 122 (1952), a suit to enjoin the use of facilities of the University of Minnesota by student religious groups was dismissed on the technical ground that the taxpayer-plaintiffs should first have taken the question to the governing body of the institution. This is in accord with what is known as the doctrine of primary jurisdiction.

48. *Tilton* v. *Richardson* and *Roemer* v. *Maryland Public Works Board*. See Robert Michaelson, "The Supreme Court and Religion in Public Higher Education," *Journal of Public Law* 13 (No. 2, 1964):343-52.

49. *McCollum* v. *Board of Education*, 333 U.S. 203, 235-36 (1948).

50. *Abington School District* v. *Schempp*, 374 U.S. 203, 225 (1963).

51. Ibid., at 300. In another concurring opinion, ibid., at 306, Justice Arthur J. Goldberg remarked that "it seems clear to me from the opinions in the present and past cases that the Court would recognize the propriety of providing military chaplains and of the teaching *about* religion, as distinguished from the teaching *of* religion, in the public schools."

52. *Engel* v. *Vitale*, 370 U.S. 421, 434 (1962). See also the remarks of Justice Abe Fortas in *Epperson* v. *Arkansas*, 393 U.S. 97, 106 (1968): "While study of religions

and of the Bible from a literary and historic viewpoint, presented objectively as part of a secular program of education, need not collide with the First Amendment's prohibition, the State may not adopt programs or practices in its public schools or colleges which 'aid or oppose' any religion."

53.   *Calvary Bible Presbyterian Church* v. *Board of Regents*, 72 Wash. 2d 912, 436 P.2d 189 (1967).

54.   The constitutional provision is as follows: "No public money or property shall be appropriated for or applied to any religious worship, exercise or instruction, or the support of any religious establishment." Wash. Cont., Art. I, Sec. 11.

55.   *Calvary* v. *Regents*, 393 U.S. 960 (1968).

56.   *Calvary* v. *Regents*, 436 P.2d 193.

57.   It is of interest to note that one judge dissented on the ground that the course in question favored the liberal, as opposed to the traditional, view of the Bible.

58.   Paul G. Kauper, "Law and Public Opinion," in *Religion and the State University*, ed. E. A. Walter (Ann Arbor: University of Michigan Press, 1958), 81.

59.   Ibid., 82. See also the remarks of Wilbur G. Katz, *Religion and American Constitutions* (Evanston, Ill.: Northwestern University Press, 1964), 52.

60.   See Robert C. Casady, "On Teaching Religion at the State University," *Kansas Law Review* 12 (March 1964):405-16; Wilber G. Katz, "Religious Studies in State Universities," *Wisconsin Law Review* (Spring 1966):297-305.

61.   Kauper, "Law and Public Opinion," 79-80.

62.   Pfeffer, *Church, State, and Freedom*, 506. See David W. Louisell and John H. Jackson, "Religion, Theology and Public Higher Education," *California Law Review* 50 (December 1962):751-99.

63.   The Court held, in *Stacey* v. *Williams*, that while a university can forbid religious services on the campus, it cannot bar speakers on religious subjects without violating the Equal Protection Clause.

64.   *Epperson* v. *Arkansas*.

65.   Ibid., at 103.

66.   Ibid., at 103-4.

67.   Ibid., at 106.

68.   Ibid., at 107.

69.   *McLean* v. *Arkansas Board of Education*, 529 F. Supp. 1255 (E.D. Ark, 1982). Summarized in *Law Week* 50:2412 and in *Science* 215 (22 January 1982):381-84. The complaining parties included the resident Arkansas bishops of the United Methodist, Episcopal, Roman Catholic, and African Methodist Episcopal Churches, the principal official of the Presbyterian Churches in Arkansas, other clergymen, taxpayer-parents of several school children, a high school biology teacher, and several educational associations, such as the Arkansas Education Association and the National Association of Biology Teachers.

70.   *McLean* v. *Arkansas*, at 1267. In *Daniel* v. *Waters*, 515 F.2d 485 (6th Cir. 1975), it was ruled that a Tennessee statute requiring the public schools to give equal attention to both evolution theory and biblical creationism, and also requiring that teachers must present evolution as being only a theory and not scientific fact, is unconstitutional. The supporting opinion was much less impressive than Judge Overton's opinion in the *McLean* case. See also *Wright* v. *Houston Independent School District*, 366 F. Supp. 1208 (S.D. Tex. 1972), aff'd *per curiam*, 486 F.2d 137 (5th Cir. 1973), cert. denied, 417 U.S. 969 (1974), which held that the teaching of the theory of evolution in the public schools did not constitute a violation of students' free exercise of religion.

   For an excellent analysis of the dispute over the teaching of evolution and "scientific creationism," see J. Greg Whitehair, "Teaching the Theories of Evolution and Scientific Creationism in the Public Schools: The First Amendment Religion Clauses and Permissible Relief," *Journal of Law Reform* 15 (Winter 1982):421-63.

71.   *McLean* v. *Arkansas*, at 1269.

72.   Ibid., at 1272.

73.   Ibid., at 1274.

74.   *Everson* v. *Board of Education*, 330 U.S. 1 (1947).

75.   *McCollum* v. *Board of Education*, at 212.

76.   *Walz* v. *Tax Commission*, 397 U.S. 664, 669 (1970). In *Lemon* v. *Kurtzman*, 403 U.S. 602, 614 (1971), Chief Justice Burger said: "Our prior holdings do not call for total separation between church and state; total separation is not possible in an absolute sense. Some relationship between government and religious organizations is inevitable. . . . Judicial caveats against entanglement must recognize that the line of separation, far from being a 'wall,' is a blurred, indistinct, and variable barrier depending on all the circumstances of a particular relationship." In *Roemer* v. *Public Works Board*, at 745-46, Justice Blackmun asserted that "the Court has enforced a scrupulous neutrality by the State, as among religions, and also as between religious and other activities, but a hermetic separation of the two is an impossibility it has never required."

77.   Laurence H. Tribe, *American Constitutional Law* (Mineola, N.Y.: Foundation Press, 1978), 823.

PART 6

RELIGION AND TAXATION

Tax Exemption and the Free Exercise of Religion

DEAN M. KELLEY

There are at least two ways to think about tax exemption, and upon the choices between them hang many implications for the freedom of churches and other voluntary, nonprofit organizations of citizens. One is the "tax expenditure" rationale and the other is the "tax base" rationale.

THE TAX-EXPENDITURE RATIONALE

The common wisdom, articulated (until recently) mainly by lower courts and some legislators, holds that exemption from taxation is an affirmative benefit extended by legislative grace to those organizations that benefit the public and is withdrawable at will from those organizations the legislature deems no longer deserving of its favor.

Thus, tax exemption is like a subsidy or grant to certain groups for performing certain services—a *quid pro quo*—that is no longer appropriate if they fail to fulfill their end of the bargain. This concept has been carried to its logical extreme by Stanley S. Surrey, who several years ago as assistant secretary of the Treasury for Tax Policy proposed that tax exemptions—like other tax immunities and preferences in the Internal Revenue Code—be viewed by Congress as "tax expenditures"—revenues foregone by the government as though granted to the exempt entity in fulfilment of legislative purposes, which the government itself might otherwise have to undertake. As a consequence of Surrey's urging, every year a list of proposed "tax expenditures" is compiled to remind Congress that in allowing such noncollection of taxes, it is in a sense (supposedly) giving such money away.[1]

There are, however, some assumptions underlying this rationale that should be examined. First, it assumes that the legislature is entitled to tax everything, and, therefore, anything it refrains from taxing is enjoying a special privilege or immunity at the expense of the rest of the community, which must then "make up for" the taxes the exempted entity does not pay.

Second, it assumes that the legislature in its wisdom can and should dispense the largesse of such exemptions only to those favored entities that—in its view—contribute to the public good or perform services the government would otherwise be obliged to perform. It also assumes that it should attach appropriate conditions to such a "grant" of tax exemption as will assure that the requisite public goods are attained or services rendered.

Finally, it assumes that tax exemptions are functionally equivalent to subsidies, overlooking several important differences in the actual operation of the two, viz.: (1) Tax exemption, unlike a subsidy, conveys no money whatever to an organization. (2) No one is compelled by tax exemption (directly) to support the organization, as they would be if a portion of their taxes were appropriated to it as a grant; rather, individuals can choose whether they wish to donate to it. (3) A tax exemption, rather than being for a specified amount, is open-ended, dependent upon the amount contributed to the exempt organization by its supporters rather than upon the decision of legislators or governmental administrators. (4) Elaborate processes of application, reporting, investigation, auditing, evaluation, regulation, and accountability are not (yet?) entailed in tax exemption as they usually or eventually are in subsidy. (5) Tax exemption does not convert the organization into an agency of "state action" as subsidy sometimes does.

The United States Supreme Court has made a similar contrast between tax exemption and subsidy in the only opinion it has issued analyzing the (property) tax exemption of churches, in *Walz* v. *Tax Commission*:

Obviously a direct money subsidy would be a relationship pregnant with involvement and, as with most governmental grant programs, could encompass sustained and detailed administrative relationships for enforcement of statutory or administrative standards, *but that is not this case.* . . . The government does not transfer part of its revenue to churches but simply abstains from demanding that the church support the state. No one has ever suggested that tax exemption has converted libraries, art galleries, or hospitals into arms of the state or employees "on the public payroll."[2]

In assuming that exemption equals subsidy, does this rationale create a corresponding implication that nonsubsidy equals taxation?

Boris Bittker, an arch-critic of the tax expenditure theory, has observed (with tongue in cheek?): "If exempting an individual from tax is equivalent to subsidizing him, excluding an individual from an expenditure program should be viewed as equivalent to taxing him. This corollary, if accepted, would greatly enlarge the circle of potential plaintiffs in 'taxpayer' suits."[3]

The application of the tax-expenditure rationale to churches is anomalous since they do not render a service that government, under the First Amendment, would or could properly supply if the churches did not. It may be that the legislature, under the First Amendment, does not have the *power* to tax the "free exercise of religion." The Supreme Court said, in *Murdock* v. *Pennsylvania,* "The power to tax the exercise of a privilege is the power to control or suppress its enjoyment . . . . Those who can tax the exercise of this religious practice [colporteuring] can make its exercise so costly as to deprive it of the resources necessary for its maintenance."[4]

In its brief *amicus curiae* in the *Walz* case, the Synagogue Council of America cited this statement and reasoned from it that property used for religious purposes, including the house of worship, the religious sanctuary, and all that is contained therein are so intimately connected with religious exercise that to levy a direct tax upon the value of such property would constitute a tax on the exercise of religion having the same effect as that tax that the Court found unconstitutional in *Murdock.*[5]

Furthermore, if the legislature were to set conditions on the tax exemption of churches to insure that they rendered supposed public services to the satisfaction of the legislature, it would be in effect creating an "establishment of religion" with respect to those churches that met the expectations of the legislature at the expense of those that did not, since the Supreme Court has held that "perferring one religion over another" is one form of violation of the prohibition against establishment of religion in the First Amendment.[6]

THE TAX-BASE RATIONALE

There is another way of looking at tax exemption that avoids these criticisms: *Nonprofit organizations are not taxed because they are not in the tax base to begin with.*

Income tax exemptions. Boris Bittker, author of the definitive five-volume work on *Federal Taxation of Income, Gifts, and Estates,* has explained the tax-base rationale as follows:

There is no way to tax *everything;* a legislative body, no matter how avid for revenue, can do no more than pick out from the universe of people, entities, and events over which it has jurisdiction those that, in its view, are appropriate objects of taxation. In specifying the ambit of any tax, the legislature cannot avoid "exempting" those persons, events, activities or entities that are outside the territory of the proposed tax. . . .

The federal income tax of current law, then, "exempts" nonprofit groups; and this quite naturally leads, on a quick glance, to the conclusion that they have been granted the "privilege" of "immunity." . . . Unless blinded by labels, however, one can view the federal income tax instead as a tax on income that inures in measurable amounts to the direct or indirect personal benefit of identifiable natural persons. So viewed, the Internal Revenue Code's "exemption" of nonprofit organizations is simply a way of recognizing the inapplicability to them of a concept that is central to the tax itself.[7]

In another article, Bittker pointed out that when Congress wrote the first modern income tax statute, the Revenue Act of 1913, only "net income" was to be taxed, thus automatically excluding all nonprofit organizations that normally have *no* net income. Cordell Hull, floor manager of the 1913 Act, remarked during the debate on it, "Of course any kind of society or corporation that is not doing business for profit would not come within the meaning of the taxing clause."[8] Bittker concluded: "The exemption of nonprofit organizations from federal income taxation is neither a special privilege nor a hidden subsidy. Rather, it reflects the application of established principles of income taxation to organizations which, unlike the typical business corporation, do not seek profit."[9]

Real property tax exemptions. A similar conclusion was reached with respect to exemption from taxes on real property by Dean Peter Swords, Columbia Law School, in a volume he prepared for the Association of the Bar of the City of New York. After extensive research into the operation of the real property tax in New York State (which is not greatly different with respect to principle from such taxes in other states), Swords concluded: (1) Since most of the proceeds of the property tax go to finance the general purposes of government rather than services directly benefiting property, it is not different in purpose from the income or sales tax.[10] (2) The initial question in imposing such a tax is: "What kinds of property ought to be in and what kinds ought to be out of the tax base," which—since people, not property, pay taxes— means, "What people or what class of people with respect to their relation to property ought in fairness to be expected to pay the property tax?"[11] (3) If nonprofit charitable organizations were to be taxed on their property, the persons who would have to pay the tax would be their contributors, who "have already paid the property tax . . . in their capacity as homeowners, consumers or investors in profit-making organizations and should not be expected to contribute additionally to the provision of government services by reason of their support of nonprofit charitable organizations from which they receive no direct benefits."[12] (4) "Only consumption and wealth accumulation ought to bear the burden of tax, i.e., be called upon to finance general government services, and . . . contributions to charitable organizations do not constitute consumption or wealth accumulation."[13] (5) The radical distinction between consumption and wealth accumulation, on the one hand, and contributions to charitable organizations, on the other hand, is that: (a) The latter provide public or collective goods that benefit all of society in such a way that their receipt by one person does not diminish the quality or quantity received by others, and that do not redound to contributors in direct and tangible benefits (e.g., profits) any more than to others in the community at large. (b) Conversely, most items of ordinary consumption benefit the consumer or accumulator alone and correspondingly lessen the supply available to others in the community.[14]

Summary of tax base rationale, whether derived from income or real property tax exemptions, with corollary considerations. The basis of taxation is wealth, and, therefore, public revenue is normally derived from the producers and amplifiers of wealth, viz., productive individuals and profit-making collectivities such as business corporations. Those not in that category are *simply not part of the revenue system*, not so much because the legislature has bestowed upon them a special privilege, but because they are impractical, unrewarding, or counter-productive objects of taxation. They are counter-productive in the sense that taxing them can be injurious to their socially constructive citizen activities and initiatives that make the community an attractive place to live and that constitute a vital and essential part of the fabric of democracy.[15]

Furthermore, each of their members is already paying his or her share of the costs of the commonwealth and should not be taxed *again* for the time, effort, interest, and money contributed to collective activities from which she or he derives no personal pecuniary gain and which may indeed benefit the community in general. One might almost say that if additional taxes are to be levied, they should fall upon the members of the community who are *not* engaged in such constructive enterprises rather than upon those who are!

Of course, any expense to the community directly attributable to such a nonprofit organization should be defrayed by its members and contributors through service charges assessed to the organization. That, however, does not apply to the undifferentiated expenses of the community in general—such as for fire and police protection—which might actually be greater if the nonprofit organization did not exist, since it not only brings funds into the community but makes it more attractive to taxpayers.[16]

Certain corollaries and implications of this rationale have consequences very different from the tax-expenditure theory. If nontaxation of nonprofit organizations is due, not to the largesse of the legislature, but to their not being part of the tax base, then the only pertinent consideration qualifying such an organization to be nontaxed is whether it is truly nonprofit. Other considerations about their mode of operation— i.e., whether they attempt to influence legislation, intervene in campaigns for public office, or conform to "public policy"— are simply not germane.

The legislature or the executive cannot properly define such organizations in or out of the tax base as cavalierly as did the New York legislature in 1971 in permitting municipalities to begin to tax the property of "bible, tract, missionary, infirmary, public playground, scientific, literary, bar association, medical society, library, patriotic or historical" organizations, which had hitherto been exempt. Swords found that the legistature was stampeded into this ill-advised measure by a committee report that predicted, on the basis of its (flawed) study of real property taxation in the state, that if present trends were to continue "one-half of the assessed value of all real property on municipal assessment rolls will be exempt within the next fifteen years."[17] The committee, however, had failed to distinguish between *public* exempt property (governmentally owned) and *private*, or to note that all of the increase in the period studied had been in the *public* sector; private exempt property had actually *diminished* slightly in that period. It was the *private* exempt sector, however, that bore the brunt of the legislature's hysteria to halt the supposed disappearance of taxable property; the real culprit—the public exempt sector— for which the legislature was more directly responsible, was not touched at all![18]

DEVELOPMENTS INCONSISTENT WITH THE
TAX-BASE RATIONALE

Life would be simpler if one or the other of these two competing rationales were consistently followed in the tax code and court decisions, but such is not the case. Congress and state legislatures shift in composition and intention from year to year, swept by the exigencies, appeals, and political cross-pressures of the moment. Even the courts are not immune from these, as will be seen. Meanwhile, the tax code has become a patchwork of mutually inconsistent fragments—"a dark, miasmic, myxomycetous sump"[19]—affording lucrative careers to the hardy practitioners of tax law who have become adept at plumbing its murky depths and tracing its meandering bayous that to mere mortals seem so convoluted and obscure.

Some meanings of "tax exemption." For one thing, when laypersons speak about an organization's "losing its tax exemption," the transaction seems simple enough, but to what does it apply? Actually, "tax exemption" (in the federal tax code alone) refers to a whole bundle of specifics, and the same rationale does not apply to all of them. It includes: deductibility from donors' gross income of charitable contributions to such organization—Section 170(c)(2) of the Internal Revenue Code; exemption from federal social security (FICA) taxes—Section 3121(b)(8)(B) of the Code, eliminated effective 31 January 1984; exemption from federal unemployment (FUTA) taxes (administered by the states)—Section 3306(c)(8) of the Code; deductibility from decedents' gross estate of charitable bequests to such organization—Sections 2055(a) and 2106(a) (2)(A) of the Code; deductibility from gift tax of charitable gifts to such organization—Section 2522(a) and (b) of the Code; and exemption from income taxation—under Section 501(a) as an organization described in Section 501(c) of the Code.

Rationales of "tax exemption." The rationale for exempting such nonprofit organizations from paying the employer's share of FICA and FUTA taxes is obscure. It might well be contended that *all employers should pay these taxes*, whether or not they are nonprofit organizations, and that is apparently what Congress thought when it recently eliminated their exemption from Social Security taxes.

The rationale for deductibility of contributions, bequests, and gifts from donors' income, estate, or gift tax is that these are *charitable* contributions that do not enrich the donor or represent the consumption, enjoyment, or accumulation of wealth. The Filer Commission on Private Philanthropy and Public Need gave this rationale for such deductibility: "The charitable deduction is a philosophically sound recognition that what a person gives away simply ought not to be considered as income for purposes of imposing an income tax . . . . it is appropriate to define income as revenue used for personal consumption or increasing personal wealth and to therefore exclude charitable giving because it is neither. . . ."[20]

The remaining element of exemption is that of an organization's net income from federal income taxation (Section 501). It is to this exclusion of nonprofit organizations from the federal income tax base that the tax-base rationale applies, and to it only. It is on this section that controversy seems to focus, however, which is ironic, since loss of Section 501 exemption would generally have little effect upon a nonprofit organization because it has little or no "net income" to be taxed. The real pinch would come with loss of deductibility of contributions (Section 170), since that would render the organization a much less attractive recipient of contributions if donors could no longer deduct them from their income tax. Section 170(c) copies the language of Section 501(c)(3) in describing an organization entitled to receive charitable contributions, so loss of status as an organization described in Section 501(c)(3) would invariably be accompanied by loss of deductibility under Section 170. The two sanctions, however, are not the same in either effect or rationale.

Added conditions of tax exemption. As has been seen, the only condition of tax exemption in the original income-tax statute of 1913 was an organization's being nonprofit. Since then, however, other conditions have been added to the most desirable category of tax exemption—the Section 501(c)(3) category, which entails in addition deductibility of contributions.

In 1934, Senator Reed of Pennsylvania added an amendment to that section that required that organizations exempt under that section should be those for whom "no substantial part of the activities . . . is carrying on propaganda, or otherwise attempting, to influence legislation."[21]

At the time of enactment, Senator Reed explained on the floor that this amendment was aimed at sham charities that were really "fronts" for the private interests of a major donor. He insisted that it was not designed to inhibit "the Society for the Prevention of Cruelty to Children or the Society for the

Prevention of Cruelty to Animals, or any of the worthy institutions that we do not in the slightest mean to affect."[22] It is,
however, precisely these genuine, "worthy institutions" that
in more recent times are the main victims of the proscription
against (substantial) lobbying.

The meaning of the qualifying modifier "substantial" has
also been a subject of some controversy. The Internal Revenue Service has never defined that term in regulations. One
court has held that 5 percent of an organization's expenditures
is not substantial.[23] Another has invoked that clause to deny a
tax exemption without using an expenditure test at all, as will
be seen later. A new section, 501(h), has been added to the
Code to permit certain Section 501(c)(3) organizations to do a
limited amount of lobbying, defining "substantial" on a slid-
ing expenditure scale proportioned to the size of the organization. Churches, however, *at their own request* are not entitled
to elect to come under that section, since they felt that any
restriction on their right to try to affect public policy is
unconstitutional, and a permit to do a *little* lobbying is no
improvement.

In 1954, Senator Lyndon B. Johnson of Texas added a
further condition to Section 501(c)(3) in equally tortured
prose: "and which does not participate in, or intervene in
(including the publishing or distribution of statements), any
political campaign on behalf of any candidate for public
office."[24] There is no margin of insubstantiality in this prohibition.

Rivalry in the courts between the two rationales. In 1972, the
Tenth Circuit Court of Appeals invoked both of these restrictions in upholding the revocation of the tax exemption of an
Oklahoma evangelist, Billy James Hargis, for intervening in
political campaigns and for substantially attempting to influence legislation. The court did not attempt to define "substantial" in expenditure terms but characterized Hargis's lobbying
activity as an "important" and "continuous" part of his work
and therefore substantial. Falling in with the tax-expenditure
rationale, the tenth circuit court upheld the revocation with
these words:

In light of the fact that tax exemption is a privilege, a matter of grace rather
than right, we hold that the limitations contained in Section 501(c)(3) withholding exemption from nonprofit corporations which engage in lobbying
do not deprive Christian Echoes of its constitutionally guaranteed right of
free speech. The taxpayer may engage in all such activities without restraint, subject, however, to withholding of the exemption, or, in the alter-

native, the taxpayer may refrain from such activities and obtain the privilege of exemption.[25]

Thus, exempt organizations (including churches?) are told by the court that they must choose between lobbying and tax exemption!

The United States Supreme Court declined to hear the Hargis case, leaving it in effect—at least in the tenth circuit. This seemed surprising in view of the fact that the tenth circuit court had contradicted the Supreme Court's *Walz* decision of two years previous in at least three respects: (1) The tenth circuit court characterized tax exemption as "subsidy"— a concept explicitly rejected by the Supreme Court in its decision in *Walz* v. *Tax Commission*, as noted above. (2) it considered tax exemption to be a privilege extended to churches in recognition of the public services they render, an idea the Supreme Court had also rejected in *Walz:* "We find it unnecessary to justify the tax exemption [of churches] on the social welfare services or 'good works' that some churches perform for parishioners and others. . . . Churches vary substantially in the scope of such services; programs expand and contract according to resources and need. . . . "[26] (3) It treated the participation by religious bodies in public affairs not as their right under the First Amendment, but as a threat to the wall separating church and state, despite the fact that the Supreme Court had said in *Walz* that such activity of churches is not only entirely proper but is their *right:* "Adherents of particular faiths and individual churches frequently take strong positions on public issues including, as this case reveals in the several briefs amici, vigorous advocacy of legal or constitutional positions. Of course, churches as much as secular bodies and private citizens have that right."[27]

The tenth circuit thus pursued its tax-expenditure rationale without correction from the Supreme Court, which seemed to have staked out some clear guideposts to the tax-base rationale in its *Walz* opinion of 1970. (It is interesting to note that the churches obtained from Congress in the Tax Reform Act of 1979 an unusual concession by way of a proviso in Section 504(c) that in enacting the new Section 501(h), it was not indicating agreement or disagreement with the court's opinions in *Christian Echoes National Ministry* v. *United States.* Thus, it was avoiding the presumption of having "re-enacted" those opinions into Section 501(c)(3) when it legislated in that area.) There is in the tenth circuit's *Christian Echoes* opinion *not even a single reference* to the Supreme Court's *Walz* opinion of two years before—an evidence of the continuing rivalry between these two competing rationales of tax exemption.

The executive grafting of the law of charities onto the nonprofit tax exemption. During the past two decades, another series of developments growing out of the effort to eliminate racial discrimination in education helped to complicate this picture further and to cloud the coherence of the tax-base rationale. Section 501(c)(3) lists an array of purposes that entitle certain nonprofit organizations to that most-favored category of exemption (most-favored because it also entails deductibility of contributions under Section 170, as was noted). Those purposes are listed disjunctively in parallel: "organized and operated exclusively for religious, charitable, scientific . . . literary *or* educational purposes. . . . " and so forth.

In 1959, the Department of the Treasury issued regulation 1.501(c)(3)-1(d)(2), which lifts up *one* of that series—"charitable"—and applies it also to the whole list. The treasury added that it is to be understood "in its generally accepted legal sense," by which it has subsequently come to be supposed that the common law of charities has now become attached to Section 501(c)(3), though Congress has never explicitly made that connection, and it scarcely makes for clarity to attribute two different meanings to the same word in the same section.

Randolph Thrower, former Commissioner of Internal Revenue, in his 1982 testimony before the House Ways and Means Committee on the subject of the tax exempt status of racially discriminatory private schools, recalled that he had set up an Advisory Committee on Exempt Organizations in 1969 that had embraced the concept that the law of charities—dating back to the English Statute of Charitable Uses of 1601—is somehow engrafted upon the exemption provided by Section 501(c)(3).

Throughout this history "charity" was used both as a narrow term denoting public welfare, as the provision of alms for the poor, and also as a broad term encompassing religion, education, public welfare and other programs of exclusively public interest and benefit. Hence, we speak in the narrow sense of donations to the poor as charity and in the broad sense of donations to churches or educational institutions as charitable contributions.

In our study together my staff and I and the members of the Advisory Committee were impressed with the fact that for the past several hundred years the legislative definitions of charity have followed the broad terms of the Statute of Charitable Uses. . . . From century to century what was char-

itable had to be determined by reference to current standards. Actions, no
matter how well motivated, which, according to standards of the day, were
illegal, anti-social or in conflict with clearly developed public policy, were
not deemed to be charitable. . . . It would be ludicrous to apply the law of
charity without this guiding light. To use a classic example, without this
standard, one might feel required to recognize as tax exempt Fagin's school
for pickpockets, provided it qualified in all other respects. And direct aid to
needy people supportive of an organized effort to violate the law could otherwise be deemed charitable.[28]

Thus does the former Commissioner of Internal Revenue
seek to justify the contention that the law of charities is
implicit in Section 501(c)(3), even though Congress has never
said so. He bulwarks this justification with two interesting
footnotes in one of which he notes that donations to organizations with "religious, charitable, scientific, literary, or educational purposes" are defined in Section 170 as "charitable
contributions"—which nobody can deny, but its relevance to
Section 501(c)(3) is not automatic. The other footnote displays
a remarkable leap of logic worthy of a true athlete of rhetoric:
"That *Congress* intended to adopt the broad common law concept of charities is reflected in income tax *regulations*, published rulings of the *Internal Revenue Service* and *decisional
law.*"[29]

He does not explain how the intent of *Congress* is demonstrated by reference to explications offered by the two *other*
branches of the federal government—the executive and the
judiciary—in regulations, rulings, and decisions in the pro-
mulgation of which Congress played no part whatever!

*The judicial grafting of the law of charities onto the nonprofit
tax exemption.* These efforts by the executive branch to read
into Section 501(c)(3) the common law of charities were ably
seconded by the judiciary. In the 1971 case that is widely supposed to have settled the matter for all time, *Green* v. *Connally*,
Judge Leventhal (for a three-judge court in the District of
Columbia) addressed the question whether private schools that
discriminate on the basis of race are entitled to tax exemption.
To resolve this question, he joined together two previously
unrelated elements. He took in one hand the recent Regulation referred to above that defined "charitable" in Section
501(c)(3)—in a way never required by Congress—and applied
to it, by "strong analogy," the "general common law of charitable trusts," with its twin corollaries of benefiting the public
and not violating "public policy." In the other hand, he took
the doctrine of *Tank Truck Rentals* v. *Commissioner* (356 U.S.

30), which prohibited the *deductibility* (under Section 162), as an ordinary and necessary cost of doing business, of state fines for overweight trucks because such deduction would offset the effect of the fines and therefore would frustrate sharply defined national or state "public policy" (against overweight trucks). He brought the two together in a remarkable match of logic enabling him to announce that racially discriminatory private schools are not entitled to tax exemption or deductibility because they are not *charitable*, since they fail to fit the criteria of the law of charities (newly) found in Section 501(c)(3) because they violate clearly defined federal public policy against racial discrimination.

He threw in the classic literary allusion to Charles Dickens's quaint portrayal of Fagin's school for pickpockets that has proved so popular with Randolph Thrower and other subsequent writers on the subject, without noting that pickpocketing, like overweight trucks, is a *criminal* activity, whereas operating a racially discriminatory school (as yet) is not. Is loss of tax exemption to be used as a sanction to punish conduct that is not reachable under the criminal code?

Judge Leventhal explicitly did not deal in his opinion with the case of "a religious school that practices acts of racial restriction because of the requirements of the religion."[30] (That issue has been working its way through the courts in cases that were decided by the Supreme Court in 1983.) The Supreme Court in 1972 affirmed *Green* v. *Connally* under the name of *Coit* v. *Green* by unsigned memorandum opinion, but noted in a subsequent case, *Bob Jones University* v. *Simon*, that its affirmance lacked "the precedential weight of a case involving a truly adversary controversy,"[31] since the Department of Justice had reversed its position and agreed with the plaintiffs on the way to the Supreme Court.

A year later, the same logic was followed by another federal court in the same district in *McGlotten* v. *Connally*, which held that the Internal Revenue Service could not accord exemption (under Section 501(c)(8)) and deductibility to *fraternal organizations* with racially discriminatory rules of membership because such tax benefits in its view constituted government support and encouragement of such discrimination. It did not, however, reach the same conclusion with respect to *social clubs* (Section 501(c)(7)), whose exemption differs only in that their investment income is taxed.[32]

As a result of this curious outcome, Congress enacted a new

section of the Code denying exemption to social clubs that
discriminate on the basis of race, color, or religion, and put it
in Section 501 as new subsection (i)—the only indication in
the Code that Congress sees a connection between racial discrimination and tax exemption.

The logic underlying this series of developments that has
undertaken to engraft the criteria of the law of charities on
Section 501(c)(3) is inconsistent with the tax-base rationale
because it assumes that tax exemption is a form of governmental support, public subsidy, or federal financial assistance and,
therefore, cannot—must not—be extended to activities
thought to be antisocial, which is a corollary of the tax-
expenditure rationale. That this is a recent development is
indicated by the debates in Congress over the Civil Rights Act
of 1964, which proposed to deny all forms of "federal financial assistance" to racial discrimination. Both opponents and
proponents of the Act listed all of the imaginable kinds of federal financial assistance that would be cut off if the Act were
adopted, *but neither side even mentioned tax exemption.* The idea
that tax exemption is a form of federal financial assistance has
emerged only more recently as a result of the injection of the
tax-expenditure rationale.

Some tax exemptions intended as incentives. The cause of consistency is further confused with respect to the tax-base rationale by the fact that there are some exemptions (usually from
property taxation) that are clearly designed—usually by temporary or partial tax remission—to induce otherwise taxpaying
entities to do something desired by the community, such as to
build low-cost housing or to locate within the district. These
incentive exemptions clearly fit the tax-expenditure rationale
and should be clearly distinguished from the kind included in
Section 501 of the Internal Revenue Code, which—as even
the McGlotten court recognized—are *not subsidies* but artifacts
of the tax structure that serve to define the meaning of
"income" for purposes of taxation, as by the phrase so often
encountered with reference to exempt organizations, "no part
of the net earnings of which inures to the benefit of any private shareholder or individual."[33]

Appropriate applications of the "law of charities." In the light
of the earlier discussion of the law of charities, one can think
of a more appropriate application of that common-law tradition to the internal revenue statute. If Congress should want
to apply the criteria of charitable trusts—that they must serve

a public purpose and must not violate public policy—to the tax code, it could do so in a way consistent with the tax-base rationale by attaching it to Section 170 rather than to Section 501(c)(3). That is, Congress could leave untouched the present basis for exempting nonprofit organizations from taxation on their net income but could say that a *charitable contribution* is one made to any organization that benefits the *public* and does not violate public policy. Therefore, any organization that *excludes* any segment of the public because of accidents of birth unrelated to the service or benefit rendered (race, sex, age, or national origin) is not eligible for contributions that are deductible as genuinely "charitable."

This stricture would apply to religious organizations as well. It would not affect their exemption from taxation nor violate their right to free exercise of religion, since it would apply to contributors rather than to the church. It would be based, not on whether the organization or the contributor's intent are religious, but on whether they are "charitable" in the sense of *benefiting the public* without exclusions due to factors over which potential beneficiaries have no control.

THE SUPREME COURT'S "TILT" TOWARD THE TAX-EXPENDITURE RATIONALE

On two successive days in May 1983, the United States Supreme Court appeared to embrace the tax-expenditure rationale rather decisively.

Taxation with representation. On 23 May, the Court announced its unanimous view in *Regan* v. *Taxation with Representation*[34] (hereinafter *TWR*) that tax exemption is equivalent to subsidy. That ruling reversed the District of Columbia Circuit Court, which had found unconstitutional the restriction on lobbying in Section 501(c)(3) of the Internal Revenue Code.

An organization seeking exemption—"Taxation with Representation"—had informed the Internal Revenue Service that one of its purposes was to seek reform of the tax code by legislation, and the Service had therefore denied its application, as it routinely does with organizations whose objectives can be attained only by changing the laws. *TWR* then went to court insisting that it could not be refused tax exemption for exercising a right guaranteed by the First Amendment—to assemble and petition Congress for redress of grievances.

The circuit court held that Congress could place such a

limitation on tax exemption if it wished, but it could not permit some organizations to lobby without losing deductibility while forbidding others to do so. Veterans' organizations are exempt from income taxation under Section 501(c)(19), but are eligible for deductible contributions under Section 170 (c)(3) in which no limitation on lobbying is included. There is such a limitation in Section 170(c)(2)(D), applying to organizations described in Section 501(c)(3), thus affording a privilege to veterans' groups denied to others—of lobbying with "soft money" and thereby violating the "equal protection of the laws" guaranteed by the Due Process Clause of the Fifth Amendment.

In an opinion written by Justice William H. Rehnquist, the Supreme Court reversed, holding that veterans' organizations are not so similar to other exempt groups that Congress cannot treat them differently if it wishes. "Our country has a long standing policy of compensating veterans for their past contributions by providing them with numerous advantages." The Court devoted only a casual penultimate paragraph to that issue. The rest of the opinion corrects *TWR*'s misguided view that it is entitled to tax exemption if it wishes to engage in attempting to influence legislation:

Both tax exemptions and tax deductibility are a form of *subsidy* that is administered through the tax system. A tax exemption has much the same effect as a *cash grant* to the organization of the amount of tax it would have to pay on its income. Deductible contributions are similar to *cash grants* of the amount of a portion of the individual's contributions. The system Congress has enacted provides this kind of *subsidy* to nonprofit civic welfare organizations generally, and an additional subsidy to those charitable organizations that do not engage in substantial lobbying. In short, Congress chose not to subsidize lobbying as extensively as it chose to subsidize other activities that nonprofit organizations undertake to promote the public welfare. [emphasis added][35]

(In ten short pages, Justice Rehnquist used the term "subsidy" or synonyms like "grants" or "largesse" thirty-one times!)

The Court then reassured *TWR* that its freedom of speech was not curtailed by the strictures on lobbying in Section 501(c)(3); it could always set up a nondeductible subsidiary to do its lobbying using "hard money." Section 501(c)(*4*) exempts "social welfare organizations," which are permitted to lobby, but they are not eligible to receive deductible contributions. In any event, Congress is not obliged to "subsidize" *TWR*'s freedom of speech.

We have held in several contexts that a legislature's decision not to subsidize the exercise of a fundamental right does not infringe the right. . . . The reasoning of these decisions is simple: "although government may not place obstacles in the path of a [person's] exercise of . . . freedom of [speech], it need not remove those not of its own creation. . . . [*Harris* v. *McRae*, 448 U.S. 297(1980)] The issue in this case is not whether TWR must be permitted to lobby, but whether Congress is required to provide it with public money with which to lobby . . . we hold that it is not.[36]

Blackmun's concurrence. In a concurring opinion, Justice Harry Blackmun, joined by Justices William J. Brennan and Thurgood Marshall, added an important corollary that bears on the much-debated subject of whether a Section 501(c)(3) organization can set up a wholly owned and controlled subsidiary under Section 501(c)(4) to do its lobbying. The IRS has seemed to think that such an arrangement permits the former to do indirectly through the latter what it cannot do directly itself. Yet if close control is not exercised by the parent organization over its subsidiary, they may drift apart and go their own ways, as happened with the National Association for the Advancement of Colored People (the Section 501(c)(4) parent) and its Section 501(c)(3) subsidiary, the NAACP Legal and Educational Fund, Inc.

Justice Blackmun did not dismiss *TWR*'s claim that unconstitutional conditions had been placed upon its tax exemption:

If viewed in isolation, the lobbying restriction contained in §501(c)(3) violates the principle, reaffirmed today, ante, at 5, "that the government may not deny a benefit to a person because he exercises a constitutional right." Section 501(c)(3) does not merely deny a subsidy for lobbying activities . . . ; it deprives an otherwise eligible organization of its tax-exempt status and its eligibility to receive tax-deductible contributions for all its activities, whenever one of those activities is "substantial lobbying." Because lobbying is protected by the First Amendment, *Eastern Railroad Presidents Conf.* v. *Noerr Motor Freight, Inc.*, 365 U.S 127, 137-138 (1961), §501(c)(3) therefore denies a significant benefit to organizations choosing to exercise their constitutional rights.

The constitutional defect that would inhere in §501(c)(3) alone is avoided by §501(c)(4). . . . A §501(c)(3) organization's right to speak is not infringed, because it is free to make known its views on legislation through its §501(c)(4) affiliate without losing tax benefits for its non-lobbying activities.

Any significant restriction on this channel of communication, however, would negate the saving effect of §150(c)(4). . . . Should the IRS attempt to limit the control these organizations exercise over the lobbying of their §501(c)(4) affiliates, the First Amendment problems would be insurmountable. It hardly answers one person's objection to a restriction on his speech that another person, outside his control, may speak for him.[37]

Justice Blackmun did not dispute the Court's view that tax exemption was equivalent to subsidization, and that "the First

Amendment does not require the government to subsidize protected activity."[38] Thus, the entire Court seems to have accepted the tax-expenditure rationale without any serious examination of its assumptions or consequences. That appearance was reinforced the next day.

Bob Jones University and Goldsboro Christian Schools v. *United States.* On 24 May 1983, the Supreme Court "dropped the other shoe." One of the most intensely awaited decisions of the Court in recent years was that in *Bob Jones University* v. *United States*, which had been combined with *Goldsboro Christian Schools* v. *United States* for hearing by the nation's highest court. Both dealt with the question of whether tax exemption could be denied a private *religious* school that discriminated on the basis of race "because of the requirements of the religion"—a question explicitly not reached in *Green* v. *Connally*.

What could have been a hard enough question of the accommodation between religious liberty and racial equality was immensely complicated by the action of the Reagan administration on 8 January 1982, which asked the Court to void the case as moot because it had decided to restore tax exemption to *all* private schools that had lost it because of discrimination—on the ground that Congress had never conditioned tax exemption on that basis. The case then became a *cause célèbre* overnight, and moral, emotional, and political cross-pressures escalated accordingly.

Although one of the parties had withdrawn, the Court did not drop the case but took the unusual step of inviting a black attorney, William T. Coleman, Jr., to argue as *amicus curiae* the position the United States had abandoned. Oral argument was heard on 12 October 1982, with William B. Ball of Harrisburg, Pennsylvania, a Roman Catholic attorney who has championed many important religious liberty cases, articulately representing Bob Jones University (but not Goldsboro).

He had an uphill task, as the "liberal establishment" had closed ranks against what they saw as a threat to the civil-rights gains since *Brown* v. *Board of Education* eliminated segregation in public schools in 1954, and leading constitutional scholars were heard in Congressional hearings proclaiming univocally—and a bit shrilly—that the issue had, too, been settled by the courts (*Green* v. *Connally*), Congress (Civil Rights Acts of 1964), and the Constitution (Equal Protection Clause of the Fourteenth Amendment).[39] Such insistence, of course, turned on several "iffy" points, such as whether the

criteria of charitable trusts attach to Section 501(c)(3) and
whether tax exemption is a subsidy, which are not as open-
and-shut as some have assumed.

The Supreme Court undertook to resolve these problems,
however, if not by persuasion, at least by assertion. In an
opinion written by the chief justice on behalf of eight justices,
the Court repudiated the administration's attempt to restore
tax exemption to racially discriminatory private schools. It ratified the full force of *Green* v. *Connally* and its linkage of tax
exemption to the criteria of charitable trusts. It rejected the
administration's contention that Congress had not endorsed
the IRS's policy resulting from *Green* v. *Connally*. After all,
reasoned the chief justice, Congress had had a dozen years in
which to correct the policy of the IRS if it did not like it, but
Congress had made no move to change it, and this "failure of
Congress to modify the IRS rulings . . . make out an unusually strong case of legislative acquiescence in and ratification
by implication of the 1970 and 1971 rulings."[40]

As a clincher, the Court referred to Section 501(i), which
Congress had added to the Internal Revenue Code in 1976 to
prohibit tax exemption for discriminating social clubs, noting
that the accompanying House and Senate reports cited *Green*
v. *Connally* and remarked that "discrimination on account of
race is inconsistent with an educational institution's tax exempt status."[41]

Several pages of the Court's opinion are devoted to demonstrating that the courts have long insisted (citing cases from
1861, 1878, and 1891) that charitable trusts must not violate
public policy—which no one was disputing. The missing link
is the one that would attach that criterion of charitable trusts
to Section 501(c)(3) of the Internal Revenue Code. The Court
quoted the House Report accompanying the Revenue Act of
1938 to the effect that "the exemption from taxation of money
and property devoted to charitable and other purposes" is justified in part "by the benefits resulting from the promotion of
the general welfare,"[42] but that statement refers to the charitable deduction in Section 170, which is a quite appropriate
place to apply the criteria of charitable trusts. It does not
resolve the question with respect to Section 501(c)(3).

The Court then explained that "when the government
grants exemptions or allows deductions all taxpayers are affected; the very fact of the exemption or deduction for the
donor means that other taxpayers can be said to be indirect

and vicarious 'donors.' Charitable exemptions are justified on
the basis that the exempt entity confers a public benefit.
. . . The institution's purpose must not be so at odds with the
common community conscience as to undermine any public
benefit that might otherwise be conferred."[43] Here the tax-
expenditure rationale—so reiteratively asserted in *Taxation
with Representation* the day before—once again made its appearance, complete with reference to Fagin's school for pickpockets (note 18). To it was coupled the criteria of charitable
trusts: that a "charity" must serve a public purpose or provide
a public benefit and must not violate public policy. All of this
was discerned in the provision for tax exemption in Section
501(c)(3), but without any explicit statement by Congress to
substantiate it.

The Court then went on to maintain that eliminating racial
discrimination in educational institutions was a clearly defined
federal public policy—which none of the parties was disputing.

Then—almost as an afterthought—the Court dealt in a few
paragraphs with the claim that racial discrimination in the
two schools was an aspect of the Free Exercise of Religion
guaranteed by the First Amendment. First, it recalled that the
free exercise of religion can be burdened in pursuance of a
compelling state interest, and then forthwith concluded that
"the government interest at stake here is compelling," and
can be subserved in no less burdensome way.[44]

Two curious comments accompanied this reasoning. The
first occurred with respect to whether religious liberty was
actually burdened: "Denial of tax benefits will inevitably have
a substantial impact on the operation of private religious
schools, but will not prevent those schools from observing
their religious tenets."[45] This was a very different view of the
possible effects of tax policy on religious liberty from that
expressed in *Murdock* v. *Pennsylvania*, noted above.

The second was a footnote that dealt with the question that
troubled the lower courts: Was Bob Jones University a church
or a school? The trial court found it equivalent to a church,
that is, not a school attached to a church but itself the seat
and repository of religious teaching and practice. The circuit
court divided two to one on the issue, with the majority holding that it was more like a school than a church. The
Supreme Court confined itself to a brief footnote (no. 29):
"We deal here only with religious *schools*—not with churches
or other purely religious institutions; here, the governmental

interest is in denying public support to racial discrimination in education.''[46]

Justice Rehnquist's dissent. The only member of the Court not persuaded by the chief justice's exposition was Justice Rehnquist, who insisted that Congress had not written a "public policy" requirement into the exemption law:

In approaching this statutory construction question the Court quite adeptly avoids the statute it is construing. This I am sure is no accident, for there is nothing in the language of §501(c)(3) that supports the results obtained by the Court.

* * * *

Perhaps recognizing the lack of support in the statute itself, or in its history, for the IRS change in interpretation, . . . the Court relies first on several bills introduced to overturn the IRS interpretation of §501(c)(3). . . . But we have said before, and it is equally applicable here, that this type of congressional inaction is of virtually no weight in determining legislative intent. . . .

The Court next asserts that Congress acted to ratify the IRS policy "when it enacted the present §501(i) of the Code. . . . "Quite to the contrary, it seems to me that in §501(i) Congress showed that when it wants to add a requirement prohibiting racial discrimination to one of the tax-benefit provisions, it is fully aware of how to do it.

* * * *

This Court continuously has been hesitant to find ratification through inaction . . . this Court has no business finding that Congress has adopted the new IRS position by failing to enact legislation to reverse it.[47]

Indeed, the majority had not asserted that there is clear language in the statute that requires their conclusion. Instead it must content itself with such lame phrases as "acquiescence" and "ratification by implication." When eight justices of the Supreme Court agree that the statute means what they think it means, however, that is the law of the United States—at least until Congress amends the statute or a new majority of the Court decides otherwise.

Justice Rehnquist contended that in adopting the exemption statute (Section 501(c)(3)), *"Congress has decided* what organizations are serving a public purpose and providing a public benefit. . . . Congress has left it to neither IRS nor the courts to select or add to the requirements of 501(c)(3)."[48] He agreed with the majority that there is a "strong national policy . . . opposed to racial discrimination," and that "Congress has the power to further this policy by denying §501(c)(3) status to organizations that practice racial discrimination. But as of yet Congress has failed to do so."[49] Therefore, he concluded, neither school had done anything that *Congress* had said should deprive them of tax exemption.

Justice Powell's partial concurrence. One other justice wrote a separate opinion. Justice Powell concurred in part and concurred in the judgment. The only part in which he concurred was the section holding that denial of tax exemption did not violate the religious liberty of the two schools! He agreed with Justice Rehnquist that the language of the statute did not necessarily support the interpretation the Court drew from it, but—unlike Justice Rehnquist—he acquiesced in the Court's view: "Indeed, were we writing prior to the history detailed in the Court's opinion, this could well be the construction I would adopt [viz., Rehnquist's]. But there has been a decade of acceptance that is persuasive in the circumstances of this case, and I conclude that there are now sufficient reasons for accepting the IRS's construction of the Code as proscribing tax exemptions for schools that discriminate on the basis of race as a matter of policy."[50] (It is unusual to find, not only Congress, but the Supreme Court acquiescing in a policy essentially arrived at by the Internal Revenue Service, a subordinate unit of the Department of the Treasury.)

One may be tempted to wonder what difference it all makes. Justice Powell's opinion is perhaps the most perspicacious in its long-range view of the troubling implications of the Court's decision:

With all respect, I am unconvinced that the critical question in determining tax-exempt status is whether an organization provides a clear "public benefit" as defined by the Court. Over 106,000 organizations filed §501(c) (3) returns in 1981 . . . I find it impossible to believe that all or even most of those organizations could prove that they "demonstrably serve and are in harmony with the public interest," or that they are "beneficial and stabilizing influences in community life. . . ."
Even more troubling to me is the element of conformity that appears to inform the Court's analysis. . . . Taken together, these passages suggest that the primary function of a tax-exempt organization is to act on behalf of the Government in carrying out governmentally approved policies. In my opinion, such a view . . . ignores the important role played by tax exemptions in encouraging diverse, indeed often sharply conflicting, activities and viewpoints. . . . Far from representing an effort to reinforce any perceived "common community conscience," the provision of tax exemptions to nonprofit groups is one indispensable means of limiting the influence of governmental orthodoxy on important areas of community life. . . .
I am unwilling to join any suggestion that the Internal Revenue Service is invested with authority to decide which public policies are sufficiently "fundamental" to require denials of tax exemptions.[51]

The majority offered a footnote to mollify Justice Powell's concern, assuring him that the Court's opinion does not invest the IRS with any such authority—though they and he seem already to have conceded such authority in this instance.

THE SUPREME COURT'S TRADE-OFFS

It is the function of courts to decide between parties in conflict, and in such decisions one party usually wins and the other loses. That is what courts are for, and they thus resolve peaceably disputes that might otherwise lead to violent conflict. Even losing parties have a stake in the peaceful resolution of disputes, just as sports competitors should be grateful that there is an umpire to call the shots, even though they may sometimes think the umpire called one wrong to their disadvantage.

In deciding for one adversary and against another where there is some justification on both sides, however, the court often makes significant trade-offs, and sometimes the interests it rejects may prove as important in the long run as those it favors. In *Scott* v. *Sandford* (the Dred Scott decision of 1857), the Supreme Court may have believed it was deciding *for* social stability, but it was wrong, since its choice contributed to the outbreak of a bloody civil war.

Likewise, in *Plessy* v. *Ferguson*, the 1896 decision that approved "separate but equal" accommodations for different races, the Supreme Court may have thought that its decision was necessary in the social climate of the time, but it saddled the nation with a half-century of "Jim Crow" segregation—until another Court in 1954 set a different direction with *Brown* v. *Board of Education*, eliminating segregation in education—at least in principle.

So in the *Bob Jones University* case, the Court has made a choice—the opposite kind of choice from the one made in *Scott* and *Plessy*—which may help to correct the legacy of racial injustice that those decisions allowed to continue. It has also made some significant trade-offs that may cause trouble in the future for other important interests.

Unconstitutional conditions. One trade-off is the seeming slippage in the doctrine of "unconstitutional conditions." The Court long has held that—even though the Constitution does not give anyone a "right" to a governmental job, unemployment compensation, or welfare benefits (or tax exemption?)—government may not withdraw or withhold such benefits—once they have been offered—from persons otherwise entitled to them as a penalty for exercising a right that the Constitu-

tion does guarantee. For instance, residence requirements for
public assistance are unconstitutional because they burden the
constitutionally guaranteed right to travel (*Shapiro* v. *Thompson*, 1969). A woman whose religion required her not to work
on her Sabbath could not be denied unemployment compensation for refusing to take jobs that entailed Saturday assignments (*Sherbert* v. *Verner*, 1963).

In the instant cases, petitioners are required to choose
between tax exemption and freedom of religion *(Bob Jones)* or
freedom of speech *(TWR)*. The Court's bland assurance that
Bob Jones's and Goldboro's loss of tax exemption "will not
prevent these schools from observing their religious
tenets"[52] has a hollow ring when compared to decisions like
Shapiro and *Sherbert*. It may not prevent them, but it will certainly *burden* them—in a fashion and to a degree much greater
than Mrs. Sherbert would have suffered for her Seventh-day
Adventist convictions if the Court had allowed the state of
South Carolina to impose such a choice on her, while offering
her the cold consolation that she was still free to observe her
religious tenets—though without either a job or unemployment compensation!

TWR was likewise assured by the Court that it was not
really losing "any independent benefit"[53] for exercising its
freedom of speech by lobbying. The only thing it was losing
was deductibility of contributions, which seems a rather heavy
price to pay for exercising one's constitutionally guaranteed
right to "assemble and petition Congress for redress of grievances."[54] The Court in *Taxation with Representation* reasserted
the doctrine of "unconstitutional conditions," but held that
TWR did not come under that doctrine. After all, it was not
denied deductible contributions for nonlobbying activity; "Congress has merely refused to pay for the lobbying out of public
monies. This Court has never held that Congress must grant a
benefit such as TWR claims here to a person who wishes to
exercise a constitutional right. . . . We again reject the 'notion
that First Amendment rights are somehow not fully realized
unless they are subsidized by the State.' "[55]

As was observed earlier, *TWR* could set up a Section
501(c)(4) "action organization" to do its lobbying with "hard
money," so what is at stake is actually deductibility, not
exemption from income taxation. Deductibility does have
about it more of the character of a "matching grant" from
government than does simple income-tax exemption. Under a

recent revision of the Code, however, an organization once having been recognized as a Section 501(c)(3) organization, and having had that status revoked for substantial lobbying, cannot then reorganize as a (c)(4) "action organization,"[56] so it does lose both deductibility *and* exemption for exercising its right of assembly and petition.

Of course, if one starts with the assumption that tax exemption is a government *grant*, then the Court's holding is logically consistent with its recent decision that poor women can be denied Medicaid payments for abortions because, though they have a constitutional right to an abortion, Congress does not have to finance the exercise of that right.[57]

If tax exemption were not viewed as a grant or subsidy, then there would not be any reason to withhold or withdraw it to avoid "subsidizing" lobbying—or racial discrimination. It *is* a benefit, however, and permitting it to be conditioned on abandonment of the free exercise of religion or speech is clearly a retreat from the Court's earlier opposition to "unconstitutional conditions." If the Court continues to maintain that people can be compelled to choose between tax exemption and the exercise of constitutional rights, everyone will be poorer.

The criteria of charitable trusts engrafted on Section 501(c)(3). As has been seen, the Court endorsed Judge Leventhal's remarkable finding in *Green* v. *Connally* that organizations exempt under Section 501(c)(3) must serve a public purpose or provide a public benefit and not violate public policy. Justice Powell was rightly troubled that this can mean that the IRS can use the threat of loss of tax exemption as a club to keep dissident or unpopular exempt organizations in line.

His concern might have been reinforced had he known that the IRS has already shown great willingness to do just that: not only did it withdraw exemption in the 1950s from organizations thought to be "communist,"[58] but it recently contended in the Ninth Circuit Court of Appeals that its revocation of the tax exemption of the Church of Scientology of California was justified by that organization's "violation of public policy" by alleged deceptive recruitment of members, keeping them in subjection by "mind-control," resisting investigation by the IRS, and misregistration of ships.[59]

Footnote 23 in *Bob Jones University*—in which the Court denied that it intended the IRS to have such power—is a thin barrier against the propensity of any administration to use such a handy weapon for stifling organized dissent. Just as the Kennedy administration pressed the IRS for the revocation of the tax exemption of Billy James Hargis's Christian Echoes National Ministry because of his virulent criticisms, so subsequent administrations have acted similarly.

Fortunately, the IRS has rarely revoked or denied a tax exemption for political reasons alone.[60] In Hargis's case, there was clear evidence of extensive lobbying and electioneering, which—under the law as then interpreted by the lower courts and now upheld in *Taxation with Representation* by the Supreme Court—justified such action. In other cases brought to the attention of the IRS by influential members of Congress or the executive branch, the IRS has made an investigation and, if it found no grounds for adverse action, eventually cleared the accused organization.[61] (This happened to the National Council of Churches, which underwent an audit by IRS from 1969 to 1972, and eventually was notified that its tax status was unchanged.[62])

Even if the IRS confines itself to revoking only those exemptions that it concludes after investigation have been forfeited by violations of the legal conditions of exemption, that leaves a rather wide area of potential vulnerability for exempt organizations. The tax law and its attendant regulations are sufficiently complex that even the most law-abiding organization can rarely be entirely sure that it has done nothing deserving of penalty.

The penalty for violating the conditions of exemption is potentially draconian. If a taxpayer errs in under-declaring income or over-declaring deductions, the error can usually be rectified by paying the tax due, plus interest and penalties. If an exempt organization errs, it can lose its entire exemption, with the various ramifications listed above—not just for the activities found to be at fault, but for *all* of its activities.

Even if the organization is eventually found blameless, the effort and expenditure required to cope with an audit by the IRS can be a severe penalty in themselves. So the prospect of incurring a tax audit can have a "chilling effect" on the exercise of First Amendment rights for an exempt organization, even if it never occurs. To be sure, some organizations are not intimidated by this prospect, but others are. The possibility of losing tax exemption is a sword of Damocles hanging over an organization all the time, which can always be invoked by hypercautious members of its board who are opposed to its taking vigorous action in the "political" realm, or doing anything that might upset the status quo, or even anything that might attract the attention of the IRS.

Such is the real mechanism behind the pressure to conformity that evoked Justice Powell's concern. With the Court's endorsement of the grafting of the criteria of charitable trusts on to Section 501(c)(3), the amplitude of possible grounds for loss of tax exemption is vastly increased, and, likewise, the arsenal of anxieties to which the apostles of prudence within an organization can appeal. The potential "chilling effect" has been doubled or trebled—a heavy trade-off indeed.

The free exercise of religion. Most troubling is the fact that none of the justices was troubled about the Court's First Amendment analysis. That was the one part of the chief justice's opinion with which Justice Powell concurred. Justice Rehnquist devoted a mere footnote to the matter in his dissent. He wrote, "I agree with the Court that Congress has the power to further the policy against racial discrimination by denying 501(c)(3) status to organizations that practice racial discrimination," and added in the margin, "I agree with the Court that such a requirement would not infringe on petitioners' First Amendment rights."[63]

The Court said at least three things on the subject: (1) denial of tax benefits will have a "substantial impact on the operation of private religious schools";[64] (2) however, that will not prevent those schools from "observing their religious tenets";[65] and (3) nevertheless, even if the free exercise of religion *is* burdened, "the governmental interest at stake here is compelling. . . . That governmental interest substantially outweighs whatever burden denial of tax benefits places on petitioners' exercise of their religious beliefs."[66]

Given the presuppositions about tax exemption with which the court began, it probably could reach no other conclusion. A different result was reached by Judge Widener, however, the dissenting judge in the fourth circuit court panel below, who felt that there ought to be room in the nation for both the important public policy of eliminating racial discrimination and the important public policy of religious liberty. He noted that a state's affording a liquor license to a fraternal lodge had been held not to constitute state action sufficient to require the lodge to follow a policy of racial nondiscrimination, and thought tax exemption also did not lend the sanction of the sovereign to the exempt entity sufficient to require a policy of nondiscrimination.[67]

One might suppose that the question could have been

treated under the rubric of *de minimis non curat lex* (the law does not concern itself with trifles), since there are few intensely religious schools like Bob Jones University and not many people of the black (or other) race clamoring to attend them. By the time the Court reached the case, however, the administration's actions had rendered it no longer *de minimis*. So the Court was obliged to respond to the larger issues injected by the administration's revoking the IRS policy with respect to *all* private schools, not just religious ones.

For many civil-rights advocates, the case could never be *de minimis*, since they not only insisted that tax exemption is a subsidy that must never be used to aid segregation, but, even if the case were confined to religious schools, they envisioned the specter of the proliferation of "segregation academies" professing to be "for whites only" because of (newly discovered) religious convictions. This very real possibility (to which Goldsboro Christian Schools lent some credibility) doubtless inhibited the Court from seeking any accommodation for the curious religious tenets of Bob Jones University, even though—unlike Goldsboro's—they long antedated the 1954 decision desegregating (public) education.

It cannot be overlooked that the logic of the Court's decisions in *Bob Jones University* and *Taxation with Representation*, if applied to churches, could lay severe restraints on the free exercise of religion. How many churches would be disposed to risk their tax exemptions by violating (current) public policy by: (1) counseling young people to refuse to register for the draft; (2) giving sanctuary to refuge-seekers from El Salvador whom the Immigration and Naturalization Service wants to deport back to mortal danger in their homeland; (3) urging a nuclear freeze in opposition to the administration's push for increased armaments; and (4) engaging in secondary boycotts against banks and other corporations doing business with South Africa, or otherwise dissenting from an incumbent administration's ideas of proper conduct?

If, as the justices all seem uncritically to assume, tax exemption *is* a subsidy, then eventually will the Court not be likely to conclude that churches are not entitled to it at all? That is exactly what some legal observers have long maintained, and they can doubtless derive much satisfaction from seeing their contentions vindicated by the Supreme Court. If the Court has tilted toward the tax-expenditure rationale of tax exemption, however, it can mean some significant losses for First

Amendment freedoms, not just for churches but for all exempt organizations, and indeed for everybody.

Of course, it may be that the Court is creating *sub silentio* a tax-exempt category unique to churches, since the *quid pro quo* doctrine voiced in both *Taxation with Representation* and *Bob Jones University* does not apply to them. If they should fail to render the function of providing religious ministry, the government could not do so in consistency with the First Amendment. Footnote 29 suggests that the Court is not ready to apply its tax-expenditure rationale to churches ("We deal here only with religious *schools*—not with churches or other purely religious institutions. . . . "). Its tax-base characterization of (property) tax exemption of churches in *Walz* ("obviously a direct money subsidy would be a relationship pregnant with involvement . . . , but that is not this case. . . . The government does not transfer part of its revenue to churches but simply abstains from demanding that the church support the state."), while not referred to in *Bob Jones University*, was not repudiated either.

The Court may not realize that this anomaly with respect to churches awaits it, or may not be prepared to deal with it until a case comes along that presents the question in a posture suitable for adjudication, but churches need to be aware of it. How should they respond? When a committee in the National Council of Churches was developing its policy statement on "Tax Exemption of Churches," it encountered the following draft paragraph: "Society may extend exemption from taxation to religious organizations on the condition that they meet certain tests, such as subscribing to loyalty oaths or refraining from political activity. Whatever may be the civil merits of this policy, Christians must determine independently whether the acceptance of such conditions will hinder their obedience to the will of God, and, if so, relinquish tax exemption."[68]

One of the members of the committee, George Harkins, then secretary of the Lutheran Church in America, said, "Nonsense! In a democracy there is an intermediate step." The paragraph quoted above was forthwith amended to read: "Christians must determine independently whether the acceptance of such conditions will hinder their obedience to the will of God, and, if so, *dispute the conditions*."[69] If churches are to dispute the terms in which tax exemption is coming to be viewed, they need to be more fully aware of the implications, which is one purpose of this type of exposition. Giving up on tax exemption should be considered only as a last resort.

TAX EXEMPTION: BUFFER OR HOSTAGE?

Tax exemption is not such a life-and-death matter for churches as some suppose. Most of them have relatively little net income to be subjected to income taxation. If any of them has accumulated a large surplus and invested it prudently in stocks, bonds, or other "passive" sources of income, they would not be mortally injured if that income were to be taxed. The churches are already taxed—at their own request—on ("active") income from any unrelated trade or business.[70] Though "religion" is by far the largest recipient of tax deductible contributions, most of those contributions are relatively small, so that loss of deductibility would be far less injurious to churches than it would be to colleges, museums, hospitals, or other charitable institutions that rely more heavily upon the incentives that deductibility affords to potential donors of large "pace-setting" gifts.

Churches have survived through many centuries, often under conditions far more adverse than loss of tax exemption, so it is not out of mere institutional self-protection that churches are concerned about tax exemption. They view it as a protection for religious liberty, not only for themselves but for everyone, and as a protection for other freedoms as well— of speech, press, assembly, and petition—which they share with nonreligious voluntary organizations. As the General Board of the National Council of the Churches of Christ in the U.S.A. put it in the policy statement referred to earlier:

In the United States, it has been a basic public policy since the founding of the nation to accord to freedom of religion, speech, press and assembly a "preferred position" at the head of the Bill of Rights. Christians support and affirm this healthful arrangement of the civil order, not solely or primarily for themselves and their churches, but for everyone. . . . Society is stronger and richer for the voluntary associations in which citizens voluntarily band together for constructive purposes independent of government support and therefore of government control. Exemption from taxation is one way in which government can and does foster such voluntary groups.[71]

As was noted earlier, what is now Section 501 of the Internal Revenue Code was originally designed to recognize that nonprofit organizations are not part of the income tax base, and, therefore, are not part of the revenue mechanism in this society. That provision created a beneficial kind of buffer zone around such centers of voluntary citizen initiative, fending off governmental scrutiny, oversight, or control. Section 501 should mean that if a group of people get together to do something of mutual interest from which they derive no personal monetary gain, their joint endeavor (so long as no laws are violated) is *simply none of the government's business* unless it comes under a few specific exceptions. The government should bear the burden of justifying any exceptions rather than the voluntary organization's having to justify its right to exist.

The exceptions (pertinent to the tax code) would include: (1) If the voluntary, nonprofit organization engages in activities that make a profit, it should pay corporate income tax on that profit (as is now the case under Section 511, the tax on income from trade or business unrelated to the exempt activity of an otherwise exempt organization). (2) If it receives "passive" income in the form of interest, dividends, rents, royalties, etc., that *could* be taxed without too great a burden on the freedom of such groups, though an argument could be made either way. (3) If it creates expenses for the community, it should pay service charges exactly equal to those expenses directly attributable to it, no more and no less. (4) If it employs people, it should pay taxes appropriate to all employers (such as FICA and FUTA taxes). (5) If it wishes to be classed as a "charity" in order to receive "charitable contributions" that donors may deduct from their taxable income, then—and only then—it may be required to meet certain additional (minimal) standards of public benefit and nonviolation of public policy. Such standards, however, should attach to Section 170 (Charitable Contributions and Gifts), not to Section 501 (Exempt Organizations). One of those requirements, as suggested earlier, might be that the services provided by the organization (and possibly its membership?) be open to all appropriate segments of the public without regard to factors over which they have no control such as race, sex, age, or national origin. (6) If it is the recipient of genuine direct governmental financial support (actual grants, loans, or contracts), then, of course, it would fall under certain canons of accountability that do not properly apply to self-supporting entities.

What if the organization engages in lobbying or electioneering? Splendid! That is exactly what citizens' organizations *ought* to do if it will help accomplish their shared purposes. It should have nothing whatever to do with their tax exemption, though it might with their deductibility because of the matching grant character of the latter. (A certain amount of legislative activity may not be inconsistent with charitable purposes for which deductibility is available, as is recognized by Section 501(h) permitting some charitable organizations to do a limited amount of lobbying without loss of deductibility—although that provision really ought to be attached to Section 170 on Deductibility of Charitable Contributions rather than to Section 501 on Exempt Organizations).

What if the organization engages in unlawful activity? Then the members responsible should pay the penalty provided by law. If the organization itself is a vehicle or instrument of such activity, then it should be fined (or dissolved?) under the civil or criminal law, not penalized by the tax law. As the Supreme Court said in 1966: "The federal income tax is a tax on net income, not a sanction against wrongdoing. That principle has been firmly embedded in the tax statute since the beginning. One familiar facet of the principle is the truism that the statute does not concern itself with the lawfulness of the income it taxes. Income from a criminal enterprise is taxed at a rate no higher and no lower than income from more conventional sources."[72] Does that still hold today? Or has the tax code now been pressed into service as a sanction to punish conduct not reachable by existing civil or criminal law?[73]

Rather than perverting the original principle of the tax statute, which is to raise revenue rather than to discourage disapproved conduct, Congress should enact clear and appropriate legal sanctions against private conduct that is injurious to others or to the community, sanctions that are effective, suitable to the offense, and consonant with the requirements of the Constitution.

It should not be the responsibility of the government to inspect, supervise, certify, and grade citizens' organizations as it does meat, especially not on the basis of their conformity to the "public policy" of the moment. After all, it is the responsibility of the citizenry, not of the government, to formulate public policy. How are they to do so wisely, creatively, or effectively unless they can organize themselves into voluntary groups around their various shared interests to explore, discuss, embrace, and advance what they believe to be desirable public policy? How are they to do that freely if the government is constantly watching over their shoulders, prepared to revoke their tax exemption if they should advocate a public policy at variance with the current public policy? That arrangement is a made-to-order strait jacket to insure that the future does not diverge to any visible degree from the past, which is not freedom, but its opposite.

Justice Powell, in his partially concurring opinion in *Bob Jones University*, was expressing somewhat mild dismay at developments that seemed to be moving in this direction, but he felt they had already moved too far to be reversed. He was echoing a concern expressed by Justice William O. Douglas, in 1972 in *Moose Lodge* v. *Irvis* (dissenting for other reasons, joined by Justice Marshall): "My view of the First Amendment and the related guarantees of the Bill of Rights is that they create a zone of privacy which precludes government from interfering with private clubs and groups."[74]

In 1958, the Court recognized that freedom of association would be impaired if the NAACP could be compelled to turn over its membership lists to the state of Alabama[75] because of sanctions the state could then impose on those members. Until recently tax exemption has provided a similar buffer between citizen activity and governmental scrutiny. With each passing year, however, the tax status of voluntary nonprofit organizations that was designed to be a protection has come to look more and more like *purdah* (the system of seclusion of highcaste women of India supposedly to protect them but actually restricting their activities to the cloistered women's quarters behind the veil or curtain called *purdah*).

To qualify for and retain tax exemption, the nonprofit organization (except churches) must submit to the government voluminous applications (Form 1023) and annual reports (Form 990)—as extensive as if they were paying taxes, perhaps more so. "Tax exemption" has come to be thought of as so special and so exotic a condition, requiring such copious justification and qualification, that a whole subchapter of the Internal Revenue Code and a whole division of the Internal Revenue Service are devoted to it. That is only exactly the opposite of the way it ought to be.

Because of this gradual shift from a tax-base to a tax-expenditure understanding of tax exemption, organizations that once found in it a buffer against state inquiries, requirements, and imposts may now begin to feel that it is some kind of hostage that they have had to give the state as a pledge of good behavior. If it is something that can be turned on or off at the will of petty administrators on the basis of whether they believe the organization's activities are meritorious or consonant with current "public policy"—whatever that may be—then it may be more bane than blessing.

Such a change will have less effect on conventional, non-controversial "charities" (and certainly less on churches) than it will on the fermentative organizations that are helping to shape a more creative and adaptive future, such as the environmental groups, the wildlife protection groups, the right-to-lifers, the abortion-righters, the peaceniks, the warniks, and all the other ideational causes and campaigns that make up the vital, vigorous fabric of democracy at the preelectoral and subrepresentational levels. It will be tragic if all of these movements that are coming into being, these potential currents of the future, must get a governmental permit to exist, report their officers, activities, and finances regularly to the government, and confine their actions to those they think the government will not disapprove as "violative of public policy."

That is not the kind of arrangement that is worthy of a nation whose commitment to the cause of liberty was once the marvel of human history and the hope of peoples living under oppressive governments elsewhere. Is freedom of voluntary citizen organization a luxury Americans no longer can afford? If so, for what great bargain was it exchanged?

NOTES

1. A classic statement may be found in *Christian Echoes National Ministries* v. *United States*, 470 F.2d 849 (10th Cir., 1972).
2. *Walz* v. *Tax Commission*, 397 U.S. 644 (1970), emphasis added.
3. Boris I. Bittker and Kenneth M. Kaufman, "Taxes and Civil Rights: Constitutionalizing the Internal Revenue Code," *Yale Law Journal* 82 (1972):51, n. 17.
4. *Murdock* v. *Pennsylvania*, 319 U.S. 105 (1943).
5. Synagogue Council of America, Brief *amicus curiae* in *Walz* v. *Tax Commission* (1970), 11.
6. *Everson* v. *Board of Education*, 330 U.S. 1 (1947). There is a special rationale for tax exemption of churches over and beyond the one set forth in this paper, which may be found, along with more extensive treatment of the rationales for tax exemption, in Dean M. Kelley, *Why Churches Should Not Pay Taxes* (New York: Harper & Row, 1977).
7. Boris I. Bittker, "Churches, Taxes and the Constitution," *Yale Law Journal* 78 (1969):1288, 1290, 1291.
8. *Congressional Record* 50 (1913):1306.
9. Boris I. Bittker and G. K. Rahdert, "The Exemption of Nonprofit Organizations

from Federal Income Taxation," *Yale Law Journal* 85 (1976):357.
10. Peter Swords, *Charitable Real Property Tax Exemptions in New York State: Menace or Measure of Social Progress?* (New York: Columbia University Press 1981), 202.
11. Ibid., 200, 206.
12. Ibid., 205, 209.
13. Ibid., 213.
14. Ibid., 215-16.
15. For further exposition of this point, see Kelley, *Why Churches Should Not Pay Taxes*, 25-36.
16. See Swords, *Charitable Real Property Tax Exemptions*, 105.
17. Ibid., 100.
18. Ibid., 138-43.
19. C. Galvin, "More on Boris Bittker and the Comprehensive Tax Base . . .," in *A Comprehensive Income Tax Base?* ed. Boris I. Bittker et al. (1968), 89, quoted in Bittker, "Taxes and Civil Rights," *Yale Law Journal* 82 (1972):64.
20. John H. Filer, chairman, *Giving in America: Toward a Stronger Voluntary Sector*, Report of the Commission on Private Philanthropy and Public Needs (1975), 128.
21. Internal Revenue Code, Section 501(c)(3).
22. *Congressional Record* 78 (1934):5861.
23. *Seasongood* v. *Commission*, 227 F.2d. 907 (6th Cir. 1955).
24. Internal Revenue Code, Section 501(c)(3).
25. *Christian Echoes National Ministry, Inc.* v. *United States*, at 857.
26. *Walz* v. *Tax Commission*, at 664.
27. Ibid.
28. Randolph W. Thrower, "Statement Before the House Ways and Means Committee on the Tax Exempt Status of Racially Discriminatory Private Schools," in *Administration's Change in Federal Policy Regarding the Tax Status of Racially Discriminatory Private Schools:* Hearing Before House Committee on Ways and Means, 97th Cong., 2d Sess., 1982.
29. Ibid. (citations omitted; emphasis added).
30. *Green* v. *Connally*, 330 F. Supp. 1150 (D.D.C., 1971).
31. *Bob Jones University* v. *Simon*, 416 U.S. 725 at 740, n.11 (1974).
32. *McGlotten* v. *Connally*, 338 F. Supp. 448 (D.D.C., 1972). This decision inspired the article by Bittker and Kaufman cited in note 3, which criticizes the contradictions and absurdities in the *McGlotten* opinion.
33. I.R.C., Section 501(c)(3).
34. *Regan* v. *Taxation with Representation* (hereinafter *TWR*), — U.S. — (1983), slip opinion, 10.
35. Ibid., 4,5.
36. Ibid., 8, 9, 10.
37. Ibid., concurring slip opinion, 2, 3.
38. Ibid., 2.
39. See testimony by Laurence Tribe, A. Rosenthal, and others in hearings cited in note 28 above. See also the report of the U.S. Civil Rights Commission, *Discriminatory Religious Schools and Tax Exempt Status*, 1982.
40. *Bob Jones University* v. *United States*, — U.S. — (1983), slip opinion, 24.
41. Ibid., 26.
42. Ibid., 15.
43. Ibid., 16, 17.
44. Ibid., 28, 29.
45. Ibid.
46. Ibid., 29, n. 29 (emphasis on original).
47. Ibid., Rehnquist dissent, slip opinion 1, 9.
48. Ibid., 4, 6 (emphasis in original).
49. Ibid., 11.
50. Ibid., Powell concurrence, 2.
51. Ibid., 4, 5, 6.

52. Ibid., majority opinion, 29.
53. *TWR*, majority opinion, 5.
54. U.S. Constitution, First Amendment.
55. *TWR*, 5.
56. I.R.C., Section 504(a).
57. *Harris* v. *McRae*, 448 U.S. 297 (1980).
58. William Lehrfeld, Testimony in Hearing on Church Audit Procedures Act, Finance Committee, U.S. Senate, 30 September 1983.
59. Brief of U.S. Internal Revenue Service in *Church of Scientology of California* v. *Commissioner of Internal Revenue*, U.S. Tax Court, Docket No. 3352-78, 30 September 1980. See also other examples of efforts by IRS to curtail "political" activities of exempt organizations during the Vietnam conflict, in Kelley, *Why Churches Should Not Pay Taxes*, 83-85.
60. Oral communication from William Lehrfeld, formerly an attorney in the Exempt Organizations branch of IRS for twelve years and now in private practice in Washington, D.C., 5 December 1983.
61. Ibid.
62. Author's personal experience.
63. *Bob Jones University* v. *United States*, Rehnquist dissent, 11, n.3.
64. *Bob Jones University*, majority opinion, 28.
65. Ibid., 29.
66. Ibid.
67. *United States* v. *Bob Jones University*, 639 F.2d 147 (4th Cir. 1980), citing *Moose Lodge* v. *Irvis*, 407 U.S. 163 (1972).
68. "Tax Exemption of Churches," Policy Statement of the National Council of Churches, Adopted 2 May 1969, First Draft, 1968.
69. Ibid., as finally adopted; amendment emphasized. Full text may be found in Kelley, *Why Churches Should Not Pay Taxes*, 140ff.
70. See Kelley, *Why Churches Should Not Pay Taxes*, 17-18, for an account of how the National Council of Churches and the U.S. Catholic Conference jointly requested that this "loophole" be closed, and it was closed in the Tax Reform Act of 1969.
71. "Tax Exemption of Churches," 2 May 1969, see note 68 above.
72. *Commissioner* v. *Tellier*, 383 U.S. 687 (1966).
73. See Bittker and Kaufman, "Taxes and Civil Rights: Constitutionalizing the Internal Revenue Code," cited in note 3.
74. *Moose Lodge* v. *Irvis*, at 179-80.
75. *NAACP* v. *Alabama*, 357 U.S. 449 (1958).

Tax Exemption and the Clergy: On Vows of Poverty and Parsonage Allowances

RONALD B. FLOWERS

In dealing with tax exemptions for the clergy, this essay will focus on two dimensions of the issue. The first of these involves vows of poverty, a very visible issue in the late 1970s and early 1980s because many "mail-order ministers" used that method as a scheme for tax avoidance. The government was able to solve that problem without impermissibly intruding into the area of defining ministry. The second dimension is parsonage housing allowances, which is afforded ministers through §107 of the Internal Revenue Code. This was an issue that did not attract much attention, but should have, since the government's administration of the law caused it unconstitutionally to define ministry, among other impermissible acts.

Vows of Poverty

Historically, in the Western world the vow of poverty has been well known. In both Roman Catholicism and Eastern Orthodoxy, monks and nuns, as they begin their vocations, take the vows of poverty, chastity, and obedience. The effect of this has been that any income earned or gifts given to the member of the order are turned over to the order for its use. The order, in turn, takes care of the personal needs of the member. Roman Catholic members of such orders began to come to America during the colonial period and there have been monastic communities that emphasized the vow of poverty for their members here since that time.

With the advent of income taxes, the question arose about the taxability of any income that might be earned by a person who had taken a vow of poverty in a religious order. Over the years the Internal Revenue Service (IRS) has worked out rules and procedures to accommodate such people and still protect the taxing power of the state. The issue is whether one who has taken a vow of poverty and works for an entity other

than the order itself and who turns his/her compensation over
to the order may exclude that amount from gross income for
tax purposes, i.e., whether the member of the order must pay
income tax on salary earned in the employ of a third party.

In response to that question, the general rule is that the
member of the order may exclude his/her salary from taxable
income if he/she is clearly under the control of the religious
order, i.e., if the order assigns and directs the member to
work for the third party. An early ruling by the IRS illustrates the point. A registered nurse was the member of a religious order, the purpose of which was to provide personnel to
missions, hospitals, schools, and social work agencies. She was
assigned by her order to take work in a hospital. For this
work she earned a salary, which she gave to her order. The
IRS concluded that the nurse worked as an agent of the religious order, consequently, the remuneration she received from
the hospital was excludable from her gross income and not
taxable.[1]

In more recent rulings, the determining factor in whether
or not a member of the order is an agent of the order is the
employer-employee relationship between the third party and
the member of the order. "Ordinarily an order is not engaged
in the performance of services as a principal where the legal
relationship of employer and employee exists between the
member and the third party with respect to the performance
of such services."[2] Consequently, if one's order instructs one
to take a position in the secular world, a position in which
one is the employee of a company or organization, then the
member becomes an agent of the employer, not the religious
order, so that the compensation is taxable in spite of the vow
of poverty the member has taken. Examples cited by IRS
Revenue Rulings are a member of an order who worked for a
law firm as a lawyer,[3] members of an order—one of whom
worked as a plumber and the other as a construction worker,[4]
and a member of an order who was a military chaplain whose
close relationship with the military made him an agent of the
military rather than his order.[5] In each of these cases, the
member was instructed by the order to find outside employment, but the close, legal relationship between the employer
and the member made the member an agent of the employer
rather than the order; thus, the member's income was subject
to taxation.

If one is instructed by one's order to work for another

agency of the supervising church, however, the employer-employee relationship is still in the service of the church, so that the member is considered a member of the order and need not include any compensation in his/her gross income for tax purposes.[6] The concept is summarized by the following two quotes: "Thus, in cases where a member of a religious order receives income as an agent of the order, and, pursuant to a vow of poverty, remits the income to the order, such income is the income of the order and not of the member."[7] "The vow of poverty itself does not cause the member to be considered an agent; rather, an agency relationship is established when it appears, based on all the facts and circumstances, that the payer of the income is looking directly to the order, rather than to the individual member, for the performances of services."[8]

Revenue Ruling 76-323, citing the Employment Tax Regulations §31.3121(b)(8)-1(d) and §31.3401(a)(9)-1(d), says that the nature of the service rendered by the member of the order is immaterial so long as it is a service one is directed to perform by one's ecclesiastical superiors. The same Rule also says that the member of the order must perform, in the outside employment, services "that are ordinarily the duties of the members of the order." In order to determine whether the work done does conform to the ordinary activities of members of the order, the IRS will examine "the established activities of the organization."[9] Consequently, in the area of traditional agencies in which people take vows of poverty, in determining whose income is taxable, the government comes to the threshhold of evaluating what kind of activity is ministry and what is not. It does not get into that forbidden area, however, because its principal criterion is whether or not the member is an agent of the order.

ABUSE OF THE VOW

In the 1970s and early 1980s, however, some people tried to use the vow of poverty concept to their personal advantage. They did this by receiving ordination to the ministry gratis (from the Universal Life Church[10]) or by purchasing it (as from the Basic Bible Church[11] or the Life Science Church[12]). These "mail-order ministers" then declared their homes to be their churches. Some then deducted as much as 50 percent of their gross income as contributions to their churches (homes) as allowed by §170(b)(A)(i) of the Internal Revenue Code.

Others wrote documents declaring a vow of poverty, thus assigning 100 percent of their salary to their churches (homes), thus avoiding the payment of any taxes. In turn, of course, in each case the church provided for all the personal needs of the "minister" and his/her family: car, shelter, food, entertainment, insurance, and so forth. Of course, the "minister" had total control over the finances of the church.

An illustration of this process, from many cases that could have been chosen, is *Robert D. and Bonnie L. Abney* v. *Commissioner of Internal Revenue.*[13] Robert and Bonnie Abney obtained ordination and a church charter from the Universal Life Church. They named their church the Dignity of Man Church. They drew up a legal document entitled "Gift of All to the Universal Life Church, Dignity of Man Chapter." In this they took a vow of poverty, in which they divested themselves of all their income and possessions, assigning them to the church. This gift to the church was irrevocable with one exception. If "secular officialdom" were to void the document creating the vow of poverty, all assets would revert to the Abneys.[14] The Abneys opened a bank account in the name of the Dignity of Man Church, changed the registration of their cars to the church, and arranged for Pan American Airways, for whom Mr. Abney was a pilot, to deposit his check directly into the church's checking account. The Abneys paid for all their housing and living expenses from the church's account, since they were its ministers (and only members, save for Mr. Abney's brother). They paid no taxes at all on their income.

Naturally, the IRS became alarmed over schemes such as this, especially since some of the ordaining churches were actively recruiting people so that they could take advantage of the tax avoidance benefits ordination provided. Between 1963 and 1980, the Universal Life Church ordained some 10 million ministers and issued fifty thousand church charters.[15] In 1979, the Church of Universal Harmony, a church founded for the purpose of spreading the gospel of tax avoidance, sold around one hundred ordinations a month.[16]

The IRS could have taken the approach mentioned above to deal with the problem of mail-order ministers because the "religious order"/church did not direct the "minister" to work for some secular organization, or because the employee/employer relationship between the "minister" and his/her employer would be such as to prevent the "minister" from being an agent of the church/order, his/her salary would not be excludable from gross income for tax purposes. This would have been especially true since the IRS will not think of a minister as having been assigned particular duties by his/her order if any of the following are true: (1) if the organization for which the minister performs services did not make specific arrangements with his/her church for him/her to do the services, (2) if the minister performs the same kinds of services that other employees, who have not been assigned by a church, perform, and (3) the minister performed the same services in the business before he/she was assigned to do them by the church.[17]

The IRS concentrated, however, on another approach afforded by §§501(c)(3) and 170(2)(B) and (C) of the Internal Revenue Code. Section 501(c)(3) establishes the rules for tax exempt status for charitable organizations and §170 articulates the requirements for such organizations to receive deductible contributions. Both sections require that organizations claiming to be religious must be organized and operated for religious purposes and that no part of their net earnings may inure to the benefit of private individuals. The IRS operates under the assumption that mail-order ministry churches, including those that employ a vow of poverty, are in reality nothing more than tax-avoidance schemes that conform to neither of these provisions of the law. The problem is that to make a judgment as to whether or not a church has a religious purpose, the government is required to make a definition of religion, which it is reluctant, if not forbidden by the Establishment Clause, to do. The regulations on §501(c)(3) do not define religion and those on §170(b)(1)(A)(i) are terribly vague as to the nature of a church.[18] Consequently, in most cases involving mail-order ministries, the case was decided on some form of the inurement concept, although that concept works in tandem with the "organized and operated" test. An organization is not organized and operated for a religious purpose if its revenues benefit private individuals. Consequently, in *Abney* v. *Commissioner* cited above, the IRS disallowed the contributions to the church and its vow of poverty because the net earnings of the church amounted to profit to the Abneys.

In summary, in dealing with vows of poverty taken by mail-order ministers, the government has to make some, but essentially minimal, examination of religious precepts and definitions of ministry. Because this method of tax avoidance on religious grounds can be handled essentially on a nonreligious basis—private inurement—the government has been able to deal with this threat to its taxing power without impermissibly entangling itself with religion.

PARSONAGE ALLOWANCES

Section 107 of the Internal Revenue Code says: "In the case of a minister of the gospel, gross income does not include—(1) the rental value of a home furnished to him as part of his compensation; or (2) the rental allowance paid to him as part of his compensation, to the extent used by him to rent or provide a home."[19]

Section 107(1) allows a minister who receives the use of a parsonage from his/her church to exclude from gross income its rental value, including utility costs, repairs and maintenance, and other costs necessary to provide oneself a home. This section has existed since 1921.[20]

Section 107(2) allows a minister who is buying or renting a home to exclude from gross income the amount used to rent or to provide a home. In existence since 1954, this section was passed to help those ministers of churches without parsonages who had to receive a higher taxable salary in order to provide a home.[21]

Early in 1983, the IRS ruled that ministers could no longer deduct mortgage interest and real property taxes and exclude parsonage allowances from gross income, as they had been able to do since 1954. Those who bought houses after 2 January 1983 could no longer deduct mortgage interest and property taxes, except for a prorated amount if the minister's housing expenses were for more than the parsonage allowance. Those who owned their homes prior to 3 January 1983 could, if they itemized their deductions, deduct interest and taxes for the years 1983 and 1984. Because of the protests of several denominations, however, the IRS extended the effective date of the rule for those in the former category until 1984 and those in the latter category until 1985.[22] These are, however, only administrative changes and do not alter the nature of §107 at all. It is the argument of this essay that §107 is unconstitutional as a violation of the Establishment Clause both in its very nature and in its application.

THE UNCONSTITUTIONALITY OF SECTION 107

Section 107 is unconstitutional because it singles out "ministers of the gospel" (and rabbis)[23] for preferential treatment.

There are housing benefits to other kinds of employees, but they are much more restrictive than those available to clergy. Section 119 provides that nonclergy taxpayers who would have a nontaxable housing allowance must show that their residence is supplied for the convenience of the employer, is located on the premises of the employer, and is required by the employer as a condition of employment.[24] Section 107 demands that clergy meet none of those requirements. As a federal court has said: "The exclusion is not provided to a broad class of persons from which petitioner is excluded solely because he is not a minister. The exclusion is granted by legislative grace to *ministers of the Gospel alone*. All persons who are not ministers are denied this grace. . . ."[25] That is precisely the statute's constitutional problem.

To be constitutional under the Establishment Clause, a law must pass three tests that have been formulated by the United States Supreme Court.[26] Section 107 does not pass any of them. The first of these tests is that a law must have a secular purpose. The purpose of a law is normally ascertained by a survey of its legislative history. The legislative history of §107 is distressingly scanty, but there is a statement from 1954 when the original 1921 statute was amended. Representative Peter Mack, Jr. of Illinois, speaking in favor of the current §107 before the House Ways and Means Committee, stated: "Certainly, in these times when we are being threatened by a godless and antireligious world movement we should correct this discrimination against certain ministers of the gospel who are carrying on such a courageous fight against this foe. Certainly this is not too much to do for these people who are caring for our spiritual welfare."[27] To give financial aid to clergy as a reward for trying to improve the spiritual condition of the country can hardly be called a secular purpose for the proposed legislation. Of course, one cannot say that all legislators who voted for the bill had the same motivation as Rep. Mack, but there does not seem to have been significant opposition to this expressed religious purpose for the bill.

Furthermore, §107 was proposed, in part, because the average income of clergy was lower than that of the labor force as a whole. One could argue that other identifiable professions were below average in income, perhaps school teachers. Congress, however, singled out ministers for tax relief. That does not seem to be a secular purpose for the legislation.[28]

The second test says that if a law has the primary effect of advancing or inhibiting religion, it is unconstitutional. In *Walz* v. *Tax Commission*,[29] a case involving the taxation of property used for religious worship, the Supreme Court approved of the tax exemption because it did not single out the property of religious institutions for the relief. Because the tax exemption was applied to the property of a wide range of charitable institutions, the fact that churches and synagogues were included in the exemption did not make that a violation of the Establishment Clause. Section 107 singles out a narrow category of persons, however, based on a religious classification, since only ordained, licensed, or commissioned ministers are eligible for the parsonage exclusion.[30] This preferential treatment of a narrow class of professionals distinguished by their religious character has the primary effect of advancing religion.

The third test prohibits excessive entanglement between religion and government. Any relationship or interaction between a religious organization and government that results in a *significant* amount of contact between the two is excessive entanglement.[31] In enforcing §107 and its accompanying regulations by determining what is the exercise of one's ministry, the government must examine the tenets and practices of the religious body to which the minister belongs to see if her/his ministry conforms to those tenets.[32] Although the government is not compelled to evaluate the truth or falsity of those doctrines or practices, it must interpret them to determine if the ministry under investigation falls within the government's guidelines. There is a long legal tradition that holds that it is not within the government's competence to interpret religious doctrine or to adjudicate cases, the outcome of which involves the definition of religion or the evaluation of denominational theology.[33] This is often a delicate matter, however, because admittedly the government must protect itself and the public from fraud or other illegal behavior that sometimes comes under religious guise, e.g., those who use proscribed drugs as a sacrament.[34] To the extent that the government is compelled to examine religious tenets and practices in its enforcement of §107, however, it can be argued that such examination is unconstitutional because of excessive entanglement.

Unconstitutionality Further Demonstrated

A test case, *Ronald B. and Leah E. Flowers* v. *United States*,[35] may demonstrate further how §107 is unconstitutional in its application. In 1975, Texas Christian University had some twenty ordained ministers on its faculty and staff. These ministers had been employed at the university for various lengths of time, but in each case, at the time of being hired, had been encouraged by the university to exclude from their gross pay a housing allowance, to which they were entitled under §107. In 1975, TCU changed the composition of its Board of Trustees in response to a perceived threat to a program dear to the university. In the early 1970s, Texas, like some other states, created a program of tuition assistance for students attending private colleges and universities. In 1971, in response to the growing difference between the amount of tuition paid by students attending private colleges and those in public colleges, a plan was implemented by which students attending private schools would receive tuition assistance from state funds, in order to make private schools more competitive in the tuition market and thus to improve their chances at viability. From the time the bill was first introduced through the 1975 session of the Texas legislature (it meets only every other year), there was strenuous opposition to the plan by some. The principal argument was that the program was a violation of the separation of church and state, as articulated by both the United States and Texas constitutions. Even though the Tuition Equalization Grant (TEG) program had become law in 1971 and implementation had begun in that year, in 1973 and again in 1975, during the debate over appropriations bills, the objections were made all over again.

The administration of TCU, in the light of the opposition to the tuition assistance plan, became convinced that if TCU appeared to be highly sectarian its students would not be eligible for the TEG funds. Consequently, the Board of Trustees at TCU voted to change its composition to be less than 50 percent members of the Christian Church (Disciples of Christ, the university's parent denomination) in order that TCU would not appear to be a sectarian institution.

When TCU changed the make-up of its Board of Trustees, the IRS responded by ruling that TCU was no longer controlled by its sponsoring church and thus was not an integral agency of the church. According to IRS regulations on §107, in most circumstances a minister must be employed by an integral agency of a church or comparable religious institution in order to be eligible for the parsonage allowance. Since

TCU was no longer an integral agency of its parent church, its ordained faculty who had been excluding amounts from their gross salary as a nontaxable housing allowance were no longer eligible to do so.

In the university's attempt to overturn the IRS' ruling, its main contention was that the university is an integral agency of its parent church. Income Tax Regulation §1.107-1(a)(2), which gives specificity to the statute, says:

In order to qualify for the exclusion, the home or rental allowance must be provided as remuneration for services which are ordinarily the duties of a minister of the gospel. In general, the rules provided in §1.1402(c)-5 will be applicable to such determination. Examples of specific services the performance of which will be considered duties of a minister for purposes of section 107 include the performance of sacerdotal functions, the conduct of religious worship, the administration and maintenance of religious organizations and their *integral agencies*, and the performance of teaching and administrative duties at theological seminaries.[36]

In the light of that, the university's principal argument was that under the congregational government of the Christian Church (Disciples of Christ), TCU is as much of an integral agency of the denomination as any local congregation, which would certainly qualify. The university contended that IRS regulations and rulings prefer a hierarchical or authoritarian church and discriminate against those churches with a congregational form of polity. Such government preference of one type of church over another was claimed to be unconstitutional under the Fifth Amendment, which guarantees due process of law, and under the First Amendment, the Establishment Clause which forbids government preference of any particular religion.

The other argument was that Flowers did indeed perform sacerdotal functions in his role as teacher at TCU. This argument was demanded by Income Tax Regulation §1.1402(c)-5(b)(2): "Service performed by a minister in the exercise of his ministry includes the ministration of sacerdotal functions and the conduct of religious worship, and the control, conduct, and maintenance of religious organizations (including the religious boards, societies, and other integral agencies of such organizations), under the authority of a religious body constituting a church or church denomination." The contention was that teaching is a sacerdotal function—a ministry. The argument for sacerdotal functions also mentioned that Flowers did counseling of students, particularly religion students who were thinking of ministry as a career, and that he occasionally performed weddings, participated in ordinations, and did church school teaching.

The court's opinion on the integral agency question was based principally on two Revenue Rulings. In Rev. Rul. 70-549, the IRS ruled that a college is an integral agency of a church if it has the following characteristics:

1. The board of directors of the college are indirectly controlled by the church because each board member must be a member in good standing of the congregation.
2. Every teacher was a member in good standing of the congregation.
3. The majority of students are members of the church.
4. All subjects taught at the college, whether in natural science, mathematics, social science, languages, etc., are taught with emphasis on religious principles and religious living.
5. The college had a department which performs all the functions for ministerial training that a seminary offers.[37]

The judge ruled that TCU did not meet the first four factors and thus is not an integral agency of the Christian Church (Disciples of Christ).[38]

In Rev. Rul. 72-606, the IRS laid down criteria to be used to determine if an institution is an integral agency of a church. (This rule is less specific than 70-549 because it does not focus on colleges.) The criteria are:

1. Whether the religious organization incorporated the institution;
2. Whether the corporate name of the institution indicates a church relationship;
3. Whether the religious organization continuously controls, manages, and maintains the institution;
4. Whether the trustees or directors of the institution are approved by or must be approved by the religious organization or church;
5. Whether trustees or directors may be removed by the religious organization or church;
6. Whether annual reports of finances and general operations are required to be made to the religious organization or church;
7. Whether the religious organization or church contributes to the support of the institution; and
8. Whether, in the event of dissolution of the institution, its assets would be turned over to the religious organization or church.[39]

Although the IRS does not require conformity with all these items for an institution to be in compliance with Rev. Rul. 72-606, the judge ruled that TCU meets only the second and seventh and thus is not an integral agency of the church.

Turning from a consideration of the Revenue Rulings, the judge accepted twenty-nine of the thirty indicia of relationship between TCU and the church mentioned in the plaintiff's brief and reviewed them to see if there were any other factors that would demonstrate the church's control over the university. There were not. He asserted that the quality of the contacts between the university and the church was more important than their quantity and then listed a number of factors that showed that the university was not controlled by the church, either directly or indirectly. Among these were the fact that the church cannot force the university to do anything, that the church does not require the faculty to be members of the Christian Church, that the church cannot control the curriculum at TCU or the manner in which professors teach their courses, and, most importantly, that the Board of Trustees was not controlled by a majority of members from the Christian Church (Disciples of Christ). Although he acknowledged that the church exercised moral persuasion over the university, that was not enough to satisfy the law. TCU is not an integral agency of its sponsoring church.[40]

TCU had tried to show that it was an integral agency of the church, to no avail. An alternative argument to that was that the IRS's regulations on §107 unconstitutionally discriminate between hierarchical and nonhierarchical churches. The court responded by simply asserting that that is not true. The judge asserted that any church, even a nonhierarchical one, may satisfy the commissioner's criteria. "Any religion can meet the requirements of the regulations and revenue ruling."[41] The effect of his argument is exactly the opposite of what he says because the meaning of the statement is that any church may meet the criteria if it becomes hierarchical.[42] "Schools and colleges can satisfy the Commissioner's criteria to become an integral agency of a non-hierarchical church. In fact, Rev. Rul. 70-549 was specifically written to give advice to nonhierarchical churches in meeting the requirements of section 107."[43] The fact of the matter is, however, that Rev. Rul. 70-549 is considerably more rigid and restrictive than the relationship of many colleges to their congregationally governed churches. The fact is that the judge and the IRS are saying that a college may comply with the criteria so long as they cast aside their own theological predilections and conform to the Commissioner's criteria. The government decides what is acceptable for churches at this point.[44]

The issue of the government's unconstitutional discrimination against nonhierarchical churches through §107 has been raised many times before. An example is *Abraham A. and Edith U. Salkov* v. *Commissioner of Internal Revenue.*[45] In that case the issue was whether Salkov, a cantor but not a rabbi, would qualify for ministerial status under §107. He did, but in the process of discussing whether or not he was ordained, the fact of Judaism's nonhierarchical, autonomous congregations came up. The tax court said: "If the statute and the regulations were so severely restrictive as to exclude ministers elected, designated, or appointed by a religious congregation, there would be a serious question in our minds as to the propriety of such an exclusion under the Constitution of the United States."[46] Here the court recognized the existence of congregational polity and its legitimacy in the ordination process. The regulations, however, do not grant the legitimacy of institutional autonomy under congregational polity in the relationship between a religious organization and its related institutions. In the words of the court, there is "a serious question in our minds" as to the constitutionality of such a statute.

Treasury Regulation 1.1402(c)-5(b)(2)(v) and 5(c)(2) combine to hold that a minister may work for an institution that is neither religious nor an integral agency of a church and still be "in the exercise of his ministry" (i.e., qualify for the parsonage allowance) if he/she is assigned to that employment by a church, but not be "in the exercise of his ministry" if he/she has not been assigned to that employment by a church. This clearly has the unconstitutional primary effect of preferring those ministers who are affiliated with a hierarchical church and penalizing those clergy who are affiliated with a church that does not have a mechanism of assignment because of a congregational polity, which usually is based upon that church's interpretation of the Bible. These regulations would not allow Flowers to be eligible for the housing allowance, conceding that TCU is not an integral agency of the Disciples Church (only for the sake of this argument), because he is a member of a church that, on theological grounds, does not have a mechanism for assigning ministers. His Methodist colleague, however, would be eligible simply because he is a member of a hierarchical church that does have a mechanism for assigning ministers. That is clearly preference for one type of religion over another.

Attention now needs to be turned to the second dimension of *Flowers*, that having to do with sacerdotal functions. This was the weakest part of the plaintiff's case. On this subject, the government pointed out that teaching is not a sacerdotal function. In saying this it interpreted "sacerdotal functions" very narrowly, rather than referring to teaching as ministry, which it is.

On the issue of the counseling of students, the government said that the counseling was because Flowers was a professor, not because he was a minister; most professors counsel students, it is not a function reserved for ordained professors. The government also noted that nonordained religion professors do exactly the same kind of counseling that Flowers does.

In ruling that teaching is not a sacerdotal function, the court relied on *James D. and Frances J. Colbert* v. *Commissioner of Internal Revenue*.[47] The statutory background for this case is Reg. §1.1402(c)-5(b)(2)(i), which reads: "Whether service performed by a minister constitutes the conduct of religious worship or the ministration of sacerdotal functions depends on the tenets and practices of the particular religious body constituting his church or church denomination." Colbert, a Baptist, worked for the Christian Anti-Communism Crusade. In that job he frequently went to churches in order to speak against "godless communism," to tell how Communists were endangering Baptist foreign missionaries and generally causing trouble in the world. The tax court ruled that in spite of Colbert's sense of ministry, anticommunism was not a tenet of the Baptist faith, so his work did not fall within the acceptable definition of sacerdotal functions. Consequently, he was denied the housing allowance. The government and the court analogized *Colbert* to *Flowers* so that even though the Christian Church (Disciples of Christ) might favor education, it is not a principal tenet or practice of the denomination, and, thus, teaching cannot be called a sacerdotal function qualifying for the ministerial housing salary exclusion. Actually, the language in *Colbert* points to a denial of the Court's holding in *Flowers*.

In presenting his case, Colbert pointed to the congregational autonomy of the Baptist church and asserted that there are no pronounced tenets and practices in that church, that ultimately each individual is responsible for deciding what is religious worship. The court rightly ruled that Colbert's assertion was too subjective. It said that the phrase "tenets and practices" used in the regulations "includes those principles which are generally accepted as beliefs and practices" within the denomination at bar.[48]

Regulation §1.1405(c)-5(b)(2)(i) and *Colbert* indicate that for the government to enforce this law it is necessary for the government to delve into theology. The government argued in *Flowers* that the resulting entanglement is not excessive and does not involve the evaluation of doctrine. Judgments have to be made, however. Given the *Colbert* test, is a particular tenet, say that teaching religion in a church-related college is as much a ministry as the pastorate, generally accepted in a denomination or held only by a few? Definitions have to be made, e.g., as in *Robert D. Lawrence* v. *Commissioner of Internal Revenue*.[49] That case hangs on the fact that Lawrence was not ordained, but in the process of deciding that he was not entitled to the parsonage allowance the court stated that a minister of Christian education is not a minister of the Gospel, a view supposedly held by the church that hired him. (There was also a vigorous dissent from that view.) Such definitions by government border on the impermissible. For example, in *David and Irene Silverman* v. *Commissioner of Internal Revenue*,[50] the court and the tax commissioner debated whether a cantor has to do all the ecclesiastical functions a rabbi does in order to be considered "a minister of the gospel"! There is a line of cases that assert that the government may not make a judgment on the truth or falsity of doctrine but may make a judgment as to whether it is sincerely held by those at bar.[51] There is another line of cases in which it is said that cases may not be decided on the basis of the interpretation of doctrine.[52] The provisions in the rules and regulations for §107 that require the government to examine the tenets and practices of religious groups in order to determine whether or not one is a minister for purposes of compliance are very close to being an impermissible entanglement of government with religion.

Finally, the government quite rightly pointed out that there are unordained professors in the Department of Religion at TCU who function exactly as Flowers does. This demonstrates that one's being an ordained minister is incidental, rather than integral, to his status as a professor. It also demonstrates, however, how discriminatory §107 is in its application. If TCU had been held to be an integral agency of the church, then Flowers would still be eligible for the housing allowance simply by virtue of being ordained whereas his unordained Religion Department colleagues, doing exactly the same things, would not be eligible.[53] That has the primary effect of advancing religion in that it gives special benefits to people simply by virtue of their having been ordained. That is

exactly the Establishment Clause claim raised in *W. Astor and
Vivian M. Kirk* v. *Commissioner of Internal Revenue.*[54] Kirk
worked for the Methodist Board of Christian Social Concerns.
Of the twelve employees of the Board, nine were ordained,
licensed, or commissioned ministers. Kirk and two others
were not. Kirk claimed that for the ordained employees to
receive the housing allowance simply by virtue of being
ordained while he could not, even though their duties at the
Board were identical, was a violation of the Establishment
Clause. Kirk was right, but neither the tax court nor a federal
district court would grapple with the issue (as so many other
courts have refused to do). Their reason was that Kirk's tax
status would not be changed whether §107 were unconstitutional or not.

In summary, §107, both on its surface and in its application,
is unconstitutional in that it violates the Establishment Clause
of the First Amendment. It singles out clergy, of all professions, for tax advantage. Furthermore, IRS interpretations
and regulations make applications that impermissibly define
what ministry is and which prefer the ministry of one kind of
religious organization (hierarchical) over that of another (congregational). For these reasons, Congress should repeal §107.
To repeal the parsonage allowance would increase government
revenues, help to equalize the tax burden among taxpayers,
and improve the public's perception of clergy. Most of all,
however, it would honor the historic concept of the separation
of church and state by eliminating an illegality based on religious discrimination in American tax law.[55]

NOTES

1. Rev. Rul. 68-123. Cf. also *Kelly* v. *Commissioner of Internal Revenue*, 62 T.C. 131
(1974).
2. Rev. Rul. 76-323.
3. Rev. Rul. 77-290.
4. Rev. Rul. 76-323.
5. Rev. Rul. 79-132.
6. Rev. Rul. 77-290. Cf. Albert Feuer, "The Taxation of Family Religious Orders,"
University of Dayton Law Review 6 (1981):19 for the view that the employer-employee
relationship is the wrong way for the IRS to determine whether the income of an
order is taxable. Cf. also George E. Reed, "Revenue Ruling 77-290—Vow of Poverty," *Catholic Lawyer* 24 (Summer 1979):217.
7. Rev. Rul. 77-290.
8. Rev. Rul. 79-132.
9. Cf. also Rev. Rul. 77-290.

10. *Universal Life Church*, v. *United States*, 372 F. Supp. 770 (1974).
11. *Basic Bible Church* v. *Commissioner of Internal Revenue*, 74 T.C. 846 (1980).
12. "Income Tax," *TRaxis: A Newsletter on Taxation and Religion* 1 (January/February 1982):7.
13. *Abney* v. *Commissioner of Internal Revenue*, 39 TCM 965 (1980).
14. Any provision that allows the assets of a church to revert to the donor in the event of the dissolution of the church shows that the donor has not given up complete control of the assets, which is itself enough to deny the tax-exempt status. Cf. Treasury Regulation 1.501(c)(3)-1(b)(4) and *Calvin K. of Oaknoll* v. *Commissioner of Internal Revenue*, 69 T.C. 770 (1978).
15. Manzanita Hensley, *The Universal Life Church* (it calls itself "The ULC Book") (Modesto, Calif.: The Universal Life Church, 1980), 14, 28.
16. Beth Ann Krier, "Spreading the Gospel of Tax Avoidance," *Los Angeles Times View*, 13 March 1980, Part 5; Steve Goolian, "Tax Avoidance Plan Pushed by Advocates," *The Tustin* (California) *News*, 22 November 1979. Both of these were distributed as reprints in the "get acquainted" packet sent by the Church of Universal Harmony and had no page numbers.
17. Rev. Rul. 78-229.
18. Treasury Reg. §1.501(c)(3)-1(d) and §1.170A-9(a). See, however, the speech by the then Tax Commissioner of Internal Revenue, Jerome Kurtz, in which he describes criteria the IRS uses to determine if an organization is a church; "Difficult Definitional Problems in Tax Administration: Religion and Race," *Catholic Lawyer* 23 (Autumn 1978):304.
19. 26 U.S.C. §107.
20. Roger H. Taft, "Tax Benefits for the Clergy: The Unconstitutionality of Section 107," *Georgetown Law Journal* 62 (1974):1267-68; Rev. Rul. 59-350.
21. Taft, "Tax Benefits for the Clergy," 1267-68; Thomas E. O'Neill, "A Constitutional Challenge to Section 107 of the Internal Revenue Code," *The Notre Dame Lawyer* 57 (June 1982): 864; Conrad Teitell, *Minister's Parsonage Allowance and Social Security* (New York: The Church Pension Fund [Episcopal], 1983), 10-11.
22. Teitell, *Minister's Parsonage Allowance*, 6-7; Rev. Rul. 83-3.
23. *Salkov* v. *Commissioner of Internal Revenue*, 46 T.C. 190 (1966).
24. 26 U.S.C. §119. Cf. Taft, "Tax Benefits for the Clergy," 1262. A large portion of this section follows Taft's argument.
25. *Kirk* v. *Commissioner of Internal Revenue*, 425 F. 2d at 495 (1970). Quoting from the same case in the Tax Court: 51 T.C. 66 at 71-72. Emphasis in original.
26. Cf. *Abington Township School District* v. *Schempp*, 374 U.S. 203 (1963) and *Walz* v. *Tax Commission of the City of New York*, 397 U.S. 664 (1970).
27. Taft, "Tax Benefits for the Clergy," 1267-68.
28. Ibid., 1268.
29. *Walz* v. *Tax Commission*, at 664.
30. Treasury Regulation 1.1402(c)-5(a)(1) and (b)(1)(i); cf. also *Salkov* v. *Commissioner*, at 190.
31. *Walz* v. *Tax Commission*, at 664; *Lemon* v. *Kurtzman*, 403 U.S. 602 (1971).
32. E.g., cf. *Colbert* v. *Commissioner of Internal Revenue*, 61 T.C. 449 (1974).
33. Cf. *United States* v. *Ballard*, 332 U.S. 78 (1944); *Presbyterian Church* v. *Hull Memorial Presbyterian Church*, 393 U.S. 440 (1969); *Serbian Eastern Orthodox Diocese* v. *Milivojevich*, 423 U.S. 696 (1976); *Espinosa* v. *Rusk*, 634 F. 2d 477 (1980), aff'd 456 U.S. 951 (1982).
34. Cf. Ronald B. Flowers, "Freedom of Religion Versus Civil Authority in Matters of Health," *The Annals of the American Academy of Political and Social Science* 446 (November 1979):149.
35. *Ronald B. and Leah E. Flowers* v. *United States*, 49 AFTR 2d 438 (1981). Leah E. Flowers was party to this action solely by virtue of having filed a joint tax return. Hereafter Ronald B. Flowers will be identified as the plaintiff.
36. Emphasis added.
37. *Flowers* v. *United States*, at 441.

38.   It is interesting to note that item 2 in this IRS rule requires just what the Texas Constitution prohibits for participation in the tuition assistance program. Cf. Attorney General's opinion H-203 (1974).

39.   *Flowers* v. *United States*, at 441.

40.   Ibid., at 441-42.

41.   Ibid., at 443.

42.   This point is well made by Dean M. Kelley, director for Civil and Religious Liberty for the National Council of Churches, in his comments about *Flowers* v. *United States*: "So the point about 'control' in the Regulations simply has the situation precisely *upside down*. Departing from the democratic principle that is supposed to govern in the political affairs of the nation, the Treasury has undertaken to impose a monarchical principle as the one and only mode of church organization that can benefit from Section 107, which is 'preferring one religion over another' in its clearest form. The judge, in upholding the IRS, made this clear while insisting the opposite: 'Any religion can meet the requirements of the regulations and revenue ruling. No religion is prohibited from having an organization, associate with the religion, from obtaining the status of an integral agency.' All they have to do is to exercise control over the agency, that is, *to become hierarchical*, and they can qualify." Dean M. Kelley, personal letter to Ronald B. Flowers, 10 December 1981.

43.   *Flowers* v. *United States*, at 442.

44.   This is a delicate point, for the government, in its posttrial briefs, pointed out that prior to 1975 TCU itself qualified because the Commissioner considered 51 percent of the Board's being members of the parent church to be the lowest limit possible for the church to have any control over the university. As long as TCU had that percent of church members on the Board, it qualified even though it was related to a nonhierarchical church. (Cf. Defendant's Post-Trial Brief, #CA4-79-376-E [9 April 1981], p. 9, and Defendant's Response to Plaintiff's Reply Brief, #CA4-79-376-E [27 April 1981], p. 2.) This is completely true in TCU's case. In order for the ordained employees of a college related to a strictly congregationally governed church that never had even a slight majority of its board members be members of the parent church to qualify, the college would have to set aside its theology and traditions and submit to the government's demands. For the government to insist on such a modification of practices on the part of nonhierarchical churches in order to gain the benefits of a program the institutions of hierarchical churches gain with no problem has the color of preferential treatment of one kind of church over another.

45.   *Salkov* v. *Commissioner*, at 190.

46.   Ibid., at 196. The tax court also recognized the existence of a strictly congregational form of polity in *Marc H. and Helga Tanenbaum* v. *Commissioner of Internal Revenue*, 58 T.C. 1 (1972) and *Silverman* v. *Commissioner of Internal Revenue*, 57 T.C. 727 (1972).

47.   *Colbert* v. *Commissioner*, at 449.

48.   Ibid., at 455.

49.   *Lawrence* v. *Commissioner of Internal Revenue*, 50 T.C. 494 (1968).

50.   *Silverman* v. *Commissioner*, at 727.

51.   Cf. note 34 and accompanying text. Cf. also *United States* v. *Seeger*, 380 U.S. 163 (1965) and *Welsh* v. *United States*, 398 U.S. 333 (1970).

52.   Cf. note 33 and accompanying text.

53.   Cf. Rev. Rul. 59-270, which makes precisely the same kind of distinctions between ordained and unordained ministers of music and ministers of education.

54.   *Kirk* v. *Commissioner of Internal Revenue*, 425 F. 2d 492 (1970), cert. den. 400 U.S. 852 (1970).

55.   The National Council of Churches has contended, for a decade and one-half, that ministerial housing allowances are unconstitutional. Cf. Dean M. Kelley, *Why Churches Should Not Pay Taxes* (New York: Harper and Row, 1977), 119-22, 140-44.

PART 7

RELIGION AND POLITICS

Religious Liberty, the Free Churches, and Political Action

FRANKLIN H. LITTELL

The American pattern of "separation" had its origin in adjustments in the interaction of religion and politics that were unique to America. On the Continent, the "Egypt" that the first settlers had left in their travel to the Promised Land, the relations of religion and politics were intimate, if not always peaceful. Beginning with Virginia, in the years of the launching of the new republic, the thirteen states took a radically different course.

Religious establishments had functioned in "Christendom" for centuries as part of the control system used by the ruling elements. Minorities, whether permanent outsiders like the Jews, or persecuted "heretics" like most radical Christian communities (Waldenses, Albigenses, Bogomili, *Taeufer*, et al.), commonly suffered contempt, repression, and periodic martyrdom.[1] When a broader toleration came, following the Enlightenment, it was often initiated by anticlericals and achieved over the bitter opposition of leaders of the religious establishments.

With the rise of militant ideologies—overtly or covertly anticlerical and anti-Semitic—in the shambles of European Christendom, "separation" frequently has been a mark for renewed persecution. The old sacral systems have, in decline, been replaced by ideological systems that continue the style of state churches. For example, the Nazi record is clear in this respect. Today, although the constitutions of Marxist governments usually have written provisions for "religious liberty," in practice such clauses simply remove religion from the centers of political power (i.e., governmental sponsorship and political privilege).[2] Under Marxist regimes, there is no concern for "the free exercise of religion"; religion is to decline and die out with other prescientific systems-of-being. The Marxist system-of-being is to supersede religion. In the meantime, the public function of religion is discouraged by all the methods once associated with the Christian state churches' treatment of Jews and "heretics."

During the colonial period in American history, the relations of church and state reflected the European pattern. Spiritually the colonies were peninsulas of the mother country, just as politically they were extensions of the sovereign's might. In the meantime, however, a force was at work that was to modify and then fundamentally alter the chartered privileges of certain churches and the supervisory authority of the bishop of London and his agents of the Society for the Propagation of the Gospel (SPG). Large numbers of the early settlers were refugees from oppression in the Old World, either as partisans of the separationist theories of the Radical Reformation or as minorities that lost out to a more powerful establishment party. Baptists and Quakers, Mennonites and Moravians, and Congregational Separatists joined with Presbyterians in undermining—some quietly, others militantly—the conservative Congregationalist and Anglican establishments.

By the time of independence, in the dissolution of New England's "Standing Order," nearly one hundred congregations had moved from establishment to Independent Congregationalist and from independency to Baptist polity. In Virginia, the Baptists and Presbyterians joined with liberal-minded Anglicans to accomplish the first effective disestablishment of a ruling church in history. The style of church-state cooperation that had been typical of European Christendom, in the *landesherrliche Kirchenregiment* as well as before the sixteenth-century magisterial Reformation, yielded place to a new pattern of benevolent neutrality and occasional creative tension. In principle, at least, government was to be free of manipulation by clerical conspiracies and cabals, and the churches were to be free of governmental intervention.

THE TWIN FOCI OF RELIGIOUS LIBERTY

These two foci of religious liberty, something quite different from toleration, were summarized in the First Amendment to the federal Constitution prohibition of an establishment of religion and the guarantee of the free exercise of religion. Of these, the second point was primary. This primacy of free exercise is clearly set forth in *Taeufer* ("Anabaptist") testimonies. The pioneers of religious liberty were those "sectarians" of the sixteenth-century Radical Reformation who were convinced that a "true church" *(rechte Kirche)* could only be restored by a return to the church's early glory. That glorious condition of primitive Christianity had been besmirched and corrupted by a "fall" at the time when a triumphalist church and the Roman Empire were united. The suffering "true church" had then become the false persecuting state-church.

In the view of the radicals, membership in the "true church" was strictly voluntary. Many of them came to signalize this perception by requiring believers' baptism; all of them were agreed that church membership, participation, and support should be a work of volunteers rather than conscripts. From this premise came the perception that good government was not sacral, but rather limited and confined to secular responsibilities.

Both voluntary religious affiliation and secular government are still disputed, even in America. The *"free* exercise of religion,"* however, plainly carries a double meaning: *government shall not* interfere and *members shall* support voluntarily. As for secular and limited government, many of the Radical Reformers of the sixteenth century were just as explicit in affirming it as the Magisterial Reformers were explicit in denying it. The state-church Reformers all perpetuated the medieval parish and territorial definition of "membership" where possible, although few went as far as Ulrich Zwingli in a simple identification of the citizens of Kanton Zürich as God's New Israel.[3] In one form or another, like the Eastern Orthodox and the Roman Catholics, the Magisterial Reformers accepted the post-Constantinian *corpus christianum* as normative.

Caspar Schwenckfeld (1489-1561) was the sixteenth century's most prolific writer for the cause of religious liberty, and in a letter to Jakob Sturm of Strassburg he explained that

civilian authority has no jurisdiction over the Kingdom of God; that government was divinely ordained for the sole purpose of maintaining an orderly life in human society, but has no right either to influence or to interfere with religious convictions; the individual is accountable to Jesus Christ as the head of the Kingdom of God. . . . Christian government, a name of recent invention, is nowhere mentioned by Paul.[4]

Sturm was Bürgermeister of Strassburg, where the city government and the Protestant preachers were more tolerant than most, but Schwenckfeld sought to convince him that it was a basic error for the government to intervene at all in religious matters. The purpose of good government was to hold back the jungle; the Word of God could and would make its own way without the assistance of the sword.

Even today, two hundred years after the Virginia burgesses broke a new path on behalf of sound religion and good government and disestablished the denomination that had enjoyed political sponsorship from 1607 to 1785, there are many who fail to perceive the difference between toleration and religious liberty. Toleration, however, is not the opposite of persecution; it is the obverse side of the coin.

Although the Declaration on Religious Freedom (De Libertate Religiosa) of the Second Vatican Council was called "the American declaration," because of the signal contributions made by John Courtney Murray and Gustave Weigel, the Declaration describes toleration rather than liberty. It was clear in stating the right of the church's proclamation and work to be free of hostile government control, but it did not encompass the perception that religious freedom of necessity implies a certain kind of church (voluntary) and a certain kind of government (limited, secular).[5]

A wise government, while sponsoring a preferred religion, may stay its hand short of persecution of dissenters and nonconformists. Toleration is a counsel of prudence. A government that has recognized religious liberty, however, which rests on a higher ground than any decision or grant of government, has made an affirmation about the nature of high religion and good government. The state constitutional conventions that ratified the First Amendment to the federal Constitution did not debate the issue from the point of departure of pragmatism, as though with so many different religions in America no other decision were possible. On the contrary, like James Madison in his "Memorial and Remonstrance," they argued the ground of high religion and good government. Madison had, in fact, already in collaboration with George Mason, set in 1776 the switches for the shift from toleration to religious liberty on the American map.[6]

Thomas Jefferson wrote the Virginia Statute of Religious Liberty (ratified in 1786) that served as a model for the First Amendment to the federal Constitution (ratified in 1791). The convictions that undergirded religious liberty, as it applies to the concept of the church and the concept of government, ring thoughout the document. A few phrases will suffice to make the point. Jefferson, who considered this contribution to liberty to be equally important to the Declaration of Independence, declared that to coerce the faith of others is "impious presumption"; that coercion of faith has led to the establishment and maintenance of "false religions over the greatest part of the world, and through all time"; that no one should be compelled to support even the teacher of his own religious persuasion; that "our civil rights have no dependence on our religious opinions, any more than our opinions in physics or geometry"; that religious preference by government "tends only to corrupt the principles of that religion it is meant to encourage"; that intrusion of the powers of the civil magistrate "into the field of opinion, and to restrain the profession or propagation of principles on supposition of their evil tendency, is a dangerous fallacy, which at once destroys all religious liberty"; and, finally, that "truth is great and will prevail if left to herself, that she is the proper and sufficient antagonist to error. . . . "[7] This classic confession of faith in truth's ability to overpower error by spiritual weapons, rather than by recourse to the dangerous expedient of coercion and suppression, stands in direct succession to John Milton's immortal *Areopagitica* (1644)—transferring the arguments for freedom of press to freedom of religious profession.

The Crisis of Religious Liberty in America

Under ordinary circumstances, it might seem unnecessary to quote extensively a document so familiar, so central to the American traditions of liberty and self-government. As two recent conferences on "Government Intervention in Religious Affairs" have made clear,[8] however, many of the principles that Americans have taken for granted are again in jeopardy— and none more so than religious liberty. As this is written, there are far more cases involving religious liberty in the courts than the sum total of all First Amendment cases in the courts from 1791 to 1980.

What has happened in America to have brought such a landslide of cases into court? How is it that lawyers, on the floor and on the bench, have moved so freely into areas that were once considered the preserve of religious officials, lay and ordained? What, to be explicit, has happened to the principle of *judicial restraint?*

It may be argued that the crisis in religious liberty arises from the general anxiety about American identity and self-definition that has been evident since the Vietnam adventure. The extent to which the undeclared Vietnam War marked a

watershed in the American loss of innocence has yet to be
fully measured. Even the question whether the monument in
Washington should be a Pieta or a heroic group finally had to
resolved by erecting both, facing each other. By whatever
measure chosen, during the last decade Americans have
shown a marked decline in self-assuredness and a striking rise
in anxiety about the direction the republic is taking. This
spiritual and emotional climate of inner insecurity has serious
implications for the successful maintenance of that delicate
balance between liberty and popular sovereignty that has been
the genius of the American constitutional experiment in representative government.

In times of anxiety, peoples tend to revert to known ways of
doing things and ancient learned responses. In the case of
Christians, this means a tendency to return to the "good old
days" of Christendom, during which government attempts to
legislate a certain morality and doctrine that the bishops,
theologians, and lay leaders consider appropriate and good. In
the case of the Jews, this means a return to the ghetto-
thinking and unilateral action that they have learned across
centuries as the only dependable survival strategy in a hostile,
gentile world.

In the presently anxious condition of the American psyche,
both tendencies are evident, and both are destructive of the
interfaith understanding and cooperation that have been slowly
emerging as the major faith communities have come to accept
pluralism and separation of the religious from the political
covenants as beneficial to each and to all.

One must remember that for thousands of years of recorded
history, as long as the mind of man runneth not to the contrary, religion and regime have cooperated intimately with
each other in a variety of control systems. That is the background in the European and Mediterranean areas. In the
American colonies, with the exception of Rhode Island and
Pennsylvania, the old pattern prevailed (to 1817 in New
Hampshire, to 1819 in Connecticut, and to 1833 in Massachusetts). As Kenneth Scott Latourette and William Warren
Sweet often pointed out, the early settlers came chiefly from
the groups of the Radical Reformation. The sixteenth-century
pioneers of religious liberty, however, left no powerful and
affirmative models of effective civil government. Their problem was simple survival, and the toll of martyrs was very
high—at the hands of both Roman Catholic and Protestant
establishments.

Not until the seventeenth century, during the debates in Oliver Cromwell's New Model Army and in the radical Puritan covenanting groups of New England, were some of the important lessons of liberty and self-government secularized and made relevant to society as a whole.[9] In sum, the period of liberty and self-government and of voluntary religion and secular government has been so short—even in American history—that in times of crisis there is a pronounced danger of losing hold of the immeasurable values of separation to both religion and government.

To create an effective and responsible style of political action, appropriate to the American situation, is made difficult by other factors besides the general reversion to axioms of racial memory in times of anxiety. The Free Church forefathers, spiritual progeny of the Radical Reformation and of Pietism and Puritanism, were very sensitive to improper invasions of their religious prerogatives by government, but often limited in their understandings of how government must function.

Many radical Protestant groups, with long memories of persecution, kept as distant from government as possible even in America. Many, such as the Mennonites and radical Pietists, would not hold public office or even vote. Their fathers on the Continent, with a foreshortened eschatology, considered the vocation of Christians to be primarily in preparation for the Lord's imminent return, and only secondarily (if at all) to give attention to the needs of the larger civil society. Others, such as the Quakers (radical Puritans) in the Pennsylvania assembly in 1756, retired from public office rather than exercise power in ambiguous circumstances. The body of teaching on which the Free Church descendants in America of the pioneers of religious liberty in Europe had to draw came from forefathers who had known only two kinds of sacral governments: those that persecuted and those that (usually temporarily) tolerated. Concerning limited and secular government, in which the populace are "citizens" (and partake of decision-making) rather than subjects, they had no body of teaching to which to turn.

Another problem in America has been the seductive appeal of the general society, along with the normalization process that occurs through the interaction of different denominations in an open society. The Free Churches—the large English-speaking churches that grew so rapidly in the nineteenth and twentieth centuries—have proven as susceptible to the myth of a "Christian America" in the past as have those churches with no tradition of religious liberty and separation in their background.

Their assimilation is shown by a relaxation of the methods of internal discipline (admonition, "fencing the table," the ban, and so forth) and also by a style of preaching in which biblical truths are curiously blended with general social values. One of those values is the memory of the "American Zion," a concept of powerful evocative appeal that is a major rallying point in American populist religion.

Two Myths of Church and State in America

There are, in fact, two contradictory myths that are widespread in America today—both of them contrary to historical evidence and destructive of a common sense approach to a healthy but nonentangled interaction of church and state.[10]

The first myth is this: that America was founded as a "Christian nation" and has been going downhill rapidly in recent years, certainly since Franklin Delano Roosevelt's New Deal. This myth appeals to those who hope to use the agencies of government to enforce their own opinions of morality and sound teaching, from "Moral Majority" preachers in Appalachia who seem to have learned the wrong lessons from New England Puritanism to Roman Catholic bishops whose denomination has but very recently accepted the principle that "error" has any political rights at all. The truth is, of course, that if government agencies could make a country "Christian" then the colonies and the states that succeeded them were—until disestablishment removed political sponsorship and control—"Christian." What Americans today, however, would openly argue that a government that sold Christian Indians and Quakers into slavery in the West Indies that undermined the "Christian Commonwealth" was truly Christian, even if it did appoint preachers, pay them with tax moneys, and give government support to a divinity school?[11]

The second myth is this: that the Founding Fathers were unbelieving deists, if not militant anticlericalists, chiefly concerned to establish a republic with a high wall of separation between church and state. In answer to this myth, the evidence is that—once the base line principle of nonmanipulation was fixed—cooperation and contractural relations between government agencies and religious agencies have flourished in America. The American Indians were educated in the custody of churches, the freedmen were educated and cared for after emancipation by church agencies, the vast majority of recent Office of Economic Opportunity contracts were negotiated, and partnership signed between the government and churches. A "high wall of separation" there has never been, and those who push projects to drive a wedge between government and the religious communities seem more inspired by bad memories of the cruel repression and persecution under European establishments than by familiarity with the unique ground rules of the American scene.

The truth is that the principle of religious liberty was enunciated with the federal Constitution, and then in the states that sooner or later adopted the federal model. The truth is that—in principle—disestablishment was official in every state by 1834. Equally true, however, is the fact that the implications of that constitutional principle have been worked out over two hundred years and are still not fixed and finished.

The truth is that America never was a "Christian nation," except in the sense of European Christendom. The truth is that the Founding Fathers were not anticlericalists—not even Jefferson, with his Marcionite Bible, paying church taxes and tithes and requiring chapel attendance at his university. Unlike the French revolutionaries, who hated "L'Infame" with a passion, the American revolutionaries esteemed high religion (voluntary) and purposed good government (limited).

RELIGIOUS LIBERTY: A PROCESS OF SELF-UNDERSTANDING

Over two hundred years some of the implications of *"free exercise of religion"* have become clear. As late as the 1940s, however, there were still Protestant chaplains of state universities preaching in chapels on state property, paid by tax moneys, in Athens, Georgia, and Columbia, South Carolina, and New Brunswick, New Jersey, and Orono, Maine. There were also official Protestant chapel services at Pennsylvania State University and many other tax-supported institutions.

Beginning with the years of World War II, Americans have become the most mobile people on the face of the earth, and they have become aware that they are religiously as well as ethnically a pluralistic society. As slowly as Americans' perceptions catch up with the facts of life, by the time they were willing to accept the cooperation of Protestants, Catholics, and Jews as normal, there were over a million Muslims in the land and one of the states had a plurality of Buddhists.

Nevertheless, 1960—when for the first time a non-Protestant was elected to the highest office in the land—marked a singular advance over 1928. Resistance to the Al Smith campaign in that year marked the high watermark of Protestant nativism. In reaction to that round of bigotry, the National Conference of Christians and Jews (NCCJ) was founded, and the NCCJ has become a useful as well as symbolic indication of a new style of political action.[12]

There is a minor tradition in America that considers religion a purely private matter, and occasionally this view has been given status by courts or by politicians. The stronger strain, however, is that which looks for religion to take its place with other organized expressions of opinion in debates on public policy. There is a feeling that religious leaders have a duty to speak out on vital matters, but that they should—like other community leaders—function with civility and courtesy towards their peers. Unhappily, there are religious leaders that find it difficult to exercise the kind of self-discipline and restraint that American politics calls for, that helps to create a genuine consensus in public affairs.

Present Unresolved Problems

In the process of working out the logic of political action under religious liberty, many areas are still needing clarification. Long after the constitutional provisions at federal and state levels, the momentum of the old Protestant hegemony and the lessons unlearned by some newer immigrants continue to put separation to the test. Two areas with danger signals today are the appropriate role of religious leaders in political controversy and the protected status of unpopular religious minorities (usually "new" or Asian faiths).

How shall a religious leader address a public issue? Members of a religious community expect their leaders to address them in the name of the Lord. They would feel deprived otherwise. Citizens who do not belong to that community, however, expect to be addressed not as communicants but as fellow-citizens. Religious leaders are entitled to be heard and to be treated with respect; otherwise they feel threatened. There is ample evidence that the magisterial style of some princes of the church—both Roman Catholic and Protestant— still carries over from earlier times in ways that give offense or evoke unhappy memories among Jews and Christians who do not belong to the denomination of these princes of the church. Moreover, the form of address appropriate to an internal religious issue is different from the form of address appropriate to an edifying discussion in the public forum.

Christian leaders risk a discreditation of the Gospel if they speak with the tone of divine authority on matters where the Spirit is still moving over the face of the waters. The affront accorded Geraldine Ferraro by the archbishop of her church in connection with the Al Smith memorial dinner in New York City was a breach of civility of the kind that Americans can do without. Eleanor Roosevelt, whose one hundredth birthday was celebrated in the fall of 1984, answered a like affront by a cleric who had forgotten that America is an open society—and not a closed "Christian" society where a few church leaders of one or two denominations declare the truth over the heads of the docile and silent masses. The cleric had, in short, forgotten that this is pluralistic America and not European Christendom.

Eleanor Roosevelt, one of the great women of the twentieth century, responded as follows:

Anyone who knows history, particularly the history of Europe, will, I think, recognize that the domination of education or of government by any one particular religious faith is never a happy arrangement for the people. . . . I assure you that I have no sense of being an "unworthy American mother." The final judgment, my dear Cardinal Spellman, of the worthiness of all human beings is in the hands of God.[13]

Precisely! The arrogant and magisterial tone of voice is out of place in an area of religious liberty and popular sovereignty.

After the anxious reversion to triumphalist Christendom and defensive ghetto, the twin reactions of inner insecurity among Christians and Jews, the most serious threat to religious liberty today is in the hysterical campaign against "sects and cults." This is much more serious than breaches of civility. On this—the crusade against "Moonies," and the followers of Hare Krishna, Scientology, the Bhagwan, and Maharishi—some Christians and some Jews seem able to effect at least an uneasy alliance, but many have not.

The passing of the Cockrell Resolution in 1984 in the European Parliament, calling upon governments to suppress movements that are misleading youth, is fitting in a setting where repression and persecution are ancient traditions. What is the logic of such crusades in America, however, where Methodists, Baptists, Quakers, Mennonites, and Mormons—

not to mention the Jews—were for many generations themselves the objects of persecution? Have Americans so soon forgotten the mob actions and political discriminations suffered
by their fathers in the faith?

The reference seems clear. Here is another indication of
how "free churches" can through accommodation and assimilation become as thoroughly "established," as thoroughly
identified with the prevailing values of a society in a certain
season, as any state-church of the old type. A religion may
become established by social adaptation as well as by law.
When it does accept such status, blessing the high places of a
society, it is susceptible to support of a program of synchroni-
zation (*Gleichschaltung*) of groups that do not float with the
prevailing tide.

A church that blends with the *Zeitgeist* is, biblically speaking, something other than the Church of Jesus Christ. This is
true whether the blending involves the *positives Christentum* of
Article 24 of the Nazi Party Program or American "civil religion." Situations of strongly supported *Kulturreligion* are especially dangerous for the Jews, who do not fit in, but the
records show that they are also dangerous for Christians who
swim against the current.

The myth that the American republic was founded in hostility to religion is bad history, but not especially dangerous to
persons. The myth, however, that the United States was
founded as a "Christian nation," and that through sinister
influences it has been perverted and corrupted, is potentially
very dangerous indeed.

These "sinister influences" may today be "liberals" and
"secular humanists," or perhaps the "sects and cults"; tomorrow, in the paranoid style of a minor strain in American politics, the "sinister influences" might be "the Elders of Zion."
All religious minorities—and here Leo Pfeffer has been far
wiser than some of his colleagues—should unite in defense of
the rights of all Americans against the single most dangerous
power of the twentieth century: idolatrous government—government that claims to deal and decide in matters affecting
ultimate commitments.

It was precisely the populist (*voelkisch*) movement, with its
mission to recover a lost "spirituality" in the nation, that gave
Nazism its popular character.[14] It is precisely the danger of
the new American "populism," called such by radical right
exponents like Howard Phillips and Richard Viguerie, that it

may move from a mythic construct of America's past to an ideological thrust to reshape America's future. Such a religious and political monolith would be dangerous not only to "sects and cults" and Jews, but to any persons of religious faith who believe—like the pioneers of religious liberty—that Christians live in the light of the Kingdom that is to come, and not in accommodation to the rules of the age that is passing away.

In the Kingdom that is to come, so it is taught, each shall speak his own language and each shall understand the other, being united in an experience of the Spirit that lifts them all above their former condition. Governmental agencies are empowered to build ziggurats. There is no evidence that they can invoke Pentecost, but when they try to deal in ultimates, they call forth spirits from which a people frees itself only with great suffering and loss.

That Americans can so soon forget that their forefathers were only a few generations ago persecuted as "sectarians," "heretics," or "deicides," that some of their church leaders conduct themselves in public affairs in ways appropriate to leaders of the *corpus christianum* rather than as messengers of the *corpus christi*, that major denominations can become identified with a populist "spirituality" even as they abandon church discipline (the *tertior nota* of a "true church")—should cause as much concern to lovers of religious liberty as the fact that the legislatures and civil courts give every evidence of eagerness to rush in and fill the vacuum.

Religious liberty—voluntary religion and secular government—is as much in danger in an age of raging ideologies and militant culture-religions as ever it was when Menno Simons traveled from congregation to congregation with a bounty on his head, or when Roger Williams was driven out of Massachusetts Bay Colony for insisting upon an adult church covenant, or when William Penn was jailed under five successive rulers of England for prophesying against the established church.

NOTES

1. The Jewish and Christian historians have seldom noticed, such is the high wall between them, that the regimes that have large records of persecution almost invariably persecute *both* Jews and Christian groups that separate from the preferred and established norm.

2.   Thus, the "religious freedom" defined in the Nazi program for the "model" area, the Warthegau, and that defined by the Communist government of East Germany are virtually identical in particulars; cf. Paul Gürtler, *Nationalsozialismus und evangelische Kirchen im Warthegau* (Göttingen: Vandenhoeck & Ruprecht, 1958), Appendix Doc. 8, and "Die Kirchen in der Deutschen Demokratischen Republik," in *Kirchliches Jahrbuch: 1958*, ed. Joachim Beckmann (Gütersloh: Gütersloher Verlagshaus Gerd Mohn, 1958), 199. "The Communists do not differ one bit from their predecessors, the National Socialists." Bishop Otto Dibelius to the triennial convention of the National Council of Churches (Denver, 1952); *RNS:Domestic* (12/12/52).
3.   Robert C. Walton, *Zwingli's Theocracy* (Toronto: University of Toronto Press, 1967), 106. "Zwingli's theory leaves no place for a believers' church," 86.
4.   Editor's summary from the *Corpus Schwenckfeldianorum* (vol. 11), cited by Selina Gerhard Schultz, *Casper Schwenckfeld von Ossig (1489-1561)* (Norristown, Pa.: Board of Publication of the Schwenkfelder Church, 1946), 311-12.
5.   Cf. commentary to *Dignitatis Humanae* in Walter M. Abbott, ed., *The Documents of Vatican II* (New York: Guild Press/America Press/Association Press, 1966), 697-700.
6.   In Article 16 of the *Virginia Declaration of Rights;* cf. Elwyn A. Smith, *Religious Liberty in the United States* (Philadelphia: Fortress Press, 1972), 36f.
7.   Harold C. Syrett, ed., *American Historical Documents* (New York: Barnes & Noble, 1960), 95-96.
8.   Cf. the report of the first conference: Dean M. Kelley, ed., *Government Intervention in Religious Affairs* (New York: Pilgrim Press, 1982); the second conference, "GIRA II," was held 3-5 September 1984 in New York City.
9.   On the application of the lessons of the church meeting to the government of the civil society, see A. D. Lindsey, *The Essentials of Democracy* (Philadelphia: University of Pennsylvania Press, 1929). For primary sources, few items can surpass John Owen's *The True Nature of a Gospel Church and Its Government . . . 1689* (London: James Clarke & Co., 1947) and John Wise, *A Vindication of the Government of New England Churches . . . 1717* (Gainesville, Fla.: Scholars' Facsimiles and Reprints, 1958).
10.   The normalization process may bring benefits as well as special problems. For example, an American Lutheran study takes a position of which no European Lutheran Church could conceive: "We shall defend both the institutional separation and the functional inter-action of church and state in the United States and Canada." *Church and State: A Lutheran Perspective* (New York: Lutheran Church of America, Board of Social Ministry, 1963), 30.
11.   Cf. Franklin H. Littell, *From State Church to Pluralism*, rev. ed. (New York: Macmillan Co., 1971), 26-31.
12.   Cf. "The Course of American Religious History: From Protestant Domination to Interfaith Cooperation," in *Contemporary Jewry: Studies in Honor of Moshe Davis*, ed. Geoffrey Wigoder (Jerusalem: Institute of Contemporary Jewry, Hebrew University, 1984), 85-96.
13.   *New York Times*, 28 July 1949.
14.   Cf. Klaus Scholder, *Die Kirchen und das Dritte Reich, I: Vorgeschichte und Zeit der Illusionen, 1918-1934* (Berlin: Propyläen Verlag, 1977), chapters 1:5 and 1:7.

Religion and the New Right in the 1980s

RICHARD V. PIERARD

The New Right, as it is popularly known, has been around for a few years and has been subjected to such intense scrutiny that the amount of literature generated is rapidly approaching the point of unmanageability.[1] Assuming, therefore, that most informed people are familiar with the contours of the New Right, this essay will forego a general descriptive discussion of it and devote attention instead to the New Christian Right, or, as commentators variously denote it, the "religious right," "new religious-political right," "evangelical right," or "born-again politics." Although this is an integral part of the wave of conservatism that has swept over the land in the post-Watergate era, space limitations necessitate that it be removed from its context and examined as a separate unit.

WHAT IS THE NEW CHRSITIAN RIGHT?

The New Christian Right in a generic sense may best be defined as encompassing a number of conservative forces that emerged in American Christianity in the 1970s and coalesced with the political right in 1979-80. It includes a number of groups, primarily fundamentalist or evangelical Protestant in orientation but with definite ties with like-minded people in the Roman Catholic, Greek Orthodox, and even Mormon churches. Much of the visible leadership is provided by preachers and television evangelists, but equally important are the publicists, political organizers, and direct mail specialists who help to enlist congregants in local churches for the cause. The leaders explicitly advocate political involvement by taking stands on public questions, helping their followers to become informed on issues, and urging them to vote accordingly.

Their politics is one of nostalgia for an earlier "Christian America" and opposition to a vague entity called "secular humanism" that they regard as the primary agent of moral decline. Like their secular counterparts, Christian rightists are firm anticommunists and join the conservative side of almost all public issues. They oppose big government (particularly

federal involvement in business and welfare matters), labor
unions, open immigration, affirmative action, school busing to
achieve racial integration, environmentalism, gun control, any
diminution of the nation's military power or position in the
world, and détente with the Soviet Union. What distinguishes
them is their deep, emotional commitment to a package of
social or "family" issues. Some of this flows from their rejection
of feminism, e.g., their opposition to abortion, to the Equal
Rights Amendment, to state-supported day-care centers for
working mothers, and to shelters for battered wives. They are,
however, also against restrictions on the power of parents to
discipline their children, legalization of homosexual conduct
and gay rights, pornography, and sex education in the public
schools. They advocate parental control over textbooks and
the content of instruction in the schools as well as the teaching of patriotism, free enterprise, "scientific creationism," and
traditional moral values. Christian rightists favor overturning
the Supreme Court rulings on Bible reading and religious
devotions in public schools through a Prayer Amendment, elimination of all state regulations governing private or
Christian schools, and provision of tuition tax credits to assist
parents who send their children to such schools. Much of this
is encompassed in the controversial Family Protection Act,
which at the time of this writing was still buried in Congress
and unlikely to achieve legislative enactment.

Some commentators find the Christian Right deeply rooted
in the past, but Martin Marty's more modest explanation is
perhaps the most convincing.[2] He points out that evangelical
Protestantism has always had a moral and, at times, a moralistic bent. The heart of the evangelical experience is conversion
to Christ (the new birth), and in America this moved followers in two closely related directions. First, they favored doctrinal orthodoxies that in turn fostered a fundamentalist movement that stressed biblical inerrancy and upheld traditional
doctrines it felt modernists were compromising. This was par-
alleled by a desire to draw boundaries that would insure their
survival in the modern, secular age. The result was a Mani-
chaean view of the world divided into dualities—God versus
Satan, the elect versus sinners, and Christians versus secularists. The latter in each case was part of a conspiracy to oppose
the good, and they turned good America into corrupt America.

Further, evangelicals became moralistic. In a nation where
church and state were separate the churches remained tax-

exempt, and in order to justify this benefit they had to demonstrate their value to the republic. Unable to appeal to the rightness of their doctrine, they had to proclaim their moral contribution to the good society. Thus, evangelicals established a multitude of charitable and reform agencies that attempted to alleviate social evils. The emergence of the social gospel, however, with its emphasis upon systemic approaches to evil, led evangelicalism to take on a more moralistic cast, advocating individual virtue as the answer to society's vice. Regardless of what the societal situation might be, the individual person had control over his or her own good actions. At the same time, conservative Protestants accepted the values of social Darwinism and tied evangelicalism to laissez-faire, free-enterprise capitalism. Accordingly, they would interpret any effort to bring about social justice through organized pressure (e.g., the civil rights movement) as the church's "meddling" in politics.

Premillennialism became a key element of conservative evangelicalism in the early twentieth century, but it did not breed as much pessimism about worldly affairs as one might think. As long as believers went about winning others and were moral in their personal lives, they could enjoy the "more abundant life" promised by Jesus. They could also survive along with the other fittest, while the weaker members of society were weeded out through capitalist competition. Further, they believed America was an elect nation, the last, best hope of the earth, which God was using as the base for missionaries who would reach people for Christ in the various nations and rescue them from their sins. It must also stand against the Soviet Union and other agents of Satan who were doing their pernicious work in the world. As a result, the supposedly otherworldly faith became very worldly indeed.

A current debate in scholarly circles is how "new" the New Right is, with the weight of opinion gravitating toward the view that the continuity within conservative thinking and action is greater than the disjunction.[3] Throughout American history religious right-wing radicalism has had little tolerance for people who dissented from their understanding of morality and right belief.[4] Leo Ribuffo brings out in his new study of Christian radicals in the 1930s and 1940s, as Erling Jorstad, John Redekop, and this author did in older works on the religious right of the 1950s and 1960s, that plenty of historical precedents exist for the extremist views of the Moral Majority

and the numerous other Christian Right organizations.[5] Gerald
L. K. Smith, Gerald Winrod, William Dudley Pelley, and
Father Charles Coughlin organized political movements in
the 1930s that captured public attention, while the next generation of rightists—the anticommunist Cold Warriors and
anti-ecumenical fundamentalist-separatists like Carl T. McIn-
tire, Billy James Hargis, Fred Schwarz, George S. Benson,
Edgar C. Bundy, Myers G. Lowman, Dan Smoot, Howard E.
Kershner, Verne P. Kaub, and their Roman Catholic counterparts, the Cardinal Mindszenty Foundation and Clarence
Manion—had less of an impact. During the McCarthy era
and again in the 1960s, they were able to generate some
enthusiasm, but the Barry Goldwater debacle revealed how little strength the Right had. The election of Richard Nixon in
1968, a seemingly conservative Republican who had close ties
with the evangelical community through Billy Graham, cut
the ground out from under the organized Religious Right.
Nixon's fall in 1974 did not help the cause any, and the
attempt of evangelical conservatives Bill Bright and Congressman John Conlan to put together an organization that would
elect conservative Christians to public office and thereby save
the nation proved abortive. Instead, they were now faced with
the born-again Baptist Jimmy Carter who openly witnessed to
his faith but espoused liberal social programs.

Two important things, however, occurred in the mid-1970s.
One was the bicentennial observance that gave the country
the opportunity to let its hair down after the traumatic experiences of Vietnam and Watergate and focused public attention once again on patriotism. Conservative evangelicals made
great capital out of this as they exulted in the country's heritage as a "nation under God" and heralded the Christian
America theme in their sermons and publications.[6] Senator
William L. Armstrong, one of the important figures in the
New Christian Right grouping in Congress, commented later
about the change that had occurred: "Something happened in
our bicentennial year—a refocusing of national thought life on
our spiritual roots."[7]

Second, secular conservative activists began to modify
their strategy. They set out to build a broad coalition that
would be autonomous from the political parties and possess a
comprehensive set of political organizations that could recruit
and train candidates, do advertising and fundraising, and
mobilize public opinion. The leaders of the so-called New

Right were careful to emphasize the vital nature of the social issues that interested the evangelical conservatives. In 1979, they assisted in creating the three groups the media most closely identified with the New Christian Right: the Moral Majority, [Religious] Roundtable, and Christian Voice. These bodies joined with other recently formed but little-known evangelical political organizations like Intercessors for America, Plymouth Rock Foundation, and the National Christian Action Coalition to do battle for the Lord. The older Christian Right groups were hardly noticeable, and the differences between the two were quite obvious. Unlike the old right, the New Christian Right made effective use of organizational strategy to mold their followers into a political movement.

The story of how television fundamentalist evangelists like Jerry Falwell, James Robison, Pat Robertson, and Charles Stanley mobilized their viewing audiences in the 1980 election campaign is well known. The same is true with the "report cards" prepared by Christian Voice and the Christian Voters Victory Fund that rated senators and congressmen on the "morality" of their voting records, the linking up with the various "right-to-life" groups and their influence on the writing of the Republican platform, the impressive Washington for Jesus Rally on 29 April 1979 that drew over two hundred thousand people to the nation's capital, and the Roundtable's National Affairs Briefing in Dallas on 21-22 August 1979 where presidential nominee Ronald Reagan was given the blessing of Christian conservatives. The New Christian Right was the subject of innumerable articles in the print media, and their figures appeared on TV interviews and the covers of leading magazines. It goes without saying that no one radiated more joy than they when Reagan triumphed in November 1980 and several liberal senators went down to defeat.

PRESIDENT REAGAN AND THE
NEW CHRISTIAN RIGHT

At first it was assumed that the Christian Right had played a crucial role in the Reagan victory, but more careful analysis of the election results soon dispelled this myth.[8] The data revealed that public disapproval of Carter's handling of the economy and foreign affairs and dissatisfaction with the existing parties and the political process as a whole were the decisive factors. A born-again bloc in fact had not materialized, and one survey showed that less than half of those polled had even heard of the Moral Majority and only a small fraction expressed approval of its goals. Little difference existed between evangelical and nonevangelical respondents on the issues listed. Moreover, there was a growing awareness that the media had considerably overestimated the strength of the New Christian Right and the figures of the viewing audience of the televangelists had been grossly inflated.[9] As a result, President Reagan backed off somewhat from his Religious Right boosters. Only one appointment of any consequence in the new administration went to a Christian Right luminary (the Moral Majority's Robert Billings), the social issues were given lesser priority as Reagan concentrated on his economic and armaments programs, and the first Supreme Court appointment went to a woman whose record on abortion was unsatisfactory to Falwell and others.

At the same time, several fundamentalists who felt Falwell's political gospel compromised the Christian message turned against him.[10] The media seemed to lose interest in the Religious Right personalities and devoted much less space and time to them. The Roundtable's attempt at a repeat performance of the National Affairs Briefing in Dallas in the summer of 1981 proved abortive. Divisions opened within the ranks of the Christian Right as several notables dropped out of the Roundtable, Christian Voice, and Moral Majority (for example, Ed McAteer's second in command, H. Edward Rowe, left to head up the Church League of America, while by 1983 two of Falwell's satraps, Greg Dixon and Tim La Haye, were busily engaged in their own rightist enterprises). Falwell personally came under intense fire for financial irregularities.[11] When Rev. Donald Wildmon announced that his Coalition for Better Television would boycott NBC, Falwell decided not to take part in it. Meanwhile, Pat Robertson of the 700 Club created his own political organization, the Freedom Council, to work toward achieving the items on the social agenda of the New Christian Right. It published its own newsletter, *The Freedom Report*, and was busily organizing local initiatives to, as a promotional brochure stated, "help defend, restore and preserve religious freedom in the United States." The conservative prima donnas found it increasingly difficult to work together even though they were all members of the Board of Governors of the Council for National Policy, an umbrella organization formed in 1981 that linked prominent figures in both the secular and Religious Right.[12]

Meanwhile, Reagan's rightist support base began eroding. Article after article in Richard Viguerie's *Conservative Digest*, in 1982 and 1983, questioned whether the president would continue to receive conservative backing if the budget deficits persisted and the social issues were neglected. In fact, the entire issue of July 1982 was devoted to criticizing the Reagan administration. In February 1983, Viguerie said openly that if Reagan "continues to move to the left, I and other conservatives don't think he should run for reelection." He was also criticized by such right-wing stalwarts as the Heritage Foundation and *Human Events*.[13] Pollster Richard Wirthlin conceded in early 1983 the president's approval rating among conservatives had fallen to 56 percent.[14] New Right achievements in the 1982 elections were less than impressive, as both NCPAC (National Conservative Political Action Committee) and Jesse Helm's Congressional Club performed poorly in electing their candidates. The anti-abortion and school prayer lobbies were noisily insisting the time had come for more forceful presidential leadership.

Reagan's lukewarmness toward the social issues was mirrored by Congressman Jack Kemp who said on CBS's *Face the Nation*, 7 November 1982, that the middle of a recession is no place for these questions which "do not rank in the importance and priority of the American electorate" and that abortion and school prayer should be put "on the back burner."[15] This attitude was undermining his position among right-wing evangelicals, and it had become necessary for him to shore up the defenses there. All along Reagan had kept lines open to them through his liaison with religious bodies, e.g., Morton Blackwell, a former Viguerie lieutenant who had edited *The New Right Report*. Blackwell told a *Christianity Today* reporter that Campus Crusade's Bill Bright, Southern Baptist luminaries Jimmy Draper and Adrian Rogers, Jerry Falwell, and Pat Robertson met frequently with the president, and Blackwell credited Robert P. Dugan, the director of the National Association of Evangelicals' Washington office, with being "immensely helpful in explaining how the evangelical community feels on a variety of issues."[16]

Reagan opened the campaign to reclaim his Christian rightist supporters with a stirring speech entitled "Believe in Her Mission" in the prestigious Alf Landon Lecture Series at Manhattan, Kansas, on 9 September 1982. Much of it was a recitation of earlier statements of religiosity, but it was cast in the classic civil religion mold with all the appropriate "God words," the identification of the nation's spiritual heritage, and the call for a crusade for national renewal. He defined the problems facing the country in the terms of the Right's social agenda—abortion, school prayer, military strength to save the world from communism, a balanced budget—and said little or nothing about poverty, racism, civil rights, or sexual and social oppression.[17] This was followed by a forceful address at the National Religious Broadcasters convention in January 1983 condemning abortion, criticizing court decisions on school prayer, and advocating tuition tax credits. The notorious "evil empire speech" at the NAE conclave in March 1983 denounced the "totalitarian darkness" of the Soviet Union and reaffirmed the package of social issues that the New Christian Right saw as important.

In 1983, Reagan did other things to curry evangelical favor, including serving as honorary chairman of the National Committee for the "Year of the Bible," giving Billy Graham the Presidential Medal of Freedom, placing his name on an article in the *Human Life Review* that reflected upon the horrors of abortion, delivering speeches in various places (e.g., the National Forum on Excellence in Education at Indianapolis on 8 December) that referred to the "expulsion" of God from the nation's classrooms, and delivering a videotaped message of greetings to the huge Campus Crusade for Christ convention in Kansas City just after Christmas that contained the usual platitudes.[18]

Although some in the New Right camp had doubts about Reagan's commitment to their cause, the president clearly could count on substantial backing from the evangelicals, and his religious advisers encouraged him to keep on stroking them. It is equally evident that by pushing the social issues and continually raising the spectre of secular humanism, the New Right was able to make significant inroads into the evangelical ranks. For example, Jerry Falwell was one of the speakers at Moody Bible Institute's Founder's Week in February 1984, while the November 1983 issue of *Moody Monthly* ran an interview with ultraconservative United States Senator Charles E. Grassley and excerpts from Cal Thomas's *Book Burning* and John Whitehead's *The Stealing of America*, two of the New Christian Right's best-sellers of the year.

The Right's biggest coup by far, however, was coopting the evangelical preacher and writer, Francis A. Schaeffer, on intellectual themes. He was welcomed to the pulpit of Falwell's Thomas Road Baptist Church in Lynchburg, Virginia, and the Moral Majority promoted his films and books, especially *The Christian Manifesto* (Westchester, Ill.: Crossway Books, 1981). The book is a pot-boiler that declares legalized abortion and secular humanism are leading America down the same path as Nazi Germany and suggests armed resistance may be required to break the hold of the tyranny fastening itself upon the nation. His social views were unveiled in a speech given at his L'Abri Mini-Seminars in 1982 spelling out the priorities for the year. They were: combating humanism (seen in the devaluation of human life through abortion and infanticide), the attack on the family (sex education, state rather than parental control of children, and no fault divorce), and the assault on the schools (in the public schools—denial of the Christians' right to speak of the Creator or to engage in voluntary prayer, and in the private schools—the state's attempt to bring in destructive humanistic teaching by gaining control of the curriculum).[19]

In another lecture, "The Secular Humanistic World View Versus the Christian World View and the Biblical Perspectives on Military Preparedness," delivered before a large assembly of prominent rightists and military figures in Washington on 22 June 1982, Schaeffer drew a close connection between secular humanism and communism and condemned unilateral disarmament as surrender to Soviet oppression and expansion.[20] Such statements show that he was on the same wavelength as the evangelists of the New Christian Right, especially that of Jerry Falwell, who by 1983 had emerged as the most outspoken defender of President Reagan's arms policy and critic of the nuclear freeze and other disarmament proposals that might leave the United States in a position of inferiority vis-à-vis the Soviet Union.

THE CHRISTIAN RIGHT CHARGES ON

The Christian Right remained active on many fronts. For one thing it stood solidly behind President Reagan's reelection, and, in the fall of 1983, Christian Voice began plying its mailing lists with literature warning people of the dire calamities facing the country if Reagan were to be replaced by any of the representatives of "the rebellious 1960 liberals who burned American flags and today subscribe to runaway federal spending, abortion and 'gay is o.k.' but refuse to support innocent school children's right to pray." Singer Pat Boone, head of the 1984 Crusade for School Prayer, asked in a national mailing for 5 million people to send postcards to their senators and congressmen urging them to support President Reagan's Prayer Amendment, as this would bring back traditional moral values.[21] The various anti-abortion and profamily groups busily cranked out literature and fund appeals as well, and some pushed for state laws mandating the teaching of "scientific creationism." The latter's sectarian nature, however, has resulted in such a long string of court defeats that it is likely to become a back burner issue for most rightists.[22]

One question that the Religious Right has been exploiting to the hilt is that of Christian schools. For over three decades, many fundamentalist churches have operated weekday educational institutions and, in the last fifteen years, their numbers have increased at an exponential rate. The curriculum centers around literal use of the Bible, moral absolutes, mastery of basic subject matter, firm discipline, and traditional teaching devices like phonics and the McGuffey readers. A leading scholar of the movement, James C. Carper, points out that this has been the first widespread secession from the public school pattern since the establishment of Catholic parochial schools in the nineteenth century. Although a few of these may be "segregation academies" created to evade racial integration measures, by and large they originate from a far different source—the growing alienation of many evangelicals from American society. Carper comments that, to these people, "the public school exemplifies the trends they deplore in the changing American social order, such as uncertainty concerning sources of authority, dissolution of standards, waning of the Judeo-Christian value system, loosening of custom and constraint, scientism, and government social engineering." They are not merely protesting the allegedly secular humanistic nature of public education and unsatisfactory academic and behavioral standards in the schools but they are also registering their disapproval of the society that sustains the educational enterprise, and in that respect they are countercultural. Carper also calls attention to the genuinely spiritual side of the enterprise, a feeling on the part of these people that all education is ultimately religious and that Christian nurture is a full-time endeavor. The schools thus constitute the third part of the triad of church and home as the basis for nurturing children in what they believe is the scriptural manner.[23]

As these schools proliferated, it was inevitable that church-state conflicts would arise.[24] Many of them refused to submit to state licensing procedures or specified minimum standards. The quality of some was open to question because of their unorthodox instructional methods. For instance, many of them used Accelerated Christian Education (ACE) packaged learning programs. Marketed out of Lewisville, Texas, this is sort of a do-it-yourself operation that utilizes television monitors, workbooks, and parents or other amateur teachers and enables any ambitious pastor to have his own school in the church basement or educational wing. Not only is the ACE curriculum "Bible-centered," but more important it indoctrinates the children in right-wing ideology.[25] Proponents of Christian schools defend them by showing their pupils score higher on national tests than the average public-school child does. This is an argument that makes no impact on professional educators since they recognize that the Christian schools have a selective clientele, that the parents are more highly motivated to see that their children achieve, and that the programmed learning modules essentially "teach for the test."

In some states like Indiana, pressure brought by fundamentalist bodies on legislators resulted in the granting of exemptions from state licensing and accreditation requirements for church schools. Often, however, the desire to be free from all regulation resulted in acrimonious confrontations between churches and local authorities and extensive litigation. Christian rightist groups, like the Moral Majority, saw these as golden opportunities to trumpet the evils of secular humanism and statism, to pose as advocates of free speech and religious liberty, and to gain followers.

One of the most notorious conflicts took place in Nebraska. The ongoing struggle there is an excellent case study of the tactics of the New Christian Right. In 1977, Everett Sileven, pastor of the Faith Baptist Church in Louisville, a rural community of one thousand inhabitants about twenty-five miles from Omaha, opened a school.[26] Before long, Sileven's Faith Christian School was cited for violating some fourteen state laws by operating as an unlicensed day school, and a county court on 11 September 1979 ordered it closed. Sileven kept it open in defiance of the mandate, and on 13 September 1981 the county sheriff was directed by the judge to padlock the church and only allow it to be open for Sunday and midweek services. A few days later the judge relented and allowed the lock to be removed. The congregation for the time being then occupied the building around the clock.

In February 1982, after the United States Supreme Court refused to hear an appeal of the case and the Nebraska legislature would not modify the education laws to allow unlicensed schools like Sileven's, the pastor was placed in the county jail at Plattsmouth for contempt of court. He was released after thirteen days when the congregation voted to close the school. In April, however, the school was reopened and after fruitless negotiations, the judge in September ordered Sileven back to jail, and the church was again locked except for services. The next month, national attention was drawn to the case when sheriff's deputies and highway patrolmen entered the church during a prayer service and evicted eighty-five laypeople and ministers who had come from around the country to demonstrate their solidarity with Sileven. Meanwhile, some parents reopened the school, but when seven of the men were charged with truancy, their wives fled the state to avoid prosecution, and the embattled pastor himself became a fugitive. The events were widely reported around the country through articles disseminated to local newspapers by the AP and UPI wire services, and the evangelical religious media gave the story extensive coverage.

Although civil disobedience was a tactic of the left that rightists had always denounced, it was now their turn. They rapidly transformed the petty conflict in an obscure community into a media event by portraying it as a cataclysmic struggle of good versus evil and a church-state issue of monumental proportions. Leading the attack was Rev. Greg Dixon, National Secretary of the Moral Majority and pastor of a large Baptist church in Indianapolis.[27] Earlier he had worked long and hard to secure exemption of Christian schools in Indiana from state requirements and to water down the state's child abuse laws. In October 1982, he mobilized several hundred pastors to descend upon Louisville (the number varies widely in the press accounts) and petition for the pastor's release and unlocking of the church. Then, on 18 October, occurred the most melodramatic event of the whole affair—the above-mentioned eviction from the closed church of local people and visiting pastors who had assembled there for a "prayer meeting." Two days later, the judge suspended his order closing the school and padlocking the church because "enforcement personnel are insufficient in numbers to cope with the potential violence" that could have resulted from another effort to clear the church, and, on 22 October, he released Sileven who agreed to a "moratorium" on reopening the school. Even President Reagan said that he was "pleased" to learn of this and that "a step toward accommodation" had been reached.

The Moral Majority was milking the Sileven affair for all the publicity value it could. It had helped raise the $250,000 that the Christian Law Association, based in Cleveland, Ohio, needed to carry out the legal defense of the school. (Its founder, Rev. Roy Thompson, was the leader of the Cleveland Moral Majority and a participant in the Louisville demonstration.) Falwell had come there a year earlier and appeared with Sileven at a rally, and the Moral Majority sent a film crew to make a "documentary" that it intended to run on prime time television. Interestingly, the camera crew was not around when the deputy sheriffs unlocked the church, but the preachers bought new padlocks and put them on the door. Then Rev. Tim Lee of Oklahoma City, a marine who had lost both legs fighting in Vietnam, wheeled up to the door with wirecutters and snapped off the lock before the whirring cameras. At a victory rally earlier that week, Lee showed up in his military uniform and wheeled around the pulpit denouncing "queers," "baby-killers," "liberal left-wingers," actress Jane Fonda, black activist Angela Davis, and Senator Edward Kennedy. "I would rather be dead than have Ted," he screamed into a microphone as the crowd responded with a chorus of amens. At the same time, the preachers set up a telephone bank in another church and bombarded state officials and legislators with around-the-clock calls in order to pressure them to exempt Christian schools from state certification. Since they were mainly outsiders, however, and the nocturnal calls aroused considerable resentment, the net result was simply to steel official resistance and embitter local residents who could not understand what all the fuss was about. They even sought to draw President Reagan's attention with a barrage of calls to the White House and that apparently evoked his comment praising Sileven's release.[28]

When the legislature refused to act and the state supreme court would not overturn Sileven's contempt conviction, he was sent back to jail to complete his four-month sentence and the situation heated up again. By now Dixon had left the Moral Majority and created a new group, the American Coali-

tion of Unregistered Churches, to fight on behalf of the
Louisville congregation and others that refused to submit to
any kind of state regulation, whether it be church-sponsored
schools, social security, IRS requirements, or whatever. Sileven also became increasingly unwilling to compromise, and,
when he was released from jail on 31 January 1983, he issued
a statement to reporters in which he asked "in the authoritative name of Jesus" that "God Almighty bind the officials of
the state of Nebraska and Cass County from further interference with the ministry of God at Faith Baptist Church and
the saints of God of Nebraska by either converting them or
restraining them or removing them or killing them."[29]

The school soon reopened and judicial proceedings were
instituted against the parents. On Thanksgiving Eve, seven
fathers refused to answer any questions about the school and
were jailed for contempt by a new judge named Ronald E.
Reagan. Their wives and Sileven fled to Iowa, while Dixon
and 150 pastors quickly converged upon Louisville and
created another media event. He called it the "greatest struggle for religious freedom since the founding of this country"
and demanded that Nebraska Governor Bob Kerrey give
"protection" to the ministers because bullets were allegedly
shot through the church windows. The request was rejected
when local authorities found the "bullets" on the church's
window ledge and they turned out to be BBs. Rushing in
from Chicago to join him was H. Edward Rowe, the new
president of the Church League of America and an experienced Christian Right organizer (Christian Freedom Foundation, Anita Bryant Ministries, and the Roundtable), who
essentially took over the show. The pastors "ran" the school,
now populated by four students, while Rowe organized regular demonstrations for the benefit of the media and had eight
phone lines installed so they could call all over the country to
elicit sympathy. The ministers carried signs bearing such slogans as: "Let Our Children Go to School" and "Don't Arrest
Our Wives." In fact, Rowe candidly admitted to Robert
Unger, a correspondent for the *Kansas City Times*: "The Christian media is our primary target, but we are also aiming at the
secular media. Are we going after public opinion? Definitely.
Are you kidding? That's what this is all about. . . . We have to
reach the people." He went on the say: "I don't know if you
like slogans, but I'll give you a few. How about 'Abolish the
Nebraska Gulag'? Another is 'Sileven, Fugitive From Injus-

tice.' We chant them at demonstrations. I've got seven of them. I wrote them myself."[30]

The rightist ministers called the jailed fathers the "Nebraska 7." They appealed to President Reagan for help, but the White House refused on 16 December to intervene in the case (an action that helped precipitate Morton Blackwell's resignation the following month). They then asked to meet with presidential candidate Jesse Jackson because, as National Christian Action Coalition President William H. Billings put it, he "is a Baptist preacher and has been involved in the civil rights movement from his days as an aide to the late Rev. Dr. Martin Luther King." Sileven began touring the country blasting "government tyranny," while Dixon brought the wives and children of the Nebraska 7 to his Indianapolis church to give their testimonies and even advertised them as "fugitives from the state of Nebraska."[31] At present the matter is far from being settled, and every so often a wire service report brings yet another episode in the continuing saga.

New Manifestations of the Christian Right

The New Christian Right is a dynamic and growing force in American politics, and it is virtually impossible for researchers to keep an eye on all the new leaders and "ministries" that are cropping up. Here are some, however, that bear watching in the years to come. Either in the beliefs espoused, methods used, or personalities involved, they have strong affinities with the New Right.

The Rutherford Institute. This is a legal organization founded in 1982 by attorney John Whitehead and Christian film producer, Franky Schaeffer V, to assist the religious community in the courts. It is named after a seventeenth-century Scottish divine who allegedly denied the divine right of kings, saying that God, not kings, makes law and that kings may be disobeyed if their laws do not conform to God's law. As a spokesman declared, the organization will help the religious community defend its freedoms and protect public morality by "sound, scholarly, and aggressive lawyering." It will intervene in cases or actually initiate lawsuits in areas like abortion, prayer and other religious practices in public schools, creationism, and government involvement in church ministries, and it will publish educational monographs on these topics.[32] The group, like most rightist organizations, operates

from the assumption that America was founded on Christian
principles and at one time was a godly nation but increasing
secularization resulted in the loosening of public morality, restriction of religious freedoms, and "persecution" of Christians. The flaws in this point of view have been excellently
exposed in a recent book by three well-known evangelical historians, Mark Noll, Nathan Hatch, and George Marsden, *The
Search for Christian America.*[33]

Theonomy. This is a comparatively unnoticed philosophical
strain of evangelicalism that has been around for a least a
quarter century. Its ideas are expounded in the voluminous
writings of a largely self-educated Presbyterian minister with
Birchite connections, Rousas John Rushdoony, and has been
popularized in recent years by Gary North and Greg
Bahnsen. Rushdoony's version, called the Christian Reconstruction Movement, publishes a scholarly journal by that
name and operates a think tank in Vallecito, California
known as the Chalcedon Foundation.[34] North, Rushdoony's
son-in-law, holds a doctorate in history and currently runs the
Institute for Christian Economics, Geneva Divinity School,
and a variety of other enterprises out of Tyler, Texas. He is
also a prolific writer and the publisher of a semiannual journal, *Christianity and Civilization.* Bahnsen is an ethicist with
conservative Presbyterian training and the author of a pond-
erous tome, *Theonomy in Christian Ethics* (Nutley, N.J.: Craig
Press, 1977.) He was bounced from a teaching post at Reformed Theological Seminary in Jackson, Mississippi for his
extreme views and now is a free-lancer associated with North.

Theonomy means being under divine law. Its votaries argue
that God set forth his immutable standards in the Pentateuch,
the first five books of the Bible, and all of creation including
mankind is subject to its jurisdiction. God's detailed commands are just as binding today as they were when he
revealed them to Moses. When any people adhere to God's
"law-order," blessing and prosperity results, while adherence
to any other "non-revelational law-order" is a demonic quest
for autonomy, a declaration of independence from God, and
disaster is certain to result. Theonomy holds to a postmillen-
nial view of the future, since it teaches that when Christians
submit to the eternal law of God, they will progressively bring
the creation under his dominion. Eventually they will arrive
at the ultimate goal of establishing the kingdom of God on
earth, the situation where all people will have turned to Christ

and placed themselves under the sovereignty and loving governance of God.

The social program of the theonomists jibes fully with that
of the New Christian Right. The family is a hierarchical institution with the subordination of the wife to the husband and a
chain of command. Abortion is a consummate evil. Education
is the responsibility of the parents and church, and children
must be taken out of the hands of the "tax-supported, state-
regulated, humanistic school system" if they are to be brought
up in the ways of God. The modern state is a "messianic
force" that preaches its own humanistic "plan of salvation."
Welfare must be for the individual and must be personal in
nature. The family and church are to care for the needy. The
state, in a biblical sense, can be the minister of God when it
suppresses violence, fraud, and "the works of Satan," but its
role must be purely negative (the protection of life and property), and its taxing power limited to no more than the tithe.
The modern welfare state functions as a substitute family and
church and asserts its "divinity" by promising people a universal insurance policy against failure and God's judgment.

The radical "Christian economics" of the theonomic system
is its most distinctive (and reprehensible) feature. Although it
is an utterly absurd marriage of laissez-faire capitalism and
social Darwinism, theonomists insist it is God's way. Gary
North boldly affirms that, as a general rule, those living under
the rule of God's law-order will prosper, and those living in
societies that are in rebellion against him will not prosper.

Long-term poverty is always a sign of God's curse. The so-called underdeveloped societies are underdeveloped because they are socialist, demonist, and
cursed. Any attempt to blame the poverty of the underdeveloped world on
the prosperity of the West is absolutely wrong. This is the old Marxist and
socialist line. It blindly fails to acknowledge the wrath of God on demonic,
tyrannical, and socialist tribal cultures. . . . The Bible tells us that the citizens of the Third World ought to feel guilty, to fall on their knees and
repent from their Godless, rebellious, socialist ways. They should feel guilty
because they are guilty, both individually and corporately. . . .

We should not be deluded about who is responsible for the lack of economic growth in the Third World. They are responsible. Their abject poverty is . . . God's economic justice. He promises that same poverty for all
nations that rebel against Him. Poverty is exactly what they deserve.[35]

Professors David Rausch and Douglas Chismar have recently sounded the alarm about the dangers of theonomy, a
cultic movement that is starting to make inroads into the
Christian community.[36] They point out how it preaches the

crassest forms of selfishness and legalism and calls for the imposition of a Puritan-style dictatorship that subverts the rights of other individuals. The brutal legalism that calls even for the stoning of unruly children and capital punishment for adulterers and homosexuals, however, is only the most egregious aspect of its belief system. Terms like socialism, statism, and humanism are thrown around in a flippant fashion, and those Christians who stress social concern are dismissed as "guilt-manipulators."[37] More important, the movement has close ties with the Rutherford group, Pat Robertson's CBN operation, and the Roundtable, and North and Rushdoony are members of the Board of Governors of the Council for National Policy.

Identity. This is a right-wing movement shrouded in obscurity. The central idea is that white Christian Americans are the spiritual and lineal descendants of the Old Testament Israelites and, thus, are God's chosen people and heirs of his promises. It is a new twist on the old British-Israel position that the Anglo-Saxon peoples came from the Ten Lost Tribes of Israel. It holds that modern Israel is a historical fraud, Jews were merely bystanders in history, and today they are the enemies of true Christians. One strain of Identity preaches a conspiratorial, racist anti-Semitism. This is the "two-seedline" or idea that throughout history two genetic groups have existed in opposition to one another, the white race favored by God subject to his laws and another race spawned by Satan in the Garden of Eden and today represented by the Jews.[38]

The other strain stresses America's uniqueness and the dangers of communism and other conspiracies. It holds that true believers will have to endure the disasters of the end-time tribulation period before they can enter the kingdom of God that will be set up at Christ's second coming. Since they believe the faithful must prepare for the imminent Satanic onslaught, many Identity adherents join survivalist groups. A noteworthy statement of this position is by Pat Brooks, a writer of charismatic books and a regular contributor to *Christian Life* magazine. She has been deeply influenced by theonomist and radical Right conspiracy theories, as evidenced by her book, *The Return of the Puritans* (Fletcher, N.C.: New Puritan Library, 1979). In her latest volume, *Hear, O Israel* (Fletcher N.C.: New Puritan Library, 1981), she adopts an unabashed identity stance. America is God's people through their descent from Israel, but they need to repent and return to him because they face the tribulation of a war with Russia in the Middle East before the Lord returns in triumph.

New Age Movement Research. Two books dealing with the so-called New Age Movement appeared in 1983 and quickly soared to the top of the evangelical charts. They were Dave Hunt, *Peace, Prosperity and the Coming Holocaust* (Eugene, Ore.: Harvest House), and Constance Cumbey, *The Hidden Dangers of the Rainbow* (Shreveport, La.: Huntington House). In spite of damning reviews in generally conservative publications, like *Christianity Today* and *Eternity*, the two books sold amazingly well. On the Christian Booksellers Association paperback best-seller list, Hunt held first place in September and Cumbey in December and neither was lower than fourth during the last quarter of 1983.[39]

Both portray in vivid detail the all-encompassing New Age conspiracy that is now at work in the world and aims at one centralized world church, government, and food authority. It will usher in an era of unparalleled prosperity under the rule of the Antichrist, and Christians will experience brutal persecution until Jesus comes and destroys the Satanic system. The New Agers are more dangerous than secular humanists because they tie together humanism, occultism, Eastern religions, Protestant liberalism, and the new fads of the day, and the movement "has successfully infiltrated nearly every segment of our personal, religious, and professional lives."[40] The New Age links may be seen in the use of such symbols as the rainbow, triangle, and circle and buzzwords like "spaceship earth," "global village," "networking," "holistic," "interdependent," and "paradigm."

Especially significant is the manner in which both writers attribute all the standard evils identified by the Right to this godless New Age Movement—lack of absolutes, self-will, drugs, occultism, selling out to the Soviets, socialism, the peace and antinuclear arms movements, environmentalism, humanism, pluralism, and feminism. Cumbey smears more liberal-minded evangelicals as New Agers or dupes of the movement. She says Tom Sine's *The Mustard Seed Conspiracy* (Waco, Tex.: Word, 1981) contains the same program as the New Age Movement and the Humanist Manifesto. The book by World Vision executive Stanley Mooneyham, *What Do You Say to a Hungry World?* (Waco, Tex.: Word, 1975), "advocates most of the political program of the New Agers." "Much that appears to be New Age-oriented" has come out of

InterVarsity Christian Fellowship in recent years. InterVarsity
Press author Ronald Sider's approach is "more New Age than
Christian." Feeding the world's hungry "through forced redis-
tribution of the world's wealth, or stated another way, through
socialism, is not a biblical imperative." Also attacked are
InterVarsity Press writer David Bryant (*In the Gap: What It
Means to Be a World Christian* [1979]), the environmental
study by the Calvin College Center for Christian Scholarship,
Earthkeeping (Grand Rapids, Mich.: Eerdmans, 1980), Sen.
Mark Hatfield, and Bread for the World.[41] The enthusiastic
reception that the two books received among the "born
again" and the authors' frequent appearance on Christian
radio and TV talk shows indicate that they are influencing
evangelicals to move right.

The Institute on Religion and Democracy (IRD). This organization is perhaps the most difficult of the new groups to
categorize. As it stands now, it could either become yet
another instrument of the New Christian Right or it may
stand as a centrist spokesman for democratic values at a time
when these are under assault from totalitarian forces on both
the left and right. Formed in April 1981, the Institute is an
interesting coalition of theologically conservative evangelicals
(Carl F. H. Henry, Richard Lovelace, Ed Robb), neoconser-
vative intellectuals (Peter Berger, Richard Neuhaus, Michael
Novak), and activists from the Social Democrats, U.S.A., a
split from the old Socialist party (David Jessup, Penn Kemble,
Paul Seabury). Its position statement affirmed the connection
between Christian faith and human freedom, especially religious freedom, the equally important connection between
human freedom and the values of liberal democracy, and the
necessity for Christians to work to advance these values in the
face of authoritarian and totalitarian opponents.[42]

Although from the outset the IRD drew flak from liberal
Protestant circles for exposing alleged leftist tendencies, it
gained national notoriety with the airing of a program entitled
"The Gospel According to Whom?" on CBS' *60 Minutes* (23
January 1983) and the publication of an article in the *Reader's
Digest.* Both of these drew upon the IRD as a prime resource
and portrayed the National Council of Churches and the
bureaucracies of the United Methodist and United Presbyte-
rian Churches as leaning "toward the Marxist-Leninist left."
Further documentation for the accusation of leftist bias was
provided in a one hundred-page booklet published by the
IRD.[43]

The liberal religious press led by *Christianity and Crisis* raised the question of whether the IRD was narrowly partisan and merely an effort to legitimize the Reagan administration's foreign policy. Peter Steinfels insisted that the IRD's position could be reduced to the following essentials: the paramount political struggle of this day is that of totalitarianism and democracy, totalitarianism is identified with Marxism-Leninism and the Soviet Union, and democracy is identical with limited, constitutional government and with the United States as well as with capitalism and the market economy. Thus, it is a "conservative-neo-conservative alliance intended to advance a distinct political agenda while claiming only a broad Christian concern."[44] An agency of the United Methodist Church commissioned a lengthy study that traced the conservative connections of its board members. Journalist Leon Howell did an in-depth analysis of its makeup, funding, and tactics that showed that its first concerns were not the defense of theological orthodoxy and promotion of ecclesiastical togetherness but rather a conservative political program.[45] Particularly telling was the revelation that, in its first two years, the IRD received 89 percent of its funding from six conservative foundations, the largest being the one controlled by Richard Mellon Scaife, one of the major financiers of the New Right.[46] Hence, the prognosis for the IRD remaining a centrist organization is not good.

THE ROAD AHEAD

In the early 1970s many assumed the Religious Right had run its course. Billy Graham, the leading evangelical, backed away from his earlier hardline anticommunism and openly proclaimed the importance of social concern, while a new generation of evangelical social activists had appeared on the scene who, through their publications and organizations, seemed to be orienting theologically conservative Protestantism in a whole new direction.[47] The events of the late 1970s and early 1980s demonstrated that this was not necessarily the case. Instead, a renewed struggle for the hearts and minds of evangelicals has broken out between the two activist groupings—the conservative, reactionary right and the progressive, socially involved left. It is too soon to tell whether the New Right will emerge victorious, but at this point in time it appears to be leading.

Still, it is doubtful that in the long run a conservative political and social ideology will really prevail over something so profoundly radical as the Bible. It has ever been the rock of stumbling for those who sought to give their political beliefs the divine imprimatur, and it will surely be so again.

NOTES

1. That can be seen from the various bibliographical works on the New Christian Right that this author has published: *Bibliography on the New Christian Right* (Terre Haute: Indiana State University History Dept., 1981); "The Religious Right: A Formidable Force in American Politics," *Choice* 19 (March 1982):863-79; "The New Religious Right: Suggestions for Further Reading," *Foundations* 25 (April-June 1982): 212-27; and "The New Religious Right in American Politics," in *Evangelicalism and Modern America*, ed. George Marsden (Grand Rapids, Mich.: Eerdmans, 1984).

2. Martin E. Marty, "Morality, Ethics, and the New Christian Right," *Hastings Center Report*, August 1981, 14-17.

3. Jerome L. Himmelstein stresses that the worldview of American conservatism as represented by the New Right today has not changed in three decades, and that it differs from the Old Right largely on matters of organizational strategy, not ideology and goals. "The New Right," in *The New Christian Right: Mobilization and Legitimation*, ed. Robert C. Liebman and Robert Wuthnow (New York: Aldine, 1983), 21.

4. This author briefly summarized that in an essay, "Radicalism of the Right and Religious Freedom," in *Conceived in Conscience*, ed. Richard A. Rutyna and John W. Kuehl (Norfolk, Va.: Donning, 1983), 21-33.

5. Leo P. Ribuffo, *The Old Christian Right: The Protestant Far Right from the Depression to the Cold War* (Philadelphia: Temple University Press, 1983); Erling Jorstad, *The Politics of Doomsday: Fundamentalists of the Far Right* (Nashville: Abingdon, 1970); John H. Redekop, *The American Far Right: A Case Study of Billy James Hargis and Christian Crusade* (Grand Rapids, Mich.: Eerdmans, 1968); and Richard V. Pierard, *The Unequal Yoke: Evangelical Christianity and Political Conservatism* (Philadelphia: Lippincott, 1970).

6. For examples, see Richard V. Pierard, "Evangelicals and the Bicentennial," *Reformed Journal* 26 (October 1976):19-23.

7. Beth Spring, "Rating Reagan," *Christianity Today* 27 (7 October 1983):47.

8. This is documented in Richard V. Pierard, "Religion and the New Right in Contemporary American Politics," in *Religion and Politics*, ed. James E. Wood, Jr. (Waco, Tex.: Baylor University Press, 1983):66-70.

9. William C. Martin, "Television: The Birth of a Media Myth," *Atlantic* 247 (June 1981):7-16; Jeffrey K. Hadden and Charles E. Swann, *Prime-Time Preachers: The Rising Power of Televangelism* (Reading, Mass.: Addison-Wesley, 1981); Tina Rosenberg, "How the Media Made the Moral Majority," *Washington Monthly* 14 (May 1982):26-34. Donna Day-Lower explodes the myth of the mass following of the Moral Majority by showing that it essentially drew from only two classes of people, the upwardly mobile who have just made it into the middle class and the economically stagnant. Because both suffered from insecurity and a lower educational level, they found the symbols of authority as wielded by Falwell to be attractive. "Who *Is* the Moral Majority? A Composite Profile," *Union Seminary Quarterly Review* 37 (No. 4, 1983):335-49.

10. For example Bob Jones, Jr., in a letter sent to the graduates of his school on 10 June 1980 denounced Falwell as "the most dangerous man in America today as far as Biblical Christianity is concerned," and his son, Bob Jones III, followed this with a blistering attack in the official Bob Jones University magazine ("The Moral Majority," *Faith for the Family* 8 [September 1980]:3, 27-28.) Falwell published the letter

and a lengthy rebuttal in the *Moral Majority Report*, 14 July 1980, 4-6. Baptist pastor James E. Singleton compiled two sizable booklets of statements from fundamentalists around the country condemning Falwell and the Moral Majority for their alleged compromises. *The Moral Majority: An Assessment of a Movement by Leading Fundamentalists*, and *The Fundamentalist Phenomenon or Fundamentalist Betrayal?* (Tempe, Ariz.: Fundamental Baptist Press, n.d.)

11.   For documentation, see Pierard, "Religion and the New Right," 66-70, 79-80.

12.   This intriguing association was created in May 1981 by more than fifty well-known conservatives, a virtual who's who of the New Right, and had the objective of educating the public on domestic and foreign policy and providing a forum for exchange of ideas relating to these concerns. They hoped they would gain the same kind of influence that liberals allegedly had through such groups as the Council on Foreign Relations. Presided over by Louisiana representative Louis "Woody" Jenkins, the promoter of the state's creationist law, the CNP to date has kept a very low profile. *New York Times*, 20 May 1981, A17; *Conservative Digest* 7 (June 1981):6-7; *Oklahoma Observer* 14 (10 May 1982):8; *Group Research Report* 20 (26 June 1981):21-22; and *Group Research Report* 21 (26 February 1982):2-3.

13.   *Washington Post*, 4 February 1983, A2.

14.   *Washington Post*, 19 February 1983, A7.

15.   *Washington Post*, 19 November 1982, A23.

16.   Spring, "Rating Reagan," 49.

17.   The best analysis of this speech is Robert D. Linder, "Reagan at Kansas State: Civil Religion in the Service of the New Right," *Reformed Journal* 32 (December 1982):13-15. For an introduction to the topic of civil religion as it relates to American evangelicals, see Robert D. Linder and Richard V. Pierard, *Twilight of the Saints: Biblical Christianity and Civil Religion in America* (Downers Grove, Ill.: InterVarsity Press, 1978).

18.   On Reagan's religiosity, see Richard V. Pierard, "Ronald Reagan and the Evangelicals: Hot and Cold," in *Fundamentalism Today: An Appraisal*, ed. Marla J. Selvidge (Elgin, Ill.: Brethren Press, 1985). At the education conference, he stated: "I just have to believe that the loving God who has blessed this land should never have been expelled from America's classrooms." *Indianapolis Star*, 9 December 1983, 30.

19.   Francis A. Schaeffer, "Priorities 1982," unpublished speech, photocopied typescript in the possession of the author.

20.   *Who Is for Peace?* (Nashville: Thomas Nelson, 1983). Schaeffer and his son, Franky, both published books in March 1984 that solidly aligned his movement on the side of the New Right. *The Great Evangelical Disaster* and *Bad News for Modern Man: An Agenda for Christian Activism* (Westchester, Ill.: Crossway Books). He died in May 1984.

21.   Brochures in the possession of the author.

22.   The problems involved in this are succinctly sketched out in James E. Wood, Jr., " 'Scientific Creationism' and the Public Schools," *Journal of Church and State* 24 (Spring 1982):231-43.

23.   James C. Carper, "The *Whisner* Decision: A Case Study in State Regulation of Christian Day Schools," *Journal of Church and State* 24 (Spring 1982):281-82; "The Christian Day School Movement," *Educational Forum* 47 (Winter 1983):135-49.

24.   For the story of a landmark Ohio case and an introduction to the extensive body of literature that is developing on the topic, see Carper, "The *Whisner* Decision," 282-303. Conservative religious publications tend to report church-state conflicts over education matters in lurid detail. An example of this genre is Clayton L. Nuttal, *The Conflict: The Separation of Church and State* (Schaumburg, Ill.: Regular Baptist Press, 1980).

25.   For an insight into the ideological stance of ACE see the book by its president, Donald R. Howard, *Rebirth of Our Nation* (Lewisville, Tex.: Accelerated Christian Education, 1979).

26.   Appreciation is expressed to James M. Dunn who graciously made available to the author the Baptist Joint Committee on Public Affairs' press clipping file on the

Sileven case. The fundamentalists' view of the affair is contained in Ed Nelson and James Singleton, *Lessons from Louisville: Observations on Christians and Confrontation* (Marlborough, N.H.: Plymouth Rock Foundation, 1983).

27.   Greg Dixon's activities and views are detailed in Richard V. Pierard and James L. Wright, "No Hoosier Hospitality for Humanism: The Moral Majority in Indiana," in *New Christian Politics*, ed. David G. Bromley and Anson Shupe (Macon, Ga.: Mercer University Press, 1984).

28.   *New York Times*, 22 October 1982, 1, 11; 12 December 1982, 38; *Cleveland Plain Dealer*, 31 October 1982; *Omaha World-Herald*, 23 October 1982; David Krajicek, "Fundamentalist Protesters Blamed for Setbacks in Church School Case," *Religious News Service*, 27 October 1982. As a footnote to this story, Thompson wrote a scathing letter to Falwell on 7 October 1983 about Sen. Edward Kennedy's speech at Liberty Baptist College four days earlier and told him either "to openly and publicly apologize for this grievous error" or dissociate himself from the Baptist Bible Fellowship, the fundamentalist group to which both belonged. Copy in the possession of the author.

29.   AP release, 1 February 1982.

30.   *Washington Post*, 3 December 1983, A3; *USA Today*, 1 December 1983, 3A; Robert Unger, "The Louisville Church School Caper: Quest for Rights or Publicity?" *Evangelical Press News Service*, 17 December 1983. Unger comments it is still remembered around town that when Falwell came in October 1981 to tape his regular TV program, his people had to find a new padlock to put on the church so it could be cut off for the camera. Sheriff's deputies had removed it three weeks before he got to Louisville. H. Edward Rowe has prepared his own account of the affair, *The Day They Padlocked the Church* (Shreveport, La.: Huntington House, 1983).

31.   *Washington Times*, 21 December 1983, 5A; *Washington Post*, 19 January 1984, A7; *USA Today*, 23 January 1984, 3A; *Indianapolis Star*, 21 January 1984, 21; and *Christianity Today* 28 (17 February 1984):32-34.

32.   Martin Mawyer, "Rutherford Institute Defends Traditional Values," *Moral Majority Report*, May 1983, 4.

33.   Mark Noll, Nathan Hatch, and George Marsden, *The Search for Christian America* (Westchester, Ill.: Crossway Books, 1983.) Ironically, the same firm publishes works by Whitehead and Franky Schaeffer V.

34.   *Group Research Report* 22 (March 1983):11; ibid. (November 1983):40.

35.   Gary North, *Unconditional Surrender: God's Program for Victory* (Tyler, Tex.: Geneva Press, 1981), 163-64. For fuller statements of the theonomic system, see also North, *An Introduction to Christian Economics* (Nutley, N.J.: Craig Press, 1973), and *The Dominion Covenant: Genesis* (Tyler, Tex.: Institute for Christian Economics, 1982); Bahnsen, *Theonomy in Christian Ethics*; Rushdoony, *The Institutes of Biblical Law* (Phillipsburg, N.J.: Presbyterian and Reformed, 1973); and articles in the various numbers of the *Journal of Christian Reconstruction* (1974-   ) and *Christianity and Civilization* (1982-   ).

36.   David A. Rausch and Douglas E. Chismar, "The New Puritans and Their Theonomic Paradise," *Christian Century* 100 (3-10 August 1983):712-15, and "Regarding Theonomy: An Essay of Concern," *Journal of the Evangelical Theological Society*, forthcoming.

37.   David Chilton, *Productive Christians in an Age of Guilt-Manipulators: A Biblical Response to Ronald J. Sider*, 2d ed. (Tyler, Tex.: Institute for Christian Economics, 1982). This is a bitter, mocking attack by a North protégé on Sider's influential *Rich Christians in an Age of Hunger* (Downers Grove, Ill.: InterVarsity Press, 1977) that even is bound in a look-alike cover. The book, *Power for Living*, which was commissioned by the Arthur S. DeMoss Foundation and distributed free to several million people to celebrate the Year of the Bible, is the most noteworthy example of theonomist influence to date. It was produced by a communications organization called American Vision that recruited writers Chilton, Ray Sutton, and others from the Institute for Christian Economics. This edition, released in October 1983, however, was suddenly shelved and extensively rewritten by the well-known charismatic

author, Jamie Buckingham, and, according to Chilton, the theonomic content was "gutted and radically changed." *Christianity Today* 28 (3 February 1984): 40-43.

38.   Philip Finch, *God, Guts, and Guns* (New York: Putnam, 1983), 66-81, is a journalistic account that contains some interesting interviews with Identity adherents. For further information on several Identity personalities and groups, see *Extremism on the Right: A Handbook* (New York: Anti-Defamation League of B'nai B'rith, 1983).

39.   Randy Frame, "Is the Antichrist in the World Today?" *Christianity Today* 27 (2 September 1983):55-56, 62-65; *Eternity* 34 (November 1983): 98. Also noteworthy are the perceptive discussions of Cumbey's and Hunt's works in the *Personal Freedom Outreach Newsletter* (P.O. Box 26062, St. Louis, Mo. 63136) 3 (July-September 1983):5-6, 8. The Christian Booksellers Association best-seller lists are published monthly in its organ, *Bookstore Journal*.

40.   Cumbey, *Hidden Dangers of the Rainbow*, 54.

41.   Ibid., 152-68.

42.   Richard John Neuhaus, *Christianity and Democracy: A Statement of the Institute on Religion and Democracy* (Washington, D.C.: Institute on Religion and Democracy, 1981).

43.   Rael Jean Isaac, "Do You Know Where Your Church Offerings Go?" *Reader's Digest* 122 (January 1983):120-25; "Warring over Where Donations Go," *Time* 121 (28 March 1983):58-59; *A Time for Candor: Mainline Churches and Radical Social Witness* (Washington, D.C.: Institution on Religion and Democracy, 1983).

44.   Peter Steinfels, "Christianity and Democracy: Baptizing Reaganism," *Christianity and Crisis* 42 (29 March 1982):80-85.

45.   Eric Hochstein and Ronald O'Rourke, "A Report on the Institute on Religion and Democracy," *IDOC International Bulletin*, no. 8-9 (1982), 17-32; Leon Howell, "Old Wine, New Bottles: A Short History of the IRD," *Christianity and Crisis* 43 (21 March 1983):74, 89-94.

46.   Howell, "Old Wine, New Bottles," 90-91; Karen Rothmyer, "Citizen Scaife," *Columbia Journalism Review* 20 (July-August 1981):41-50.

47.   Richard V. Pierard, "From Evangelical Exclusivism to Ecumenical Openness: Billy Graham and Sociopolitical Issues," *Journal of Ecumenical Studies* 20 (Summer 1983):425-46; Robert Booth Fowler, *A New Engagement: Evangelical Political Thought, 1966-1976* (Grand Rapids, Mich.: Eerdmans, 1983).

PART 8

RELIGION AND WORLD ORDER

Alternatives to Separation of Church and State in Countries Outside the United States

SAMUEL KRISLOV

LEO PFEFFER AND THE AMERICAN SYSTEM OF SEPARATION

Leo Pfeffer is probably *sui generis*. There are a score or so of lawyers who have litigated the majority of cases by their chosen area of expertise in front of the United States Supreme Court. A few of these have written extensively in the same area. No one comes to mind, however, to rival Pfeffer's intellectual dominance over so vital an area of constitutional law for so extensive a period in this combination of pleading and intellectualizing. His corpus of work comes close to meeting the components this author once suggested for a successful constitutional reform movement—articulated theory, extensive litigation over time, pragmatic flexibility, and patient and persistent step-by-step strategy. Remarkably, this was achieved by a one-man "repeat player," albeit one rooted in an organizational pattern that helped and sustained his efforts.

Pfeffer's predominance is perhaps best acknowledged in a brief extract from a recent review of a book highly critical of Pfeffer: "The book is a frontal attack on the opinions of Leo Pfeffer as expressed in *Church, State and Freedom* and *God, Caesar and the Constitution*. [Robert L.] Cord picked his target with good reason, for Pfeffer has argued roughly half the Establishment Clause cases to come before the Supreme Court. It is his version of that clause's meaning more than others that forms the Court's reasoning in this area."[1]

This acknowledgment of Pfeffer's constitutional handicraft is, of course, two-edged. Cord is neither the first nor the last, the ablest nor the weakest, critic of the church-state balance that the Supreme Court precariously maintains. Certain problems with that balance are clearly evident; the "wall of separation" seems in some areas an unbridgeable chasm, in other areas, it is a rather flimsy plyboard. So prayers may, with Supreme Court approval, open sessions of state legislatures but never in schools. To avoid submitting sincerity of religious faith to legal judgment, society permits palpable frauds to hide beyond the First Amendment. The children of Amish parents may be exempted from compulsory high school, but newer sects are not so privileged. Perhaps symbolizing problems more than any other, the Court's abortion decision, in seeking to avoid religious implications in defining life, has offended the sensibilities of a conscious and determined religious minority.

The separation doctrine, as currently practiced, is quite clearly flawed. Virtually every legal doctrine, however, is flawed *ab ovo* and, if not, it ultimately finds its level of inapplicability. "All rights tend to declare themselves absolute to their logical extreme. Yet all, in fact, are limited by the neighborhood of principles . . . strong enough to hold their own when a certain point is reached," so Oliver Wendell Holmes developed his Peter principle for legal principles.[2] The test must be rather: Are there better or comparable alternatives? In general those alternatives considered are, by worldwide terms, rather narrow—partly a practical assessment of the limits of constitutional adaptation. It is also, however, partly an acknowledgment of the close match between present-day American society and the pattern of accommodation now prevailing.

Still, a consideration of the range of world practice might lead to an appreciation of those factors and contradictions that are endemic in this difficult interrelation that has perplexed societies for centuries. It might also give some perspective on the problems of other approaches—perspectives that might impel society to bear the ills it now has, rather than move to others whose problems are demonstrably not less.

Separation in Different Countries: A Summary of Summaries

The fundamental difficulty in arriving at a stable balance is quite simply that state and religion have unstable boundaries. Those religions that operate in states that fuse politics and moral force still have predominantly some separate structures for differing elements and subsequent rivalries. Those states that attempt to separate the two domains find demarcation less than complete. God and Caesar do not normally conveniently limit their claims upon the individuals involved. As these lines were written, the pope's 1983 visit to Poland dramatically underscored the message that what is a "religious" duty and need to one entity may emerge as emphatically political to another.

Separation is largely a doctrine of Western civilization, but even among its religions there are considerable differences on this score, as Bernard Lewis has vividly and recently reminded us.[3] The three major Middle Eastern religions are significantly different in their relations with the state and their attitudes to political power. Judaism was associated with the state and was then disentangled from it. Its new encounter with the state at the present time raises problems that are still unresolved. Christianity, during the first formative centuries of its existence, was separate from and indeed antagonistic to the state with which it only later became involved. Islam from the lifetime of its founder *was* the state, and the identity of religion and government is indelibly stamped on the memories and awareness of the faithful from their own sacred writings, history, and experience.[4] Similarly, Hinduism has successfully instilled its views pervasively throughout society, while Buddhist attitudes about control of politics vary from country to country.

Politics also vary enormously in their orientations. A 1978 study of written constitutions (computer analyzed no less) indicates that forty-three (or 30 percent) of those analyzable provided for a national religion and ninety-nine (or 70 percent) did not. Thirty-three countries specified religion, most notably for the office of religious minister. All but twenty had some reference to church or religion. Sixty-one (or 43 percent) guaranteed freedom of religion, while sixty-four (or 47 percent) guaranteed both religious freedom and the right to affiliate religiously. Only ten (or 7 percent) have no constitutional provision of this type. Provisions for freedom of religion are much more common than provisions for freedom of thought; indeed, the frequency is almost double that of what Alexander Meiklejohn has called "political freedoms."[5] Such generalized labels can be misleading. Ivo Duchacek, in a less mechanistic study, points out that the Indian constitution specifies a secular polity but prohibits slaughtering of cows and calves and permits Sikhs to carry daggers. The Swiss constitution of 1848 guarantees freedom of worship but prohibits the Society of Jesus or Kosher slaughtering. Duchacek lists the following as having established religions: England, the Scandinavian countries, Ireland, Spain, Portugal, most Latin American countries, Greece, Burma, the former countries of Cam-

bodia and Laos, Ceylon, Nepal, Malaysia, Pakistan, and most
Moslem countries. He suggests as secular: the United States,
France, and all Communist countries. Others are seen as having mixed characteristics.[6] Duchachek notes that in most
Communist societies one could suggest that atheism is elevated to the status of an established religion. In Yugoslavia,
however, multiple churches are expressly permitted and aided.
In most Communist systems, the comparative lack of private
funds is exacerbated by regulations on fund-raising adding to
tighter government control.

Duchacek notes, too, the wide range of ingenuity of constitution drafters. The primacy of Islam is unamendable in the
Moroccan constitution, while the Ugandan constitution
uniquely protects the right of the individual to change religions.

A United Nations study of minority rights adds indirect
evidence on these patterns. The rapporteur, Francesco Capotorti, notes that all states, including establishment countries,
offer minority protection by law if not by constitutional provision. The *Study on the Rights of Persons Belonging to Ethnic,
Religious, and Linguistic Minorities* focuses on individual protections rather than patterns of interaction.[7] Still, it highlights
such considerations as those states that require prior government recognition for juridical purposes (e.g., Japan or Austria)
or those that may operate independently.

In short, as one penetrates formalism one finds layers of
behavior and complexity in these relationships.

CORRELATES OF SEPARATION

From previous studies certain distinguishing variables can
be identified: (1) religious composition of the country; (2)
degree of religious homogeneity; (3) geographic location,
including the possible presence of a "dominant" exemplar
country; (4) ideology of dominant group at moment of independence, or other significant point for regime identification;
(5) the state of industrial (and arguably "cultural") development; and (6) internal political leadership or history of leadership.

These are not entirely helpful for two reasons: the variables
are difficult to operationalize while the differential conclusions
are not really impressive; and these variables are both obviously and also in more subtle ways highly interrelated. For
example, religions spread by diffusion. That means the varia-

ble of geographic proximity of countries with more (or less) separation of state and religion coincide to a marked degree with parallel patterns of religious faith. So Western Europe and North America have heterogeneous religious groupings, with a multiplicity of Protestant sects. Their fundamental political values were in each country largely set by the Enlightenment and the French Revolution experience, and the countries are geographically compact and are mutually and interactively influencing, one upon the other.

Previous studies seem to support the following, somewhat disappointing conclusions.

Religions and their attitudes. In almost all countries where its members constitute a majority, Islam retains much of its rigorous and tenacious hold on the state. While Turkey has "laicized" its society and dissolved the nexus with Islam, only Egypt and Morocco (and at one time Iran) have followed that example with any significant departures from traditional personal law. The Egyptian regime under both Gamal Abdel Nasser and Anwar Sadat has actually tightened its grip upon Mosque personnel and policies to try to control resistance to modernization policies.[8] Most of the Middle East retains the "millet" system established by the Turks in accordance with traditional Islamic practice. Those nonconforming groups recognized by the Koran and Islamic tradition as monotheistic may carry on with their own personal law administered by their community authorities. Interaction with Islamic citizens is governed by Islamic law and the other *millas* must acknowledge a secondary (and often overtly humiliating) status.

The one Jewish state, Israel, unable to secure constitutional agreement, perpetuates the *millet* (or separate community) arrangement for personal law but has (1) given orthodox Judaism much the status described above for Islam in other Middle Eastern countries; (2) passed legislation on personal law affecting all religions (e.g., minimum ages for marriage); and (3) continued and expanded secularization with universalistic laws for commercial and other aspects of society.[9] The inability to achieve easy consensus on religion has resulted in Israel's "status quo" formula: public transportation officially does run on the Sabbath in Haifa as was the British mandatory practice. It is not permitted in the rest of the country, however. Religious communities supported by Israel are precisely those recognized by the British. Thus, the Karaites, regarded by Rabbinic Judaism as heretical for centuries, is

subsidized while Conservative Judaism, which claims continuity with the Rabbinic tradition, has no standing at all.

Countries with predominantly Christian populations present
the most variegated pattern, and by far the most conspicuously
secularized societies. Further, there is a distinct difference
between heavily Protestant and Catholic countries in that
respect. The difference, however, is diminishing. This is to be
expected as Catholic Church attitudes toward equal treatment
of other religions has veered from the severe condemnation of
Quanta Cura and *Immortale Dei* to contemporary positive
approval, especially among the ecumenical elements of the
Church.

While Buddhism is essentially nonprogrammatic in countries where it is a minority, it claims and fuses political
authority in majority countries like Burma. While in Tibet
the state and religion are completely fused, in Burma the
Sangha (Buddhist monastic order) is separate and independent.[10] While constantly intervening in politics, the Sangha is
free to pursue theological independence.

Concentration. The one clear pattern that emerges is that the
extent of predominance or relative balance of religious populations has sharp and obvious consequences for degrees of secularization or merger of religion and polity. Even Islam had to
adjust to the complex honeycomb of faith and sects that constitute Lebanese society. The balance of populations in the
Netherlands had produced a no less intricate solution, negotiated at the turn of the century, under which each religious
grouping may operate a school system with pupil-based support. This, traditionally buttressed by separate newspapers,
Boy Scout troops, and other social institutions, resulted in a
society characterized by Dutch sociologists as "pillarization"—
parallel societies coexisting. Arend Lijphart dubbed it a "consociational society," and, in many ways, the description is of a
somewhat segmented drastic millet system.[11] Korean politics
try to skirt any Buddhist-Christian issues of the type that
plagued the last years of the Diem and Thieu regimes in
Vietnam.

Homogenous populations or dominant groupings produce
greater interinvolvement. Heterogenous groups develop conflict or accommodation.

Location. Policies of neighboring states have obvious influence upon each other, though, as has been noted, it is difficult
to separate this phenomenon from other causes that tend to

operate across borders as well. The many states of Latin America, Catholic in composition, which attempt varying degrees of separation, are an example. They also illustrate the force of the "modal" state—the United States in Latin America and France in the early nineteenth century. Britain's established churches, as examples for its dominions, and the antichurch attitude of Eastern European socialist countries are other illustrations. There may also be in this an integrated holistic set encouraged by adoption of a system, but this is conjectural. For example, the Soviet attitude toward their churches was in the first place determined by Marxist-Leninist atheism. It may be perpetuated by the jealousy of the system of any semiautonomous groups in society. Similarly, separation of church and state may be linked to a laissez-faire system in some deep way—as is probably the Anglo-Saxon bias for letting the litigants dominate legal proceedings, a fight (or self-initiated) theory of justice over truth values.

In any event, the world clusters sharply with each of the various continents dominated by one or two religions. There is a parallel pattern of religion interacting with the state, and each continent has relatively few patterns of such interactions. A very few countries, like Cuba and to some degree Albania, have deviant patterns from that of any of their neighbors, but in general the diffusion of church-state patterns is remarkably monotonic.

Ideology or critical events. The time of regime formation tends to have great impact on the resulting system. The early establishment of the Anglican Church has continued to influence Great Britain, a state that also has the Church of Scotland as part of a unique system of dual churches. Even as modernity has required accommodation, not just of nonconformist Christianity or Catholicism and Judaism but also of Islam and other African influences, retention of the two-way link between the established church and traditional British governance is marked. Only recently was the Anglican Church freed from (largely theoretical) Parliamentary control of its prayer book, and the Church still is represented in the House of Lords.[12] Tony Benn, who has been in political semiseclusion for a few years, has grown more interested in religion and argued for separation in a lecture at St. James Church in 1983. His extensive list of necessary changes and that of the *London Times* leader criticizing his position give some idea of the remaining scope of involvement.[13] (Interest-

ingly, the *Times* concedes that the system would not be created
from choice today, but argues it would not be worth attempting to undo it.)

The rationalist faith (or lack of faith) of the Enlightenment
was transmuted in a set of political moves in the half-century
after the French Revolution into new regimes that generally
moved sharply to secularize or, to use the French term, laicize
society in accordance with liberal precepts. Most of the European continent took these standards as their own though
not Catholic countries other than France. The pace was also
rather slower in the homogenous Lutheran, Scandinavian
countries and in Britain, and these countries have mitigated
the effects of establishment while clinging to the forms.

Before the liberal wave more-or-less burnt itself out in the
last quarter of the twentieth century, it had considerable
impact in South America. The Bolivian model of liberal nationalism was one followed throughout the continent (e.g.,
Colombia and Uruguay). Similarly, Italian unification began
under such auspices (Giuseppe Mazzini, Camillo Benso di
Cavour) but ended with continued acquiescence to Catholicism's particular role. The path of laicization was to Kamal
Ataturk the road to modernity, and the establishment of the
current regime in Turkey was the triumph of this point of
view. The instability of this effort was literally underscored by
the emergence of the reactionary regime of Ayatollah Khomeini and repudiation of the Shah's unabashed Westerniza-
tion. This has obvious parallels with backlash regimes in
Indonesia and Pakistan, putting considerable restraint on
modernizers in Egypt and Morocco.

More recently, avowedly athestic regimes in Eastern Europe
have provided models not only in that region, but also for
Africa and other countries. While thorough-going hostility
toward religion has occasionally emerged in countries with a
liberal bent—most prominently in Mexico from the 1920s—
Soviet-type antagonism is standard for Eastern bloc countries.
Its ingredients include: (1) official antireligious propaganda;
(2) heavy-handed control of religious premises, meetings, and
printed religious materials to discourage believers; and (3) outlawing some forms of religious practice (e.g., most foreign
contacts), limits on religious education, and other dissemination effects.

It is clear that the initial tone of relations for a regime is a
dominant influence and a predictor of the future in this

domain. Gradual changes do occur that may ultimately affect basics, but over centuries rather than decades. A drastic change in relationships usually goes hand in hand with a crisis—a change in dominant elites rather than as of a product of normal political processes or gradualism. A period of religious conflict may be ended, however, by a conscious act of accommodation and compromise, as in the Lebanese agreement of 1926-28 and the Dutch settlement of 1913-17. Those were extra-political social concordats but were ratified through normal constitutional means with only moderate accommodation to political elites, not radical transformation.

Leadership initiative and idiosyncracy. At moments of crisis, leadership can be of special importance. Kamal Ataturk's attitudes determined the sweeping extent of Turkish reform that was enacted while a more cautious leader might have been less thoroughgoing. Whether the social consequences, measured by influence of family law or interpersonal behavior, were much greater than would have been the case had more modest reforms been embraced is conjectural. Clearly the law is far more secular and "advanced" than personal behavior throughout Turkey, especially in rural communities. With respect to ending the direct linkage of mosque and state, however, the consequences are quite clear.[14] Financing of mosques and religious practices is no longer a state function.

Similarly, the comparative success at minimizing religious life in countries once quite devout, achieved by a relatively small cadre of doubters, is a quite remarkable feat of social engineering. Eastern Europe was traditionally a stronghold of Catholic and Orthodox religions, with the church's wielding temporal power and commanding worldly goods. While religion lives on, it does so partly on internal strength and partly on sufferance. Regimes have found excessive pressure to be counterproductive. As everywhere, marriage and family relations are conservative and resistant to even repressive efforts. Continued pressure, however, is sufficiently erosive over time. Whether Cuba would revert to traditional Catholic predominance or Russia again be swayed as formerly by Eastern Orthodoxy if the regimes changed tomorrow is most doubtful.

At the same time, the formidable example of Cardinal Stefan Wyszysinski in Poland reminds one of the force of personality in resisting change as well as in developing it. Those who believe in historical inevitability might argue plausibly that it was most likely Poland (or Hungary) that would

oppose most militantly Soviet supremacy. It was not inevitable
that the chosen instrument of that resistance be the church.
The fortuitous choice of a Polish pope further underscored
the element of change in determining at least the specific
form in which relations are expressed and the influence of
such institutions is acted out.

FORMS OF INTERACTION:
THE UNDERLYING COMPLEXITY

The range of church-state relations spans the logical possibilities: the state may embrace or throttle religion, ignore it or
dominate it. As indicated earlier, the "macro" question—establishment—may mask quite a variety of practices; similarly, the
practice of oppositionist regimes with respect to religion may
ease to a situation of benign neglect.

There are three major dimensions of interaction of religion:
degree of interinvolvement, attitude toward religion, and
power and control. Hostile regimes require considerable subordination of religion and usually, therefore, are deeply en-
meshed in religious affairs. Similarly, the Nasser-Sadat regimes' moves toward secularization were accompanied by
stricter controls over mosques and the clergy. The inclusion of
a provision by Eamon De Valera in the Irish Constitution,
however, recognizing the "special position" of the Catholic
Church, having no clear legal consequences, has been symbol-
ically of considerable significance and may even have led to
less religion-state interaction in the glow of that semiestab-
lishment clause.[15]

Scope of interaction: political initiatives. Theoretically, religion
and polity could be coterminous (i.e., overlap) or religion
could be nonexistent. In practical terms, neither is quite
achievable.

Some religions aspire to comprehensiveness in scope (e.g.,
Islam and Judaism), but life manages to focus on gaps in such
systems. Futhermore, even in what Donald Smith labels as
"organic" societies, where the two are regarded as coterminous, there is a differentiation of personnel and structure,
leading to something less than absolute identity.[16]

Total elimination of religion is not achievable either. At
least in the private recesses of the mind forbidden impulses
can survive even the most ruthless persecution. It is easy to be
over glib, as is implicit in Benjamin Jowett's response to
whether one may remain a Christian while tortured on the

rack. "Yes, if one is a very good Christian, and it is a very bad rack." Still, the case of private defiance in practice acts as a brake upon sensible regimes and leads to some accommodation based upon controlled observance. Even here, such extremes as the Pol Pot regime, which has transcended any norms of sensibility, have been seen. There are also periods of intensive strife that may test these bounds.

Additionally, other constraints must be noted. Decision makers generally appreciate the contribution of religious morality to civic virtue. The Soviet reliance on religion in the World War II struggle against Nazism illustrates the point. Religious institutions must operate, however, within a polity and overtly or covertly require public support. In the modern world, the polity supplies most of the basic welfare and safety needs of the population. Many social systems share educational functions with the church's and some share its health or welfare function. Rarely throughout history have religious institutions been militarily self-sufficient or even fully capable of domestic policing. (It may even be speculated that there is sufficient discordance between religious teaching and the use of force, that the two will over time become disjunctive however potent the two combined are in a temporary situation, as with Joan of Arc, for example.) The deep dependency of such religious institutions on force is often camouflaged, much as the Swiss guards stand before the Vatican, but the Italian Army stands as the real guarantor of tranquility.

States that permit a religion to assume wide social powers do not follow a standard pattern. Even Islamic states have long had variations on this point. Sunni states generally have a strong political system in which the rulers are seen as the caliph (religious and civil surrogate) of Mohammed with the right to adjust laws within Islamic tradition and subject to influence and criticism from the religious and scholarly community, the *Ullama*. This permits secular dominance of a sort, although the balance varies in place and time. Shiites generally take more literally the completeness of Islamic law, preempting much secular legislation. In the modern era, even Shiite or fundamentalist regimes have legislated extensively, with wholesale borrowing of Western regulations on industry and technology. This has created a dynamic in which minor adjustments on more close-to-the-bone problems, such as family relations, would occur (a limit on plural marriages or an increase in age of consent). The final step—enactment of comprehensive secular legislation, albeit largely in accordance with *shariya*—has been taken in only a few states.

This presents a remarkable contrast even with Catholic or Protestant states with "establishment" clauses. Such countries generally do not delegate authority over a domain to the church *pro tanto*. Rather it is expected that the secular law enacted will be in conformity with the dictates of church teaching. Again, the intensity of tutelage and control of church leadership intervention varies. The pattern that law is state-promulgated and religious power is demonstrated in the content of law, however, is in contrast to the often deadly struggle simply to laicize or secularize Islam in form or content.

One domain that retains fluid boundaries in Western society is the field of education and, as in the United States, this is a battleground in many countries. There are remarkable variations in the systems of control and delegations. Rejectionist states of the modern socialist type forbid not only religious control of secular instruction but also religious instruction except under highly (and usually increasingly) restrictive conditions. It is rare for Western states to restrict religious education, but there are quite different patterns on allowing religious institutions to provide secular instruction.[17] Some churches regard this as a vital right for it permits considerable control over interpretation of secular information on a day-to-day basis even where curriculum is controlled by the state. Since curriculum is additionally maleable, this (a strong monopoly on interpretation) is buttressed by control over time spent on directly religious studies.

Modern Western establishment states that authorize religious conduct of schools generally permit minor sects the same privilege, though this is not always easy for minority religions, especially since administrative obstacles may be interposed. Not infrequently there are legal restrictions on proselytizing or offending believers in the established religion without equivalent restrictions on the majority. As in the United States, there is a tendency for these restrictions to fall into desuetude and eventually be removed.

The detailed implementation of plans of instruction varies enormously. Most instruction in "Anglican" England takes place in secular governmental schools; these are required by law to provide religious instruction in a regular class. A committee of clerics of those religions deemed by the local authorities appropriate to their district guides the schools; usually, of course, the local Anglican clergy dominate.[18] The instruction, however, is often colorless and inoffensive. In contrast, nominally Protestant Netherlands has a system of education that has been evaluated by one writer as probably the most satisfactory to Catholic authorities.[19] Within general standards for achievement and examination, religious schools operate with equal payment for students to all types of school systems including secular state and other schools. This support pattern extends to the university level where both Catholic and hardline Calvinist universities have full support. Except for requirements to protect religious minorities in locales where it is not reasonable to establish their own schools, religious instruction is unfettered.[20]

Both establishment and nonestablishment Western states permit or even encourage church-related union, welfare, and health arrangements. Those do not, however, generally achieve monopoly positions, and there are rival secular, and even anticlerical, structures in most countries.

The United States is the most insistent upon nonintrusion of the two domains. Practice, however, is much more complex than sloganizing. Tax exempt "contributions" are the life and blood of all religious institutions in the United States, and their legitimacy has barely been challenged except in the domain of schools. To be sure, the secular universal public school has an important meaning, a centrality that has been stressed by Horace Mann, for example, but this centrality has not been constitutionally rooted.

Still, most governments fund church-related educational and welfare programs even more directly, generally providing only a basic subvention rather than full costs. Indeed, totally stateborne costs often reflect a desire for state control on suspicion between the systems.

As in the U.S., there may be specific allocations for specified activities granted by formula. Cultural programs may be supported—drama, music, and art. In the Netherlands, both television channels are allocated to associations more or less corresponding to the modern Pillars who have both general and propagandistic programs, though the latter are increasingly muted.

Governments also lend their collection machinery to religion. In some German states the church tax is voluntary, but those who choose to pay it know it goes to the sect of their choice. In the Netherlands, denominations are merely provided with income tax information to permit uniform assessments. Many Eastern bloc countries directly subsidize most religious activities. In Poland, Sunday School teachers in all churches are eligible to receive a stipend from the state. Austria subsidizes religious activities as part of the Independence Treaty of 1955.[21] Government fiscal controls are generally not extensive even where collection is governmentally aided. Identification of responsible officials for each community or association is vital, however, particularly where governmental funds are to be paid.

Governments sometimes permit and sometimes restrict broad social structures under the aegis of religion. The most significant of these are labor unions. Standard socialist regimes forbid independent unions, as have some South American regimes of right-wing and even Marxist types. Particularly in Western Europe, religious and secular unions compete with one another, and industry coordination becomes a problem for union effectiveness and management efficiency.

There are limited survivals of traditions of sanctuary. The Vatican's special status in Italy and diplomatic status for its agents are cases in point. In practice more than by law, monasteries and churches are given rather wide berths by authorities. Recognition of the priest's vow of silence as to the confession is a nonterritorial application of the same notion. Exemption of clergy from military service is quite common. Religious conscientious objection to war is a fairly common basis for draft exemption. Similarly, laws repugnant to a religion may be modified for limited populations. Thus, the slaughtering of animals under Jewish ritual requirements (Kashruth) is exempted in the U.S. and others from a requirement that stunning of the animals precedes killing. (Conversely, comprehensive slaughtering regulations have been used by Polish, Swiss, and Nazi governments at least in part for anti-Semitic harassment.)[22] A dramatic instance of such exemptions was the Supreme Court decision exempting Amish communities from compulsory high school attendance laws, where the education was seen as destructive to "the old ways" and when the community had demonstrated over the years its ability to provide for its own members. In extending these rights not to individuals but to a tightly defined type of community, the Court attempted to confine the exemption.[23]

Systems must wrestle with protecting their boundaries,

however, and, in general, insist upon obedience to law even where there are religious objections. This is easily justified where religious behavior jeopardizes others. Thus, vaccination requirements are universally enforced and cults of assassins are not countenanced even when religious tenets support them. More problematic are moral questions when no immediate physical threat obviously exists. The outlawing of plural marriages in Utah that was sustained by the United States Supreme Court in *Reynolds* v. *United States* was criticized by the late Harold Laski as an invasion of Mormon religious freedom.[24] (Today the Mormon Church itself bans such marriages.) Where the threat is to the "social fabric" or social order rather than a physical one, societies waver. Where it is clear that only consequences for the individual are involved, there is even more room for exemption. Still, few societies relax drug laws or permit snake charmer rites in the name of developing religious ecstasy.

As indicated earlier, two key questions evolve defining "religion" and preventing fraud in its name. Most societies define religions pragmatically rather than abstractly, using numbers of adherents of the organization and duration as unstated major distinguishing marks. In many countries, there is rigidity of classification, and newer sects are at a considerable disadvantage. The Netherlands and Germany, however, are quite generous in requirements for qualifying for recognition.

Even in the United States, where courts strenuously avoid trying to define or to choose leadership, conflicts over property rights or power within the religion may force the authorities, especially the courts to decide. Rather specious religious orders quickly develop, e.g., the church that ordains as ministers anyone who sends a donation. The problem of how one can define religion without curtailing new and sincere forms of expression becomes quite acute. The greater the special protection of religion afforded by the law, the graver the problem.

The United States with its more abstract approach to the problem of definition therefore has difficulties with the concept of fraud. In the light of *United States* v. *Ballard* (1944),[25] sincerity of belief is not to be a legal issue. Hence, the "church of gastronomy" organized to permit public eating in a state with Sunday closing laws, which would be dismissed without ado in almost any other country, becomes a complex issue here. At the same time, the danger of arbitrary denial to any group by administrative fiat is minimized.

Religion as definer. The scope of religious-secular interaction is not just a one-sided product of the attitude of the polity or society. Religious quietism or social activism by the faithful helps delimit the zone of interaction. For example, the Islamic requirement of the religious charitable institution, the *Waqf*, necessarily involves secular authority, and its financial sums often tempt rulers to try to influence expenditures. Buddhist priests in the Sangha beg daily for their food and are socially and politically active even as they emphasize personal quietism.

Similarly, attitudes may vary as to political stands by the clergy. The Catholic bishops in the Netherlands, for example, before the invasion had indicated that known Nazis were not to be offered communion. While this probably had little practical effect, its symbolic stand was clear. The reiteration of the stand under occupation in 1940 was quite remarkable.[26] The historical, universal prohibition of Catholic membership in the Masonic order helped crystallize its ultimate antichurch stand. Again, the Catholic hierarchy has been active in several conflicts in Ireland over such issues as joining trade unions. Baptist and Methodist churches, among others, have often been active in prompting prohibition, as have religious groups in India. The degree to which religions see their role as oriented inwardly or outwardly, individual morality, and/or social morality is only partly conditioned by basic teachings and partly by external situations. The primary focus is on social policy rather than religion, but the reciprocal effect cannot be ignored.

Governmental attitude toward religion as a variable in policy. The argument advanced above is essentially that the scope of interinvolvement is generally greater at both ends of the spectrum—promotion or opposition to religion. This section essays the range of polity attitudes, as well as to indicate that a regime's basic stance is easily modified in any direction and that there are a wide variety of well-established techniques for doing so.

The apparently similar policy may be pursued for quite opposite ends. Thus, in Sweden to leave the church rolls and be on the civil register, one must request the action in a letter of explanation. (This was actually a liberalization of an old requirement of personal appearance before a committee.) The

German Democratic Republic has formalized a church-withdrawal rite and, for some offices, one must go through such a ceremony.[27] Of course, one action is intended to discourage withdrawal, the others to promote it.

The evolution and subtle variations from step-to-step of Soviet policy toward religion illustrates how the same general attitude is implemented in accordance with prevailing conditions. Implementing a policy entails moving toward an objective as much or more than formulating the end. The Soviet constitution originally (1918) guaranteed freedom of both religious and antireligious propaganda. Subsequently, only freedom of worship is guaranteed while antireligious propaganda may continue. "Cults" are also severely restricted; religious worship, mutual assistance, education, library, and educational services are forbidden.[28] The pattern of gradual encirclement and choking off of functions allows one to interpret the original "evenhandedness" as the first step in "Salami tactics" characteristic of Soviet tactics. Satellites have varied in their limitation of the Russian antireligious stand, and some seem benignly to permit much greater freedom.

Similarly in Malaysia, a non-Muslim may not hand a Muslim a non-Islamic religious work except by request. Nor may one utter in open-air meetings any teachings contrary to Islam if Muslims are present. (In closed meetings, a Muslim who is present is assumed to have consented to listen.) Movies may not portray non-Muslims as holy or saintly. The correlative regulations are absent; Muslims are permitted to proselytise and propagandize.[29] Such "badges of inferiority" make unmistakable the intent of the authorities.

Those attitudes are more significant in understanding the operative relationship than generalizations or global terms like "freedom of worship" or separation. The incidence of such administration and legislation affect both organizational freedom and individual lives more than pious declarations of equality. This complicates analysis, for no authorities claim to be denying fundamental freedoms or wish to be classified as bigoted.

Donald Eugene Smith has distinguished between religiously-oriented societies that are organic—where political and religious institutions are fused—and the "church" model where the two are seen as separate.[30] Islam, as is known, requires an "organic" society for the caliph is viewed as both the religious and temporal substitute for the prophet. Christian countries generally operate with a church model.

While others have followed Smith's distinction and Smith has himself attempted to build upon it,[31] there has been little use in recent years and no elaboration. An obvious linking is to concepts of power and penetration.

Again, it may be noted that intentions of rulers are meaningful, mostly in conjunction with their ability to deliver. Furthermore, as society moves toward individual, internalized values, control becomes more problematic. As noted above, family law is often the test of power and control.

An illustration of this point is the continual European conflict on secular marriage. In the battle to achieve the option of secular marriage, secularists insisted upon making it the official marriage and a requirement, whether or not it was to be followed by a religious ceremony.[32] This anomaly persists to this day even though the bitterness it reflects is long gone.

History seems to record the dominance that flows to the nonreligious secular authority figures under organic societies. Of course, this varies with the talent and drive within the differing structures. At times in history, of course, religious centers have dominated through their control over education and sources of mobility. The prominence of cardinals as rulers in France, or the remarkable power of the Catholic hierarchy of Argentina in its early history, is matched by the contemporary role of the Buddhist priests in Burma. A special instance is the dominance of clergy during crusades and other moments of national regeneration. Such moments in history are, however, fleeting and, in the long run, Savonorolas and Joan of Arcs lose out as religious ecstasy wanes. Leaders small of soul generally succeed to such moralizers, and seldom have had religious pretensions. (Presumably there is some lesson here for post-Khomeini Iran.)

Islam suggests the truth of the proposition that organic unity strengthens secular rather than religious power. This is particularly true of Sunni societies that have in fact given rulers a relatively wide set of religious powers. Arguably that dominance might have brought religious institutions under even greater temporal control if Islam had a hierarchy to aid in transmission of control.[33] This dimension of power, reflecting Vladimir Lenin's question, "Who, whom," and the dominance of one partner or another in a relationship of church and state can be asked of both separatist and fused societies. Shared power is more easily achieved through one and dominance the other, but those represent tendencies rather than sharp differences.

CONCLUSIONS

"Separation" of church and state is an artificial concept not really capable of easy implementation or logical achievement. "Involvement" of state with religion, however, creates equally deep questions with respect to boundary lines. The spreading of a governmental mantle over religions often involves power narrowly to define religion. A close relation permits control and suggests a struggle for power. History here suggests secular authorities' power is more likely to prevail with power tending to accrue to those who most value it rather than to people and institutions' oriented to more transcendental issues.

The study of emergence of separatist and independent institutions remains of major importance for a world that accepts the need for such freedom but really has not yet learned how to create them or buttress their existence. The patterns of their existence suggest that society is on the verge of creating a reasonable taxonomy of such relationships.

NOTES

The author acknowledges the generosity of the University of Minnesota in granting a sabbatical and the Bush Foundation and Netherlands Fulbright program for grants permitting a year of research facilitating this study.
1.   Paul J. Weber, review of Robert L. Cord, *Separation of Church and State* in *Journal of Church and State* 24 (Autumn 1982):605.
2.   *Hudson County Water Company* v. *United States*, 209 U.S. 350 (1908).
3.   Bernard Lewis, "The Return of Islam," in *Religion and Politics in the Middle East*, ed. Michael Curtis (New York: Westview Press, 1981), 11-12.
4.   Ibid.
5.   Hen C. Van Moorseven and Ger Van der Tan, *Written Constitutions: A Comparative Computer Study* (Dobbs Ferry, N.Y.: Oceana Publishers, 1978), 65-66, 109-10, 127, 135, and 149.
6.   Ivo Duchacek, *Rights and Liberties in the World Today* (Santa Barbara, Calif.: ABC-Clio Books, 1973), 22, 35, 61-64, 98-99. See also M. Searle Bates, *Religious Liberty* (New York: International Missionary Council, 1945), though out of date and written from an evangelistic viewpoint, it remains useful.
7.   Francesco Capotorti, *Study on the Rights of Persons, Belonging to Ethnic, Religious and Linguistic Minorities* (New York: United Nations, 1979), 68-75. For older country-by-country accounts, which range from useless to superlative but fortunately tend toward the latter, see Hans Mol, ed., *Western Religions* (The Hague: Mouton, 1972), and Carlo Caldarola, *Religions and Societies: Asia and the Middle East* (Berlin: Mouton, 1982).
8.   For the best analysis of this development, see Monroe Berger, *Islam in Egypt Today* (Cambridge: Cambridge University Press, 1970), esp. 9ff and 45ff.

9. See, e.g., Ervin Birnbaum, *The Politics of Compromise* (Rutherford, N.J.: Farleigh-Dickenson University Press, 1981), 75-113, and Robert E. Eisenman, *Islamic Law in Palestine and Israel* (Leiden: E.J. Brill, 1978), 50ff.

10. Carlo Calderola, "Thailand" in his edited collection, Calderola, *Religions and Societies*, 397.

11. Arend Lijphart, *The Politics of Accommodation* (Berkeley: University of California Press, 1968), 102ff. See also, Val R. Lorwin, "Segmented Pluralism," *Comparative Politics* 3 (1971): 141-75.

12. Gavin White, "No one is Free from Parliament. The Worship and Doctrine Measure in Parliament," in *Religion and National Identity*, ed. Stuart Mews (Oxford: Basil Blackwell, 1980), 557ff.

13. *London Times*, 3 March 1983, 1 and 13.

14. The classic works on this process that speak eloquently on current developments throughout Islam are Bernard Lewis, *The Emergence of Modern Turkey* (London: Oxford University Press, 1969), and Niyazi Berkos, *The Development of Secularism in Turkey* (Montreal: McGill University Press, 1964). See also Leonard Binder, *Religion and Politics in Pakistan* (Berkeley: University of California Press, 1961).

15. See J.H. Whyte, *Church and State in Modern Ireland* (London: Gill and Macmillan, 1971), 55-56 and 349-50.

16. See Donald E. Smith, *Religion and Political Development* (Boston: Little Brown, 1970), esp. 7-8, as well as his contribution in his *Religion and Political Modernization* (New Haven: Yale University Press, 1974), 116ff.

17. Capotorti, *Study on Rights*, 74-75, lists seven states forbidding secular schools by religious or other groups and gingerly discusses states such as Sri Lanka and Sudan that impose restrictions on religious schools but avoids any discussion of Eastern bloc countries except Poland.

18. St. John A. Robill, "Religious Freedom as a Human Right within the United Kingdom," *Human Rights Review* 6 (1981):91ff. Keith Roberts, "Religion and Identity in Modern British History," in *Religion and National Identity*, 468ff.

19. Whyte, *Church and State in Ireland*, 16.

20. Lijphart, *Politics of Accommodation*, 105-10, describes this well. See also, J.P. Kruit, "The Netherlands: The Influence of Denomination on Social Life and Organizational Problems," in *Consociational Democracy*, ed. K.D. McRae (Toronto: McClelland and Stewart, 1974), 92ff. The overwhelming majority of the Netherlands population is educated in at least nominally denominational schools.

21. Capotorti, *Study on Rights*, 73.

22. See Samuel Krislov, "'Church,' State and Kashruth," *Jewish Social Studies* 25 (July 1963):174-85.

23. *Wisconsin* v. *Yoder*, 406 U.S. 205 (1972).

24. *Reynolds* v. *United States*, 98 U.S. 145 (1828). Harold Laski, *Liberty in the Modern State*, rev. ed. (New York: Viking Press, 1930, 1948), 98-99.

25. *United States* v. *Ballard*, 322 U.S. 78 (1944).

26. J.H. Boas, *Religious Resistance in Holland* (London: Allen and Unwin, 1945), 12-20; Werner Warmebrunn, "The Netherlands Under German Occupation 1940-1945" (Ph.D. diss., Stanford University, 1955), 16, 238-39.

27. Compare Berndt Gustafson, "Sweden," in *Western Religion*, 481, with Bernard Wilhelm, "Germany: The Democratic Republic," in *Western Religion*, 222.

28. Robert Conquest, *Religion in the USSR* (London: The Bodley Head, 1968), 13-22, gives a concise summary of the process of increasing control.

29. See Gordon P. Means, "Malaysia," in Calderola, *Religions and Societies*, 465-70.

30. Smith, *Religion and Political Development*, 7-8.

31. Smith, *Religion and Political Modernization*, 116ff.

32. See Lennart Pelsson, "Marriage and Divorce," in *The International Encyclopedia of Comparative Law*, 17 vols. (New York: Oceana, 1976-82), 3:44ff.

33. Donald Eugene Smith, *South Asian Politics and Religion* (Princeton: Princeton University Press, 1966), 1966.

The UN Declaration on the Elimination of Religious Intolerance and Discrimination: Historical and Legal Perspectives

SIDNEY LISKOFSKY

On 25 November 1981, the United Nations General Assembly adopted a "Declaration on the Elimination of All Forms of Intolerance and of Discrimination Based on Religion or Belief."[1] This event was the culmination of almost a quarter century of persistent efforts by a small, dedicated group of representatives of several governments, abetted and encouraged by a number of nongovernmental organizations, both religious and secular.

The idea of universal human rights, including freedom of religion, was assumed in the UN Charter in 1945. One of the principal purposes of the new world organization was to promote fundamental freedoms without discrimination on grounds of race, sex, language, or religion. Although the founding members could not agree to include an international bill of rights in the body of the Charter, they did begin to work on it shortly thereafter. Over the next twenty years, the UN completed a three-part international bill of rights, consisting of the Universal Declaration of Human Rights, adopted in 1948, and two legally binding pacts: the Covenant on Economic, Social, and Cultural Rights and the Covenant on Civil and Political Rights, both adopted in 1966.

In 1959, the UN Subcommission on the Prevention of Discrimination and the Protection of Minorities, with a mandate from its parent body, the Commission on Human Rights, prepared a "Study of Discrimination in the Matter of Religious Rights and Practices," written by Arcot Krishnaswami, a member designated as special rapporteur for the project.[2] This study generated a proposal to formulate a special declaration and/or convention on the elimination of all forms of religious intolerance. After many postponements and decades of tortuous drafting, the Declaration finally came into being.

Like most other UN pronouncements, the Declaration was the product of political compromise. Its eventual adoption by consensus is all the more remarkable in view of the diverse ideological outlooks and political difficulties that had to be reconciled or overcome. For example, the Soviet Union, opposed in principle to all forms of religion, contended that the issue of religious freedom had been raised as a Cold War maneuver. For most Muslims, Islamic law held supremacy over any other religious or secular law. The black African states—generally tolerant in religious matters, but deeply concerned with colonial, racial, and economic issues—were not convinced that a special declaration on religion was of primary importance.

Its adoption resulted from a fortuitous convergence of favorable circumstances. The personal commitment of the Senegalese chairman of the Human Rights Commission's working group, and of several dedicated Western representatives, was an important factor as was the vigorous support by nongovernmental organizations. Inadequate coordination among the opponents, especially the Communist and Muslim blocs, which for separate and opposite reasons did not want the Declaration, is probably part of the explanation.

The Declaration is a moral and political document rather than a legally binding instrument. Though flawed in some respects by exceptions, generalities, and omissions, it helps to clarify and to reinforce principles in the binding instruments, particularly the Covenant on Civil and Political Rights. Like other UN human rights declarations, it does not provide for implementation, although it can be cited in proceedings under the Covenant on Civil and Political Rights, as well as other international agreements. Again, like other declarations, it required separate decisions to initiate follow-up activity. In focusing on the specific issue of religious freedom, it made it easier to create special UN programs and to encourage citizen activities in this area.

Whether the Declaration's potential will be realized or not depends largely on what the UN and other intergovernmental bodies do to promote it and, above all, on the zeal with which governments and religious and other nongovernmental organizations, including academic institutions, advocate it and teach about it. In the UN, some steps have already been initiated: to translate it into all the official languages, disseminate it widely, conduct a comprehensive worldwide study of current dimensions of religious intolerance and discrimination, and convene a seminar under the UN's human rights advisory services.

This study (actually a compilation) provides an overview of the provisions pertaining to religion in the principal international instruments concerned with human rights: the Universal Declaration, the Covenant on Civil and Political Rights, the three main regional instruments (the American and European human rights conventions and the Helsinki Final Act), and especially the 1981 UN Declaration, which is discussed in detail. The analysis is preceded by a brief account of the philosophical and historical background from which the general idea of natural—or human—rights and the specific idea of religious freedom evolved, and the place of this freedom in the present ideologically divided system of international human rights. Clearly, these are very complex subjects, and this account is intended merely to highlight some of the important issues that they involve.

I.   The Idea of Universal Human Rights

PRE-TWENTIETH CENTURY PRECEDENTS[3]

Greek philosophers held, in essence, that justice and moral values are part of the natural order. The Judeo-Christian tradition holds that moral law is divinely inspired. This belief, that nature, God, or both, are the source of morality and law and are valid universally, was central to the development of the doctrine of natural law in Thomas Aquinas and other medieval scholastics. In the early modern period, it was transposed into the idea of natural rights, which later became interchangeable with human rights.

During the seventeenth and eighteenth centuries, when philosophers of the Enlightenment in England and France explained natural rights, they stressed the individual's freedom from encroachment by the state. John Locke, for example, argued that before entering organized society the individual possessed natural rights, which he did not relinquish under the original "social contract." His view of natural rights exerted an important influence on the American and French revolutions and declarations of rights two hundred years ago, and through these declarations on later important national and international human rights documents.

Natural rights are most often discussed as "negative" rights, centering on the individual's right to be "left alone," to be

protected against arbitrary acts by the state. These rights, such
as the right to freedom of religion, are considered to be inherent in man's nature, regardless of differing cultures, and to be
suitable for adoption as universal norms. By contrast, "positive" rights may not be so deemed because they entail a role
for the state in serving the material and social needs of the
citizenry; and, therefore, the rights of individual citizens will
vary according to the structures and programs instituted by
government to serve these needs. Some philosophers, however, would also consider certain basic economic necessities
requiring an activist government role as natural rights, such
as the rights to food and shelter.

The theory of natural rights has been challenged on both
philosophical and historical/cultural grounds. Citing differing
moral concepts in different times and cultures, some critics
say it is patronizing and that it may do real harm to impose
universal standards on viable societies that function very well
under their own moral systems. The theory of natural rights,
however, also has its defenders who cite reliable evidence that
dissimilar societies have many common moral values. Some
defenders insist that without a transcendent belief persons and
nations have no solid basis for a human rights ethic; indeed,
they attribute today's widespread decline in personal morality,
as well as domestic—even international—lawlessness to a growing disbelief in a "higher" source of moral guidance. Pragma-
tist supporters of universal human rights assert that they can
produce empirical evidence that human beings are better off
in societies that respect the purported universal human rights
than in those that do not. They observe that "God has been
enrolled under all banners," and they see no need for religious or metaphysical justifications.

Locke and other philosophers of the Enlightenment who
subscribed to the idea of natural rights profoundly influenced
the United States' founding fathers, many of whom described
themselves as deists. The Declaration of Independence speaks
of the "laws of nature and nature's God," "self-evident"
truths, and "inalienable" rights. Although the federal Constitution did not use this language, the assumption that persons
have natural rights is implicit in the Bill of Rights, in the first
ten amendments annexed to the Constitution. The Declaration of the Rights of Man and the Citizen adopted by France
in 1789 and annexed to its constitutions of 1793 and 1795 is
based on the same assumption.[4] "In the nineteenth century it

[i.e., the natural rights assumption] became part of the law of nearly all European states . . . the French Constitution of 1848 recognized 'rights and duties anterior and superior to positive laws.'"[5]

The existence of natural rights is assumed in subsequent international human rights documents, notably the Universal Declaration, adopted exactly a century later, whose preamble opens with a reference to the "equal and inalienable rights of all members of the human family." The idea of natural rights is stated explicitly in the preamble to the American Declaration of the Rights and Duties of Man, adopted by the Ninth International Conference of American States the same year, 1948: "The essential rights of man are not derived from the fact that he is a national of a certain state, but are based upon attributes of his personality." This is explained in the official Organization of American States' Handbook of Existing Rules Pertaining to Human Rights: "The American states recognize that when the state legislates in this field, it does not create or concede rights but rather recognizes rights that existed prior to the formation of the state, rights that have their origins in the very nature of the individual."[6]

FROM THE LEAGUE OF NATIONS TO THE UNITED NATIONS

After World War I, the victorious powers did not want to incorporate into the League of Nations' Covenant the general idea of universal human rights, a detailed international bill of rights, or even the concepts of religious freedom and racial equality.[7] The League, however, did serve as guarantor of human rights protections for national and religious minorities included in Minorities Treaties imposed by the Allied Powers on the newly independent successor states of the defeated Austro-Hungarian and Turkish empires.

During World War II, influential persons and religious and civic organizations, chiefly American, urged that one of the victors' main goals be the safeguarding of human rights everywhere, and that the safeguards take the form of an international bill of rights. This goal was articulated in several historic pronouncements, notably one by United States President Franklin D. Roosevelt in his Annual Message to Congress in January 1941, almost a year before the country officially entered the war. The "four essential freedoms" that must be made secure, he said, are freedom of speech and expression,

freedom of every person to worship God in his own way everywhere in the world, freedom from want, and freedom from
fear.[8]

In 1945, the UN Charter became the first international
agreement to incorporate the idea of universal human rights.
Among the new organization's principal purposes was the
encouragement of "respect for human rights and fundamental
freedoms for all without distinction as to race, sex, language,
or religion" (Article 1). The Charter pledged all Member
States, jointly and separately, to pursue this goal (Articles 55
and 56).

Although the Soviet Union participated in formulating the
Charter, the human rights purpose of the UN, indeed the
very idea of a world organization, derived mainly from Western internationalist idealism. Given the ideology of the USSR,
it could participate in the human rights undertaking only
with fundamental reservations; it could hardly cooperate
wholeheartedly if it believed that under capitalism, freedom
and democracy are illusory, and that they can truly exist only
in a "classless" society.[9]

The participation of the Western countries, however, the
United States included, was not unqualified, nor were these
nations altogether clear about the long-term import of the
human rights undertaking. Like the Soviet Union, the nations of the West were reassured by the generalities in the
Charter's human rights clauses, by their limitation to "promotion" rather than "protection" of human rights, and, especially, by Article 2 (7), which barred UN intervention in
"matters which are essentially within the domestic jurisdiction
of any state."

THE UN AND HUMAN RIGHTS: ACCOMPLISHMENTS AND DIFFICULTIES

When it was adopted, the UN Charter was faulted by many
people for not including an international bill of rights that
would spell out the rights and freedoms it would promote. A
process of accomplishing this, however, began almost at once
and has continued to the present day.[10] The Universal Declaration was adopted in December 1948 with only the Eastern
bloc and Saudi Arabia (eight members in all) abstaining in the
General Assembly vote. With the addition to this document of
two legally binding covenants—on civil and political rights
and on economic, social, and cultural rights—the goal of an
international bill of rights was finally achieved in 1966. The

Universal Declaration was followed over the next three decades by conventions, declarations, and other norm setting statements focused on particular rights or issues: racial discrimination, refugees, stateless persons, slavery and slave-like practices, women's and children's rights, discrimination in education and occupation, torture, treatment of prisoners, medical ethics, and others.

More recently, norm setting efforts were begun on many other subjects: the rights of the mentally ill, enforced disappearances, arbitrary and summary executions, the rights of human rights "defenders," rights during states of emergency, the rights of indigenous peoples, ethnic, religious, and linguistic minorities, genetic engineering, and data protection. There have also been proposals for new categories of rights, called "solidarity" or "third generation" rights, such as the right to development and the right to peace. (The civil and political rights were called "first generation" rights, and the economic and social rights were called "second generation" rights.) Proposals have been advanced for new international economic, informational, cultural, and humanitarian "orders." Underlying some proposals for new rights and new "orders" are ideologically motivated desires of authoritarian regimes of both left and right for legitimation of enlarged state authority over economic, information, and other segments of the private sectors in their countries as well as of claims to various forms of international distributive justice.

This proliferation of new and proposed norms has added to the doubts of many, already skeptical, about the utility of the UN's human rights enterprise. Apart from the lack of a shared ideological basis and religious and cultural heritage to serve as a sound foundation for it, many cite basic flaws in the accumulated jurisprudence—among others, blurred distinctions between binding and nonbinding rules, gaping loopholes created by permissible limitations attached to individual freedoms, and formulations susceptible to contradictory interpretations.

There is also skepticism about the feasibility of international implementation, particularly in the framework of the UN, which includes too many authoritarian members that violate human rights systematically. The Charter-based committees dealing specifically with South Africa, the Israeli-occupied territories, and Chile and certain other Latin American countries are rudimentary and subject to political influence, as are the procedures of general applicability based on Charter authority as well as those established under the major human rights conventions (e.g., the Covenant on Civil and Political Rights, the Convention on Racial Discrimination). Their formal rules (e.g., secrecy) and their realities (e.g., nonindependence of many of their members despite election in a personal rather than a representative capacity) do not remotely conform to accepted standards of procedural fairness.

Other observers, though cognizant of the shortcomings, are more hopeful. They point, for example, to the universal acceptance of the civil and political rights, even if hypocritically on "paper" by the states that often violate them. The world would be darker and the future even grimmer, it is argued, but for the latter's formal endorsement of the international documents affirming these rights. Though differences remain in regard to the "second generation" economic and social rights, and especially the vaguer "third generation" rights, trends in population growth, scientific discovery, communications and other technological innovations, economic relationships, weaponry, and the world's material, social, and political environment mandate that they not be dismissed out of hand. The Western and other democracies cannot avoid taking part in international debates over issues and proposals in these areas. They should do so with minds open to the legitimate claims of others while repulsing cynical manipulation of human rights symbols and semantics for regressive ends. Whether and in what respects the division over these proposals may be bridged is hard to foresee.

Despite limited accomplishments in matters of implementation, optimists observe that the UN procedures have contributed to some degree to the promotion and protection of human rights. Without doubt, "selective morality" (manifested among other ways in overconcentration on some countries, while overlooking more egregious human rights denials elsewhere) persists, but the UN has actually extended its coverage beyond the threesome of South Africa, Israel, and Chile to include problems in parts of Africa and Asia, and even (although barely) in Eastern Europe. This has occurred in the standing committees with general mandates as well as in the efforts of special committees, working groups, rapporteurs, and representatives designated to deal with special types of problems (slavery, disappeared persons, summary executions, and so on). Initiatives have also been taken to investigate situations in particular countries.

In the UN's early period, when it was Western-dominated, the emphases in its norm setting efforts were on civil and political rights. This pattern changed in the late sixties and early seventies with the admission of a large number of African and Asian states, which joined the Soviet bloc in sidetracking projects in these areas in favor of activities centered on colonial, racial, and economic issues, with particular attention to South Africa and the Israeli territories. In the late fifties, the Subcommission on Discrimination and Minorities commissioned a series of studies on the right to leave any country and to return, political rights, and religious rights, among others. The study on religious rights was intended to spell out the right to freedom of thought, conscience, and religion that had been stated in broad terms in the Universal Declaration and the Covenant on Civil and Political Rights. Follow-up of the recommendations in these studies, especially adoption of norm setting declarations and/or conventions, was stalled by the Soviet Union abetted by various African and Asian states. Twenty years elapsed before advocates of a special instrument on religious rights, chiefly the Western democracies, were able to convince the General Assembly in November 1981 to adopt the Declaration on Religious Intolerance.

II.   THE CONCEPT OF RELIGIOUS FREEDOM: HISTORICAL AND LEGAL DEVELOPMENT

Arcot Krishnaswami's introduction to his 1959 study reviewed the history of the concept of freedom of thought, conscience, and religion. While noting that "not frequently, horrors and excesses have been committed in the name of religion," he found in all religions "voices in favor of tolerance and religious freedom"—from King Asoka, patron of Buddhism twenty-three hundred years ago, the biblical Book of Leviticus, and Mohammed, to such Catholic scholars as Thomas Aquinas in the thirteenth century and the Jesuit Francisco Suarez in the sixteenth century. Historians have cited other examples, among them the Jewish Khazar kings in the Crimea from the sixth to the tenth centuries, and King William the Silent of Holland in the sixteenth century.[11]

These "voices," however, did not tolerate the same things. Aquinas, for example, was relatively easy on the heathens or pagans but altogether intolerant of heretics.[12] It has often been observed that the most advanced and difficult level of tolerance is a group's willingness to bear with its own dissenting members.

Martin Luther's appeal to conscience in the first half of the fifteenth century did not encompass the notion of religious pluralism.[13] Nor did the Treaty of Augsburg in 1555—and the Treaty of Westphalia in 1648, marking the end of the thirty years of religious wars in Europe, which incorporated the Augsburg principle—include the idea. The solution to the religious conflicts arising from the Reformation was, "He who rules the territory determines its religion." If the ruler opted for Lutheranism, the Catholic inhabitants were to have the choice of conversion or emigration, and vice versa.[14]

RECOGNITION IN NATIONAL LAW

The principle of religious freedom and equality was only gradually recognized, at first with regard to a few religions, and later, with setbacks on the way, for all religious groups. In France, Calvinists and Jews were granted equal religious freedom with Catholics only through the Revolution of 1789. The Declaration of the Rights of Man and the Citizen provided: "No person shall be molested for his opinions, even such as are religious, provided that the manifestations of opinions do not disturb the public order established by the law."[15] The Constitution adopted in 1791 assured all citizens, regardless of religion, equality before the law.[16] Moreover, while the Constitutional Charter of 1814, under Napoleon Bonaparte, recognized Roman Catholicism as the state religion, it extended the principle of religious freedom from France to the rest of Europe, except for Russia.[17] That achievement survived, in law, the return of the ancien régime in France after Napoleon's defeat, and throughout Europe in the constitutions adopted after the 1830 and 1848 revolutions. Despite the twenty years of reaction that followed, religious freedom became an integral part of virtually all Western legal systems.

In England, two concurrent events in 1698—John Locke's famous Letter of Toleration and the Toleration Act—gave important impetus to the idea of religious liberty. Locke argued: "If solemn assemblies, observations of festivals, public worship be permitted to any one sort of professors, all these things ought to be permitted to the Presbyterians, Independents, Anabaptists, Armenians, Quakers, and others with the same liberty. Nay, if we may openly speak the truth . . . neither pagan nor Mohametan nor Jew ought to be excluded from the civil rights of the commonwealth because of his religion. . . ."[18]

The Toleration Act exempted Protestant dissenters from certain legal penalties, while maintaining the privileged status of the Church of England; only its adherents could hold public offices. The rights granted Protestant dissenters were extended to Roman Catholics by the Catholic Emancipation Acts of 1829 and 1832, and extended to Jews by the Religious Disabilities Act of 1846, although in fact Catholics and Jews were not really free and equal under law until decades later.

North America, in the colonial period, was fertile soil for the idea of religious freedom notwithstanding the established religions and the restricted freedom of religious minorities in the mother countries of England, France, and Spain. It is true that most colonists did not themselves really believe in religious freedom, but discriminated against Jews, as they had in the Old World, and even persecuted Catholics, Quakers, and Baptists. Nevertheless, the idea gathered momentum. The theological postion of most religious groups was that since God is the Lord of all, humans are obliged to depend on Him alone, whatever the state's demands. Also, the colonists came from many different lands and cultures and settled in geographically scattered communities. These influences and the fact that wide sectors of the commercial class belonged to nonconformist groups created a climate conducive to both religious dissent and indifference. Interdenominational strife, too, made mutual tolerance imperative. These factors, as well as the liberal influence of such advocates of religious freedom as Roger Williams and William Penn, advanced a general movement toward religious freedom in all the American colonies.[19]

Though the desire of the mother countries to populate their colonies was the main motivation, Jewish settlers in the New World were among the beneficiaries of the movement toward religious freedom. Jews who came to America from Holland and England were granted equal rights in the seventeenth and eighteenth centuries, long before they had such rights in Europe, and colonial precedents in turn contributed to the eventual removal of legal obstacles in the mother countries.[20]

The example of Surinam is noteworthy. In 1665, when the island was still an English colony, a decree provided that every Hebrew resident be "considered as Englishborn," enjoy the same liberties and privileges granted to citizens and inhab-

itants of the colony, and be permitted "in the most ample
manner possible . . . to practice and perform their religion,
according to their usages. . . ."[21] The Plantation Act of 1740,
whose declared purpose was to increase the wealth and population of the English colonies, provided for the naturalization
of "Foreign Protestants and Others" already settled or expecting to settle there. It specifically exempted Jews from reciting
the words "upon the full faith of a Christian" in the naturalization oath, a legal obstacle to equal status that was later
gradually abolished in England.[22]

The U.S. Constitution did not even mention religion, except to prohibit any religious qualification for election to federal office. The principles of separation of church and state
and of the free exercise of religion were added in 1791 with
the enactment of the Bill of Rights, whose First Amendment
provides that "Congress shall make no law respecting an
establishment of religion, or prohibiting the free exercise
thereof. . . ."[23]

In Czarist Russia, as Krishnaswami noted, the dominant
Russian Orthodox Church pressed the public authorities to
oppose dissenters, and in turn the authorities used the
Church's influence to stamp out minority cultures and "to
foster religious and national antagonisms . . . to eliminate opposition to the established régime." Five months after the
February 1917 Revolution, the provisional government enacted
a law guaranteeing freedom of conscience in the former Russian Empire. In January 1918, following the Bolshevik Revolution the previous October, a new decree provided for "separation of the Church from the State and the School from the
Church." Committed ideologically to atheism and to the disappearance of religion, however, the Soviet authorities, despite
constitutional guarantees and international treaty commitments, pursued a policy of discrimination and even persecution against religious groups.[24]

Although there were state religions in India, such as Buddhism in the third century B.C.E. under Emperor Asoka, and
Islam from the tenth to the mid-eighteenth centuries, Krishnaswami found that religious exclusion and persecution were
rare. When the British made Christianity the state religion in
India, they did not interfere in the religious affairs of the
indigenous population. In 1950, three years after India became
an independent state, freedom in religious matters was constitutionally guaranteed.[25] Unhappily, this constitutional guaran-

tee, which Krishnaswami did not point out, was a weak protection against the volcanic religious and ethnic tensions between the Hindu majority and India's Muslim, Sikh, and other minorities. These tensions erupted into mass violence on the heels of independence in 1947, and again many times afterward, up to the recent anti-Sikh mob violence after the assassination of Prime Minister Indira Gandhi.

INTERNATIONAL RECOGNITION OF THE
PRINCIPLES OF RELIGIOUS FREEDOM

Protection of minority religious groups (mainly Christian) by special treaty agreements antedates guarantees of religious freedom in national law, having appeared "long before the idea of systematic protection of civil and political rights was developed." A treaty between France and Turkey in 1536 granted religious freedom to French merchants in Turkey and, later on, became a model for similar agreements (known as the "capitulations" system).[26] The Treaty of Westphalia in 1648, provided for a degree of mutual toleration between Protestant and Catholic minorities, but did not guarantee religious freedom for all other groups.[27] In 1773, treaties concerning the partition of Poland assured religious freedom to Catholics, and a 1774 agreement between Russia and Turkey obliged Turkey to protect the Christian religion. In 1815, the Congress of Vienna agreed that Christian religious parties would enjoy civil and political rights, and even committed the Diet of the German Confederation to look into improving the civil status of Jews. The Diet failed, however, to follow up that commitment in regard to the individual German states.[28]

The 1878 Congress of Berlin following the Russo-Turkish War was convened by the Austrian Empire with British encouragement to prevent Russian domination of the Balkans. The principal participants were the Big Powers, including Austria-Hungary, Britain, France, Italy, and Turkey, with representatives of the Balkan countries—Rumania, Serbia, Montenegro, and Bulgaria (created by the Congress)—allowed to attend solely to present their countries' views concerning their respective interests. Also present, but unofficially, were representatives of Jewish organizations to urge inclusion in the peace treaty under consideration guarantees of equal civil and political rights for members of all religions. The ensuing treaty conditioned recognition of the independence of the four countries on their agreeing to such guarantees. Though all

four agreed, Rumania took advantage of a constitutional loophole in its constitution to evade this guarantee with respect to
its Jewish population.[29]

The Covenant of the League of Nations was concerned
primarily with the achievement of international peace and
security. Although the victors in World War I proclaimed
worldwide democracy as their goal, the idea of universal
human rights was not incorporated in the Covenant.[30] Nor
were the allies willing to recognize religious freedom as a
goal, largely because it was linked to an even less acceptable
request by the Japanese that racial equality be recognized as
well. Instead, in a series of separate Minority Protection Treaties, the allies imposed obligations concerning religious freedom and equality only on the newly created multinational
states in Central and Eastern Europe, the Middle East, and
Africa. It was not long before some of the new states protested
that these obligations not only infringed on their sovereign
equality (the Big Powers and other states did not assume
comparable obligations), but encouraged their minorities to
look to powerful neighbors for protection. This purported
flaw in the minority protection system—that is, the obligee
states' injured pride over their unequal position, which gave
them an excuse to evade the obligations—later spurred American and other nongovernmental groups to work for a universally applicable system of human rights.[31]

With some variations, the Polish Minority Treaty of 1919
was typical of other treaties imposed on the new states.
Among other things, it guaranteed to "all inhabitants of
Poland . . . the free exercise, whether public or private, of any
creed, religion or belief, whose practices are not inconsistent
with public order or morals"; and to "all Polish nationals . . .
the civil and political rights without distinction as to race,
language or religion." It included specific guarantees concerning minorities' languages and religious and educational institutions.[32] Treaties, or special declarations to the League of
Nations, imposed comparable commitments on Czechoslova-
kia, Greece, Rumania, Yugoslavia, Austria, Bulgaria, Hungary, Turkey, Estonia, Latvia, Lithuania, Finland (the Aaland
Islands), and Iraq. The only provision on religious liberty in
the body of the League's Covenant concerned the Mandates
system. The Covenant specified that the power responsibile

for administering the Central African territory was to "guarantee freedom of conscience and religion, subject only to the maintenance of public order and morals" (Article 22).

III.   NONDISCRIMINATION AND FREEDOM IN THE MATTER OF RELIGION OR BELIEF

THE UNIVERSAL DECLARATION OF HUMAN RIGHTS AND
THE COVENANT ON CIVIL AND POLITICAL RIGHTS

While the UN Charter was being drafted, Chile, Cuba, New Zealand, Norway, and Panama suggested detailed provisions on the right to freedom of thought, conscience, and religion. The suggestion was not adopted; but the Charter prohibited *discrimination* on the ground of *religion*, race, sex, and language (Article 1). Religious discrimination was also proscribed in subsequent human rights agreements. The Universal Declaration, adopted in December 1948, entitles everyone to all the rights specified in it, "without distinction of any kind, such as race, colour, sex, language, *religion*, political and other opinion, national or social origin, property, birth or other status" (Article 2). The Genocide Convention, adopted in December 1948, defines the international crime of genocide as certain intentionally committed acts designed to destroy "in whole or in part, a national, ethnical, racial or *religious* group, as such" (Article 2) (emphasis added).

With regard to religious discrimination, almost identical wording as in the Universal Declaration may be found in the Covenant on Economic, Social and Cultural Rights (Part II, Article 2 [1]), and the Covenant on Civil and Political Rights (Part II, Article 2 [1]), both adopted in 1966. The United Nations Educational, Scientific, and Cultural Organization (UNESCO), the Convention Against Discrimination in Education (Article 1), and the American and European regional human rights conventions (Articles 14 and 1, respectively), also include religion among other prohibited grounds of discrimination.

The right to *freedom* of religion or belief was recognized in the Universal Declaration and the Covenant on Civil and Political Rights (emphasis added). In fact, the first article of the 1981 Declaration on Religious Intolerance is taken nearly unchanged from Article 18 of the Covenant, whose first paragraph corresponds, with minor differences, to Article 18 of the Universal Declaration. The latter reads: "Everyone has the right to freedom of thought, conscience and religion; this right includes freedom to change his religion or belief, and freedom, either alone or in community with others and in public or private, to manifest his religion or belief in teaching, practice, worship and observance."

The Covenant's Article 18 (second paragraph) also proscribes "coercion which would impair" this freedom; subjects (third paragraph) freedom to "manifest" religion or belief "only to such limitations as are prescribed by law and are necessary to protect public safety, order, health or morals or the fundamental rights and freedoms of others"; and requires (last paragraph) that contracting states "have respect for the liberty of parents . . . to ensure the religious and moral education of their children in conformity with their own convictions." The Universal Declaration's Article 26 (3) gives parents a "prior right to choose the kind of education that shall be given their children."

Combining "thought" and "conscience" with "religion" in both the Universal Declaration and the Covenant, terms not defined nor even extensively discussed in the drafting, was a compromise intended, without saying so explicitly, to embrace atheists and other nonbelievers. According to one authority, the terms include "all possible attitudes of the individual to the world, toward society, and toward whatever determines his fate and destiny in the world, be it a divinity, a superior being, reason and rationalism, or chance." "Thought" encompasses "political and social thought," and "all morality" is included in "conscience."[33]

When the 1981 Declaration was being drafted, the right "to change" one's religion was one of the main divisive issues, as it had been in the past. Although the Universal Declaration had incorporated that term over Muslim opposition, a few years later the Covenant (first paragraph) substituted "have or adopt" for "change"—a reflection of increased influence of the Muslim states in the UN. The 1981 Declaration went a step further by eliminating the word "adopt." This modification, however, was mainly symbolic, for it was generally agreed that the right to change is already implied in the phrases "freedom of conscience" and "freedom from coercion," and in the provision (Article 8) preserving the rights as previously defined in the Universal Declaration and Covenant. The Covenant's Article 18 (3) permits states' parties to limit such manifestations of religion or belief as "worship, observance, practice and teaching," in order to protect "public safety, order, health or morals of the fundamental rights and freedoms of others." In contrast, the Universal Declaration deals with limitations in omnibus Article 29, applicable to all the freedoms it sets forth.

Both the Universal Declaration's Article 29 and the Covenant's Article 18 require that limitations be set forth in law and be "necessary." Article 29 permits limitations on all the individual freedoms, including that on religion, in order to protect "the rights and freedoms of others"; the Covenant's Article 18 requires that these "rights and freedoms of others" be "fundamental." Article 29 permits limitations to protect "public order," whereas the Covenant's Article 18 speaks of "public safety" and "order." It is generally agreed that "public order" does not refer to the broad, flexible notion of "national public policy" ("ordre public"), but to the prevention of "public disorder." Neither article allows limitation on grounds of "national security." Finally, the Universal Declaration, but not the Covenant, cites "the general welfare in a democratic society" as a permissible ground for limiting manifestations of religion or belief.[34]

The Covenant's Article 18 (4), which obliges states' parties to respect the freedom of parents to decide their children's religious and moral education, is weaker in its assertion of parental and children's rights than Article 26 (3) in the Universal Declaration. Taken as a whole, Article 18 in the Covenant would give individual freedom to manifest religion or belief "great weight against the public interests asserted." This is evidenced by its inclusion (along with the right to life and the prohibitions against slavery and torture) in the Covenant's Article 4 (1,2) on "derogations," as rights that may not be diminished even in times of public emergency.[35]

Although the Universal Declaration, the Covenant, and the 1981 Declaration all guarantee the right to manifest religion or belief, however, none requires that there be separation between church and state. As Soviet proposals to consider the establishment of religion as discriminatory in itself were rejected, all of these instruments permit the existence of state religions, provided they do not impinge on the rights of non-established religious groups. Thus, these groups must accept the reality that established churches may enjoy certain practical advantages, but they know also that such advantages can be challenged if they significantly harm the rights of others.

Organization of American States (OAS). The 1948 Charter of the Organization of American States affirms the fundamental rights of the individual irrespective of creed, race, nationality, or sex. Also enacted in 1948 was the American Declaration of the Rights and Duties of Man, whose thirty-eight articles define both the rights protected and the duties they entail.[36]

In 1959, the Consultation of Foreign Affairs Ministers of the OAS Member States established the Inter-American Commission on Human Rights and mandated it to prepare a draft convention on human rights and a draft statute for a regional human rights court. In 1965, the Commission was empowered to examine human rights communications and other information, from private as well as governmental sources, and to report and submit annual recommendations to the Inter-American Conference (or to the Consultation of Foreign Affairs Ministers), on steps needed to give effect to the rights in the American Declaration. The Convention was adopted a decade later, in November 1969, in San José, Costa Rica, and entered into force in 1978. That year, the Commission was made a principal organ of the OAS. In 1979, the Inter-American Court formally came into being as an "autonomous judicial institution whose purpose is the application and interpretation of the American Convention," with adjudicatory and advisory jurisdiction.

Article 3 of the American Declaration guarantees everyone "the right freely to profess a religious faith, and to manifest and practice it in public and in private." With minor differences, Article 12 of the American Convention is patterned on the UN Covenant. Like the Universal Declaration, this Convention guarantees the right to change one's religion or belief. The right to manifest religion or belief is subject to essentially the same permissible limitations as in the Covenant. Unlike the Universal Declaration and Covenant, "thought" is not combined with "conscience and religion" as in the Covenant clause, "freedom of thought, conscience and religion." Parents "have the right to provide for the religious and moral education of their children or wards that is in accord with their convictions."

Council of Europe. The European Convention on Human Rights, which came into force in September 1953, three years after its adoption in Rome, is the most important of the conventions concluded under the auspices of the Council of

Europe.[37] Its implementing measures, including a Commission, Court, and Committee of Ministers, are more advanced than those under any other international human rights instrument. The Commission is empowered to examine not only charges brought by one state against another but also complaints from individual victims of human rights violations, even against their own governments, providing the state complained against has agreed to submit to this procedure. Most Council members have so agreed. The European Convention's antidiscrimination provision, in Article 14, includes religion among the proscribed grounds. These are identical with those in Article 2 of the Universal Declaration and the Covenant (except for adding "association with a national minority" to the prohibited grounds).

The European Convention reproduces in Article 9 (2) almost verbatim the Universal Declaration's Article 18, including the right to change religion or belief (which it took over in 1950 from an early draft of the Covenant) and the freedom to manifest them "in worship, teaching, practice and observance." The freedom to manifest may be limited on grounds similar to those in the Covenant, namely, prescription by law, and necessity in a democratic society. (As noted above, the reference to a democratic society is included in the Universal Declaration but not in the Covenant.) The right of children to education, and of parents to ensure their children's education in accordance with their religious and philosophical convictions, is not included in Article 9 of the European Convention, but it is guaranteed in Article 1 of the First Protocol to this Convention.

Helsinki Final Act (1975). The 1975 Helsinki Final Act's Declaration on Principles Guiding Relations Between the Participating States provides that these states "will respect the freedom of the individual to profess and practice, alone or in community with others, religion or belief acting in accordance with the dictates of his conscience."[38] In this Declaration, the section on "Human Contacts" (in the part on "Cooperation in Humanitarian and Other Fields") confirms "that religious faiths, institutions and organizations, practising within the constitutional framework of the participating states, and their representatives can, in the field of their activities, have contacts and meetings among themselves and exchange information."

Two conferences were held, one in Belgrade in 1977-1978

and the second in Madrid, beginning in November 1980, to review compliance with the provisions elaborated in Helsinki. The Concluding Documents of the prolonged Madrid conference that ended in the summer of 1983 essentially reaffirmed the principles and commitments of the Final Act, which the participating states agreed to pursue "by continuous implementation, unilaterally, bilaterally and multilaterally." Regarding religion, they reaffirmed the promise "to take the action necessary to ensure the freedom of the individual to profess and practice, alone or in community with others, religion or belief, acting within the dictates of his own conscience"; "to consult, whenever necessary, the religious faiths, institutions and organizations, which act within the constitutional framework of their respective countries"; to "favorably consider applications by religious communities of believers . . . to be granted the status provided for in their respective countries for religious faiths, institutions and organizations"; and to "further implement" the Final Act's relevant provisions "so that religious faiths, institutions, organizations and their representatives can, in the field of their activity, develop contacts and meetings among themselves and exchange information."

In addition to keeping alive the Helsinki process and airing specific cases and situations, the main accomplishment in human rights of the Madrid conference may have been the decision to hold follow-up meetings, among them a meeting of experts in Ottawa, Canada, in May 1985, to discuss "respect, in their states, for human rights and fundamental freedoms, in all their aspects, as embodied in the Final Act." Questions concerning religious freedom will undoubtedly be raised at that meeting. The Madrid conference also agreed to "consider favorably" the holding of voluntary "bilateral" round-table meetings on human rights issues.

IV.   THE UN DECLARATION ON THE ELIMINATION
OF ALL FORMS OF INTOLERANCE AND DISCRIMINATION
BASED ON RELIGION OR BELIEF

As its full title indicates, the 1981 Declaration deals with both intolerance and discrimination on grounds of religion or belief.[39] Here, the UN has followed the established practice of singling out rights previously recognized in general terms in the Universal Declaration and the Covenants on Human Rights, and dealing with them in detail in special instruments that set standards for governmental and private conduct. In the case of conventions (e.g., on racial discrimination), provision is frequently made for complaints and reporting mechanisms. With regard to declarations—and also conventions—UN bodies and agencies, regional intergovernmental organizations, governments, and nongovernmental organizations are encouraged to undertake supportive educational programs. Since UN declarations do not usually contain implementing provisions, such encouragement is especially important.

HOW THE DECLARATION CAME TO BE ADOPTED

Originally, the UN's efforts against racial and religious discrimination were linked. They were combined, for example, in the conventions on discrimination in employment and education adopted in 1958 by the International Labor Organization (ILO) and UNESCO, respectively. In 1960, the Human Rights Commission, reacting to outbreaks of swastika smearing in Europe and the United States the previous year, adopted a resolution on "Manifestations of Anti-Semitism and Other Forms of Racial Prejudice and Religious Intolerance." Two years later, the General Assembly (Res. 1781 [17]) called on the Commission to draft separate declarations and conventions on the racial and religious issues.[40] The Soviet Union and some other states that pressed for separation hoped thereby to delay and eventually to prevent action on the religious issue altogether.

Action on the racial question was indeed swift. With the energetic support of the African states, the General Assembly adopted a declaration in November 1963, followed in December 1965 by a convention containing far-reaching substantive provisions and relatively strong implementation measures. In contrast, efforts to advance religious freedom and nondiscrimination moved exceedingly slowly and all but petered out. In 1960, the Commission's Subcommission on Discrimination and Minorities proposed a set of draft principles for possible incorporation into both a declaration and convention. The drafts, based on Special Rapporteur Arcot Krishnaswami's seminal study on religious discrimination as well as on recommendations by governments and religious and other nongovernmental organizations, became a point of departure for subsequent work on this issue. In 1962, the Assembly asked the Commission for such drafts; two years later, six articles of a declaration were ready. A draft convention, including a preamble and thirteen articles, including possible implementing provisions, was submitted in 1967.[41] The draft convention's definition of "religion or belief," which included "theistic, nontheistic and atheistic beliefs," evoked strong opposition from the Islamic states, the Catholic Church, and other religious groups. By 1968, however, the Assembly could only— and even then with many abstentions—adopt a controversial preamble for the convention. No further work was done on either the convention or the declaration until 1972, when the Assembly set aside the convention to concentrate on the declaration.

As in many other areas of the UN's human rights work, international political issues, particularly in the Middle East, inevitably intruded. In 1967, for example, while the Assembly was reviewing the Commission's draft convention, a proposed amendment to one of its articles, requiring that states institute educational and informational measures to combat prejudices, would have added, "as, for example, anti-Semitism and other manifestations which lead to religious intolerance. . . ." The USSR and several Arab states, with Libya in the forefront, put forth a subamendment referring to "nazism, Zionism and fascism" as additional examples of prejudice. This strategem was devised to block the reference to anti-Semitism by making it conditional on the inclusion of an invidious reference to Zionism. The dispute was resolved by a compromise decision to omit all specific examples of prejudice, including anti-Semitism.[42] There is no doubt, however, that anti-Semitism is covered by the general prohibitions in the proposed convention on religious intolerance, as also by those in the 1965 convention on racial discrimination and in other UN instruments. The debates were an ominous portent of things to come. In 1975, the General Assembly was to pass a resolution equating Zionism with racism.[43]

The Soviet Union resisted the very idea of a special instrument on religious intolerance, and many Third World members were disinclined to be involved in what they viewed as an East-West issue. So the Commission's efforts to carry out the Assembly's latest request to work first on a declaration, were again stalled. By 1978, the preamble to a declaration, but not a single operative article, had been agreed on. During these bleak years, except for a few Western governments, only the nongovernmental organizations kept insisting on the need for action. In 1979, the Commission's Western members reluctantly agreed to bypass the prevailing understanding that decisions to formulate human rights and other norm setting instruments be made only by consensus. In doing so, they prevented a filibuster that might have blocked the whole undertaking. Three operative articles put to a vote and approved were not innovative, for they were largely adaptations of earlier UN instruments, but the logjam was broken.[44]

Several public events provided additional impetus, among them a conference on the proposed UN Declaration, held in November 1979 under the auspices of the University of Santa Clara, a leading Catholic institution in California, and a UNESCO-sponsored consultation on religion and human rights, held the following month in Bangkok, Thailand.[45] Finally, on 10 March 1982, the Human Rights Commission adopted a seven-article draft Declaration, by a vote of thirty-three in favor, none against, and five abstentions.[46] That autumn, the General Assembly's Third Committee, after making a few revisions and adding an eighth article, approved the Declaration as a whole by consensus; it was adopted by the Assembly in plenary on 25 November 1981.[47]

PROVISIONS OF THE DECLARATION

The new Declaration reaffirmed and spelled out Article 18 in both the Universal Declaration and the Covenant on Civil and Political Rights, which relates to freedom of religion or belief, including nonreligious belief. It was originally titled "Declaration on the Elimination of All Forms of Religious Intolerance," to parallel the title of the prior declaration and convention on the "Elimination of All Forms of Racial Discrimination." Communist delegates and several African and Asian representatives, however, objected that this designation, by linking the word "intolerance" only to religion and not to other beliefs, demonstrated a bias toward religion. Contending also that the term lacked juridical meaning, they wanted to limit the content of both the proposed declaration (and any parallel convention) to "discrimination." The compromise affirmed by the Assembly's Third Committee in 1968, became, "Elimination of All Forms of Intolerance and Discrimination Based on Religion or Belief."

As finally adopted, the Declaration comprises a ten-paragraph preamble and eight substantive articles on three main groups of issues: prohibition of both state-imposed and private discrimination based on religion or belief; freedom to manifest a religion or belief without unwarranted government interference, even if applied without such discrimination; and the commitment of governments to adopt both legal and educational measures to eliminate intolerance and discrimination.

Preamble. The Preamble recalls the relevant principles in the Universal Declaration and the Covenant on Civil and Political Rights.[48] It "considers" that "infringement" of the right to freedom of "religion or *whatever* belief" has precipitated wars and great suffering, "especially where they serve as a means of foreign interference in the internal affairs of other States and amount to kindling hatred between people and nations" (emphasis added). This provision is a softened version of a Soviet proposal, which had stated that religion "continues to serve in this manner." The modifier "whatever" was added by the Assembly to the term "belief" at the request of the Soviet Union to emphasize that belief includes atheism, which the Commission, in the face of strong Muslim and Catholic opposition, had declined to say explicitly.

The Preamble notes that for anyone professing religion or belief, it is "*one* of the fundamental elements in his conception of life," and should be fully respected and guaranteed. This, too, was language watered down to accommodate Soviet objections to "*a* fundamental element" in the original draft (emphasis added).

It is essential also, the Preamble asserts, to promote religious tolerance and ensure that religion or belief is not used for ends inconsistent with the UN Charter and the principles of the present Declaration. Finally, the Preamble expresses the conviction that religious freedom should contribute to peace, justice, and friendship among peoples and to eliminating "ideologies or practices of colonialism and racial discrimination." Again the language is softened from more provocative wording advocated by the Soviet Union, which had alluded to the need to prevent exploitation of religion for political ends and to impede efforts to eliminate colonialism and racism.

Article 1. Article 1 contains the essence of the Declaration.[49] After affirming the right of all persons to freedom of thought, conscience, and religion, it specifies that this right includes not only the freedom "to have" a religion or belief of one's choice, but also "to manifest" it, i.e., to express it openly, "either individually or in community with others and in public or private," by means of "worship, observance, practice and teaching." At the insistence of the Islamic states, the reference in the Universal Declaration to the right to "change," and in the Covenant to the right to "adopt," a religion or belief was not carried over to this article. Article 8 was added as a compromise to placate those who opposed the deletions.

As in the Universal Declaration and the Covenant, "religion or belief" is defined neither in Article 1 nor elsewhere in the Declaration (nor in the regional instruments, nor for that matter in national constitutions). The Soviet Union and other East European states repeatedly demanded that this term be defined, purportedly to protect atheists. Given the diversity of religions and beliefs, however, and the hornet's nest of theological, legal, and political disputes any definition would open up, any attempt to define "religion or belief" would be fruitless at best. At the same time, the legislative history of Article 18 in both the Universal Declaration and the Covenant, the prefacing of "belief" with the modifier "whatever" in the 1981 Declaration's Preamble and Article 1, and the express statement of understanding by the Commission's working group chairman (as well as the terms "thought" and "conscience") leave no doubt that "atheism" has been covered. It seems clear that the Soviet demand for a definition was meant to frustrate the search for consensus on the entire Declaration.

The article guarantees not only the absolute freedom to "have" a religion or belief, that is, to maintain it within the mind's privacy, but also the more limited freedom to "manifest" it. Governments cannot limit manifestations arbitrarily, however, for the limits must be "prescribed by law" and "necessary." Because the criterion of necessity is vague, only independent courts or administrative agencies operating by rules approximating due process, as well as an alert and assertive public, can be an effective counterforce to the arbitrary exercise of government authority. In the main, the discussion over criteria for balancing the individual right to manifest religion or belief with the community's collective concern for "public safety, order, health or morals or the fundamental rights and freedoms of others" recapitulated arguments and understandings during debates over the Covenant's Article years earlier.

Proposals to add "national security" to these permissible limitations were not accepted. Even so, the limitations mentioned in Article 1 already offer governments the widest loopholes and have too often been cited in UN or other international forums in defense of denials of individual rights.

Article 2. Proscribing discrimination "by any state, institution, group of persons or person on grounds of religion or other belief," covers both the public and the private spheres.[50] In language adapted from Article 5 of the Convention on Racial Discrimination, "intolerance and discrimination based on religion or belief" are defined to mean "any distinction, exclusion, restriction or preference based on religion or belief having as its purpose or as its effect nullification or impairment of the recognition, enjoyment or exercise of human rights and fundamental freedoms on an equal basis." As in the racial area, the article raised difficult questions of interpretation, for example, on the issues of reverse (or "benign") quotas and other kinds of affirmative action.

Article 3. Essentially hortatory, Article 3 rejects religious discrimination as an affront to human dignity, a contradiction of the UN Charter, a violation of the Universal Declaration and the Covenant, and an obstacle to peaceful interstate relations.[51]

Article 4. Article 4 calls on states to "take effective measures to prevent and eliminate discrimination on the grounds of religion or belief . . . in all fields of civil, economic, political, social and cultural life."[52] The United Kingdom representative had proposed citing examples like those in the Convention on Racial Discrimination, pertaining to employment, the professions, citizenship, voting, public office, and so on. The proposal was rejected on Byelorussia's objection, but even so, there is no doubt that they are covered by the article. States are required to "make all efforts to enact or rescind legislation where necessary to prohibit such discrimination, and to take all appropriate measures to combat intolerance on the grounds of religion or other beliefs. . . ." Thus, they are mandated to take legislative steps ("where necessary") as well as educational and other means to counteract religious discrimination and bigotry.

Article 5. Article 5 ensures parents the right "to organize the life within the family in accordance with their religion or belief," including the child's "moral education" (Par. 1).[53] The child, in turn, has the right to have access to religious education in accordance with the wishes of his parents, and not to be "compelled to receive teaching against" their wishes. The "guiding principle" in this provision is the "best interests of the child" (Par. 2). Who decides, however, what are the "best interests" of the child—the parents, the teacher, a psychiatrist, or a state social agency? This troubling question is left unanswered. If a child is not in the care of his parents, "due account shall be taken of their expressed wishes" (or other proof thereof) regarding religion or belief; again, "the best interests of the child" is "the guiding principle."[54]

Article 5 stipulates also that the practices stemming from religion or belief in which the child is raised "must not be injurious to his physical or mental health or to his full development." Of these three requirements, injury to physical health would seem to be the least subjective, and in fact, the article's drafting history demonstrates that the supporters were thinking of such problems as the parents' refusing to permit a medically recommended blood transfusion or other treatment for minors, in which case the parents' wishes would not prevail. More problematic is the term "mental health" (which replaced "moral harm" in an earlier draft) and, even more, the term "full development."

The provision concerning the child's right "to have access to religious education" has been faulted because it does not say where and how. It does not mention, for example, the right to establish the religious schools that would make such instruction possible. In this connection, it is noteworthy that another international instrument, the UNESCO Convention Against Discrimination in Education (1960), does expressly recognize the right, for religious reasons, to establish "separate educational systems or institutions offering an education which is in keeping with the wishes of the pupil's parents." Attendance must be optional and instruction must conform to state-approved standards for secular education (Article 2). The Covenant on Economic, Social, and Cultural Rights also obliges states parties "to respect the liberty of parents . . . to choose for their children schools, other than those established by the public authorities" (again, with conformity to minimum state standards), and "to ensure the religious and moral education of their children in conformity with their own convictions" (Article 13 [21]).[55] Article 8 of the 1981 Declaration states that in case of conflict between any of its provisions and a right in the legally binding Covenants on Human Rights, the latter would prevail; therefore, this provision in the Economic and Social Covenant would prevail over a contrary rule in the Declaration.

Article 6. Article 6 enumerates nine specific freedoms, included in the right to "freedom of thought, conscience, religion or belief," which may be manifested "individually or in community with others and in public or private," subject only to the limitations already mentioned.[56] The list is clearly not meant to be exhaustive and implies other freedoms, left unspecified. Although it fails to include some rights recommended by the Subcommission on Discrimination and by nongovernmental organizations over the past twenty years, the provision is more far-reaching than even optimists had expected. To avoid polarization that might have jeopardized the entire undertaking, some proposals had been rejected by the Commission outright or withdrawn by their advocates. The Soviet Union and its allies had wished to delete the list of particulars altogether, and made its customary try for language stating that the freedoms set forth in the Declaration would be exercised "in accordance with national legislation." The USSR and other East Europeans almost always propose such a clause when human rights instruments are being drafted, in order to neutralize obligation. As usual, this effort failed.

Credit for Article 6, probably the most significant in the Declaration, because of its particularity, belongs to Canada, the Netherlands, the United Kingdom, and, to be sure, the United States, which offered the initial text. These nations stood firm when other Western members of the Commission, worn down by Soviet tactics, would have accepted a truncated document.[57] Some of the disputed issues are indicated in the article's nine subparagraphs, which include:

—Freedom to "worship or assemble" in connection with a religion or belief, and to establish and maintain "places" for such purposes. The original wording was the right to "places of worship or assembly," but the Soviet representative insisted that these be defined. In Communist countries, the state owns "places" outside private homes. Religious groups did not like the ambiguity introduced by this change that seemed to give the Soviet authorities a basis for relegating believers to any manner of "place" to worship or assemble.

—Freedom to "establish and maintain appropriate charitable or humanitarian institutions." The reference to "educational institutions," contained in the initial U.S. draft, is gone. The Soviet Union objected that in the USSR "only the state provided for education." Also omitted is the right to send students abroad for religious training.

—Freedom to "make, acquire and use to an adequate extent" necessary articles and materials related to religious rites or customs. A conspicuous omission here, as a compromise with the Soviets, is the right to import such materials if they are not available locally. Such a phrase was part of the U.S. draft and had been approved by the Commission's working group. "Acquire" was substituted for "distribute and import." All the same, it is possible to argue that "acquire" implies the right to import a needed article if it is not available domestically.

—Freedom to write and disseminate "relevant" religious publications. There is no mention of acquiring, much less importing, such publications as Hebrew Bibles or other religious works. The modifier "relevant" was suggested by Argentina to replace "appropriate," which Byelorussia had proposed, presumably because the latter is more susceptible to arbitrary application.

—Freedom to teach a religion or belief, in "places suitable for these purposes." The right to establish private religious schools, in addition or as an alternative to state schools, is omitted, although (as indicated) it is recognized in the UNESCO Convention Against Discrimination in Education and in the Covenant on Economic, Social, and Cultural Rights. The limiting term "suitable" was inserted after Byelorussia pointed out that in some countries "public education was secular and there was no provision for religious education."

—Freedom "to solicit and receive voluntary financial and other contributions from individuals and institutions." The term "voluntary" was inserted to meet the objections of the Soviet Union, which vigorously fought the entire provision. Its suggestion, however, to add the qualification, "not motivated by political considerations," was turned down.

—Freedom "to train, appoint, elect or designate by succession appropriate leaders called for by the requirements" of one's religion or belief. The clause "in adequate numbers," was deleted on Nigeria's motion from the Commission's working group draft. The Soviet Union's proposal to add the phrase, "including leaders of atheist organizations," was rejected.

—Freedom to observe religious days of rest, holidays, and ceremonies "in accordance with the precepts of one's religion or belief." This provision is in the interest both of religious

believers in antireligious countries with only secular days of
rest and of adherents of minority religions in countries where
only the majority religion's day of rest (Friday, Saturday, or
Sunday) is recognized.

—Freedom to communicate in religious matters "with individuals and communities at the national and international levels." For years, nongovernmental groups had urged that the
right to form and participate in the activities of local, regional,
and international associations or federations be recognized;
but given the Soviet Union's resistance even to the present
weaker provision, there was no chance to win anything more
far-reaching.

All the freedoms listed in Article 6 were approved in the
Commission's working group by consensus, except for those
relating to financial and other contributions, training and
choosing religious leaders, and communicating on the national and international levels, to which the Soviet Union
objected. Several other specific freedoms, suggested but not
included in the list, had appeared in the Subcommission's
draft principles or in the Commission's draft convention, or
both. Among these were the freedom to make pilgrimages to
holy sites inside or outside the country; to teach and learn the
sacred languages of one's religion; to be married or divorced
according to the prescriptions of one's religion; to be buried
according to religious prescriptions, and for burial sites to be
protected; to be free from compulsion to participate, against
one's convictions, in a religious ceremony or to take a religious oath; and to be protected against discrimination in
regard to subsidies, taxation, and exemptions.

Another freedom recommended, unsuccessfully, for inclusion in Article 6 was the right "to express the implications of
one's religion or belief in public life," a principle repeatedly
affirmed by the World Council of Churches and the Vatican,
and by many other religious bodies as well.[58] Although this
principle was not incorporated as such in Article 6 or elsewhere in the Declaration, it is implicit. The question of religious groups' involvement, on the basis of the right to freedom of thought, conscience, and religion, in the political
issues of the day, is likely to loom large in future polemics
over the Declaration. Disapproving governments will tend to
charge that such involvement is politics disguised as religion.[59]

Even as the General Assembly's Third Committee was
about to conclude the drafting of the Declaration, the Soviet

Union wanted a new article to say: "The state shall not interfere in the internal (devotional or canonical) affairs of the
church, and the church shall not interfere in the affairs of the
state." The USSR also proposed that both the school and the
state be separated from the church, to legitimize the prohibition of church-related schools; and it requested a provision
specifying the right to criticize religion. These proposals were
not accepted, nor was another by some Western nongovernmental groups for a prohibition of incitement to hatred
against adherents of a religion or belief. Such a provision,
prohibiting incitement to violence, discrimination, and hatred,
had been included in the Convention on Racial Discrimination (Article 4). (Civil libertarians in the United States, however, would be concerned lest governments be motivated to
stifle mere critical comment concerning a religious group's
practices or pronouncements, on the pretext of preventing
incitement to hatred.)

Article 7. Article 7 calls for the enactment of national legislation to enable the individual "to avail himself . . . in practice" of the Declaration's freedoms.[60] This U.S.-sponsored
article, underscoring the intent to prevent the Declaration's
provisions ending up as paper promises, was also approved
over Soviet objections.

Article 8. Article 8 states that "nothing in this Declaration
shall be construed as restricting or derogating from any right
defined in the Universal Declaration of Human Rights and
the International Covenants on Human Rights."[61] The intent
of this article, proposed by the Netherlands, was to declare
indirectly the continuing validity of the right to "change"
one's religion or belief as provided in the Universal Declaration, or the essentially equivalent right to adopt a religion as
provided in the Covenant. As noted earlier, the Muslim members conditioned their agreement on the 1981 Declaration on
the exclusion of these provisions. This concession disturbed
Sweden and several other Western members. To retain their
support, Article 8 was added to confirm by implication the
continuing validity of the right to "change" or "adopt" a
religion, as well as other relevant provisions in these or other
international instruments that may be more liberal than those
in the Declaration. The device of covering over irreconcilable
differences by including provisions geared to both sides of an
issue is a common practice in international documents.

A proposal for an article on enforcement mechanisms, such

as national tribunals to adjudicate complaints of violations of
religious freedom, analogous to Article 6 in the Convention
on Racial Discrimination, was not approved. This provision
obligated contracting states "to assure everyone within their
jurisdiction effective protection and remedies, through the
competent national tribunals and other state institutions
against any acts of racial discrimination. . . ."

<small>POST-VOTE "UNDERSTANDINGS" IN THE GENERAL ASSEMBLY</small>

A number of states, particularly the hostile Soviet bloc and
the reluctant Islamic group, issued statements of understanding, or reservations, regarding the Declaration after it was
voted in the Assembly's Third Committee.[62] The Soviet delegate said the document gave a "one-sided" version of freedom
of conscience, but that he had not voted against it on the
understanding that it protected the right to profess not only a
religion, but also atheist beliefs and the right "to conduct atheist propaganda." Official Soviet policy is to propagate atheism
vigorously, whereas religion may only be "professed," at least
in theory. More important was the Soviet objection to the
whole of Article 6, which spells out the rights embraced by
the freedom to manifest religion or belief.

Other Communist representatives echoed the Soviet position. The Polish and Vietnamese delegates repeated the
charge that the Declaration disregarded the rights of nonreligious persons; the East German representative asserted that
the right to profess and practice one's religion "must not be
used to keep citizens from fulfilling their civic duties." The
Czechoslovak said that the Declaration must "not be a pretext
for interference in the internal affairs of countries." The
Rumanian objected that Article 5, giving parents the right to
determine their children's education, was inconsistent with
Rumanian law. Syria objected to Article 7, which requires
that states reflect the Declaration's rights and freedoms "in
national legislation." Speaking for the Islamic group, the Iraqi
representative took exception to any provision inconsistent
with the principles of, or legislation based on, the *shariya* (the
Islamic law). The Iraqi president of the General Assembly
expressed his personal view, however, at a press conference
after the close of the session, that "there is absolutely no justification for any kind of discrimination whatsoever based on
religion and faith. If you do not solve that problem, it is very
difficult to have the kind of society that the charter of the UN

calls for. I think that the full freedom of belief and religion should long ago have been enshrined as an instrument which should have been adopted and should be lived up to by all Member States." In a different vein, the Swedish member emphasized that the Declaration must not lower the level of protection established by prior norm setting agreements. He had joined the consensus on the understanding that the Declaration "in no way restricted already recognized rights, including the right to change one's belief."

The fact that the African states did not actively come out in favor of the Declaration during the years of its tortuous drafting was not based, in the case of most, on principled opposition. "A key aspect of African society is the widespread religious tolerance. Virtually all African countries are characterized by religious pluralism."[63] The Africans remained passive because they felt the UN should concentrate its attention on racial and economic issues, and because they viewed the issue of religious freedom as but another facet of the East-West conflict. In the final stages of the Assembly's deliberations, however, several black African states expressed support for the Declaration; in endorsing it, the delegates of Madagascar, Sierra Leone, Ghana, Liberia, Malawi, and Uganda referred to their nations' constitutions and positive traditions in this area.

U.S. LAW AND SOME IMPLICATIONS OF THE DECLARATION

Like the Universal Declaration and the Covenant on Civil and Political Rights, the 1981 Declaration accepts the reality of a world in which many countries of diverse political and social orientations, including democracies like the United Kingdom, Ireland, and Norway, as well as Israel and most Islamic countries, maintain state religions. In contrast, separation of church and state in the United States is mandated by the First Amendment, which prohibits both "an establishment of religion" and "interference with the free exercise thereof."[64] Since the Declaration prohibits the latter but not the former, it could not be invoked to proscribe policies, such as subsidizing religious schools through money grants or tax-exemptions, giving religious authorities exclusive jurisdiction over matrimonial matters, or enforcing Sabbath closing laws, simply on the ground that the "wall of separation" has been breached. If these policies were adversely to affect minority religious groups or nonbelievers, however, they could be challenged on the basis of the Declaration's antidiscrimination provisions.

To come under the protection of the First Amendment, American courts require that activities or practices motivated by conscience or nonreligious beliefs be connected by some rationale to the notion of "religion."[65] In contrast, the Declaration clearly covers nonreligious beliefs. Therefore, its protection is applicable also to individuals or groups acting from conscientiously held beliefs not connected to a deity or an organized religion.

Perhaps most contentious will be the activities of religious groups to influence social or human rights conditions or political situations inside countries. The boundary between affairs of state and church will always be disputed, within churches as well as between church and state. Since most religions involve world views with implications for the larger national and even international society, it is all but impossible to draw the line between the religious and the secular and political domains. That is why the proposed Soviet provision that state and church shall not interfere in each other's affairs was rejected.

The difficult issues are those indicated in the Declaration's Article 1 (3), which permits the state to limit the right to manifest religion or belief on the basis of the society's collective interest in public safety, order, health, or morals or the fundamental right and freedoms of others. As noted, these concepts provide governments disposed to curtail freedom with broad loopholes through which to constrain individual or group manifestations of religion or belief. Clearly, the best protections against abuse of these permissible limitations are independent judiciaries and informed and assertive citizen organizations.

V.   Follow-up: UN Decisions and Proposals

With the adoption of the Declaration, its supporters in governments and nongovernmental organizations turned their attention to educational and promotional activities that could make it into a living document, both within and outside the UN. In fall 1982, the General Assembly asked the secretary-general to issue the text in the UN's six official languages and "disseminate it widely as a matter of priority in as many other languages as possible." To date it has been printed in English, French, and Spanish, but not in Arabic, Chinese, and Russian, an omission not unrelated to resistance on the part of the countries involved. The Assembly also invited governments to publicize the Declaration and asked the Human Rights Commission to consider measures needed to "implement" it, a term on which the East European and certain Muslim states looked with disfavor.[66]

In spring 1983, the Human Rights Commission, endorsing a recommendation of its Subcommission on Discrimination, asked the secretary-general to convene a seminar in 1984-85 on "the encouragement of understanding, tolerance and respect" in matters of religion and belief. It would focus on educational programs, taking into account how the universal spiritual and human rights principles underlying all the major world religions have been expressed in social teachings, now and in the past, as well as the root causes of existing intolerance and discrimination.[67] The Commission also approved the Subcommission's appointment of its Costa Rican member as special rapporteur to produce a comprehensive study of the manifestations of intolerance and discrimination on the grounds of religion or belief in the world, using the Declaration as a standard. Basing her study on information from governments and regional intergovernmental organizations as well as from nongovernmental organizations, she was also to identify the "root causes" of the manifestations and to recommend specific remedial measures, especially in education.[68]

Nongovernmental organizations and some Western governments have offered suggestions for additional UN activities.[69] Among them is the idea that the General Assembly proclaim 25 November, the date of the adoption of the Declaration, as annual Religious Freedom Day, to be observed throughout the world with appropriate ceremonies and programs by UN bodies and agencies, national governments, nongovernmental organizations, churches, and other institutions. Another suggestion is that the Commission or Subcommission set up working groups (analogous to those that monitor cases of disappeared persons or slavery) to review annually official and nongovernmental information on denials of religious freedom, and to intercede with offending governments. Even now, notwithstanding the limitations of politicized forums, existing Commission and Subcommission procedures provide some opportunities to call attention to such denials as do the procedures under the Covenant on Civil and Political Rights, UNESCO's human rights committee, and other UN conventions and committees. One suggestion is to request those states that have ratified the Covenant on Civil and Political Rights to include information on their laws and practices bearing on the questions of religious intolerance and discrimination in the compliance reports they periodically submit to the Covenant's Human Rights Committee.

Finally, it has been suggested that the Declaration be developed into a legally binding convention following the precedents set in connection with other human rights declarations. Some believe this effort should be initiated at once, but others advocate that it be postponed. The latter contend that some states might try to attach many more exceptions and other escapes to a legally binding instrument than they have to the Declaration, thus diminishing the value of both. They also fear that the long drafting process of a convention would permit elements hostile to the Declaration to argue against discussing reported denials of religious freedom until there is agreement on the terms of the convention.

CONCLUSION

Already more than two decades ago the General Assembly had called for both an international declaration and a legally binding convention to protect religion and belief. The convention has yet to be achieved.

Some had questioned the need for special instruments on religion on the ground that the right to protection from discrimination and to freedom in matters of religion or belief is covered, expressly or by implication, in the Universal Declaration, the Covenant, and other international instruments. For example, apart from Article 18 in both the Universal Declaration and the Covenant, freedom to assemble for religious purposes is implied in the Covenant's provision on freedom of assembly, and freedom to establish charitable institutions in the provision on freedom of association. Freedom to write and disseminate religious publications and to communicate about religious matters with individuals and communities is encompassed within freedom of opinion and expression. The Covenant's Article 19 guarantees the freedom "to receive and impart information and ideas through any media regardless of frontiers." Freedom to teach a religion or belief is embraced by the right of ethnic, religious, or linguistic minorities "to enjoy their own culture, to profess and practice their own religion, or to use their own language."

The availability of a special declaration on religious freedom, however, offers important benefits by the very fact of its focus on this issue, by particularizing some general principles previously agreed upon and by providing a basis for special educational and promotional programs under UN, governmental, and nongovernmental auspices.

One authority, Karl Josef Partsch, has enumerated specific avenues for exercising the influence of the Covenant's Article 18. The Declaration can enhance that influence. Referring to Article 18, Partsch explained:

Like all rights recognized in the Covenant, the guarantees of freedom of thought, conscience and religion are interpreted by various bodies, both national and international; by governments considering adherence to the Covenant and possible reservations; in national parliaments comparing the national legal order with the requirements of the Covenant; by officials required to give effect to the Covenant; and by national courts in those states where the provisions of the Covenant are directly applicable. Increasingly they are, and will be interpreted also by states parties reporting on their compliance to the Human Rights Committee established under the Covenant, by states complaining to the Committee of violations by other states (pursuant to Art. 41), and by individuals transmitting communications to the Committee under the Protocol to the Covenant; the Human Rights Committee will interpret the Covenant in its deliberations and reports.[70]

Some UN declarations as well as historic human rights documents have, of course, become standards for measuring law and practice, and have had a momentous impact on public values and events. One need only mention, among others, the French Declaration of the Rights of Man and the Citizen, Franklin Delano Roosevelt's Four Freedoms, and the Universal Declaration of Human Rights.

Only time will tell the efficacy of the Declaration, and the convention if it ever materializes, in preventing religious discrimination and overcoming religious intolerance. Jeremy Bentham and more recent political theorists have been skeptical of high-minded moral and political declarations. Bentham observed almost two hundred years ago, "A great abundance of words only seems to hide the poverty and falsity of ideas." Michael Novak, a former U.S. representative to the UN Human Rights Commission, has observed that "if human rights consisted of words on paper, all would be well. . . ." Self-deception arises, first, from believing, naively, that mere words make human rights real. It arises, second, from believing, naively, that all countries understand the concepts in similar ways."[71]

Whatever the ultimate significance of the Declaration, it

will have little impact unless religious and other national and
international groups promote it energetically through education and advocacy programs. If it is allowed to gather dust on
library shelves, it will be nothing more than a footnote for
scholars and students, but if it is used thoughtfully and effectively, it can be made to advance the cause of those who still
must struggle to achieve their basic right to freedom of religion and conscience. By expressing the solemn aims and sentiments of the word community, the Declaration, instead of
remaining a collection of "mere" words, can dramatize the
contrast between the real and the ideal, expose violations of
this freedom, give hope to victims, shame their oppressors—
and, indeed, inspire remedial action. All this can come true
even if the Declaration is not soon followed by a convention,
despite the reservations and the "understandings," even the
hypocrisy, of some of the states that joined in adopting it.

NOTES

1.   GA Res. 55, 25 November 1981, General Assembly Official Record (hereafter
cited as GAOR), Supp. 48, A/36/48/1981. Hereafter cited as the 1981 Declaration or
simply as Declaration.
2.   Arcot Krishnaswami, "Study of Discrimination in the Matter of Religious Rights
and Practices," UN Doc. E/CN.4/Sub 2/200/Rev. 1 (1960), UN Pub. No. 60 XIV 2.
Published under the title, "The Status of Religions in Relation to the State," *Journal
of Church and State* 2 (May 1960):44-60. See also "The United Nations Proposed
Code on Religious Liberty," *Journal of Church and State* 2 (May 1960):61-64.
3.   Hersh Lauterpacht, *An International Bill of the Rights of Man* (New York:
Columbia University Press, 1945), 16-25, 104-7; David Sidorsky, "Contemporary
Reinterpretations of the Concepts of Human Rights," in *Essays on Human Rights:
Contemporary Issues and Jewish Perspectives*, ed. David Sidorsky (Philadelphia: The
Jewish Publication Society of America, 1979), 88-109; Yoshikazu Sakamoto, "Human
Rights Are Universal," *UNESCO Courier* (August-September 1982); Jack Donnelly,
"Human Rights as Natural Rights," *Human Rights Quarterly* 4 (Summer 1982):391-
405; Adamanta Pollis, "Liberal, Socialist and Third World Perspectives of Human
Rights," in *Towards a Human Rights Framework*, ed. Peter Schwab and Adamanta
Pollis (New York: Praeger, 1982), 1-26; American Anthropological Association,
"Statement on Human Rights," *American Anthropologist* 47 (October-December
1947):539-43; Cornelius F. Murphy, Jr., "Objections to Western Conceptions of
Human Rights," *Hofstra Law Review* 9 (Winter 1981):433-47; Henry Shue, "In the
American Tradition, Rights Remain Unalienable," *The Center Magazine* 17 (January-
February 1984):6-17.
4.   Walter Laqueur and Barry Rubin, eds., *The Human Rights Reader* (New York:
New American Library, 1979), 106-9, 118-20.
5.   Lauterpacht, *An International Bill of the Rights of Man*, 24.
6.   Organization of American States, *Handbook of Existing Rules Pertaining to Human
Rights in the Inner-American System* (updated to July 1983), General Secretariat, OAS;
OEA/ser. L/V/11.60. doc. 28, rev. 1, 1 September 1980, p. 8.
7.   The Covenant of the League of Nations (with amendments in force, 1 February
1935), published by World Peace Foundation, New York.

8. Lauterpacht, *An International Bill of the Rights of Man*, 6.

9. Laqueur and Rubin, "The Marxist Critique," in *The Human Rights Reader*, 179-92.

10. Egon Schwelb, *Human Rights and the International Community: The Roots and Growth of the Universal Declaration of Human Rights* (Chicago: Quadrangle Books, 1964); *Human Rights Documents, Compilation* (Washington, D.C.: U.S. House of Representatives, Committee on Foreign Afairs, Subcommittee on Human Rights and International Organizations, 1983); Jean-Bernard Marie, "International Instruments Relating to Human Rights: Classification and Chart Showing Ratifications as of January 1, 1984," *Human Rights Journal* 4 (July 1983):503-28; L. Sohn and T. Buergenthal, *International Protection of Human Rights*, 2 vols. (Indianapolis: Bobbs-Merrill, 1973); H. Hannum, *Guide to International Human Rights Practice* (Philadelphia: University of Pennsylvania Press, 1984); and Sidorsky, *Essay on Human Rights*. See also: Moses Moskowitz, *The Political and Dynamics of Human Rights* (Dobbs Ferry, N.Y.: Oceana Publications, 1968); idem, *The Roots and Decisions of United Nations Actions* (Netherlands: Sijthoff and Noordoff, 1980); Julian R. Friedman, "Human Rights Internationalism: A Tentative Critique" in *International Human Rights: Contemporary Issues*, ed. J. L. Nelson and V. M. Green (Standfordville, N.Y.: Human Rights Publishing Group, 1980), 29-42; Rosemary Righter, "The Political Challenge to the Western Press: Another New Order?" *The World Today* 35 (April 1979): 167-75; H. Tolley, Jr., "Decision Making at the United Nations Commission on Human Rights, 1972-1979," *Human Rights Quarterly* 5 (Winter 1983):27-57; and Sidney Liskofsky, "Coping with the Question of the Violation of Human Rights and Fundamental Freedoms: Highlights of the 31st Session of the United Nations Commission on Human Rights, Geneva, February 3-March 7, 1975," *Revue des Droits de l'Homme* 8 (1975):883-914.

11. Krishnaswami, "Study of Discrimination," 1-12. See also Salo W. Baron, *A Social and Religious History of the Jews*, 24 vols. to date, 2d ed. (New York: Columbia University Press, 1952-).

12. Robert Gordis, "Judaism and Religious Liberty," in *Religious Liberty in the Crossfire of Creeds*, ed. Franklin H. Littell (Philadelphia: Ecumenical Press, 1978), 29.

13. Luther was not thinking of "a society of religious pluralism, within which many varieties of belief, and even of disbelief, would live side by side in comparative harmony"; Jaroslav Pelikan, "The Enduring Relevance of Martin Luther—500 Years After His Birth," *The New York Times Magazine*, 18 September 1983, 103.

14. John A. Garraty and Peter Gay, eds., *The Columbia History of the World* (New York: Harper and Row, 1972), 536-38, 590.

15. Raphael Mahler, *Jewish Emancipation: A Selection of Documents*, Pamphlet Series on Jews and the Post-War World, No. 1 (1942), published by the Research Institute on Peace and Post-War Problems of the American Jewish Committee, New York City, 25.

16. Ibid.

17. Ibid., 37.

18. Krishnaswami, "Study of Discrimination," 3.

19. Robert T. Handy, "The American Tradition of Religious Freedom: A Historical Analysis," *Journal of Public Law* 13 (1964):247-66; Littell, "Foundations and Traditions of Religious Liberty," in *Religious Liberty in the Crossfire of Creeds*, 4-7.

20. Mahler, *Jewish Emancipation*, 9.

21. Ibid., 11-13.

22. Ibid., 13-14.

23. Laqueur and Rubin, "The Age of Democratic Revolutions," 115.

24. Krishnaswami, "Study of Discrimination," 6. See also European Parliament, "Political Affairs Committee Report on Human Rights in the Soviet Union," 16 May 1983. This report is published in *Human Rights Journal* 4 (July 1983):110-23.

25. Krishnaswami, "Study of Discrimination," 7.

26. Ibid., 11.

27. Ibid.

480 RELIGION AND THE STATE

28. Mahler, *Jewish Emancipation*, 37-38.
29. Ibid., 61; Laqueur, "The Issue of Human Rights," in *Essay on Human Rights*, 140; *Encyclopedia Judaica*, 4:655-56.
30. Covenant of the League of Nations, see note 7.
31. Sohn and Buergenthal, *International Protection of Human Rights*, 213-335; Jacob Robinson et al., *Were the Minorities Treaties a Failure?* (New York: American Jewish Congress, Institute of Jewish Affairs [Antin Press], 1943).
32. See text of "Minorities Treaty with Poland," in Robinson, *Were the Minorities Treaties a Failure?* 313-17; Mahler, *Jewish Emancipation*, 67-70; Laqueur and Rubin, "The Marxist Critique," 151-56.
33. Karl Josef Partsch, "Freedom of Conscience and Expression, and Political Freedom," in *The International Bill of Rights: The Covenant on Civil and Political Rights*, ed. L. Henkin (New York: Columbia University Press, 1981), 213-14.
34. Alexandre Kiss, "Possible Limitations on Rights," in *The International Bill of Rights*, 290-310.
35. Partsch, "Freedom of Conscience and Expression," 212, 214.
36. T. Buergenthal and R. Norris, *Human Rights—The Inter-American System* (Dobbs Ferry, N.Y.: Oceana Publications, 1982); Organization of American States, *Annual Report of Inter-American Commission on Human Rights, 1982-1983*; OEA/Ser. L/V/11.61, Doc. 22 rev. 1, 27 September 1983; OAS *Handbook*.
37. *What Is the Council of Europe Doing to Protect Human Rights?* (Strasbourg: Council of Europe, 1977), 15-28; *Report of Council of Europe to the International Conference of Human Rights, 1968* (Strasbourg, 1967). Text of First Protocol, 102-4; discussion of Article 9, 25-26. See also Sir Humphrey Waldock, "The Effectiveness of the System Set Up by the European Convention on Human Rights," *Human Rights Journal* 1 (1980):1-12; Jochen A. F. Bielefeld, "The European and American Convention on Human Rights—A Comparison," ibid., 44-65.
38. *Helsinki Final Act, 1975*. U.S. Department of State Bulletin, 1 September 1975, Department of State Bureau of Public Affairs; T. Buergenthal, ed., *Human Rights International Law and the Helsinki Accord* (Montclair, N.J.: Universe Books, 1977), 203. For the text of the Final Act including the Declaration on Principles Guiding Relations Between Participating States, see Appendix, 161-99. See also Sidney Liskofsky, "The Belgrade Conference," *American Jewish Year Book, 1979* (New York and Philadelphia: The American Jewish Committee and the Jewish Publication Society of America, 1978), 152-59. For the position of Soviet Jewry, 1977-80, see *Report on Implementation of the Helsinki Final Act Since the Belgrade Follow-up Conference*, prepared on behalf of the Ongoing Presidium and Steering Committee of the World Conference on Soviet Jewry in Cooperation with the Jewish Communities Concerned, 1980 ("The State of the Jewish Religion in the U.S.S.R.," 15-21). See *Concluding Document* of the 1983 Madrid Conference; and the *Special Edition* of the CSCE Digest (Commission on Security and Cooperation in Europe), United States Congress, Washington, D.C., 12 October 1983. At this meeting, the U.S. and other Western delegates raised questions concerning the repression of advocates of religious, cultural, and linguistic freedom. Many of them were members of monitoring groups in the U.S.S.R. and other Eastern-bloc countries, including Andrei Sakharov. The clause in the Declaration on Principles, "within the constitutional framework," is a variant of an "escape" clause the Soviet Union routinely seeks for most of its human rights undertakings, to make sure its domestic law retains priority over its international commitments. The promise to "favorably consider applications by religious communities . . . to be granted the status provided for in their respective countries . . . ," was aimed at the Soviet Union. Its practical significance is unclear. On the one hand, such status may enable groups to claim certain entitlements they were previously denied; on the other hand, governmental authorities may also use this status as an instrument of control. Apparently, the proponents believed the benefits would outweigh the disadvantages.
39. Sidney Liskofsky, *Eliminating Intolerance and Discrimination Based on Religion or Belief: The UN Role, Reports on the Foreign Scene* (New York: American Jewish Com-

mittee, 1968), gives an account of early UN efforts in this field, including text of draft convention in the version formulated by the Commission on Human Rights as of 1967. See also "Elimination of All Forms of Religious Intolerance," *Note by Secretary-General* prepared in accordance with Sub-Commission Res. 1982/28, E/CN .4/Sub. 2/1982/29, 17 May 1983; Homer Jack, "The UN Declaration for Religious Freedom: The Results of Two Decades of Drafting" and "How the UN Religious Declaration Was Unanimously Adopted" both mimeographed (New York: World Conference on Religion and Peace, 1981 and 1982); Nathan Lerner, "Toward a Draft Declaration Against Religious Intolerance and Discrimination," *Israel Yearbook on Human Rights* 11 (1981):82-105; Roger S. Clark, "The United Nations and Religious Freedom," *New York University Journal of International Law and Politics* 11 (1979):197; and James E. Wood, Jr., "The Proposed United Nations Declaration on Religious Liberty," *Journal of Church and State* 23 (Autumn 1981):413-22. For the complete UN document, see "Text of the United Nations Declaration on the Elimination of All Forms of Intolerance and of Discrimination Based on Religion or Belief," *Journal of Church and State* 24 (Winter 1982):201-4.

40.   GA Res. 1781, 17 GAOR, Supp. 17, UN Doc. A/4217 (1962).

41.   Commission on Human Rights (CHR), *Report on 23rd Session*, ESCOR, Supp. 6, E/4322; E/CN.4/940, 13-40. Liskofsky, *Eliminating Intolerance and Discrimination.*

42.   GA Res. 2295, Press Release GA/3570 (GA Round-up), 15 December 1967, Part V, 13.

43.   Daniel P. Moynihan, "The Significance of the Zionism-as-Racism Resolution for International Human Rights," in *Essays on Human Rights*, 37-45; S. Liskofsky, "UN Resolution on Zionism," *American Jewish Year Book, 1977*, 97-125.

44.   CHR, *Report on 35th Session*, 1979 ESCOR, Supp. 6, E/1979/36; E/CN.4/1347, 69-76.

45.   See UNESCO, *Meeting of Experts on the Place of Human Rights in Cultural and Religious Traditions*, Bangkok (Thailand), 3-7 December 1979; Final Report, SS-79/Conf. 607/10, Paris, 6 February 1980.

46.   CHR, *Report on 37th Session*, 1981 ESCOR, Supp. 6 E/1981/25; E/CN.4/1475.

47.   GA Res. 55, 36 GAOR, Supp. 48, A/36/48 (1981), Press Release GA/6546, 332-35.

48.   CHR, *Report on 32nd Session*, 1976 ESCOR, Supp. 3, E/5 768, E/CN.4/1213, 37-41; CHR, *Report on 33rd Session*, 1977 ESCOR, Supp. 6, E/5927, E/CN.4/1256, 43-48.

49.   CHR, *Report on 34th Session*, 1978 ESCOR, Supp. 4, E/1978/34, E/CN.4/1292, 56-65.

50.   CHR, *Report on 34th Session*, ibid., CHR, *Report on 35th Session*, 1979 ESCOR, Supp. 6, E/1979/36, E/CN.4/1347, 69-76.

51.   Ibid.

52.   CHR, *Report on 36th Session*, 1980 ESCOR, Supp. 3, E/1980/13; E/CN.4/1408, 108-18.

53.   Ibid.

54.   Circumstances during World War II and the Holocaust created the sensitive postwar issue of Jewish orphans who had been hidden by non-Jews and raised as Christians. At the time that the Universal Declaration and Covenants were being drafted, Jewish nongovernmental organizations recommended including a provision to deal with their cases. One such proposal was: "Children whose parents were killed in a war or other catastrophe shall be brought up in the religion of their parents," implying unqualified recognition of the presumption that the murdered parents would have wanted their children brought up as Jews. These nongovernmental organizations objected to weaker terms like giving priority to the "objectively ascertained wishes of the child," or providing that the parents' wishes be merely "taken into account," or making the guiding principle "the best interests of the child," which in practice would most likely be decided by a state agency. Now, with the passage of time, however, the issue of orphan children of the Holocaust is moot. Isaac Lewin, *Toward International Guarantees for Religious Liberty: Addresses Before the United Na-*

tions (New York: Shengold Publishers, 1981), Chaps. 7 and 19.

55. *Human Rights: A Compilation of International Instruments*, ST/HR/1 Rev. 1, UN, N.Y. 1978: UNESCO Convention Against Discrimination in Education (1960), 35; Covenant on Economic and Social Rights (1966), 6.

56. CHR, *Report on 37th Session*, 1981 ESCOR, Supp. 5, E/1981/25, E/CN.4/1475, 138-54.

57. Committee on Foreign Affairs and its Subcommittee on Human Rights and International Organizations, House of Representatives, 97th Cong., 2nd Session, *Hearings: Religious Persecution as a Violation of Human Rights*, prepared statement of Thomas A. Johnson, Office of the Legal Adviser, Department of State, 844.

58. See the World Council of Churches' "Declaration on Religious Liberty," adopted in Amsterdam in 1948. It provided that "every person has the right, in addition to expressing his religious beliefs in worship, teaching and practice," to proclaim "the implications of his beliefs for relationships in a social or political community." The WCC's 1975 "Statement on Human Rights and Religious Liberty" affirms, "Religious freedom should also include the right and duty of religious bodies to criticize the ruling powers when necessary, on the basis of their religious convictions." The "Declaration on Religious Freedom," adopted by Vatican Council II in 1965, states: "It comes within the meaning of religious freedom that religious bodies should not be prohibited from freely undertaking to show the special value of their doctrine in what concerns the organization of society and the inspiration of the whole of human activity." Walter M. Abbott, *The Documents of Vatican II* (New York: Guild Press, 1966), 675-87.

59. For example, *Pravda*, the Slovak Communist newspaper, accused Pope John Paul II of using religion as a political tool for subverting the Communist governments of the Soviet bloc, *New York Times*, 7 October 1983. The Khomeini regime has claimed that its anti-Bahai measures were directed at a political group masquerading as a religion.

60. CHR, *Report on 37th Session*.

61. Ibid.

62. A/36/864, *Report of the Third Committee*, 19 November 1981, Elimination of All Forms of Religious Intolerance; Summary Records, Third Committee, 27-30 October 1981.

63. Edward Kannyo, *Black Africa and the UN Declaration on the Elimination of Religious Intolerance and Discrimination* (New York: The American Jewish Committee, 1982), a brochure prepared for the Jacob Blaustein Institute for the Advancement of Human Rights.

64. Leo Pfeffer, *God, Caesar and the Constitution: The Court as Referee of Church-State Confrontation* (Boston: Beacon Press, 1975); Milton R. Konvitz, *Religious Liberty and Conscience: A Constitutional Inquiry* (New York: Viking Press, 1968).

65. Ibid. See also M. R. Konvitz, "Church and State: How Separate?" *Midstream* (March 1984):32-37.

66. GA Res. 187, 37 GAOR, Supp. 51; A/37/51 (1982), Press Release GA/6787 (4 January 1983), 402.

67. CHR, *Report on 39th Session*, 1979 ESCOR, Supp. 3, E/1983/13; E/CN .4/1983/60, 101-2; Res. 40, 173. The seminar was scheduled for December 1984.

68. E/CN.4/Sub. 2/1984/3; E/CN.4/Sub. 2/1983/43, 46-47, 98-99. As of the time of writing, the study was in its initial stages.

69. Committee on Foreign Affairs and its Subcommittee on Human Rights and International Organizations, House of Representatives, 97th Cong., 2nd Session, *Hearings: Religious Persecution as a Violation of Human Rights*, 10 February, 23 March, 25 May, 27 and 29 July, 5 and 10 August, 23 September, and 1 and 14 December 1982. See the following presentations: Rev. J. Bryan Hehir, director, Office of International Justice and Peace, U.S. Catholic Conference, 1 December 1982, 698-722; Jerome J. Shestack, former U.S. Ambassador to UN Commission of Human Rights, 14 December 1982, 795-823; T. Johnson, U.S. Mission to the UN, 14 December 1983, 824-64; and S. Liskofsky, Director, Division of International Organizations,

American Jewish Committee, 14 December 1982, 684-74.
70.   Partsch, "Freedom of Conscience and Expression," 214.
71.   *New York Times*, 20 October 1981.

PART 9

LEO PFEFFER

An Autobiographical Sketch

LEO PFEFFER

In 1911 (I was then two years old), my father, an Orthodox
rabbi, left my birthplace, a small ghetto town in Austria-
Hungary, to explore the possibilities of obtaining a pulpit in
the United States. Within six months he was successful, and
the family, consisting of three daughters and two sons (I was
the youngest), emigrated to America to settle in the lower east
side of New York City.

The apartment in which we lived was necessarily close to
the synagogue that my father served as rabbi. It was, however,
about a mile from the closest yeshivah, known officially as the
Rabbi Jacob Joseph Elementary School. For that reason, I
was sent to Public School 15, located but two short streets
from our apartment. There are only two things relating to my
attendance at the school that I remember. The first was the
daily Bible reading in the assembly. The reading was done by
the school's principal, Miss Knox—as far as the pupils knew
that was her full name. She was gray-haired and probably a
Protestant. The reading was limited to the book of Psalms,
which I assume was from the King James version. I assume,
too, that the limitation was based upon the reality that almost
all the pupils in the school were Jewish.

The second experience was also related to my future career.
In the middle of my 4A term, the first semester of the fourth
year, the public school educational authorities received and
were considering a proposal to introduce released-time religious instruction into the schools. This was long before the
Supreme Court's decision in *McCollum* v. *Board of Education*,[1]
and I think that the proposed program would have been based
upon in-school instruction. Whatever the case might be, in
the end the proposal was not adopted. My parents, however,
did not wait for that. I was immediately withdrawn from Public School 15 and enrolled in the yeshivah.

Upon graduation from elementary school, I was enrolled in
a yeshivah for secondary school students, known as the Rabbi
Isaac Elchonon Talmudical Academy, which later expanded
into the arena of higher education under the name Yeshivah
University. My collegiate education was received at the City

College of New York, and my law degree was granted by
New York University in 1933. I was admitted to the bar in
December of that year. In 1937, I married Freda Plotkin,
whom I met when we were both members of Young Israel
Synagogue of Manhattan. It was because of her, by sheer
chance as a coconspirator, that I later entered the field of
church-state relations.

In 1944, our first child, Alan, was born. Our other child,
Susan, was born three years later. Freda was then employed as
a secretary in the Women's Division of the American Jewish
Congress, and, after an effort of several months to continue
her career while mothering a child, she gave up and resigned
from her position. She informed me that the organization was
expanding its committee on law and legislation and had open-
ings for lawyers. I applied for a position, was accepted as a
staff member of the Commission on Law and Social Action
(CLSA), and started work on 1 October 1945.

The American Jewish Congress had started as a loose committee of Jewish organizational representatives who assembled
in Philadelphia in December 1918 for the purpose of commis-
sioning a joint delegation to the Peace Conference in Ver-
sailles. Its function was to present Jewish interests and concerns to the Conference and it was to dissolve after submitting
its report at the second and last session in Philadelphia in
1920. At the conclusion of the Conference, however, a number
of the delegates decided to continue the organization as a
permanent association committed to the protection of Jewish
rights. In the 1930s, it became a leading force in the anti-Nazi
movement and organized a boycott against German goods and
services.

For almost all of the period from its formation until his
death in 1949, Rabbi Stephen S. Wise was the president of
the American Jewish Congress. A cofounder of both the
National Association for the Advancement of Colored People
and the American Civil Liberties Union, he committed his
life to the protection of civil liberties and the achievement of
social justice for the economically disadvantaged. In 1945, the
American Jewish Congress converted its legal committee into
a Commission on Law and Social Action, under the joint
leadership of Will Maslow and Alexander H. Pekelis, designated respectively as director and chief consultant.

My first assignment as a staff member of the Commission
on Law and Social Action was to prepare a memorandum on

the pros and cons of released time for religious instruction. The American Jewish Congress was considering whether to take a position on the subject and, if so, what position to take. Why I was selected for the assignment, I do not know. It may be that I was the only member of the staff who had a religious education. It may be that in my application for employment I noted that I had written some articles that were published in religious-oriented Jewish periodicals. Or it may have been purely a matter of chance. If the last option was the fact, then chance was very good to me, for the memorandum I prepared setting forth both sides of the controversy indicated quite clearly that I opposed the released-time program primarily, though not exclusively, on constitutional grounds. This is hardly surprising in view of my childhood experience with the released-time proposal. In any event, the memorandum resulted in my being assigned responsibility for litigation involving religious freedom and church-state issues.

The issue reached the United States Supreme Court in the 1948 case of *McCollum* v. *Board of Education* and again, four years later, in *Zorach* v. *Clauson*.[2] Before considering these cases, perhaps it is appropriate for me to relate my experiences with Sunday Closing Laws, since my involvement in this area, as president of the Young Israel of Manhattan, antedated my joining the Commission's staff. New York's statute, in the 1940s, made no exception for persons whose religious conviction forbade engaging in commercial activities on the seventh day of the week. This put Orthodox Jews who owned retail stores in a difficult economic dilemma. If they kept their stores open for business on Sunday, they were summoned to court and fined. If they closed their stores on both Saturdays and Sundays, they were at a serious economic disadvantage in competing with storekeepers who closed only Sundays.

Efforts to amend the law so as to permit stores to be open for business on Sundays if their owners observed another day as the religious day of rest were consistently unsuccessful, even though from time to time the law was amended to expand nonreligious exceptions. Thus, for example, newspapers could be sold on Sundays, but not books or periodicals; sales of bread, milk, and eggs were permissible all day, but butter and cheese could not be sold in grocery stores after 10 A.M., although they could be obtained in delicatessen stores between the hours of 4:00-7:30 P.M. Sale of beer for on-premises consumption was unlawful, but it could be purchased for off-premises consumption before 3 A.M. and after 1 P.M. Fruit could be obtained all day, but vegetables only up to 10 A.M.

These are only some of the crazy-quilt patterns of inclusions and exemptions that accumulated over the years. During my research in preparation for a suit challenging the constitutionality of the law, I learned, among other things, that if a substantial contribution was made to both political parties, observers of the Jewish Sabbath "might" obtain an exemption. I say "might" because exemption would be opposed, openly by the Lord's Day Alliance (which did not matter since its political power was negligible) and not so openly by merchants' associations that could make considerably larger contributions to political party treasuries. I learned also that if you made appropriate contributions (in bills, no checks) to local party leaders and/or police lieutenants or plainclothesmen, the policemen on the beat or the plainclothesmen would suffer from defective vision and not notice that your store was open, while your noncontributing neighbor would regularly receive a summons for Sunday law violations.

This was the situation when I was authorized by the American Jewish Congress officers to seek judicial review on the issue of unconstitutionality. Two owners of small kosher butcher stores, Sam Friedman and Sam Praska, each of whom received a summons, retained me (after being assured that there would be no costs to them) to defend them literally "up to the Supreme Court."

The defendants were found guilty, and each was sentenced to pay a fine of $10 or serve a sentence of two days in the city prison. The fines were promptly deposited and appeals were taken to New York's higher courts, which, without opinion and without dissent, affirmed the convictions. I then sought an appeal to the Supreme Court, setting forth four grounds for unconstitutionality: (1) the New York law violated the First Amendment's prohibition of laws respecting an establishment of religion; (2) on its face, the crazy-quilt pattern of inclusion and exclusion violated the Fourteenth Amendment's guarantee of the equal protection of the law; (3) the erratic enforcement of the statute violated the same provision; and (4) as enforced against Sabbatarians, the statute infringed upon the Free Exercise Clause of the First Amendment since it imposed a disadvantage on those whose religion forbade engaging in business on Saturdays.

The effort was in vain. In *Friedman* v. *New York*,[3] the Supreme Court dismissed my appeal for want of a substantial federal issue—which means that the complaint of constitutional violation was so lacking in merit that it would be a waste of the Court's time to listen to argument.

Ten years later, in the 1961 decisions on joint appeals in cases arising in Massachusetts, Pennsylvania, and Maryland, known collectively as the Sunday Law Cases, the Court found sufficient merit in exactly the same arguments as to warrant a hearing, and spent two days listening to arguments in open Court. (Simultaneously, I also presented the arguments in a friends-of-the-court brief, also known as an amicus curiae brief, on behalf of the Synagogue Council of America[4] and the National Community Relations Advisory Council.)[5] The net result, however, was the same. Accompanied by lengthy concurring opinions and some dissents, the Court rejected all the arguments on the ground that while Sunday statutes undoubtedly originated as religious laws, they had by now become secular laws aimed at insuring a day of rest and relaxation for all persons, owners of stores as well as their hired help. The Court disposed of the Sabbatarians' argument that a day of rest on Saturday was as salutory as one on Sunday; it ruled that the difficulty of policing laws that had different applications to stores on the basis of the religions of their owners justified applying the same law to all.

Between the time of the Court's decision and today, Sunday Closing Laws have come to an end almost everywhere in the country, not by the bang of a Supreme Court decision, nor even by a whimper from the Lord's Day Alliance or other Christian groups, but by the potency of American capitalism that could not sanction a day in which people were not allowed to spend money. Sunday laws today, where not repealed, have, for all practical purposes, largely become dead letter laws.

Like *Friedman* v. *New York*, *Heisler* v. *Board of Review*[6] was disposed of by the United States Supreme Court in 1954 through its refusal to accept an appeal because my challenge under the Free Exercise Clause was so lacking in merit that it would be a waste of the Court's time to hear the arguments. Mary Jane Heisler was an Orthodox Jew, who was denied unemployment insurance benefits because she would not accept a proffered job that would require her to work on the Sabbath. Unlike *Friedman*, however, the ultimate outcome in respect to claims such as hers was a happier one. In *Sherbert* v. *Verner*,[7] the Court heard the arguments and held that a denial of benefits for refusal by reason of religious conscience was unconstitutional. The appeal that Adell Sherbert asked the Supreme Court to hear was based on the claim that the unemployment insurance board's rejection of her claim deprived her of religious freedom. With this, the Supreme Court (twelve years after *Heisler*), agreed in interpreting and applying the First Amendment to require the state to award her unemployment compensation benefits.

As indicated earlier, my first assignment with the Commission on Law and Social Action was with released-time programs. The principles applied in the *McCollum* (1948) and *Zorach* (1952) cases were formulated by the Supreme Court in *Everson* v. *Board of Education* (1947)[8] a year before *McCollum* was decided. In that case, Arch Everson, a New Jersey taxpayer, brought a suit challenging under the Establishment Clause a law providing state funds to finance bus transportation to parochial (as well as public) schools. When the case reached the Supreme Court, I recommended to Will Maslow that the American Jewish Congress intervene as amicus curiae supporting the challenger. Maslow took the matter up with the organization's officials but informed me that they had decided against it. The reason, he said, was political. Henry Epstein, a prominent Jewish lawyer who had previously been solicitor-general of the State of New York and now held high office in our organization, was the Democratic candidate for the office of associate judge of New York's highest court. I do not know whether Epstein himself asked us to stay out of the appeal or the idea came from some other source, but the reason given was that our intervention would alienate Catholic voters and this might cause him to lose the election.

Whatever the case, we did not intervene, but Epstein lost the election anyway. At that time, Epstein was the American Jewish Congress representative in the National Community Relations Advisory Council and was serving as its chairman. It was, therefore, natural that when, after the election, the National Community Relations Advisory Council decided to file a brief jointly with the Synagogue Council in the *McCollum* appeal, he should be designated as the attorney representing the two organizations and I should write the brief.

At first, the American Jewish Committee and the Anti-Defamation League vigorously opposed intervention in the

McCollum case, because they felt it would aggravate anti-Semitism and provide ammunition for those who considered all or most Jews to be atheists, particularly in view of the fact that the plaintiff in the case, Vashti McCollum, was generally considered to be an avowed atheist. With almost no backing for this position, either in the National Community Relations Advisory Council or the Synagogue Council, the American Jewish Committee and the Anti-Defamation League had no choice but either to go along with or withdraw from the National Community Relations Advisory Council. Both reluctantly elected the former, and agreed, with equal reluctance, that Epstein should be attorney of record.

To ease the unhappiness of the American Jewish Committee and the Anti-Defamation League, it was decided (over my urging to the contrary on the ground that we had nothing for which to apologize) that I draft a few paragraphs disassociating ourselves from Mrs. McCollum and her ilk and expressing regret that she chose this case as a medium for the dissemination of her atheistic beliefs. The brief asserted, however, that we had concluded that to abstain from filing a brief would constitute an inexcusable dereliction in our duty to American Jewry.

In respect to one delicate but, to me, critical aspect of our brief, I did prevail. The trial record disclosed that the religious teaching in the released-time instruction given to the Protestant pupils (and there is no reason to believe that the situation was different in the Catholic classes) dealt with the crucifixion of Jesus and Jewish responsibility for it. In my book, *Church, State, and Freedom*,[9] published five years later, I was able to expand on this point and quote from the trial testimony. In the brief, however, over initial objection by the American Jewish Committee and the Anti-Defamation League representatives, I was permitted to include in the "Interest of the Amici" portion of the brief reference to the stigmatizing effect of teaching Jewish participation in the crucifixion, particularly where, as the record showed, it was done in the presence of the regular public school teacher.

In my brief, I argued that Illinois, through its local school board, violated the First Amendment in aiding religion, preferring some religions over others, influencing or compelling children to attend religious instruction, rendering financial aid to religious instruction by allowing public school classrooms to be used for that purpose, and by implicitly, if not expressly, participating in the instruction.

There is generally no way in which one can judge whether a brief amicus affects the Court's decision in any particular instance. An exception may be *Epperson* v. *Arkansas* (1968).[10] There the Supreme Court ruled violative of the Establishment Clause a statute forbidding teachers in tax-supported schools to teach any theory that contradicted Genesis and to teach instead that man descended from a lower order of animals. The establishment argument was not urged or even suggested by counsel for Susan Epperson but appeared only in an amicus brief that I had written for joint submission by the American Jewish Congress and the American Civil Liberties Union. In basing its decision on the Establishment Clause, the Court blithely ignored its oft-repeated statement that it would not consider any contention not previously presented in the lower courts.

In the *McCollum* decision, invalidating the released-time program as violative of the establishment provision, Justice Felix Frankfurter's concurring opinion did point out in a footnote that "the divergent views expressed in the briefs submitted here in behalf of religious organizations, as *amicus curiae* in themselves suggest that the movement has been a divisive and not an irenic influence in the Community." Beyond this, however, none of the opinions in the case referred to our brief even indirectly. That, however, did not prevent the Jewish organizations from claiming substantial credit for the outcome. More important to the American Jewish Congress and, of course, to me personally was that after *McCollum* I became de facto counsel for the National Community Relations Advisory Council and the Synagogue Council in all briefs submitted to the courts in the arena of church-state relations and religious freedom.

One year after the *McCollum* decision, the American Jewish Congress decided to present a brief amicus to the Supreme Court in the case of *Stainback* v. *Mo Hock Ke Lok Po*.[11] (Offhand, the Court's ultimate decision in this case had no patent significance in the area of civil rights or religious freedom, inasmuch as it avoided passing upon the plaintiff's complaint on the purely technical ground that the case should have been decided by a one-judge rather than three-judge tribunal.) The suit challenged the constitutionality of a Hawaiian statute, enacted in 1943, forbidding school teaching of any foreign language to pupils before they passed the fourth grade in elementary school. By its terms it encompassed not only the Japanese language, which, in the hysteria following the attack on Pearl Harbor, was its obvious target, but all foreign languages—the plaintiff in the case was a Chinese rather than a Japanese school—including Hebrew.

The statute reflected two significant tendencies in American history. The first was a general aversion to the culture, particularly as reflected in language, of a wartime enemy. During World War I, sauerkraut became liberty cabbage and frankfurters became hot dogs, and laws were enacted (and held unconstitutional in *Meyer* v. *Nebraska* [1925])[12] forbidding the teaching of foreign (meaning German) languages in private and parochial schools. The second was a specific aversion to and fear of what William Randolph Hearst had termed the "Yellow Peril" that had manifested itself in restrictive immigration laws and denial of naturalization to persons of Chinese and Japanese descent.

When *Stainback* v. *Mo Hock Ke Lok Po* reached the Supreme Court, I recommended that we file a brief amicus curiae in support of the parents. Nominally, the challenged law applied to all foreign language schools, including Jewish religious schools that taught the Hebrew language, although in the period of anti-Semitism at its worst in Nazi Germany, it may be assumed that this was the last thing the Hawaiian legislature intended. Nor was there any likelihood that it would be enforced against Jewish schools. Nevertheless, the act could be applied against these schools and there was no guarantee that in order to meet charges of prejudice against the "Yellow" race this might not occur. In recommending our intervention, I pointed out that as close by to us as Mt. Kisco, New York, and as recently as November 1948, an application of a former famous European Talmudic college to conduct a vocational training school in connection with its seminary was granted on condition that English become the language of secular instruction.

Moreover, the Hawaiian law could not be reconciled with the concept of cultural pluralism, to which we were committed, and, accordingly, when our entry into the case was approved, the brief I drafted relied heavily upon the premise that the uniqueness and promise of American culture lay in its diversity. For this, I referred not only to court decisions and legal authorities, the usual procedure in court briefs, but also to the writings of historians, social scientists, and philosophers such as Horace Kallen, himself an active member of the American Jewish Congress, and Robert MacIver, who was later to recommend to the National Community Relations Advisory Council that primary responsibility for resort to law in protecting Jewish communal interests be allocated to the Commission on Law and Social Action. This was a recommendation that led to the temporary withdrawal of the American Jewish Committee and the Anti-Defamation League from the National Community Relations Advisory Council. I also resorted to the field of literature, citing Alphonse Daudet's classical story, "The Last Lesson," based upon Alsatian resistance to German attempts to outlaw the French language after the 1870 Alsatian defeat.

Resort to nonjudicial sources in a brief to the Supreme Court was neither original nor novel; it could be traced back at least to the "Brandeis brief" submitted in the case of *Muller* v. *Oregon* (1908),[13] which contained two pages of legal argument and over a hundred pages of economic and sociological material showing that long factory working hours were dangerous to women's health, safety, and morals. Nor was the analogue between Hawaii's foreign language schools and the Jewish schools original with me. An article by Milton Konvitz (a contibutor to the present volume) stated: "Before Pearl Harbor there were in Hawaii large schools teaching the Chinese and Japanese languages, in the afternoon, after the regular schools had adjourned—a pattern followed in the continental United States by the Jewish schools known as Talmud Torahs."[14]

What I think was original in respect to my brief was the resort to Jewish law from the Torah, Talmudic, and post-Talmudic authorities (such as Moses Maimonides, Moses of Coucy, and writings such as the *Shulchan Aruch, Jire Deah*, compiled by Joseph Coro and Moses Issules) to support the argument that the challenged statute impaired the religious freedom of Jews. The authorities cited dictated that every child be taught the Bible and prayers in the Hebrew tongue, and that Jewish communities conduct elementary schools for that purpose.

An illustration of how I later resorted to Talmudic authorities is a brief amicus curiae that I submitted in behalf of the Synagogue Council and the American Jewish Congress in the 1972 case of *Furman* v. *Georgia*.[15] Urging in the brief that the death penalty constituted an affront on the dignity of man, did not comport with civilized standards, and could not be sustained under the Eighth Amendment's ban on cruel and unusual punishment, I quoted from the Talmud that a Sanhedrin (court of law) that executes a criminal once in seven years is called a "court of destroyers." Rabbi Eliezer ben Azariah stated that this is so even if it executes one every seventy years. Rabbi Tarphon and Rabbi Akiba stated that if they had been members of the Sanhedrin, no one would ever have been executed.

One rabbi, Simeon ben Gamliel, expressed a contrary view reflecting the most common justification for capital punishment, namely, its deterrent effect. If the views of Rabbi Tarphon and Rabbi Akiba were to prevail, he said, "they would increase murders in Israel." Maimonides and other later commentaries noted, however, that Rabbi Simeon's was a minority view and that the others expressed the normative opinions of the Talmudic Rabbis.

Although within the American Jewish Congress I was the staff's specialist in the First Amendment's religion clauses and, thus, the lawyer assigned responsibility for the *McCollum* and *Stainback* briefs and prosecution of the Sabbath observers case, the then importance—or, more accurately, unimportance—of that area of constitutional law in the organization's scheme is manifest in a law review student-prepared article that appeared in 1949 in the *Yale Law Journal*.[16] The article, entitled "Private Attorneys-General: Group Action in the Fight for Civil Liberties," was an analysis of the American Jewish Congress, the National Association for the Advancement of Colored People, and the American Civil Liberties Union. In the first footnote of the article, the author expressed his appreciation to the staff members of these three organizations for their cooperation in providing the necessary information. The American Jewish Congress lawyers named were Will Maslow, the Commission on Law and Social Action director, and Joseph Robison, a member of the Commission's staff. In the article itself, I was mentioned only as coauthor of a survey entitled "The 'Distinctive Name' Method of Determining Jewish Enrollment in Medical Schools." There was a footnote mention of the brief in *McCollum*, but nothing was said about the subject of the case, and no mention at all was made of religious freedom or church-state separation in the article. In view of the fact that the First Amendment's religion clauses were later to become by far the most important area of concern of the Commission on Law and Social Action, one is reminded of the Psalmist assertion that "the stone which the builders refused is become the head stone of the corner."[17]

Nevertheless, my reputation as somewhat of an authority in church-state matters was beginning to be recognized, first among Jewish organizations, and later, beyond that. In 1948, the *Lawyers Guild Review* carried an article by me, entitled "Religion, Education, and the Constitution," and later that same year, *The Standard*, a publication of the American Ethical Union, published an article by me, entitled "The Fight Against Released Time."[18] More significant than either of these was the paper I read the following year at a conference on religion in state universities, sponsored by the University of Minnesota in Minneapolis.

The significance of that appearance lay not in what happened, but in what did not happen. The conference and my address were well publicized and there were no untoward reactions. Prior thereto, it was not uncommon for officers of synagogues at which I agreed to speak to keep my appearance a secret from all but members of the congregation. I was generally picked up at the airport or railroad station, driven to the synagogue where I delivered my lecture, and driven back to the station for my return to New York. There was great fear that my opposition to religion in the public schools or appropriation of tax-raised funds to support parochial schools would be interpreted as being anti-Christian or anti-Catholic, with unhappy consequences such as economic boycotts of the synagogue's congregants or even, perhaps, violence.

Remnants of that fear were manifested when the case of *Zorach v. Clauson* was instituted a few months after the *McCollum* decision was handed down. At the urging of the American Jewish Congress, the Jewish organizations in the National Community Relations Advisory Council agreed to sponsor a suit challenging New York state's system of released time for religious instruction given, not in the public schools, but in nearby churches or parochial schools. The American Jewish Committee, with obvious reluctance, agreed to go along with this provided that the lead attorney and the lead plaintiff (those whose names were listed first) be non-Jews. It was agreed that the former should be Kenneth Greenawalt and the latter, Tessim Zorach, a well-known sculptor, both non-Jews with, however, names that to many would sound Jewish. Zorach in biblical Hebrew means shone (as e.g., in Deut. 33:2).

Greenwald is a common Jewish surname; the editor of my father's posthumous book was Rabbi Ykutial Judah Greenwald. Greenawalt, a partner in the Wall Street firm of Davies, Auerbach, and Cornell, had written the American Civil Liberties Union brief amicus in the *McCollum* case, and was willing to accept our invitation, provided that I agreed to prepare all the legal papers and draft the briefs, since his obligations to his firm and his clients made it impossible for him to assume any part of that task. When the case reached the Supreme Court, Greenawalt suggested that I share the argument with him, but the idea was quickly vetoed by the American Jewish Committee and Anti-Defamation League attorneys on the strategy committee.

Our complaint and our briefs in *Zorach* stated expressly that although the plaintiffs' children did not participate in the released-time program, all regularly attended Protestant Episcopal or Jewish schools for religious instruction at times other than the hours in which public schools were in session—an allegation legally unnecessary but insisted upon by the strategy committee to distinguish the plaintiffs from the atheistic Vashti McCollum. This homage paid to religiosity was echoed in Justice William O. Douglas's opinion for the majority of the Court distinguishing the *Zorach* from the *McCollum* decision and upholding the New York practice of released time off school grounds. Said Justice Douglas (who was later to be the sole dissenter in *Walz* v. *Tax Commission*,[19] which upheld the constitutionality of property tax exemption for church-owned buildings): "We are a religious people whose institutions presuppose a Supreme Being. . . . When the state encourages religious instruction or cooperates with religious authorities by adjusting the schedule of public events to sectarian needs, it follows the best of our traditions." There is no evidence in the record, Justice Douglas said, to support the plaintiffs' claim that coercion was used to get public school students into religious classrooms, and there was, therefore, no violation of either the Free Exercise or Establishment Clauses of the First Amendment. He did, however, refer in a footnote to the New York court's refusal to grant a trial on that issue because the plaintiff had not properly raised this claim in the manner required by state practice.

My book, *Church, State, and Freedom*, published a year after the *Zorach* decision, set forth in full affidavits by parents, pupils, and teachers relating to the testimony that had been ex-

cluded by the trial court. For example, Esta Gluck, coplaintiff
in the suit, deposed in an affidavit that Miss Jeffries, the
teacher in her child's class, had said to a sick student "that
she did not object to looking at the vomit as much as she
objected to looking at the student's face because he did not
participate in the released time program." A former pupil
swore that the "Jewish students in the class did not participate
in released time and the released students assumed that anyone
remaining in the school during the released time hours was
Jewish, which was not true in my class since I am an Episcopalian." Another former pupil swore that because she did not
participate in the program, her classmates called her by "such
names as 'Christ killer' and 'dirty Jew.'"

    Church, State, and Freedom received a generally, but by no
means unanimous, favorable reception by scholars, judges,
and lawyers. Anson Phelps Stokes, author of the three-volume
Church and State in the United States,[20] welcomed the book as a
valuable contribution to the field of church-state studies. Others went further, some designating it as indispensable to
anyone involved as teacher or practitioner in the areas covered.
Judge (later Chief Judge) Charles S. Desmond of New York's
highest state court, however, writing in the *Harvard Law
Review*, attacked the book as reflecting anti-Catholic bias.[21]
Professor Paul Kauper, in a generally favorable review article
in the *Michigan Law Review*,[22] found fault with my analysis of
the *McCollum* and *Zorach* decisions. My article, entitled "Released Time and Religious Liberty: A Reply," appeared in the
succeeding issue of the *Michigan Law Review*, only to be followed by Professor Kauper's response, entitled "Released
Time and Religious Liberty: A Further Reply."[23] As was to
be expected, when the dialogue was over, neither of us had
persuaded the other.

    Church, State, and Freedom was by no means the first book
to deal with the constitutional aspects of church-state relations. Stokes's work was historical rather than legal or analytical; and the same was true of Sanford Cobb's *Rise of Religious
Liberty in America. Separation of Church and State in the United
States*, by Alvin Johnson and Frank Yost, preceded my book
by five years, and so did William Torpey's *Judicial Doctrines of
Religious Rights in America*.[24] It was, however, the largest work
on the subject, and fairly well established for me a reputation
as a leading authority on the subject. This, as will be indicated shortly, was a mixed blessing, since my interest in con-

stitutional law was not limited to the Establishment and Free Exercise Clauses of the Constitution but extended to the whole field of civil rights and liberties, secured not only by the initial Bill of Rights but also by the Fourteenth Amendment guarantee of equality.

In June of 1957, it became known that the Bureau of the Census was considering and was favorably inclined, for the first time in American history, to include in the 1960 census a question regarding religion or religious affiliation. There was much to favor the idea. It would help church groups in planning and recruitment (the Supreme Court had said in the *Zorach* case that "we are a religious people," and there was, therefore, no reason why information helpful to religion should not be procured by the government for use by religious groups); it would help demographers and social scientists; Canada includes a question on religion in its census with no ill effects; a trial run had been conducted by our government in four Wisconsin counties and, according to the bureau, "very few persons" objected to the inclusion of the question or refused to answer it; and there were always a few people who object to any questions in a census, even those relating to a person's name, age, and place of residence.

Public reaction to the proposal appeared to be unanimously favorable. The first public expression of disapproval, as far as I remember, was set forth in a letter that I drafted and was printed in the *New York Times* and the *Washington Post* under the signature of Israel Goldstein, then president of the American Jewish Congress. Even among our own organization's policy makers, there was some disapproval of my recommendation that we express opposition to the proposal and urge other organizations to do the same. I remember that when I quoted Thomas Jefferson's statement, "I never will, by any word or act, bow to the shame of intolerance, or admit a right of inquiry into the religious opinion of others," a member replied that the census taker would not question people as to their religious opinions or beliefs, but only as to their affiliation, or actions, i.e., whether they were members of or attended religious worship at any church or synagogue.

The letter, and an article under my own name that appeared in *The Christian Century*,[25] made four principal arguments against the proposal: (1) the Supreme Court had expressly and repeatedly ruled that under the First Amendment the government had no power to compel any person to profess a belief or

disbelief in any religion; (2) it was alien to our concepts and
traditions to divide and classify Americans in categories of
religion and nonreligion and subcategories of sect and denomination; (3) the guarantee of church-state separation would be
violated if the instrumentalities of government were used for
church purposes; and (4) inclusion of the question would constitute an unwarranted impingement upon the privacy of
Americans. By that time, my reputation as an absolutist in the
area was well established, and it was, therefore, not surprising
that my article asserted unconstitutionality even if response to
the religion question would be voluntary.

It is, I believe, a fair assumption that the letter and *The
Christian Century* article sparked an expression of opposition
by other Jewish religious associations, the American Civil
Liberties Union, the Seventh-day Adventists, the Baptist Joint
Committee on Public Affairs, and others. It is also fairly certain that these expressons impelled the census bureau to issue
a statement, dated 12 December 1957, that the 1960 census
would not include an inquiry on religion because of its
"recognition of the fact that at this time a considerable number of persons would be reluctant to answer such a question,"
although it had earlier pointed to the Wisconsin inquiry to
support its proposal.

As of the present writing, the situation has not changed.
There was little effort to include a question on religion in
either the 1970 or 1980 census. Whether an effort to revive it
will be made in later census years cannot be predicted. Until
fairly recently, I was confident that, should it be successful,
the Supreme Court would rule unconstitutional any criminal
prosecution of persons who refused to respond. Today, in the
light of its recent church-state decisions, I no longer have that
sense of confidence.

It was to escape the narrow limitation of my concerns to the
church-state arena that I wrote *The Liberties of an American* in
1956,[26] and *This Honorable Court: A History of the Supreme
Court* in 1965.[27] Independent of this, however, two fortuitous
events mandated my involvement in civil liberties beyond the
church-state scene. The first was my promotion, in 1958, to
the directorship of the Commission on Law and Social Action,
replacing Will Maslow, who had been appointed executive
director of the American Jewish Congress. The second was
my appointment, six years later, to professorship and political
science department chairman at the Brooklyn Center of Long

Island University. As the Commission on Law and Social Action director, I had responsibility in respect to its entire program and not merely church-state litigation. As a professor, I was equally obligated to teach political science beyond the range of the First Amendment religion clauses.

At the time of my promotion, the Supreme Court had accepted jurisdiction in the case of *National Association for the Advancement of Colored People* v. *Alabama*.[28] Involved was a lawsuit instituted by the state's attorney-general in a state court to enjoin the Association from conducting any business in the state and from furnishing legal help and financial assistance to persons challenging racial segregation at the University of Alabama and on the buses in the state capital because of its failure to register as a foreign corporation as required by the state's laws.

The National Association for the Avancement of Colored People offered to comply with the registration statute and the court's order to register as a foreign corporation except to the extent that it mandated the listing of members who reside in Alabama. The trial court deemed this insufficient, fined the organization $100,000, and ordered it to cease all further activities in the state. When the NAACP filed its appeal to the Supreme Court, I requested and received authority from the American Jewish Congress to submit a brief amicus curiae in its behalf and that of other civil rights organizations willing to join in it.

The brief was drafted by me and Joseph Robison, then assistant director of the Commission on Law and Social Action. Thirteen other national organizations, including the American Civil Liberties Union, the American Friends Service Committee, the American Veterans Committee, the Board of Home Missions of the Congregational Church, the United Church of Christ, and the Japanese American Citizens League joined in the brief. On completion, copies were sent to the counsel for the National Association for the Advancement of Colored People and the State of Alabama with a request for consent to its submission to the Court. As was expected, the NAACP granted consent, but Alabama refused to do so, thus necessitating a motion to the Supreme Court for permission to file.

In earlier periods, such motions were usually granted, at least when they were made by recognized responsible organizations, and this is the case in the more recent years. In the

mid and late fifties, however, the Court became more stringent and almost uniformly denied leave to file unless the brief
was presented by a federal or state agency. In a substantial
sense, this stringency represented an exercise in futility (which
may explain its abandonment after a short period of experi-
mentation) for at least two reasons. In the first place, with an
agreement for reciprocity, the parties did usually consent to
filing. Secondly, if they did not, the motion for leave to file
had to be accompanied by the brief itself, and it is a fair
assumption that if the justices themselves did not initially read
the tendered briefs, their law assistants did, and, in all likelihood, passed on to the justices briefs they felt would be useful
to them in making their decisions on the merits of the appeals.

In any event, in our case, it was a certainty that the one
part of our brief that had not already been presented to the
Court in the *NAACP* case was read by all the justices. It dealt
with the place of anonymity as an aid to free expression in a
democratic society, and cited such instances as Benjamin Franklin's use of the name "Silence Dogwood," Thomas Paine's
use of the name "Humanus," the use by New York's Governor George Clinton of the name "Cato" in opposing ratification of the Constitution, and, above all, the anonymity resorted
to by protagonists of the Constitution in publishing "The
Federalist" essays. Our motion to file was denied before the
expiration of the NAACP's time to file its reply brief, and
what its counsel did was simply to take this part and, after
devoting three paragraphs to respond to a point raised in the
state's brief, incorporated practically verbatim the anonymity
argument from our rejected brief.

My involvement in civil rights was not limited to the filing
of briefs in the Supreme Court. The early sixties was the
period in which the charismatic Martin Luther King, Jr.
organized the Southern Christian Leadership Conference and
launched a campaign of nonviolent resistance to racial segregation. The effort attracted a large number of college students, particularly from New England and the mid-Atlantic
states, who, during midterm recesses and the summer vacation
period, came South to participate in the campaign. One of the
means used to achieve desegregation in cafeterias and restaurants was for small groups of local blacks and the white college students to enter and seat themselves at tables reserved
for whites rather than eating while standing or sitting in the
section set aside for blacks. The same tactic was used in

cinemas, buses, trains, and even beaches, all of which had separate sections for whites and blacks. The consequence was often violence visited particularly upon the intruders from the North, followed by their arrest for inciting to riot or disturbing the peace. A more civilized approach was to arrest them for alleged minor traffic violations and to hold them for bail in amounts obviously beyond their ability to provide. For example, failure to signal on making a turn, punishable by a fine of $5, resulted in an arrest and a bail set at $5,000. Our most effective means of meeting such actions was to apply to the federal courts for relief by reducing the bail to reasonable amounts, such as $50, which could be met.

All this, however, required lawyers, and these were not easily obtainable in the South in those days. There were few black lawyers (only one in Mississippi), and fewer white lawyers who would risk losing white clients by defending Northern white enemies of the South. There was no lack of lawyers (mostly from the National Association for the Advancement of Colored People and the NAACP Legal Defense and Educational Fund) to handle cases that raised new principles of constitutional law and were headed for ultimate decision by the Supreme Court. What was sorely needed were lawyers to handle traffic violations and prosecutions for disturbing the peace and obstructing traffic, cases not likely to reach the Supreme Court.

It was to fill this need that a group of lawyers, who (with the exception of Robert Drinan, then dean of Boston College Law School) were professionally associated with civil rights organizations, formed the Lawyers Constitutional Defense Committee (LCDC). I was elected president of the organization; the other officers and directors of the board were John M. Pratt of the National Council of Churches, Carl Rachlin of the Congress for Racial Equality, Melvin Wulf of the American Civil Liberties Union, Edwin Lukas of the American Jewish Committee, Robert L. Carter of the National Association for the Advancement of Colored People, Jack Greenberg of the NAACP Legal Defense and Educational Fund, Clarence B. Jones, counsel to the Reverend Martin Luther King, Jr., and Howard Moore, Jr. of the Students Non-Violent Coordinating Committee.

Our purpose was to enlist lawyers from the North who would volunteer to spend at least two weeks in the half dozen or so Southern cities in which we opened offices to provide

legal defense services for persons engaged in a coordinated
campaign to end racial segregation. While many, if not most,
of these were local blacks organized by the Reverend King,
Jr., a substantial number were white college students from the
North who cooperated in the effort and white law school students, also from the North, who assisted our lawyers.

The Lawyers Constitutional Defense Committee operated
independently for about two years, until its financial resources
were no longer sufficient to continue the project. Thereafter,
the program was taken over by the American Civil Liberties
Union, which engaged as a member of its own staff, our
executive secretary, Henry Schwarzschild (brother of Steven
Schwarzschild, editor of the American Jewish Congress's
quarterly journal, *Judaism*). In the course of its operations, a
number of the lawyers and law students who came to the
South to assist our lawyers suffered physical injuries and frequent arrests on charges of disturbing the peace, obstructing
traffic, violating traffic regulations, and resisting arrest.

In respect to the law students, one gratifying note should be
added. Before applicants to the bar are admitted, they must
persuade the states' committees on character and fitness that
they are of good character and must disclose all criminal
offenses, whether felonies or misdemeanors, of which they
may have been convicted. Criminal offenders faced denial or
at least long delay in receiving the necessary endorsement
from the committees. The Northern committees, with the
approval of the courts, adopted rules that in the absence of
other circumstances, arrests and convictions of law students
aiding the Lawyers Constitutional Defense Committee and
other civil rights organizations in the campaign against racial
segregation and discrimination in the South, were not to be
considered in adjudging fitness of character.

In 1964, I received an invitation to accept the chairmanship
of the political science department on the Brooklyn campus of
Long Island University. Earlier, I had served for a year as visiting professor of constitutional law at Yeshivah University
and had given a course at the New School for Social Research,
both in New York City, and, in 1958, I gave a series of lectures at Mt. Holyoke College in an interdepartmental course
on "Religion and the State." Later, in 1965, I gave a course
in church-state relationships at Rutgers Law School in New
Jersey. I very much enjoyed teaching, but did not want to
retire from the arena of litigation in respect to the First

Amendment religion clauses. Fortunately, both the university and the American Jewish Congress were willing to accede to my suggestion that I accept the offer and, thereafter, work halftime for the American Jewish Congress with the title of special (rather than, as formerly, general) counsel, and half-time for Long Island University.

The outcome was one that many seek but few achieve—that is, to enjoy the best of two worlds. In 1980, I had to make two adjustments by reason of my age; at Long Island University, I had to retire from the departmental chairmanship and continue as a professor emeritus, teaching one graduate course each semester; at the American Jewish Congress, I continued as special counsel but waived salary or other compensation and limited myself to activities involving church-state relations.

In 1964, moving from Woodmere, Long Island, to an apartment in University Towers, a building complex owned by the university, required a change in synagogue affiliation, and, in that year, my wife and I became members of Congregation Mt. Sinai, just a few streets from our apartment. The synagogue was a short distance from the borough hall and court section of Brooklyn, and was visited regularly on Yom Kippur and, to a lesser extent, on other Jewish holy days, by judges—federal, state, and city—other government officials, and politicians. They usually made their appearance, shook hands with as many congregants as they could, and left. Over a period of time, the neighborhood, originally upper middle class to wealthy, gradually changed to the lower middle and, at the fringes, poverty classes. There was considerable crime, not only in the streets but even in the halls and elevators of apartment houses. In a period of less than two years, my wife, my son, and I were assaulted on the building grounds.

The resulting migration of residents from the neighborhood culminated in a drastic reduction in synagogue membership and worshipers. At our synagogue, a committee of car owners was formed to drive members home safely, and the synagogue building itself, for want of funds, became dilapidated and unsafe in many parts. By what to the overwhelming majority, if not to all, was a stroke of pure luck or a miracle from heaven, an offer to purchase the building was made by the ISKCON Corporation, a Hari Krishna group (unfavorably deemed by many to be a "cult") with the intent to use it for their religious services. Somehow or other this became known and was reported in the press, with the consequence of virulent attacks upon the synagogue officers by a local newspaper and by what was known as The Task Force on Cults, an agency of the Jewish Community Council of New York.

It did not matter that there was no hope for the synagogue; that if the sale did not go through, the building would go to ruin and the congregation fade away; that with the money received, the officers, in reliance upon the sale, had been able to negotiate and obtain a long-term lease on premises in Brooklyn Heights, an upper-class neighborhood within walking distance for many of its members, and were awaiting completion of necessary alterations to accommodate the congregation in a new location.

The attack proved futile. With the strong approval of the rabbi, Joseph Potasnik, the contract was ratified by the congregation, and a deed was executed and given to the purchasers. Until the new premises became ready in 1984, ISKCON permitted the congregation to use one part of the building for religious services, while the other part was used by them for their religious services. In the interim, there had been no bolt from heaven signifying disapproval from the divinity of either the Jews or the "cults."

My own views in respect to "cults" are set forth in my letter to the editor of the *New York Times*. The letter reads:

My initial reaction to the Sept. 26 Op-Ed article "Countering the Cults," by A. J. and M. R. Rudin, was to consider it a hoax along the lines of [Daniel] Defoe's "Shortest Way With Dissenters." Rereading it impelled me to conclude that, alas, the authors were in earnest.

They recognize that "some legal observers" might find First Amendment difficulties with what they propose in their list of 10 ways to dispose of "cults." They urge, however, that First Amendment guarantees "must be weighed against cult abuses," and that such weighing leads to a determination of constitutionality.

Governor Carey has recently vetoed for unconstitutionality a bill seeking to impose "conservatorships" on the person and property of converts to cults, but that measure was as indefensible in First Amendment terms as some of the Rudins' 10 proposals.

It is doubtful, for example, that any court is likely to sustain a law defining "minors" for purposes of protection against conversion as persons under the age of 21, even though they may be self-supporting, married, and, since their 18th birthday, subject to compulsory military service. (It cannot be argued that the cultists are not of sound mind and memory, since, if that were so, the 21-year age provision would be meaningless.)

Efforts to use the instrumentalities of law to accomplish what parents have been unable or unwilling to do, that is to secure the religious upbringing of their children, are hardly new; proposals to return prayer to the public-school classrooms are a current illustration of that. Nor is there anything new in resorting to facially neutral laws, such as those relating to tax exemption as a means of countering unpopular sects. Indeed, historically there is hardly a well-established and fully respected faith which has not been to a greater or lesser extent subjected to some degree of persecution by legislation such as that proposed by the Rudins: Catholics, Jews, Mormons, Jehovah's Witnesses and Black Muslims, to name but a few, can testify to this.

The history of these and other "cults" which in time have become acceptable religions leads to the conclusion that persecution, whether by physical force or by law, is counter-productive; it is more likely to insure than to terminate their survival.

Of course, revenue, health, sanitation and consumer-protection laws should be enforced against "cults," as they should in respect to all other groups; but to single out "cults" as particular subjects for enforcement cannot easily be reconciled with the First Amendment's free-exercise guaranty, nor with the 14th Amendment's mandate relating to the equal protection of the laws.

The crux of the matter is that our Constitution does not recognize any distinction between accepted religions and hated "cults," and that use or abuse of law to destroy the latter threatens the security of the former and of all persons committed to First Amendment values.[29]

For years now, I have pleaded and argued with the officers and members of Jewish organizations, religious and secular, urging abandonment of a policy that I deemed violative of the First Amendment. I asserted that of all people Jews have the most to fear from any weakening of the Constitution's protection of religious minorities. Until recently, the effort was all in vain.

A breakthrough, however, came in my own organization, the American Jewish Congress. In November 1981, it submitted a brief amicus curiae in a case before New York's highest court[30] involving the denial of tax exemption to the Holy Spirit Association of the Unification Church (known popularly as "the Moonies," after its leader, the Reverend Sun Myung Moon). Denial was based on a determination by the lower court that because political and economic theory is such a substantial part of the Association's doctrine, it could not claim that its primary purpose was religious.

The amicus brief, in support of the Association's claim, was followed in March of 1982 by the American Jewish Congress's submission of a statement to the New Jersey legislature in opposition to a measure authorizing judicial appointment of guardians for adults who join "cults." The statement was based upon the ground that such a law violated the First Amendment's guaranty of religious freedom. (I had previously presented statements in my own behalf and in behalf of the

American Civil Liberties Union to the governors of New York and New Jersey urging vetoes on constitutional grounds of similar measures. In all instances the measures were vetoed on those grounds.)

As of this writing, only one other Jewish organization has joined the American Jewish Congress in its actions. The American Jewish Committee participated as a co-plaintiff in a suit by the Church of Scientology seeking to invalidate an ordinance aimed at cults. I have no doubt that in due course the position will be adopted by most if not all the major Jewish organizations. That has been our experience in many previous similar controversies such as those relating to religion in the public schools, religion in the census, and imposition of the death penalty.

"Cults" was not the only arena in which the American Jewish Congress did not at first accept my recommendations. I was equally unsuccessful in respect to one aspect of the struggle involving abortion.

Here, as in the efforts toward adoption of the Equal Rights Amendment, our organization's policy was clear: we opposed governmental restrictions on a woman's right to abortion except as in the case of all other medical services, to the extent necessary to insure the safety of the procedure. Our position was shared by the Conservative and Reform constituents of the Synagogue Council, but was opposed by the Orthodox.

In 1979, I was asked by the Religious Coalition for Abortion Rights, a group of some twenty-seven religious organizations, including the American Jewish Congress and numerous mainline Protestant groups, to prepare and submit on behalf of those members of the Coalition that would go along, a brief amicus in the case of *Harris* v. *McRae*,[31] which challenged on a variety of grounds, an act by Congress that terminated medicaid benefits for abortions other than those necessary to preserve the woman's life. My argument was that the denial to poor women of medicaid benefits for abortions by reason of the fact that the procedure is condemned as sinful by particular religious groups (primarily, though not exclusively, the Roman Catholic Church) violated both the Establishment and Free Exercise Clauses of the First Amendment. I had presented the argument two years earlier in an amicus curiae brief submitted on behalf of the American Jewish Congress and a number of other organizations in the case of *Poelker* v. *Doe*,[32] but the Court had not addressed itself to this issue. In the *McRae* case, counsel for the women who brought the suit decided to present this claim, among others, to the Court. The brief I prepared was limited to the religion issue and was ready to go to the printer when the Philadelphia chapter of the American Jewish Congress expressed its opposition, asserting that the claim was unsound and would unnecessarily evoke negative reactions from Catholic and Orthodox Jewish spokesmen. The matter was presented to our Commission on Law and Social Action board, which, with one dissent (that of Esther Polen, who was also a member of the Philadelphia chapter) argued against submission of the brief. My response was that omitting the issue would be like playing Hamlet without the Dane inasmuch as withdrawal by the Catholic Church of opposition to the measure would, as in the case of artificial birth control, end the controversy.

None of the other twenty-six organizations expressed any opposition to the brief and it was, therefore, submitted in their names. The Religious Coalition on Abortion Rights reprinted and distributed it among its constituent organizations and other interested groups.

On its face, the ultimate outcome was not a happy one for me, for the Religious Coalition, or for the organizations whose counsel argued the case in behalf of the women who brought the suit. In a few paragraphs, the Court set forth the establishment argument and, with no dissent on this point, ruled it invalid.

In the church-state arena, I argued the case of *Torcaso* v. *Watkins*[33] before the Supreme Court in 1961. It involved a Maryland statute, going back to colonial times, requiring all persons seeking state office, whether by election or appointment, to take an oath that they believed in the existence of God. Such a law could not apply to federal office in view of the prohibition of religious tests in Article VI of the Constitution. In arguing before the Court an appeal by an atheist who was denied a license to serve as a notary public because of his refusal to take the oath, I urged that the statute violated the Establishment Clause not only because it preferred religion over nonreligion but also because it preferred some religions over others, noting that there were some religions such as Buddhism, Taoism, and Ethical Culture, whose faiths were nontheistic, i.e., not based upon belief in a personal deity.

Without dissent, the Court ruled the statute unconstitutional on the ground that it violated the First Amendment's mandate of neutrality between religion and nonreligion. In addition, Justice Hugo Black, who wrote the Court's opinion, noted in a footnote that among religions that were not based upon "belief in the existence of God are Buddhism, Taoism, Ethical Culture, Secular Humanism and others." As I noted in an article published in *Free Inquiry*,[34] addition of "Secular Humanism" evoked a reaction that I am sure Justice Black never intended. Protagonists of religion in the public schools and governmental aid to religious schools have since demanded that either their claims be accepted or that the public schools cease teaching subjects such as biology, history, and others that, to them, clearly were predicated upon the religion of "Secular Humanism."

Epperson v. *Arkansas*, or perhaps more accurately its aftermath, illustrates this. Like the *Scopes* case, it involved a challenge to an Arkansas law that forbade public school teaching of the "theory or doctrine that mankind ascended or descended from a lower order of animals." Susan Epperson, a public school teacher, challenged the law on the ground that it violated the First Amendment's guarantee of freedom of speech, which encompasses freedom to teach and to learn, but did not mention the Establishment Clause. I raised that issue in a friends-of-the-court brief I submitted in behalf of the American Jewish Congress and the American Civil Liberties Union. What my brief urged and what the Court adopted in ruling for Epperson was the assertion that a penal statute forbidding teachers of a secular subject to instruct their students about a widely held scientific explanation of man's origin solely because some might consider it inconsistent with the biblical account of the creation, was not an act of neutrality but a specific aid to religion and, therefore, a violation of the First Amendment's Establishment Clause.

Recognizing the unlikelihood of the Court's reversing itself, Protestant fundamentalists have resorted to the "fairness principle" that mandates equal time for opponents of positions endorsed in television or radio broadcasts. With the endorsement of President Ronald Reagan and the Reverend Jerry Falwell's Moral Majority, they have succeeded in having two states (Arkansas and Louisiana) enact laws declaring that in any public school in which evolution was taught equal time must be provided for the Genesis account of the Creation and the great flood in Noah's time. To avoid the ban against religious instruction imposed in the *McCollum* case, the program was given the name "Creation-Science," and the laws were entitled "Balanced Treatment for Creation Science and Evolution Science Act." Lawyers for the American Civil Liberties Union, assisted by lawyers of the New York firm of Paul, Weiss, Rifkind, Wharton, and Garrison (including my son, Alan) have been engaged in litigation challenging the constitutionality of these laws.

Protagonists of these measures (and others still being considered in quite a few other states) base considerable reliance upon the "Secular Humanism" footnote in *Epperson*, and urge that if the Court is not prepared to outlaw the teaching of evolution on that ground, at the very least it should mandate equal time for creationism. At the present writing, it is fairly certain that it will take a number of years before litigation (so far inconclusive in the lower courts) will reach the Supreme Court.

The issue of teaching religion in the public schools had been resolved by the Supreme Court in the *McCollum* case in 1948. Unresolved by that decision, however, were the cognate questions of Bible reading and prayer recitation. One aspect of the Bible issue did reach the Supreme Court in the case of *Tudor* v. *Board of Education*[35] in 1954. The suit challenged the constitutionality of the widespread practice of Gideon Bible distribution in the public schools. After the public school authorities in Rutherford, New Jersey had rejected complaints by a Jewish and a Catholic parent (the latter because the Bible was the King James version), I was retained by a parent of each faith to sue for an injunction. Although the local priest and rabbi joined in sponsoring the suit, the former was overruled by higher ecclesiastical authorities, with the result that the Catholic parent, Ralph Lecoque, withdrew, leaving the Jewish parent, Bernard Tudor, as the sole plaintiff.

At the trial, I presented evidence to show that the Gideon Bible was not a nonsectarian book, that the assertion of voluntariness in accepting or rejecting the book was not realistic, and that the distribution of the book was harmful to Jewish children and to the aims and purposes of public education. These points were made through expert testimony by clergymen, educators, and psychologists, a practice later often followed in cases involving religion in the public schools.

The New Jersey Supreme Court (one of whose members was William Brennan, later to be elevated to the United States Supreme Court) unanimously ruled the practice uncon-

stitutional as inconsistent with both the Establishment and
Free Exercise Clauses of the First Amendment. The opinion
relied heavily upon the expert testimony and quoted much of
it in support of its finding involuntariness in violation of the
Free Exercise Clause. The Gideon Association joined as a
defendant to the suit, sought to appeal to the United States
Supreme Court but its petition for certiorari was denied. Thereafter, the *Tudor* decision was uniformly followed in other
states when the issue arose, with the result that distributors of
the Gideon Bible are now instructed not to enter the public
schools, but to offer the Bible to students after they reach the
street.

It was a decade later that the Supreme Court definitively
ruled on the constitutionality of Bible reading in the public
schools in *Abington School District* v. *Schempp* (1963).[36] A year
earlier, in the case of *Engel* v. *Vitale*,[37] it had found it necessary to pass upon the question of prayer in the schools. The
case involved a challenge to a resolution by the board of education in a suburb of New York authorizing recitation of a
twenty-two word prayer, formulated by the state board of
regents, which read: "Almighty God, we acknowledge our
dependence upon Thee, and we beg Thy blessings upon us,
our parents, our teachers and our country." With but one dissent, the Supreme Court held that the school board's action
violated the Establishment Clause, and, thereby, invoked upon
itself an imprecatory assault by fundamentalist ministers,
Southern politicians, and Catholic cardinals. The last would
seem somewhat surprising. As I noted in the revised edition of
Church, State, and Freedom, for more than a century opposition
to prayer in the public schools had come almost exclusively
from the Catholic Church, since the prayer most often recited
was the Lord's Prayer according to the (Protestant) King
James version, recitation of which was deemed sinful.

What affected me personally was an editorial that appeared
several months after the decision in the national Jesuit weekly,
America, entitled "To Our Jewish Friends."[38] It remarked
that following the decision "there have been disturbing hints
of heightened anti-Semitic feeling," and that "all necessary
steps should be taken to prevent an outbreak of anti-Semitism." It then continued:

We should recognize that full responsibility for the decision in *Engel* is not
to be pinned on the Jewish community. Along with that well-publicized
Jewish spokesman Leo Pfeffer, and such organizations as the American

Jewish Congress responsibility for the concerted opposition to the New York prayer—and to other forms of religious practice in the public schools and public life—belongs to the American Civil Liberties Union, the Ethical Culture Society, the Humanist Association, some Unitarians, many atheists and certain other groups with doctrinaire views on the meaning and application of the principle of separation of Church and State.

The editorial charged further that "one long-range objective" of this "sector of the Jewish community" was to "create a 'climate of opinion' in which the Supreme Court (could) more readily continue to make decisions in consonance with the principle of separation of church and state as that principle (had) been interpreted in absolutistic terms by Leo Pfeffer, by the American Jewish Congress, and by the Supreme Court in the *McCollum* case of 1948."

It would be most unfortunate [the editorial continued], if the entire Jewish community were to be blamed for the unrelenting pressure tactics of a small but overly vocal segment within it. . . . Conceivably with help from some important Jewish groups, the recitation of the Lord's Prayer, as well as the reading of passages from the Bible in the public schools, can and may, in the near future be declared unconstitutional. We wonder, therefore, whether it is not time for provident leaders of American Judaism to ask their more militant colleagues whether what is gained through the courts by some victories is worth the breakdown of community relations which will inevitably follow them. What will have been accomplished if our Jewish friends win all the legal immunities they seek, but thereby paint themselves into a corner of social and cultural alienation? The time has come for these fellow citizens to decide among themselves precisely what they conceive to be the final objective of the Jewish community in the United States—in a word, what bargain they are willing to strike as one of the minorities in a pluralistic society. When victories produce only a harvest of fear and distrust, will it all have been worth-while?

Two weeks after the initial editorial appeared, *America* published a second editorial on the subject. In this editorial, entitled, "The Main Issue," the editors said:

This fall the Supreme Court will rule on a number of cases relative to religious practices in the schools. If, as they are now bending every effort to do, Leo Pfeffer and his fellow campaigners succeed in winning Supreme Court decisions that strike down the Lord's Prayer and Bible reading in school classrooms, there will be once again—as there was at the time of the *Engel* decision, only more so—an intensely unfavorable public reaction. When and if such decisions are handed down, then unless it has been made clear that Dr. Pfeffer and the American Jewish Congress do not speak for the whole of American Jewry, Jews in general will be unfairly blamed for what in fact will have been accomplished by a mere handful of militants, allied with an assortment of humanist groups, ethical culturists, Unitarians, secularists and atheists.

In singling me out as the arch villain who exercises Svengalian influence on all the Jewish organizations, rabbinical, congregational, and secular, the editors of *America* manifested surprising ignorance of American Jewry; as I have noted earlier, I could not get more than one member of the American Jewish Congress governing council to agree with my position on the religious issue in abortion. The editors also disregarded many non-Jewish and nonatheistic voices that supported the Court's decision, including *The Christian Century*, the Baptist Joint Committee on Public Affairs, the Seventh-day Adventists, Martin Luther King, Jr., and, somewhat later, the National Council of Churches of Christ. Perhaps most significant was a petition that, though drafted and circulated by me, was signed by 343 constitutional law professors and practitioners throughout the nation urging Congress not to pass a resolution for a Constitutional amendment that would void *Engel* v. *Vitale* and sanction the return of prayer to the public schools.

Most egregious of the editors' errors was their bland ignoring of the two real villains in the drama—the plantiffs who brought the suit and the Supreme Court that decided it. (As to the former, I should, however, note that at some point in the proceedings one of the five plaintiffs—I do not remember which one—told me that what impelled him or her to join in the suit was a reading of the chapter in the first edition of *Church, State, and Freedom* dealing with religion in the public schools.)

An even broader assignment of responsibility is found in the following sentence in Robert L. Cord's recently published book, *Separation of Church and State*: "The Pfeffer school of thought—including its adherents in the United States Supreme Court—relies on historical evidence to prove the validity of its interpretation of the Establishment Clause."[39]

Somewhat surprising, in view of the intense Catholic condemnation of the *Engel* decision, has been the response of the United States Catholic Conference to President Reagan's call for a constitutional amendment nullifying the decision and returning prayer to the public schools. While endorsing the proposal, the Conference stated that it would prefer an amendment that would overrule the *McCollum* decision and allow pupils to attend released-time religion in school premises during school hours. Even more surprising, however, is *America's* response to the president. The penultimate paragraph of an article by the associate editor, John W. Donahue, entitled "Prayer in the Schools: The Unanswered Question," reads:

Since the President made his announcement in the Rose Garden last May, there has been fairly general agreement among commentators that school prayer will rarely be voluntary because classrooms are rarely protected against coercion. But if the wisdom of school prayer is doubtful, the wisdom of cranking up the enormous mechanism of a constitutional amendment to make such prayer possible is even more so.[40]

If the 1962 editors of *America* had any realistic expectation or even hope that their editorials condemning the Jewish organizations that joined in the *Engel* brief or the Supreme Court justices who decided the case would mend their ways in respect to public school recitation of the Lord's Prayer and devotional readings from the Bible, they were soon disillusioned in respect to both. In *Abington School District* v. *Schempp*, which came to the Court within a year after *Engel*, the Jewish organizations authorized me to file a brief in their behalf, and the Supreme Court, citing its decision in *Engel*, ruled both practices to be unconstitutional. Moreover, in the 1980 case of *Stone* v. *Graham*,[41] the Jewish organizations directed me to file an amicus brief in a case asserting the unconstitutionality of a Kentucky law authorizing the posting of the Ten Commandments on the walls in public school classrooms, and the Supreme Court so ruled, summarily, that is, without hearing argument by the attorneys in the case.

The year 1968 marked the beginning of a new era in the history of constitutional law relating to the Establishment Clause as it affects governmental aid to parochial schools. *Everson* had dealt with the subject twenty years earlier and the issue remained dormant during the ensuing period while the Supreme Court dealt with the problem of religion in the public schools. Two decisions on the issue handed down in 1968 seemed to point in opposite directions. In one, *Board of Education* v. *Allen*[42] (an American Civil Liberties Union suit), the Court upheld the constitutionality of a New York statute authorizing the loan of public school textbooks for use in parochial schools. In the other, *Flast* v. *Cohen*,[43] it ruled that a taxpayer had the right to challenge in the federal courts legislation aiding such schools.

In *Allen*, I submitted an amicus curiae brief in behalf of the American Jewish Congress and a number of other Jewish organizations supporting the American Civil Liberties Union contention. In it, I argued that accepting the theory that the purpose and primary effect of the statute were not to aid the schools but rather the children who attended them (an argu-

ment often called the child benefit theory) could lead to constitutional justification of public financing of all costs of
parochial and sectarian schools, with the possible exception of
costs relating to the direct teaching of religious dogma and
practices. Justice Byron White, who wrote the majority opinion upholding constitutionality, agreed with this, as is evidenced by the fact that every subsequent Supreme Court decision invalidating laws financing parochial school operations
has been accompanied by a dissent from Justice White.

Flast v. *Cohen* was a suit I brought on behalf of a number of
taxpayers challenging the constitutionality under the Establishment Clause of a provision in the Federal Elementary and
Secondary Education Act of 1965 that included "private elementary and secondary schools" (a euphemism for religious or
parochial schools) as beneficiaries of the financial aid accorded
by the statute. The defendant, Secretary of the Department of
Health, Education and Welfare, successfully challenged the
suit in the federal district court on the ground that the plaintiffs, who were merely taxpayers not having any specific interest in the controversy other than that possessed by all taxpayers, lacked the requisite "standing" to bring the suit. The
Supreme Court, however, ruled to the contrary and announced
the principle upon which has been based all subsequent judicial challenges to federal expenditures supporting aid to religious schools. Realistically speaking, the Court ruled that taxpayers could sue, if they wanted to, but, in view of the *Allen*
decision, they could not win (which may explain why Justice
White concurred in the *Flast* decision). Because of this, I
decided not to pursue the *Flast* case further unless and until
later decisions indicated a better chance of prevailing.

What happened later in this controversy was the commission by me of an act of negligence so gross as to have warranted a suit for damages had my clients suffered any financial
loss as a result. I will explain this after I recount intervening
events.

Although in *Church, State, and Freedom* I sought to present
as impartially as I could the arguments for and against particular issues in church-state relationships, I left the reader in no
doubt as to my own position on each issue. On rare occasions,
my position was too "absolutist" or "extremist" (terms often
applied to me) even for the American Jewish Congress,
although it never sought in the slightest to censor what I
wrote or taught. Tax exemption for church or synagogue

owned property used for religious purposes was one instance of this. In my book, I expressed the view that exemption could not be reconciled with the principles of church-state separation as expressed in all the Supreme Court's decisions from *Everson* on, but predicted nevertheless that at least in the foreseeable future the Court would not invalidate exemption.

When the case of *Walz* v. *Tax Commission* reached the Supreme Court in 1971, I proposed that the American Jewish Congress submit a brief amicus in support of the plaintiff's First Amendment challenge to the state's exemption law. I had no expectation that the proposal would be accepted, but I anticipated (correctly) that the difference of opinion within the organization would result in the compromise that no brief would be submitted on either side, notwithstanding the fact that generally ardent separationist organizations, such as the National Council of Churches, the Synagogue Council, and even Americans United for Separation of Church and State would be submitting briefs in support of constitutionality. Initially, Americans United's counsel prepared and printed a brief in support of Walz's position, but, on instruction by the organization's executive director, discarded it and wrote and filed a new brief in opposition to *Walz*. I did agree to prepare a brief for submission by the American Civil Liberties Union, provided that my name did not appear on it, to avoid possible embarrassment to the American Jewish Congress, although I disclosed my authorship to its officers. (They would have guessed it anyway, in view of the frequent references to my writings in it.)

Since the publication of *Church, State, and Freedom*, I had from time to time received requests from other organizations to represent them as an individual practitioner in church-state litigation. In most of these I received no fee for my services; in a few, I did, and as an expert, my fees were fairly substantial. (Actually, my first professional—and unsuccessful—argument in the United States Supreme Court in the case of *Lanza* v. *New York* [1962][44] had no relevance to church-state relations. It dealt with the right of a prisoner—who had been convicted of racketeering—to confer privately with visitors and without eavesdropping by police authorities.) In my capacity as a church-state specialist, I accepted an invitation from the American Civil Liberties Union two years after *Walz* to prepare a brief in my own name and argue an appeal to the Supreme Court in *Diffenderfer* v. *Central Baptist Church of*

Miami.[45] That suit challenged the constitutionality of a Florida law that accorded exemption to religious institutions even in respect to income from the unrelated business operations of owning and operating a parking lot in downtown Miami exclusively for congregants on Sundays, but as a commercial enterprise during the other days of the week.

I urged in my brief that the *Walz* decision did not go beyond upholding constitutionality in respect to properties used exclusively for religious purposes, but that a law allowing exemption in respect to properties used for profit-making purposes constituted impermissible aid to religion. Counsel for the church argued that the *Walz* decision applied to all church-owned properties if, as in the present case, the ensuing income was used only to maintain the church and finance its religious functions. Coincidentally, and somewhat amusingly, my adversary, Charles Whelan, a Catholic priest who taught law at Fordham University and was associate editor of the Jesuit magazine *America*, was likewise appearing in his individual capacity. There was, however, one difference between us. While the American Jewish Congress had never taken any position on tax-exemption, the United States Catholic Conference had stated, in its amicus brief in the *Walz* case, that it did "not defend exemptions from taxation accorded church properties used or operated for commercial purposes and had so advised Congress and the public."

Somewhat amusing, too, was the outcome of the case. Between the time I filed my brief and the day of argument, the Florida legislature amended the exemption statute to exclude church-owned properties to the extent that they were used for commercial purposes. Accordingly, the Supreme Court dismissed the appeal as moot or academic, a rare instance of winning my case before arguing it.

Organizations that had cooperated in financing *Flast* v. *Cohen* and whose officers joined as individual taxpayers were, besides the American Jewish Congress, the United Parents Association, the United Federation of Teachers, and the New York Civil Liberties Union. Recognizing the need to carry on, primarily through litigation but also through efforts to defeat proposed legislation, I sent a letter to these and other like-minded organizations inviting them to send representatives to a meeting to consider coordinating our efforts in the defense of the Establishment Clause in its relation to education.

At the ensuing meeting held in the office of the American Jewish Congress, we agreed to form a permanent organization that, when fully established, consisted of some thirty-five associations concerned with education and church-state separation. We called it the New York Committee for Public Education and Religious Liberty. Joseph Robison, my successor as the Commission on Law and Social Action director, noted the acronym of PEARL and it was thereafter often used (even in Supreme Court opinions) to identify the organization. Accordingly, in all subsequent litigation I, as counsel, named PEARL as the first plaintiff, although, being tax exempt, it did not qualify as a taxpayer, and for that reason was often stricken by the courts when my adversaries made a motion for that purpose. This did not bother me at all since, on appeals all the way to the Supreme Court, I continued to use the title (a procedure entirely appropriate) until the particular suit was ultimately decided.

Similar organizations, sometimes using the title PEARL (as Missouri PEARL), and sometimes somewhat similar names, such as Public Funds for Public Schools of New Jersey, were formed in other parts of the country. In 1974, I convened a meeting of representatives of those and a number of national organizations (including the American Association of School Administrators, the American Civil Liberties Union, the Baptist Joint Committee on Public Affairs, Americans United for Separation of Church and State, the United Methodist Church, and the National Education Association) for the purpose of forming a National PEARL. We met in Washington and did form an organization but, for reasons I never learned, named it the National Coalition (rather than Committee) for Public Education and Religious Liberty (National PEARL). The persons who were selected and agreed to serve as officers included Dean Willard Heckel of Rutgers Law School, Dean Jefferson Fordham of the University of Pennsylvania Law School, Rabbi Robert Gordis of New York, Florence Flast, James E. Wood, Jr., then executive director of the Baptist Joint Committee on Public Affairs, and Stanley McFarlane of the National Education Association. We selected as our executive director, Joanne Goldsmith, a member of the Maryland School Board. Here, too, I was selected to be general counsel.

One incident in the life of National PEARL merits recounting here. In 1981, the Supreme Court accepted an appeal in a case *Plyler* v. *Doe*[46] involving the constitutionality of a

Texas law requiring parents (primarily Mexicans) who were illegally in the United States to pay tuition for the education of their children in the public schools. I recommended that we submit an amicus curiae brief in support of the Mexican parents and received approval from a majority of National PEARL constituents.

My justification pointed to the fact that our organizational purpose was to protect public education *and* religious liberty, and the former was clearly endangered by the Texas law. I was under no illusions as to the soundness or the unsoundness of my position; logically, it would mean that we could intervene in any case involving religious liberty, including, for example, those relating to conscientious objection to draft registration or anti-"cults" legislation. Strong objection to our entering the Texas case was expressed by Professors Heckel and Fordham and I had no doubt that my recommendation had been in large measure motivated by the treatment of blacks in the South. In any event, while pride prevented me from acknowledging the soundness of the objection, I informed our constituents that in view of the objections we would not file a brief in the case, but this, of course, did not prevent any of them from filing briefs independently of PEARL.

The Supreme Court ruling in *Flast* v. *Cohen* had made possible taxpayers suits challenging federal financing of sectarian schools and assured challenges to similar state statutes. The first of these to reach the Supreme Court were respectively *Tilton* v. *Richardson* on the college level and *Lemon* v. *Kurtzman* and *Earley* v. *DiCenso* on the elementary and secondary schools level.[47] The Court's practically complete turn-around on the constitutionality of aid was expressed first in the single opinion covering both the *Lemon* and *DiCenso* suits. The basic question in all three cases, and the many similar cases that followed them, was whether secular instruction could be constitutionally separated from religious thereby rendering religious and public schools equally eligible to receive tax-raised funds.

Lemon involved the constitutionality of a Pennsylvania statute permitting contracts between the state and private school authorities under which they would sell their secular educational services to the state and deliver these services by teaching similar subjects to the children in their particular schools. *DiCenso* challenged a Rhode Island law authorizing supplementing the salaries of teachers of secular subjects in nonpublic schools by paying directly to each teacher 15 percent of his or her current annual salary.

Both of these cases were instituted under the auspices of the local chapters of the American Civil Liberties Union. In both cases, I participated as cocounsel with local American Civil Liberties Union attorneys, in Rhode Island with Milton Stanzler and in Pennsylvania with Henry Sawyer (the successful attorney in the *Schempp* prayer case). Sawyer took over the appeal to the Supreme Court in *Lemon* and I submitted a brief amicus curiae on behalf of the American Association of School Administrators, American Vocational Association, Association for Supervision and Curriculum Development, Horace Mann League of the United States, National Association of Elementary School Principals, National Education Association, National School Boards Association, and Rural Education Association. I handled the *DiCenso* appeal on the basis of a trial record that sought to establish indivisability of parochial school instruction in respect to religious and secular subjects. I quoted, for example, a provision in the 1965 edition of the *Handbook of School Regulations* of the Diocese of Providence that read: "Religious formation is not confined to formal courses, nor is it restricted to a single subject area. It is achieved through the example of the faculty, the tone of the school, the manner in which the curriculum is taught, and religious activities."

I also quoted a statement by Bishop (later Cardinal) Joseph L. Bernadin, then general secretary of the United States Catholic Conference, that "Catholic educators have always maintained that a Catholic school is not one which teaches religion only during one period every day. Rather the whole atmosphere of the school is to be a Christian one, animated by a community of faith—the children, the teachers and the parents."

I presented considerable other evidence in support of our contentions that the purpose and effect of aid to parochial schools are to aid religion, and that the result is inevitably entanglement of church and state, including that which would be necessary to assure that the Establishment Clause is not violated.

The establishment argument was based on the *Walz* decision, handed down a year earlier. It was the entanglement aspect that the Court adopted in ruling the Rhode Island law unconstitutional. Although there had been no trial record in

Lemon, the lower court having dismissed the complaint without a trial, the Supreme Court held that the entanglement
fault was equally inherent in the Pennsylvania statute thereby
rendering it unconstitutional on its face.

One aspect of the *Lemon* and *DiCenso* cases merits mentioning. When I drafted the complaint in the *DiCenso* suit, I
included a paragraph asserting that governmental financing of
nonpublic schools would enable middle class white parents,
who otherwise might not be able to afford to send their children to such schools to do so, with the ultimate result of
promoting two schools systems—a public school system predominantly black, poor, and inferior, and a nonpublic school
system predominantly white, affluent, and superior. I had
made the same allegation in a companion case to *Lemon* v.
Kurtzman, also brought in a federal court in Philadelphia, but
the lower courts in both cases held that since all the plaintiffs
in both cases were white, they had no standing to assert this
claim.

In my brief to the Supreme Court in the *DiCenso* case, I
repeated this argument, but the Court did not find it necessary to pass upon it since it found the laws unconstitutional on
the ground of entanglement. Nevertheless, I think that the
validity of this argument is supported by almost unanimous
opposition among black organizations and spokesmen to the
current (Bob) Packwood-(Daniel) Moynihan measure, endorsed
by President Reagan, to accord credit for tuition in parochial
and other private schools.

On the same day in June 1971 that the Court handed down
its decision in *Lemon-DiCenso*, it also decided *Tilton* v. *Richardson*. In that suit, I challenged the inclusion of sectarian colleges in the Higher Education Facilities Act of 1963, two
years before enactment of the Federal Elementary and Secondary Education Act. The law provided federal construction
grants for college facilities, public and private, except facilities
to be used for sectarian instruction or religious worship or
were part of a school or department of divinity. The law also
provided that if this exclusion were violated within twenty
years the government could recover the amount of its grant,
but after that period the institution could use the facility for
any purpose it wished, including religious purposes.

I challenged the constitutionality of this law in a case
involving four church-related colleges in Connecticut, on the
same grounds as those I set forth in *DiCenso* and *Lemon*. The

Court, however, reached a contrary result, noting that, unlike elementary and secondary schools, church-related colleges do not have religious indoctrination as a substantial purpose and there was, therefore, less likelihood that religion would permeate the area of education. The Court stated also that non-ideological character of the aid made entanglement through surveillance less likely, particularly where the aid given is a one-time single purpose construction grant. It did, however, invalidate the provision in the law allowing the college to use the financed structure for any purpose, including religious ones such as use of a chapel, after twenty years, since the restrictive obligations of the Establishment Clause do not expire while the building has substantial value.

Two years later, I argued the case of *Committee for Public Education and Religious Liberty* v. *Nyquist*.[48] Involved was a three-part statute enacted in New York that provided "health and safety" grants to nonpublic schools to help them comply with state regulations on safety, lighting, and sanitary facilities, reimbursement of tuition to low income parents of children in nonpublic schools, and a modification of gross income in computing state income taxes of middle-income parents whose children attended nonpublic schools.

Within three hours after the measure was signed into law by Governor Nelson Rockefeller, I instituted a lawsuit challenging all three parts of the law, and within thirteen months I was able to get a definitive decision from the Supreme Court. Relying on the effect aspect of the three-prong purpose-effect-entanglement test of unconstitutionality, the Court held all three parts of the statute unconstitutional.

The decision was reported over the radio on 25 June 1973. At that time, I was suffering from what my physician had diagnosed as congestive heart failure. My wife thought the news of the Court's decision would be helpful to me. Accordingly, she sent my son, Alan, to Long Island University (across the street from my apartment) so that I could be informed of the good news immediately. I was in the middle of my lecture when Alan knocked on the classroom door and for a moment scared me out of my wits. When I opened the door, I do not know whether the good news had any beneficial effect on my cardiac condition, but if it did it was not enough to make unnecessary the radical heart surgery I underwent a year later.

In 1975, the Court handed down a decision, *Meek* v. *Pit-*

tenger,[49] for which I had been waiting since 1968, when the Court simultaneously ruled that taxpayers could challenge federal laws appropriating tax-raised funds for the support of church-related schools, but that such a suit would probably be unsuccessful insofar as it provided federal funds to finance provision of textbooks for parochial school use, and probably unsuccessful if appropriated to finance "auxiliary services" of the type provided for in the Elementary and Secondary Education Act of 1965. In *Meek* v. *Pittenger*, I challenged the constitutionality of a Pennsylvania law to finance the provision of textbooks and other "instructional materials and equipment, useful to the education" of nonpublic school children. The other, and major part of the statute, authorized the use of tax-raised funds to finance "auxiliary services" provided in those schools.

Emboldened perhaps by the victories achieved in *Lemon* v. *Kurtzman*, *PEARL* v. *Nyquist*, and other cases involving aid to religious schools, I challenged the constitutionality of both parts of the Pennsylvania statute, hoping that in respect to the textbook provision the Court might overrule the *Allen* decision, and, in respect to the "auxiliary services" clauses, invalidate it on the basis of the claim I had presented in the complaint in *Flast* v. *Cohen*.

When the decision came down in 1975, I found that unlike my efforts in *Nyquist* I did not get all I wanted; but I did get substantially all I could have realistically hoped for. I had asked the Court to overrule *Allen* and invalidate the Pennsylvania Act in its entirety, but on this point I was able to persuade only Justices William J. Brennan, William O. Douglas, and Thurgood Marshall. As to the rest of the statute, the Court, over the dissent of Chief Justice Warren Burger and Justices Byron R. White and William H. Rehnquist, ruled against constitutionality. It refused to extend *Allen* to encompass loans of "instructional materials and equipment" such as projectors, recording and laboratory equipment, maps, charts, globes, and all other materials provided for use in public schools—all of which, it should be noted, were to be loaned, not to the schools or its teachers, but to the children attending the schools.

More important were the sections dealing with state financing of "auxiliary services" provided in nonpublic schools, defined to include, among others, guidance, counseling and testing services, services for the educationally disadvantaged, "and such other secular, neutral, nonideological services as are of benefit to nonpublic school children and are presently or hereafter provided for public school children of the Commonwealth." The language used was almost exactly that contained in the Elementary and Secondary Education Act challenged in *Flast* v. *Cohen*, and its purpose was to supplement the moneys received from the government under the federal law.

Relying upon the entanglement ban as applied in *DiCenso* and *Lemon*, the Court ruled the Pennsylvania statute unconstitutional. It seemed to me that the ban on the establishment of religion in the First Amendment could not mean less in respect to the federal government than it does in respect to the states (particularly since it is applicable to the states only because it is incorporated into the Fourteenth Amendment). Accordingly, I wrote to the Department of Health, Education, and Welfare calling upon it to comply with the supreme law of the land and discontinue financing educational services to religious schools. This did not mean that the federal law was unconstitutional; tax-raised funds could constitutionally be used to finance purchase of textbooks, transportation to religious schools, and provision of noninstructional services such as meals and medical and dental care.

The department politely acknowledged my letter and assured me that it would be given consideration. I waited many months before I finally received the department's answer; it would continue the existing practice until the Supreme Court directed it to do otherwise. In view of the response, it was clear that the only remedy was a suit against the department. I accordingly instituted such a suit on behalf of National PEARL and federal income-tax payers.

A trial was held in a three-judge district court in Manhattan and ultimately a decision came down upholding constitutionality and dismissing my complaint. The next step was to file a notice of appeal in the district court after serving copies upon all the attorneys who appeared in the suit. I prepared such a notice, but then committed the stupid error to which I earlier referred: instead of going down to the district court to file the notice in person and receive a receipt for it, I mailed it to the clerk and mailed copies to all the attorneys. For some reason, the notice was either not received by the court clerk or (as often happens) was misfiled by him, although the copies were received by counsel for all three defendants.

The law requires that a notice of appeal be filed within ninety days after the judgment appealed from was entered. The relevant Supreme Court decisions were to the effect that timely filing was a jurisdictional requisite for an appeal to the Supreme Court, which means that it cannot be extended either by the lower court or the Supreme Court. The net result was an order by the Supreme Court dismissing my appeal.

In the interim, between the beginning of my suit and its dismissal by the Supreme Court, Congress, by amendment, abolished three-judge tribunals in cases such as mine. This meant that in order to get the issues to the Supreme Court it would be necessary to start a new action, appeal if necessary to the Court of Appeals, and then appeal (again) to the Supreme Court. Realistically, a final ruling by that Court would take at least two or three years, in view of the delaying tactics employed by the defendants in the PEARL cases.

Stanley Geller, a member of the advisory council of the Commission on Law and Social Action, undertook to institute a new case (in Brooklyn rather than Manhattan and on behalf of taxpayers who were not plaintiffs in the first case) provided that I act as cocounsel and prepare all the necessary legal papers and briefs. Unfortunately, shortly after the new suit was started, I was stricken with what was diagnosed as pneumonia, and, in a period of not much more than a year, I had to enter the hospital three times.

After my last discharge from the hospital, I grew progressively weaker and lost considerable weight (from more than 140 to less than 125 pounds). My weakness necessitated my resignation as counsel of both New York and National PEARL. Soon thereafter tests ordered by my physician revealed that my illness was not pneumonia but cancer of the stomach. Fortunately, an operation removing half of my stomach proved successful and I was later able to resume in some part my career as lawyer, teacher, lecturer, and writer, including authorship of *Religion, State, and the Burger Court*, published in early 1985.[50]

Lawyers and scholars cognizant in the field of free exercise of religion and church-state relations are aware that I am frequently characterized as an absolutist or extremist or doctrinaire or unrealistic or uncompromising. Even if I would, I could not challenge the thrust of the characterizations. My briefs, writings, and lectures manifest my commitment to absolutism in respect to all First and Fourteenth Amendment rights.

Like other civil liberties defenders, I recognize that absolute freedom of religion or of speech or of assembly is not possible, but that hardly proves anything. The reality that no person is immortal does not mean that the medical and pharmaceutical professions should be abolished.

Aside from my deep commitment to the religion clauses as a matter of sincerely held principle, pragmatic considerations impel me to defend an absolutist position. "The same authority," James Madison said, "which can force a citizen to contribute three pence only of his property for the support of any one establishment may force him to conform to any other establishment in all cases whatsoever."[51] Absolutists serve an important function in church-state law; any compromise becomes too often the starting point for further compromises. The recent compromise that led to the enactment of a law accepting prayer at the secondary school level will most assuredly not end the crusade for the return of religion to all public schools of whatever level.

During the thirty years since I submitted my first Supreme Court brief in the *McCollum* case until the present writing, the Supreme Court has had three chief justices—Fred M. Vinson, Earl Warren, and Warren E. Burger. In respect to this period, we realistic absolutists could hardly have been happier. The Court did allow released-time religious instruction off public school premises, and somewhat restricted state financing of church-related colleges, but in the main, church-state separationism was triumphant. So, too, was the principle of free exercise, and, in respect to this aspect, the Supreme Court has done more than quite well.

The more recent history of the Establishment Clause during the Burger period has been different. Indeed, it is as if there were two Burger Courts: Burger Court I in the seventies and Burger Court II in the eighties. In 1970, the Court upheld the constitutionality of the tax exemption privilege accorded to churches. In view of the reality that the privilege had long existed when the Constitution was adopted, and that it has continued to exist without interruption in the federal government and all the states in the Union, it would have been completely unrealistic to have expected the Court to decide otherwise.

More important, in his opinion upholding the statute, Burger interpreted the Establishment Clause in a way that delighted the most doctrinaire of separationists. The clause, he said, invalidated a law if its purpose was to advance religion or if its effect (intended or not) was to advance religion, or if it resulted in excessive governmental entanglement with religion. The decisions in the next decade of Burger Court I indicate that in the *Walz* case it had meant what it said and not what it did. During that period with but one or two rather minor exceptions, it uniformly struck down under the Establishment Clause a variety of statutes enacted with the purpose of finding a way to finance parochial schools that the Court would accept. It was the Burger Court, which for the first time in American history, ruled unconstitutional laws appropriating funds to finance the operations of religious schools.

At the turn of the present decade, Burger Court II began handing down decisions pointing in the direction exactly opposite to that of the preceding decade. With two exceptions, however—one dealing with the posting of the Ten Commandments in public schools, and the other a very minor one dealing with the proximity to churches of restaurants serving intoxicating beverages—Burger Court II (which came into existence by reason of Justice Lewis F. Powell's conversion from absolutism to accommodationism) handed down rulings that made the separationists grieve and the accommodationists smile. Like probably all other strict separationists, I suffered a period of despondency, convinced that all that I and other absolutists had strived for in the seventies would be vitiated case by case in the eighties.

My period of acute despondency came to an end when I suddenly realized that Burger Court II had not overruled the absolutist decisions of Burger Court I. It had not, for example, overruled decisions ruling unconstitutional tax credits for parochial school tuition costs, or appropriations to finance instruction in those schools, or the posting of the Ten Commandments in public schools. It consistently rejected appeals from decisions outlawing prayer on public school premises before and after instructional hours. Instead, it limited itself to applying its laissez faire approach to fact situations that had not been passed upon by Burger Court I (e.g., allowing tax deductions for parochial school tuition payments, or prayer on college premises, or financing a crèche displayed during the Christmas season).

One can only speculate why Burger Court II contented itself with this compromise, rather than overruling the unhappy decisions of Burger Court I. Perhaps compromise was the price that had to be paid for Justice Powell's conversion.

Perhaps the Court did not want to emulate the recklessness of the Roosevelt-packed New Deal Court in overruling the decisions of its conservative predecessors. Indeed, it is even possible (but to political scientists, not likely) that the majority really believed that the Burger Court I cases were correctly decided, and so, too, were those of Burger Court II.

Whatever the explanation, the rulings of Burger Court I are still the supreme law of the land. Of course, as a strict separationist, I am not happy with this compromise. Then neither are protagonists of tax credits for parochial school tuition or school-sponsored prayers at the elementary and secondary school level, or teaching of creationism in the public school, or the prohibition of abortions. These prostrict separationist decisions still stand intact.

It may well eventuate that the reluctance of the 1980 Burger Court to overrule the 1970 Court decisions will not be shared by a new majority in which, like Sandra Day O'Connor, Republicans will replace Brennan and Marshall, and Burger Court III will follow the practice of the Roosevelt Court in not hesitating to overrule prior decisions it does not like. For the time being, however, the situation is not as tragic as we strict separationists have thought it to be.

NOTES

1. *McCollum* v. *Board of Education*, 333 U.S. 203 (1948).
2. *Zorach* v. *Clauson*, 343 U.S. 306 (1952).
3. *Friedman* v. *New York*, 341 U.S. 907 (1951).
4. The Synagogue Council of America is a coordinating body consisting of the organizations representing the three divisions of Jewish religious life, Orthodox, Conservative, and Reform, on the rabbinic and congregational levels.
5. The National Community Relations Advisory Council (now National Jewish Community Relations Advisory Council) is a coordinating body comprised of the major Jewish organizations, American Jewish Committee, American Jewish Congress, Anti-Defamation League of B'nai B'rith and others, and more than a hundred local councils concerned with American Jewish community relations.
6. *Heisler* v. *Board of Review*, 343 U.S. 939 (1952).
7. *Sherbert* v. *Verner*, 374 U.S. 398 (1963).
8. *Everson* v. *Board of Education*, 330 U.S. 1 (1947).
9. Leo Pfeffer, *Church, State, and Freedom*, rev. ed. (Boston: Beacon Press, 1967).
10. *Epperson* v. *Arkansas*, 393 U.S. 97 (1968).
11. *Stainback* v. *Mo Hock Ke Lok Po*, 336 U.S. 368 (1949).
12. *Meyer* v. *Nebraska*, 262 U.S. 390 (1923).
13. *Muller* v. *Oregon*, 208 U.S. 412 (1908).
14. Milton Konvitz, "Pursuit of Liberty," *Common Ground* 9 (Winter 1949):99-101.

15.   *Furman* v. *Georgia*, 408 U.S. 238 (1972).

16.   "Private Attorneys-General: Group Action in the Fight for Civil Liberties," *Yale Law Journal* 58 (March 1949):574-98.

17.   Psalms 118:22.

18.   Pfeffer, "Religion, Education, and the Constitution," *Lawyers Guild Review* 8 (May-June 1948):387-99; "The Fight Against Released Time," *The Standard* 35 (November 1948):4-10.

19.   *Walz* v. *Tax Commission*, 397 U.S. 664 (1970).

20.   Anson Phelps Stokes, *Church and State in the United States*, 3 vols. (New York: Harper & Brothers, 1950).

21.   Charles S. Desmond, "Church, State, and Freedom," *Harvard Law Review* 67 (January 1954):536-38.

22.   Paul Kauper, "Church, State, and Freedom: A Review," *Michigan Law Review* 52 (April 1954):829-48.

23.   Pfeffer, "Released Time and Religious Liberty: A Reply," *Michigan Law Review* 53 (November 1954):91-98; Kauper, "Released Time and Religious Liberty: A Further Reply," *Michigan Law Review* 53 (November 1954):233-36.

24.   Sanford Cobb, *Rise of Religious Liberty in America: A History* (New York: Cooper Square Publishers, 1968); Alvin Johnson and Frank Yost, *Separation of Church and State in the United States* (Minneapolis: University of Minnesota Press, 1984); and William Torpey, *Judicial Doctrines of Religious Rights in America* (Chapel Hill: University of North Carolina Press, 1948).

25.   Pfeffer, "Is It the Government's Business?" *The Christian Century* (30 October 1957):1281-83.

26.   Pfeffer, *The Liberties of an American: The Supreme Court Speaks* (Boston: Beacon Press, 1956).

27.   Pfeffer, *This Honorable Court: A History of the Supreme Court* (Boston: Beacon Press, 1965).

28.   *National Association for the Advancement of Colored People* v. *Alabama*, ex rel. Patterson, 357 U.S. 449 (1958).

29.   Pfeffer, "Countering the Cults—and the Constitution," *New York Times* (8 October 1980), A26.

30.   *Holy Spirit Association for the Unification of World Christianity* v. *The Tax Commission of the City of New York*, 55 NY 2d (1982).

31.   *Harris* v. *McRae*, 448 U.S. 297 (1980).

32.   *Poelker* v. *Doe*, 432 U.S. 519 (1977).

33.   *Torcaso* v. *Watkins*, 367 U.S. 488 (1961).

34.   Pfeffer, "The Supreme Court and Secular Humanism," *Free Inquiry* 2 (Spring 1982):24-27.

35.   *Tudor* v. *Board of Education*, 348 U.S. 816 (1954).

36.   *Abington School District* v. *Schempp*, 374 U.S. 203 (1963).

37.   *Engel* v. *Vitale*, 370 U.S. 421 (1962).

38.   Editorial: "To Our Jewish Friends," *America* 107 (1 September 1962):665-66.

39.   Robert L. Cord, *Separation of Church and State: Historical Fact and Current Fiction* (New York: Lambeth Press, 1982), 19.

40.   John W. Donahue, "Prayer in the Schools: The Unanswered Question," *America* 147 (25 September 1982):146-50.

41.   *Stone* v. *Graham*, 449 U.S. 39 (1980).

42.   *Board of Education* v. *Allen*, 392 U.S. 236 (1968).

43.   *Flast* v. *Cohen*, 392 U.S. 83 (1968).

44.   *Lanza* v. *New York*, 370 U.S. 139 (1962).

45.   *Diffenderfer* v. *Central Baptist Church of Miami, Florida*, 404 U.S. 412 (1972).

46.   *Plyler* v. *Doe*, 457 U.S. 202 (1981).

47.   *Tilton* v. *Richardson*, 403 U.S. 672 (1971); *Lemon* v. *Kurtzman*, 403 U.S. 602 (1971); and *Earley* v. *DiCenso*, 403 U.S. 602 (1971).

48.   *Committee for Public Education and Religious Liberty* v. *Nyquist*, 413 U.S. 756 (1973).

49. *Meek* v. *Pittenger*, 421 U.S. 349 (1975).
50. Pfeffer, *Religion, State, and the Burger Court* (Buffalo, N.Y.: Prometheus, 1985).
51. Appendix to *Everson* v. *Board of Education*, at 65.

The Writings of Leo Pfeffer

PREPARED BY FREDA PFEFFER

BOOKS AND PAMPHLETS

Released Time: A Study from the Jewish Viewpoint. New York: American Jewish Congress, 1945. A pamphlet.

"Religion and the Public Schools." *Jewish Affairs* 2 (15 December 1947). Rev. in 3 (15 February 1949). A pamphlet.

Church, State and Freedom. Boston: Beacon Press, 1953. Rev. ed., 1967.

The Common Core of Religious Teachings. New York: American Jewish Congress Office of Jewish Information, 1954. A pamphlet.

The Liberties of an American. Boston: Beacon Press, 1956. 2nd ed., 1963.

Creeds in Competition. New York: Harper and Row, 1958.

Church and State in the United States (with Anson Phelps Stokes). New York: Harper and Row, 1964.

Save the Bill of Rights. New York: Jewish Advisory Committee of Synagogue Council of America and National Jewish Community Relations Advisory Council, 1964. A pamphlet.

This Honorable Court. Boston: Beacon Press, 1965.

God, Caesar, and the Constitution. Boston: Beacon Press, 1974.

Freedom and Responsibility. New York: National Project Center for Film and the Humanities, Inc., 1974. A pamphlet.

The Bill of Rights: A Tale of Two Centuries. New York: National Project Center for Film and the Humanities Inc., 1975. A pamphlet.

Religious Freedom. Skokie, Ill.: National Textbook Co., 1976.

Religion, State, and the Burger Court. Buffalo, N.Y.: Prometheus, 1985.

ARTICLES AND BOOK REVIEWS

1944

"The Council for Religious Observance." *Young Israel Viewpoint* (June 1944):9-10.

"The Sunday Law and the Sabbath Observer." *Jewish Forum* 27 (July 1944):131-32.

1945

"New York's Anti-Discrimination Law." *Jewish Forum* 28

(October 1945):246-49.

"How Free Shall Speech Be?" *Congress Weekly* 12 (7 December 1945):6-8.

1946

"Defense Against Group Defamation." *Jewish Frontier* 13 (February 1946):6-8.

"Columbia's Restricted Clientele." *Jewish Spectator* 11 (July 1946):25-28.

1947

"A Little Case Over Bus Fares." *Congress Weekly* 14 (21 March 1947):5-7.

Review of *Religion in Public Education*, by V. T. Thayer. *The Standard* 33 (April 1947):259-61.

1948

"Religion Before the Supreme Court." *Congress Weekly* 15 (9 January 1948):10-11.

"Religion, Education, and the Constitution." *Lawyers Guild Review* 8 (May-June 1948):387-400.

"The Fight Against Released Time." *The Standard* 35 (November 1948):4-10.

1949

"The Meaning of the First Amendment." Address delivered at First National Conference on Church and State, Americans United, Washington, D.C., 27 January 1949. In *Liberty* 44 (Second Quarter 1949):5-10.
ter 1949):5-10.

"The Dixon Case in New Mexico." *American Jewish Congress CLSA Reports* (30 June 1949):1-3.

"The Church Says No." *Jewish Frontier* 16 (October 1949): 9-12.

"The Church Says No." *American Jewish Congress CLSA Reports* (October 1949):1-4.

1950

Review of *Separation of Church and State in the United States*, by Alvin W. Johnson and Frank H. Yost; *Religion and Education Under the Constitution*, by J. M. O'Neill; and *The First Freedom*, by Wilfred Parsons, S.J. *Columbia Law Review* 50 (January 1950):117-22.

"Sunday Law and Sabbath Observance." *Congress Weekly* 17 (3 February 1950):9-11. Reprinted in *Liberty* 45 (Second Quarter 1950):17-21; and in newspapers in Canada, Chile, England, and Germany.

"Constitutional Aspects of Religion in State Universities." In *Religion in the State Universities: An Initial Exploration*, edited by Henry E. Allen, 44-52. Minneapolis: Burgess, 1950. Paper originally presented at Conference on Religion in State Universities, University of Minnesota, Minneapolis, 28 October 1949.

1951

"The Supreme Court as Protector of Civil Rights: Freedom of Religion." *The Annals of the American Academy of Political and Social Science* 275 (May 1951):75-85.

"Judgment by Attack and Default." *Congress Weekly* 18 (25 June 1951):7-8.

"Heresy, American Democracy and 'The Miracle.'" *Jewish Frontier* 17 (August 1951):14-18.

"The Supreme Court as Protector of Freedom of Religion." *Liberty* 7 (Fourth Quarter 1951):21-28.

"Church and State: Something Less than Separation." *University of Chicago Law Review* 19 (Autumn 1951):1-29; reprinted in *Liberty* 47 (First Quarter 1951):36-50 under the title, "Church-State Tensions in Public Education: The Meaning of the First Amendment." Paper originally presented at University of Chicago Law School, 10 May 1951.

1952

"In Defense of the Public School." *The Standard* 38 (February-March 1952):83-86.

"Victims of Sectarian Conflict." *Congress Weekly* 19 (3 March 1952):17-19.

"Summary of Argument Before the United States Supreme Court in 'The Miracle' Case." *American Jewish Congress CLSA Reports* (28 April 1952):1-8.

"'The Miracle' Case: Shall the State Suppress Heresy?" *Congress Weekly* 19 (28 April 1952):9-11.

"Summary and Analysis of Decisions in 'Miracle' and 'Pinky' Cases." *American Jewish Congress CLSA Reports* (10 June 1952):1-4.

"The Outlook in the Struggle for Church-State Separation." *Jewish Education* 23 (Fall 1952):24-28. Paper presented at Institute on Religion in Public Education, Central Conference of American Rabbis, New York, 7 May 1952.

1953

"No Law Respecting an Establishment of Religion." *Buffalo Law Review* 2 (Spring 1953):1-17.

"Setback for Religious Liberty." *Congress Weekly* 20 (25 May 1953):9-11.

"The Prospect in Church-State Relations." *Jewish Education* 23 (Fall 1953):24-28.
"The Gideons March on the Schools." *Congress Weekly* 20 (5 October 1953):7-9.
Review of *America's Way in Church, State and Society*, by Joseph M. Dawson. *The Annals of the American Academy of Political and Social Science* 290 (November 1953):166-67.

1954

Review of *The Russian Church and the Soviet State*, by John S. Curtiss, and *The Irish and Catholic Power*, by Paul Blanshard. *Congress Weekly* 21 (3 May 1954):15-16.
"Released Time and Religious Liberty: A Reply." *Michigan Law Review* 53 (November 1954):91-98.
"A New Religion in the Schools?" *Congress Weekly* 21 (8 November 1954):8-10.
Review of *Man Against the Church: The Struggle to Free Man's Religious Spirit*, by Duncan Howlett. *The Annals of the American Academy of Political and Social Science* 296 (November 1954):193-94.
Review of *Catholicism in America*, by Editors of *Commonweal; The Catholic Church in World Affairs*, edited by Waldemar Gurian and N. A. Fitzsimons; and *Religion Behind the Iron Curtain*, by George N. Shuster. *Congress Weekly* 21 (1 November 1954):14-15.

1955

"Blasphemy on the Potomac." *The Christian Register* 134 (March 1955):11-13.
Review of *Bill of Rights Reader* (Cornell Studies in Civil Liberty), by Milton R. Konvitz. *The Annals of the American Academy of Political and Social Science* 298 (March 1955): 188-89. Reprinted in *Jewish Frontier* 22 (February 1955):42.
"Religion by Compulsion." *Congress Weekly* 22 (25 April 1955):5-7.
"Secularizing the Ketubah." *The Jewish Horizon* 17 (June 1955):7-8.
"Religion in the Upbringing of Children." *Boston University Law Review* 35 (June 1955):333-93. Paper presented at Civil Rights Seminar, Yale Law School, New Haven, Connecticut, December 1954.
"Church and National Policy." *The Christian Century* 72 (21 September 1955):1086-88. Paper originally presented at annual meeting of Americans United, Washington, D.C., 19 January 1955.

Review of *The American Legal System*, by Lewis Mayers. *The Annals of the American Academy of Political and Social Science* 301 (September 1955):215-16.

"Religious Freedom in the United States." *Congress Weekly* 22 (28 November 1955):12-16; and in *Liberty* 51 (Third Quarter 1956):11-14 under title "The Meaning of Separation of Church and State"; 51 (Fourth Quarter 1956):18-21 under title "Establishment of Religion"; and 52 (First Quarter 1957):14-16 under title "Judicial Application of the Separation Doctrine." Originally presented to Subcommittee on Constitutional Rights, U.S. Senate Committee on the Judiciary, Washington, D.C., 3 October 1955, under the title "Freedom of Religion and Separation of Church and State."

"Should Our Public Schools Teach Religion?" *Hadassah Newsletter* 35 (December 1955):1,13.

1956

"American Individualism and Horace Kallen's Idea." In *Cultural Pluralism and the American Idea*, edited by Horace M. Kallen, 159-60. Philadelphia: University of Pennsylvania Press, 1956.

"Issues that Divide." *The Journal of Social Issues* 12 (1956): 21-39.

Review of *Scrolls from the Dead Sea*, by Edmund Wilson; *The Dead Sea Scrolls*, by Millar Burrows; and *The Jewish Sect of Qumran and the Essenes*, by A. Dupont-Sommer. *Congress Weekly* 23 (9 January 1956):13-14.

Review of *Nine Men*, by Fred Rodell. *New York University Law Review* 31 (January 1956):242-48.

Review of *Nine Men*, by Fred Rodell. *The Annals of the American Academy of Political and Social Science* 303 (January 1956): 208-9.

Review of *The Growth of the Pentateuch*, by Immanuel Lewy. *Congress Weekly* 23 (27 February 1956):13-14.

"The Outlook in Church and State." *Congress Weekly* 23 (16 April 1956):8-11.

"Qumran and Christianity." *Congress Weekly* 23 (30 April 1956):8-10.

Review of *Who Crucified Jesus?* by Solomon Zeitlin. *Congress Weekly* 23 (23 June 1956):16-17.

Review of *The New Testament and Rabbinic Judaism*, by David Daub. *Judaism: A Quarterly Journal of Jewish Life and*

Thought 5 (Fall 1956):373-75.

Review of *The Essenes and the Kabbalah*, by Christian D. Ginsburg. *Congress Weekly* 23 (8 October 1956):15-16.

Review of *The Meaning of the Dead Sea Scrolls*, by A. Powell Davies; *The Dead Sea Scrolls and the Originality of Christ*, by Geoffrey Graystone; *The Qumran Community*, by Charles T. Fritsch; and *Treasure From Judean Caves*, by R. B. Scott. *Congress Weekly* 23 (19 November 1956):12-13.

1957

"Judicial Applications of the Separation Doctrine." *Liberty* 52 (First Quarter 1957):14-16.

"A New Religion in America." *The Churchman* 173 (April 1959):9-10. Paper originally presented at convention of Women's Division of American Jewish Congress, Washington, D.C., 7 May 1957.

"Review of *Discovery in the Judean Desert*, by Geza Vermes; *The Dead Sea Scriptures in English Translation*, by Theodore H. Gaster; and *The Dead Sea Scrolls*, by J. M. Allegro. *Congress Weekly* 24 (20 May 1957):13-14.

"Is It the Government's Business?" *The Christian Century* 74 (30 October 1957):1281-83.

1958

"Church and State: The Case for Separation." In *Religion in America*, edited by Earl Cogley, 52-94. New York: Meridian Books, Inc. 1958. Paper originally presented at Seminar on Religion and the Free Society, Fund for the Republic, New York City, 5-9 May 1958.

"Are Sunday Laws Religious Laws?" *Liberty* 53 (Fourth Quarter 1958):16-20.

1959

"Church and State: A Jewish Approach," *The Princeton Seminary Bulletin* 53 (October 1959):37-48. Also in *Jews in the Modern World*, edited by Jacob Freid, 1:207-23. New York: Twayne Publishers, Inc., 1962. Paper presented at Convocation of Faculty and Students, Princeton Theological Seminary, Princeton, New Jersey, 22 April 1959.

Review of *The Ancient Library of Qumran and Modern Biblical Studies*, by Frank M. Cross, Jr. *Judaism* 8 (Winter 1959): 89-91.

1960

"Sunday Laws Are Religious Laws." *Liberty* 55 (January-February 1960):9,30-31.

"Changing Relationships Among Religious Groups." *The*

Journal of Intergroup Relations 1 (Spring 1960):81-93; and in *Minority Problems*, edited by Arnold M. Rose and Caroline B. Rose, 33-41. New York: Harper and Row, 1965. Paper originally presented at Conference of National Association Intergroup Relations Officials, New York City, 21 January 1960.

"State Sunday Laws Violate the First Amendment." *Liberty* 55 (March-April 1960):15-16, 26-27.

"Sunday Laws—An Unconstitutional Exercise of Police Power." *Liberty* 55 (May-June 1960):15-16, 27-28.

"Freedom and Separation: America's Contribution to Civilization." *Journal of Church and State* 2 (November 1960):100-111; and in *Religious Conflict in America*, edited by Earl Rabb, 152-63. Garden City, N.Y.: Doubleday, Anchor Books, 1964. Paper originally presented at First Annual J. M. Dawson Lectures on Church and State, the Institute of Church-State Studies, Baylor University, Waco, Texas, 28 April 1960.

1961

"Federal Aid to Public Grade and High Schools." *Congress Weekly* 28 (17 April 1961):7-8. Statement submitted to U.S. House Committee on Education and Labor, 29 March 1961.

"New Frontiers in Social Action," *Jewish Heritage* 4 (Winter 1961-62):46-49. Under title "The Synagogue and Social Action," address at Convention, National Federation of Jewish Men's Clubs, Liberty, New York, 16 May 1961.

"The United States Supreme Court Decisions in the Sunday Law Cases." *American Jewish Congress CLSA Reports* (8 June 1961):1-19.

"The Sunday Law Decisions." *Congress Bi-Weekly* 28 (26 June 1961):7-9.

"Federal Aid for Private and Parochial Schools? No." *Current History* 41 (August 1961):77-81.

"Supreme Court's Changing Interests." *The Nation* 193 (23 September 1961):180-81.

"An Analysis of Federal Aid to Parochial Schools." *Journal of Church and State* 3 (November 1961):137-48.

"Some Current Issues in Church and State." *Western Reserve Law Review* 17 (December 1961):9-33.

1962

"Federal Funds for Parochial Schools? No." *Notre Dame Lawyer* 37 (March 1962):309-22.

Review of *The Bible, Religion and the Public School*, by Donald
E. Boles. *Yale Law Journal* 71 (March 1962):801-4.
"The Jewish Rationale for Social Action." *American Jewish
Congress CLSA Information Bulletin* 1 (1 May 1962):1-4.
Also in *A Reader in Jewish Community Relations*, edited by
Ann G. Wolfe, 206-10. New York: KTAV Publishing
House, Inc., 1975.
"Literacy and the Right to Vote." *American Jewish Congress
CLSA Information Bulletin* 2 (15 May 1962):1-4.
"Court, Constitution, and Prayer." *Rutgers Law Review* 16
(Summer 1962):735-52.
"Religious Confusion and Public Education." *American Juda-
ism* 11 (Summer 1962):7-9.
"Shared Time." *American Jewish Congress CLSA Information
Bulletin* 3 (1 June 1962):1-4.
"Censorship—Public and Private." *American Jewish Congress
CLSA Information Bulletin* 4 (15 June 1962):1-4.
"Second Thoughts on Shared Time." *The Christian Century* 79
(20 June 1962):779-80.
"Non-Citizens and Not Quite Full Citizens." *American Jewish
Congress CLSA Information Bulletin* 5 (15 July 1962):1-4.
"State Sponsored Prayer." *Commonweal* 76 (27 July 1962):
417-19. Also in *American Government: The Clash of Issues*,
edited by James A. Burkhart et al., 174-76. Englewood
Cliffs, N.J.: Prentice Hall, 1962. Rev. ed., 1964.
"Who's Who in the Prayer Controversy." *American Jewish
Congress CLSA Information Bulletin* 6 (15 August 1962):1-4.
"Dialogue in Jerusalem." *American Jewish Congress CLSA In-
formation Bulletin* 7 (4 September 1962):1-4.
"'America' v. The Jews." *American Jewish Congress CLSA
Information Bulletin* 8 (17 September 1962):1-4.
"The Faceless Accuser." *American Jewish Congress CLSA In-
formation Bulletin* 9 (1 October 1962):1-4.
"The Sorry Record of the 87th Congress-or-Much Ado About
Less Than Nothing." *American Jewish Congress CLSA In-
formation Bulletin* 10 (15 October 1962):1-4.
"What and Why is the NCRAC?" *American Jewish Congress
CLSA Information Bulletin* 11 (1 November 1962):1-4.
"The New York Regents' Prayer Case." *Journal of Church
and State* 4 (November 1962):150-59.
"Agenda for the 88th Congress." *American Jewish Congress
CLSA Information Bulletin* 12 (15 November 1962):1-4.
"Counterreflections on Church and State." *Midstream* 8
(December 1962):15-23.

"The Fifth Amendment." *American Jewish Congress CLSA Information Bulletin* 13 (December 1962):1-4.

"Catholics and the Secular Public School." *American Jewish Congress CLSA Information Bulletin* 14 (17 December 1962):1-4.

Review of *Render unto Caesar: The Flag Salute Controversy*, by David R. Manwaring. *Fordham Law Review* 31 (December 1962):405-8.

1963

"Religious Tests for Public Office." *New Catholic Encyclopedia.* New York: McGraw Hill, 1971. 12:332-35.

Review of *Render Unto Caesar: The Flag Salute Controversy*, by David R. Manwaring. *The Annals of the American Academy of Political and Social Science* 345 (January 1963):154-55.

"Sunday Law and Sabbath Observers." *American Jewish Congress CLSA Information Bulletin* 15 (2 January 1963):1-4.

"Federal Aid to Church-Related Colleges?" *American Jewish Congress CLSA Information Bulletin* 16 (1 March 1963):1-4.

"The President's Civil Rights Program." *American Jewish Congress CLSA Information Bulletin* 17 (15 March 1963): 1-4.

"Religion-Blind Government." *Stanford Law Review* 15 (March 1963):389-406.

"The Pros and Cons of Group Libel." *American Jewish Congress CLSA Information Bulletin* 18 (1 April 1963):1-4.

"Recent Developments in Sunday Laws." *American Jewish Congress CLSA Information Bulletin* 19 (17 April 1963):1-4.

"Assault on Court and Constitution." *American Jewish Congress CLSA Information Bulletin* 20 (1 May 1963):1-4.

"Church and State in 1963." *Conservative Judaism* 17 (Spring-Summer 1963):1-38. Paper presented at annual convention, Rabbinical Assembly, Greenfield Park, New York, 8 May 1963.

"Why Fight for Church-State Separation?" *American Jewish Congress CLSA Information Bulletin* 21 (15 May 1963):1-4.

"Posthumous Assault on Civil Liberties." *American Jewish Congress CLSA Information Bulletin* 22 (3 June 1963):1-4.

"The President's Second Message on Civil Rights." *American Jewish Congress CLSA Information Bulletin* 23 (19 June 1963):1-4.

"Aftermath of the Bible Decision—Chapter I." *American Jewish Congress CLSA Information Bulletin* 24 (15 July 1963): 1-4.

"Quotas, Compensation, and Unlawful Demonstrations—Part I." *American Jewish Congress CLSA Information Bulletin* 25 (15 August 1963):1-4.

"Quotas, Compensation, and Unlawful Demonstrations—Part II." *American Jewish Congress CLSA Information Bulletin* 26 (1 September 1963):1-4.

Review of *Religion and the Law: Of Church and State and the Supreme Court*, by Philip B. Kurland. *Review of Religious Research* 5 (Fall 1963):57-58.

"Aftermath of the Bible Decision—Chapter 2." *American Jewish Congress CLSA Information Bulletin* 27 (1 October 1963): 1-4.

"A Suggested Program for a Lawful Revolution—Part I." *American Jewish Congress CLSA Information Bulletin* 28 (15 October 1963):1-4.

"A Suggested Program for a Lawful Revolution—Part II." *American Jewish Congress CLSA Information Bulletin* 29 (1 November 1963):1-4.

"This Honorable Court." *American Jewish Congress CLSA Information Bulletin* 30 (15 November 1963):1-4.

"The Schempp-Murray Decision on School Prayers and Bible Reading." *Journal of Church and State* 5 (November 1963): 165-75.

"Federal Aid and Judicial Review." *American Jewish Congress CLSA Information Bulletin* 31 (1 December 1963):1-4.

1964

"A Momentous Year in Church and State." *Journal of Church and State* 6 (Winter 1964):36-43.

Review of *The Hebrew Scriptures: An Introduction to Their Literature and Religious Ideas*, by Samuel Sandmel. *Judaism* 13 (Winter 1964):121-28.

"A Momentous Year in Church and State." *American Jewish Congress CLSA Information Bulletin* 32 (1 January 1964): 1-4.

"Protective Silencing." *American Jewish Congress CLSA Information Bulletin* 33 (15 January 1964):1-4.

"The Courts and De Facto Segregation: Part I." *American Jewish Congress CLSA Information Bulletin* 34 (1 February 1964):1-4.

"From Religious Monism to Pluralism in the United States." *Congress Bi-Weekly* 31 (10 February 1964):7-8,13.

"The Becker Amendment." *American Jewish Congress CLSA*

Information Bulletin 35 (15 February 1964):1-4.
"Protestants Look at Church and State." *American Jewish Congress CLSA Information Bulletin* 36 (1 March 1964):1-4.
"The Courts and De Facto Segregation: Part II." *American Jewish Congress CLSA Information Bulletin* 37 (15 March 1964): 1-4.
"Conscientious Objectors and the Constitution." *American Jewish Congress CLSA Information Bulletin* 38 (1 May 1964): 1-4.
"A Decade in Civil Rights." *American Jewish Congress CLSA Information Bulletin* 39 (1 June 1964):1-4.
"A City in Terror: Part I." *American Jewish Congress CLSA Information Bulletin* 40 (1 July 1964):1-4.
"A City in Terror: Part II." *American Jewish Congress CLSA Information Bulletin* 41 (1 August 1964):1-4.
"A Decade in Civil Liberties." *American Jewish Congress CLSA Information Bulletin* 42 (1 September 1964):1-4.
"The Becker Amendment." *Journal of Church and State* 6 (Autumn 1964):344-51.
"The Civil Rights Act of 1964." *American Jewish Congress CLSA Information Bulletin* 43 (1 October 1964):1-4.

1965
"The Price We Pay for Federal Aid." *Midstream* 11 (March 1965):38-42.
"Contract and Status in Religion and Law." *Church-State Relations in Ecumenical Perspective*, edited by Elwyn Smith, 218-27. Duquesne: Duquesne University Press, 1966. Paper originally presented at Duquesne University, Pittsburgh, Pennsylvania, 2 November 1965.
Review of *Religion in American Public Law*, by David Fellman. *The Annals of the American Academy of Political and Social Science* 362 (November 1965):143-44.

1966
"Reflections on Conversion." *Congress Bi-Weekly* 33 (24 January 1966):5.
"The 'Child Benefit' Theory and Church-State Separation." *Church and State* 19 (April 1966):6-7; also published as a pamphlet: Washington, D.C.: Americans United, 1966. Paper originally presented at National Conference on Church and State, Americans United, Nashville, Tennessee, 22 February 1966.
"Portent or Sport?" *Congress Bi-Weekly* 33 (4 April 1966):5-6.

"Intellectual Integrity." *Congress Bi-Weekly* 33 (25 April 1966): 6-7.

"Constitutional Confrontation in New York State." *The Christian Century* 83 (13 July 1966):885-87.

"The Supreme Court and the Bill of Rights: Freedom of Expression." *The Nation* 203 (3 October 1966):315-18.

"The Supreme Court and the Bill of Rights: Justice for the Accused." *The Nation* 203 (10 October 1966):351-54.

"The Supreme Court and the Bill of Rights: Discovery of Equality." *The Nation* 203 (17 October 1966):385-88.

"Is the First Amendment Dead?" *Congress Bi-Weekly* 33 (7 November 1966):4-7.

"Is the First Amendment Obsolete?" In *A Reader in Jewish Community Relations*, edited by Ann G. Wolfe, 195-99. New York: KTAV, 1975. Paper originally presented as position paper at Conference on Religion in the Census, National Jewish Community Relations Advisory Council, Synagogue Council of America, and Council of Jewish Federations and Welfare Funds, New York City, 16 October 1966.

Review of *The Garden and the Wilderness: Religion and Government in American Constitutional History*, by Mark DeWolfe Howe. *Political Science Quarterly* 81 (December 1966): 655-56.

"The Supreme Court and the Bill of Rights." Brooklyn, N.Y.: Long Island University Press, 1966. Paper originally presented at Conference on the Bill of Rights Today and Tomorrow, Long Island University, Brooklyn, New York, 9 December 1966.

1967

"What Price Federal Aid?" *Saturday Review* (21 January 1967):59-60,80. Reprinted in *Contemporary American Issues and Problems*, edited by Maurice Boyd and Donald Worcester, 285-88. Boston: Allyn & Bacon, Inc., 1968.

"Church and School." *The Nation* 205 (23 October 1967): 389-90.

1968

"Commentary on Bellah's Essay: Civil Religion in America." In *The Religious Situation*, edited by Donald R. Cutler, 360-65. Boston: Beacon Press, 1968.

Review of *Religion, Politics, and Diversity: The Church-State Theme in New York History*, by John W. Pratt. *Journal of Church and State* 10 (Winter 1968):117-19.

1969

"Crisis in Catholicism." *Congress Bi-Weekly* 36 (13 January 1969):8-11.

"Should Churches Be Taxed?" *Congress Bi-Weekly* 36 (24 March 1969):11-14.

"Church, State, and American Jewry." In *A Reader in Jewish Community Relations*, by Ann G. Wolfe, 179-85. New York: KTAV, 1975. Paper originally presented at plenary session of National Jewish Community Relations Advisory Council, Pittsburgh, Pennsylvania, 30 June 1969.

Review of *Expanding Liberties: Freedom's Gains in Postwar America*, by Milton R. Konvitz. *Jewish Social Studies* (October 1969):345-46.

"The Intolerable Death Penalty." *Congress Bi-Weekly* 36 (13 October 1969):10-12.

Review of *Prayer in the Public Schools: Law and Attitude Change*, by William K. Muir, Jr. *Political Science Quarterly* 84 (December 1969):666-67.

1970

Review of *School Prayer: Congress, the Courts, and the Public*, by John J. Laubach. *Journal of Church and State* 12 (Winter 1970):135-37.

"What Hath God Wrought to Caesar: The Church as a Self-Interest Interest Group." *Journal of Church and State* 13 (Winter 1971):97-112. Paper presented at Joint Annual Meeting of American Academy of Religion, Society for the Scientific Study of Religion, and Society of Biblical Literature, New York City, 22 October 1970.

"Ready, Aim, Pray." *Commonweal* 93 (11 December 1970): 274-76.

1971

"The Right to Religious Liberty." In *The Rights of Americans*, edited by Norman Dorsen, 336-47. New York: Pantheon Books, Random House, 1971.

"No Public Funds for Parochial Schools." *Church and State* 24 (March 1971):10.

"The Parochiaid Decision." *Today's Education* 60 (September 1971):63-64,79.

"The Misguided Prayer Amendment." *Congress Bi-Weekly* 38 (29 October 1971):5-6.

1972

"Quotas, Compensation, and Open Enrollment." *Congress Bi-Weekly* 39 (25 February 1972):4-9.

"Political Religion Is Dangerous." *Sh'ma* 2 (19 May 1972):99.

Review of *The Sectarian College and the Public Purse: Fordham— A Case Study*, by Walter Gellhorn and R. Kent Greenawalt. *Texas Law Review* 50 (August 1972):1288-91.

"Aid to Parochial Schools: A Chess Game with the Constitution." *Reform Judaism* 1 (October 1972):5.

"American Jewry and National Politics." *Our Age* 14 (5 November 1972):4-5.

1973

"The Supremacy of Free Exercise." *Georgetown Law Journal* 61 (May 1973):1115-42.

"Background," "Discussion Guide," and "Bibliography," for *Abandon Ship* (a film by Richard Sale). New York City: Center for Film and the Humanities, Inc., 1973.

Review of *Self-Incrimination in Jewish Law*, by Aaron Kirschenbaum. *Judaism* 22 (Winter 1973):107-14; and in *Israel Yearbook on Human Rights* 2 (1972):365-72.

1974

"Aid to Parochial Schools: The Verge and Beyond." *Journal of Law and Education* 3 (January 1974):115-21.

"Who Is Worthy to Lead Us in Prayer?" *Sh'ma* 4 (22 February 1974):59-60.

"The Legitimation of Marginal Religions in the United States." In *Religious Movements in Contemporary America*, edited by Irving I. Zaretsky and Mark P. Leone, 9-26. Princeton, N.J.: Princeton University Press, 1974. Paper originally presented at Conference on Marginal Religious Movements in America, Princeton University, Princeton, New Jersey, 5 April 1971.

"A Modern Prayer." *Sh'ma* 4 (6 September 1974):127.

"Where Do I Stand Now?" *Judaism* 23 (Fall 1974):449-52.

1975

"The Illegitimacy of Illegitimacy." *Congress Monthly* 42 (March 1975):12-14.

"Feminism and Judaism." *Congress Monthly* 42 (June 1975): 12-14.

"The 'Catholic' Catholic Problem." *Commonweal* 102 (1 August 1975):302-30.

"The Fading of the Blue Laws." *Congress Monthly* 42 (September 1975):7-9.

"Uneasy Trinity: Church, State, and Constitution." *Civil Liberties Review* 2 (Winter 1975):138-61.

"Taxes: The Price of a Civilized Society." *Liberty* 71 (November-December 1975):16.

1976

Articles on "Joseph Bradley," "Davis Josiah Brewer," "Harold Hitz Burton," "Pierce Butler," "John Archibald Campbell," "John Catron," "John Hessin Clarke," "Nathan Clifford," "Benjamin Robbins Curtis," "William Cushing," "Peter Vivian Daniel," "Clarence Seward Darrow," "William Rufus Day," "Morris Leopold Ernst," "Stephen Johnson Field," "Abe Fortas," "John Marshall Harlan," "James Iredell," "Robert Houghwout Jackson," "Karl Nickerson Llewellyn," "Meyer London," "Horace Harmon Lurton," "George Sutherland," "Smith Thompson," "Thomas Todd," *"Granger Cases,"* and *"Texas* v. *White"* in *Encyclopedia Americana.* New York: Americana Corp., 1976.

"State's Blue Laws: The Penultimate Chapter." *New York Law Journal* 23 (June 1976):1.

"Abortion and Religious Freedom." *Congress Monthly* 43 (June 1976):9-12. Statement originally submitted to Subcommittee on Civil and Constitutional Rights, U.S. House Committee on the Judiciary, 24 March 1976, and reprinted as a pamphlet, *Abortion and Religious Freedom,* by Religious Coalition for Abortion Rights.

"Is the Conlon Amendment Unconstitutional?" *The Humanist* 31 (September-October 1976):9-10.

1977

"Church-State Relations Today." *Congress Monthly* 44 (February 1977):8-11.

"The Case Against Parochiaid." *Church and State* 30 (April 1977):14-17.

"Fair Employment for Sabbath Observers." *Congress Monthly* 44 (May 1977):8-10.

"Abortion Rights for the Poor: A Serious Setback." *American Jewish Congress CLSA Reports* (June 1977):1-3.

"Setback for Sabbath Observers." *American Jewish Congress CLSA Reports* (June 1977):1-3.

"The United States Supreme Court Decision in *Wolman* v. *Walter." American Jewish Congress CLSA Reports* (June 1977): 1-4.

"The Case for Keeping Separation Private." *Sh'ma* 7 (30 September 1977):153-55.

"The Supreme Court and Religion." *Congress Monthly* 44

(September 1977):9-12.

"Issues That Divide: The Triumph of Secular Humanism." *Journal of Church and State* 19 (Spring 1977):203-16. Paper originally presented under the title "Religious Pluralism in America: Issues That Divide—Twenty Years Later," at Joint Annual Meeting, Society for the Scientific Study of Religion, Religious Research Association, and Association of Professors and Researchers in Religious Education, Philadelphia, Pennsylvania, 29 October 1976.

"Parochiaid, the Supreme Court, and the Constitution." *Church and State* 30 (October 1977):9-11.

"Workers' Sabbath: Religious Belief and Employment." *Civil Liberties Review* 4 (November-December 1977):52-56.

"The United States Supreme Court Decision in *New York* v. *Cathedral Academy.*" *American Jewish Congress CLSA Reports* (December 1977):1-3.

"The Special Constitutional Status of Religion." In *Taxation and the Free Exercise of Religion*, edited by John W. Baker, 7-10. Washington, D.C.: Baptist Joint Committee on Public Affairs, 1977. Paper presented at Religious Liberty Conference, Baptist Joint Committee on Public Affairs, Washington, D.C., 3 October 1977.

1978

"Close Encounters: Church and State." Interview by Aron Hirt-Manheimer and Lisa von Valtier. *Keeping Posted* 23 (February 1978):20-23.

"United States Supreme Court Decision in *McDaniel* v. *Paty.*" *American Jewish Congress CLSA Reports* (May 1978):1-7.

"American Jews and Aid to Parochial Schools." *Congress Monthly* 45 (June 1978):34.

"Why Are We So Silent on Begin's Policies?" *Sh'ma* 8 (29 September 1978): 175-76.

Review of *Religion and Politics: The Intentions of the Authors of the First Amendment*, by Michael J. Malbin. *Church and State* 31 (September 1978):10-13.

"Church, State, and the Jewish Community." *Sh'ma* 8 (13 October 1978):185-87.

"Religion: A Precise Liberty Impossible to Define." *New Conversation* 3 (Fall 1978):4-7.

1979

"United States Supreme Court Decision in *NLRB* v. *Catholic Bishop of Chicago.*" *American Jewish Congress CLSA Reports* (April 1979):1-8.

"Sabbatarians and the Courts." *Civil Rights Digest* 2 (Spring 1979):28-33.

"Religious Freedom and the American Community." *Judaism* 28 (Spring 1979):137-46.

"Equal Protection for Unpopular Sects." *New York University Review of Law and Social Change* 9 (1979-80):9-15. Paper originally presented at Conference on Alternative Religions, Government Control, and the First Amendment, New York University, New York City, 3 November 1979.

"The Current State of the Law in the United States and the Separationist Agenda." *The Annals of the American Academy of Political and Social Science* 446 (November 1979):1-9.

Review of *Why Churches Should Not Be Taxed*, by Dean M. Kelley. *Journal of Church and State* 21 (Winter 1979): 114-15.

1980

"Freedom and/or Separation." *University of Minnesota Law Review* 64 (March 1980):561-84. Reprinted in *Union Seminary Quarterly Review* 38 (1984):337-59. Paper originally presented at Symposium on From Religious Toleration to Religious Freedom, Columbia University Department of Religion, Newport, Rhode Island, 24 May 1978.

"Priorities for the AJC." *Congress Monthly* 47 (June 1980):19-22. Paper originally presented at Annual Convention, American Jewish Congress, Washington, D.C., 1 May 1980.

"Unionization of Parochial School Teachers." *St. Louis University Law Journal* 24 (September 1980):273-94; reprinted in *Specialty Law Digest* 1 (August 1981):5-27.

"Public School Prayer—and What Next?" *The Christian Century* 87 (15 October 1980):958-59.

1981

"The Deity in American Constitutional History." J. M. Dawson Lecture on Church and State, Institute of Church-State Studies, Baylor University, Waco, Texas, 31 March 1981. *Journal of Church and State* 23 (Spring 1981):215-39.

"Public School Scientific Creationism." *Sh'ma* 12 (13 November 1981):161-63.

"Amici in Church-State Litigation." *Law and Contemporary Problems* 44 (Winter 1981):83-110.

1982

The Separation of Church and State." In *Speak Out Against*

the New Right, edited by Herbert F. Vetter, 75-82. Boston: Beacon Press, 1982.

"The Supreme Court and Secular Humanism." *Free Inquiry* 2 (Spring 1982):24-27.

"Jews and Jewry in American Constitutional History." In *Jews, Judaism, and the American Constitution*, edited by Jacob R. Marcus, 20-34. Cincinnati, Ohio: Hebrew Union College—Jewish Institute of Religion, 1982.

Review of *Jewish Justice and Reconciliation: History of the Jewish Conciliation Board of America 1930-1968*, by Israel Goldstein. *Judaism* 31 (Fall 1982):499-501.

"The Future of First Amendment Provisions Regarding Church-State Relations." In *The Future of Our Liberties: Perspectives on the Bill of Rights*, edited by Stephen C. Halpern, 111-29. Westport, Conn.: Greenwood Press, 1982. Paper originally presented at Conference on the Future of the Bill of Rights, Buffalo Civil Liberties Union and New York State Council for the Humanities, Buffalo, New York, 16 October 1978.

1983

"The Bible, the President and Church-State Separation," *Free Inquiry* 3 (Summer 1983):20-24. Paper originally presented at Symposium on Religion in American Politics, Washington, D.C., 16 March 1983.

1984

"Religious Exemptions." *Society* 21 (May-June 1984):17-22.

"Leo Pfeffer: Champion of Religious Liberty." Interview by Aron Hirt-Manheimer and Steven Schnur. *Reform Judaism* 13 (Fall 1984):8-9,29.

1986

"United States Constitution and Religion: First Amendment Issues." In *The Encyclopedia of Religion*. New York: Free Press, 1986.

1987

Articles on "American Jewish Congress," "Child Benefit Theory," "Cults (Religious) and the Constitution," "Government Aid to Sectarian Institutions," "Released Time," "Religion and Fraud," "Religion in Public Schools," "Religious Liberty," "Religious Tests for Public Office," and "Religious Use of State Property." In *The Encyclopedia of the American Constitution*. New York: Macmillan Co., 1987.

COURT BRIEFS
(p=brief for party in case; a=brief for amicus curiae)

1946

Davidescu v. *Rubenfeld* (p), 159 F.2d 147, aff'g 66 F.Supp. 747 (1946). Deportation of Jewish stowaway.

Goldstein v. *Mills* (a), 270 (N.Y.) App. Div. 930 (1946). Religious discrimination and tax exemption.

Kut v. *Bureau of Unemployment Compensation* (p), 146 Ohio St. 522 (1946). Unemployment compensation for Sabbatarians.

1948

Bull v. *Stichman* (a), 298 N.Y. 516 (1948). Taxpayer's standing to sue.

Kemp v. *Rubin* (a), 188 N.Y. Misc. 310 (1948). Housing discrimination.

McCollum v. *Board of Education* (a), 333 U.S. 203 (1948). Religious education in the public schools.

Takahashi v. *Fish & Game Commission* (a), 334 U.S. 410 (1948). Anti-Japanese discrimination.

1949

Hughes v. *Superior Court* (a), 339 U.S. 460 (1949). Racial quotas.

Stainback v. *Mo Hock Ke Lok Po* (a), 336 U.S. 368 (1949). Ban of foreign languages.

1951

Kelly v. *Inhabitants of Dover* (a), 100 N.E.2d 1751 (Mass. 1951). Zoning.

Friedman v. *New York* (p), 341 U.S. 907 (1951). Sunday laws.

1952

Burstyn v. *Wilson* (a), 343 U.S. 495 (1952). Censorship.

Doremus v. *Board of Education of New Jersey* (a), 342 U.S. 429 (1952). Standing to sue.

Gally, Petition of (a), 107 N.E.2d 21 (1952). Interreligious adoption.

Heisler v. *Board of Review* (p), 343 U.S. 939 (1952). Unemployment compensation for Sabbatarians.

Zorach v. *Clauson* (p), 343 U.S. 306 (1952). Released time.

1953

Barrows v. *Jackson* (a), 346 U.S. 249 (1953). Housing discrimination.

1954

Gideons International v. *Tudor* (p), 348 U.S. 816 (1954). Bible distribution.

Rice v. *Sioux City Memorial Park Cemetery* (a), 348 U.S. 880

(1954). Racial restrictive covenant.

Roman Catholic Welfare Corp. v. *City of Piedmont* (a), 289 P.2d 438 (Calif., 1954). Zoning.

Swenson v. *Michigan Employment Security Commission* (a), 65 N.W.2d 709 (1954). Unemployment compensation for Sabbatarians.

Tary v. *State of Ohio* (a), 119 N.E.2d 56 (1954). Unemployment compensation for Sabbatarians.

1955

Goldman v. *Fogarty* (p), 348 U.S. 942 (1955). Interreligious adoption.

1956

Diocese of Rochester v. *Planning Board of Town of Brighton* (a), 1 N.Y.2d 508 (1956). Zoning exclusion of churches.

Lynch v. *Uhlenhopp* (a), 78 N.W.2d 491 (Iowa, 1956). Divorce decree requiring wife to raise child as Catholic.

Miller, In the Matter of (a), 91 S.E.2d 24 (N.C., 1956). Unemployment compensation for Sabbatarians.

1957

Matter of Application of St. Matthew Episcopal Church and Mission School (a). Submitted to Albuquerque, N.M. City Board of Adjustment, in behalf of American Jewish Congress at request of Church. Not officially reported (1957). Zoning exclusion of churches.

1958

Baer v. *Kolmorgan* (p), 170 N.Y.S.2d 40 (1958). Nativity scene.

National Association for the Advancement of Colored People (NAACP) v. *Alabama* (a), 357 U.S. 449 (1958). Freedom of association.

Speiser v. *Randall* (a), 357 U.S. 513 (1958). Loyalty oath.

1959

Camacho, Matter of v. *John Doe* (a), 7 N.Y.2d 762 (1959). Literacy test in Spanish for voting qualification.

Petition and Appeal to Commissioner of Education, *Matter of Paulus* (a). Not officially reported. Racial segregation in public schools.

1960

Martin v. *City of New York* (a), 22 N.Y. Misc. 2d 389 (1960). Housing discrimination.

Talley v. *California* (a), 362 U.S. 60 (1960). Anonymous handbills ban.

1961

American Jewish Congress v. *Carter* (p), 9 N.Y.2d 223 (1961).

Religious discrimination for employment in Saudi Arabia.

Anonymous, Matter of (a), 10 N.Y.2d 740 (1961). Religious discrimination in admission to the bar.

Gallagher v. *Crown Kosher Supermarket* (a), 366 U.S. 617 (1961). Sunday laws.

Torcaso v. *Watkins* (p), 367 U.S. 488 (1961). Religious test for public office.

1962

Carlson v. *Dickman* (p), 371 U.S. 823 (1962). Religious school aid.

Engel v. *Vitale* (a), 370 U.S. 421 (1962). State sponsored school prayer.

Lanza v. *New York* (p), 370 U.S. 139 (1962). Prisoner's right to privacy.

1963

Abington School District v. *Schempp* (a), 374 U.S. 203 (1963). Prayer and Bible reading in the public schools.

Orange County Board of Public Instruction v. *Brown* (p), 155 S.2d 371 (Fla., 1963). Bible distribution.

Sherbert v. *Verner* (a), 374 U.S. 398 (1963). Unemployment compensation for Sabbatarians.

1964

Balaban v. *Rubin* (a), 14 N.Y.2d 193 (1964). Housing discrimination.

Chamberlin v. *Dade County* (p), 377 U.S. 402 (1964). Prayer and Bible reading in the public schools.

Davis v. *Mann* (a), 377 U.S. 678 (1964). Reapportionment.

Maryland Committee for Fair Representation v. *Tawes* (a), 377 U.S. 656 (1964). Reapportionment.

Reynolds v. *Sims* (a), 377 U.S. 533 (1964). Reapportionment.

WMCA v. *Lomenzo* (a), 377 U.S. 633 (1964). Reapportionment.

1965

O'Hare v. *Detroit Board of Education* (a), 106 N.W.2d 538 (Mich., 1965). Public funds and religious schools.

United States v. *Seeger* (a), 380 U.S. 163 (1965). Conscientious objection.

1966

Abel v. *Lomenzo* (a), 25 N.Y. App. Div. 2d 104 (1966). Housing discrimination.

Brown v. *Heller* (p), 51 Misc. 2d 660 (1966). Public funds and religious schools.

Cardona v. *Power* (a), 384 U.S. 672 (1966). Literacy test.

Horace Mann League v. *Board of Public Works* (p), 385 U.S. 97 (1966). Public funds and religious schools.

1967

Garber v. *Kansas* (a), 389 U.S. 51 (1967). Compulsory school attendance.

Worrell v. *Matters* (p), 226 A.2d 53, cert. denied 389 U.S. 846 (1967). Public funds and religious schools.

1968

Alexander v. *Bartlett* (p), 14 Mich. App. 177 (1968). Public funds and religious schools.

Board of Education v. *Allen* (a), 392 U.S. 236 (1968). Public funds and religious schools.

Epperson v. *Arkansas* (a), 393 U.S. 97 (1968). Evolution and the public schools.

Flast v. *Cohen* (p), 392 U.S. 83 (1968). Standing to sue.

Jones v. *Mayer* (a), 392 U.S. 409 (1968). Housing discrimination.

Levy v. *State of Louisiana* (a), 391 U.S. 68 (1968). Illegitimacy.

1969

Bermen v. *Board of Election* (a), 420 F.2d 684 (1969). Literacy test for voting.

Maryland and Virginia Eldership of Churches of God v. *Church of God at Sharpsburg, Inc.* (a), 393 U.S. 528 (1969). Church dispute.

1970

Allen v. *Hickel* (a), 424 F.2d 944 (1970). Crèche in public park.

Eugene Sand & Gravel, Inc. v. *Lowe* (p), 397 U.S. 1042 (1970). Religious symbols on public property.

Maxwell v. *Bishop* (a), 398 U.S. 262 (1970). Death penalty.

1971

Burke, Matter of Adoption by (p), 59 N.J. 36 (1971). Religion in adoption.

Clayton v. *Kervick* (p), 285 A2d 11 (N.J., 1971). Public funds and religious schools.

De Martino v. *Scarpetta* (p), 404 U.S. 805, cert. denied from 269 N.E.2d 787 (1971). Religion in adoption.

Earley v. *DiCenso* (p), 403 U.S. 602 (1971). Public funds and religious schools.

Jiminez v. *Naff* (a), 400 U.S. 986 (1971). Literacy test for voting.

Lemon v. *Kurtzman* (p and a), 403 U.S. 602 (1971). Public funds and religious schools.

Second United Presbyterian Church of Johnstown v. *Presbytery of Albany* (p), 404 U.S. 309 (1971). Inter-church conflict.

Tilton v. *Richardson* (p), 403 U.S. 672 (1971). Public funds and church colleges.

1972

Aikens v. *California* (a), 406 U.S. 813 (1972). Death penalty.

Brusca v. *State Board of Education* (p), 405 U.S. 1050 (1972). Public funds and religious schools.

Diffenderfer v. *Central Baptist Church of Miami* (p), 404 U.S. 412 (1972). Tax exemption.

Furman v. *Georgia* (a), 408 U.S. 238 (1972). Death penalty.

Laird v. *Anderson* (a), 409 U.S. 1076 (1972). Chapel attendance at U.S. military academies.

Oliver v. *Postel* (p), 30 N.Y.2d 171 (1972). Excluding reporters from criminal trial.

Wisconsin v. *Yoder* (a), 406 U.S. 205 (1972). Compulsory school attendance and religion.

1973

Committee for Public Education and Religious Liberty (PEARL) v. *Nyquist* (p), 413 U.S. 756 (1973). Public funds and religious schools.

Levitt (Levitt I) v. *Committee for Public Education and Religious Liberty (PEARL)* (p), 413 U.S. 472 (1973). Public funds and religious schools.

Sloan v. *Lemon* (p), 413 U.S. 825 (1973). Public funds and religious schools.

1974

Franchise Tax Board v. *United Americans for Public Schools* (p), 419 U.S. 890 (1974). Public funds and religious schools.

Jones v. *Butz* (p), 419 U.S. 806 (1974). Humane slaughtering.

Marburger v. *Public Funds for Public Schools* (p), 417 U.S. 961 (1974). Public funds and religious schools.

1975

Meek v. *Pittenger* (p), 421 U.S. 349 (1975). Public funds and religious schools.

Minnesota Civil Liberties Union v. *Minnesota* (p), 224 N.W.2d 344 (1975). Public funds and religious schools.

Roe v. *Norton* (a), 422 U.S. 391 (1975). Abortion.

Wheeler v. *Barrera* (p), 417 U.S. 402, modified 422 U.S. 1004 (1975). Public funds and religious schools.

1976

Commonwealth v. *Edelin* (a), 359 N.E.2d 4 (Mass., 1976). Abortion.

Kennedy v. *Sloan* (p), 429 U.S. 862 (1976). Public funds and religious schools.

Roemer v. *Board of Public Works of Maryland* (a), 426 U.S. 736 (1976). Public funds and church colleges.

1977

Committee for Public Education and Religious Liberty (PEARL) v. *Court of Claims* (p), 354 N.Y.S.2d 370 (1977). Public funds and religious schools.

Committee for Public Education and Religious Liberty (PEARL) v. *Levitt (Levitt II)* (p), 433 U.S. 902 (1977). Public funds and religious schools.

First Presbyterian Church of Schenectady v. *United Presbyterian Church in the U.S.A.* (p), 430 F.Supp. 450 (1977). Church dispute.

Key v. *Doyle* (a), 434 U.S. 59 (1977). Death bed bequest.

Parker Seal v. *Cummins* (a), 433 U.S. 903 (1977). Unemployment compensation for Sabbatarians.

Poelker v. *Doe* (a), 432 U.S. 519 (1977). Abortion.

TransWorld Airlines v. *Hardison* (a), 432 U.S. 63 (1977). Religion in labor law.

Wolman v. *Walter* (a), 433 U.S. 229 (1977). Public funds and religious schools.

1978

McDaniel v. *Paty* (a), 435 U.S. 618 (1978). Religious test for public office.

National Coalition for Public Education and Religious Liberty (PEARL) v. *Califano* (p), 489 F.Supp. 1248 (1978). Public funds and religious schools.

1979

Beggens (Byrne) v. *Public Funds for Public Schools of New Jersey* (p), 422 U.S. 907 (1979). Public funds and religious schools.

Holy Spirit Assn. v. *Harper & Row* (p), 101 Misc.2d 30 (1979). Libel.

Meltzer v. *Board of Public Instruction of Orange County Florida* (p), 439 U.S. 1089 (1979). Public funds and religious schools.

National Labor Relations Board v. *Catholic Bishop of Chicago* (a), 440 U.S. 490 (1979). Religion in labor law.

Yott v. *North American Rockwell Corp.* (a), 602 F.2d 904 (1979). Religion in labor law.

1980

Committee for Public Education and Religious Liberty (PEARL)

v. *Regan* (p), 444 U.S. 646 (1980). Public funds and religious schools.

Gavin v. *Peoples Natural Gas Co.* (a), 613 F.2d 482 (1980). Refusal to raise flag.

Harris v. *McRae* (a), 448 U.S. 297 (1980). Abortion.

National Coalition for Public Education and Religious Liberty (PEARL) v. *Hufstedler* (p), 449 U.S. 808, dismissing appeal in 489 F.Supp. 1248 (1980). Public funds and religious schools.

Margaret S. v. *Edwards* (a), 488 F.Supp. 181 (1980). Abortion.

Ring v. *Grand Forks Public Schools* (a), 483 F.Supp. 272 (1980). Posting Ten Commandments in the public schools.

Worldwide Church of God v. *California* (a), 446 U.S. 987 (1980). Government intrusion in church finances.

1981

Brandon v. *Board of Education of Guilderland* (a), 454 U.S. 1123 (1981). Prayer in the public schools.

Stone v. *Graham* (a), 599 S.W.2d 157, reversed 449 U.S. 39 (1981). Posting of Ten Commandments in the public schools.

Thomas v. *Review Board* (a), 450 U.S. 707 (1981). Unemployment compensation.

1982

Mueller v. *Allen* (a), 676 F.2d 1195 (1982). Public funds and religious schools.

1983

Secretary of the United States Department of Education v. *Felton* (p), on appeal from — F.2d —, reversing 489 F.Supp. 1248 (1983). Religious school aid.

UNPUBLISHED DOCUMENTS AND MANUSCRIPTS

1946

"Legal and Constitutional Aspects of Released Time." Paper presented at Conference on Religious Instruction and the Public School, National Jewish Community Relations Advisory Council and Synagogue Council of America, New York City, 11 November 1946.

1947

"Federal Aid to Education (S. 80, 170, 199, 472)." Statement to U.S. Senate Subcommittee on Education, Washington, D.C., 25 April 1947.

"Constitutional, Statutory, and Judicial Aspects of Sectarianism in Education in the U.S.A." Paper presented at Con-

ference on Sectarianism in Public Schools, Synagogue
Council of America and National Jewish Community Relations Advisory Council, New York City, 10 June 1947.

1948

"Statement in Opposition to Proposed Regulation Restricting
Privilege of Temporary Sojourn to the U.S.A." (with W.
Maslow). Submitted to United States Immigration and
Naturalization Service, February 1948.

"Privilege to Become a Naturalized Citizen (H. Res. 5004)."
(with S. Bolz). Statement submitted to U.S. House Judiciary Committee, Washington, D.C., 16 April 1948.

"Civil Rights Legislative Program." Statement submitted to
Missouri Equal Rights Committee, St. Louis, 1 November
1948.

1949

"Legislation for Federal Funds to Parochial Schools (S. 246)."
Statement to Subcommittee on Education, U.S. House
Committee on Education and Labor, Washington, D.C., 2
June 1949.

1950

"Catholic-Protestant Relations in the United States." Paper
presented at Plenary Session, National Jewish Community
Relations Advisory Council, Atlantic City, New Jersey, 27
May 1950.

"Church-State in Crisis." Paper presented at Biennial Convention of American Jewish Congress, New York City, 18
November 1950.

1952

"Funds for Trips to Museums from Non-Public Schools."
Testimony to New York City Board of Estimate, July
1952.

"Freedom and Patriotism." Paper presented at Institute for
Religious and Social Studies, University of Chicago and
Jewish Theological Seminary, Chicago, 25 November 1952.

1953

"Memorandum in Support of Proposal re Sunday Law Amend-
ment to Allow Sabbatarians to Do Business on Sunday."
Submitted to Joint Legislative Committee, New York
State Legislature, Albany, 15 January 1953.

1954

"Religion and Public Education: Implications for American
Jewry." Paper presented at meeting of Synagogue Council
of America and National Jewish Community Relations

Advisory Council, St. Louis, 16 January 1954.
"Statement Against Zoning Regulations Relating to Religious
Institutions." Presented to New York City Planning Commission, 17 February 1954.
"Statement and Testimony in Opposition to Christian Amendment to Constitution to Include Acknowledgment of 'The
Law and Authority in the Lord Jesus Christ.'" (S. Res.
87). Presented to U.S. Senate Judiciary Committee, Washington, D.C., 17 May 1954.
"Sunday Laws." Statement presented to New York Democratic State Committee, 13 July 1954.
"The Teaching of a 'Common Core' of Religion." Paper
presented at Conference on the Role of the Public School
in Dealing with Religion, Joint Advisory Committee of
Synagogue Council of America, and National Jewish Community Relations Advisory Council, New York City, 25
October 1954.

1956

"Humane Slaughtering of Livestock and Poultry (S. 1636)."
Statement submitted to the Subcommittee of the U.S.
Senate Committee on Agriculture and Forestry, Washington, D.C., 10 May 1956.
"Church, State, and Child Welfare." Paper presented at
meeting on Religion in the Public Schools, National Conference of Jewish Communal Service. St. Louis, Missouri,
30 May 1956.
"The Development of Moral and Spiritual Ideals in the Public Schools." Statement presented at Public Hearing of the
New York City Board of Education, 17 September 1956.

1957

"Public School Display of Ten Commandments." Memorandum of Law submitted to New York State Commissioner
of Education, 2 February 1957.
"Constitutionality of Metcalf-Baker Fair Housing Practice
Bill." Memorandum submitted to New York State Legislature, Albany, 1 March 1957.
"Federal Employees Security Program." Statement submitted
to Commission on U.S. Government Security, Washington, D.C., March 1957.
"Humane Slaughtering (H. Res. 176, etc.)." Statement to Subcommittee on Livestock and Feed Grains. U.S. House
Committee on Agriculture. Washington, D.C., 2 April
1957.

"Religious Identity in Custody, Guardianship, and Adoption."
Statement submitted to the Temporary State Commission
on the Constitutional Convention of New York State, 14
June 1957.

"Immigration Act (H. Res. 1050)." Statement submitted to
U.S. House Committee on the Judiciary, Washington,
D.C., 17 July 1957.

1958

"Jenner-Butler Bill to Limit Appellate Jurisdiction of United
States Supreme Court (S. 2646)." Statement submitted to
Subcommittee of U.S. Senate Judiciary Committee, Wash-
ington, D.C., 3 March 1958.

"Immigration (H. Res. 8439)." Statement submitted to U.S.
Senate Committee on the Judiciary, Washington, D.C., 16
April 1958.

"Interreligious Relationships: Conflict or Competition?" Paper
presented at convention of American Jewish Congress,
Miami, Florida, 16 May 1958.

"Interreligious Relations in America Today." Paper presented
at Plenary Session of National Jewish Community Relations Advisory Council, Boston, Massachusetts, 16 June
1958.

"Proposed Affiliation Agreement of Jersey City Medical Center and Seton Hall University." Statement submitted to
City Commissioner of Jersey City, New Jersey, 1 July
1958.

"Sunday Laws." Statement submitted to Platform Committee,
New York State Democrats and Republicans, 18 August
1958.

"Bills Concerning Wiretapping." Statement submitted to the
Constitutional Rights Subcommittee, U.S. Senate Judiciary
Committee, Washington, D.C., 4 December 1958.

"The Court and Its Critics." Paper presented at Boston University Law School, 10 December 1958.

1959

"Memorandum in Support of Fair Sabbath Law (S. I. 1317
and A. I. 1691)." Submitted to Joint Legislative Committee of New York State Legislature, Albany, 29 January
1959.

"Humane Slaughter of Animals (S. 5 H. 2007)." Statement
submitted to Joint Committee on Agriculture, General
Assembly of State of Connecticut, Hartford, 10 February
1959.

"A Bill to Repeal the Loyalty Oath Requirement in the National Defense Act of 1958 (S. 819)." Statement submitted to the Subcommittee on Education of the U.S. Senate Committee on Labor and Public Welfare, 7 May 1959.

"Fair Sabbath Law." Statement to Joint Legislative Committee, Legislature of State of New York, Albany, 19 May 1959.

"Pennsylvania Sunday Laws (S. 405)." Statement submitted to Committee on Rules, Pennsylvania House of Representatives, Harrisburg, 24 June 1959.

"American Passport Policy." (with P. Baum). Statement submitted to U.S. Senate Committee on Foreign Relations, Washington, D.C., 15 July 1959.

"New Concepts of 'Church and State.'" Commentary on Church and State Relations in Social Welfare. Board of Social and Economic Relations, New York East Conference of the United Methodist Church, Tuxedo Park, New York, 9 September 1959.

"Fair Sabbath Law." Memorandum of Law submitted to New York State Democratic Committee, 10 December 1959.

"Religion, the Public Schools, and the Jewish Community: A Thirteen-Year Review." (with J. Cohen). Paper presented at Conference of Synagogue Council of America and National Jewish Community Relations Advisory Council, New York City, 13 December 1959.

1960

"The Relationship of Church and State as It Affects Religion in Public Education." Paper presented at Institute on Church and State, Detroit Jewish Community Council, Detroit, Michigan, 20 April 1960.

"Anti-Semitic Action and Agitation: Counteraction by Law and Legislation." (with Paul Annes). Paper presented at Plenary Session, National Jewish Community Relations Advisory Council, Philadelphia, Pennsylvania, 23 June 1960.

"The Living Constitution—Church and State." "The Open Mind," WNBC-TV, New York City, 27 November 1960. Rebroadcast 9 July 1961, 1 October 1961, and 26 December 1962.

1961

"Memorandum of Law on Interpretation of Section 6 of the Unemployment Insurance Law in Relation to Disqualification for Benefits for Refusal to Accept a Position Requiring Violation of Religious Conscience." Submitted to State of Maryland Department of Employment Security, 21 February 1961.

"Federal Aid to Parochial Schools." Debate with Rev. Neil G. McCluskey on "The Nation's Future," WNBC-TV, New York City, 18 March 1961.

"Wiretapping (S. 1086, 1221, and 1495)." Statement submitted to Subcommittee on Constitutional Rights, U.S. Senate Judiciary Committee, May 1961.

"The Eichmann Judgment." "The Open Mind," WNBC-TV, New York City, 17 December 1961.

1962

"The Legal Climate in Church-State Relations." Address at Annual Conference of Americans United, Chicago, Illinois, 6 February 1962.

"Proposed Amendments to State Sunday Law to Exempt Sabbath Observers." Statement submitted to Committee on Codes, New York State Assembly, Albany, 14 March 1962.

"Bills Concerning Wiretapping." Statement submitted to U.S. House Committee on the Judiciary, June 1962.

"Our Most Precious Heritage." Statement on Proposed Amendments to the United States Constitution Concerning Prayers in Public Schools submitted to U.S. Senate Committee on the Judiciary (signed by 132 Deans and Professors of Law and Political Science at American Universities), 7 November 1962. Resubmitted with 223 signatories, 8 June 1964, and with 343 signatories, 2 November 1971.

1963

"Supreme Court Decisions on Church and State." Paper presented at Plenary Session, National Jewish Community Relations Advisory Council, Atlantic City, New Jersey, 28 June 1963.

"Federal Aid to Education (S. 580)." Testimony and Statement to U.S. Senate Subcommittee on Education, 14 June 1963.

1964

"Shared-Time Education (H. R. 6074)." Statement and Testimony to Ad Hoc Subcommittee on Study of Shared-Time Education of the U.S. House Committee on Education and Labor, Washington, D.C., 28 February 1964.

"The School, the Church, and the State: Fallacies and Realities on Federal Aid to Parochial Schools." Paper presented at annual convention, National School Boards Association,

Houston, Texas, 28 April 1964.

"The First Amendment to the United States Constitution with Respect to Bible Reading and Prayers in Public Schools (H. J. Res. 693)." Statement and Testimony submitted to U.S. House Committee on the Judiciary, Washington, D.C., 30 April 1964.

"The Vatican Schema and the Jews." Paper presented at national conference, American Jewish Congress, New York City, 11 November 1964.

1965

"Aid to Elementary and Secondary Education (H. R. 2361 and 2362)." Testimony at Hearings of General Subcommittee on Education, U.S. House Committee on Education and Labor, Washington, D.C., 2 February 1965.

"Proposed Regulations Relating to the Elementary and Secondary Education Act of 1965 (Public Law 89-10)." Memorandum submitted to U.S. Commissioner of Education, Washington, D.C., 28 June 1965.

1966

"The Hausbeck Humane Slaughter Bill." "Barry Gray Show," WMCA Radio, New York City, 12 January 1966.

"The Public Mission of the Private University." Paper presented at 40 Anniversary Charter Day Seminar, Long Island University, Brooklyn, New York, 2 February 1966

"Constitutionality of Utilizing Church-Related Institutions in Carrying Out the Provisions of the Economic Opportunities Act." Memorandum submitted to the United States Office of Economic Opportunities, 10 February 1966.

"A Bill to Provide for Judicial Review of the Constitutionality of Grants or Loans under Certain Acts (S. 2097)." Testimony at Hearings before the Subcommittee on Constitutional Rights of the U.S. Senate Committee on the Judiciary, Washington, D.C., 8 March 1966.

"Elementary and Secondary Education Act of 1966 (S. 3046, 2278, 2928, 3012)." Testimony before the U.S. Senate Subcommittee on Education, 19 April 1966.

"Article Eleven, Section Three of the New York State Constitution." Statement submitted to the New York State Temporary Commission on the Constitutional Convention, 11 October 1966.

"The Church, the State, and the School." Paper presented at Conference of New York School Boards Association, Syracuse, New York, 25 October 1966.

"Amending the First Amendment to the United States Constitution with Respect to Bible Reading and Prayers in Public Schools (S.J. Res. 148)." Statement submitted to the U.S. Senate Subcommittee on Constitutional Amendments, 4 December 1966.

1967

"To Defend Our Schools." Paper presented at New York State Council of Churches' Annual Legislative Seminar, Albany, New York, 28 February 1967.

"Constitutionality of Baccalaureate Services Held in the Minnesota Public Schools." Memorandum of Law (with D. Kresge) submitted to the Attorney General of Minnesota, 3 August 1967.

"Statement in Support of a Ruling Permitting Pupils to Keep Their Heads Covered in Class if Their Religion So Requires." Submitted to the State of New Jersey Department of Education, 29 September 1967.

"Should the Proposed New Constitution for the State of Maryland Include a Provision Forbidding the Expenditure of Tax-Raised Funds in Support of Sectarian Educational Institutions?" Statement on Constitutionality submitted at invitation of the Maryland Constitutional Convention, 3 October 1967.

1969

"Church and State: The Constitutional Problem." Paper presented at National Conference on Church and State, Americans United, New York City, 28 January 1969.

1971

"Extend Economic Opportunity Act (H. Res. 40 and 6354)." Testimony to U.S. House Committee on Education and Labor, 4 May 1971.

1972

"Man in Office." Interview by Joseph Michaels, WNBC-TV, New York City, 5 March 1972.

"Parochiaid: The Courts, the Legislature, and the Executive." Paper presented at National Conference on School Finance, National Education Association, New York City, 27 March 1972.

"The Many Meanings of the Yoder Case." Paper presented at Symposium on Conscience and Society, Eastern Mennonite College, Harrisonburg, Virginia, 8 December 1972.

1976

"Religious Pluralism in America." Paper presented at Plenary Session, National Jewish Community Relations Advisory Council, Louisville, Kentucky, 27 June 1976.

"Church Schools and the First Amendment," "Firing Line," WOR-TV, New York City, 14 August 1976.

1977

"Church State Relations and Religious Freedom." Paper presented at Plenary Session, National Jewish Community Relations Advisory Council, Miami Beach, Florida, 23 January 1977.

1978

"Proposed Tuition Tax Credit Act." Statement submitted to Subcommittee on Taxation and Debt Management, U.S. Senate Finance Committee, Washington, D.C., 18 January 1978.

"The Religious Needs of Employees as They Relate to the Scheduling of Work." Statement submitted at Hearing of the United States Equal Employment Opportunity Commission, New York City, 6 April 1978.

1979

"Jonestown, Guyana: Religious Sacrifice Incident." Statement submitted to U.S. House Committee on Foreign Affairs, Washington, D.C., 26 March 1979.

1980

"Prayers in Public Schools (S. 450 and 210)." Statement submitted at Hearing before Subcommittee on the Courts, Civil Liberties, and the Administration of Justice, U.S. House Judiciary Committee, Washington, D.C., July 1980.

"California Senate Bill No. 1493." Statement presented to Senate Legislative Committee reviewing Bill, Sacramento, California, 25 November 1980.

1981

"Church-State Relations in the Reagan Administration: A Preview." J. M. Dawson Lecture on Church and State, Institute of Church-State Studies, Baylor University, Waco, Texas, 1 April 1981.

"Oversight on Private Schools." Testimony at Hearings Before Subcommittee on Elementary, Secondary, and Vocational Education, U.S. House Committee on Education and Labor, Washington, D.C., 13 May 1981.

"A Liberal's View." Jerome W. Sidel Memorial Lecture, American Jewish Congress of St. Louis and St. Louis University Law School, 28 October 1981.

"Temporary Guardians for Cultists (A. 7912 S. 6614)." State-

ment presented to the Hon. Hugh Carey, Governor of
New York, and members of the New York Legislature, 1
November 1981.

1982

"An Act Concerning Limited Guardians for Cultists (S. 488)."
Statement to New Jersey Legislature, 1 November 1982.

"Government Intrusion into Religion: The Problem and the
Solution." Paper presented at Religious Freedom and Interfaith Dialogue Conference, Church of Scientology, Clear-
water, Florida, 6 November 1982.

1983

"Church-State Relations: New Challenges to Old Principles."
Paper presented at First Annual Fred Krinsky Lecture,
Claremont College, Claremont, California, 24 April 1983.

1984

"Religion in Politics: New Threats to the Separation of
Church and State." Paper presented at General Assembly,
Council of Jewish Federations, Toronto, Canada, 14
November 1984.

CONTRIBUTORS

JAMES C. CARPER is Associate Professor of Foundations of Education, Mississippi State University. Coauthor of *Religious Schooling in America* (1984), his articles have appeared in scholarly journals such as *Journal of American History, Educational Forum*, and *Journal of Church and State*.

NEAL DEVINS is Attorney and Member of General Counsel, U.S. Commission of Civil Rights. His articles have appeared in *Notre Dame Law Review, William and Mary Law Review, Vanderbilt Law Review, Journal of Law and Politics*, and *Journal of Church and State*.

DAVID FELLMAN is Emeritus Vilas Professor of Political Science, University of Wisconsin. Founding editor of *Midwest Journal of Political Science*, he is the author of *The Censorship of Books* (1957), *The Constitutional Right of Association* (1963), *Religion in American Public Law* (1965), and *The Defendant's Rights Under English Law* (1966). His articles have appeared in *Minnesota Law Review, Temple University Law Quarterly, American Political Science Review*, and *Wisconsin Law Review*.

RONALD B. FLOWERS is Professor of Religion, Texas Christian University. Coauthor of *Toward Benevolent Neutrality: Church, State, and the Supreme Court* (1982) and author of *Religion in Strange Times: The 1960s and 1970s* (1984), his articles have appeared in scholarly journals such as *Journal of Church and State, Religion and Life*, and *Annals of the American Academy of Political Science*.

EDWIN SCOTT GAUSTAD is Professor of History, University of California at Riverside. An author and editor of many books including *The Great Awakening in New England* (1957), *A Religious History of America* (1974), *Historical Atlas of Religion in America* (1976), and *Documentary History of Religion in America* (2 vols., 1982-83), his articles have appeared in *Church History, Journal of the American Academy of Religion, The William and Mary Quarterly*, and *Journal of Church and State*.

KENT GREENAWALT is Cardozo Professor of Jurisprudence, Columbia School of Law. He is author of *Discrimination and Reverse Discrimination* (1983) and coauthor of *The Sectarian College and the Public Purse* (1970). His numerous articles have appeared in scholarly journals including *Columbia Law Review*,

William and Mary Law Review, *Virginia Law Review*, and *Wilson Quarterly*.

A. E. DICK HOWARD is White Burkett Miller Professor of Law and Public Affairs, University of Virginia School of Law. Author of *The Road from Runnymede: Magna Carta and Constitutionalism in America* (1968), *Commentaries on the Constitution of Virginia* (2 vols., 1974), and *State Aid to Private Higher Education* (1977), his articles have appeared in *Virginia Law Review*, *Wilson Quarterly*, *American Oxonian*, and *American Bar Association Journal*.

DEAN M. KELLEY is Director of Civil and Religious Liberty, National Council of the Churches of Christ in the U.S.A. He is author of *Why Conservative Churches Are Growing* (1972) and *Why Churches Should Not Pay Taxes* (1977) and editor of *Government Intervention in Religious Affairs* (1982). His numerous articles have appeared in *Journal of Church and State*, *The Christian Century*, *Liberty*, and *Annals of the American Academy of Political Science*.

MILTON R. KONVITZ is Professor Emeritus of Law and of Industrial and Labor Relations, Cornell University Law School. Author of *Fundamental Liberties of a Free People* (1957), *First Amendment Freedoms: Selected Cases on Freedom of Religion, Speech, Press, Assembly* (1963), *Expanding Liberties* (1966), *Religious Liberty and Conscience* (1968), and *Judaism and the American Idea* (1978), he is Chairman of the Editorial Board of *Midstream* and a member of the Editorial Board of *Journal of Law and Religion*.

SAMUEL KRISLOV is Professor of Political Science and Adjunct Professor in Jewish Studies and South Asian and Islamic Studies, University of Minnesota. He is the author of *The Supreme Court in the Federal Process* (1965), *The Supreme Court and Political Freedom* (1968), *Compliance: A Multi-Disciplinary Approach* (1972), and *Forecasting the Impact of Legislation on Courts* (1980). His essay was supported by a Bush Foundation Fellowship for 1982-83.

LEONARD W. LEVY is Professor of History, Claremont Graduate School. He is the author of *Legacy of Suppression: Freedom of Speech and Press in Early American History* (1960), *Jefferson and Civil Liberties* (1963), *Origins of the Fifth Amendment: The Right Against Self-Incrimination* (1968), and *Treason Against God—A History of the Offense of Blasphemy* (1981), and the editor of the forthcoming *Encyclopedia of the American Con-*

stitution (4 vols., 1987). His numerous articles have appeared in various scholarly journals including *American Historical Review*, *Columbia Law Review*, *The William and Mary Quarterly*, and *Political Science Quarterly*.

SIDNEY LISKOFSKY is Director of the Jacob Blaustein Institute for the Advancement of Human Rights of the American Jewish Committee. He is a coeditor of *The Right to Leave and the Right to Return* (1976) and *Essays on Human Rights* (1979). A contributor to *World Politics and the Jewish Condition* (1970) and *Human Rights in the Inter-American System* (1982), his articles have appeared in numerous publications such as *American Jewish Yearbook*, *Reports on the Foreign Scene*, and *Human Rights Journal*.

FRANKLIN H. LITTELL is Professor of Religion, Temple University, and Adjunct Professor, Hebrew University Institute of Contemporary Jewry. He is author of *The Free Church* (1957), *The Church and the Body Politic* (1969), *The Crucifixion of the Jews* (1975), *The Atlas History of Christianity* (1976), and *Religious Liberty in the Crossfire of Creeds* (1978), and is editor of and contributor to *Reflections on the Holocaust* (1980). His articles have appeared in numerous scholarly journals such as *Journal of Ecumenical Studies, Journal of Church and State, Church History, Mennonite Quarterly Review*, and *Journal of Holocaust and Genocide Studies*.

DAVID LITTLE is Professor of Religious Studies, University of Virginia. Author of *Religion, Order, and Law: A Study in Pre-Revolutionary England* (1969) and *Comparative Religious Ethics* (1978), his articles have appeared in *Union Seminary Quarterly Review, Journal for the Scientific Study of Religion, Religious Education, The Christian Century*, and *Christianity and Crisis*.

FREDA PFEFFER is wife of and assistant to Leo Pfeffer.

LEO PFEFFER is Emeritus Professor of Political Science, Long Island University. He is author of *Church, State, and Freedom* (1953; rev. ed., 1967), *God, Caesar, and the Constitution: The Court as Referee of Church-State Confrontation* (1975), and *Religion, State, and the Burger Court* (1985), and coauthor of *Church and State in the United States* (1964). A member of the Editorial Council of *Journal of Church and State*, his numerous articles have appeared in such periodicals as *Catholic World, The Christian Century, The Churchman, Commonweal, Nation, Saturday Review*, and *Journal of Church and State*.

RICHARD V. PIERARD is Professor of History, Indiana State University. He is author of *The Unequal Yoke: Evangelical Christianity and Political Conservatism* (1970) and coauthor of *Twilight of the Saints: Biblical Christianity and Civil Religion in America* (1978). His articles have appeared in various scholarly journals such as *Journal of Church and State, Journal of Ecumenical Studies, Contemporary Education*, and *Fides et Historia*.

NORMAN REDLICH is Dean and Judge Edward Weinfeld Professor of Law, New York University School of Law. He is the editor of *Confronting Injustice: A Compilation of the Ratings of Edmond Cahn* (1967), author of *Professional Responsibility: A Problem Approach* (1976), and coauthor of *Constitutional Law, Cases and Materials* (1983). His numerous articles have appeared in such journals as *Journal of Legal Education, The Nation, American Bar Foundation Research Journal*, and *New York University Law Review*.

JOHN M. SWOMLEY is Professor of Christian Ethics, Saint Paul School of Theology. Author of *Military Establishment* (1964), *Religion, the State, and the Schools* (1968), *American Empire: The Political Ethics of Twentieth-Century Conquest* (1970), and *Liberation Ethics* (1972), his articles have appeared in *The Nation, The Christian Century, The National Catholic Reporter*, and *The Progressive*.

JAMES E. WOOD, JR. is Simon and Ethel Bunn Professor of Church-State Studies, Baylor University. Founding editor of *Journal of Church and State*, he is coauthor of *Church and State in Scripture, History, and Constitutional Law* (1958), author of *Nationhood and the Kingdom* (1977), and editor of and contributor to *Baptists and the American Experience* (1976), *Religion and Politics* (1983), and *Religion, the State, and Education* (1984). His articles have appeared in numerous scholarly journals including *Annals of the American Academy of Political Science, Ecumenical Review, Journal of the American Academy of Religion*, and *Religious Education*.

SHARON L. WORTHING is Attorney, New York City. She has contributed to *Government Intervention in Religious Affairs* (1982) and *Religion, the State, and Education* (1984). A member of the Editorial Council of *Journal of Church and State*, her articles have appeared in *Annals of the American Academy of Political Science, Christianity and Crisis, Journal of Church and State, Fordham Law Review*, and *Liberty*.

INDEX

DATE DUE